269

*Literacy
Lesson*

The Bicycle Man

This lesson illustrates the concepts of vocabulary development using a delightful book, *The Bicy-cle Man* (Say, 1982). You will see how words were selected for direct teaching and how the de-cisions were made about when and how to teach vocabulary. The plan uses the literacy lesson concept presented in Chapter 2.

Before Reading the Plan

1. Think about what you have learned about vocabulary development from this chap-ter. Review any portions that you may have forgotten or that may have been unclear.
2. Recall the parts of the literacy lesson plan. (See Chapter 2 if you need review.)
3. Read *The Bicycle Man* (Say, 1982).
4. Read and study the Teacher Preparation section to see the decision making in-volved in planning the vocabulary activities for this book.

---

288   Chapter 5 • Developing Vocabulary: Words and Meanings Beyond the Beginning Literacy Level

*Literacy
Lesson
continued*

Teacher Preparation

The literacy lesson for *The Bicycle Man* was developed for a class of third graders who were mak-ing good progress in developing their literacy. They often had difficulty with comprehension but were beginning to develop more independence. This book was one that I wanted the entire class to experience. A great deal of independent reading and self-initiated writing went on in this class, and the students' vocabularies were expanding because of the extensive reading and writing and the emphasis on vocabulary. My preparation for this lesson proceeded as follows:

1. I read *The Bicycle Man* and wrote out a rough story map for it:
   • *Setting:* Japanese school after World War II.
   • *Characters:* Main—person telling the story (I), the principal, Mrs. Morita (teacher), red-headed soldier, black soldier. Secondary—Mr. Oka (art teacher).
   • *Problem:* Japanese people are afraid of the American soldiers (inferred, p. 17).
   • *Action:* (1) Students prepare the school grounds for a sportsday. (2) Parents arrive with lunch boxes and [...] (3) Principal, Mr. Morita, begins sportsday with a speech about sports[...] [...] to winners. (5) Children and par[...] ers; everyone is havi[...] dier is black. (8) Sol[...] of soldiers. (9) Black[...] on bicycle and delig[...]
   • *Outcome:* Everyone [...]
   • *Theme:* Getting to k[...]

2. Next, I reviewed the sto[...] (See page 239 for a dis[...] words were directly rela[...] *ers, emperor,* and *cham[...]*

3. I then thought about th[...] preparing the lesson. I[...] cause we had read *The[...]* of all the emphasis ou[...] *sportsmanship* are wo[...] use the context, their[...] knowledge. I decided[...] fore reading.

4. I decided to use thre[...]
   • *Semantic mapp[...]* knowledge and[...]
   • *Preview and pr[...]* tivation and pur[...]
   • *Vocabulary self[...]*

5. Finally, I decided to[...] cooperative and in[...] the support they c[...] be free to move a[...] by reading aloud a[...]

---

290   Chapter 5 • Developing Vocabulary: Words and Meanings Beyond the Beginning Literacy Level

*Literacy
Lesson
continued*

ACTIVITY	PROCEDURE	NOTES
Making predictions: using preview and predict	1. Ask students to predict what they think will happen in this story.	Flows naturally from all activities that have been done.
	2. Refer students to the preview and predict poster, if needed.	See Chapter 3, page 106
	3. Have students record predictions in their journals.	Sets purpose for reading.
Reading and Responding to *The Bicycle Man*		
Teacher read-aloud	1. Read aloud the first two pages as students follow along.	Gives all students the sup-port they sometimes need to get started reading.
	2. Stop and ask students what they think is going to happen. Discuss whether they want to change any predictions.	
	3. Encourage students to make changes in their predic-tions.	Continues active process of predicting and confi[...]
Making journal notes	Remind students to note any words or ideas they want to talk about in their journals.	Supports the process of responding during reading.
Student-selected mode of reading: Cooperative (oral or silent) Independent	1. Have students select the mode of reading they want to use for the remainder of the story.	Gives students a choice in meeting their own needs. (See Chapter 2 on modes of reading.)
	2. Remind students to continue to check whether their predictions were confirmed or changed.	Continues focus on reading for a purpose.
	3. As students read, observe each pair or trio; stop and ask questions or prompt those who need extra help.	
Individual written responses	After they complete the story, ask students to write about it in their journals. Display the following response chart for those who need more support:	Gives all students a chance for personal response. (See Chapter 6 on responding.)

Excerpt from an extended
Literacy Lesson

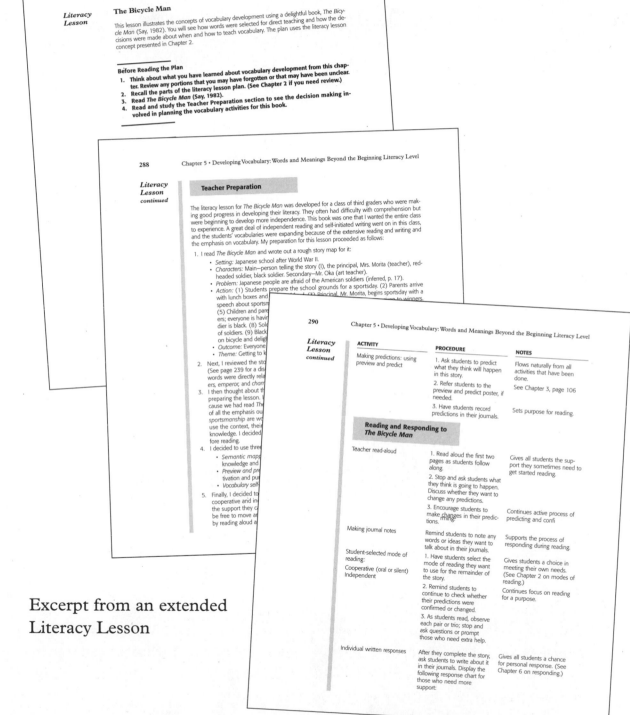

Literacy

Helping Children Construct Meaning

Fourth Edition

J. David Cooper

Ball State University

with an introduction by

Kathryn H. Au

Houghton Mifflin Company   Boston   New York

To Isabelle, Melissa, and Michael

Senior Sponsoring Editor: Loretta Wolozin
Senior Associate Editor: Janet Edmonds
Senior Project Editor: Kathryn Dinovo
Senior Manufacturing Coordinator: Marie Barnes
Senior Marketing Manager: Pamela J. Laskey

Cover design: Catherine Hawkes, Cat & Mouse
Art direction: Susan Beebe and Catherine Hawkes
Front cover image: Michael, Dallin School, Arlington, Massachusetts
Back cover image: Hannah, Dallin School, Arlington, Massachusetts

Contents

3 Activating and Developing Prior Knowledge   91

6 Responding and the Construction of Meaning 295

7 Writing and the Construction of Meaning   331

8 Teaching Strategies for Constructing Meaning   389

9 Constructing Meaning Across the Curriculum   429

10 Organizing and Managing the Balanced Literacy Classroom   467

11 Assessment and Evaluation in the Balanced Literacy Classroom 521

HANDBOOK RESOURCE

Word Skills: Phonics and Structural Analysis for Teachers   565

Preface

Success in literacy learning for *all* children continues to be an important national goal and priority (Learning First Alliance, 1998; Snow, Burns, & Griffin, 1998). Evidence supporting a balanced literacy program as the way to achieve this goal continues to mount. *Literacy: Helping Children Construct Meaning,* 4th Edition, was written to support *all* preservice and inservice teachers' learning—to help them provide balanced literacy instruction for *all* students.

Background for this Edition

Literacy: Helping Children Construct Meaning, 4th Edition, builds on the extremely successful third edition. Not only was the third edition used in many college classrooms but it was also used as an inservice study group text for many elementary and middle schools. The practical nature of the fourth edition with its many sample lessons provides preservice and inservice teachers a wealth of ideas from which to develop their own instructional strategies.

Preservice and inservice teachers are becoming more and more aware of the need for research-based instructional programs and strategies. Preservice and inservice teachers are becoming more and more convinced that *all* children can learn to read and write. Therefore, the major goal for the fourth edition of this text was to provide *all* teachers of balanced literacy instruction strategies that are well grounded in the research.

Strategies and Lessons for Direct and Indirect Instruction

This text provides strategies and sample lessons for both direct and indirect instruction. Four complete pieces of literature are provided with updated sample lessons: (1) *Jamaica Tag-Along;* (2) *Mummies, Tombs, and Treasure;* (3) *My Brown Bear Barney;* and (4) *The Bicycle Man.* These lessons serve as models to help teachers develop their own lessons for a balanced literacy program. A new literacy lesson using a technology program, *The Little Planet and the Magic Hats,* is also provided.

Revisions in This Edition

The major thrusts of the revisions in this edition are in six major areas:

1. *Balanced Literacy Instruction*—The concept of balanced literacy instruction is maintained and updated throughout this text. A model for the balanced beginning literacy program presented in Chapter 4 shows how the beginning literacy program needs to differ from the program at grades 3 and beyond.

2. *Technology*—The use of technology has been woven into lessons and strategies throughout the text. Where appropriate, chapters conclude with a listing of technology resources. A new literacy lesson in Chapter 7 derives its instruction on prediction from *The Little Planet and the Magic Hats,* part of a literacy curriculum on a technology platform. In today's emergent technology explosion, it remains essential to put instructional goals first when evaluating the uses of materials now housed in technology.

3. *Direct and Indirect Instruction*—Strategies for both direct and indirect instruction are presented with emphasis on how they fit into a balanced literacy program. Instructional strategies with large and small groups and individual children are often a seamless combination and flow of approaches chosen by the expert teacher as a response to students' needs.

4. *Beginning Literacy Instruction*—A completely new chapter is provided on beginning literacy instruction. Numerous examples support all teachers' needs to give today's children grounding in word knowledge.

5. *Word Skills: Phonics and Structural Analysis for Teachers*—A new resource handbook at the end of the book helps all teachers learn the basic content of phonics and structural analysis. Its easy-to-find tabbed pages make it a handy reference.

6. *Spelling and Grammar*—Sample lessons for systematic and direct teaching of spelling and grammar connected to writing are included.

Text Features to Support All Litercy Instructors: Preservice and Inservice Teachers, Related Personnel, Family, and Community Members

Literacy: Helping Children Construct Meaning was written as a text for preservice and inservice teachers. A variety of instructional formats are provided to make the text user friendly:

- A graphic organizer for each chapter includes page numbers for ease of locating information.

- Both direct and indirect teaching strategies are presented with a clear explanation of the research and rationale behind the strategy.

- Photographs specifically taken for this text clearly illustrate key concepts and strategies.

- Fully developed literacy lessons, minilessons, and specific teaching strategies serve as models for developing additional lessons.

- Figures and tables bring out important strategies and information in an easy-to-use format.

- Examples of students' work are presented where appropriate.

- A bibliography of technology resources is presented at the end of appropriate chapters.

- Suggestions for additional reading are provided at the conclusion of each chapter to help teachers study areas of interest in more detail.

▶ A bibliography of all literature cited in each chapter is included to help teachers locate literature for classroom use.

▶ A complete list of references throughout the text is found at the conclusion of the book.

Organization and Scope of the Text

The eleven chapters and teacher resource handbook provide comprehensive coverage of topics important in helping teachers develop a balanced literacy program that utilizes both direct and indirect instruction.

Chapter 1, "Understanding Literacy: Learning and Constructing Meaning," provides background on the changing views of reading, literacy learning, language acquisition, prior knowledge, and schema theory. Emphasis is placed on the appropriate roles of phonemic awareness, phonics, and decoding as they relate to the construction of meaning.

Chapter 2, "Developing a Balanced Literacy Program," presents the concept of a balanced literacy program and develops the need for both direct and indirect instruction using thematic units, literacy lessons, and minilessons. A sample literacy lesson is provided.

Chapter 3, "Activating and Developing Prior Knowledge," presents background material supporting the importance of schema and prior knowledge for literacy development. It suggests strategies for helping students achieve independence in activating their own prior knowledge. A sample literacy lesson focusing on prior knowledge development is presented.

Chapter 4, "Beginning Literacy: Learning to Read and Spell Words and Construct Meaning," is a totally new chapter focusing on the framework for a balanced beginning literacy program. The importance of heavier emphasis on decoding in the beginning literacy program is stressed. A set of instructional routines especially useful in kindergarten, first grade, and second grade is presented along with a sample literacy lesson.

Chapter 5, "Developing Vocabulary: Words and Meanings Beyond the Beginning Literacy Level," focuses on how students develop vocabulary and emphasizes strategies leading to student independence. A sample literacy lesson is provided.

Chapter 6, "Responding and the Construction of Meaning," presents responding as a source for student assessment and the development of students' abilities to construct meaning. Techniques and strategies from journals to literature circles are presented.

Chapter 7, "Writing and the Construction of Meaning," focuses on how to promote and support writing within the balanced literacy classroom. Emphasis is placed on how to teach spelling and grammar related to writing.

Chapter 8, "Teaching Strategies for Constructing Meaning," shows elementary and middle school teachers how to directly and systematically model strategies for students. Five strategies supported by the research are presented.

Chapter 9, "Constructing Meaning Across the Curriculum," applies many concepts developed in earlier chapters to the entire curriculum, and it gives a plan for developing cross-curricular thematic units.

Chapter 10, "Organizing and Managing the Balanced Literacy Classroom," presents guidelines for planning and managing the literacy classroom at the elementary and middle school levels. Procedures for developing student routines are presented.

Chapter 11, "Assessment and Evaluation in the Balanced Literacy Classroom," focuses on assessment as an integral part of instruction. A variety of alternatives and techniques for assessment are presented.

The Handbook Resource, "Word Skills: Phonics and Structural Analysis for Teachers," is a new feature designed to help teachers develop a basic knowledge of the content of phonics and structural analysis. A practice exercise is provided for teachers to check their own knowledge.

Instructor's Resource Manual

The Instructor's Resource Manual that accompanies this text contains many ideas for using it in preservice courses as well as inservice training. The Instructor's Resource Manual was developed in conjunction with Dr. Nancy D. Kiger of the University of Central Florida. For each chapter of the text, the manual provides organizing tools such as chapter outlines and summaries, questions and activities to encourage class discussion and active learning, and pedagogical aids such as transparency masters to reinforce key concepts in the text. The manual was developed as a flexible tool to complement individual instructors' unique teaching styles.

Acknowledgments

This text continues to be a reflection of my continuing efforts to help preservice and inservice teachers do a more effective job of teaching *all* children to read and write. There are many people who have provided strong support and assistance in developing this fourth edition:

- Thousands of children and teachers over the last twenty years have provided many ideas and reactions that helped formulate my understanding of effective literacy instruction.

- Michael D. Robinson, Title I Instructional Specialist, read and reacted to every chapter and gave many valuable suggestions.

- Irene Boschken, K–6 Language Arts Coordinator; Janet McWilliams, literacy consultant; and Lynne Pistochini, Curriculum Resource Teacher, all gave many valuable suggestions for the new Chapter 4 on beginning reading.

- Dr. William Valmont, University of Arizona, made very helpful suggestions for the new Chapter 4.

- Dr. Nancy Kiger, professor, author, and special friend, not only developed the Instructor's Resource Manual but gave many helpful suggestions for Chapter 4 and the Handbook Resource.

- Brenda Stone Anderson, my assistant, worked endless hours to input manuscript, proofread, and develop charts and tables. This project would not have been possible without her.

Ali Sullo, Editor-in-Chief and Vice President, Reading Language Arts at Houghton Mifflin, provided unbelievably strong support in revising this text. She read the entire manuscript in an efficient and thorough manner, offering many suggestions that helped focus the text. She also made it possible to continue the use of full pieces of literature as a basis for sample lessons. Her support reflects her continuing dedication to teachers and children.

Janet Edmonds, Development Editor, gave valuable suggestions for the revisions of each chapter. She provided solid leadership in developing the new technology focus. Nancy Benjamin, of Books By Design, saw the manuscript through production to a final user-friendly book. Loretta Wolozin, Senior Sponsoring Editor, continued to provide the strong support she has given me for fifteen years with this and earlier editions of this text.

The manuscript was also reviewed by college and university professors from across the country who gave valuable suggestions for improvements: Susan L. Brenner, Clarion University; Janie Knight, The University of Memphis; Jan LaBonty, The University of Montana; Karen M. Moore, California State University, Sacramento; and Jo-Ann Snyder, Wayne State University.

To all of the individuals mentioned—THANK YOU!

Finally, I find myself reflecting on the effort and time that I have put into this edition. I know that *all* children can learn to read and write if we provide good instruction. If we continue to provide balanced literacy instruction and avoid quick pendulum swings and fads, it is possible to have all children become successful readers and writers.

J. David Cooper

Introduction

Two groups of students in Jo Ann Wong-Kam's fifth-grade class were reading *Sing Down the Moon* by Scott O'Dell. The morning I observed, they were in the process of learning to conduct their own literature discussions. Jo Ann had the students prepare for these discussions by writing questions for their group to address. The students had discovered that some questions fostered discussion while others cut it short.

Jo Ann called the two groups together to discuss what they were learning about questions. Nicole said that some questions were just too easy. An example of such a question was, "Who was Bright Morning?" These questions only had one answer, Thomas pointed out.

Kanani said that harder questions seemed to work better. An example of such a question was, "What was the theme?" Renee stated that these questions had many answers and that you had to think about the whole book in order to answer them. Kanani observed that these questions forced you to explain why you chose your answer.

Jo Ann called the students' attention to the way certain questions started. The students decided that questions beginning with *why* usually required considerable discussion, while those beginning with *who* or *where* did not. Kanani suggested starting questions with *how come,* and Jo Ann noted that this was another way of saying *why.* Several students thought it best to avoid questions that could be answered with a *yes* or *no,* but Kona pointed out that a *yes* or *no* question was all right if it also made you give reasons for your answer.

It was a struggle for the students to compose their own discussion questions, and Jo Ann wanted to be sure they understood the purpose of the activity. "When I do all the questions, who's doing the thinking?" Jo Ann asked. "You are," the students replied. "Yes," Jo Ann said, "and when you ask the questions, who's doing the thinking?" "We are," the students answered.

In the fourth edition of *Literacy: Helping Children Construct Meaning*, J. David Cooper shows teachers how to help students do their own thinking about text, as Jo Ann was doing with her students. Creating opportunities for students to read, write, and make their own discoveries about literacy is an important first step. However, when the goal is higher-level thinking about text, even the most capable students benefit from a teacher's expert guidance. The least capable students absolutely require such guidance if they are to read and write well. Instruction and guidance provided by well-prepared teachers is the key to having students achieve the third of America's National Education Goals, which emphasizes higher-level thinking, including reasoning ability, problem solving, application of knowledge, and effective communication.

David recognizes that constructivist approaches leading students to higher-level thinking are much more complex and demanding for teachers than earlier skills-oriented, behaviorist approaches to literacy instruction. In writing this textbook, he has translated his wealth of knowledge about current research and effective practice into teaching strategies, minilessons, and plans for units, all easily understood and readily applied in actual classroom settings.

David argues for a balanced literacy program. The need to understand the importance of balance is especially acute in the area of beginning literacy, the most controversial of topics in our field. This edition features a timely and sensible new chapter on beginning literacy. Traditionally, advocates of code-emphasis approaches have been pitted against advocates of meaning-emphasis approaches. In taking a balanced view, David shows why both decoding (or word identification) and meaning making (or comprehension) are necessary parts of beginning literacy instruction. In keeping with the consensus emerging in the field, he believes that children are best served when we provide them with both skill instruction and motivating contexts for real reading.

What needs to be balanced in literacy instruction? David highlights the need for a balance between the affective dimension, including motivation, and the cognitive dimension in the teaching of literacy. He emphasizes a balance between time spent teaching reading and time spent teaching writing, as well as opportunities to integrate the two. He stresses the importance of teacher-led instruction and modeling while pointing out that the teacher's support must gradually be withdrawn, to lead students to independence. He calls our attention to strategies and skills in areas such as word identification, spelling, grammar, and vocabulary, while placing these strategies and skills in the larger context of purposeful reading and writing. He argues for the value both of responding to literature and of reading for information. A balanced literacy program reflects a consideration of all these factors.

The movement toward balanced, constructivist approaches and away from skills-oriented approaches can be a cause of concern to those unfamiliar with the benefits of the new forms of instruction. About a week after I had made the observations in Jo Ann's fifth grade class, I received a phone call from a staff member at the Hawaii state legislature. The staff member wanted to know why teachers had stopped teaching phonics. He expressed the opinion that classrooms today were undisciplined when compared to those of the past, with far too much noise and activity. In his day, he said, teachers had enforced discipline and made sure that students sat quietly and listened. No, I replied, teachers had not stopped teaching phonics. Yes, I admitted, classrooms today were noisier and more active than in the past. Then I explained why students who learn nothing but phonics and do nothing but sit quietly and listen are not going to be excellent readers and writers.

This encounter reminded me of why we must spread the word about the virtues of a balanced literacy program. Our lives as literacy educators would be a lot easier if those simpler, skills-oriented models had worked. But they have not proved equal to the task of preparing students to do their own higher-level thinking about text.

To date, only constructivist, balanced approaches have shown the potential for leading students to become thoughtful readers and writers. We must guard against the mistaken notion that a return to the past will enable us to address the challenge of teaching reading and writing to the diverse population of students in today's schools. Instead of looking back, we must move forward, applying the powerful new ideas now available. By making balanced literacy instruction understandable and practical for all teachers, this new edition of David's well-regarded textbook brings us closer to our goal of high-level literacy for all students.

Kathryn H. Au

Understanding Literacy Learning and Constructing Meaning

1

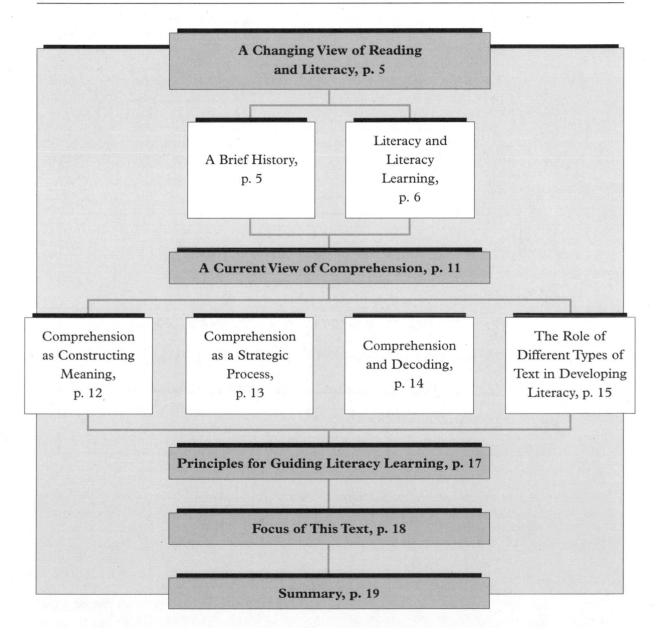

A Changing View of Reading and Literacy, p. 5

A Brief History, p. 5

Literacy and Literacy Learning, p. 6

A Current View of Comprehension, p. 11

Comprehension as Constructing Meaning, p. 12

Comprehension as a Strategic Process, p. 13

Comprehension and Decoding, p. 14

The Role of Different Types of Text in Developing Literacy, p. 15

Principles for Guiding Literacy Learning, p. 17

Focus of This Text, p. 18

Summary, p. 19

A look at how some fourth graders are working with the book Flossie and the Fox *(McKissack, 1986) will help us begin to think about what happens in balanced literacy classrooms to help students develop their abilities to read and write.* Flossie and the Fox *is a wonderful book, written in dialect, about how a little African American girl from the South outsmarts a fox.*

Fourth graders Eddie, Andrew, Lisa, Christina, Jose, Terri, and Gil were each huddled in their own special place in the classroom reading Flossie and the Fox*. When Lisa finished, she wrote in her journal how she felt about Flossie. When Gil finished, he drew a picture of his favorite part and wrote, "Flossie is so-o-o smart!!!" As each reader finished, journal writing began.*

Soon Mrs. Miller asked for everyone who was reading Flossie and the Fox *to meet in a discussion group. On the wall hung a chart like the one shown below. The students began by sharing their personal responses from their journals. Everyone was so eager to share that Mrs. Miller had to encourage them to take turns.*

After the students shared their personal responses, Mrs. Miller asked, "How did we do with our predictions?" Students discussed which predictions had been confirmed in their reading and which had not. For example, Terri said she found out right away that what she had predicted didn't happen.

> ## Our Predictions About
> ## <u>Flossie and the Fox</u>
>
> 1. The fox is going to eat Flossie's eggs.
> 2. Flossie is going to trick the fox.
> 3. A fox is smart. I think the fox will trick Flossie.

Mrs. Miller then asked the children whether the first prediction on the chart had been confirmed. Three students said it had not, but the others were not sure. Terri suggested, "We could look back in our books to see if it was true." After several students responded, Mrs. Miller directed the group to page 9. She asked them to think about the first prediction as she read the page aloud. Then she modeled the thinking involved in using the skill of evaluating predictions by saying, "This section begins to tell me that Flossie is not going to be tricked by the fox. This leads me to believe that our first prediction may not be confirmed. In fact, it leads me to think I should change the original prediction that we made because I have gotten more information about Flossie and how she thinks."

A discussion followed that focused on predictions and how they change as one gathers more information during reading. After all the predictions were discussed, Mrs. Miller asked the group to talk about how making predictions had helped them understand the book. After a short discussion, she then asked the students what they would like to do with the story now that they had finished it. Lisa, Jose, Gil, and Eddie wanted to take parts and make a play. The others wanted to add examples of Flossie's dialect to the class language wall (part of the class language project Mrs. Miller had started to help children develop an appreciation and understanding of different dialects and cultures).

THESE FOURTH GRADERS and their teacher were developing literacy. The book they were discussing was an original work, not one that had been adapted or rewritten. The group had previewed the story and predicted what they thought would happen. They then revisited the story to think about how their predictions had been confirmed or changed as they read. When Mrs. Miller realized that students were having difficulty with one prediction, she used a think-aloud process to model how she might have changed her thinking about the first prediction. The students then discussed how each prediction had been confirmed, changed, or rejected. After the discussion, the children and their teacher reflected on how making predictions helped them to understand the story.

These students made personal responses to *Flossie and the Fox;* they responded by doing the types of things one usually does after reading a story. They did not just answer questions, a form of response that occurs only in school. Instead, Mrs. Miller encouraged the children to choose their own forms of response, just as real readers do in real life. Finally, the students decided what they wanted to do with this story after they had completed it.

The scene described in Mrs. Miller's room now occurs more and more in classrooms throughout the country:

- Students read original works of literature.
- Reading and writing activities are developed and used together.
- Personal and creative responses are encouraged and respected.
- Students and teacher work together to formulate an understanding of the book.
- The teacher teaches skills and strategies as needed.
- The teacher strives to foster positive attitudes and maintain a high degree of motivation.

Contrast Mrs. Miller's classroom with the one more commonly seen when the first edition of this text (Cooper, 1986) was written:

- The teacher taught the group a reading skill. Sometimes the skill was modeled using passages of text.
- Students then practiced the skill on a worksheet or in a workbook.
- Students read stories that had been adapted to conform to a particular readability formula.

In this literacy-centered classroom, where children are actively engaged, literacy learning develops in part through different experiences. © *Michael Zide*

▶ Students answered questions about the story on worksheets; then they usually discussed the story.

▶ Students then usually completed more skill activities.

Comparing and contrasting these two classrooms shows how reading instruction is changing. Teachers, reading specialists, and researchers have learned a great deal about how children and young adults learn to read and write, or become literate. Recent research on literacy clearly supports the idea of providing a balanced literacy program that is designed to help all children succeed in developing literacy (Snow, Burns, & Griffin, 1998). This program incorporates the best elements of both holistic instruction and direct instruction.

A major part of this new way of thinking about literacy includes technology. New ways of using computers, exciting software, and the use of the Internet make it possible for you to meet a greater range of students' needs within a balanced literacy program (Grabe & Grabe, 1998). This ensures that chldren of all abilities from a variety of backgrounds will have the best opportunities to become literate. Failure will be prevented for a majority of students.

A Changing View of Reading and Literacy

Since before the turn of the century, educators and psychologists have tried to understand what really happens when an individual learns to read (Huey, 1908, 1968; Robinson, Faraone, Hittleman, & Unruh, 1990; Smith, 1965). Though this interest has intensified in recent years, the process of reading itself has not changed. Two things that have changed are (1) our understanding of what reading is and how it takes place and (2) the literacy demands of society. Today's technological world has brought an escalating need for literate, critical thinkers who can fully participate in society.

A Brief History

Emphasis on Decoding

During the 1960s and 1970s, a number of reading specialists believed that reading was an end product of decoding (Fries, 1962); if students could name the words, comprehension would occur automatically. However, as teachers placed greater emphasis on decoding, they found that many students still did not understand what they read. Comprehension was *not* taking place automatically.

Asking Questions

Educators then began to speculate that perhaps teachers were asking the wrong types of questions. The emphasis in reading instruction shifted, and teachers began asking students a greater variety of questions at levels differing according to some taxonomy, such as the Barrett Taxonomy of Reading Comprehension (Clymer, 1968). Research on the use of questions in classroom practices and in basal readers supported the view that asking questions was just checking comprehension, not teaching it (Durkin, 1978, 1981a). Current thinking supports teachers using questions as prompts to focus students' attention on the important aspects of a text (Beck & McKeown, 1981; Shake & Allington, 1985).

Comprehension "Skills"

During the late 1960s, 1970s, and early 1980s, educators began to believe that the best way to develop reading comprehension was to identify a set of discrete skills called "comprehension skills" (Otto et al., 1977). The focus of reading instruction in many classrooms then became the teaching and practicing of each individual skill, even though previous researchers and educators had questioned the efficacy of these practices (Goodman, 1965).

The research does not clearly support the identification of any set of comprehension skills (Rosenshine, 1980); current research supports the idea that readers need to learn key comprehension strategies as a part of their process of becoming effective readers (see Chapter 8).

A Transactional Approach

During the 1970s and 1980s, researchers in education, psychology, and linguistics began to theorize about how a reader comprehends and then attempted to verify certain aspects of their theories through research (Anderson & Pearson, 1984; Smith, 1971; Spiro, 1979). Rosenblatt was the first researcher to propose that reading is a transaction between the reader and the text; she established the belief that readers have the right to, and do, establish or construct their own meanings (Rosenblatt, 1938/1983, 1978).

The research and theories of the 1970s and 1980s broadened the thinking of many educators and led them to focus on a literacy perspective rather than the isolated elements of reading, writing, speaking, listening, viewing, and thinking. The work of the Russian psychologist Lev Vygotsky (1978) has provided a basis for the concept that children learn by being supported by adults and peers. At the same time, researchers established the idea that children learn language holistically rather than in bits and pieces (Halliday, 1975). Today the work of these researchers and others has led educators to focus on reading in the broad perspective of *literacy learning* (Clay, 1979, 1982, 1985, 1991; Teale & Sulzby, 1986). The result of this period came to be known as *whole language*.

A Balanced Approach

The work with whole language programs during the 1980s and 1990s again revealed that there is no one way to think about literacy learning. Researchers found that it was important to teach certain prerequisite skills at the beginning stages of reading (Adams, 1990). It became clear that a balanced approach was needed, using a combination of direct instruction and authentic reading and writing experiences to teach children to be literate (Snow et al., 1998).

Literacy and Literacy Learning

Literacy is often viewed as the ability to read and write (Teale & Sulzby, 1986). However, researchers have found that literacy involves much more than reading and writing. A classic study found that literacy in the "real world" involves such things as reading signs, advertisements, and bumper stickers; writing letters; reading newspapers and magazines; and giving oral and written messages to others or leaving them for oneself (Heath, 1983). In school-based settings, however, students spend more time on learning isolated reading skills than on learning the types of literacy skills they are likely to use in real life (Guthrie & Greaney, 1991). In fact, researchers have found that potential employers want their employees to have mastered two aspects of literacy often omitted from school curricula: listening and speaking (The Secretary's Commission on Achieving Necessary Skills [SCANS], 1991).

Literacy also involves communicating through technology (Thornburg, 1992). Therefore, expanding our concept of literacy to include technology (computers, CD-ROMs, and the World Wide Web) will influence how we prepare our students for the real world (Association for Supervision and Curriculum Development, 1994). *Given what we have learned, we must view literacy as the ability to communicate in real-world situations, which involves the abilities of individuals to read, write, speak, listen, view, and think.* Viewing is the process whereby one looks critically at some visual information such as a movie, television show, video, and so forth. As one engages in any one of these aspects of literacy, other aspects also come into play.

For example, reading and listening both involve thinking, and responding to something heard involves both thinking and speaking.

When thinking about helping students develop literacy, it is important to remember that reading, writing, speaking, listening, viewing, and thinking do not develop as separate components and should not be taught as separate subjects. All aspects of literacy develop simultaneously and interactively (Freeman & Hatch, 1989; Strickland, 1990). Thus, students develop literacy as they encounter many authentic, or real, literacy experiences in which they are able to approximate the real tasks of literacy (Cambourne, 1988). *Children learn to read, write, speak, listen, view, and think by having real opportunities to read, write, speak, listen, view, and think as opposed to completing contrived exercises that involve marking, circling, and underlining. As they have these real opportunities to develop literacy, children get support (instruction) along the way from more experienced individuals; these individuals may be parents, peers, or teachers.*

For example, the young child who writes a note such as the one in Figure 1.1 is having an authentic, or real, literacy experience. She is learning to form letters and to construct and convey meaning. This child is developing a major understanding about the functions of print (to convey meaning) as well as about the forms or conventions of print (to form letters, to construct sentences). Her attempt to write a note is her approximation, her trial, of a complete note. As she continues to have such experiences, she will get more feedback and her approximations will come closer and closer to a more accepted form of note writing.

Going through approximations such as these is exactly how we all learn anything. Think back to when you learned to ride a bicycle. You had seen other people ride a bike, so you had models to emulate. You probably began by getting on the bike and trying to make the pedals move while someone held on to you or the bike. (This was a part of the scaffold, or support, that children need as they learn. Gradually, the scaffolding is taken away [Au, Mason, & Scheu, 1995].) You knew what real bike riding was supposed to be, but your first few approximations were not perfect. You continued to get feedback from yourself and others each time you tried to ride the bike, and each approximation allowed you to test another hypothesis that you had about bike riding. Thus, your mistakes were essential to your learning. Gradually, over a period of time, your approximations came closer and closer to skillful bike riding until you finally achieved your task and rode off alone!

Literacy learning follows similar patterns: learners go through various approximations as they strive to develop their own literacy (Cambourne, 1988; Wells, 1990). Think about how you became a reader. Someone probably read to you or you saw or heard others read, so you had models of reading. When you found a book or a story that you liked, you began to pretend to read it. As time went on, you gradually began to associate ideas with each page and the print on it. Through instruction and experiences over many years, you became a reader. Your early attempts were not perfect: it was through your partial, or incomplete, approximations and repeated contacts with "real reading" provided through models from adults and peers that you grew into literacy and became a reader. Even before this, you had already developed some of your abilities to listen, speak, and think in this manner. This description of the complex process of literacy learning is oversimplified,

FIGURE 1.1

SAMPLE OF A KINDERGARTNER'S WRITING

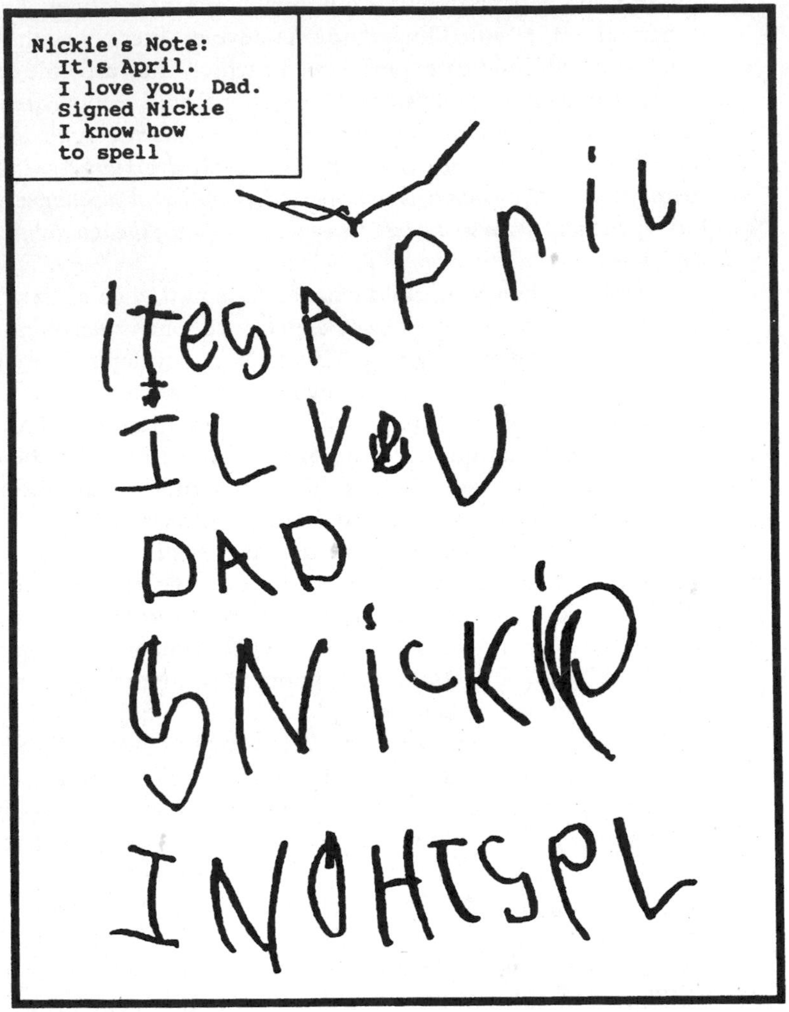

but it illustrates the type of process all learners undergo as they develop their abilities to construct meaning.

These conclusions about how literacy learning takes place have developed over many years of research and study. Research on emergent literacy, language acquisition, schema theory, and phonemic awareness has shed much more light on these ideas.

Emergent Literacy

Emergent literacy is the idea that children grow into reading and writing with no real beginning or ending point, that reading and writing develop concurrently, interrelatedly, and according to no one "right" sequence, or order (Strickland, 1990; Teale & Sulzby, 1986). Instead, learners are always emerging. Moreover, this process begins long before children enter school, through the activities and experiences in their everyday lives and through their interactions with peers and adults (Goodman, 1986; Harste, Woodward, & Burke, 1984; Heath, 1983; Sulzby, 1985). Literacy learning involves all elements of the communication process: reading, writing, speaking, listening, viewing, and thinking. Quite simply, children develop their ability to construct meaning by having meaningful literacy experiences, which might include sharing books or sitting on a grandparent's lap tapping the keys on the computer.

The concept of emergent literacy has not always been the one accepted by schools. Before the 1960s, educators talked about "reading readiness" (which is *not* the view supported in this text). Essentially, the reading readiness concept assumed that all children must master *just* a sequence of skills before they can begin to read; there was no focus on writing.

The concept went virtually unchallenged until the mid-1960s, when Durkin's (1966) classic study, *Children Who Read Early,* showed that it was simply not viable. This study was followed by investigations into language acquisition and the literacy habits of young children (Clay, 1967) that led to the formation of the concept known as *emergent* (emerging) *literacy* (Clay, 1967; Teale & Sulzby, 1986). This new view of literacy has led to many changes in reading and writing instruction.

Language Acquisition

As described so far, the process of acquiring language is continuous and unending; each of us continues to acquire new aspects of language through our interactions and experiences. Therefore, language acquisition is first and foremost a social process (Cook-Gumprez, 1986; Wells, 1990). Taylor and Dorsey-Gaines (1988), in their award-winning book *Growing Up Literate,* report that inner-city families "use literacy for a wide variety of purposes (social, technical, and *aesthetic* purposes), for a wide variety of audiences, and in a wide variety of situations" (p. 202). Thus, all children come to school with a language base, and this base may or may not match the base on which the school is trying to build. Since a strong connection between oral language and reading has been clearly established (Cazden, 1972; Loban, 1963; Menyuk, 1984; Ruddell, 1963; Snow et al., 1998), it is important that schools build literacy experiences around whatever language a child has developed.

There are many theories of language acquisition. *Nativists* believe children acquire language innately without practice or reinforcement (Chomsky, 1965; Lenneberg, 1967; McNeil, 1970). Those who hold the *cognitive development* point of view stress that children acquire language through their various activities (Piaget & Inhelder, 1969). Vygotsky, mentioned earlier, proposes a concept known as a *zone of proximal development,* a range in which a child can perform a task only with the help of a more experienced individual (Vygotsky, 1978).

Halliday (1975) views language acquisition as an active process in which children try out their language and make approximations of real language. We should therefore accept errors during literacy development, because it is through these approximations that children gradually develop their perfected forms of language.

All of these theories contribute to our understanding of how children acquire language. Basically, we know that children acquire language

1. When they have a need that is meaningful and real
2. Through interactions with peers and adults
3. By making approximations of real language
4. At varying rates and in various stages, even though they all go through similar phases of development

This understanding provides a solid basis on which to develop a literacy program that fosters comprehension development. At no time during children's acquisition of oral language do they stop to learn an isolated part or piece of language. From the outset, the process is whole, meaningful, supportive, and continuous.

Prior Knowledge, Schemata, Background, and Comprehension

Another area that has contributed to our increased understanding of literacy learning and reading comprehension is schema and schema theory. Schemata (plural of *schema*) are structures that represent the generic concepts stored in our memory (Rumelhart, 1980). Schema theory explains how these structures are formed and related to one another as we develop knowledge.

Children develop schemata through experiences. If readers have had no experience or limited experience with a given topic, they will have no schemata or insufficient schemata to recall, and comprehension will be limited or impossible. Many studies on comprehension, schemata, and background have shown that prior knowledge greatly influences comprehension (Adams & Bertram, 1980; Durkin, 1981b; Pearson et al., 1979). (Researchers and educators use the terms *prior knowledge* and *background* interchangeably.) Readers' backgrounds seem to have a greater influence on the comprehension of implied or inferred information than on directly stated information, probably because readers understand implied information only when they can relate it to their prior knowledge and experiences.

The process of comprehension depends on the reader's schemata. The more closely those schemata match the schemata intended by the author, the easier it is to comprehend the text. An example will help to illustrate this point.

Example 1.1

Read the following paragraph:

Andrew was having a great time at his birthday party. He was playing games and opening presents. When it came time to blow out the candles on the cake, he blew and blew but they would not go out. As soon as he thought he had blown out the candles, they would light up again.

To comprehend this paragraph, you must have a schema about birthday parties. However, if that schema does not include anything about trick candles, you will not understand what has happened to Andrew. From the information in the paragraph, you can tell that Andrew was having a birthday party, and your schema for birthday parties helps you understand most of what was taking place at the party. However, to understand what type of candles were on Andrew's cake, you must rely even more heavily on your schema because the text does not tell you what kind of candles they were. Therefore, to fully comprehend this paragraph, you have to use both your schema and clues from the text.

Readers use both their schemata and clues from the text in varying amounts as they comprehend (Spiro, 1979). In fact, effective comprehenders use an *interactive* process, both relying heavily on their schemata and obtaining information from the text. Even though these two processes appear to occur simultaneously, it is the reader's schemata that provide the structure needed to associate meaning with text (Anderson & Pearson, 1984).

In summary, schemata are the categories of knowledge (concepts, information, ideas) that form in readers' minds through real or vicarious experiences. As reading comprehension occurs, readers relate the ideas from the text to their acquired or prior knowledge—their schemata. If they do not already have schemata for a particular topic or concept, they may form a new schema for it if enough information is provided. As they construct new knowledge by relating new information to already stored information, their schemata continuously expand. Schema theory is discussed further in Chapter 3.

Phonemic Awareness

Phonemic awareness is the knowledge that words are comprised of sounds. Research in this area has contributed greatly to our understanding of beginning literacy development (Adams, 1990; Snow et al., 1998). There is a need for systematic, explicit instruction in phonemic awareness as a part of beginning balanced literacy instruction. A more detailed discussion of this aspect of literacy development is given in Chapter 4.

A Current View of Comprehension

In light of what we have learned over the past several decades, we can now formulate a better definition of reading comprehension. *Comprehension is a strategic process by which readers construct or assign meaning to a text by using the clues in the text and their own prior knowledge.* In the broad sense this is also a definition of reading, since reading is comprehending, or constructing meaning. This meaning comes primarily from our own existing knowledge.

Two major perspectives should help us understand the process of comprehension more clearly and help us formulate appropriate learning experiences that foster comprehension growth: comprehension as constructing meaning and comprehension as a strategic process.

Comprehension as Constructing Meaning

Comprehension is a process by which the reader constructs or assigns meaning by interacting with the text (Anderson & Pearson, 1984). Reading and writing are both constructive processes that are mutually supportive (Pearson & Tierney, 1984; Tierney & Shanahan, 1991).

The understanding that readers achieve during reading comes from their prior knowledge, experiences that are triggered as they identify the author's words, sentences, and paragraphs. Although readers need not be able to orally decode every word on a page, they must be able to use the variety of cues provided in printed text to decode words. The interaction, or transaction, between the reader and the text is the foundation of comprehension (Rosenblatt, 1938/1983). In the process of comprehending, readers relate the new information presented by the author to old information stored in their minds (schemata). Let's consider an example.

Example 1.2

> Read the following sentence:
>
> The lazy, old cat spent his whole day curled up asleep by the fireplace.

What did you think about when you read this sentence? You probably had no difficulty comprehending it. Maybe you immediately pictured in your mind an old cat you had seen, known, or heard about. Using your schemata about cats, you may have thought of all the qualities and characteristics of this cat and could picture it asleep by the warm fire. Although the writer of this sentence intended to convey a certain meaning to you, the reader, the exact meaning you constructed related to the knowledge, information, feelings, and attitudes about cats that you have in your mind. You constructed your meaning from within your experiences (Pearson & Tierney, 1984). It is this interaction between the reader and the text that is the process of comprehending. As Anderson and Pearson (1984) note, "To say that one has comprehended a text is to say that she has found a mental 'home' for the information in the text, or else that she has modified an existing mental home in order to accommodate that new information" (p. 255).

To comprehend the written word, readers must be able to (1) understand how the author has structured or organized the ideas and information presented in the text and (2) relate the ideas and information from the text to ideas or information stored in their minds (schemata). That is exactly what you did as you read the sentence about the cat. *The meaning the reader constructs or assigns does not come from the printed page; it comes from the reader's own experiences that are triggered or activated by the ideas the author presents.*

Of course, readers are usually presented with more material to read than a single sentence. As they proceed through the text, they gain additional information, which in turn activates other ideas from their schemata and helps them construct further meaning. An example will help to illustrate how this process works.

*Example
1.3*

> Read the following two sentences:
>
> I ran quickly through the tunnel trying to escape my captors. As I rounded a turn, the ground seemed to disappear beneath me.

What did you think of as you read these two sentences? You probably gained some idea that the paragraph is about someone who is in trouble. You probably pictured a person running through a tunnel. At this point, you can't be sure what the writer means by the ground disappearing. You have constructed your meaning for the two sentences, but your understanding seems incomplete.

Now read the complete paragraph to see what happens to the meaning you constructed.

*Example
1.4*

> I ran quickly through the tunnel trying to escape my captors. As I rounded a turn, the ground seemed to disappear beneath me. I seemed to fall for hours. Just as I saw the ground approaching, a voice called, "Wake up! It's time for breakfast."

After reading the complete paragraph, your understanding of what is happening has changed because new information from the author has helped you construct a different meaning.

To summarize, as readers gather additional information from the text, they relate that information to the information stored in their memory and in this way construct meaning. No matter how long or short the text, the process occurs in the same manner.

Comprehension as a Strategic Process

Comprehension can also be viewed as a strategic process in which readers adjust their reading to suit their purpose and the type of text they are reading. (Anderson, Hiebert, Scott, & Wilkinson, 1985). Both processes, constructing meaning and strategic adjustment, operate simultaneously. Strategic readers are also able to monitor their thinking while reading. Each time you read, you have a purpose. If you are reading for fun and enjoyment, you will read differently than if you are reading to study for a test or to follow the directions for putting a toy together. Strategic readers are also able to adjust their reading to the type of text at hand. The book *Inspirations: Stories About Women Artists* (Sills, 1989), which presents factual accounts, is likely to be approached differently than *Ronald Morgan Goes to Bat* (Giff, 1988), a humorous story about a young boy learning to play baseball.

Part of this process of adjustment is understanding the organization of the text, or what is known as *text structure*. There are two basic types of text structure: narrative and expository. *Narrative text* tells a story and is the type usually found in short stories and novels. *Expository text* provides information and facts and is the type usually found in textbooks, informational books, and directions or instructions for doing something (often referred to as *procedural text*). Text structure is discussed more fully in Chapter 3.

Teachers have known for years that students do not and should not read science material in the same way they read a story. Narrative and expository writings are organized differently, each with their own particular vocabularies and concepts. Thus, readers must use their comprehension processes differently when reading these different types of text. Indeed, evidence shows that teaching students strategies for focusing on text structure will enhance their comprehension (Beach & Appleman, 1984; Taylor & Beach, 1984).

Strategic readers are also able to use their metacognitive processes while reading. *Metacognition*, which refers to the knowledge and control students have over their own thinking and learning activities (Brown, 1980), appears to involve two basic components (Baker & Brown, 1984a):

1. Awareness of the processes and skills needed to complete a task successfully
2. The ability to tell whether one is performing a task correctly and to make corrections during the task if needed, a process termed *cognitive monitoring* or *comprehension monitoring*

Both aspects of metacognition play an important role in reading comprehension. Helping readers learn to become aware of and develop their metacognitive processes is an important part of helping them learn to construct meaning (Mier, 1984; Pearson & Dole, 1987; Schmitt, 1990).

Comprehension and Decoding

Effective comprehenders are able to identify words automatically (Adams, 1990; Perfetti, 1985); however, they do not have to be able to identify every word or know the meaning of every word in a text to understand it. In summarizing the research on how many unknown words a student can handle in a text, Nagy (1988) points out that readers beyond the beginning stages of reading may be able to "tolerate text in which as many as 15 percent of the words are not fully known." He goes on to conclude that "students do not have to know *all* of the words in a text to read it with a high level of comprehension" (p. 29).

Traditionally, the term *decoding* has been used to describe the process of identifying words without emphasizing their meanings. Decoding, however, is the ability to get the intended meaning from a printed message by analyzing the graphic symbols. Since identifying words is a means to this end, learning any system of identification (context, phonics, structural analysis) helps in constructing meaning. In other words, the goal of any literacy experience is always the construction of meaning.

Throughout the history of education, educators have debated the role of word identification, and especially phonics, in reading instruction (Chall, 1967, 1983; Flesch, 1955, 1981). This debate has ranged from political controversy to outright rage. A recent attempt to bring clarity and sanity to the controversy has been Adams's book *Beginning to Read: Thinking and Learning About Print* (1990), a scholarly, technical work that has been summarized into a shorter piece by Stahl, Osborn, and Lehr (1990). But even this work has met with controversy (Weaver, 1990b).

The collective body of research over the past 30 years leads to the conclusion that effective readers should be *explicitly taught* letter-sound associations (phonics) as a significant part of their beginning reading program (Adams, 1990; Anderson et al., 1985; Bond & Dykstra, 1967; Chall, 1967, 1983; Snow et al., 1998). This instruction in phonics must be combined with many meaningful text experiences.

The meaningful texts for early listening and reading experiences should be highly predictable in terms of rhyme and sound patterns and plot. These texts might include such books as *Sheep in a Jeep* (Shaw, 1986), *The Three Billy Goats Gruff* (Galdone, 1973), or *There's a Wocket in My Pocket* (Seuss, 1974). Through repeated read-alouds, the sound elements are modeled for children. Children develop their abilities to use various decoding strategies, including phonics, through explicit direct instruction in phonics plus meaningful reading and writing experiences. Chapter 4 discusses this area in more detail.

The Role of Different Types of Text in Developing Literacy

Since literacy is viewed broadly as communicating in "real-world" situations (see page 6), literature must also be viewed in a broad context. Throughout this text, all discussions about literature refer to stories, informational texts, magazines, newspapers, brochures, maps, stories on CD-ROMs, Web sites, and any other materials that can be read. The texts of "real" or "authentic" literature have not been rewritten to make them conform to some readability procedure or any other guidelines to control their difficulty. The language is the original language of the author.

A second type of text is needed to help beginning readers develop independence in reading. This type of text is known as *decodable text,* text that has been written to provide students practice with the phonics skills and high-frequency words they have been taught. These short books give students immediate practice and application of what they have learned. (See Chapter 4 for a complete discussion of decodable texts.)

As soon as readers have developed independence in decoding, they should shift from reading decodable texts to reading authentic literature. Even at the beginning stages of learning to read when students are reading created, decodable texts, they should also experience real literature through teacher read-alouds. There are three reasons for using real literature in the literacy program:

1. Real literature is motivating, captivating, and engaging for students of all ages.
2. Real literature provides learners with a natural base for developing and expanding their language.
3. Real literature is often easier to understand than text that has been developed to conform to grade-level standards.

Real Literature Motivates, Captivates, and Engages

A major part of helping children develop their ability to construct meaning is to keep them motivated and excited about learning. The use of real literature has that power. For example, the young preschooler finds a favorite book and asks someone to read it again and again. Whether the book is Dr. Seuss's *Green Eggs and Ham* (1960) or Margaret Wise Brown's *Goodnight Moon* (1947), that child is motivated, captivated, and engaged in learning and the love of literature. This young child is experiencing a book that has natural language and is not written to conform to given grade-level standards. In reality, literature has no grade level. It is, *in part,* how literature is approached that makes it easy or difficult for students to read and experience it and to construct meaning.

This same motivation can be created in classrooms by placing real literature at the core of literacy learning. Studies have shown that in classrooms that use real literature, children are motivated to read stories again and again and to read them with "passionate attention" (Sanders, 1987). All learners need this type of engagement to help them construct meaning. It might be created by using Julie Brinckloe's *Fireflies!* (1985), Betsy Byars's *The Summer of the Swans* (1970), or exciting magazines such as *Ranger Rick* (National Wildlife Federation), *National Geographic World* (The National Geographic Society), or *American Girl* (Pleasant Company Publications). Louise Rosenblatt (1938/1983) concludes,

> When there is active participation in literature—the reader living through, reflecting on, and criticizing his own responses to text—there will be many kinds of benefits. We can call this "growth in ability to share discriminatingly in the possibilities of language as it is used in literature." But this means also the development of the imagination: the ability to escape from the limitations of time, place and environment, the capacity to envisage alternatives in ways of life and in moral and social choices, the sensitivity to thought and feeling and needs of other personalities. (pp. 290–291)

Real Literature Provides Natural Language

Real literature also provides children with models of natural language that continually help them develop and expand their own language structures (Sawyer, 1987). This expansion is the foundation for all meaning construction. Real literature provides opportunities to experience many language structures and an ever-increasing vocabulary. The beauty of language expressed in words and through the art of magnificent illustrations gives students the basis for expanding their language, their experiences, and their schemata. Texts that have been created to conform to grade-level standards are unable to accomplish this goal in the same way (Huck, 1991).

Real Literature Is Easy to Understand

Many children come to school with a sense of story (Applebee, 1978), especially if they have been read to regularly. They understand the predictability and patterns in texts. Therefore, it seems only logical that school experiences should begin by building on this knowledge. The use of real literature as a basis for literacy learning will capitalize on what most students already know when they come to school and will expand those existing structures. Even beginning readers, while they are developing their abilities of decoding by reading controlled texts, develop comprehension skills and strategies through listening to and/or shared reading of such books as *Skip to My Lou* (Westcott, 1989) or *My Brown Bear Barney* (Butler, 1988). (See Chapter 4 for more discussion of beginning readers and writers.)

Referring to some published materials designed for use with beginning readers, *Becoming a Nation of Readers* notes, "Many stories for the early grades do not have a predictable structure. In fact many of these selections do not actually tell a story" (Anderson et al., 1985, p. 66). Rewritten texts often confuse children and prevent them from understanding or enjoying the stories (Routman, 1988). In fact, research has shown that when texts are rewritten to conform to grade-level standards or a readability formula, they are frequently more difficult for students to read (Simons & Ammon, 1989).

In summary, real literature is critical to successfully developing students' ability to construct meaning. However, in the beginning stages of literacy development, it must be accompanied by *decodable texts* for the immediate practice and application of the decoding skills students are learning.

Principles for Guiding Literacy Learning

Constructing meaning is the ultimate goal of all literacy instruction. This chapter has developed a basic point of view about reading and literacy learning that results in five principles for guiding literacy development (see Table 1.1):

1. *Reading, writing, speaking, listening, viewing, and thinking develop simultaneously as learners grow into literacy.* The research on literacy learning, emergent literacy, and language acquisition clearly shows that all aspects of the language arts develop together as learners become literate. Therefore, the major focus of instruction should be developing activities that promote the authentic use of reading, writing, speaking, listening, viewing, and thinking using real literature as the basis for learning. These are the types of activities that will promote students' abilities to construct meaning.

2. *Individuals develop literacy by having real literacy experiences combined with direct instruction of needed strategies and skills.* No evidence supports the idea that students develop literacy by being taught only discrete skills. Readers and writers become readers and writers by reading and writing; individuals become listeners by listening. As students have these real literacy experiences, they are supported by more experienced individuals such as parents, peers, or teachers; in school, this support takes on the many forms of instruction (see Chapter 2).

3. *Prior knowledge and background are major elements in one's ability to develop literacy and construct meaning.* The theory and research about prior knowledge, schemata, and background knowledge clearly support the principle that background influences the ability to construct meaning. The literacy program must incorporate instructional procedures that help learners activate, or develop and relate, that background to what they read as well as what they write.

4. *A variety of types of materials are needed to help all students effectively develop literacy.* These materials should include such things as real literature, decodable texts, CD-ROMs, and computer software. The effective use of the materials within the framework of approachable instruction is critical to the success of every student.

5. *Comprehension is the process of constructing meaning by relating ideas from a text to one's prior knowledge and background.* Helping learners construct meaning

TABLE 1.1 \ PRINCIPLES FOR GUIDING LITERACY DEVELOPMENT

1. Reading, writing, speaking, listening, viewing, and thinking develop simultaneously as learners grow into literacy.
2. Individuals develop literacy by having real literacy experiences combined with direct instruction of needed strategies and skills.
3. Prior knowledge and background are major elements in one's ability to develop literacy and construct meaning.
4. A variety of types of materials are needed to help all students effectively develop literacy.
5. Comprehension is the process of constructing meaning by relating ideas from a text to one's prior knowledge and background.

involves helping them to focus on the relevant features of a text and to relate those features to their prior experiences. This includes using real literature, which provides students with models of different types of text. Since constructing meaning is a personal process, each reader will develop his or her own meanings from any text that is read.

These five principles form the basis for all of the ideas for developing literacy that are presented in this text. Teachers who use these ideas to guide their thinking about literacy development will be effective teachers in the schools of the future.

A Few Words About Technology

As you are no doubt aware, technological advances are changing and will continue to change our understanding of literacy development. As yet, however, no large body of research exists to guide us through the integration of technology and literacy. That research is emerging, and in time we will be much better informed about how children and adults develop literacy through electronic reading and writing. We will also know more about how classrooms will change. Already we know that electronic and printed texts are different. Just how different they are we shall discover as we explore and use the new technologies (at the end of this chapter, you'll find readings and Web site addresses of organizations and companies with products and resources you may wish to explore). What we also know now is that in the midst of this transforming revolution, the five principles above remain timely, relevant, and flexible.

Focus of This Text

Literacy: Helping Children Construct Meaning is written for preservice and inservice classroom teachers and literacy specialists. Two major themes are developed throughout this text:

1. Understanding the process of constructing meaning from a literacy perspective
2. Creating interactive, child-centered classrooms that facilitate the construction of meaning from a balanced literacy perspective

The remaining chapters in this book will help you further develop the knowledge and skills needed to support students in developing literacy:

▶ Chapter 2 develops the concept of a balanced literacy program that focuses on meaningful blocks of instruction.

▶ Chapter 3 discusses the role of prior knowledge and background and presents strategies and procedures for helping students become independent in activating their prior knowledge for any literacy experience.

▶ Chapter 4 shows how the balanced beginning literacy program needs to have a slightly different focus from the program for students beyond the beginning stages of literacy.

▶ Chapter 5 examines the role of vocabulary and decoding in the construction of meaning beyond the beginning literacy stage.

▶ Chapter 6 focuses on how to use responding to literature as part of helping students develop their ability to construct meaning.

▶ Chapter 7 emphasizes the role of writing as it relates to teaching spelling and grammar.

▶ Chapter 8 presents a detailed discussion of modeling.

▶ Chapter 9 pulls together many of the concepts developed in the first eight chapters and relates them to the construction of meaning across the curriculum.

▶ Chapter 10 provides guidance in organizing and managing the balanced literacy classroom.

▶ Chapter 11 presents ideas for dealing with assessment in the classroom literacy program.

Summary

Reading instruction is changing. More and more teachers are providing a balanced approach to instruction that includes a combination of authentic experiences, direct instruction, and the use of technology.

Educators now view reading as a process of constructing meaning by interacting with a text. The changes taking place in classrooms and in our thinking about reading, have resulted from four major areas of study and research on literacy and literacy learning: emergent literacy, language acquisition, prior knowledge, and decoding.

Reading is inseparable from the broad concept of literacy. Literacy includes all aspects of communicating in real-world situations—reading, writing, speaking, listening, viewing, and thinking—which develop concurrently and interrelatedly as children grow into literacy. Therefore, constructing meaning must be viewed according to this broader perspective of literacy learning.

Individuals become literate by having real literacy experiences and receiving instruction along the way. Through such experiences children develop their literacy abilities, first approximating the real tasks they are trying to achieve.

Students' schemata are the basic categories of knowledge stored in their minds. These schemata, which are a part of the student's prior knowledge, develop and change as a result of experiences. Schemata form the basis on which construction of meaning takes place.

As a result of current research, reading is now seen as a strategic process of constructing meaning. While effective readers must be able to identify words, the end result of word identification is constructing meaning. It is not necessary for a reader to pronounce or know the meaning of every word to read with a high degree of comprehension.

Literature encompasses stories, informational texts, and any other materials that can be read. The use of a variety of types of literature is important in developing students' literacy and their ability to construct meaning.

Five basic principles should guide you as you support children in developing literacy:

1. Reading, writing, speaking, listening, viewing, and thinking develop simultaneously as learners grow into literacy.
2. Individuals develop literacy by having real literacy experiences combined with direct instruction of needed strategies and skills.
3. Prior knowledge and background are major elements in one's ability to develop literacy and construct meaning.
4. A variety of types of materials are needed to help all students effectively develop literacy.
5. Comprehension is the process of constructing meaning by relating ideas from a text to one's prior knowledge and background.

Literature

Brinckloe, J. (1985). *Fireflies!* New York: Macmillan.

Brown, M. W. (1947). *Goodnight moon.* New York: Harper.

Butler, D. (1988). *My brown bear Barney.* Auckland, New Zealand: Reed Methuen.

Byars, B. (1970). *The summer of the swans.* New York: Viking Penguin.

Galdone, P. (1973). *The three billy goats gruff.* New York: Clarion.

Giff, P. R. (1988). *Ronald Morgan goes to bat.* New York: Viking Kestrel.

McKissack, P. C. (1986). *Flossie and the fox.* New York: Dial Books.

The National Geographic Society. *National Geographic World,* published monthly.

National Wildlife Federation. *Ranger Rick,* published monthly.

Pleasant Company Publications. *American Girl,* published bimonthly.

Seuss (1960). *Green eggs and ham.* New York: Beginner Books, Random House.

Seuss (1974). *There's a wocket in my pocket.* New York: Random House.

Shaw, N. (1986). *Sheep in a jeep.* Boston: Houghton Mifflin.

Sills, L. (1989). *Inspirations: Stories about women artists.* Niles, IL: Albert Whitman.

Westcott, N. B. (1989). *Skip to my Lou.* Boston: Little, Brown.

For Additional Reading

Morrow, L. M. (1989). *Literacy development in the early years: Helping children read and write.* Englewood Cliffs, NJ: Prentice-Hall.

Strickland, D. S., & Morrow, L. M. (Eds.). (1989). *Emerging literacy: Young children learn to read and write.* Newark, DE: International Reading Association.

For Exploration: Electronic Products and Resources

Helping all children succeed in developing literacy has always required that teachers spend time keeping up with new materials, new practices, and new research. The following Web sites will help you keep up with and learn about changes in a variety of areas of educational interest, especially technology.

Educational Resources Information Center

The Educational Resources Information Center (ERIC) is a national information network of education information from all sources. The database and ERIC document collections are housed in about 3,000 locations worldwide, including most major public and university library systems. ERIC offers a variety of publications and AskERIC, an electronic question-answering service for teachers. **www.ed.gov/EdRes/EdFed/ERIC.html**

International Reading Association

The International Reading Association (IRA) provides resources for teachers, reading specialists, tutors, and others concerned about literacy. Topics range from performance-based assessment to classroom discussion strategies, integrated instruction, motivation for reading, and teaching English as a Second Language. Visit the IRA's Web site to learn about books, journals, videos, and multimedia products about reading comprehension and literacy. You may be particularly interested in the IRA's five professional journals:

- *The Reading Teacher*—for preschool, primary, and elementary teachers
- *Journal of Adolescent & Adult Literacy*—for teachers of middle school, high school, and adult learners
- *Reading Research Quarterly*—a journal of reading research
- *Lectura y vida*—Spanish language journal for all teaching levels
- *Reading Online*—an electronic journal using the Web to explore research, instruction, and communication

www.ira.org

International Society for Technology in Education

The International Society for Technology in Education (ISTE) helps K–12 teachers and administrators share effective methods for enhancing student learning through the use of new classroom technologies. The Web site offers information about publications as well as conferences and workshops. **www.iste.org**

Learning Technology Center at Peabody College

The Learning Technology Center (LTC) at Vanderbilt University is a collaborative, multidisciplinary group of approximately 70 researchers, designers, and educators internationally known for their work on technology in education. Members of the LTC are currently working on a variety of projects in the areas of mathematics, science, social studies, and literacy. All LTC projects are research-based and all products undergo extensive evaluation before being implemented. Explore the Young Children's Literacy Project and the Middle School Literacy Project on their Web site.

peabody.vanderbilt.edu/ltc/general/

National Council of Teachers of English

The National Council of Teachers of English (NCTE) is devoted to improving the teaching of English and the language arts at all levels. NCTE publishes a member newspaper, three monthly journals, and ten quarterlies. It also publishes position papers, teaching ideas, and other documents on professional concerns such as professional standards. Explore the Web site to learn more. The following journals may be of particular interest to you.

- *Language Arts*—for elementary teachers and teacher educators
- *Primary Voices K–6*—a journal written by different teams of elementary educators
- *School Talk*—a newsletter for classroom teachers
- *Voices from the Middle*—for middle school teachers

www.ncte.org

National Educational Computing Association

The National Educational Computing Association (NECA) sponsors The National Educational Computing Conference (NECC). It provides education professionals with an annual forum to learn, exchange, and survey changes in education technology. Through workshops, lecture-format and interactive "short" sessions, discussions with key industry speakers, and the largest vendor exhibition of its kind, participants have the unique opportunity to discover and share what they need to develop the appropriate use of technology in their classrooms, districts, and universities.

www.neccsite.org

U.S. Department of Education

The U.S. Department of Education's Web site features current news and events, publications and products, technology, and links to a variety of other online educational resources.

www.ed.gov/

Developing a Balanced Literacy Program

2

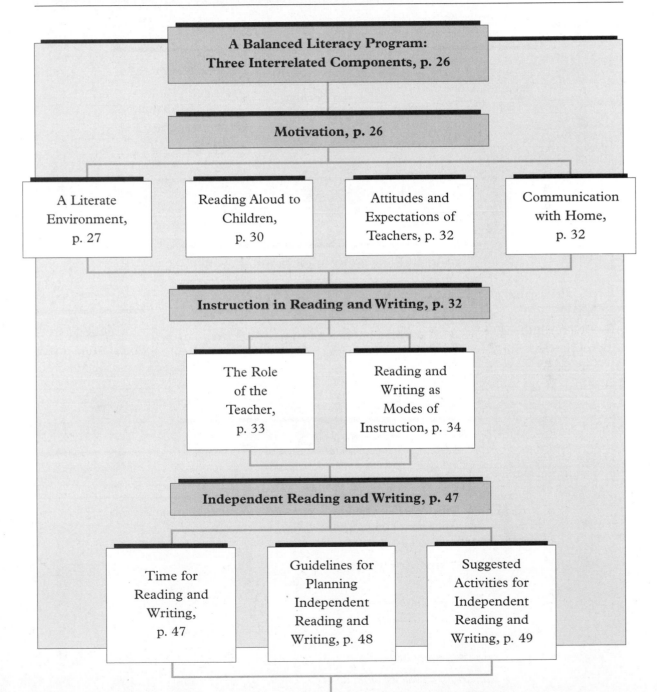

A Balanced Literacy Program: Three Interrelated Components, p. 26

Motivation, p. 26

A Literate Environment, p. 27

Reading Aloud to Children, p. 30

Attitudes and Expectations of Teachers, p. 32

Communication with Home, p. 32

Instruction in Reading and Writing, p. 32

The Role of the Teacher, p. 33

Reading and Writing as Modes of Instruction, p. 34

Independent Reading and Writing, p. 47

Time for Reading and Writing, p. 47

Guidelines for Planning Independent Reading and Writing, p. 48

Suggested Activities for Independent Reading and Writing, p. 49

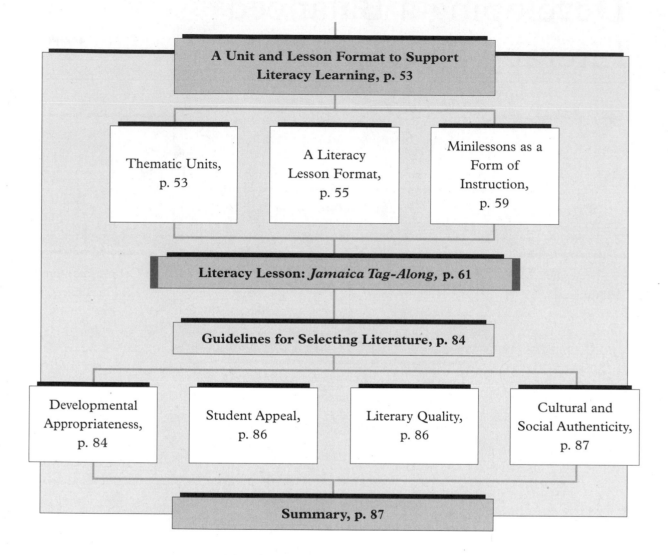

A Unit and Lesson Format to Support Literacy Learning, p. 53

Thematic Units, p. 53

A Literacy Lesson Format, p. 55

Minilessons as a Form of Instruction, p. 59

Literacy Lesson: *Jamaica Tag-Along*, p. 61

Guidelines for Selecting Literature, p. 84

Developmental Appropriateness, p. 84

Student Appeal, p. 86

Literary Quality, p. 86

Cultural and Social Authenticity, p. 87

Summary, p. 87

*L*et's begin by looking at how Graeme Base invites readers into his magnificent mystery, The Eleventh Hour *(Base, 1988)*:

A book is read, a story ends, a telling tale is told.

But who can say what mysteries a single page may hold?

A maze of hidden codes and clues, a clock at every turn,

And only time will tell what other secrets you may learn . . .

In The Eleventh Hour, *the story of Horace's eleventh birthday party, someone has stolen the feast that Horace had prepared for his guests. As the celebration draws to a close, the guests are surprised to discover that even though the feast has been stolen, Horace has hidden the birthday cake in another place. However, the mystery is not solved. The book concludes:*

*Then, as they sat and ate their lunch,
there came one last surprise,*

*When Horace asked for everyone
to kindly close their eyes.*

*And there it was—the Birthday Cake!
The Guests all clapped and cheered.*

*He'd kept it in the kitchen, and it
hadn't disappeared!*

*And so they picnicked on the lawn
until the evening fell,*

*And everyone left satisfied—the
day had finished well.*

*But in the end, although the thief
was someone they all knew,*

*They never found out who it was
that stole the feast—can you?**

BEAUTIFUL BOOKS SUCH as *The Eleventh Hour* and stories presented on CD-ROMs (electronic books) are the basis for successful literacy learning. By reading and responding to such books, children continue their literacy growth (Huck, 1989). However, simply exposing students to wonderful books will not in and of itself make them better readers and writers. As Wells (1990) says, "Children learn most effectively through participation in meaningful, joint activities in which their performance is assisted and guided by a more competent member of the culture" (p. 15). To this end, Chapter 2 will help you develop

1. A clear concept of a *literacy program*
2. A flexible thematic unit plan and *literacy lesson format* supported by minilessons that will work throughout the literacy program

Both formats, the literacy program and the literacy lesson supported with minilessons, will help you see the importance of long-range planning and understand how to achieve the balance in your classroom that will help all students develop literacy. It is important that we understand the necessity of a balanced program in which students have opportunities for both discovery and direct instruction. This is especially important as we create programs for children from diverse cultural back-grounds (Delpit, 1995).

◼ A Balanced Literacy Program:
Three Interrelated Components

Teachers should develop a concept of a literacy program and know how the components of this program work together. In recent years, many teachers have thought of their published textbooks or basal readers as their reading program (Winograd, Wixson, & Lipson, 1989). But *published textbooks do not constitute a program,* even though some of them may be appropriate resources. What, then, is a literacy program?

A program is a plan for getting something done. *A literacy program, therefore, is a plan for supporting children as they develop their ability to read, write, speak, listen, view, and think or grow into literacy.* Figure 2.1 shows the three interrelated components of a literacy program for the classroom and/or school:

1. Motivation (see page 26)
2. Instruction in reading and writing (see page 32)
3. Independent reading and writing (see page 47)

These three components continually interact with one another in the dynamic, literacy-centered classroom. When one observes such a classroom, one will not (and should not) see them as isolated elements, even though their presence will be evident as the children engage in learning to read and write. Chapters 2 and 10 present models to help you organize and manage a balanced literacy program for beginning readers and writers and beyond.

◼ Motivation

Motivation, the act of providing an incentive or a reason for doing something, is the key to learning—or doing anything—successfully. When individuals are highly motivated and their experiences are meaningful and purposeful for them, they learn more readily (Guthrie & Wigfield, 1997).

Sometimes motivation comes from within students; at other times it is fostered by the teacher, other students, or experiences. Motivation is *not a single activity* that a teacher conducts; it involves a complex set of ongoing attitudes and activities that occur in the classroom environment and lead to the creation of a community of learners, including the teacher, who are excited about all aspects of literacy and *want* to learn.

Within this environment, students take ownership for their learning: that is, they come to believe they have the right to choose what they want to learn and to manage that learning in cooperation with their peers and teacher. In the literacy program, motivation is crucial to creating learning experiences that promote positive attitudes about reading and writing and literacy in general and sustain keen interest and enthusiasm. Motivation has four important aspects: (1) a literate environment, (2) reading aloud to children, (3) attitudes and expectations of teachers, and (4) communication with parents and other caregivers.

FIGURE 2.1

A LITERACY PROGRAM

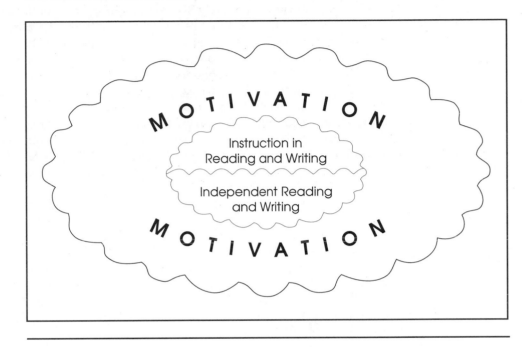

A Literate Environment

A teacher begins to build motivation by creating a literate classroom environment rich in language and print. Such an environment stimulates authentic learning and promotes the concept of the class as a community of people who are learning together. This type of environment, which is basic to every classroom at every grade level, provides part of the motivation needed to encourage all learners to want to construct meaning.

The literate environment should include a variety of areas or centers, each with a specific focus. The contents, organization, and arrangement of these areas will vary from classroom to classroom and from grade level to grade level. *It is most important to place these special areas where they will be readily accessible to the children.* Often this should be in the center of the room, but in many classrooms space is at a premium and this will not be possible. Therefore, you will need to think about how to arrange these special areas to make the best use of your available space. Limited space need not be a deterrent to creating a literate environment.

The areas or centers in the classroom should include the following: (1) a library area, (2) a writing and publishing area, (3) a listening, speaking, and viewing area, (4) a sharing area, (5) a creative arts area, (6) a group meeting area, and (7) a display area.

Library Area

The major purpose of the library area is to promote and support independent reading (see page 47). It should include many books of varying levels and interests, books on tapes, books on CD-ROMs, magazines, newspapers, brochures, and posters, all organized and displayed attractively. To promote the concept of the children as both readers and writers, this area should also include books that have been "published" by the students themselves (see Chapter 7 for a discussion of publishing).

Change or add to the collection of books in the library area frequently. Books may be borrowed from the school library, local library, or bookmobile; brought in by the children; or donated by parents or community groups.

The library area should have some appropriate seating, such as an old rocker, beanbag chairs, a bathtub with pillows, or tables and chairs. There should also be a bulletin board where you might display book jackets or children might display an advertisement for their favorite book. For example, a child who has just finished reading *El Chino* (Say, 1990), a book about the first Chinese bullfighter, might want to make a poster to advertise and sell the book to other children.

If your school has a central library staffed with a librarian, media specialist, or some other type of support person, you will want to work with this person as you create your classroom library area. It is important to view the school library as an extension of the classroom library, since both it and the librarian are valuable resources for your program. For example, the librarian can help you select books (see page 84) and plan units, and the school library should become a place where students can come and go freely to select books and other resources.

Writing and Publishing Area

The writing and publishing area is the place where you promote writing and display some of the children's writing. Furnish it with tables and chairs and some of the tools for writing, including paper (unlined for beginners), pencils, markers, crayons, scissors, and tape. If possible, include an old typewriter or, even better, a computer with the appropriate word-processing program for your grade level. You can locate popular software programs by attending conferences and conventions, and by browsing through magazines and Web sites for educators (Grabe & Grabe, 1998).

You can learn about new software from magazines such as *Electronic Learning* (902 Sylvan Avenue, Englewood Cliffs, NJ 07632) and *Learning and Leading with Technology* (formerly *The Computing Teacher,* International Society for Technology in Education, 1787 Agate Street, Eugene, OR 97403). For a detailed discussion of the use of word processing in writing and other topics about educational technology, see Grabe and Grabe (1998) in the For Additional Reading section at the end of the chapter.

The writing area should also have a place where each child can store writing ideas and products. This might be an individual file folder or some type of box for each child.

To help children publish their books, you should include in this area materials for making book jackets, such as old wallpaper, cardboard, construction paper, yarn, and brads. For more discussion of writing and the use of the writing area, see Chapter 7.

Listening, Speaking, and Viewing Area

This area should contain a listening post with headphones, a tape recorder, and/or a compact disc player. There should be tapes of books and stories to which students can listen, as well as blank tapes for students to record their own stories. For viewing, the area needs personal filmstrip viewers. Many schools now have video players and recorders, making it possible to use the educational videos that are becoming available. Some schools have computers with CD-ROM drives that allow students to practice literacy skills with electronic books and a wide variety of instructional technology.

Sharing Area

An important part of learning to construct meaning is sharing what you have read or written and approximating authentic reading and writing experiences (Holdaway, 1979). For this reason, children need a place to get together to share what they are reading and writing. This area should include tables and chairs or other comfortable seating and some places for students to display some of the products they have developed. The author's chair (see page 50) might be kept in this area or in part of the library or writing area.

Creative Arts Area

Drama, art, and music are important to children as they respond to their reading and writing and share it with others. Therefore, there should be some area that includes puppets and items students can use for costumes and props for giving plays, retelling stories, or giving reader theater performances. (For a discussion of the readers theater, see Chapter 6 and the For Additional Reading section at the conclusion of this chapter.)

A portion of this area might have materials for painting, drawing, paper sculpture, or other art activities. If space is available, develop a separate area for art. Make available some simple musical instruments, such as a recorder, autoharp, or xylophone. Using music with pieces of literature such as *Ben's Trumpet* (Isadora, 1979) or *Song and Dance Man* (Ackerman, 1988) is appropriate at many different grade levels (Lamme, 1990). A teacher does not have to be musically inclined to help children carry out many of these activities.

Group Meeting Area

You will also need an area where you can meet with small groups for discussions and instruction. This area might contain a chalkboard, an overhead projector, and other materials you will need for teaching, such as books and charts.

Display Area

Displays of items related to topics of study, art pieces, photographs, and posters all help to motivate students and expand their backgrounds. The display area should be changed frequently and include material brought in by students. For example, a class reading or listening to *Where the Red Fern Grows* (Rawls, 1961) might create a display of photographs of pets that have meant a great deal to the children, as Old Dan and Little Ann meant to Billy.

A literate environment not only is motivating but is also a vital part of developing oral language, expanding prior knowledge, and creating an atmosphere that promotes opportunities for authentic reading and writing experiences that children are able to share with all members of the classroom community. Figure 2.2 presents a checklist you can use to evaluate the literate environment in your classroom.

Reading Aloud to Children

The second important element of motivation is reading aloud to children. When teachers read aloud a favorite book such as *The Best Town in the World* (Baylor, 1982), they convey their love and excitement for both reading and learning. Some consider such reading to be "the single most important activity for building the knowledge required for eventual success in reading" (Anderson et al., 1985, p. 23). Indeed, research shows that preschool children who learn to read on their own generally have had an adult read to them repeatedly (Clark, 1976; Durkin, 1966). The overall value of reading aloud to children at home has been clearly documented (Cain, 1996; Strickland & Taylor, 1989). As teachers, we should encourage all parents to read to their children as much as possible.

Research also verifies the value of reading aloud to children as a part of the classroom program (McCormick, 1977). It not only helps to motivate students but also provides a basis for expanding oral language and prior knowledge (Feitelson, Kita, & Goldstein, 1986), especially for those children who have not had these experiences at home. Reading aloud also influences children's writings (Dressel, 1990). When children actually hear a great variety of stories, they reflect many story features in their own writing.

Certainly there is no substitute for reading to children at home; however, classroom read-aloud periods can provide some of the same benefits (Strickland & Taylor, 1989; Taylor & Strickland, 1986), especially for those children who have not been read aloud to at home. Following are some guidelines that should be helpful as you plan the read-aloud periods in your classroom:

▶ *Read aloud every day.* Select a consistent time so that children will look forward to it. Many teachers prefer to read aloud first thing in the morning because it gets the day off to a positive start. If you have a few unexpected extra minutes throughout the day, use them for additional read-aloud time. These extra times may be necessary when you work with children who have different language backgrounds or who generally lack prior knowledge background.

▶ *Have a comfortable, inviting place in the classroom for reading aloud.* Use the library area if it is large enough, and use a favorite or special chair such as a rocker.

▶ *Select books that both you and the children will enjoy.* Some books may relate to specific themes or topics of study, but they do not have to. If you find you have selected a book the class is not enjoying, stop reading it and take some time to discuss why you have stopped. You should also vary the types of books you read and be sure to include some poetry, since children of all ages enjoy poetry that rhymes and has humor (Terry, 1974; Thomas, 1989). Two favorite

FIGURE 2.2

A CHECKLIST FOR EVALUATING THE CLASSROOM LITERATE ENVIRONMENT

	Yes	No	Needs Work
1. Do I have the following areas or combinations of areas in my classroom?			

- Library area
- Writing and publishing area
- Listening and viewing area
- Sharing area
- Creative arts area
- Group meeting area
- Display area

2. Do I change or improve areas within reasonable time frames?
3. Do students utilize certain areas more than others?

   Which ones? _____

   _____

4. Areas that I need to add:

   _____

   _____

5. Areas that I need to improve or change:

   _____

   _____

poets of most children are Shel Silverstein and Jack Prelutsky. Here are some of their best-known works:

Where the Sidewalk Ends (Silverstein, 1974)

A Light in the Attic (Silverstein, 1981)

The New Kid on the Block (Prelutsky, 1984)

Ride a Purple Pelican (Prelutsky, 1986)

Tyrannosaurus Was a Beast (Prelutsky, 1988)

Poems of A. Nonny Mouse (Prelutsky, 1989)

Beneath a Blue Umbrella (Prelutsky, 1990)

Something Big Has Been Here (Prelutsky, 1990)

There are also many good anthologies that include poetry. You might want to consider the following:

> *A New Treasury of Children's Poetry: Old Favorites and New Discoveries* (Cole, 1984)
>
> *Random House Book of Poetry for Children* (Prelutsky, 1983)
>
> *The Poetry of Black America: Anthology of the 20th Century* (Adoff, 1973)
>
> *A Child's Garden of Verses* (Stevenson, 1885/1981)

▶ *Read with expression and feeling.* Make the book come alive for children. Trelease (1989) suggests adding a real-life dimension to your read-alouds; for example, if you are reading *Blueberries for Sal* (McCloskey, 1948), have a bowl of fresh blueberries for children to taste.

▶ *Allow time for discussion during and after each read-aloud period.* If students have questions during reading, take time to discuss them, and use the discussion to talk about favorite parts, feelings, or reactions. Also, be sure to share your own thoughts about a book or story.

▶ *Don't allow the discussion to become a time to "test" children on the book.* Direct the discussion so that children get to share their thoughts but also stay on the topic.

▶ *Allow students to write or draw as they listen.* Some may find it easier to pay attention if they are allowed to write or draw while listening. Of course, they should not be completing work assignments at this time.

▶ *The New Read-Aloud Handbook* (Trelease, 1989) might be helpful in planning read-aloud periods.

Attitudes and Expectations of Teachers

The third aspect of motivation involves your attitudes and expectations. The teacher who is enthusiastic and positive about reading, writing, and learning and conveys these feelings to the students does a great deal to motivate. If you believe all students can learn and share these feelings both directly and indirectly, you set up expectations for success for all students (Wigfield & Asher, 1984).

Communication with Home

Finally, communication with parents and other caregivers is an important part of motivating students (Vukelich, 1984). If you send home newsletters and have school meetings where parents are invited to attend, you keep caregivers involved and informed about what you are doing in the classroom, which helps to create and maintain a higher degree of motivation for learning. You can also help them see the importance of supporting their children in many positive ways. This support, in turn, leads to better motivation.

Instruction in Reading and Writing

The second component of the literacy program is instruction. In a balanced literacy program, instruction is both direct and indirect. In *direct instruction,* the teacher systematically and explicitly teaches and models a particular skill, strategy, or process related to reading or writing. For example, a first-grade teacher explicitly models a phonic skill for the class or group (see Chapter 4). In *indirect instruction,* the teacher creates the circumstances that allow students to learn by themselves from each other; the teacher monitors the students and provides input as needed. For example, a fifth-grade teacher creates discussion groups to allow students to respond to a piece of literature they have read (see Chapter 6).

The Role of the Teacher

The teacher creates the circumstances and conditions within the classroom that let instruction take place. In many instances, teachers direct the activities. In lessons or minilessons, they may use *modeling;* that is, they may show or demonstrate for students how to use the processes of reading or writing or how to use particular strategies that might help in constructing meaning. For example, when teachers read a story to the class, they are modeling reading; when they write a group story with the class, they are modeling writing. Many times, modeling involves the use of "think-alouds," sessions in which teachers share the thought processes they have gone through in formulating the meaning of a text (Clark, 1984; Meichenbaum, 1985). (For a detailed discussion of modeling and sample lessons using think-alouds, see Chapter 8.)

In other instances, the teacher may set up an activity where students work together on a task. This is known as *cooperative* or *collaborative learning.* The teacher observes the activity while students are working and provides directive support through questions and/or suggestions. (For further reading on cooperative learning, see the For Additional Reading section.)

Instruction also involves opportunities for students to respond to their reading and writing. *Responding* is the essence of literacy: constructing personal meanings (Rosenblatt, 1938/1983, 1978). It includes activities such as reacting to, talking about, or doing something appropriate with a piece of literature children have read or listened to or a story children have written. For example, after writing a mystery, a student might want to read it aloud to some classmates or have it read and reacted to by others. Students who have read a piece such as *Bridge to Terabithia* (Paterson, 1977) might respond to it by getting together in a group or literature circle for a discussion. Such responding must be authentic in that it must be the type of activity one naturally does with reading and writing. It may take place before, during, or after students read or write. See Table 2.1 for examples of responding.

From an instructional point of view, the teacher's role is to plan and support the activities and experiences that encourage responding. Teachers should include lessons that involve reading many kinds of books, all the time prompting students to respond in ways of their own choosing or directing them by offering suggestions for the types of responses they might make. Posting a reading response chart such as the one on page 50 is one way to accomplish this.

Instruction begins with the reading of literature in a variety of ways. The support the teacher provides while students are involved in any aspect of reading or writing can be thought of as *scaffolding* (Collins, Brown, & Newman, 1986). This might be questioning that helps students understand what they have read or modeling to show

TABLE 2.1

EXAMPLES OF RESPONDING

- *Before reading:* Students might look at a book and predict what will happen in it. This is the beginning of responding.
- *During reading:* As students are reading, they might have a reaction to a particular character and write a note about it in their journal.
- *After reading:* Because students loved the book they read, they may select another book by the same author or may choose to retell the story to someone else.

students how to think through a particular piece of text or to learn a strategy. As students become increasingly competent, the teacher begins to remove the scaffolding and provides less and less support. This is what Pearson (1985) calls the "gradual release of responsibility." In other words, the teacher gradually gives more responsibility to the students. This process can be observed in any learning situation. For example, young children who learned to read before going to school learned in this way: first someone read to them, and then gradually that person read less and less and the children read more and more.

Instruction may be planned or unplanned (Durkin, 1990), and both types are necessary. However, once you have learned how to provide quality planned instruction, you are more likely to be comfortable seizing the "teachable moment," responding spontaneously to a situation that arises unexpectedly during a lesson or an activity. For example, suppose the children have read *Today Was a Terrible Day* (Giff, 1980). In the discussion that follows, you realize that several children do not understand why Ronald Morgan is feeling so unhappy in school. Therefore, you begin by directing them to the first unhappy incident, when Ronald Morgan dropped his pencil. By questioning and discussing, you help the children see how the event of dropping the pencil and Miss Tyler's response made Ronald unhappy. You continue through the story, looking at all events that take place in this way. You are providing the support or scaffold, when it is needed, to help the children construct meaning.

Reading and Writing as Modes of Instruction

An important part of the instruction in a balanced literacy program is to use different types of reading and writing to scaffold the support that students need. In this section we will look at different modes of reading and writing with a focus on how and when to use them. Knowing how to use different modes of reading and writing along with explicit, direct instruction provides you with a powerful combination of teaching tools that will ensure that *all* students achieve success in reading and writing.

Modes of Reading

Students may access or read a piece of literature in a variety of ways, depending on their reading abilities and current levels of performance as well as the complexity of the literature being read. No one mode is exclusively for the at-risk reader or the advanced reader. Rather, decisions as to which mode to use in a given lesson or instructional situation should be made by the teacher and/or students on the basis of the literature, the students' reading abilities, and the particular lesson or situation. The primary concern for you as the teacher is to be aware of each of the possible ways to approach reading and when, why, and how to use them. We will discuss five reading modes: independent reading, cooperative reading, guided reading, shared reading, and reading aloud.

Independent Reading.   During independent reading, students read an entire selection or part of a selection by themselves. (As a mode of instruction, independent reading should not be confused with the independent, self-selected [voluntary] reading portion of the literacy program discussed later in this chapter [see page 47].) Since independent reading involves the least support possible, it is used when students have sufficient ability to read a piece of literature without any support from the teacher or peers or for rereading after students have received sufficient support through other modes of reading. Unfortunately, we know that at-risk learners frequently get few, if any, opportunities to read whole pieces of quality literature independently (Allington, 1977, 1983; Allington & Walmsley, 1995). *All students at all levels need to have instructional experiences in independent reading.*

Cooperative Reading.   Cooperative reading uses the principles of cooperative learning (Slavin, 1990). Pairs of students take turns reading portions of a piece of literature aloud to each other, or read silently to a designated spot, and then stop to discuss what they have read. The students then predict what they think will happen next and continue reading the next portion of the text, either aloud or silently, and stop again for discussion. This pattern continues until they have finished the book or selection.

Cooperative reading is sometimes called *buddy reading, partner reading,* or *paired reading* (Tierney, Readence, & Dishner, 1990). It should be used when students need *some* support and are not quite able to handle an entire selection independently. The guidelines in Table 2.2, based in part on the successful reciprocal teaching model (Palincsar & Brown, 1986), should be helpful for using cooperative reading in your classroom. You may want to model this process for your students.

When using cooperative reading, students may take turns reading a sentence, paragraph, or page. Be sure they are allowed to pass when their turn comes if they do not feel prepared to read the text.

Guided Reading.   There are two basic types of guided reading—observational and interactive. Observational guided reading (this author's term) is the type discussed by Fountas and Pinnell (1996). In observational guided reading, students read a text with a minimal number of new concepts and skills. The teacher introduces the text; students make some predictions. As the students read, the teacher observes and coaches students in their uses of strategies. The text being read is usually a short book or text that is read in its entirety. Detailed use of observational guided reading is discussed in Chapter 4.

With interactive guided reading, the teacher carefully guides, directs, or coaches students through the silent reading of a meaningful chunk of text by asking them a

TABLE 2.2

GUIDELINES FOR COOPERATIVE READING

1. *Preview and predict.* Have the students look through the text and examine the illustrations and/or pictures; ask them to read the beginning portion of the text and predict what they think will happen or what they will learn.
2. *Read orally or silently.*

ORAL VERSION	SILENT VERSION
• *Skim silently.* Each student skims the text silently before beginning oral reading. • *Read orally.* One student reads aloud the first part of the text while the other(s) follow along. • *Discuss, respond, and check predictions.* The students stop and retell and/or discuss how they feel about what they read. They talk about whether they have verified or need to change their overall predictions. • *Predict and read.* The students then predict what they think will happen or what they will learn in the next section. The second student then reads aloud the next section. This pattern continues until the selection is completed.	• *Read.* Each student reads the same portion of text silently, keeping in mind the predictions made. • *Discuss, respond, and check predictions.* The students stop and retell or summarize what they have read. They tell how they feel about what they have read or what they have learned, and they talk about whether their overall predictions were verified and/or need to be changed. • *Predict and read.* The students then predict what they think will happen next or what they will learn. They continue reading the next section silently. This pattern is followed until the entire piece has been completed.

3. *Summarize and respond.* After completing the entire selection, the students summarize what they have read. They respond by discussing how they feel about what they have read and deciding what they might do with it (tell someone about it, write their own summaries, use art to share what they read, and so forth).

question, giving prompts, or helping them formulate a question that they then try to answer as they read the designated section of text. Sometimes the teacher helps students make predictions. At the conclusion of each section, the students stop and discuss with the teacher the answer to the question or their predictions, as well as other points. The teacher also encourages students to reflect on the strategies they have used and discuss how those strategies have helped them construct meaning. At each stopping point, the teacher encourages students to respond to what they have read. Interactive guided reading, as the name implies, is interactive, with students and teacher each participating in the process.

Interactive guided reading is used when students need a great deal of support in constructing meaning from the text because of either the complexity of the text or students' limited abilities. This approach also allows the teacher to adjust the support, or scaffold, according to students' needs. For example, suppose your students are reading *Matilda* (Dahl, 1988) and you are guiding them through the first chapter, "The Reader of Books." After reading the first portion of the chapter, you realize the students do not have the appropriate or sufficient background needed to construct meaning from it. For example, students cannot relate to a child who can go to school reading as well as Matilda does. Therefore, you introduce into the discussion the background points they need. This is the type of unplanned instruction that uses the "teachable moment." The lesson scenario using interactive guided reading might go as follows. Use the annotations in parentheses to help you see what is happening.

(Relate prior knowledge to first chapter.)

Teacher:	We have previewed the book *Matilda* and know that it is about a little girl who is gifted. We are now ready to read the first chapter. Who can find it in the book and read the title?
Sammy:	"The Reader of Books."

(Get students to think about what might happen.)

Teacher:	What do you think that title tells you about Matilda?
Megan:	She might read books.
Beth Ann:	I think the teacher reads books.
Teacher:	Let's turn through the chapter and look at the illustrations that Quentin Blake, the illustrator, drew. What does Matilda seem to be doing?
Tara:	She's reading lots of books.
Sammy:	It looks like she is in the library.
Juro:	Maybe she just looks at the pictures. She's so young to read.

(Guide students to predict. Help students set purpose for reading.)

Teacher:	What would you predict is going to happen in this chapter?
Sammy:	Matilda is going to read a lot of books.
Juro:	Matilda is a little girl, but she reads a bunch of books.
Teacher:	(Records predictions on chalkboard.) Let's read pages 7, 8, and 9 silently to see if either of these predictions is correct.
	(Students read.)

(Follow up by having students check predictions. This is all a part of the scaffolding.)

Teacher:	Were either of our predictions confirmed?
Larry:	No. The author just told us that some parents think their kids are geniuses.

(Support students in clarifying.)

Teacher:	Did he mean the kids really are geniuses?
Juro:	No. Parents just think they are.
Teacher:	How can you tell that Roald Dahl is making fun of these types of parents?
Analise:	Because of the funny things he would write about the kids.
Teacher:	Like what?
Beth Ann:	He said he would write that Maximillian is a total washout and that he hopes there is a family business for him.
Sammy:	That's funny.
Teacher:	Why?

Sammy:	Because it just is. Maximillian must be lazy or dumb.
Megan:	No, he isn't. Roald Dahl is just being funny.

(Coach students to notice how authors motivate readers.)

Teacher:	Do you think he is trying to get us interested in his book?
Most students:	Yes.

(Encourage personal response.)

Teacher:	How did these pages make you feel?
Larry:	They were kind of funny.
Beth Ann:	Sad. I hope a teacher wouldn't really write those things.

(Support students in thinking about their predictions.)

Teacher:	Do you think we should change our predictions?
Juro:	No, we haven't read enough yet.

(Support students in having a purpose for reading.)

Teacher:	Let's read pages 10 and 11 silently and think about our predictions.

(Follow up on purpose for reading.)

Larry:	She's smart.
Juro:	She's a little kid.
Analise:	Her mother and dad don't like her.
Juro:	That's sad.
Teacher:	It *is* sad. Why do you think they feel that way?
Sammy:	Because she is so smart and wants to read.
Teacher:	Are there books for her to read?
Beth Ann:	No. Just one on cooking.

(Support students in keeping predictions in mind and setting their own purpose for reading.)

Teacher:	Have we learned whether our predictions are true?
Megan:	No, but maybe Matilda is going to the library.

(Support students to read to check the predictions they have made. Begin to help students monitor their own reading.)

Teacher:	Let's find out. Read pages 12 through the top of page 15.
	(Students read silently.)
Teacher:	What did she do?
Juro:	She went to the library. Her dad wouldn't get her any books.
Teacher:	Were our predictions true?
Analise:	Yes, she read all the children's books.

(Provide a purpose for reading.)

Teacher:	Now read pages 15, 16, 17, and to the end of the last full paragraph on 18 to see if she reads anything else.
	(Students read silently.)

(Follow up on purpose for reading.)

Teacher:	What did she read next?
Larry:	I think she read some books, but I never heard of them.

(Students' responses show they don't know the books.)

Tony:	Me either!
Teacher:	The books listed on page 18 are novels that adults usually read.
Megan:	That's why I don't know 'em.
Teacher:	Maybe your parents might read some of these books.
Beth Ann:	Not mine!

(A teachable moment! Build concept of novel.)

Teacher:	What is a novel?
Sammy:	Is it a story?
Teacher:	Yes. What else can you tell me about a novel?
Juro:	Is this book a novel?
Megan:	Does a novel have chapters?
Teacher:	Yes, it does. *Matilda* is a novel like the ones listed on page 18.
Juro:	Is a novel true?
Teacher:	No, but it may be realistic. A novel is what we call fiction. There are many types of fiction. We'll talk about those later. Let's go on with our discussion. Was Matilda taking her books home to read?
Sammy:	No.
Teacher:	Why not?
Analise:	I'll bet she was afraid of her dad.
Larry:	No, she wasn't.
Teacher:	Why do you think that, Larry?
Larry:	She just didn't seem to be afraid of him. I'm not afraid of my dad.

(Help students set own purpose by predicting.)

Teacher:	What would you predict she's going to do about her books?
Juro:	Read them in the library.
Analise:	Maybe she'll take them home.

(Draw students back to the chapter and focus them on their predictions.)

Teacher:	Let's finish the chapter and see if our predictions are true.
	(Students read silently.)

(Follow up on purpose.)

Teacher:	What did Matilda do about getting books to read?
Sammy:	She started taking them home from the library.
Teacher:	What did she do with her books?
Juro:	She took a trip.
Teacher:	Did she really go on a trip?

Megan:	No. She just read stories about places.
Teacher:	How did you think this book might take us other places?
Tony:	We don't know much about English schools. This'll be like a trip.
Teacher:	Does anyone have any questions?

(Students are encouraged to ask about anything they don't understand.)

Beth Ann:	What is Bovril or Ovaltine?
Teacher:	Does anyone know?
Most students:	No.

(Begin to use teachable moment.)

Teacher:	Any clues?
Analise:	It must be something you drink or eat. It says she took a hot drink to her room.
Teacher:	It is! Ovaltine is like hot chocolate.

(Encourage more personal responses and get students thinking about the remainder of the book.)

Teacher:	Think about how this chapter makes you feel about Matilda. Before we start the next chapter, you can share your thoughts about your feelings for Matilda.

Interactive guided reading is a flexible tool; you can provide more support for students at the beginning of the reading and gradually release the responsibility to students as the reading progresses. In this process, you control the amount of support through (1) the types of questions you ask or prompts you give before reading and during discussion, (2) the amount of text you have students read, and (3) the type of discussion held between reading sessions. When more support is needed, you can direct the discussion; then, as you give students more responsibility, they may carry out and direct the discussion with a partner.

Throughout interactive guided reading, be aware of the role of questions and prompts. Simply asking children about what they have read is not going to teach them how to construct meaning (Durkin, 1978, 1981a, b; Herber & Nelson, 1975). However, we do know that the questions asked and the prompts given during interactive guided reading can help if they are of the appropriate types (Beck, 1984; Beck, Omanson, & McKeown, 1982). Effective questions or prompts meet the following criteria:

▶ Questions or prompts given *before* reading should lead students to the important ideas in the text. In narrative text, they should focus on the setting of the story (time and place), the major characters, the story problem, the action, the resolution, and the overall moral or theme. In expository text, they should focus on the main ideas. For example,

> *Narrative text:* Who are the two important characters that are introduced in the story, and what do they do?

> *Expository text:* Think about the important things we know about plants.

▶ Questions and prompts used during discussion *between* the reading of sections should pull together ideas brought out in reading and should help build relationships among ideas. For example,

> *Narrative text:* Who were the two characters? What did you learn about them and how they usually work together?

> *Expository text:* What was the first important thing you found out about plants? How is this likely to help people?

▶ Questions and prompts should be given in an order that follows the order of the text.

By using these guidelines, you will help students develop what Beck calls an overall mental picture of the text being read (Beck, 1984). An example illustrating the use of interactive guided reading appears in the literacy lesson on page 61.

A monitoring guide can be used independently by students who still need structured support during reading. Sometimes called a *study guide* by content-area teachers, this is a sheet that poses questions and gives activities that carefully guide students through the reading of the text. Although often used in content classes, it can be used in reading any text. Figure 2.3 shows a portion of a monitoring guide that could be used by students reading the first chapter of *Matilda* (Dahl, 1988).

Shared Reading.   Holdaway (1979) developed a procedure known as the "shared book experience" for introducing beginners to reading by using favorite stories, rhymes, and poems. In this procedure, the teacher reads aloud a story and invites children to join in the reading or rereading when they feel comfortable. Stories are read several times, and children receive many opportunities to respond through writing, art, drama, discussion, and so forth. In Holdaway's early description of this procedure, some of the children's favorite books were enlarged for group study; this is the basis for the "big book" concept used by many teachers.

Shared reading provides very strong support for learners. It allows for the modeling of real reading and accounts for the ways "natural readers" have learned to read by being read to, reading along with an adult or older child, and ultimately reading on their own. Although shared reading can be used for beginning reading, it can also be used with students at other levels. For a detailed discussion and a sample lesson on how to use shared reading, see Chapter 4.

Reading Aloud.   Sometimes the best way to help children understand a particular piece of literature is to first read it aloud and discuss it with them. This type of reading helps to activate already acquired knowledge and develop background vocabulary and concepts. It also is a way to model real reading.

Reading literature aloud for instructional purposes (not to be confused with reading aloud for motivation, as discussed earlier) provides very strong teacher support for students. It is used when a particular piece of literature has many difficult concepts or words, would be hard for students to decode, or is difficult to follow. After the teacher has read a piece aloud, students may read it under the teacher's guidance, cooperatively, or independently.

FIGURE 2.3

PORTION OF A MONITORING GUIDE FOR *MATILDA*

by Roald Dahl, illustrated by Quentin Blake
Chapter 1, "The Reader of Books," pages 7–21

Previewing and Predicting
- Try to get an idea about this chapter
  —Look at the illustrations
  —Read page 7
- Write your prediction about what you think will happen in this chapter:

_____

_____

Reading Pages 7–11
- Now read pages 7–11 to see if your prediction was verified. Maybe you will want to change your prediction. As you read, make notes about any thoughts you have about the chapter.

- Notes: _____

_____

_____

After Reading Pages 7-11
- What did you learn about your prediction?

_____

_____

- Complete this chart showing what you learned about Matilda. Add other ovals if you need them.

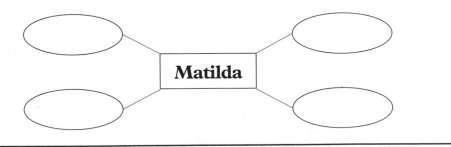

Combinations of Reading Modes.   Table 2.3 summarizes the five modes of reading we have discussed. Figure 2.4 shows how varying these modes of reading provides different amounts of support or scaffolding for students. Frequently it is appropriate to combine several modes of reading at once. For example, if your students are reading a short story or a chapter in a book, you might begin by reading aloud the first portion of a chapter and discussing it with them. Next, you might put students into

TABLE 2.3

Modes of Reading

Mode	Description	When to Use
Independent reading	Students read text alone without support, usually silently.	When students are likely to have no difficulty with the text or are highly motivated about the text or text topic.
Cooperative reading	Students read with a partner or partners, either orally or silently.	When students' abilities show need for some support. May also be done just for fun.
Guided reading	Teacher talks, coaches, and walks students through sections of text with questions and student predictions.	When text or students' abilities show need for much support. May be used for variety.
Shared reading	Teacher reads aloud as students view the text. Students chime in when they are ready to do so.	When students need a great deal of support for reading. Often used with beginning readers.
Reading aloud	Teacher reads aloud text. Students usually do not have a copy of the text.	Used when text is too difficult, when background needs to be developed, for fun, or for variety.

pairs and have them do the oral version of cooperative reading. Finally, you might complete the chapter by having each student read a small portion of the text independently; in this way, each child would also have the opportunity to read alone. This combined instructional reading strategy can be called *read aloud, read along, read alone*. Notice that by combining these forms of reading, you provide a scaffold for learning that gradually releases some responsibility to the students. At the same time, you activate prior knowledge, develop background, and model real reading.

Remember that you can create different combinations as you work to meet the differing needs of your students in relation to the literature they are reading. You should also give them the opportunity to select their own mode of reading (see pages 55–56). Finally, you may vary the mode of reading just to add fun and variety to your instruction.

Modes of Writing

Throughout the literacy program, students will also be writing in response to literature (see Chapter 6) and for other purposes. When they write, they will frequently do process writing; that is, they will follow the same steps used by effective writers (Graves, 1983; Hillocks, 1987a, b): selecting the topic, drafting, revising, proofreading, and publishing. Chapter 7 discusses the writing process along with spelling and grammar.

Five basic modes of writing may be used as a part of instruction and learning: independent, collaborative/cooperative, guided, shared writing, and write aloud.

FIGURE 2.4

VARYING MODES OF READING PROVIDES DIFFERING AMOUNTS OF INSTRUCTIONAL SUPPORT

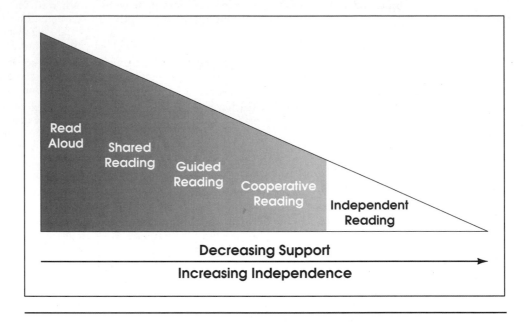

Independent Writing.   Independent writing is what students do when they write alone. It assumes students are able to develop their products with little or no support. Independent writing builds power and fluency in writing.

Collaborative/Cooperative Writing.   When students write collaboratively/cooperatively, they work with a partner or partners on a single product, often taking turns doing the actual writing. This mode of writing (comparable to the cooperative reading mode) gives students support by letting them work together and share ideas. It is often a good way to support the writer who is unmotivated.

Guided Writing.   Guided writing is comparable to guided reading. Students work on their own products, and the teacher is available to guide them through prompting and questioning. Routman (1991) suggests that this is the heart of the writing program.

Shared Writing.   Just as there is shared reading, so can there be shared writing (McKenzie, 1985). This is sometimes called *interactive writing*. In this type of writing, teacher and students work together to write a group story on the chalkboard, a chart, or the overhead projector, following the steps of process writing. In the be-

FIGURE 2.5

SAMPLE OF A SHARED WRITING EXPERIENCE

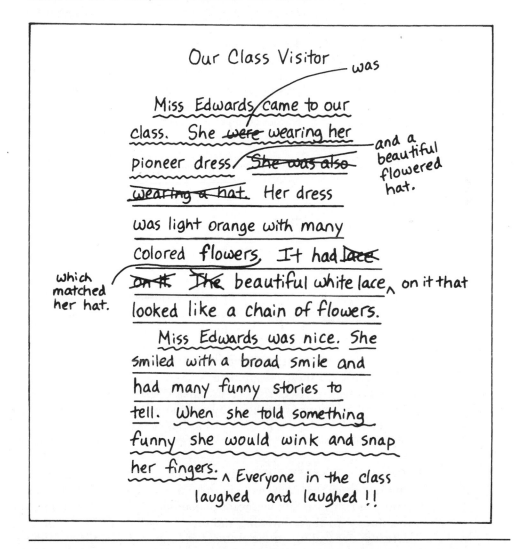

ginning you might do the actual writing, but as you progress different students might take turns writing parts of the story. You may also choose to build into the experience problems that you know students are having in their own writing. In this way, you can model a particular aspect of grammar or spelling for a group of students without pointing out those problems in their writing. At the same time, you model the full process of writing and can share the thinking processes involved in the construction of meaning.

TABLE 2.4

MODES OF WRITING

MODE	DESCRIPTION	WHEN TO USE
Independent	Students write alone.	Students need little or no support.
Collaborative/ cooperative	Students write with a partner or partners on single product.	Students need limited support in their writing.
Guided writing	Students write their own product; teacher prompts and guides.	Students have had models of writing but need support in learning how to write their own product.
Shared	The group or class writes together, working with the teacher.	Students need a large amount of support in their writing or you see the need to focus on a particular writing convention.
Write aloud	Teacher writes at chart or overhead, sharing thinking of the process being used.	Students need to have the process of writing modeled for a particular type of writing.

Write Aloud.   This mode of writing allows the teacher to model the thinking process during writing. As the teacher writes at a chart or overhead, he/she thinks aloud to tell students his/her thought process during writing. Students listen and read what is being written. This is a modeling process for writing and may be used at any grade level to teach writing. (See Chapter 7.)

Figure 2.5 shows a sample of shared descriptive writing that the teacher and students have revised. You can use shared writing when you think students need a great deal of support to help them expand their writing abilities. It is a powerful vehicle for developing minilessons to help students overcome problems in writing at all grade levels.

Combinations of Writing Modes.   Table 2.4 summarizes the five modes of writing just discussed. You may use these modes with any students at any grade level, and you may also find you want to combine them. For example, you might begin a product with shared writing and move to collaborative/cooperative, independent writing, depending on the amount of support you believe students need. Keep in mind that *all students at all levels* need to have the experience of independent writing to develop independence. You will need to vary the modes of writing you use with students in light of their needs and growth stage. Figure 2.6 shows that by changing the mode of writing you use with students, you change the amount of support you give them. Just as you can give students choices of reading modes, you can give them the opportunity to select the mode of writing they use. For example, you might suggest that students write a story independently or collaboratively. As when they read, you should encourage students to select the mode of writing that most appropriately meets their current needs.

FIGURE 2.6

VARYING MODES OF WRITING PROVIDES DIFFERING AMOUNTS OF INSTRUCTIONAL SUPPORT

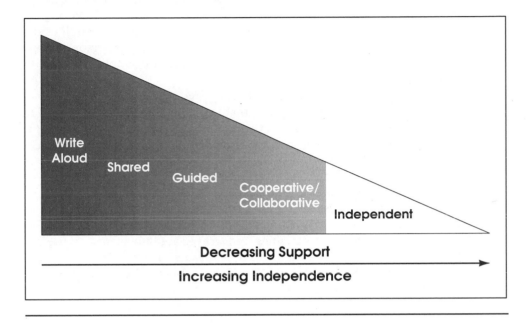

Independent Reading and Writing

The third component of the literacy program is independent or voluntary reading and writing. *Every day, in every classroom, students should have time for self-selected reading and self-initiated, independent writing.*

Time for Reading and Writing

Research consistently supports the importance of giving students time for indepen-dent reading (Anderson, Wilson, & Fielding, 1988; Cunningham, Hall, & Defee, 1998; Elley & Mangubhai, 1983; Fielding, Wilson, & Anderson, 1986; Morrow, 1987; Snow, Burns, & Griffin, 1998; Taylor, Frye, & Maruyama, 1990). Existing evidence indicates that independent reading does the following for students:

▶ *Enhances their reading comprehension*

▶ *Provides them with a wide range of background knowledge*

▶ *Accounts for one-third or more of their vocabulary growth*

▶ *Promotes reading as a lifelong activity* (Center for the Study of Reading, n.d., p. 1)

Similarly, researchers have verified the importance of extended writing as the major way in which students develop their ability to use grammar and learn to spell

(Anderson et al., 1985; Hillocks, 1987a, b). Independent reading and writing help to make literacy learning an exciting process and also provide students with many authentic experiences—the basis for all literacy learning. Existing research offers guidelines and suggestions that should help teachers create and maintain this component in their classroom (Anderson et al., 1988; Graves, 1983; Graves & Hansen, 1983; Morrow & Weinstein, 1982, 1986; Taylor et al., 1990).

The amount of time for independent reading and writing needs to be seriously considered when planning the literacy program. Research evidence suggests some guidelines to follow for independent reading (Anderson et al., 1985; Taylor et al., 1990) but offers little or no guidance for the amount of time devoted to independent writing.

Becoming a Nation of Readers: The Report of the Commission on Reading (Anderson et al., 1985) suggests that two hours of independent reading per week should be expected of children by the time they are in third or fourth grade; this would include both in- and out-of-school reading. However, a more recent study suggests that in-school independent reading may be more significant than out-of-school reading, *even though both are important* (Taylor et al., 1990). This study found that an average of 16 minutes per day of independent reading in school for fifth and sixth graders was significantly related to their reading growth; the out-of-school reading time was approximately 15 minutes per day.

Independent reading and writing are important because children are learning to do what we want them to do: *read* and *write*. They are thinking and expanding their schema and prior knowledge, which is the basis for their literacy learning. In the process, they are developing and using what Clay (1985) calls a "self-improving system."

Guidelines for Planning Independent Reading and Writing

In light of existing research findings and good classroom practices, several guidelines should be considered in planning the independent reading and writing component of the literacy program:

- Create a program that will promote both in-school and out-of-school independent reading and writing.

- Begin the program in kindergarten. Ideally, good reading habits will have been modeled for children before this time through at-home read-aloud opportunities; even if this has not happened, this will be a good beginning.

- Allow 10 to 15 minutes per day for independent in-school reading from kindergarten through grade 2. Allow approximately 20 to 30 minutes per day for independent writing.

- In grades 3 through 5, increase the amount of time for in-school independent reading to 15 to 20 minutes per day. Provide 30 to 45 minutes per day for independent writing.

- Above grade 5, continue to increase the amount of independent reading and writing. Because of the middle school or junior high structure at these levels, this time may need to be provided during a homeroom time or rotated through different classes. The main thing to keep in mind is that independent reading and writing should not occur just during the reading or English class in the middle school or junior high.

▶ Be flexible about the amounts of time devoted to independent reading and writing. Gradually build up the time. When independent reading and writing are going well in class, extend the time if possible.

▶ Have designated periods or times for independent reading and writing. These do not have to be back to back.

▶ Give your independent reading and writing periods names that appeal to the students, such as SQUIRT (Sustained Quiet Uninterrupted Reading Time), DEAR (Drop Everything And Read), or WART (Writing And Reading Time).

▶ Encourage students to share what they have read or written during their independent reading and writing time. Make this a pleasant experience that will encourage them to want to participate, but do not demand sharing.

▶ During independent reading and writing time, *you should also be reading and writing* for the first 5 minutes or so. This provides an adult model and says that you also value these activities. After your own reading or writing, you should move around the class to prompt and support those who need assistance. During sharing, you should also share what you have read and written. Sharing can take place in pairs or small groups.

There are many exciting ways to promote and encourage independent reading and writing. Often, however, teachers overlook this important aspect of the literacy program for a number of reasons, none of them valid:

▶ *Not important.* The research we have discussed clearly shows this is not true.

▶ *Not enough time.* Research shows how important this area really is. Therefore, we must *make* enough time.

▶ *Not enough books in my room.* Even though some classrooms may have limited resources, these can be built. Use the school library, public library, book clubs and book club bonuses, students' books brought in from home, and so forth.

▶ *Students will read at home.* This may or may not happen. Recall that some researchers report that in-school independent reading time may be more important than out-of-school time (Taylor et al., 1990).

Suggested Activities for Independent Reading and Writing

The following activities are just a few ways to develop and support independent reading and writing as a part of your literacy program.

Journals. Have students make a reading journal in which they keep track of the books they have read. Suggest that they include the title, author, and date completed. Then have them record how they have responded to the book. A reading response chart similar to the one presented in Figure 2.7 is a good way to encourage personal responses to reading. Change charts frequently, and always include the "Other" category to get students to create their own response activities. For a detailed discussion of journals and response charts, see Chapter 6.

FIGURE 2.7

SAMPLE READING RESPONSE CHART

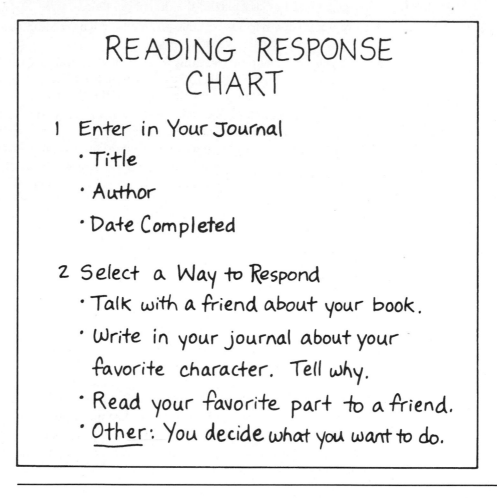

READING RESPONSE CHART

1 Enter in Your Journal
   • Title
   • Author
   • Date Completed

2 Select a Way to Respond
   • Talk with a friend about your book.
   • Write in your journal about your favorite character. Tell why.
   • Read your favorite part to a friend.
   • Other: You decide what you want to do.

Records of Books Read or Time Spent Reading.   Use other types of reading records to help students see the amount of reading they are doing. For example, use a thermometer such as the ones pictured in Figure 2.8 to have students keep track of books read or the number of minutes spent reading independently at home and at school.

Author's Chair and Reader's Chair.   Designate a chair where students who have written something and are ready to share it can sit as they read it to a group or the whole class. This chair is known as the "author's chair" and is a very effective way to encourage students to share what they have written (Graves & Hansen, 1983). Another chair, designated the "reader's chair," can be the place where stu-

FIGURE 2.8

SAMPLE READING THERMOMETERS

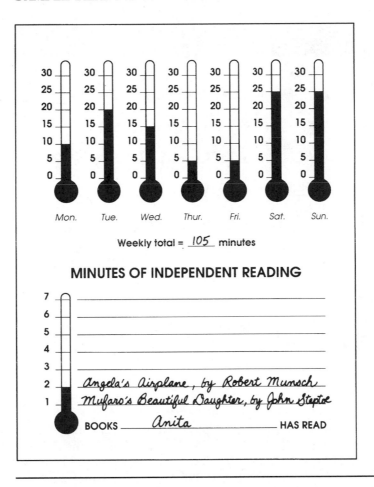

Weekly total = _105_ minutes

MINUTES OF INDEPENDENT READING

BOOKS _Anita_ HAS READ

Angela's Airplane, by Robert Munsch
Mufaro's Beautiful Daughter, by John Steptoe

dents sit when they have a story or book they would like to read, retell, or just talk about with a partner or group.

Home Reading and Writing Programs. Programs that promote independent reading and writing at home are important to the success of the literacy program. These can range from a simple system, in which children take home a favorite book they have read in school to read aloud to a family member, to more elaborate programs.

One simple system for encouraging at-home reading can consist of having books in plastic bags that children take home to read on their own or to a family member.

FIGURE 2.9

CERTIFICATE VERIFYING HOME READING

Home Reading Certificate

This verifies that **Troy Brown**

read **The Secret in the Matchbox**

(**X** *aloud to* **Angela** / _____ *alone*)

on **December 17, 1999** .

Angela Brown

Sister

The person to whom the book has been read then completes a certificate to be returned to school. (If the child reads the book alone, some designated person still fills in the certificate.) Figure 2.9 shows a sample completed certificate for the book *The Secret in the Matchbox* (Willis, 1988). When the certificate is returned to the school, the child is recognized for the accomplishment and the certificate is placed in her or his reading folder. You can devise your own variation of this type of program. For example, Farris (1987) has created a successful at-home reading program using magazines that were sent home with activities to promote family reading.

Similar programs can be used to promote at-home independent writing. Reutzel and Fawson (1990) have created "The Traveling Tales Backpack," which contains materials for writing with suggestions for getting students to write their own stories at home. Many teachers have used a similar idea with a briefcase. Linda Vaile, a first-grade teacher from Green Bay, Wisconsin, puts writing materials in an old briefcase and makes it a special event for children to take it home to do independent writing. Students take turns carrying the briefcase home and sharing their writing when they return to the class.

You can encourage independent reading and writing at school and at home in a variety of ways. Use a combination of procedures and activities to keep motivation high. Whatever techniques you use should motivate and reward individual students rather than compare students to one another.

These sections of Chapter 2 have developed the concept of the balanced literacy program: (1) motivation, (2) instruction in reading and writing, and (3) independent reading and writing. These three components interact with one another continuously. By ensuring that all of them are present in your classroom and/or school, you develop a balanced program that helps students develop literacy and construct meaning, promotes and fosters student ownership of literacy learning, and builds a love for reading and writing. In the remainder of this chapter, we focus on developing a unit and lesson format for use in the literacy program.

A Unit and Lesson Format to Support Literacy Learning

To plan the appropriate instruction to help your students grow and develop in their ability to construct meaning, you need some type of format to help you organize what you do. This section presents

- ▶ A simple, easy-to-use thematic unit plan
- ▶ A literacy lesson format that you can use alone or throughout the thematic unit
- ▶ A minilesson concept and format that you can use to support literacy lessons as needed

Thematic Units

A thematic unit is a framework based on a particular topic, idea, author, or genre. Each unit has outcomes, or goals, that specify what you want students to accomplish as a result of the unit experiences and lessons. One way to think about the unit outcomes is to consider them in terms of the two overall goals of literacy learning: constructing meaning and developing positive attitudes and habits. Constructing meaning is what this text is all about; this overall outcome tells you what understanding(s) you expect your students to obtain as a result of reading the literature in a unit. Attitudes and habits are the feelings, beliefs, and routines related to reading and writing that you hope students develop through the unit experiences. Table 2.5 presents some sample unit outcomes for thematic units from various grade levels.

Thematic units usually consist of several pieces of literature around which the teacher develops lessons and experiences. These themes may involve a number of curricular areas, such as science, art, music, or math, even though the focus of the unit is developing students' ability to read and write. (See Chapter 9 for a detailed discussion of planning cross-curricular units.) For example, a thematic unit on understanding families and family relationships might include books such as *Number the Stars* (Lowry, 1989) and *Where the Red Fern Grows* (Rawls, 1961). Though very different, both stories show how different circumstances reveal the relationships, courage, and feelings within families.

TABLE 2.5

THEMATIC UNIT OUTCOMES FROM SELECTED GRADE LEVELS

THEME	GRADE LEVEL	CONSTRUCTING MEANING OUTCOME	ATTITUDE AND HABITS OUTCOME
Friendship	Kindergarten	Use events from stories and own experiences to make predictions about friendship.	Share favorite stories about friends with others and talk about the importance of friendship.
Folktales	Grade 1	Understand how folktales use sequence of events and repetitive language.	Choose a favorite folktale to share.
Byrd Baylor (author theme)	Grade 3	Understand how an author develops characters in realistic stories.	Independently read and share books by another favorite author.
Learning from Outer Space	Grade 5	Generate and answer own questions about outer space.	Develop an appreciation for space exploration.
Adventure Writing	Grade 7	Understand how characters respond to various tests of courage in adventure.	Develop an appreciation for adventure literature.

The theme plan consists of three parts:

▶ *Introducing the thematic unit:* This portion of the unit activates and assesses prior knowledge for the theme and develops any additional background needed to understand it. At this time, you let students know what they will do during the unit and have them participate in deciding what they would like to accomplish.

▶ *Lessons and activities:* These are the specific experiences of the unit developed around each piece of literature.

▶ *Closing the thematic unit:* This section consists of activities that pull together the major learnings in the unit and allow children to share and celebrate their successes.

There are several advantages to using a thematic unit plan:

1. By incorporating several different pieces of literature focused on a common theme, you enable students to thoroughly account for and develop their prior knowledge and background on a particular subject, which is an essential part of meaning construction (Paris, Wasik, & Turner, 1991).
2. The thematic unit allows for a variety of experiences and lessons that promote literacy learning as an active, constructive process, which in turn fosters the community of learners concept (Pappas, Kiefer, & Levstik, 1990).
3. The unit plan allows the teacher to provide differing levels of support (or scaffolds for learning) based on a common body of literature for the class; this, in

turn, makes the classroom a community for learning, a place where all children can learn and have similar experiences and successes.

4. All students get a great deal of practice with many aspects of literacy through independent activities.

Lessons need to be planned around each piece of literature included in each unit. The next section focuses on how to develop these specific lessons and activities.

A Literacy Lesson Format

Various formats have been suggested for lesson plans to guide children in learning to read. These include the DRTA—Directed Reading-Thinking Activity (Stauffer, 1969), the DRA—Directed Reading Activity (Harris & Sipay, 1985; Burns, Roe, & Ross, 1988), and the DRL—Directed Reading Lesson (Cooper, 1986; Cooper, Warncke, Ramstad, & Shipman, 1979), among others. Although these plans differ somewhat, they are similar in that they focus primarily on reading. The following lesson format focuses on both reading and writing and helps the teacher and students relate both activities as integrated literacy learning processes. It has three simple parts: introducing the literature, reading and responding to the literature, and extending the literature.

Introducing the Literature

When you introduce each piece of literature, two things must happen:

1. Students' prior knowledge must be activated and assessed, and pertinent additional background must be developed. *Sometimes* this may include the development of key concept vocabulary.
2. Students must develop their purpose(s) for reading.

These two things are accomplished in a variety of ways and with differing levels of teacher support, depending on the literature and the students' needs. Sometimes you may want to teach a few words that are key to understanding the literature. Or you might use artwork: for example, if students in a second-grade class are going to read *The Art Lesson* (de Paola, 1989), you might have them preview the story by looking at the pictures and discussing what they think the book will be about. Their purpose for reading then becomes seeing whether their predictions will be verified. Throughout, you provide support according to their needs. Many times you may incorporate writing into this phase of the lesson; for example, you may have students do a "quick write" (an activity in which students are given a topic and a short time to write on it) to activate prior knowledge or to write predictions that will be checked during and after reading.

Reading and Responding to the Literature

Reading and responding to literature take place concurrently; that is, students respond while they are reading as well as after they have read.

Different pieces of literature will need to be read using different modes of reading (see page 34 for modes of reading), depending on the literature and students' abilities. Beginning readers and writers and those having difficulty learning need more teacher support than those who are making effective progress. Moreover, some pieces of literature are more complex than others and require more teacher support even for students who are progressing well.

The primary focus of this part of the lesson is reading and getting to know the piece of literature. While students are reading, they should be reminded and helped to monitor their reading by asking themselves whether what they are reading makes sense; if it does not, they should know and use appropriate strategies to help overcome the problem and construct meaning. (See Chapter 8 on modeling strategies for reading.) This aspect of metacognitive development is a vital part of constructing meaning and comprehension (Paris et al., 1991).

It is not necessary that you always select the mode of reading students will use. This decision can and should be made, in part, by the students. When you give students the opportunity to choose their own modes of reading, they select those that are most appropriate for their own needs and take greater ownership of their learning.

When responding to the literature, students need to do something: *think about it, talk about it, write about it, or do something creative with it involving art, music, or drama.* Responses should be personal and creative, because construction of meaning is an individual matter. Another important part of responding is summarizing what was read. Again, some students and some pieces of literature will require more teacher support than others. By observing carefully how students respond, you can determine whether they need additional support or minilessons that go directly back to the literature (see page 59 on minilessons).

Let's suppose your class is now ready to read *The Art Lesson* (de Paola, 1989). This book seems easy enough for all students in your class to read independently. However, you offer them the option to read it independently or cooperatively. You remind students to check whether their predictions were verified or changed as they read and encourage them to make running notes about their feelings or reactions in their journals. After-reading responses could involve forming small groups to retell the story and share their favorite parts. From the responses, you may discover that some students do not understand why Tomie was upset about the art lessons. You then go back to the book and model how Tomie's expectations for art lessons had been built up and how he became disappointed in school. You can do this by developing a graphic organizer such as the one shown in Figure 2.10.

Throughout the reading-and-responding component, students should be encouraged to reflect on both the meanings they have constructed and how various strategies they have used helped them construct meaning.

Extending the Literature

Extending the literature is where more instruction and integration of the language arts and cross-curricular connections take place. Students are encouraged to use what they have learned in various appropriate ways or in different curricular areas such as science, social studies, art, music, or writing. Many minilessons may be taught at this point as well as at other places in the lesson.

The teaching of writing may be tied directly to the literature by having the literature serve as a model for a certain type of writing. For example, a natural writing extension for *The Art Lesson* is writing a story. Of course, you would vary the

FIGURE 2.10

CHART MODELING TOMIE'S DISAPPOINTMENT IN *THE ART LESSON* (DE PAOLA, 1989)

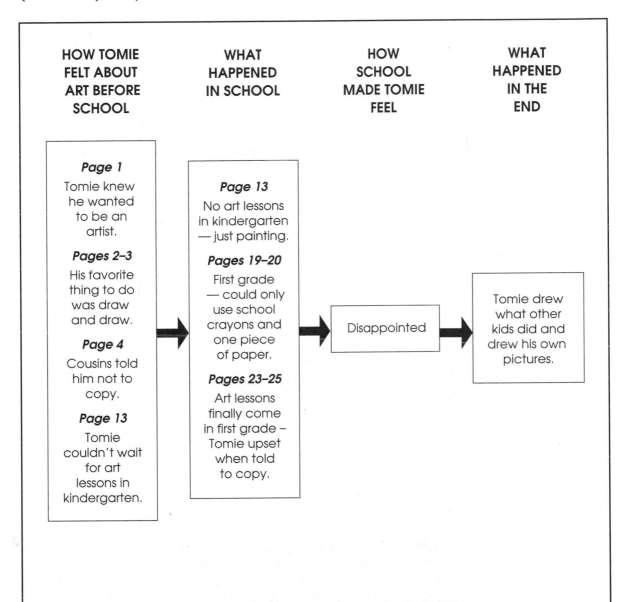

HOW TOMIE FELT ABOUT ART BEFORE SCHOOL	WHAT HAPPENED IN SCHOOL	HOW SCHOOL MADE TOMIE FEEL	WHAT HAPPENED IN THE END
Page 1 Tomie knew he wanted to be an artist. *Pages 2–3* His favorite thing to do was draw and draw. *Page 4* Cousins told him not to copy. *Page 13* Tomie couldn't wait for art lessons in kindergarten.	*Page 13* No art lessons in kindergarten — just painting. *Pages 19–20* First grade — could only use school crayons and one piece of paper. *Pages 23–25* Art lessons finally come in first grade – Tomie upset when told to copy.	Disappointed	Tomie drew what other kids did and drew his own pictures.

TABLE 2.6

SUMMARY OF THE LITERACY LESSON

LESSON PART	PURPOSES	REMARKS
Introducing	Activate and assess prior knowledge and develop background Help students set purposes for reading	The amount of teacher support provided will depend both on the literature and on the students' needs. Sometimes the support will include development of key concepts and vocabulary. Activities used will incorporate reading, writing, speaking, listening, and thinking.
Reading and responding	Read and have access to the entire selection Do something creative and personal during and/or after reading the selection	The mode for reading the selection is determined by students' needs and the literature. This portion of the lesson focuses on the personal construction of meaning.
	Summarize what has been read	By observing students' responses, you will be able to determine the need for additional support or minilessons using the literature as the vehicle for instruction.
	Reflect on the literature and how various strategies helped in constructing meaning	This part of the lesson helps students develop their metacognitive abilities, which leads to more effective comprehension or construction of meaning.
Extending	Use the understandings and ideas gained from the literature Use the literature as a model for writing	Extension of the literature will utilize the knowledge gained in many creative ways or in other curricular areas. Writing may be taught using the literature as a model for the type of writing being developed. (See Chapter 7 on writing.)

mode of writing according to students' needs. (See page 43 for modes of writing. Chapter 7 contains more about writing and the writing process.)

This simple, easy-to-use literacy lesson is flexible and can be used throughout all grades. Make adjustments and variations in accordance with the developmental levels of the students, the literature being read, and the needs of the individual students. Table 2.6 summarizes the parts of the literacy lesson. A sample lesson using *Jamaica Tag-Along* (Havill, 1989) appears on page 61 of this chapter.

Minilessons as a Form of Instruction

Throughout all literacy lessons that you develop, you will need to provide different levels of support to help students continue their process of learning to read and write. Sometimes you will provide this support when *introducing* the literature, sometimes while students are *reading and responding,* and sometimes as they are *extending* the literature. *You will provide support in many forms and ways.* Minilessons are one effective way to provide the systematic direct instruction that is an important part of a balanced literacy program. The minilesson concept helps you to break down instruction into smaller units or "chunks," which is a critical element of effective instruction.

You can use minilessons that go directly back to the literature or to the students' own writing to model the construction of meaning, a skill, or a strategy. These minilessons may take place before, during, or after reading or writing. You determine the need for a minilesson by observing how students read and respond to the literature or how they write and respond to their writing. Thus, minilessons should be used to directly and explicitly model a skill, a strategy, or some aspect of constructing meaning. Figure 2.11 shows how all of these elements fit together.

Minilessons may be informal and formal. For example, suppose your students are reading *Mufaro's Beautiful Daughters: An African Tale* (Steptoe, 1987), which tells a different version of Cinderella. As they are responding and discussing the fairy tale, you realize they have not understood that the snake, the hungry little boy, and the old woman are all the same person—the king, Nyoka. You immediately go back to the story and have them locate the places where each character appeared and show them that these are all the king, who has changed himself into these characters. This is a minilesson that takes place immediately when the "teachable moment" arises.

Most minilessons will be more formal and more carefully and thoroughly planned. A typical planned minilesson incorporates the following steps:

1. *Introduction:* Let the students know what they will learn, and relate it to the literature or their writing (set goals).
2. *Teacher modeling:* Model the element being taught using the literature or writing to show examples. Incorporate think-alouds as needed. (See Chapter 8 for a discussion of think-alouds.)
3. *Student modeling and guided practice:* Guide students in modeling and using what is being taught by finding other examples of what they have learned in the literature or in their writing.
4. *Summarizing and reflecting:* Help students summarize what they have learned and talk about how and when they might use it.

The follow-up for the minilesson should include the following:

1. *Independent practice:* Have students read or write using what has been taught.
2. *Application:* Give students repeated opportunities to immediately use or apply what they have learned in other reading and writing experiences.
3. *Reflecting about use:* After students have had several opportunities to apply what was taught, encourage them to talk about how they have used what they have

FIGURE 2.11

MODEL OF READING AND WRITING WITH MINILESSONS

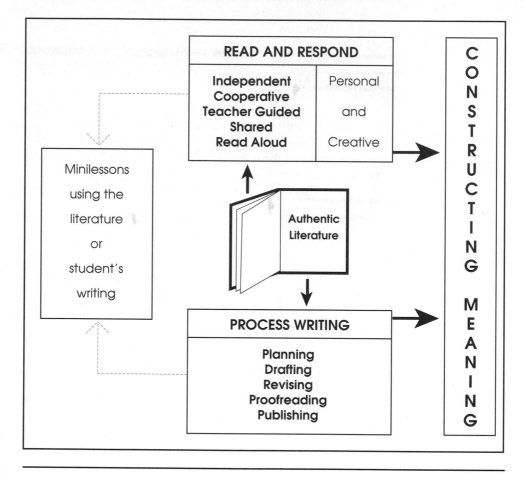

learned and what they might do to improve it. Again, this promotes metacognitive development, which leads to better construction of meaning.

Research shows that directed lessons such as the type being suggested here do help some students learn to read and write (Pearson & Dole, 1987). These lessons should always go back to the literature or sample of writing for examples of what is being taught, and all practice and application should be in the form of reading and writing, not filling blanks, marking, circling, or underlining on a worksheet. A minilesson to accompany the literacy lesson appears in the next section of this chapter. (Minilessons are discussed in more detail in Chapter 8.)

*Literacy
Lesson*

Jamaica Tag-Along

This section presents a sample literacy lesson and minilesson based on the discussions on pages 55–60 of this chapter and the book *Jamaica Tag-Along* (Havill, 1989), a delightful story about a little girl who wants to tag along with her older brother and realizes she is treating a little boy on the playground like her older brother has treated her. Juanita Havill has also written another book about Jamaica entitled *Jamaica's Find* (1986); children love both books because they can so easily relate to Jamaica and her problems.

The literacy lesson plan presented here has been used with children and illustrates the concepts and ideas about literacy learning developed throughout this text. Many of its ideas have been discussed in the first two chapters, but some will be discussed later. The plan for *Jamaica Tag-Along* would be suitable for a thematic unit on growing up, which might be used in late first grade or early second grade. The "notes" presented throughout the plan explain why each activity was selected and give references to sections of this text that explain the rationale behind what was done. The minilesson on inferencing on page 81 should be used only if students have demonstrated a need for such support.

Before Reading the Plan

1. **Think about what you have learned about constructing meaning and literacy learning.**
2. **Review the parts of a literacy lesson (page 58) and of a minilesson (page 59).**
3. **Read *Jamaica Tag-Along* to determine the problem, action, and outcome in the story.**

While Reading the Plan

1. **Keep in mind that your purpose in reading this plan now is to get a big picture of the plan. The notes in the last column will help you understand why each step was done as it was.**
2. **Think about the literacy lesson plan and how the parts were carried out.**
3. **Think about why each part was done as it was. Note any questions you might have.**
4. **Think of other ways you might have developed this lesson.**
5. **Think about which activities would help you know when to use the minilesson.**

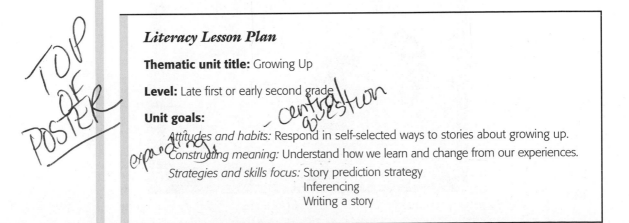

TOP OF POSTER

Literacy Lesson Plan

Thematic unit title: Growing Up

Level: Late first or early second grade

Unit goals:

~ central question

expanding

Attitudes and habits: Respond in self-selected ways to stories about growing up.
Constructing meaning: Understand how we learn and change from our experiences.
Strategies and skills focus: Story prediction strategy
  Inferencing
  Writing a story

Jamaica ran to the kitchen to answer the phone. But her brother got there first.

"It's for me," Ossie said.

Jamaica stayed and listened to him talk.

"Sure," Ossie said. "I'll meet you at the court."

Illustrations by Anne Sibley O'Brien

Jamaica Tag-Along

Juanita Havill

Ossie got his basketball from the closet. "I'm going to shoot baskets with Buzz."

"Can I come, too?" Jamaica said. "I don't have anything to do."

"Ah, Jamaica, call up your own friends."

"Everybody is busy today."

"I don't want you tagging along."

"I don't want to tag along," Jamaica said. "I just want to play basketball with you and Buzz."

"You're not old enough. We want to play serious ball."

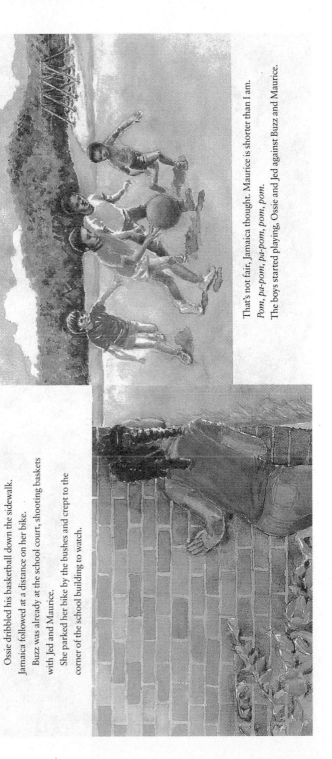

Ossie dribbled his basketball down the sidewalk, Jamaica followed at a distance on her bike.

Buzz was already at the school court, shooting baskets with Jed and Maurice.

She parked her bike by the bushes and crept to the corner of the school building to watch.

That's not fair, Jamaica thought. Maurice is shorter than I am.

Pom, pa-pom, pa-pom, pom, pom.

The boys started playing, Ossie and Jed against Buzz and Maurice.

Jamaica sneaked to the edge of the court.
Maurice missed a shot and the ball came bouncing toward
her. Jamaica jumped. "I've got the ball," she yelled.
  "Jamaica!" Ossie was so surprised he tripped over Buzz. They
both fell down.
  Jamaica dribbled to the basket and tossed the ball. It whirled
around the rim and flew out.

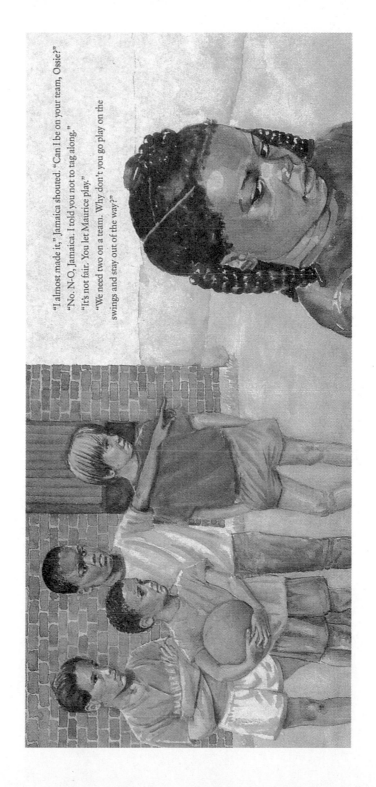

"I almost made it," Jamaica shouted. "Can I be on your team, Ossie?"

"No. N-O, Jamaica. I told you not to tag along."

"It's not fair. You let Maurice play."

"We need two on a team. Why don't you go play on the swings and stay out of the way?"

"I still think it's not fair." Jamaica walked slowly over to the sandlot.

She started to swing, but a little boy kept walking in front of her. His mom should keep him out of the way, Jamaica thought.

She looked up and saw a woman pushing a baby back and forth in a stroller.

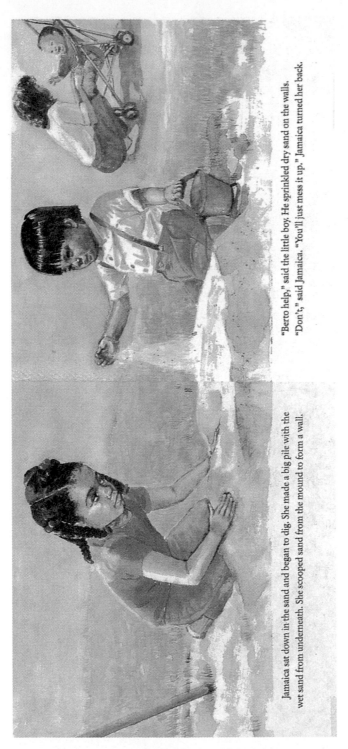

Jamaica sat down in the sand and began to dig. She made a big pile with the wet sand from underneath. She scooped sand from the mound to form a wall.

"Berto help," said the little boy. He sprinkled dry sand on the walls. "Don't," said Jamaica. "You'll just mess it up." Jamaica turned her back.

She piled the wet sand high. She made a castle with towers.

She dug a ditch around the wall.

Jamaica turned to see if Berto was still there. He stood watching. Then he tried to step over the ditch, and his foot smashed the wall.

"Stay away from my castle," Jamaica said.

"Berto," the woman pushing the stroller said, "leave this girl alone. Big kids don't like to be bothered by little kids."

"That's what my brother always says," Jamaica said. She started to repair the castle. Then she thought, but I don't like my brother to say that. It hurts my feelings.

Jamaica smoothed the wall. "See, Berto, like that. You can help me make a bigger castle if you're very careful."

Jamaica and Berto made a giant castle. They put water from the drinking fountain in the moat.

"Wow," Ossie said when the game was over and the other boys went home. "Need some help?"

"If you want to," Jamaica said.

Jamaica, Berto, and Ossie worked together on the castle.

Jamaica didn't even mind if Ossie tagged along.

Literacy
Lesson
continued

Introducing *Jamaica Tag-Along*

ACTIVITY	PROCEDURE *what?*	NOTES *How? (Don't have to write on poster)*
Brainstorming about experiences	1. Ask children in small groups (three to five) to list problems they have had with older siblings. Encourage discussion about their feelings. 2. Make a class summary chart.	Activates pertinent prior knowledge and gets children thinking about the central problem. Students for whom this lesson is planned do not need vocabulary instruction before reading.

> | *Problems with Older Brothers and Sisters* | *How We Feel* |
> |---|---|
> | | |

ACTIVITY	PROCEDURE	NOTES
Previewing *Jamaica Tag-Along* Strategy: story map prediction	1. Show the book *Jamaica Tag-Along*. Read the title, author, and illustrator. Have children look through the book to see what they think will happen. 2. Show the story map prediction strategy chart. Briefly discuss the meanings of setting, characters, and problem in a story. 3. Ask children to predict the setting, characters, and problem. Record group predictions. (For children who have difficulty predicting, model how to make predictions about setting; then have children predict the other parts.)	The story map prediction strategy chart helps students see how to predict. The chart and the discussion help to support them as they begin to construct meaning. Predictions become the purpose for reading. For a discussion of the story map prediction strategy, see Chapters 3 and 8.

STORY MAP PREDICTION

Setting: *Time*   *Place*

Characters:

Problem:

Action:

Outcome:

Reading and Responding to *Jamaica Tag-Along*

ACTIVITY	PROCEDURE	NOTES
Student selection of reading mode	Suggest that this story might be read independently or with teacher support (teacher-guided/independent reading). Encourage students to select the method they prefer.	Gives students choices and helps them take part in meeting their own needs. (Some may need suggestions on which way to read the story.)
Independent reading (for children who select to read this independently)	Have them read it to verify their predictions.	Most children can read this book independently because it is easy enough for them to understand.
Making notes and responding while reading independently	Remind children to make notes and respond in their journals as they read, if they choose to do so.	This will encourage natural responding.

Literacy Lesson continued	ACTIVITY	PROCEDURE	NOTES
	Interactive-guided/ independent reading (for children who select it)	Guide children who select this mode through part of the story and then have them read the remainder independently. Direct them through three parts of the story to verify the predictions they made.	The different modes of reading provide varied levels of support to meet individual needs.
		Discussion questions: pages 1—2: Who were the characters we met? Where is this story taking place?	Helps children construct meaning by checking their predictions, building a mental map of the story, and responding personally as they read.
		Predicting: What do you think Ossie is going to do? Why?	Helps children develop their ability to monitor by continuously making, verifying, and changing predictions.
		pages 3—9: Were your predictions correct? What is the problem in this story? How do you feel about Jamaica and Ossie right now?	Checks predictions and brings out story problem. Predictions help students relate their own knowledge to the reading and monitor their reading.
		Predicting: How do you think the boys will treat Jamaica now? Why?	
		pages 10—17: Was your prediction correct about how the boys would treat Jamaica? Whom did Jamaica meet? How did Jamaica react to Berto when he tried to help her?	Checks predictions and brings out story action.
		Predicting: What do you think will happen in the remainder of the story?	Sets purpose for reading remainder of story.
		pages 18—28: Have children read remainder of story independently to see if their predictions are verified.	

Literacy
Lesson
continued

ACTIVITY	PROCEDURE	NOTES
Children-selected responses	Display the after-reading response chart and ask children to select how they wish to respond in their journals. Children may share their responses in the discussion circles.	Allow all children to respond in the manner that is best for them. Ideas are on the chart. For a discussion of the importance of responding to literature, see page 55 and Chapter 6.

> *After-Reading Response Chart*
>
> 1. Enter in your journal
>   - Title
>   - Author
>   - Response
> 2. Select a way to respond
>   - Write about your favorite character. Tell why you picked this character.
>   - Draw a picture about your favorite part. Write about it.
>   - Decide what you can do to respond.

ACTIVITY	PROCEDURE	NOTES
Literature discussion circles	1. Divide the class into literature discussion circles. Display the discussion circle chart and go over the procedures before children begin.	Literature discussion circles (or literature circles) are another form of responding to literature. The chart guides children and thus helps structure this experience. See Chapter 6 for a further discussion of literature circles.

> *Discussion Circle Chart: Story Prediction*
>
> 1. Talk about the predictions made before reading.
> 2. Retell the story.
> 3. Share your response with the group.

	2. As children work, move from group to group to monitor and support the activity.	Observe how well children can make predictions and inferences. For children who need extra support with inferencing, use the minilesson on inferencing (see end of this plan). For a discussion of minilessons, see page 59. For a discussion of observing, see Chapter 11.

Literacy
Lesson
continued

ACTIVITY	PROCEDURE	NOTES
Whole-group discussion: Summarizing the story and checking the unit focus	1. Discuss the points covered on the discussion circle chart.	
	2. Have children talk about what Jamaica and Ossie may have learned from this experience.	
	3. Have children relate Jamaica's experiences to their own.	
Reflecting	Ask children to talk about how their predictions helped them understand the story.	Assists metacognitive development.

Extending *Jamaica Tag-Along*

ACTIVITY	PROCEDURE	NOTES
Theme mural on growing and changing	Some children may draw a picture about how Jamaica and/or Ossie changed and then write a caption for their picture; these can become part of a mural.	Allows children to construct personal meaning in another way. Helps to continue to pull together the theme.
Process writing: Writing a story, brainstorming	Begin story writing by having children brainstorm to compile a list of possible topics for a story that they will write during this theme unit. Writing will continue throughout the unit.	This is a very strong example of a good story. The use of the prediction strategy will have helped children focus on the elements of a story. For more discussion of process writing, see Chapter 7.

Minilesson on Inferencing

Thematic unit: Growing Up

Book: *Jamaica Tag-Along*

Focus: Using story clues to make inferences

When to Use: Use only when children have demonstrated through responding that they need more directed support on inferencing and constructing meaning in this book.

Literacy Lesson *continued*	ACTIVITY	PROCEDURE	NOTES
	Introduction: let children know what they will learn	Tell children that sometimes authors give you a clue to what they mean without really saying it. (Give example from a story children know.) In this lesson, they will revisit Jamaica to look at how the author has done this.	It is important to let children know what they will learn. This focuses their attention and gives them a purpose for the lesson. The term *inferencing* may be used. See page 59 for a discussion of minilessons.
	Teacher modeling of inferencing	1. Ask children to discuss how Jamaica felt in the story. 2. Have children open their books to pages 6–7 and to follow along as you read the pages aloud. Then *think aloud* with children:	Modeling using the literature children have already read gives them a meaningful starting point. For a discussion of modeling, see page 33 and Chapter 8. If more than one modeling experience is needed, use page 8 in the same manner as pages 6–7.

> *Think Aloud:*
>
> ``These pages tell me that Jamaica really wants to play with the older boys. She is getting upset because Maurice is shorter than she is. I use the author's clues and my own knowledge to begin to figure this out. The story doesn't say this directly."

	Student modeling and guided practice	page 8: Have children read this page to tell how the boys feel about Jamaica. Then ask them to explain how they were able to tell. Did the author say it?	This activity begins to release the responsibility for inferencing to the children. Some may need several examples. This modeling helps to develop metacognitive abilities.
	Summarizing and reflecting on how to inference	Help children summarize what they have learned about inferencing: Did the author tell you everything about Jamaica? How were you able to figure out that the boys were getting upset with Jamaica? When do you think you will use this strategy?	Children need to summarize in their own words what they have learned. Guiding them with questions is a good way to do this. It is important to get children to put into their own words what they have done and when they might use it. This

	ACTIVITY	PROCEDURE	NOTES
Literacy Lesson continued	Summarizing and reflecting on how to inference *(continued)*		helps to create better conditions for transfer to other books they will read by developing their metacognitive abilities.
	Independent practice using inferencing	1. Using the story clues chart, ask children to go through the remainder of the book to locate other places where they used story clues to learn something that the author didn't say directly.	This type of practice puts the process of inferencing in meaningful text and continues to release the responsibility of inferencing to the children. See pages 33–34 on the importance of releasing responsibility.

Story Clues

Page	Clue	What Was Learned
--	---------------- ---------------- -----	----------------------- ----------------------- ----------------------- ----------------------- ----- ----------------------- ----------------------- -----

		2. Summarize the activity after children have completed it.	
	Application of inferencing	In the next book in the theme, ask children to look for clues authors give to suggest things they don't really say. Have them be ready to share these clues and explain how they could tell what was meant.	Application of this process in reading is important. If children have difficulty using it, further modeling will be needed.

After Reading the Plan
1. **Review and discuss the plan with some of your peers who have also studied it.**
2. **Select a piece of literature that you know well, and develop a literacy lesson plan of your own. Share and discuss your plan with some of your peers.**

Guidelines for Selecting Literature

Selecting the appropriate literature for the literacy program is both a critical and a challenging decision, but it can be fun and rewarding if you have some guidelines in mind.

What constitutes "good literature" is a much-debated topic (Goodman & Goodman, 1991). Although this judgment is generally a personal matter, it is possible to select a variety of quality literature for your students. Since thousands of new books are published annually, literature selection is an ongoing process that should involve you, other teachers, the librarian or media specialist, students, parents, and other interested persons.

There are four basic criteria to consider in selecting literature: developmental appropriateness, student appeal, literary quality, and cultural and social authenticity.

Developmental Appropriateness

For years, selections for reading instruction have been based on their readability as determined by one of several formulae that yield a grade-level score. However, serious questions have been raised about the validity of such formulas (Klare, 1984; Weaver & Kintsch, 1991). In addition to lacking validity, such prescriptions actually cause problems (Routman, 1988; Simons & Ammon, 1989). The literature is in essence destroyed, watered down, or made more difficult by such procedures. Moreover, when the natural language patterns are altered and controlled vocabulary is used, the reader lacks the appropriate clues to read the text with ease and fluency.

Remember that beginning learners (kindergarten, first, and second grade) need highly predictable literature that offers the richness, rhyme, and pattern of the language (Bridge, Winograd, & Haley, 1983; Goodman & Goodman, 1991). For example, the book *Mary Wore Her Red Dress and Henry Wore His Green Sneakers* (Peek, 1985) has a predictable language pattern:

> *Mary wore her red dress, red dress, red dress,*
> *Mary wore her red dress all day long.*
>
> *Henry wore his green sneakers, green sneakers, green sneakers,*
> *Henry wore his green sneakers all day long.*
> [and so forth]

Bridge et al. (1983) have identified seven patterns of predictability in literature:

1. Phrase or sentence repeated (example: *Mary Wore Her Red Dress and Henry Wore His Green Sneakers* [Peek, 1985])
2. Repetitive-cumulative pattern in which a word, phrase, or sentence is repeated (example: *Nobody Listens to Andrew* [Guilfoile, 1957])
3. Rhyming patterns (example: *Sheep in a Jeep* [Shaw, 1986])
4. Familiar cultural sequences, cardinal and ordinal numbers (example: *Over in the Meadow* [Keats, 1971])
5. Familiar cultural sequences, alphabet (example: *Dr. Seuss's A B C* [Seuss, 1963])

Teachers and the librarian work together to stay abreast of new literature. © *Michael Zide*

6. Familiar cultural sequences, days, months, colors (example: *Monday, Monday, I Like Monday* [Martin, 1970])
7. Predictable plots (example: *Mr. Gumpy's Outing* [Burningham, 1970])

These patterns should be considered when selecting literature for the beginning levels. The more difficulty children are having learning to read and write, the more highly predictable the literature needs to be.

To determine the developmental appropriateness of a book beyond the beginning reading levels, look at the concepts and general complexity of the text. Are the concepts ones your students will know? Have they had experience with them? Is the text written in a clear style that your students will find easy to understand? These are the types of questions that can guide your selection.

The general nature of the guidelines just described may prompt you to think that determining developmental appropriateness is a very arbitrary process. However, recall that literature has no grade level. Therefore, there is no one single grade for which a book may be assumed to be absolutely appropriate. Rather, a book may be used in different ways at different grade levels. For example, *Ira Says Goodbye* (Waber, 1988) may be read aloud to children in kindergarten but may be read independently by second or third graders.

Student Appeal

Student appeal may well be one of the most important aspects to consider in selecting literature for the literacy program. The books selected need to appeal to students, captivate their imaginations, and entice them to want to read more and more. Appeal may best be determined by the students themselves. However, when you cannot consult with each student, you should consider such sources as "Children's Choices" and "Young Adults' Choices," published annually each fall in *The Reading Teacher* and the *Journal of Reading,* both publications of the International Reading Association. These listings present favorite books voted on by children and young adults. *The Reading Teacher* also publishes an annual list of teachers' choices. You may want to consider earlier editions of all of these listings.

Literary Quality

The books you select should be of high literary quality. Watch for elements of plot, characterization, setting, theme, style, and point of view that create memorable stories. You may want to read Norton's (1991) chapter, "Evaluating and Selecting Literature for Children," listed in the For Additional Reading section for a detailed discussion of how high-quality literature incorporates these elements.

Determining the literary quality of books is a large task for a busy teacher. The following sources can help you evaluate new books as they become available:

The WEB describes how books on specific topics may be used in the classroom. Published four times a year by Martha L. King Center for Language and Literacy, The Ohio State University, 29 Woodruff Avenue, Columbus, OH 43210-1177.

The Horn Book Magazine reviews books from many perspectives. Write to The Horn Book Magazine, Park Square Building, 31 St. James Avenue, Boston, MA 02116.

The New Advocate provides articles and book reviews. Published four times a year by Christopher-Gordon Publishers, Inc., 480 Washington Street, Norwood, MA 02062.

Book Links presents reviews of books that have been grouped by thematic areas. Published bimonthly by the American Library Association, 50 East Huron Street, Chicago, IL 60611.

In addition, the following professional journals review literature in each edition:

The Reading Teacher (elementary), published by the International Reading Association

Journal of Adolescent and Adult Literacy (middle school, junior high school, high school), published by the International Reading Association

Language Arts (elementary), published by the National Council of Teachers of English

You can keep up with reviews of new books or books about children's literature by writing the National Council of Teachers of English (NCTE) Web site at www.ncte.org and the International Reading Association (IRA) Web site at www.ira.org.

Cultural and Social Authenticity

The literature selected for the literacy program must include selections that are both culturally and socially authentic. "Through multicultural literature, children of the majority culture learn to respect values and contributions of people in other parts of the world. . . . The wide range of multicultural themes also helps children develop an understanding of social change" (Norton, 1991, p. 531). In essence, reading and writing about a variety of real cultural and social situations helps students develop an appreciation and understanding of how people from a variety of cultures and social settings live and work together. Books such as *The Patchwork Quilt* (Flournoy, 1985), *Hawk, I'm Your Brother* (Baylor, 1976), *Felita* (Mohr, 1979), and *The Rainbow People* (Yep, 1989) are examples of the types of literature that should be a part of every literacy program. You may also want to read Norton's (1991) chapter on multicultural literature listed in the For Additional Reading section.

Another source for literature is published literature anthologies. Many people still refer to these as *basal readers*. Over the years, basals have been highly criticized for both their content and their instructional suggestions (Goodman, Freeman, Murphy, & Shannon, 1988). Although many of the criticisms have been valid, they often related more to how basals were used than to what was in them, and publishers have now begun to look more critically at what goes into such texts. In fact, many publishers now incorporate authentic, unadapted literature into their series and resources. When selecting a basal series, therefore, you should apply the same criteria suggested for selecting books. In addition, you should keep the following points in mind:

▶ The literature should be authentic and unadapted. It should not be rewritten to conform to a readability score.

▶ The literature anthology is a resource, not a recipe book. Choose the pieces of literature that are best for your students. *You do not have to use all the selections provided.*

Selecting literature is a big job, but by using some of the suggestions given here, you will make the task more manageable.

Summary

This chapter developed two important frameworks: the literacy program and a thematic unit plan supported by literacy lessons and minilessons. The balanced literacy program has three important parts: (1) motivation, (2) instruction in reading and writing, and (3) independent reading and writing. These three components interact in helping children learn to construct meaning and grow into literacy.

A thematic unit and literacy lesson format were suggested as a way to plan and organize instruction throughout the literacy program. In each literacy lesson, a work of literature is introduced, read and responded to, and finally extended in some way. Different modes of reading and writing are used throughout the lessons to vary support for students as needed. Within the framework of the literacy lesson, minilessons can be used to more directly model strategies and the processes of constructing meaning. The chapter presented a literacy lesson for *Jamaica Tag-Along,* along with a minilesson on inferencing, and suggested criteria for selecting literature for thematic units and literacy lessons.

Literature

Ackerman, K. (1988). *Song and dance man.* New York: Knopf.

Adoff, A. (Ed.). (1973). *The poetry of black America: Anthology of the 20th century.* New York: Harper and Row.

Base, G. (1988). *The eleventh hour.* New York: Harry N. Abrams.

Baylor, B. (1976). *Hawk, I'm your brother.* New York: Scribner's.

Baylor, B. (1982). *The best town in the world.* New York: Scribner's.

Burningham, J. (1970). *Mr. Gumpy's outing.* London: Henry Holt.

Cole, J. (Ed.). (1984). *A new treasury of children's poetry: Old favorites and new discoveries.* New York: Doubleday.

Dahl, R. (1988). *Matilda.* London: Jonathon Cape.

de Paola, T. (1989). *The art lesson.* New York: G. P. Putnam.

Flournoy, V. (1985). *The patchwork quilt.* New York: Dial.

Giff, P. R. (1980). *Today was a terrible day.* New York: Viking.

Giff, P. R. (1988). *Ronald Morgan goes to bat.* New York: Viking Kestrel.

Guilfoile, E. (1957). *Nobody listens to Andrew.* Cleveland: Modern Curriculum Press.

Havill, J. (1986). *Jamaica's find.* Boston: Houghton Mifflin.

Havill, J. (1989). *Jamaica Tag-Along* Boston: Houghton Mifflin.

Isadora, R. (1979). *Ben's trumpet.* New York: Greenwillow Books.

Keats, E. J. (1971). *Over in the meadow.* New York: Scholastic.

Lowry, L. (1989). *Number the stars.* Boston: Houghton Mifflin.

McCloskey, R. (1948). *Blueberries for Sal.* New York: Viking.

Martin, B. (1970). *Monday, Monday, I like Monday.* New York: Holt, Rinehart and Winston.

Mohr, N. (1979). *Felita.* New York: Dial.

Munsch, R. (1983). *Angela's airplane.* Toronto: Annick Press.

Paterson, K. (1977). *Bridge to Terabithia.* New York: Crowell.

Peek, M. (1985). *Mary wore her red dress and Henry wore his green sneakers.* New York: Clarion.

Prelutsky, J. (Ed.). (1983). *Random House book of poetry for children.* New York: Random House.

Prelutsky, J. (1984). *The new kid on the block.* New York: Greenwillow Books.

Prelutsky, J. (1986). *Ride a purple pelican.* New York: Greenwillow Books.

Prelutsky, J. (1988). *Tyrannosaurus was a beast.* New York: Greenwillow Books.

Prelutsky, J. (1989). *Poems of A. Nonny Mouse.* New York: Knopf.

Prelutsky, J. (1990). *Beneath a blue umbrella.* New York: Greenwillow Books.

Prelutsky, J. (1990). *Something big has been here.* New York: Greenwillow Books.

Rawls, W. (1961). *Where the red fern grows.* New York: Bantam.

Say, A. (1990). *El Chino.* Boston: Houghton Mifflin.

Seuss (1963). *Dr. Seuss's A B C.* New York: Random House.

Shaw, N. (1986). *Sheep in a jeep.* Boston: Houghton Mifflin.

Silverstein, S. (1974). *Where the sidewalk ends.* New York: Harper and Row.

Silverstein, S. (1981). *A light in the attic.* New York: Harper & Row.

Steptoe, J. (1987). *Mufaro's beautiful daughters: An African tale.* New York: Scholastic.

Stevenson, R. L. (1885/1981). *A child's garden of verses.* New York: Checkerboard Press, a Division of Macmillan.

Waber, B. (1988). *Ira says goodbye.* Boston: Houghton Mifflin.

Willis, V. (1988). *The secret in the matchbox.* New York: Farrar, Straus and Giroux.

Yep, L. (1989). *The rainbow people.* New York: Harper and Row.

For Additional Reading

Educational Leadership. (1990). Volume 47, Number 4. Entire issue on cooperative learning.

Grabe, M., & Grabe, C. (1998). *Integrating technology for meaningful learning,* 2nd ed. (Chapters 3 and 5). Boston: Houghton Mifflin.

Johnson, D. W., Johnson, R. T., & Holubec, E. (1988). *Cooperation in the classroom.* Edina, MN: Interaction Book Company.

Norton, D. E. (1991). Evaluating and selecting literature for children. In *Through the eyes of a child: An introduction to children's literature* (3rd ed., pp. 83–126). New York: Macmillan.

Norton, D. E. (1991). Multicultural literature. In *Through the eyes of a child: An introduction to children's literature* (3rd ed., pp. 529–605). New York: Macmillan.

Pearson, P. D. (1985). Changing the face of reading comprehension instruction. *Reading Teacher, 38,* 724–738.

Tierney, R. J., Readence, J. E., & Dishner, E. K. (1990). Readers theater. In *Reading strategies and practices: A compendium* (3rd ed.) (pp. 190–195). Boston: Allyn and Bacon.

Trelease, J. (1989). *The new read-aloud handbook.* New York: Penguin.

Walmsley, S. A., & Walp, T. P. (1990). Integrating literature and composing into the language arts curriculum: Philosophy and practice. *Elementary School Journal, 90*(3), 251–274.

For Exploration: Electronic Products and Resources

A variety of multimedia products can be integrated into a balanced literacy program. These products may include video, software, the Internet, and interactive technology on CD-ROM. The following companies or organizations create educational materials in language arts for a variety of grade levels. Explore their Web sites to learn what the technology offers, evaluate new teaching and learning tools, and investigate resources for educators. Some sites also offer resources and activities for students.

Broderbund
www.broderbund.com/education

The Learning Company
www.learningco.com

Little Planet
www.littleplanet.com/

Micrograms Software
www.micrograms.com/

Sunburst
www.sunburst.com

Activating and Developing Prior Knowledge

3

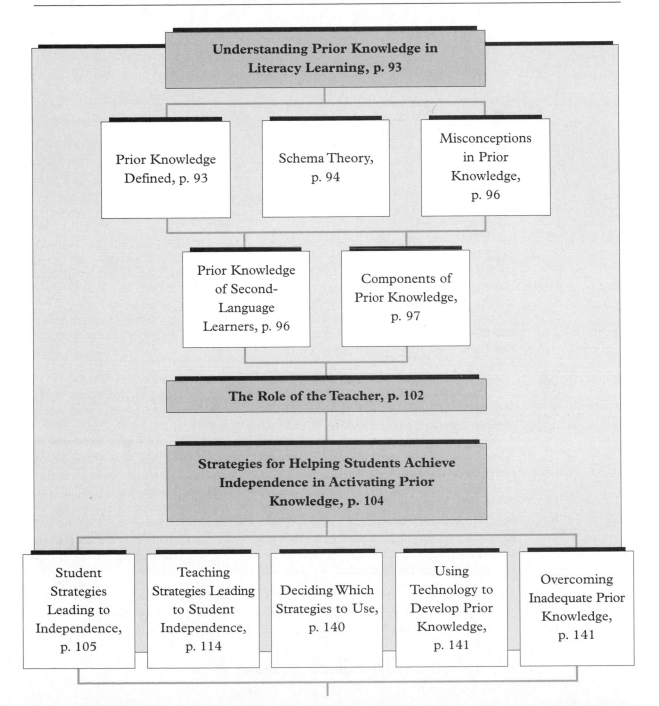

Understanding Prior Knowledge in Literacy Learning, p. 93

Prior Knowledge Defined, p. 93

Schema Theory, p. 94

Misconceptions in Prior Knowledge, p. 96

Prior Knowledge of Second-Language Learners, p. 96

Components of Prior Knowledge, p. 97

The Role of the Teacher, p. 102

Strategies for Helping Students Achieve Independence in Activating Prior Knowledge, p. 104

Student Strategies Leading to Independence, p. 105

Teaching Strategies Leading to Student Independence, p. 114

Deciding Which Strategies to Use, p. 140

Using Technology to Develop Prior Knowledge, p. 141

Overcoming Inadequate Prior Knowledge, p. 141

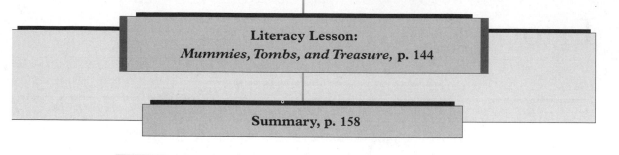

Literacy Lesson:
Mummies, Tombs, and Treasure, **p. 144**

Summary, p. 158

*L*et's drop in on a fourth-grade classroom where the teacher is actively engaging students in beginning a unit on Abraham Lincoln.

Mr. Willett had given his class five minutes to write what they knew about Abraham Lincoln. Displaying a chart labeled K-W-L (Figure 3.1), he then told the class they were going to begin a thematic unit on Abraham Lincoln. To get started, they were going to use the strategy known as K-W-L to think about what they knew about Lincoln and what they would like to learn about him.

Mr. Willett then divided the class into small groups and asked them to use the paragraphs they had written as a basis for brainstorming ideas to go in the "know" column of the K-W-L chart. After about five minutes of small-group discussion, Mr. Willett brought the entire group together to summarize what they had listed. One student served as recorder and listed on the chalkboard the points given by various class members.

Mr. Willett could tell by the students' responses that most of them knew a great deal about Lincoln, but he could also tell that some had very little or erroneous knowledge that they needed to expand and/or correct.

IN THIS EXAMPLE, Mr. Willett was activating his class's prior knowledge before starting the theme on Abraham Lincoln. Through his observations, he was able to assess how much the students knew and to determine what additional background he needed to develop before introducing the first book they would read, the Newbery Award winner *Lincoln: A Photobiography* (Freedman, 1987). Mr. Willett used four different techniques for activating prior knowledge: a quick writing exercise, brainstorming, the K-W-L strategy (Ogle, 1986), and small- and large-group discussion.

In Chapter 1 of this text, we established the importance of prior knowledge to successful literacy learning. In Chapter 3, we examine this area in more detail and focus on techniques and strategies that help students activate and develop their prior knowledge in thematic units and literacy lessons. Throughout this chapter, two major points are stressed:

▶ *Purpose:* Students must have a purpose for reading and writing; in part, this purpose is created by activating and developing prior knowledge.

▶ *Independence:* Students must become independent in activating their own prior knowledge if they are to construct meaning effectively.

All of the strategies presented in this chapter lead to these two goals.

FIGURE 3.1

K-W-L STRATEGY CHART

K	*W*	*L*
What we *know* about Abraham Lincoln	What we *want* to learn about Lincoln	What we *learned* about Lincoln

Understanding Prior Knowledge in Literacy Learning

Research over the past two decades has clearly established that the process of constructing meaning through reading, writing, speaking, and listening is based on the prior knowledge that individuals bring to the situation (Adams & Bertram, 1980; Anderson & Pearson, 1984). After reviewing extensive research, Tierney and Cunningham (1984) concluded that "intervention research has supported the existence of a causal relationship between background knowledge and comprehension" (p. 612). More recent researchers have drawn similar conclusions, even though many questions about prior knowledge and literacy learning remain unanswered (Barr, Kamil, Mosenthal, & Pearson, 1991). Researchers and educators use the terms *prior knowledge, background, background knowledge or information,* and *world knowledge* interchangeably; in this text, we will use the term *prior knowledge* when referring to all of these areas.

Prior Knowledge Defined

The concept of prior knowledge is not new to educators. For many years, educators have recommended that teachers ensure that readers have the appropriate background for reading a given selection because such background was believed to enhance learning (Smith, 1965). Essentially, prior knowledge is "the sum of a person's previous learning and development; experience; . . . experiences which precede a learning situation, story, etc." (Harris & Hodges, 1981, p. 29). The information Mr. Willett gained from his students through quick writing, discussion, and the use of K-W-L constituted their collective prior knowledge about Abraham Lincoln.

Schema Theory

Our understanding of the importance of prior knowledge in literacy learning has developed through research based on schema theory (plural *schemata*), which assumes that individuals develop a cognitive structure of knowledge in their minds (Bartlett, 1932; Rumelhart, 1980). As individuals experience the world, they add new information to their schemata, which are divided into various interrelated categories. One way to picture this concept more concretely is to think of the mind as a large system of file folders. As one gains new knowledge and information, the mind creates a new file folder, or schema, or adds the information to an existing schema (Anderson & Pearson, 1984; Rumelhart, 1980). Then, as individuals develop and expand their schemata, they construct meaning by drawing from various schemata and building connections among them; that is, they make inferences (Anderson & Pearson, 1984). This process goes on continuously while a person engages in literacy tasks. Example 3.1 illustrates how the experience of reading expands one's schemata.

Example 3.1

> You are going to read a magazine article about the pleasures of automobile racing. As you begin to read, you think about what you know about automobile racing; in the process you activate your schemata, which probably formed over many years of experience. If your schemata include positive, pleasant ideas, you will read the article differently than if they included negative, unpleasant ideas. If you have no schema or very limited schemata for automobile racing, you will begin to form a schema as you read the article, and you will relate the information you gain to any other schemata you have about cars. For example, you may have a schema that relates auto racing to danger; if you read about how training reduces the dangers, you may form a new, broadened schema. Throughout the process of reading, you take the information from the text and either relate it to an existing schema or form a new schema (see Figure 3.2).

Schema theory contends that individuals understand what they read only as it relates to what they already know. Anderson, Reynolds, Schallert, and Goetz (1977) demonstrated this very clearly through their research. They asked students in an educational psychology class and students in a weightlifting class to read the following passage and tell what they thought it was about. Read this passage for yourself and see what you think:

Rocky slowly got up from the mat and planned his escape. He hesitated a moment and thought. Things were not going well. What bothered him the most was being held, especially since the charge against him had been weak. He considered his present situation. The lock that held him was strong but he thought he could break it. He knew, however, that his timing had to be perfect. Rocky was aware that it was because of his early roughness that he had been penalized so severely—much too severely from his point of view. The situation was becoming frustrating; the pressure had been grinding on him far too long. He was being ridden unmercifully. Rocky was getting angry now.

FIGURE 3.2

READER INTERACTING WITH THE TEXT TO ACTIVATE AND EXPAND SCHEMA

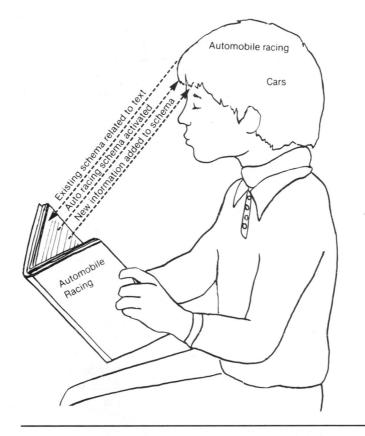

He felt he was ready to make his move. He knew that his success or failure depended on what he did in the next few seconds. (p. 372)

What was the focus of this paragraph? What topic came to your mind as you read? Most psychology students interpreted the passage as a prison escape, whereas the weightlifting students related it to a wrestling match. Thus, research supports the idea that individuals construct meaning in light of their prior knowledge and interests. Construction of meaning is an individual and personal matter (Rosenblatt, 1938/1983). Research in emergent literacy further supports this conclusion (Sulzby, 1989). For in-depth reading on schema theory, see the For Additional Reading section at the conclusion of this chapter.

Misconceptions in Prior Knowledge

Although research has documented the significance of prior knowledge in students' abilities to construct meaning, there is also evidence that some students bring incomplete or erroneous ideas to certain learning tasks. Such misconceptions can interfere with meaning construction (Driver & Erickson, 1983; Lipson, 1982, 1983), and numerous researchers have attempted to look at how this happens (Alvermann, Smith, & Readence, 1985; Dole & Smith, 1989; Hynd & Alvermann, 1986; Pace, Marshall, Horowitz, Lipson, & Lucido, 1989). In all instances, they have found that an individual's interpretation of the text was definitely influenced by erroneous or incomplete prior knowledge. Various attempts to alter students' misconceptions have met with some success (Alvermann & Hynd, 1987; Dole & Smith, 1989; Maria, 1988). Although most of this research has been conducted using scientific material, it has assumed that misconceptions can interfere with the construction of meaning in narrative and expository texts as well. Strategies for overcoming misconceptions are discussed later in this chapter.

Prior Knowledge of Second-Language Learners

In classrooms throughout the country, many children are learning English as a second language; such children are often referred to as multilingual, ESL (English as a Second Language) students, or LEP (Limited English Proficiency) students. More recently, they have been called Students Acquiring English because that is what they are actually doing and this label has a positive connotation.

Regardless of the term used, these are all students whose native language is not English. Some may have learned to read in their native language. Research has been shown that second-language learners are able to learn to read in their native language and in English at the same time (Barrera, 1983). They develop literacy and the ability to construct meaning through essentially the same process first-language learners use, the only differences being language structure, knowledge of the language, and cultural prior knowledge (Weber, 1991). Since second-language learners have an extensive base of prior knowledge that has not been developed around English and the cultural traditions of English, their prior knowledge needs to receive special attention.

Rigg and Allen (1989) have proposed five principles regarding the literacy development of second-language learners:

1. *People who are learning another language are, first of all, people.*
2. *Learning a language means learning to do the things you want to do with people who speak that language.*
3. *A person's second language, like the first, develops globally, not linearly.*
4. *Language develops best in a variety of rich contexts.*
5. *Literacy is part of language, so writing and reading develop alongside speaking and listening.* (p. viii)

You will notice that these principles do not differ significantly from what we already have said about helping all students learn to construct meaning. Second-language learners bring their own language and prior knowledge to the classroom, which we must build on and expand. As Rigg and Allen (1989) conclude, "We should offer our second-language students a rich bath of language, not a string of language beads, one bead at a time" (p. xi). For further reading on this topic, see Rigg and Allen (1989) and Au (1993), listed in the For Additional Reading section at the end of this chapter.

What does all of this mean for you as a teacher? Given the vast quantity of research related to schema theory and prior knowledge, you need to remember these points as you develop and conduct your literacy program:

▶ Prior knowledge is crucial to the successful construction of meaning for *all* learners.

▶ Some students will have incomplete or erroneous prior knowledge related to a topic; it is therefore important to assess a student's state of knowledge, if possible, before any learning experience.

▶ When students have erroneous or incomplete prior knowledge, it is possible to alter it and help them construct meaning more successfully.

In the remainder of this chapter, we focus on how to help students achieve independence in activating their own prior knowledge.

Components of Prior Knowledge

Within the literacy program, prior knowledge needs to be thought of in two ways: as overall prior knowledge and as text-specific or topic-specific prior knowledge.

Overall prior knowledge is the entire base of knowledge that students possess as a result of their accumulated experiences both in and out of school, such as being read to, taking trips, watching television, or seeing movies. Since this is facilitated by extensive reading and writing, the *independent reading and writing* component of the literacy program is critical for expanding this knowledge base (Center for the Study of Reading, n.d.). The more students read and write, the more extensive prior knowledge they build, which in turn improves their ability to construct meaning.

Text-specific or topic-specific prior knowledge is the specific information needed for a particular theme or experience. For example, if students are going to read *The Boys' War* (Murphy, 1990), a book about the Civil War and the experiences of the young boys who fought in it, they will need specific information about the Civil War as well as knowledge about the structure of this type of text (see Figure 3.3).

As you develop thematic units and literacy lessons, you need to be concerned about two major components of text-specific or topic-specific prior knowledge: knowledge about the type of text (understanding that a story or an article has certain elements) and knowledge about the topic (for example, having some knowledge about mountains before reading a book about the Alps). Both play an important role in helping students construct meaning (Paris, Wasik, & Turner, 1991).

Knowledge About the Text

Recall from Chapter 1 that there are two basic types of text: narrative and expository. Since students need some knowledge about both types of text, it is important that you have some basic understanding about them.

Narrative Texts.   Narrative texts tell a story and are organized into a sequential pattern that includes a beginning, a middle, and an end. Within this pattern, any

FIGURE 3.3

OVERALL PRIOR KNOWLEDGE DEVELOPMENT

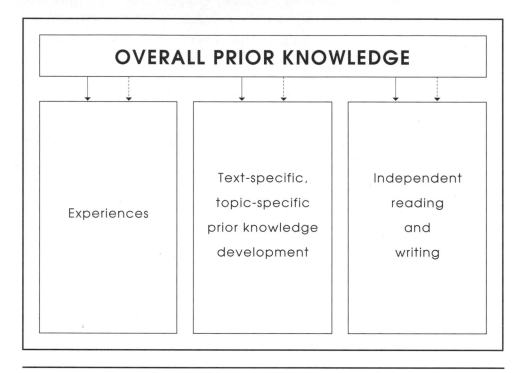

given narrative may be composed of several episodes, each consisting of characters, a setting, a problem, action, and a resolution of the problem (the outcome). These elements are the story's grammar, or basic plan. A graphic representation of these elements is called a *story map,* which can take many different forms (Freedle, 1979). The exact map for a story depends on the story's structure.

The *theme* of a story is the basic idea, stated or unstated, around which the whole story is written. In good literature the theme is most often unstated, requiring the reader to infer it. The *plot* is the way in which the story is organized; it is made up of episodes. The *setting* is the place and time at which the story occurs. The *characters* are the people or animals who carry out the action in the story. The *problem* is the situation or situations that initiate, or lead to, other events in the story. Finally, the *action* is what happens as a result of the problem; it is composed of events that lead to the solution of the problem, which is called the *resolution,* or outcome.

A story map of "The Three Pigs" appears in Figure 3.4. As you can see, you need only the essential elements to understand the story. Each episode leads to the next, leading to the overall understanding, or the theme, of the story. Notice that three of the episodes have essentially the same problem, but the third ends with a different resolution.

FIGURE 3.4

STORY MAP OF "THE THREE PIGS"

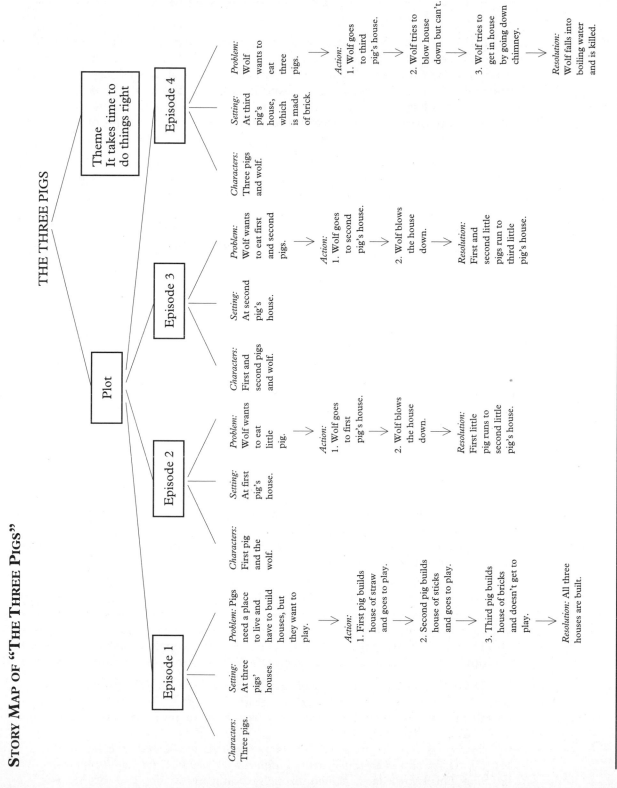

THE THREE PIGS

Theme
It takes time to do things right

Plot

Episode 1

Characters: Three pigs.

Setting: At three pigs' houses.

Problem: Pigs need a place to live and have to build houses, but they want to play.

Action:
1. First pig builds house of straw and goes to play.
2. Second pig builds house of sticks and goes to play.
3. Third pig builds house of bricks and doesn't get to play.

Resolution: All three houses are built.

Episode 2

Characters: First pig and the wolf.

Setting: At first pig's house.

Problem: Wolf wants to eat little pig.

Action:
1. Wolf goes to first pig's house.
2. Wolf blows the house down.

Resolution: First little pig runs to second little pig's house.

Episode 3

Characters: First and second pigs and wolf.

Setting: At second pig's house.

Problem: Wolf wants to eat first and second pigs.

Action:
1. Wolf goes to second pig's house.
2. Wolf blows the house down.

Resolution: First and second little pigs run to third little pig's house.

Episode 4

Characters: Three pigs and wolf.

Setting: At third pig's house, which is made of brick.

Problem: Wolf wants to eat three pigs.

Action:
1. Wolf goes to third pig's house.
2. Wolf tries to blow house down but can't.
3. Wolf tries to get in house by going down chimney.

Resolution: Wolf falls into boiling water and is killed.

Expository Texts.   Expository texts present information organized around main ideas. These are the types of materials commonly found in informational books, textbooks, the World Wide Web, CD-ROMs, newspapers, and magazines. Students generally have more difficulty reading expository texts than narrative texts because they have had less experience with them and because these texts may not follow a clear-cut pattern; instead, the organization depends on the type of information and purpose of the text. There are five frequently used patterns of expository writing (Meyer, 1975; Meyer & Freedle, 1984):

▶ *Description* presents information about a particular topic or gives characteristics of the topic. Unlike the other types of expository text structure, descriptive passages do not provide readers with clue words to aid in comprehension; therefore, readers must use the basic strategies they have learned for noting details and selecting the important information from the passage. However, the structure of descriptive passages can help the reader anticipate the type of content that is likely to follow.

▶ *Collection* presents a number of ideas or descriptions in a related group. Since the writer is presenting lists of related points, this structure is often called a *listing* or *sequence,* and the author frequently uses clue words such as *first, second, next,* and *finally* to introduce the points. Readers must infer the relationship between the listed points and the overall topic, noting details and identifying the sequence of ideas.

▶ The *causation,* or cause-effect, type of expository structure presents ideas so that a causal relationship is either stated or implied. This structure is frequently used in content area textbooks and in newspaper and magazine articles. The author often uses clue words: *therefore, consequently, because, as a result of, since,* or *the reasons for.* The reader must identify the elements being related and either recognize or infer the cause-effect relationships.

▶ The *response* structure presents a problem, question, or remark followed by a solution, answer, or reply. This type of structure is often used in mathematics, science, and social studies. Sometimes (as in mathematics) the reader is expected to provide the solution. The author may use clue words such as *the problem is, the question is, one reason for the problem is, a solution is,* or *one answer is.*

▶ *Comparison* requires the reader to note the likenesses and differences between two or more objects or ideas. This type of structure is frequently found in social studies and science texts. The author uses clue words and phrases such as *like, unlike, resemble, different from, same as, alike,* or *similar to* to make comparisons. The reader must recognize the objects or ideas being compared and the points of similarity or difference among them. Often these points are not directly stated.

Table 3.1 presents an example of each of the five types of expository text structure. Remember, however, that one paragraph is not sufficient to determine the overall structure of a particular text. Moreover, within a given expository text, several of these structures may be present.

Students need to know enough about text structure to understand the basic differences between narrative and expository texts and to realize how this will help them construct meaning. This knowledge is gained through reading and writing and through mini-

TABLE 3.1

EXAMPLES OF EXPOSITORY TEXT STRUCTURES

EXPOSITORY STRUCTURE	EXAMPLE
Description	The tiger is the master of the Indian jungle. It stalks its prey in deadly silence. For half an hour or more, it carefully watches and then slowly, placing one foot softly in front of the other, closes in.
Collection	As master of the Indian jungle, the male tiger plays many roles. First, he is the hunter of prey who stalks in deadly silence. He is the beauty of the jungle, an expert at doing nothing so that he can rest to be ready for his hunt. Finally, the lord of the jungle is the active seeker of mates, who begins his mating with a nuzzle but ends with a roar.
Causation or cause-effect	We observed the tiger from our vehicle as it stalked the herd of deer. As a result of the slight noise from our running camera, the tiger turned and knew we were there. This didn't stop it from returning to its intended prey. Slowly and carefully it moved forward, not making a sound. The deer were initially unaware of its presence, but because of the shifting winds they caught the tiger's scent. This was enough to scare them away.
Response, problem-solution, question-answer, or remark-reply	One problem to be resolved in tiger watching is transportation. How is it possible for observers to get close enough to a tiger without scaring it away or being attacked? Nature has helped solve this problem by making the tiger and the elephant friends. It is possible for an elephant carrying several people to get very near a tiger without even being noticed. If it weren't for this natural friendship, tiger watching would be virtually impossible.
Comparison	The power of the great tiger is like that of no other animal in the jungle. With one steady lunge, it can destroy its prey, seemingly without any effort at all. Unlike other predators, the tiger basks in the sun after an attack to prepare for its next kill. The actions of the tiger resemble those of no other animal in the Indian jungle.

lessons, if needed. Knowledge of text structure will assist you in helping students activate the appropriate type of prior knowledge; it will also help you identify which words are key to understanding a selection (see Chapter 5) and the types of questions to ask when using interactive-guided reading (see Chapter 2).

Knowledge About the Topic

The second component of text-specific or topic-specific prior knowledge is knowledge about the topic of the materials to be read, which includes the key concepts and key terminology. This knowledge must be activated along with knowledge of text structure.

If your students were reading *Ronald Morgan Goes to Bat* (Giff, 1988), you might think you needed to activate prior knowledge of baseball, but this book is narrative. The problem is that Ronald really wanted to play baseball, but he

Example
3.2

> ### Incorrect Method of Activating Prior Knowledge
>
> Today we are going to read the article "Birds in Winter." Have you ever seen birds during the winter? What kinds of birds do you usually see in winter? How do birds get food in winter?

couldn't catch or hit. The prior knowledge that is most likely to improve students' ability to construct meaning from this text is what it is like to really want to do something even though one is not very good at it. This is what Beck (1984) refers to as *schema-directed prior knowledge development.* If the students had been preparing to read an expository text about baseball, the focus of the prior knowledge activation and development would have been the main ideas about baseball. Strictly topical prior knowledge activation and development without consideration of the actual structure of the text does not improve students' ability to construct meaning (Beck, Omanson, & McKeown, 1982).

The prior knowledge needs for narrative text are determined by the story line. The needs for expository text are determined by the topic, main ideas, and structure of the text.

Suppose your students are about to read an article entitled "Birds in Winter," which describes the survival of birds during a blizzard. To construct meaning from this article, students must understand the concepts of *survival* and *blizzard*. Study Examples 3.2 and 3.3 to see the incorrect and correct ways to activate prior knowledge.

Notice that the discussion in Example 3.2 is topical and general. It does not include background development related to the main point or key concepts of the article. The discussion in Example 3.3, in contrast, clearly requires students to use whatever past experiences or schemata they have developed about birds and winter to make predictions. The teacher develops what students already know by relating that information to the concepts of *survival* and *blizzard*. Key-concept vocabulary is developed within the context of the background development. Finally, the teacher guides the students in summarizing the key points to make sure they have a schema for reading that relates directly to the article's main point.

▣ The Role of the Teacher

When using thematic units and literacy lessons, it is important to think about two things in relation to prior knowledge:

1. What prior knowledge probably needs to be activated and/or developed for the overall theme, for each book to be read during the theme, and for writing to be done?
2. How independent are your students in using strategies to activate their own prior knowledge?

To make the first decision effectively, you must consider three elements: (1) the theme goals, (2) the theme topic, and (3) the literature.

Example 3.3

> **Correct Method of Activating Prior Knowledge (schema directed)**
>
> Today we are going to read the article "Birds in Winter." Before we read it, I want you to think about some important ideas that will help you understand what you read. From the title, what would you say this article is going to be about? (Record student responses; discuss them.) This article is about how birds survive during a blizzard. (Relate the students' predictions to surviving in a blizzard.) What is a blizzard? (Students respond. Write a sentence on the chalkboard that contains the word *blizzard,* and discuss its meaning.) What does it mean to survive in a blizzard? What kinds of problems might birds have surviving during a blizzard? (Discuss these questions; list students' responses on the board, and discuss them. Add your own points to the discussion.)
>
> Example:
>
> 1. A blizzard is a bad snowstorm with high winds.
> 2. Birds could have many problems surviving in a blizzard. These could include
>   getting food.
>   not freezing to death.
>   having water to drink.
>   having a place to sleep that is protected from the wind.

You begin by considering what you want your students to accomplish in relation to the theme. This constitutes your theme goals related to students' attitudes and habits and their ability to construct meaning (see Chapter 2).

Next, you think about the theme topic. What are the big ideas or concepts that students need to understand? For example, for a science fiction theme, do students know what science fiction is? Have they had prior experiences with it?

Then you think about each book to be read. Are the books narrative or expository? What are the story lines for the narratives? What are the main ideas of the expository texts? Knowing this will help you determine the prior knowledge that is most likely to help students construct meaning.

To judge students' independence, you must think about the students in relation to the theme goals, the topic, the literature to be read, and their ability to use various strategies. You can make this assessment by observing your students and using the strategies and techniques suggested in the next section of this chapter. Assessment of students' prior knowledge is not separate from instruction. *Good instruction incorporates assessment, and every instructional activity can also be used for assessment.* Therefore, the assessment of prior knowledge becomes a natural part of instruction.

Holmes and Roser (1987) have identified and compared five techniques for assessing prior knowledge during instruction:

▶ *Free recall:* "Tell me what you know about _____."

▶ *Word association:* "When you hear the words *thief, stolen,* and *detective,* what do you think of?"

❧ *Recognition:* Displa the following key terms (phrases or sentences may be used), and ask students to tell which ones they think may be related to the book they are about to read, *The Polar Express* (Van Allsburg, 1985): *train, North Pole, wagon, train, conductor, sand, snow.*

❧ *Structured question:* In preparation for reading the book *Martin Luther King, Jr.: Free at Last* (Adler, 1986), ask students a set of prepared questions that will help you assess prior knowledge: "Who was Martin Luther King, Jr.?" "What was Martin Luther King's concern in life?" "How did Martin Luther King try to reach his goal in life?"

❧ *Unstructured discussion:* "We are going to read about outer space. What do you know about it?"

Holmes and Roser (1987) found the last procedure, unstructured discussion, to be *least* effective and useful for assessing prior knowledge. Note that each of these techniques is designed to activate, or access, as well as *assess* prior knowledge. (Assessment is discussed in detail in Chapter 11.)

One issue that concerns most teachers is how to assess and develop each student's prior knowledge when working with many students at the same time. It may not be possible to know everything about every student's prior knowledge of a particular theme, but you can get a good sense of what the group knows and the group's level of independence by using the types of teaching strategies suggested in the next section and by helping students develop independence in activating their own prior knowledge. The sample lesson presented at the conclusion of this chapter illustrates the process of selecting prior knowledge for a theme and for one book. You might want to look at that lesson now before reading the remainder of the chapter to get an overview of how the lesson functions (see page 144).

Strategies for Helping Students Achieve Independence in Activating Prior Knowledge

There are many ways to help learners become more strategic and independent readers (Paris et al., 1991), and prior knowledge activation and development may occur at three points:

1. When introducing the theme, at which time the focus is on the broad concepts and ideas needed to understand the theme
2. When each piece of literature is introduced within the lessons
3. Throughout the theme when you observe that certain students need more prior knowledge to better understand what they are reading or writing

This section of the chapter presents student and teaching strategies you can use to activate and develop prior knowledge in various places throughout the thematic unit. A strategy is a plan selected deliberately to accomplish a particular goal (Paris, Lipson & Wixson, 1983; Paris et al., 1991). When students reach the point where they can use a strategy automatically, they have achieved independence in its use. A student strategy is one that students can use on their own to construct meaning. A

TABLE 3.2

STUDENT STRATEGIES FOR ACTIVATING AND DEVELOPING PRIOR KNOWLEDGE

STRATEGY	TYPE OF TEXT	COMMENTS
Preview and predict • Story map prediction • Preview and self-question	Narrative or expository Narrative Expository	For all students; variations may be used to increase motivation and interest in using the strategy.
K-W-L	Expository	For all students; good for introducing a thematic unit.

teaching strategy is a plan or an activity that the teacher can use to accomplish a desired outcome.

Student Strategies Leading to Independence

Two basic strategies students can use to activate their prior knowledge and set their own purposes for reading are preview and predict and K-W-L. Table 3.2 presents an overview of these strategies and indicates when they should be used.

Preview and Predict

Description.   This strategy combines the processes of previewing and predicting, both of which have been shown to be effective in helping students construct meaning (Fielding, Anderson, & Pearson, 1990; Graves & Cooke, 1980; Graves, Cooke, & LaBerge, 1983; Hansen, 1981). Students look over the material to be read and then predict what they think will happen (narrative text) or what they will learn (expository text). This is the first step in inferencing, which is ongoing in the process of constructing meaning. As they read or after completing the reading, students decide whether or not their predictions have been confirmed, verified, or changed.

Procedures.   Students begin by reading the title. Then they look at the pictures or illustrations to get a sense of what will be covered. They decide whether this is a story or informational text. Using their prior knowledge and the information gained from their preview, students then predict what will happen or what they will learn. For beginning readers and primary children, the preview should be very simple, focusing on the title and illustrations. Older students can read the first few paragraphs of the text and/or captions under the illustrations.

After completing the preview, students read to verify predictions. It is important to stress that students will be constantly thinking about their predictions and changing them as they read (or monitoring their reading). See Chapter 8 for a discussion of monitoring strategies.

One effective way to help students learn and remember to use this as well as other strategies is to display a strategy poster (Paris, Cross & Lipson, 1984). Figure 3.5

FIGURE 3.5

STRATEGY POSTER FOR PREVIEW AND PREDICT

presents a strategy poster for preview and predict. Adjust the wording on the poster for different grade levels. All strategies must be modeled to be learned effectively (Pressley et al., 1990). Chapter 8 discusses modeling in detail.

When to Use.   The preview and predict strategy is effective with both narrative and expository text. As students begin to use the strategy independently, be sure to distinguish between the two types of text. Preview and predict is most effective when students have some knowledge of the topic. With second-language learners or students having difficulty constructing meaning, this strategy works better under the teacher's direction and/or in combination with another strategy. A limited amount of research has suggested that, generally speaking, any type of previewing strategy is more effective in helping students recall story information when carried out with teacher guidance (Neuman, 1988). This is most likely to be true when students are just beginning to learn the strategy.

Assessment Value.   By observing students' responses during the preview and predict process, you should be able to assess the status of their prior knowledge before reading a text. From this information, you can decide on the need for additional prior knowledge development activities.

Comments.   The preview and predict strategy will help students activate their prior knowledge and set their own purposes for reading. The real power of this strategy will become evident when students use it on their own. If students do not see its importance or refuse to use it, it is critical that you discuss and model its importance. This is most likely to succeed when students have repeated successful opportunities to use the strategy.

One variation of preview and predict is story map prediction, which is specifically for narrative texts. Training in the use of story maps has proven to be effective in helping students improve their comprehension (Pressley et al., 1990). Figure 3.6 presents a strategy poster for story map prediction.

Beginning readers should predict about one or two elements of the story map. As they become more sophisticated, they can focus on more elements. Of course, you won't ask students to predict all the action in a story, because this is usually not possible; furthermore, even if it could be done, there would be little point to reading the story.

A variation, preview and self-question, is used with expository texts. Students preview the text and then pose questions they think they can answer from their reading. Figure 3.7 presents a strategy poster for preview and self-question, which is similar to the question-generating strategy discussed in Chapter 8.

K-W-L Strategy

Description.   K-W-L is another strategy for activating students' prior knowledge and helping them determine their purpose for reading expository texts. Remember that it requires students to focus on three questions, two before they read and one after they read: what I *know* (K), what I *want* to learn (W), and what I *learned* and still need to learn (L). This strategy, developed by Ogle (1986), is the one Mr. Willett

FIGURE 3.6

POSTER FOR THE STORY MAP PREDICTION STRATEGY

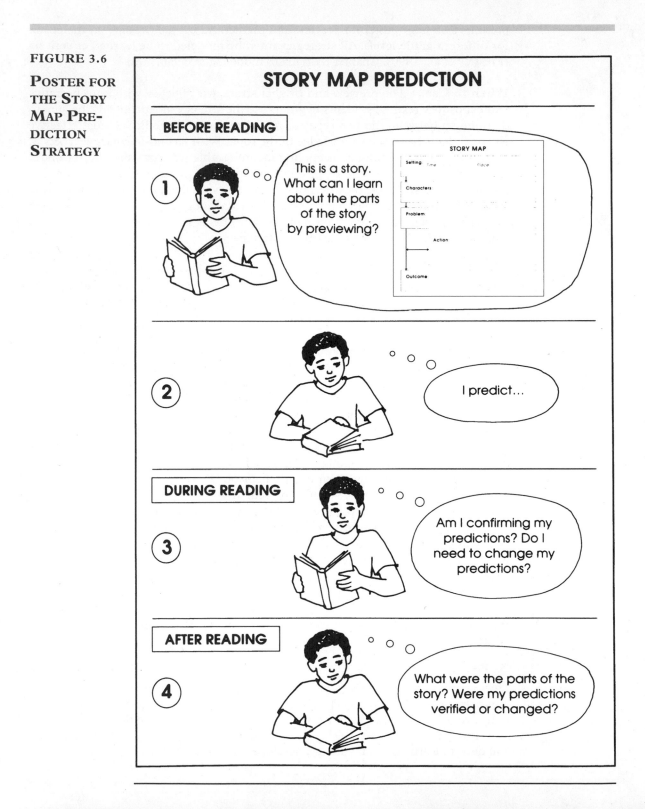

FIGURE 3.7

POSTER FOR PREVIEW AND SELF-QUESTION STRATEGY

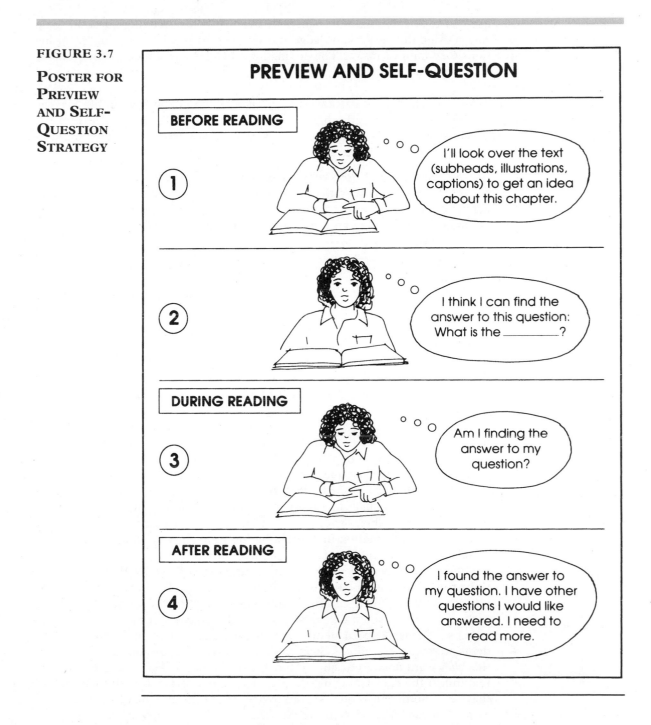

was using at the beginning of this chapter. The two before-reading questions help students activate their prior knowledge and set their purposes for reading by raising questions they want to answer. The driving force behind this strategy is the students and their ideas and questions.

Procedures.   Each student has a worksheet such as the one in Figure 3.8. For the first two steps, the teacher leads students in a discussion of the topic relative to the book they are going to read. During the last step, students write down their answers to the questions posed before reading.

1. *Step K—what I know* begins with students brainstorming what they know about the topic. In keeping with the need to have schema-directed prior knowledge activation and development, the teacher selects a topic specifically related to the main ideas and key concepts of the material students will read. Ogle (1986) states the following:

   When the class will read about sea turtles, use the words sea turtles *as the stimulus, not "What do you know about animals in the sea?" or "Have you ever been to the ocean?" A general discussion of enjoyable experiences on the beach may never elicit the pertinent schemata. . . . If there appears to be little knowledge of sea turtles in your students' experiences, then ask the next more general question, "What do you know about turtles?"* (p. 565)

   Students record what they know on their worksheet and add to it as they share their ideas. Meanwhile, you should also record these ideas on a larger version of the worksheet on the chalkboard, chart, or overhead projector. To broaden and deepen students' thinking during the discussion, Ogle suggests that the teacher ask students such questions as "Where did you learn that?" or "How might you prove it?" When disagreement occurs, students must look for answers in the reading. If they seem to have little knowledge about the topic, you should ask more specific questions to draw out what information they do have.

   The second part of the brainstorming involves identifying *categories of information* students might find in the material they will read. You might ask students to look over their list of what they know to see if any of the items fit into categories of information that might be found in their reading: for example, "foods turtles eat" or "use of sea turtles by humans."

2. *Step W—what I want to learn* is a natural outgrowth of step K. As students continue to share ideas, areas of uncertainty or lack of knowledge will arise, and you can then help them turn these into questions they may answer by reading the text. As the discussion continues, students may think of other questions about sea turtles. Record all questions on the group chart. Just before the students are ready to read, ask them to write several questions on their worksheet that *they* want answered. This step helps students set their own purposes for reading. If the text is long or complex, you may preview it with them before they read. Sometimes you will want to have students read the text in parts.

3. *Step L—what I learned* requires students to write the answers to their questions after reading; this helps them determine which questions they still need to answer or whether they have additional questions. It also helps to take students beyond the reading of a single selection.

FIGURE 3.8

K-W-L Strategy Sheet

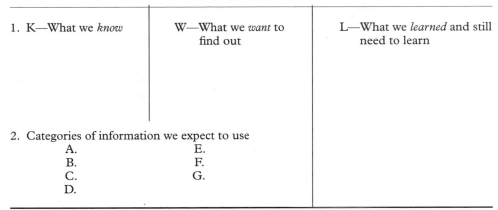

K-W-L Strategy

1. K—What we *know*	W—What we *want* to find out	L—What we *learned* and still need to learn
2. Categories of information we expect to use 　A.　　　　　E. 　B.　　　　　F. 　C.　　　　　G. 　D.		

The following transcript of a lesson involving K-W-L shows the type of interaction that takes place (Ogle, 1986, pp. 567–569). The italicized annotations have been added to draw attention to what is happening in the lesson.

(Starting the K step. Teacher also helps students relate to information they already have.)

Teacher:　Today we're going to read another article about animals. This one is about a special kind of spider—the Black Widow. Before we begin the article, let's think about what we already know about Black Widows. Or if you aren't familiar with this kind of spider, think about some things you know about spiders in general, and we can then see if those are also true for the Black Widow. (Teacher writes *Black Widow spider* on the board and waits while students think about their knowledge of spiders. Next she elicits ideas from children and writes their contributions on the board.)

(Students interact.)

Tony:　Spiders have six legs.

Susan:　They eat other insects.

Eddie:　I think they're big and dangerous spiders.

(Teacher directs and deepens thinking.)

Teacher:　Can you add more about what you mean when you say they're big and dangerous?

Eddie:　They, they, I think they eat other spiders. I think people are afraid of them, too.

Steph:　They spin nests or webs to catch other insects in.

Tom:　My cousin got stung by one once and almost died.

(Teacher focuses responses.)

Teacher: You mean they can be dangerous to people?

Tom: Yah, my cousin had to go to the hospital.

(Teacher draws in other students.)

Teacher: Does anyone else know more about the Black Widow? Tammy?

Tammy: I don't think they live around here. I've never heard of anyone being stung by one.

Teacher: Where do Black Widows live? Does anyone know? (She waits.) What else do we know about spiders?

John: I think I saw a TV show about them once. They have a special mark on their back. I think it's a blue triangle or circle, or something like that. If people look, they can tell if the spider's a Black Widow or not.

Teacher: Does anyone else recall anything more about the way they look? (She waits.) Look at what we've already said about these spiders. Can you think of other information we should add?

John: I think they kill their babies or men spiders. I'm not sure which.

(Teacher focuses students to begin to think about sources of information.)

Teacher: Do you remember where you learned that?

John: I think I read an article once.

(Beginning to think about questions.)

Teacher: OK, let's add that to our list. Remember, everything on the list we aren't sure of we can double check when we read.

(Teacher directly focuses on categories of information.)

Teacher: Anything more you think we should know about these spiders? (She waits.) OK, before we read this article let's think awhile about the kinds or categories of information that are likely to be included. Look at the list of things we already know or have questions about. Which of the categories of information have we already mentioned?

Peter: We mentioned how they look.

(Teacher informally models the concept of categories of information.)

Teacher: Yes, we said they're big and have six legs. And someone said they think Black Widows have a colored mark on them. Good, description is one of the main categories of information we want to learn about when we read about animals or insects. What other categories of information have we mentioned that should be included?

Anna: Where they live; but we aren't sure.

Teacher: Good, we should find out where they live. What other kinds of information should we expect to learn from the article? Think about what kinds of information we've learned from other articles about animals.

Diane: We want to know what kind of homes they make.

Raul: What do they eat?

Andy: How they protect themselves.

Cara: How do they have babies? How many do they have?

(Focus shifts to more questions to be answered.)

Teacher: Good thinking. Are there other categories of information we expect to learn about? (She waits.) We've thought about what we already know and what kinds of information we're likely to learn from an article on Black Widow spiders. Now what are some of the questions we want to have answered? I know we had some things we weren't sure about, like where these spiders live. What are some of the things you'd like to find out when we read?

Cara: I want to know how many baby spiders get born.

Rico: Do Black Widows really hurt people? I never heard of that, and my dad knows a lot about spiders.

Andy: Why are they called Black Widows? What's a widow?

(Students identify their own specific questions.)

Teacher: Good question! Does anyone know what a widow is? Why would this spider be called a "Black Widow"? (After eliciting questions from several students, the teacher asks each child to write their own questions on their worksheet.) What are the questions you are most interested in having answered? Write them down now. As you read, look for the answers and jot them down on your worksheet as you go, or other information you don't want to forget. (The students read the article.)

(Teacher encourages personal response to the article and gets students to think about what they have learned.)

Teacher: How did you like this article? What did you learn?

Raul: The Black Widow eats her husband and sometimes her babies. Yuck! I don't think I like that kind of spider!

Steph: They can live here—it says they live in all parts of the United States.

Andy: They can be recognized by an hourglass that is red or yellow on the abdomen.

(Focus on vocabulary development and expansion.)

Teacher: What is another word for abdomen? (She waits.) Sara, please look up the word *abdomen.* Let's find out where the hourglass shape is located. While Sara is looking the word up, let's check what we learned against the questions we wanted answered. Are there some questions that didn't get answered? What more do we want to know?

(The discussion continues in this manner.)

When to Use.   K-W-L is used with expository texts. Even though the research using this strategy has involved students in the middle grades, it could be used with students of any age. Primary children and students experiencing difficulty constructing meaning may need a more simplified version that focuses just on the K-W-L without thinking about sources of information. This strategy is a good way to initiate a thematic unit, because it sets students up to continue to read several selections on a given topic. It is also useful when reading chapters in textbooks in areas such as science, social studies, or health.

All students will profit from using this strategy; because it is so interactive, it gives students many opportunities to learn from one another. K-W-L is especially strong for second-language learners and students experiencing difficulty constructing meaning, because it immerses them into a natural discussion and offers a strong scaffold provided by teacher support and student interaction. Sometimes it will be necessary to incorporate other teaching strategies, such as previewing and the use of concrete materials, to further develop prior knowledge.

Assessment Value.   K-W-L affords many opportunities to assess students' prior knowledge during all three steps. During the K and W steps, you can tell whether students have prior knowledge relative to the topic and how accurate it is. During the L step, you can tell whether students have gained new knowledge and how well they have integrated that knowledge with what they already know.

Comments.   K-W-L has a sound theoretical research base (Ogle, 1986). However, additional research evaluating its effectiveness is still needed.

Initially, the teacher should model the use of the strategy (see Chapter 8). Repeated opportunities to use the strategy under teacher direction are important.

Even though K-W-L was designed as a teaching strategy, students can learn to use it as an independent study strategy in working alone or cooperatively. A poster such as the one shown in Figure 3.9 may be helpful.

Teaching Strategies Leading to Student Independence

This section discusses twelve teaching strategies in terms of their value for supporting students in *becoming independent* in activating their prior knowledge and setting their purpose(s) for reading. Table 3.3 describes when to use these strategies. Remember that your goal should always be to move students toward independence as quickly as possible.

Discussion

Description.   Discussion is one of the most widely used strategies for activating students' prior knowledge before reading or writing. However, much of what is done in the name of discussion is nothing more than teacher assessment of students' comprehension (Durkin, 1978, 1981a) or conducting of a recitation period (Dillon, 1984). Such unstructured discussions have been found to be ineffective in activating appropriate prior knowledge (Holmes & Roser, 1987).

A discussion is an interactive procedure whereby the teacher and students talk about a given topic; it is not simply the teacher telling students a body of information. According to Alvermann, Dillon, and O'Brien (1987), discussions must meet three criteria:

- *Discussants should put forth multiple points of view and stand ready to change their minds about the matter under discussion;*
- *students should interact with one another as well as with the teacher;*
- *and the interaction should exceed the typical two or three word phrase units common to recitation lessons.* (p. 7)

FIGURE 3.9

K-W-L STRATEGY **P**OSTER

Procedures.   Conducting an effective discussion for activating and developing prior knowledge before reading requires careful planning on the part of the teacher as well as on-the-spot decisions during the discussion. The following guidelines should be helpful in carrying out this process:

1. *Review the text to be read.* Determine the story line or main ideas to help you decide what key background concepts are needed to comprehend the text. For

TABLE 3.3

TEACHING STRATEGIES FOR ACTIVATING AND DEVELOPING PRIOR KNOWLEDGE

STRATEGY	TYPE OF TEXT	COMMENTS
✓Discussion	Narrative or expository	For all students.
✓Brainstorming	Narrative or expository	Use when students have some knowledge of topic; for all students.
Quick writing	Narrative or expository	For all students; often needs to be combined with other strategies.
Picture walk/text walk	Narrative or expository	For students requiring a very structured framework for what they are going to read.
Semantic mapping	Most effective with expository; can be used with narrative	For all students; gives a visual picture of concepts.
✓Prequestioning and purpose setting	Narrative and expository	For beginning learners or those having difficulty constructing meaning; usually combined with other strategies.
Anticipation guides	Best with expository; may be used with narrative	Useful for overcoming misconceptions in prior knowledge. For all students.
Structured previews	Narrative or expository	Especially for second-language learners or students experiencing difficulty constructing meaning.
✓Reading aloud to students	Narrative or expository	Good to use when students have limited or erroneous knowledge; for all students, especially second-language learners.
Role playing	Narrative; sometimes expository, especially in social studies	For students needing more concrete prior knowledge development.
Projects	Narrative or expository	For all students; develops long-term prior knowledge throughout a theme.
Concrete materials and real experiences	Narrative or expository	For students with limited prior knowledge.

example, if your class is going to read the expository text *Monarch Butterfly* (Gibbons, 1989), focus your discussion on what students know about monarch butterflies (or, if nothing is known, butterflies) and their life cycle. If, on the other hand, your students are reading the story (narrative) *Imogene's Antlers* (Small, 1985), the discussion should focus on how they might react if a strange or unusual circumstance occurred in their lives.

2. *Ask questions that require students to respond with more than* yes *or* no. Questions should require students to elaborate on and explain their answers. Teachers who are just learning to lead a discussion should plan such questions in advance. The suggested guidelines that accompany basal readers, content texts, or some trade books can be helpful.

3. *Encourage students to raise their own questions about the topic or about other students' answers.* It is a good idea for the teacher to model such behavior and tell students that they can ask similar questions of the teacher or other students.

4. *Call on individual students to answer questions; don't always wait for volunteers to answer.* You want to encourage maximum participation by all students, even those who are sometimes reluctant to respond.

5. *When calling on individual students to answer questions, ask the question before calling on the student.* This practice encourages everyone to listen.

6. *After asking a question, give students sufficient time to answer.* Students need varying amounts of time to think.

7. *Participate in the discussion and model good questioning and question-responding behavior.* Encourage students to ask questions in a discussion in the same manner you do.

8. *Keep the discussion focused on the topic.* A short, lively discussion is better and more motivating than a lengthy one.

9. *Conclude the discussion by having students summarize the points that were made.* For the discussion to be of value to them, students must be able to internalize and verbalize the points that were developed.

Discussions may be planned for the whole class or small groups. Sometimes it is useful to begin with small-group discussions and then use the whole-class format to pull together the ideas discussed in each group. This is a natural way to lead to a summary and to involve all students in a more interactive lesson. In either instance, the preceding nine guidelines apply. It is also a good idea to develop with students a set of guidelines or suggestions to follow during discussions. Figure 3.10 presents a sample set of guidelines developed by a group of fifth graders and their teacher.

When to Use.   Discussion is a teaching strategy you can use with any group at any time to activate and develop prior knowledge. When students have limited or incorrect knowledge or difficulty constructing meaning, combine discussion with other strategies to make prior knowledge activation and development more concrete. For example, a group that has limited prior knowledge about frogs will profit from a discussion combined with photographs, a film, or a filmstrip on frogs. To

FIGURE 3.10

**SAMPLE DISCUSSION GUIDELINES DEVELOPED
BY ONE FIFTH-GRADE CLASS**

Our Discussion Guidelines
1. Stick to the topic.
2. Pay attention to the person talking.
3. Ask questions about ideas given.
4. Give everyone a chance to participate.
5. Think about what is being said.
6. Try not to interrupt others.

help students move toward independence, encourage them to take the lead in small-group discussions.

Assessment Value.   Discussion is an excellent way to assess students' prior knowledge; however, it must not be unstructured (Holmes & Roser, 1987). Students' responses and interactions will reveal their knowledge and their misconceptions.

Comments.   Discussion is a powerful technique for activating and developing prior knowledge. Chapters 6 and 7 focus on the use of discussion in other ways, such as constructing meaning through responding to reading and writing. For more about discussion, see the For Additional Reading section at the conclusion of this chapter.

An important factor in using discussion is knowing the cultural rules that guide the entire process of asking and answering questions. Mason and Au (1990) found that Hawaiian children responded best when the teacher asked a question and all children were allowed to respond if they had something to say. Several children spoke at once, and the teacher then repeated the highest-quality response for the group. Mason and Au point out that this pattern reflects the Hawaiian emphasis on the group rather than the individual (pp. 49–50).

Your job is to try to match your teaching strategies and procedures to fit not only the students' language base but also their cultural values. This is true, of course, for all teaching strategies.

Brainstorming

Description.   Brainstorming requires students to tell all they know about a particular topic or idea, which begins to activate their prior knowledge.

Procedures.   Students can work individually or in pairs, first generating all of the ideas they have for a particular topic and then sharing their ideas with the group.

The teacher lists the ideas on the chalkboard, and then they are discussed. By hearing others' ideas, students may activate additional information in their memories or learn new information. The following steps offer one way to carry out a brainstorming activity:

1. Provide cards on which students can record information.
2. Tell students they are to write any words, ideas, or phrases they know about the given topic. Provide a time limit.
3. Have students read their lists aloud to the group as you record all of their ideas on the chalkboard or overhead projector.
4. Discuss the information recorded, pointing out ideas that directly relate to the selection students are going to read. If incorrect information is on the list, you may leave it until after reading; through discussion and responding, students may correct themselves. However, if the error is significant and is likely to interfere with meaning construction, discuss it at this point.
5. Direct the discussion of the ideas generated by the students to the story line or main ideas of the selection. Conclude the discussion by helping the students set a purpose for reading or giving them a purpose for reading.

When to Use.   Use brainstorming when students have some knowledge of the topic. It is useful as an opening activity for a thematic unit or for reading a story or informational text. For example, if your sixth graders are going to read *Cousins* (Hamilton, 1990), brainstorming will help them think about what might happen when conflicts between cousins arise.

The following script shows how a teacher used brainstorming to introduce an article about whales.

(Teacher focuses the brainstorming.)

Teacher: Today we are going to read an article about whales and why they are in trouble. I want you to write on this card all the things you can think of about whales. Don't worry about spelling. (The ideas of two students were pictured on the accompanying cards. After a few minutes, the teacher asked the students to stop writing.)

Ted

Whales are mammals.
Whales live in the ocean.
These are killer whales.
Whales can talk.

```
┌─────────────────────────────────┐
│  Elsie                          │
│                                 │
│    fish                         │
│    big                          │
│    eat people                   │
│                                 │
└─────────────────────────────────┘
```

Teacher: I want each of you to read what you have written on your card, and I will write your ideas on the board. (The teacher accepted all responses from each student, unless it was a duplicate.)

(Students are looking for incorrect information.)

Teacher: Let's look at our list of ideas to see if there is anything that is incorrect.

   Whales are mammals

   Whales live in the ocean

   There are killer whales

   Whales can talk

   Fish

   Big

   Eat people

   Can be made into oil

   Can be eaten

   Are hunted by fishermen

Student: Whales aren't fish.

Teacher: Whales live in the ocean; they look like fish, but they are much bigger. We will learn why they are not fish in our reading. (The teacher removed *fish* from the list.)

Teacher: You know that dinosaurs once lived on the earth, but for many reasons they disappeared. The same thing is happening to whales. Look at this list to see if you can identify any reasons why whales might be in danger of disappearing. (The students responded. The teacher discussed their answers and identified those items the students missed.)

Teacher: We are going to read the article entitled "Disappearing Whales." Based on the information we have just discussed about whales and why they might be in danger of disappearing, what do you think would be a good thing for us to think about or look for as we read?

Student: Maybe we could look to see if our reasons about why whales disappear are right, and maybe we can find some others.

(Setting a purpose for reading.)

Teacher: That's a good idea. (The teacher wrote the student's response on the board and had students read the article silently, telling them they would later discuss the article based on that purpose.)

Assessment Value. Brainstorming is an excellent way to assess students' prior knowledge. As you can see in the preceding dialogue, the teacher was able to identify and *begin* to correct errors in students' prior knowledge about whales.

Comments. It is important to keep the brainstorming focused without controlling it. If students have a limited amount of knowledge about the subject, the small-group activity may be more effective because it will enable them to learn from one another.

Like the other strategies presented in this chapter, brainstorming is often more effective if used in conjunction with another strategy, such as preview and predict or purpose setting. Not only will you more effectively meet individual needs; you will also keep interest high by varying your teaching strategies.

Quick Writing

Description. Writing has been shown to be an effective way to activate prior knowledge before students read (Marino, Gould, & Haas, 1985; Moore, Readence, & Rickleman, 1989). Quick writing is structured by the teacher and is done in a brief amount of time.

Procedures. The procedures are general because they depend on the selection being read and what is to be written. The following guidelines should be helpful:

1. *Select what you want students to write about.* This should relate directly to the story line or main ideas in the text. For example, if students are going to read *The Stupids Have a Ball* (Allard & Marshall, 1978), you might ask them to pretend they are a person who does everything the opposite of normal, telling funny things that might happen to them. (The characters in this story do just that.) Quick writing can focus on a character, on the story problem, or on the major topic developed in an expository text.
2. *Have students write.* Allow students 3 to 5 minutes to complete the writing. Remind them that these papers are not to be evaluated and graded.
3. *Invite students to share what they have written.* Direct students in a discussion of the ideas shared.
4. *Help students formulate a purpose for reading.* For example, they can now read *The Stupids Have a Ball* to see how the Stupids are like the characters they have written about.

When to Use. Writing can be used as soon as students begin to be able to write and express their ideas. If you know students have limited prior knowledge relative to the topic, it will be best to use some other technique that will more concretely develop the concepts and ideas needed. Second-language learners should, in most instances, have an activity that introduces key words and phrases prior to writing;

discussion combined with more concrete materials such as pictures would accomplish this goal.

Assessment Value. Although writing is a valuable way to assess students' prior knowledge, you must be cautious about drawing conclusions from a response to a written task, since students may be hampered by limited writing skills or a dislike for writing rather than by limited prior knowledge. A good rule is to make no firm conclusion about a student's prior knowledge on the basis of a single sample *from any source.* It is always wise to look at two or more samples from different sources.

Comments. Quick writing is an important element in the overall process of constructing meaning and helps students build the connections between reading and writing, but it does not replace other kinds of writing. For more discussion of writing, see Chapter 7.

Picture Walk/Text Walk

Description. A picture walk or text walk is a technique whereby the teacher guides students through a piece of literature to be read, using the pictures, illustrations, or other graphics to develop the "big picture" of what the text is about. This technique has been used in New Zealand (Goldenberg, 1991) in regular classrooms and in special support programs such as Reading Recovery in both New Zealand (Clay, 1985) and the United States (DeFord, Lyons, & Pinnell, 1991; Hiebert & Taylor, 1994). The advantage of this technique is that it sets the reader up to succeed with the text by developing key concepts, vocabulary, and a general picture of the text before it is read. Clay (1985) says that carrying out this type of procedure before reading ensures that "the child has in his head the ideas and the language he needs to produce when prompted in sequence by printed cues" (p. 68). The term *picture walk* is usually used when referring to a story, and *text walk* is used when referring to an informational text.

Procedures. You may adapt the following procedures to any level, including middle school or high school content classes:

1. Before working with students, read the text to get a picture of important ideas developed, the story line, key terms, and so forth.
2. If appropriate, show students the cover and have them predict what the text is likely to be about or what is going to happen.
3. Turning through the pages and using the pictures, illustrations, or graphics as prompts, tell key things that will happen in the text or have students predict what is likely to happen. As you tell the major elements of the text, use some of the key words students will encounter in the text.
4. In most instances, you tell the entire text that is to be read. In some cases, however, you may only tell enough to develop a framework without giving away a surprise or exciting ending.

When to Use. Picture walk or text walk is especially helpful when working with students who need a great deal of extra support to successfully construct meaning. However, you can use it any time students are going to read a text when you think

Fifth graders take a "text walk" with their teacher before reading a social studies chapter.
© *Michael Zide*

they need very structured scaffolding to help them understand the material. For example, students reading a social studies chapter in grade 4 may need the structured support of text walk to help them understand the chapter.

Assessment Value.   As students respond during the picture walk/text walk, you can get a sense of their prior knowledge, their ability to make predictions, and their general ability to express themselves orally. Throughout the use of this teaching strategy and others, observe and listen to students' responses. For more information on using observation, see Chapter 11.

Comments.   By sharing with students what they are going to read before they read it, you set them up for success when they read.

Semantic Mapping

Description.   Pearson and Johnson (1978) describe a strategy called *semantic mapping* that can help students activate and develop prior knowledge by seeing the relationships in a given topic. A semantic map is a visual representation of a particular

FIGURE 3.11

SEMANTIC MAP FOR PINE TREES USING GUIDELINES 1

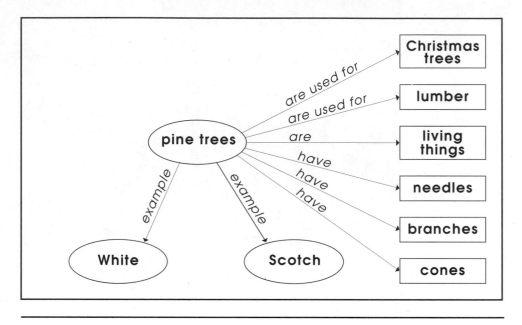

concept. Ovals are used to represent the concepts, and lines with arrows and words written above them represent the relationships. The relationships depicted on a map can be *class* (pine trees), *example* (white pine), or *property* (needles). Figure 3.11 shows a semantic map created with a group of third graders who were preparing to read an article about the uses of pine trees.

Procedures.   There are many ways to use semantic mapping. The first set of guidelines that follows is structured and directed by the teacher; the second set is also teacher directed, but it incorporates brainstorming followed by grouping and labeling of concepts. The second set uses many of the ideas suggested by Taba (1967) many years ago, as described by McNeil (1987); the Taba lesson was known as List-Group-Label and was suggested for social studies, but it can be used in many more situations.

Guidelines 1

1. Write the major concept being discussed on the chalkboard or overhead, and draw an oval around it. (In Figure 3.11, the concept is pine trees.)
2. Ask students to think of words to describe the topic. Write those words in boxes, and link them with arrows to the main concept oval. Above the arrows, write words and phrases such as *have* or *are used for* to indicate the relationship between the main concept and the boxed words.

FIGURE 3.12

SEMANTIC MAP FOR PINE TREES USING GUIDELINES 2

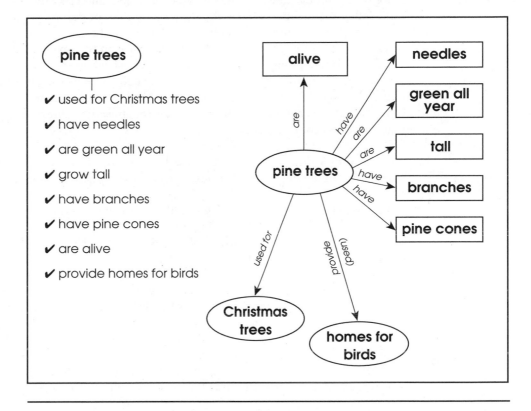

3. Ask students to give some examples of the topic, and write these in ovals with arrows indicating examples.

Guidelines 2

1. Present the concept to be discussed by placing it in an oval on the chalkboard or overhead.

2. Ask students to brainstorm words or ideas related to the concept. If necessary, probe for additional information.

3. Guide students in grouping the words or ideas to create the semantic map for the concept. Use different shapes to depict the different categories of information: rectangles for uses or descriptions, circles for examples, and squares for other types of information. Figure 3.12 shows how this process worked in one class.

There is no one right way to develop a semantic map. The words written on the arrows to show relationships will vary according to the topic being discussed.

When to Use.   Semantic mapping is most effective when used with expository texts. It can also be used with narratives, but you must be certain that the concept used for activating prior knowledge is central to the story line.

You can use semantic mapping with all students; it helps them visualize the relationships among ideas. Second-language learners and students with limited prior knowledge may respond best when the second set of guidelines is used, because they start out on a more global basis and move on to categorizing. You should always keep the activity focused on the central ideas in the text.

Semantic mapping is a good procedure to use when students will read several sources related to the same topic. The teacher and students can start the map before students begin the reading, then can add to it as they gain new information while they read. After they have completed their reading, they can return to the map to make additions or changes.

Assessment Value.   As you use semantic mapping with students, you are able to assess their understandings of various concepts and relationships.

Comments.   Semantic mapping has also been suggested for many other uses in helping students construct meaning; these include summarizing the text, expanding their vocabulary, and writing (Noyce & Christie, 1989; Stahl & Vancil, 1986; Weisberg & Balajthy, 1985).

A variation of the semantic mapping strategy is semantic webbing, in which students generate ideas and/or words related to a given topic and then talk about how those ideas/words are related; lines are drawn showing these relationships. Figure 3.13 shows a semantic web created with a group of students to activate their knowledge about what it is like to be the oldest child in a family. (Although webbing can be used this way, this author has found that it often takes students too far afield from the text.) Webbing is also a good way to brainstorm for writing.

Semantic mapping is discussed in more detail in Chapter 5.

Prequestioning and Purpose Setting

Description.   Asking a question or giving students a topic to think about that will continue to focus their attention as they read has been shown to be effective in activating prior knowledge and in improving construction of meaning (Tierney & Cunningham, 1984).

Procedures.   Following are some simple guidelines that should be used flexibly with various reading tasks.

1. Examine the text to determine the story line or main ideas.
2. Decide what prior knowledge students are likely to need.
3. Formulate a question(s) or a statement of purpose for students to think about before reading. These should focus students on the big ideas.

Recall the article "Birds in Winter" discussed earlier. The focus of that article was on the survival of birds during a blizzard, and the main point was that birds often have to depend on humans to survive under extreme winter conditions. The following prequestions would be useful for this article:

FIGURE 3.13

SEMANTIC WEB

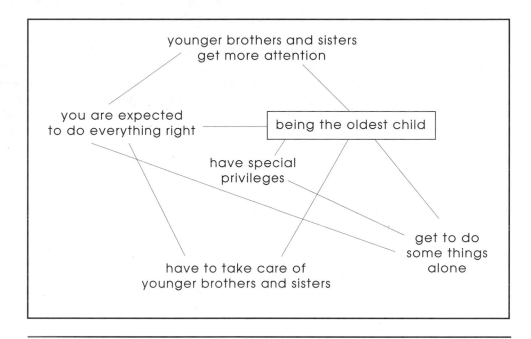

How do the problems the birds in this article face compare to the problems you have seen birds experience during bad winter storms?

On the basis of "Birds in Winter" and of your own experience, why do you think it is important for people to help birds during winter storms?

The following would be an appropriate purpose-setting statement:

You have discussed some of the problems that birds can have surviving in winter. Read this article to find out if there are other reasons why birds have difficulty surviving in blizzards.

Notice that the only real difference between this purpose statement and the questions is the form in which the purpose is stated.

The following prequestions would *not* be appropriate because they focus on specific points rather than the overall text. Furthermore, these questions do not require readers to draw from their prior knowledge:

What two birds have the greatest difficulty surviving during blizzard conditions?

What three reasons does the author give to justify why people should help birds during blizzards?

4. Have students read the text to answer the question or to accomplish the purpose given.

5. After reading, return to the question or purpose statement to see if students have achieved their goals and to discuss what they found. Research has demonstrated that returning to check the purpose for reading is important in helping students construct meaning (White, 1981).

When to Use.   This strategy should be used when students are just beginning to learn to construct meaning and cannot yet formulate their own purposes or prequestions or when the text is extremely difficult. Keep in mind, however, that your real goal should be to get students to use the independent strategies discussed in the first portion of this chapter. Usually you should combine prequestions and purpose statements with other strategies, such as discussion or brainstorming, to activate prior knowledge.

Assessment Value.   Prequestions and purpose statements are not as helpful as other strategies in assessing students' immediate prior knowledge relative to a topic or an idea. Their assessment value comes after reading, when students respond and show how well they have constructed meaning.

Comments.   Prequestions and purpose statements are an effective strategy for providing the scaffold for learning that some students need, and you will find you frequently use them when you employ the teacher-guided reading mode discussed in Chapter 2. One variation is to put them in monitoring guides or study guides (discussed in Chapter 2). These are discussed further in Chapter 9.

Anticipation Guides

Description.   An anticipation guide is a series of statements about a particular text that students are going to read. Students indicate whether they agree or disagree with the statements before reading and return to them after reading to do the same. This strategy, developed by Readence, Bean, and Baldwin (1981, 1985, 1989), is designed to activate prior knowledge and to give students a purpose for reading.

Procedures.   Readence, Bean, and Baldwin (1981, 1985, 1989) suggest eight steps in constructing and using anticipation guides:

1. *Identify major concepts.* Review the text to identify the major concepts or main ideas to be learned.

2. *Determine students' prior knowledge of these concepts.* Drawing on your experiences with your students, think about what they know about these concepts or ideas.

3. *Create statements.* Using the information gained from steps 1 and 2, write out four to eight statements for students to react to that relate to the concepts to be learned and the students' prior knowledge. The exact number of statements will depend on the amount of text to be read, the number of concepts in the text, and the age of the students. The statements should reflect information

about which students have some knowledge but not complete knowledge. They should not be just a true-false type of check. Some good statements for a chapter on food and nutrition might be the following:

An apple a day keeps the doctor away.

If you wish to live a long life, be a vegetarian.

Three square meals a day will satisfy all your body's nutritional needs.

Calories make you fat. (Tierney, Readence, & Dishner, 1990, p. 48)

4. *Decide on the statement order and presentation mode.* Sequence the statements to follow the text, inserting spaces for responses. Create a set of directions. Finally, decide whether the guide is to be presented individually or in a group mode such as on the chalkboard or overhead.

5. *Present the guide.* Tell students they are to react to each statement by indicating whether they agree or disagree with it. Tell them they will share their responses with the group.

6. *Discuss each statement briefly.* Encourage students to share their opinions and tell why they feel as they do. You can tally the responses to each item.

7. *Direct students to read the text.* Have students read the text, keeping their opinions in mind. As they read, they should think about how the text relates to the statements on the guide.

8. *Conduct a follow-up discussion.* First ask students to respond to each statement in light of what they have read. Then have them discuss the statements, focusing on what they have learned and how their opinions and ideas have changed. Figure 3.14 presents a sample anticipation guide for a social studies chapter on transportation.

When to Use.   Anticipation guides may be used for any students at any level. They are generally more useful for expository texts, but may also be used with narrative texts. Figure 3.15 presents a guide to be used with *Today Was a Terrible Day* (Giff, 1980).

This type of strategy is effective when students have misconceptions in prior knowledge; by interacting with the text and comparing opinions with what was learned from reading, students are likely to correct their misconceptions.

Assessment Value.   The anticipation guide is an excellent diagnostic tool. By looking at and listening to students' responses, you can tell the state of their prior knowledge and easily recognize their misconceptions. Then, by looking at the after-reading responses, you can tell whether those misconceptions have changed.

Comments.   Construction of an anticipation guide is sometimes challenging. The statements must require students to think. Though the theory underlying this strategy is solid, this author is unaware of any controlled research.

Structured Previews

Description.   We discussed the value of previewing a text before reading earlier in this chapter, but some students may need to have the previewing process structured

FIGURE 3.14

ANTICIPATION GUIDE FOR SOCIAL STUDIES

Chapter 6, Transportation

Directions: Read each statement. Mark *A* for agree or *D* for disagree. Do the same after reading the chapter.

Before Reading		After Reading
_____	1. Travel has not changed much in the last 25 years.	_____
_____	2. The car is still the best way to travel.	_____
_____	3. The safest way to travel is by air.	_____
_____	4. Large cities need to have more parking garages for increased populations.	_____
_____	5. Cars should be banned from the central business district of large cities.	_____

more carefully. A structured preview is carefully guided by the teacher and often involves some type of graphic display of information to help students see the ideas that are forthcoming in the text and how they are organized. The concept is based on research showing that students' prior knowledge needs to be directed toward the story line (Beck, 1984; Beck, Omanson, & McKeown, 1982). To be helpful to students, this process needs teacher guidance (Neuman, 1988).

Procedures. The procedures for conducting a structured preview are different for narrative texts and for expository texts, though there are similarities.

Narrative Structured Preview

1. Look through the book to get a sense of the story line. Identify the setting, characters, problem, action, and outcome.
2. Formulate questions or statements that will direct students to read the title and the opening paragraph or two (depending on the level) and look at the first few illustrations. Have students share what they learn.
3. Display the story map (see Figure 3.16) and discuss with students the elements in the story. For beginning learners and those having difficulty constructing meaning, focus on only one or two elements. Include other elements later.
4. Ask students to predict what they can about the story elements from their preview, keeping students focused on the story line.
5. Have students read the story silently in its entirety or in sections. Then return to the story map to help them see whether their predictions were verified or changed. Together, complete the story map.

FIGURE 3.15

ANTICIPATION GUIDE FOR *TODAY WAS A TERRIBLE DAY* (GIFF, 1980)

Today Was a Terrible Day

Write *A* for agree or *D* for disagree after each statement below.

1. Kids who get into trouble at school don't care what others think of them. _____
2. You shouldn't be friends with people who get into trouble at school. _____
3. Teachers don't like kids who get into trouble at school. _____
4. Kids who get into trouble at school don't like their teachers. _____
5. Kids who have trouble learning to read are dumb. _____

Source: Sample Anticipation Guide for *Today Was a Terrible Day* (Giff, 1980) developed by Molly McLaurin, I. S. Klein; D. Klein, Texas. Used by permission of the author.

The steps involved in the structured preview must always be adjusted to fit the story content, illustrations, and level. The primary focus of the preview should always be to get students to begin to think about the particular story problem and relate what they already know to it. If your third-grade students are going to read *Wilfrid Gordon McDonald Partridge* (Fox, 1985), a book about how a young boy helps an elderly woman in an old people's home get her memory back, you begin the structured preview by having the children look at the cover and tell who they think this book is going to be about. Next, while looking through the first three or four pages, you ask children to talk about old people's homes and the types of things that might be problems for people living in them, focusing on the idea that some people forget things as they get older. You then complete the preview by presenting the story map and asking the children to predict the characters and the possible problem in the story.

Expository Structured Preview

The narrative structured previews are similar because all narrative texts have the same basic structure. The expository structured preview will vary more because such text has varying text structures. Therefore, you will need to adapt the following guidelines to fit the structure of the text.

1. Review the text to determine the main ideas. Try to identify a graphic organizer that will help students see how the information fits together. For example, if the text has three main ideas, the graphic organizer might be like the one shown in Figure 3.17. However, many texts do not lend themselves to such a neat outline.
2. Formulate questions and statements to use in helping students preview the text by using such things as reading the title, looking at the illustrations and captions, and reading subheads.

FIGURE 3.16

STORY MAP FOR STRUCTURED PREVIEW

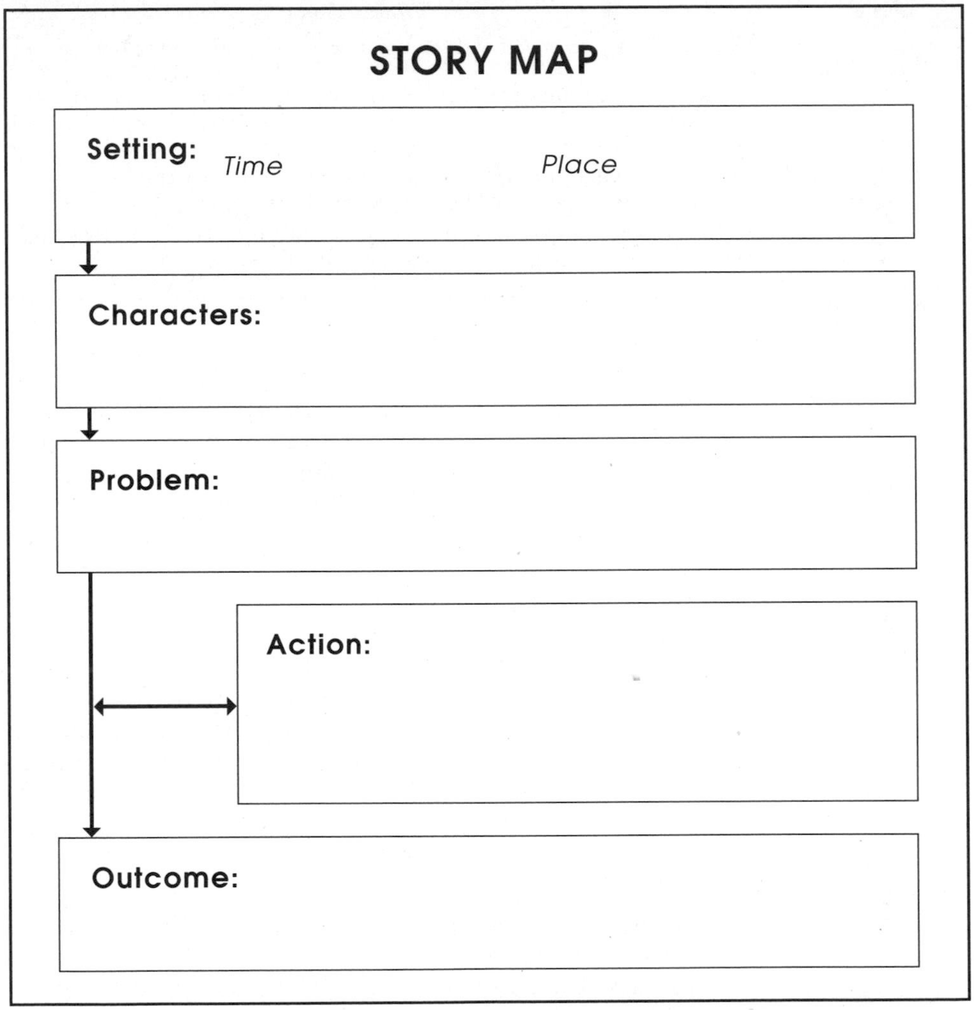

STORY MAP

Setting: *Time*   *Place*

Characters:

Problem:

Action:

Outcome:

3. Guide students through a preview of the text, having them begin to predict the type of information they will learn.
4. Present the graphic organizer, and tell students that the ideas in this text are organized in the pattern shown.
5. Have students read the text to look for the main ideas depicted in your organizer. As they become more sophisticated readers, they can also identify the information that supports the main ideas.

FIGURE 3.17

GRAPHIC ORGANIZER SHOWING THREE MAIN IDEAS IN AN EXPOSITORY TEXT

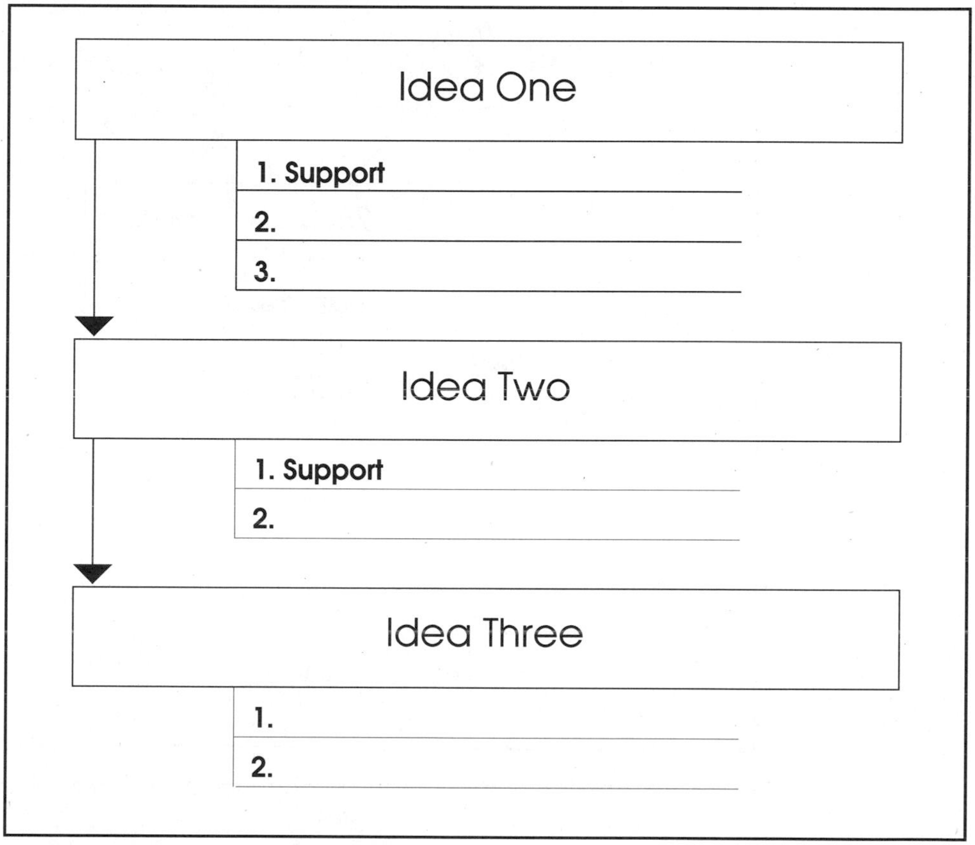

In conducting a structured preview for an expository text, you must pay close attention to how the main ideas are presented in the text. For example, if your second graders are going to read *Fiesta!* (Behrens, 1978), you should note that this work has only one main idea with many facts given about it. Figure 3.18 shows how this idea with its supporting facts might be depicted. When conducting your preview, you should present only the basic outline of the graphic organizer, telling students they will learn one big idea about fiesta and six areas of information about what happens during fiesta. This type of structured preview activates prior knowledge about the topic and also gives students a framework to use in thinking about how the information is organized.

FIGURE 3.18

GRAPHIC ORGANIZER FOR STRUCTURAL PREVIEW OF *FIESTA!*

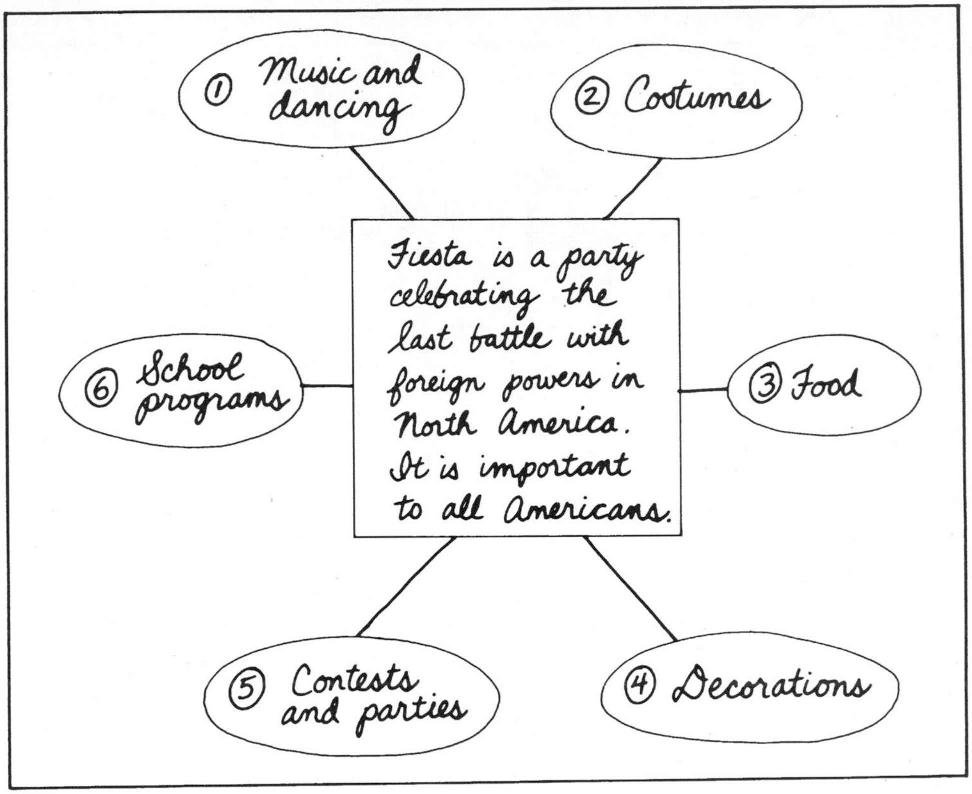

When to Use.   Structured previews are useful on a number of occasions:

▶ When the text is particularly difficult

▶ When students are second-language learners

▶ When students are having difficulty constructing meaning

▶ When you know students have limited prior knowledge about the topic or about the type of text

Assessment Value.   Students' responses during the preview session will help you determine the status of their prior knowledge and what they are gaining from the preview. Since the preview is so teacher directed, you may be limited in what you can tell about what students know and are thinking. Select this strategy only if you are sure your students need this type of scaffold.

Comments.   The use of structured previews and graphic or semantic organizers is not new (Pehrsson & Robinson, 1985), and they can be very helpful to students, but they can also be unnecessarily complicated. Therefore, you should keep your structured previews as simple as possible, making certain that any graphic organizers used actually *do* help students see how the text is organized. The structured preview may be combined with many of the other strategies discussed in this chapter.

Reading Aloud to Students

Description.   The importance of reading aloud to students was well established in Chapter 2. In this strategy, the reading is specific to a thematic topic or selection.

Procedures.

Reading Aloud Background Material

Use the following guidelines to carry out this strategy:

1. Select a book, article, or other background material that relates to the topic or selection.
2. Tell students what it is about and why you are reading it.
3. Give students a purpose for listening. For example, have them listen to identify some important idea or concept to retell an important part of the story. As an alternative, you can also ask them to make predictions about what they expect to learn as they listen.
4. After the read-aloud, discuss the material by checking the purpose for which students were to listen, or discuss whether predictions were confirmed.

Reading Aloud a Portion of a Selection

Guidelines for using this strategy are as follows:

1. Decide on the story or article students will read.
2. Identify how much of the initial part of the selection you are going to read aloud.
3. Introduce the selection and give students a purpose for listening.
4. Read aloud the selected section.
5. Discuss the portion read aloud, checking the purpose given for listening.
6. Have students predict what they think will happen or what they will learn in the remainder of the text.
7. Have students read silently to check their predictions.
8. Discuss the entire selection, focusing on students' predictions.
9. Have students respond to the selection in their own way.

You may vary this second read-aloud strategy by reading aloud part of the text and alternating these sessions with students reading cooperatively or independently. The amount of reading aloud you do will depend on the students' needs and the text. This is a variation of the read aloud, read along, read alone strategy discussed in Chapter 2.

When to Use.   The read-aloud strategy is excellent to use when you know students have limited or erroneous prior knowledge. It is also good for second-language learners because it helps to develop oral language.

Assessment Value.   By reading aloud to students, you can generally tell how they comprehend through listening. You can tell how well they remember and organize ideas without being concerned about decoding or their ability to figure out words. It is more difficult to use the read-aloud strategy as a way to assess students' specific prior knowledge.

Comments.   Reading aloud is an excellent way to build students' background and increase motivation, and it should not be overlooked for helping *all* students. Reading aloud is also useful in building prior knowledge for writing.

Role Playing

Description.   In role playing, students take parts and act out a situation. The purpose of this strategy is to get students to think about a problem or circumstance and bring their prior knowledge to bear on it.

Procedures.   Role playing can be fun, but it requires careful planning to make it a valuable experience for prior knowledge activation.

1. Select the book you want students to read. Determine the story line.
2. Select a situation that would be easy and fun for children to role-play. Make sure it relates to the story line but does not give away the story.
3. Describe the situation to the children. Divide them into small groups to decide on parts and determine how they will act out their situations.
4. Have each group perform and discuss the situations, focusing the discussion on the book to be read, not on an evaluation of their performances.
5. Have students read the book to compare their experience with that described in the book.

Suppose your sixth graders are going to read *Wayside School Is Falling Down* (Sachar, 1989), a hilarious book about the adventures of children in Louis Sachar's imaginary school. You could ask children to role-play the strangest and funniest thing they could imagine happening in school. As each group performs, you then discuss the incident, leading the children to focus on the book by directing them to see how their experiences compare with those of the Erics and other children in Wayside School.

When to Use.   Role playing is a good strategy to use for students who need concrete experiences. Often second-language learners who are reluctant to talk out individually in an open discussion will relate to and interact with their peers in a role-playing situation. Although role playing is often used with narrative texts, it may also be useful with expository texts, especially social studies.

Assessment Value.   Observing students in a role-playing situation can give you a sense of their prior knowledge as well as the ways they think and solve problems. For more discussion about observations, see Chapter 11.

Comments.   Too often prior knowledge activation is handled only through discussion. Remember that many children enjoy role playing and are more likely to "be themselves" and use what they actually know in this activity. At the same time, some students may be too shy to participate, in which case you may consider using simple puppetry to accomplish the same purpose.

Projects

Description.   A project is a task undertaken to achieve a particular goal; it is usually long term, and because of its goal you can tell when it is completed (Ward, 1988). For example, students might construct a model of a Native American village during a thematic unit on Native Americans of the Southwest. This project would be developed throughout the thematic unit and would focus continuously on activating prior knowledge and integrating new knowledge.

Procedures.   The following guidelines should be helpful:

1. *Identify the project.* Decide what the project will be; usually it will relate to a particular theme or area being studied. Some possible projects might include the following:
   - Making a birdhouse
   - Developing a family tree
   - Constructing a simple machine
   - Writing a book comparing the characters of a particular author

   You may select the project, but students often have their own ideas and should be encouraged to use them. This helps to foster students' ownership in their learning and increases motivation.
2. *Select resources.* Decide what resources you want students to use—the library, an encyclopedia, interviews, the Internet, and so on. As students improve their ability to construct meaning, they will be able to identify the resources they need.
3. *Make a plan to carry out the project.* Both you and the students need a plan. It should include what they will do and when they will do it, thus giving both you and them a way to monitor the project.
4. *Plan how to share the project.* It is important that students share their projects because interaction with peers is a part of their authentic learning experience. Therefore, they need to have an idea of how they will do this. Will sharing take place through a book that is developed, a display, a show, or some other means?

To be of value, projects must be clearly focused. Having a plan will help to make this happen. A project sheet such as the one in Figure 3.19 should help you with this planning and monitoring process.

When to Use.   Projects may be used with any students at any grade level as long as they match the students' abilities and work habits. Since projects involve developing and integrating long-term prior knowledge over a thematic unit, they are not the most efficient way to activate and develop prior knowledge before reading a particular text.

FIGURE 3.19

PROJECT PLANNING AND MONITORING SHEET

Project Plan

I. Project, Title, and Focus

_____

_____

II. Resources to Be Used

_____   _____

_____   _____

_____   _____

_____   _____

III. Action Steps

                          Step   *Date Completed*

1. _____   _____

   _____

2. _____   _____

   _____

3. _____   _____

   _____

IV. Sharing Plans

_____

_____

_____

Assessment Value.   All of the activities that take place during a project can help you determine the status of students' prior knowledge by observing how they respond. However, because of the long-term and independent nature of projects, they do not lend themselves to easy observation of activities. They do, however, provide authentic experiences that show what students know and what they can do.

Comments.   Projects do much more than activate prior knowledge. They also help students learn new strategies and skills and gain new information. Projects often create the need for students to read and do research. They help students integrate new knowledge with old knowledge, learn to work cooperatively and independently, develop critical thinking, and learn new skills and strategies. Students may do projects independently or in groups, depending on their purposes. They should

FIGURE 3.20

THEME PROJECT CHART

Projects for the Fairy Tale Theme

1. Write your own fairy tale.
2. Create a diorama of your favorite fairy tale.
3. Make a collection of favorite fairy tales.
4. Plan your own project. You decide what you would like to do in this unit.

be encouraged to select and plan their own projects through the use of a theme project chart such as the one shown in Figure 3.20.

Be cautious when using this strategy. Sometimes students get so caught up in completing a project that it replaces most, if not all, of the reading and writing they should be doing.

Concrete Materials and Real Experiences

Description.   Often the best way to activate and develop students' prior knowledge is to use concrete materials and real experiences. These could include pictures, films, filmstrips, videos, field trips, or classroom planned experiences. For example, a classroom science experiment involving treating three plants differently—one gets water and no light, one gets light and no water, and one gets water and light—would be a good way to develop prior knowledge before starting a theme on plants or on air and water.

Procedures.   The only procedure to follow is to ensure that the materials or experiences actually help to activate and develop prior knowledge that is relevant to the theme, the text to be read, or the writing experience. Always be sure that what you are using really helps students to more effectively construct meaning.

When to Use.   Concrete materials and real experiences are most important when students lack prior knowledge on a particular topic. Second-language learners and children who have limited background often need this type of support. This strategy is also useful for introducing a new topic to all students.

Assessment Value.   Since concrete materials and real experiences are used to *develop* prior knowledge, they will have limited assessment value. However, as in all learning experiences, students' responses will give you an indication of what they know and what they are learning.

Comments.   Real experiences may seem to lack a clear connection to the instruction, so you should always introduce such experiences by letting children know their purpose. After the experience, you and the students should talk about what was learned and how it relates to the topic or theme being covered. For example, in preparation for a thematic unit on wild animals, students should make predictions about certain animals before going to the zoo. Then they can discuss which predictions were confirmed and summarize what they learned about the animals. This knowledge will help them as they work in this unit.

Deciding Which Strategies to Use

Each of the fourteen strategies—two student strategies and twelve teaching strategies—with variations just discussed has as its primary focus activation and/or development of prior knowledge, leading students to set their purpose for reading. As the teacher, you must continuously make decisions about which strategies to use. Some lessons will call for combining several strategies, and others will require only one strategy. Some will require heavy teacher support, others almost none. The following guidelines should help you decide which strategies to use and when to use them.

Motivation and Interest

The amount of student motivation and interest for a topic or book will directly influence the amount of prior knowledge activation and development needed. Usually students who select their own topics or books are either very highly motivated or have good prior knowledge about the topic. If they are highly motivated to read or write about a certain topic but have little prior knowledge about it, they will need support in developing this knowledge. Those who know a great deal about the topic will need little or no support.

It is important to consider students' needs in planning prior knowledge activation. Too many activities keep students from what they really want to do: *read* or *write*. When prior knowledge is not activated, you should observe as children read and write to see whether it is needed. Even when you select the books students read, the amount of student motivation and interest should guide you in deciding how much prior knowledge you need to activate.

The Text

You must also know the type of text (narrative or expository) and its difficulty when deciding which strategies to use. With narrative text, focus on the story line; for expository text, focus on the main ideas.

When topics or texts have complex concepts, ideas, or structures, more prior knowledge activation will be needed, and some strategies will be more useful than others. Refer back to Tables 3.2 and 3.3 for a summary of when to use the strategies presented in this chapter.

Student Needs and Level of Independence

As you become familiar with your students, you will know which ones need the most prior knowledge support. Students who have achieved independence may need no support, but keep in mind that this need will change from situation to situation. Again, refer to Tables 3.2 and 3.3 for guidance.

Lesson Variety

A final factor to consider is lesson variety. Using the same strategies over and over again becomes boring to both you and the students. Vary your strategies to keep interest and motivation for learning high.

Using Technology to Develop Prior Knowledge

More and more classrooms have greater access to technology including VCRs, computers, CD-ROMs, and the Internet. These resources can be used to build background as well as activate prior knoweldge.

Students can view videos related to topics being studied or books being read. These experiences build background and help students develop concepts needed for successfully constructing meaning.

CD-ROM programs provide interactive experiences that help meet the prior knowledge needs of individual students before reading a selection. For example, *GREAT START!* from Houghton Mifflin Company develops key concepts and ideas based on students' needs prior to reading.

Visiting various Web sites can also be helpful in developing background and prior knowledge. For example, students involved in a unit of study on the presidency of the United States might visit the Web site on the White House to develop prior knowledge about the President's home.

If your school has a media specialist, he/she can help you locate many of the technology resources available. The public library in your area is another good source for this information.

Overcoming Inadequate Prior Knowledge

Students who experience difficulties in constructing meaning often have limited or erroneous prior knowledge (Lipson, 1984). These students often need more prior knowledge development that is *directed specifically to the reading or writing task* they are expected to perform. You can use all of the strategies presented in this chapter to help in these circumstances, but you will need to approach them systematically and somewhat differently than for other students.

Limited Prior Knowledge

All students come to school with prior knowledge; however, it may not match what the school community expects them to have. If they lack experience with the world in general and with literacy events, they may have had limited life experiences or may not have been read to at home. Or they may come from homes where the concept of and motivation for literacy learning are different from those of the school (Taylor & Dorsey-Gaines, 1988). Regardless of the circumstances, *it is our goal to help them take whatever prior knowledge they bring to school and expand and build on it.*

Within the framework of the literacy program, there are many opportunities to expand students' world knowledge and knowledge and experience with literacy events. You must do this systematically, always emphasizing the value of each individual and what he or she brings to school. The following suggestions should be helpful in planning classroom experiences that will help expand students' prior knowledge.

Sharing and Talking.   Create many opportunities for students to share and talk about their own experiences and backgrounds. This says, "What you know is good and of value." Opportunities for these experiences can be provided in opening morning exercises, sharing times, or throughout the day. Students of all ages like the opportunity to talk about what is important to them.

Sharing should also give students time to talk about books they have read or things they have written. This is a good time to make use of the author's chair or reader's chair discussed in Chapter 2.

Read-Aloud Time.   Reading aloud to children is one of the best ways to broaden their prior knowledge and language experiences. If children have not been read to at home, this activity is even more significant in school. See Chapter 2 for guidelines on reading aloud to students.

Independent Reading and Writing Time.   Students who have limited prior knowledge need *more time to read and write independently.* See Chapter 2 for suggestions.

Provide Access to the Internet.   Some students with inadequate prior knowledge will be motivated to seek information on the Web and to share that information in meaningful ways with peers.

Plan Lessons and Experiences to Develop Prior Knowledge.   Use the strategies suggested in this chapter and those you learn from other sources to systematically develop prior knowledge when you start a new theme, when students read a selection, or when they begin a writing experience. Use the literacy lesson format presented in Chapter 2 with the strategies that lend themselves to more concretely developing prior knowledge for students.

Students who have limited prior knowledge often need continued support throughout their reading lessons to develop and relate this knowledge to what they read.

Misconceptions in Prior Knowledge

Correcting misconceptions or erroneous prior knowledge is difficult, but research indicates it is possible to make these corrections and improve students' ability to construct meaning (Alvermann & Hynd, 1987; Alvermann et al., 1985; Dole & Smith, 1989; Hynd & Alvermann, 1986; Maria, 1988). Although research presents no hard-and-fast guidelines, it does give some suggestions that lead to the following guidelines.

Activate and Assess Prior Knowledge.   First, you must find out what students know and/or think about the topic, using many of the strategies discussed in this chapter. As students respond, note misconceptions or errors.

Decide on the Best Time for Correcting the Error or Misconception.   This is not an easy decision to make. Research suggests that changing students' misconceptions is a long-term process that takes place through reading and writing over a period of time. Minor errors or misconceptions may be corrected before reading, but more serious ones will need to be viewed in the long-term process of instruction. Brainstorming and discussion may be natural strategies for correcting minor misconceptions before reading (Flood & Lapp, 1988). However, Maria (1990) cautions that too heavy a focus on correcting errors or misconceptions before reading may deter students from wanting to read.

FIGURE 3.21

THINKSHEET BASED ON DOLE AND SMITH (1989) RESEARCH

Matter Unit Thinksheet

Central Questions	① Everyday Ideas I Know or Believe	② Scientific Ideas from My Textbook	③ Text Ideas Same as Everyday Ideas	④ Text Added Information	⑤ Text Conflicted with Everyday Ideas	⑥ Text Was Confusing
1. What are objects made of?						
2. What happens when water freezes/ evaporates?						
3. What happens when a nail rusts?						

Select the Strategies to Be Used.   Whereas all the strategies discussed in this chapter might be useful in correcting minor misconceptions, those that involve longer-term thinking processes are more likely to be effective in overcoming more deeply rooted misconceptions. One such strategy is the anticipation guide presented on page 128.

Another strategy designed and used in research specifically for the purpose of correcting misconceptions in prior knowledge is the "thinksheet" (Dole & Smith, 1989; Maria, 1988). Figure 3.21 presents a sample thinksheet that employs the Prior Knowledge Monitoring and Integrating (PKMI) strategy, which works as follows:

1. Introduce the topic and have a general discussion about it.
2. Present the thinksheet and have students record their ideas in column ①.
3. During reading, have students complete column ② and place a check in the appropriate column (③–⑥).

4. After reading, have students discuss their thinking about the central questions and what they learned from reading.

PKMI was effective in changing fifth-grade students' thinking about a text (Dole & Smith, 1989); however, much more research is needed before this strategy can be considered completely viable.

Research on the role of misconceptions in prior knowledge and the construction of meaning is just beginning to accumulate. Although the guidelines presented here are certainly supported by the limited amount of research that exists, you should be on the lookout for new information in this area.

Literacy Lesson

Mummies, Tombs, and Treasure

At the conclusion of Chapter 2, you read a literacy lesson for narrative text, *Jamaica Tag-Along* (Havill, 1989). That lesson used two strategies when introducing the book to activate and develop prior knowledge: brainstorming (a teaching strategy) and story map prediction (a student strategy). You might want to look back at that lesson now to see how those strategies were used.

This lesson focuses on introducing a theme and introducing one of the books to be read during the theme. You will see how global prior knowledge is activated and developed when introducing the theme and how text-specific prior knowledge is activated and developed for the first chapter.

This portion of the sample unit is based on a thematic unit plan on "ancient Egypt" designed for fifth, sixth, or seventh graders in which one of the books to be read is *Mummies, Tombs, and Treasure* (Perl, 1987). The sample presented here focuses on introducing the theme and gives a literacy lesson for the first chapter in the book.

Before Reading the Plan

1. Think about what you have learned about prior knowledge activation and development.
2. Recall the parts of a thematic unit plan and a literacy lesson. (See Chapter 2 if you need to review.)
3. Read "The First Egyptian Mummies," Chapter 1 of *Mummies, Tombs, and Treasure.*
4. Read and study the teacher preparation section to see how I decided which prior knowledge to activate for the theme and the literacy lesson.

While Reading the Plan

1. Notice how prior knowledge was activated and developed for this theme and lesson.
2. Think about why each strategy was used. Note any questions.
3. Think of other ways you might have activated and developed prior knowledge for this theme and lesson.

Contents

MUMMIES, TOMBS,
AND TREASURE
Secrets of Ancient Egypt

BY LILA PERL

Illustrated with photographs · Drawings by Erika Weihs

CLARION BOOKS

1
The First Egyptian Mummies

What is a mummy, and why do we find mummies so fascinating? We've all heard of old-time horror movies with names like *The Mummy's Hand, The Mummy's Ghost,* and *The Mummy's Tomb.* And then there is "the mummy's curse." Even today there are people who believe that anyone who has ever gone near a mummy will meet with sudden misfortune.

Yet a mummy is nothing more than a dead body, either human or animal. Perhaps the reason mummies fill some of us with fear and fire up our imaginations is that they are so lifelike. Many Egyptian mummies are thousands of years old. But they still have their hair, their fingernails and toenails, and even their eyelashes. Their flesh and their features are well preserved. In looking at photographs taken when these mummies were discovered, in recent times, we can tell them apart and recognize their faces.

A mummy, of course, is a dead body that has been

The 3000-year-old mummy of an ancient Egyptian priest

I

sues of once-living things, returning them to nature in other forms.

But sometimes nature springs a surprise or two on us. One such surprise took place long ago in the vast North African desert country of Egypt. Before the beginning of recorded history — perhaps seven or eight thousand years ago — people began to settle on the banks of the Nile River, which runs through the Egyptian desert. The ribbons of well-watered land that bordered the Nile provided precious soil for growing food crops. So, in selecting a place to bury their dead, the Egyptian farming people avoided the river shore. They chose instead the hot, barren sands that lay beyond it.

The people dug small shallow graves. Usually they buried their dead in a crouched position. They placed them on their sides with their knees drawn up to their chests. That way their bodies took up as little space as possible.

The Egyptians hoped that in some magical way the dead were not really dead. Perhaps their spirits lay beneath the sand along with their limp, unclothed bodies. Perhaps a spirit might wish to eat or drink just as the living did. So the families of the dead included some clay pots of food and jars of water in the shallow pit graves. And sometimes they added a man's favorite tool or spear of sharpened stone, a woman's beads of shell or bone, or a child's toy.

Then the family covered the grave with sand and piled some rocks on top of it. The rocks helped to mark the grave. They also made it difficult for jackals and other wild animals of the desert to reach the body inside it.

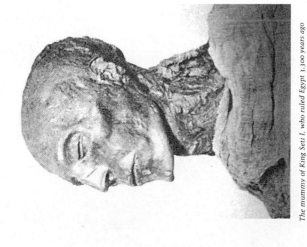

The mummy of King Seti I, who ruled Egypt 3,300 years ago

preserved — either accidentally by nature or on purpose by humans. Without preservation, dead animal matter usually decays very quickly. This is true of plant matter, too. A dead bird or cat, a piece of rotting fruit, can show us some of the stages of decay. Decay is caused by bacteria. These microscopic organisms break down the tis-

The hot dry sand of the shallow unlined graves did an amazing thing: it preserved the bodies of the early Egyptians wonderfully well. Moisture helps bacteria in bringing about decay. And the human body contains about seventy-five percent water. By rapidly absorbing the body's moisture, the hot sand acted as a natural preservative. The skin and other organs dried instead of decaying, and the first Egyptian mummies were born!

Similar accidents of nature have taken place in other parts of the world. But the early Egyptians had no way of knowing about those.

We know today, for example, that bodies can be naturally preserved by dry cold as well as by dry heat. In Siberia in northern Asia, woolly mammoths — huge prehistoric animals that resembled hairy elephants — have been found well preserved in ice. Their mummified bodies are at least ten thousand years old, for that is when the last of the mammoths died out.

Dry cold has also preserved the bodies of the Incas of Peru. The people of that far-reaching Indian empire lived in the high Andes Mountains of South America. Until they were conquered by Spanish explorers about five hundred years ago, they placed their dead in rock shelters. They arranged the bodies in a sitting position with knees drawn up, and bound them into bundles, wrapped in cloth, grass, and fur. In the dry, crisp mountain air, the Inca dead were soon transformed into mummies.

The early Egyptians must have been pleased when they somehow discovered the naturally mummified bodies of their dead. Soon they looked for ways to improve their graves. They lined the burial pits with straw

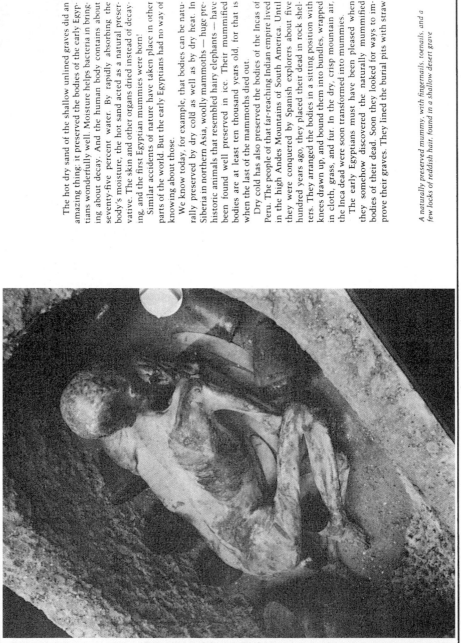

A naturally preserved mummy, with fingernails, toenails, and a few locks of reddish hair, found in a shallow desert grave

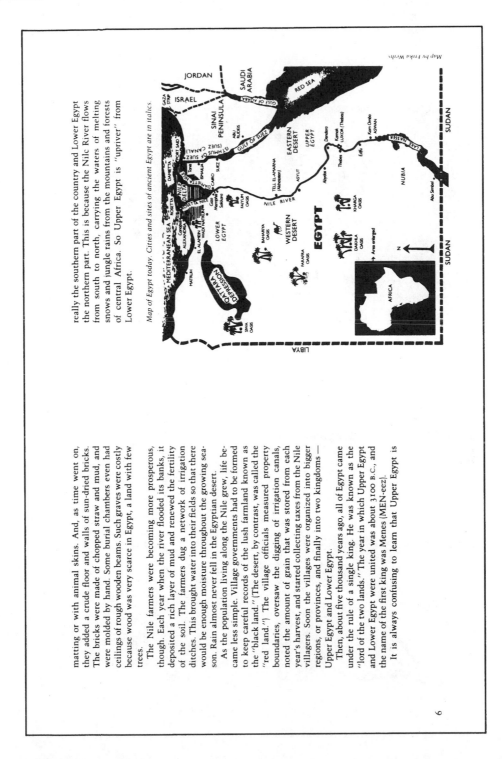

Map of Egypt today. Cities and sites of ancient Egypt are in italics.

Map by Erika Werlis

matting or with animal skins. And, as time went on, they added a crude floor and walls of sun-dried bricks. The bricks were made of chopped straw and mud, and were molded by hand. Some burial chambers even had ceilings of rough wooden beams. Such graves were costly because wood was very scarce in Egypt, a land with few trees.

The Nile farmers were becoming more prosperous, though. Each year when the river flooded its banks, it deposited a rich layer of mud and renewed the fertility of the soil. The farmers dug a network of irrigation ditches. This brought water into their fields so that there would be enough moisture throughout the growing season. Rain almost never fell in the Egyptian desert.

As the population living along the Nile grew, life became less simple. Village governments had to be formed to keep careful records of the lush farmland known as the "black land." (The desert, by contrast, was called the "red land.") The village officials measured property boundaries, oversaw the digging of irrigation canals, noted the amount of grain that was stored from each year's harvest, and started collecting taxes from the Nile villagers. Soon the villages were organized into bigger regions, or provinces, and finally into two kingdoms — Upper Egypt and Lower Egypt.

Then, about five thousand years ago, all of Egypt came under the rule of a single king. He was known as the "lord of the two lands." The year in which Upper Egypt and Lower Egypt were united was about 3100 B.C., and the name of the first king was Menes [MEN-eez].

It is always confusing to learn that Upper Egypt is

really the southern part of the country and Lower Egypt the northern part. This is because the Nile River flows from south to north, carrying the waters of melting snows and jungle rains from the mountains and forests of central Africa. So Upper Egypt is "upriver" from Lower Egypt.

6

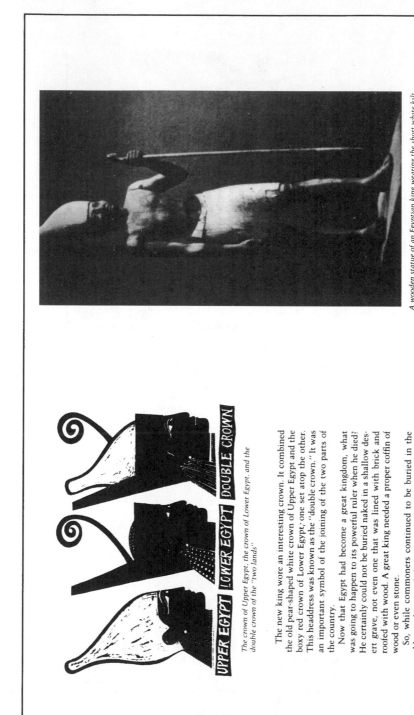

UPPER EGYPT   LOWER EGYPT   DOUBLE CROWN

The crown of Upper Egypt, the crown of Lower Egypt, and the double crown of the "two lands"

A wooden statue of an Egyptian king wearing the short white kilt and the white crown of Upper Egypt

The new king wore an interesting crown. It combined the old pear-shaped white crown of Upper Egypt and the boxy red crown of Lower Egypt, one set atop the other. This headdress was known as the "double crown." It was an important symbol of the joining of the two parts of the country.

Now that Egypt had become a great kingdom, what was going to happen to its powerful ruler when he died? He certainly could not be buried naked in a shallow desert grave, not even one that was lined with brick and roofed with wood. A great king needed a proper coffin of wood or even stone.

So, while commoners continued to be buried in the old way, kings and their queens, and other nobles were

8   9

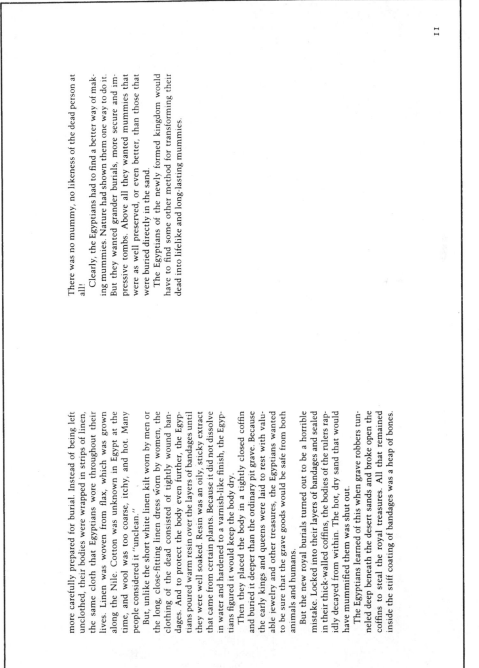

more carefully prepared for burial. Instead of being left unclothed, their bodies were wrapped in strips of linen, the same cloth that Egyptians wore throughout their lives. Linen was woven from flax, which was grown along the Nile. Cotton was unknown in Egypt at the time, and wool was too coarse, itchy, and hot. Many people considered it "unclean."

But, unlike the short white linen kilt worn by men or the long, close-fitting linen dress worn by women, the clothing of the dead consisted of tightly wound bandages. And to protect the body even further, the Egyptians poured warm resin over the layers of bandages until they were well soaked. Resin was an oily, sticky extract that came from certain plants. Because it did not dissolve in water and hardened to a varnish-like finish, the Egyptians figured it would keep the body dry.

Then they placed the body in a tightly closed coffin and buried it deeper than the ordinary pit grave. Because the early kings and queens were laid to rest with valuable jewelry and other treasures, the Egyptians wanted to be sure that the grave goods would be safe from both animals and humans.

But the new royal burials turned out to be a horrible mistake. Locked into their layers of bandages and sealed in their thick-walled coffins, the bodies of the rulers rapidly decayed from within. The hot, dry sand that would have mummified them was shut out.

The Egyptians learned of this when grave robbers tunneled deep beneath the desert sands and broke open the coffins to steal the royal treasures. All that remained inside the stiff coating of bandages was a heap of bones.

There was no mummy, no likeness of the dead person at all!

Clearly, the Egyptians had to find a better way of making mummies. Nature had shown them one way to do it. But they wanted grander burials, more secure and impressive tombs. Above all they wanted mummies that were as well preserved, or even better, than those that were buried directly in the sand.

The Egyptians of the newly formed kingdom would have to find some other method for transforming their dead into lifelike and long-lasting mummies.

Teacher Preparation

The theme "Ancient Egypt" was selected because it has high student appeal and is a topic of study usually found in grades 5, 6, or 7. Preparation proceeds as follows:

1. I selected books for the theme. *Mummies, Tombs, and Treasure* (Perl, 1987) would be read by all students, and other books would be self-selected from the school library.
2. I then identified my major outcomes in terms of attitudes and habits and constructing meaning:

   - *Attitudes and habits:* Develop an appreciation of influences from the past on the present.
   - *Constructing meaning:* Understand how previous civilizations have influenced our lives today.

   I decided that the strategies and skills focus would be on the following:

   - Preview and self-question
   - Summarizing information from different sources
   - Using library resources

   This theme and text naturally lend themselves to focusing on these areas.
3. Next, I thought about the major background concepts students needed to have for a theme on ancient Egypt. I concluded that they needed to know where it was, when it existed, and what the climate was like.
4. I then read *Mummies, Tombs, and Treasure* and determined that the first chapter has two main ideas with a strong cause-effect structure.

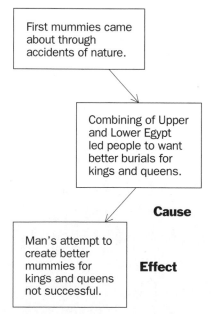

Main ideas

First mummies came about through accidents of nature.

Combining of Upper and Lower Egypt led people to want better burials for kings and queens.

Cause

Man's attempt to create better mummies for kings and queens not successful.

Effect

This graphic organizer would help students see the structure in the first chapter and prepare them for the remainder of the book.

5. Next, I reviewed Chapter 1 to see if there was any key-concept vocabulary related to the main ideas. Four words seemed important: *mummy, bacteria, decay,* and *coffin. Mummy* and *bacteria* were defined in the text, and students would know decay from their experiences with teeth and *coffin* from their television experiences. Therefore, I decided not to preteach any vocabulary. Vocabulary would be the focus of an extension activity after reading, if needed.

6. Finally, I decided to use the following teaching strategies to introduce the theme:

   • *Brainstorming and discussion* (using a photograph of a mummy and a map): This would help bring out what students knew and give them a general idea of where Egypt is.

   • *Anticipation guide:* This would help students think about what they believed before the unit and see how their beliefs changed after the unit.

   • *Project:* Students would plan a project during the theme. This would help them integrate what they were learning. They would use the book we were reading together, as well as self-selected books from the library.

For the first literacy lesson, I decided to use a structured preview because this would give students a sense of how the book was organized and would help them think about constructing meaning as they read. I also planned to use the preview and self-question strategy because it is appropriate for expository text and I wanted students to continue to become more independent.

Thematic Unit and Literacy Lesson Plan

Thematic unit title: Ancient Egypt

Level: Grades 5, 6, or 7

Unit focus:

Attitudes and habits: Develop an appreciation of influences from the past on the present.

Meaning construction: Understand how previous civilizations have influenced our lives today.

Strategies and skills focus: Preview and self-question
Summarizing (and synthesizing)
   information from different sources
Using library resources

Literacy
Lesson
continued

Introducing the Theme

ACTIVITY	PROCEDURE	NOTES
Brainstorming and discussion about Egypt	1. Show students mummy photograph and ask them where they think this is from. Discuss.	Motivates students.
	2. Divide class into small groups. Have students share what they know about ancient Egypt.	Activates global prior knowledge. Gives teacher a chance to assess prior knowledge.
	3. Bring class together and discuss what is known, focusing on • where Egypt is • what it is like (desert) • when it existed	
	4. Display a map and have students locate Egypt; continue discussion on above points.	
Anticipation guide	1. Tell students that they will be learning about ancient Egypt.	Continues to activate prior knowledge. Focuses students' thinking on the unit outcomes.
	2. Distribute the anticipation guide and ask students to read each statement and indicate whether they agree or disagree. Students will return to this after the unit is completed.	Will allow students to see how their knowledge and beliefs change during the unit.

Ancient Egypt

Before the Unit		After the Unit
_____	1. All that we know about burial was learned from the mummies.	_____
_____	2. Studying history is not a good idea.	_____
_____	3. Not many treasures of the past exist today.	_____
_____	4. What we know today is based only on new scientific discoveries.	_____

Literacy Lesson *continued*	ACTIVITY	PROCEDURE	NOTES
	Introducing the theme project	1. Tell students that during the theme they will be doing a project on Egypt. They can pick a suggested one or design their own. Students can decide after reading a chapter or two in the book.	Provides a way for students to integrate new knowledge with what they already know.

> *Possible Projects*
>
> 1. Write a book about Egypt.
> 2. Make a miniature mummy.
> 3. Create visual display showing how things from Egypt have influenced our lives.
> 4. Conduct a television news show about discoveries in ancient Egypt.
> 5. You decide. Plan your own project.

		PROCEDURE	NOTES
		2. Discuss selecting other books to use for the project. Encourage students to share.	Begins to focus on using library resources. This will continue later in the unit.

Introducing *Mummies, Tombs, and Treasure*

	ACTIVITY	PROCEDURE	NOTES
	Using preview and self-question strategy	1. Display the preview and self-question poster (see page 109). 2. Have students preview *Mummies, Tombs, and Treasure* and list questions in their journals they would like to answer while reading. Encourage them to make notes as they read.	Activates prior knowledge related specifically to the book and makes students take responsibility for their own learning by having them raise questions they want answered; these become their purpose for reading. Students have learned to use this strategy in previous units. If more modeling is needed, provide it here (see Chapter 8).
	Structured preview of Chapter 1, "The First Egyptian Mummies"	1. Invite students to locate Chapter 1 and read the title and captions for each illustration. 2. Ask students what they think they will learn in this chapter. Discuss briefly. 3. Display the graphic organizer for Chapter 1. Tell students that this chapter has two main ideas and a cause-effect organization.	The structured preview activates and develops prior knowledge specific to the chapter. I decided to use this because I felt this class needed this type of support in beginning the book.

Literacy
Lesson
continued

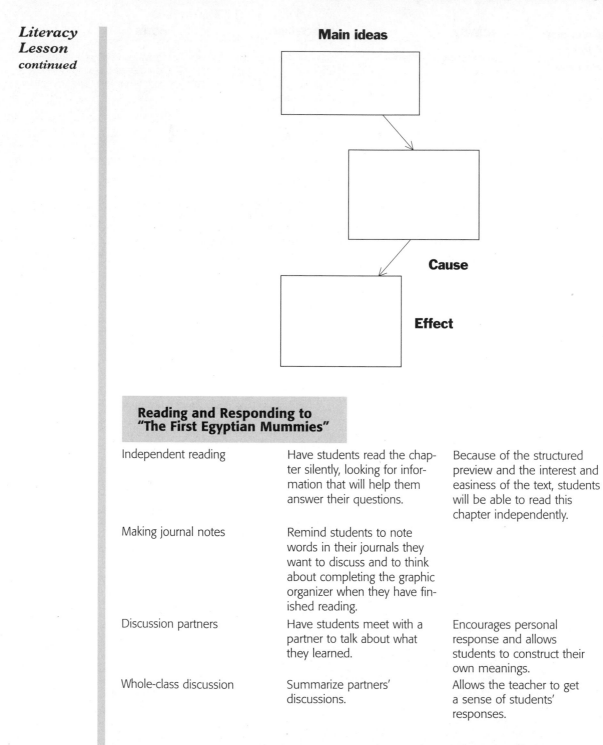

Main ideas

Cause

Effect

Reading and Responding to "The First Egyptian Mummies"

Independent reading

Have students read the chapter silently, looking for information that will help them answer their questions.

Because of the structured preview and the interest and easiness of the text, students will be able to read this chapter independently.

Making journal notes

Remind students to note words in their journals they want to discuss and to think about completing the graphic organizer when they have finished reading.

Discussion partners

Have students meet with a partner to talk about what they learned.

Encourages personal response and allows students to construct their own meanings.

Whole-class discussion

Summarize partners' discussions.

Allows the teacher to get a sense of students' responses.

	ACTIVITY	PROCEDURE	NOTES
Literacy Lesson *continued*	Completing the graphic organizer chart	Display the graphic organizer chart. Ask students to help complete the chart. Discuss the two main ideas and the cause-effect structure.	This experience will help students formulate main ideas and see how certain events cause other things to happen. If students have difficulty with this, the teacher models how to identify these points (see Chapter 8 on modeling).
	Discussing journal notes and vocabulary	Invite students to share any notes or words they wrote in their journals. Ask them to look at their original list of questions to see if they can answer any of them yet.	Allows a way to teach any words causing difficulty; also, a good assessment opportunity to identify students who will need more support while reading the remainder of this book.

Extending "The First Egyptian Mummies"

Students are likely to be excited about getting on with the reading of this book; therefore, no additional activities are planned, and students will read the remainder of the book independently. We will stop for discussion after every two chapters or more frequently if needed. If some students need teacher support (determined through responses to Chapter 1), I will meet with them in small groups and guide their reading and/or have them do cooperative reading. The project will be started after students have read several chapters; then meetings in the library will be planned. Throughout the reading of this book, I will conduct conferences with students to give them needed support in constructing meaning. See Chapter 10 for information on conferencing.

After Reading the Plan
1. **Review and discuss the plan with some of your peers who have read it, focusing on how prior knowledge was activated and developed throughout the lesson.**
2. **Assume you have a group of students who need much more prior knowledge development for the book *Mummies, Tombs, and Treasure*. Work out a plan showing how you will do this for Chapter 1.**

◼ Summary

This chapter focused on the importance of activating and developing prior knowledge for the effective construction of meaning. It presented information about how to use prior knowledge to help all students develop their ability to construct meaning. Second-language learners, students with limited prior knowledge, and students with misconceptions need special support. Fourteen strategies, two student strategies and twelve teaching strategies, were described, with emphasis on how and when to use them. *The ultimate goal of the literacy program is to get students to use strategies independently and to call up their own prior knowledge to determine their purpose for reading.* The chapter concluded with a sample lesson illustrating the process of planning a lesson that focuses on prior knowledge.

Literature

Adler, D. A. (1986). *Martin Luther King, Jr.: Free at last.* New York: Holiday House.

Allard, H., & Marshall, J. (1978). *The Stupids have a ball.* Boston: Houghton Mifflin.

Behrens, J. (1978). *Fiesta!* Chicago: Childrens Press.

Fox, M. (1985). *Wilfrid Gordon McDonald Partridge.* New York: Kane/Miller.

Freedman, R. (1987). *Lincoln: A photobiography.* New York: Clarion.

Gibbons, G. (1989). *Monarch butterfly.* New York: Holiday House.

Giff, P. R. (1980). *Today was a terrible day.* New York: Viking.

Giff, P. R. (1988). *Ronald Morgan goes to bat.* New York: Viking Kestrel.

Hamilton, V. (1990). *Cousins.* New York: Philomel.

Murphy, J. (1990). *The boys' war.* New York: Clarion.

Perl, L. (1987). *Mummies, tombs, and treasure.* New York: Clarion.

Sachar, L. (1989). *Wayside School is falling down.* New York: Lothrop, Lee & Shepard.

Small, D. (1985). *Imogene's antlers.* New York: Crown.

Van Allsburg, C. (1985). *The polar express.* Boston: Houghton Mifflin.

For Additional Reading

Alvermann, D. E., Dillon, D. R., & O'Brien, D. G. (1987). *Using discussion to promote reading comprehension.* Newark, DE: International Reading Association.

Anderson, R. C., & Pearson, P. D. (1984). A schema-theoretic view of basic processes in reading comprehension. In P. D. Pearson (Ed.), *Handbook of reading research* (pp. 255–291). New York: Longman.

Au, K. H. (1993). *Literacy instruction in multicultural settings.* Ft. Worth, TX: Harcourt Brace.

Graesser, A., Golding, J. M., & Long, D. L. (1991). Narrative representation and comprehension. In R. Barr, M. L. Kamil, P. Mosenthal, & P. D. Pearson (Eds.), *Handbook of reading research* (Vol. 2, pp. 171–205). New York: Longman.

Leu, D. J. Jr. (Ed.). (1998). Exploring literacy on the Internet. *The Reading Teacher 51*(8), 694–700.

Rigg, P., & Allen, V. G. (1989). *When they don't all speak English.* Urbana, IL: National Council of Teachers of English.

Weaver, C. A., III, & Kintsch, W. (1991). Expository text. In R. Barr, M. L. Kamil, P. Mosenthal, & P. D. Pearson (Eds.), *Handbook of reading research* (Vol. 2, pp. 230–245). New York: Longman.

For Exploration: Electronic Products and Resources

Without activated prior knowledge or background information, students cannot construct meaning from texts. Teachers can activate students' prior knowledge and help them become independent in activating their prior knowledge with strategies discussed throughout this chapter. More and more, we can expect to see a variety of technology applications play a part in activating students' prior knowledge and setting their own purposes for reading.

The Education Connection

The Education Connection is the creation of a partnership between Vanderbilt University, Little Planet Publishing, and Computers for Education. This site provides resources and links for educators, parents, and students. Resources for educators provide links to resources for K–12. Explore these resources for effective materials to use in activating prior knowledge. Explore the student resources also. **www.asd.com/asd/edconn/page5nf.htm**

Check multimedia products created by educational software companies, and keep an eye on the publications sections of organizations and associations devoted to education. These sites (see addresses at the end of Chapter 1) will help you stay aware of new ways to activate prior knowledge among students at all levels.

Beginning Literacy: Learning to Read and Spell Words and Construct Meaning

4

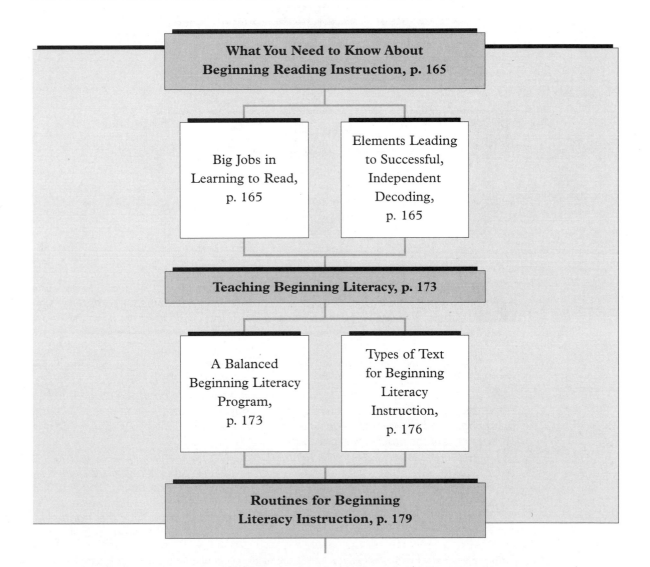

What You Need to Know About
Beginning Reading Instruction, p. 165

Big Jobs in
Learning to Read,
p. 165

Elements Leading
to Successful,
Independent
Decoding,
p. 165

Teaching Beginning Literacy, p. 173

A Balanced
Beginning Literacy
Program,
p. 173

Types of Text
for Beginning
Literacy
Instruction,
p. 176

Routines for Beginning
Literacy Instruction, p. 179

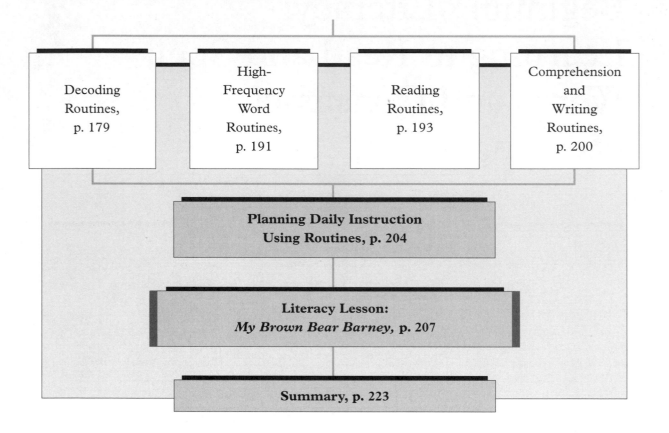

B*eginning readers must learn to read words quickly, accurately, and automatically; this ability is critical to the process of constructing meaning, or comprehension (Adams, 1990). A look at how two different first-grade teachers approach reading will help you begin to understand this process.*

Mr. Paredes and his students were rereading aloud the book The Lady with the Alligator Purse *(Westcott, 1988). As Mr. Paredes read, the children chimed in: "Miss Lucy had a baby, / His name was Tiny Tim. . . ." After rereading the whole book, the children talked about their favorite parts and found pages to show examples. Luanda said, "I like the pizza page" and showed the page where the characters are eating pizza in the bed. Mr. Paredes encouraged every child to respond.*

After the discussion, Mr. Paredes returned to the first page and said, "Let's reread this page together: 'Miss Lucy had a baby, / His name was Tiny Tim.'" All the children joined in. Mr. Paredes said, "What was the baby's name?" The children responded, "Tiny Tim." Mr. Paredes wrote the name on the chalkboard and said, "What is the beginning letter of the baby's name?" Several children responded, "t". Mr. Paredes underlined the T *and said, "This letter stands for /t/."* Then he said, "We are going to talk about the /t/ sound today."*

*When a letter is set off in slash marks, /t/, you are to give the sound for the letter. It is difficult to give the sound of a consonant without adding a schwa sound. Be aware of this difficulty and try to keep the sound as pure as possible. For example, the sound for *t* is not /*tuh*/; it is /t/ with quick, breathy sound.

"Does anyone in our class have a name that begins with the /t/ sound?" he asked. As the children called out names, Mr. Paredes listed them under Tiny Tim. *He then asked different children to come up and underline the* t *and give the sound it stood for:*

Tiny Tim
Terry
Tom
Tanisha
teacher

One child said, "Lisa." Instead of telling the child she was wrong, Mr. Paredes listed the name to the side of Tiny Tim *and said, "Let's compare these two beginning sounds. Which one begins with /t/?" "Tiny Tim." "Which one begins with /l/?" "Lisa." "Are these the same sound?" asked Mr. Paredes. "No," the children chorused. Then he said, "Let's look at our lists on the wall to see if we have one where Lisa's name will fit."*

The children did not find a list for the letter L *because it had not been taught yet. Mr. Paredes tore off a long strip of paper, wrote* Lisa *at the top, and underlined the* L. *He said, "We will talk about this letter another day."*

Mr. Paredes returned to the list of t *words, reread it with the children, and said, "Now we are going to play our game, EVERYONE SHOW. When I say a word, if it begins with the* t *sound /t/, everyone show the t-card. If it doesn't begin with /t/, show your* No *card. (Mr. Paredes read* teacher, top, dog, say, tiger, tap, run, toss. *He had a checklist of names where he noted any child having difficulty for reteaching later.) He then directed children back to the big book,* The Lady with the Alligator Purse, *and had the group reread it with him. He then asked the children to read several pages and locate and read aloud words that began with /t/. He gave each child a little book he had written and duplicated called* Tip at the Top. *This book contained many t-words and used only CVC (Consonant-Vowel-Consonant) words that children could decode and sight words they already knew. He said, "Here is a book that will let you apply what we have learned about the letter* t. *It uses only skills and words you have learned. Read it to yourself to tell the others in the group what happened to the bird in the story."*

Compare Mr. Paredes's class to Ms. Anderson's class.

"Boys and girls, we are going to meet a new phonics character today," said Ms. Anderson. "His name begins with this letter. What is this letter?" (Ms. Anderson printed the letter B *on the board.) The group called out "B." "Yes," said Ms. Anderson. "Here is a picture of our character. What is he?" (Ms. Anderson showed a picture of a bear.) "A bear," responded the children. "Our character's name is Boris Bear. You say it." (The children all replied* Boris Bear.) *"Boris Bear is our character for the* b *sound. Listen to the /b/ sound at*

the beginning of his name—/B/-/B/-Boris /B/-/B/-Bear. You say it." (Children responded /B/-/B/-Boris /B/-/B/-Bear.)

"Now we are going to learn to read words that begin with /b/." (Ms. Anderson printed the word book on the board. She modeled for the children how to read the word aloud. She placed her hand under the b and said:) "This letter stands for /b/ and I remember /o͞ok/; /b/-/o͞ok/. I blend it faster /b/-/o͞ok/—book. I can read the word. Now you will practice reading words together. I will point to the letter or letters and say SOUND. You say the sound; then I will say BLEND. You will blend the sounds to say the word. Let's try it again with book."

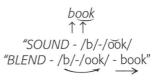

(Ms. Anderson repeated the SOUND/BLEND process using bag, bug, boy, bump.)

"Boys and girls, now take out your magic slates. We are going to learn to spell words that begin with /b/. Number 1 to 5 down the side. I will say five words. Write b beside the number if the word I say begins with /b/ as in Boris Bear." (Ms. Anderson read 1. cap, 2. box, 3. baby, 4. sing, 5. bunny. She walked around looking to see who was having problems so she could give them help later.)

"Now we are going to read a story using what you already know and what you have learned about the sound for b." (Ms. Anderson passed out copies of a little book titled Bing, which is part of her published reading program.) "Read this story silently to find out who the main character is and what he does. Remember, use the sound at the beginning of Boris Bear and what you already know to figure out the words." After silent reading, children discussed the story and read it aloud as a group.

MR. PAREDES AND MS. Anderson were each teaching students to read words. Look back over the examples and think about how these two teachers were alike and different. Compare your ideas to the following:

- Mr. Paredes started with a big book and returned to that big book after students had been taught the sound. Ms. Anderson started by teaching the individual sound.
- Both Mr. Paredes and Ms. Anderson explicitly modeled the sound being taught by isolating it for students.
- Ms. Anderson modeled for children how to sequentially read words.
- Ms. Anderson had the children learn to spell words using the sound being taught.
- Both teachers had children immediately practice reading a book that was controlled by containing only the sounds and words that had been previously taught.
- Both teachers were using procedures and practices that could be defended from current research. (See the remainder of this chapter.)

In this chapter, you will learn the *basic* background about how beginning readers learn to identify words, including using phonics; you will also learn the *basics* about how to teach beginning reading. You will have a better understanding of why Mr. Paredes and Ms. Anderson taught the lessons as they did.

What You Need to Know About Beginning Reading Instruction

Effective beginning reading instruction is critical for the success of all children. All teachers need to understand the process in order to adequately teach students of any age. Research from the last several decades has led us to some very clear conclusions about beginning reading.

Big Jobs in Learning to Read

Learning to read is not a simple process. Many factors and elements interact as a child learns to read (Juel, 1991). However, within the process, two big jobs work together—*decoding* and *comprehension*. Figure 4.1 shows how these jobs change in emphasis from beginning reading to mature reading.

Decoding is the process of translating written language into verbal speech (oral reading) or inner speech (thinking the words in one's head) (Eldredge, 1995). Many people equate decoding with reading; they are not equal. Decoding is necessary but not sufficient for reading.

Reading, however, does not occur unless an individual comprehends. Comprehension is the process whereby the reader constructs meaning by interacting with the text (Anderson & Pearson, 1984; Cooper, 1986). (See discussion of comprehension in Chapters 1 and 3.) Decoding and comprehension interact as individuals learn to read.

Refer to Figure 4.1. Notice that as an individual moves from beginning reading to mature reading, the emphasis in learning shifts from more focus on decoding to more focus on comprehension. Comprehension is *always* a part of the process and decoding is *always* a part of the process. However, as students become mature readers, their primary focus is on comprehension or constructing meaning. This process is not as smooth and linear as the diagram shows; it is what Cooper and Kiger (in press) call a "jerky continuum."

Figure 4.1 does show, however, that the instructional emphasis on the "big jobs" of reading needs to shift from the beginning to the mature stages. In other words, the two jobs (decoding and comprehension) are not equal at the various stages; the amount of instructional emphasis shifts from one component to another with *both always being included*. Let's focus on the "big job" of beginning reading—decoding.

Elements Leading to Successful, Independent Decoding

The ultimate goal of reading words is fluency. *Fluency is the process of automatically, accurately, and rapidly recognizing words* (LaBerge & Samuels, 1976; Perfetti, 1985; Stanovich, 1980, 1986). As children become fluent readers, they build a stockpile of *sight words* or words that they recognize instantly. If readers come to words they

FIGURE 4.1

CHANGING EMPHASIS IN LEARNING TO READ

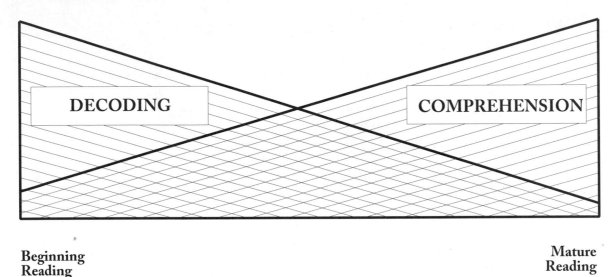

Beginning
Reading

Mature
Reading

do not recognize as sight words, they must use decoding to hypothesize the pronunciation of the word (orally or silently). In other words, children must be *independent decoders* and have the skills and strategies to figure out words on their own.

In the beginning stages of learning to read, a child must depend heavily on his or her decoding abilities to pronounce words. As the child has repeated practice in reading, he or she learns to recognize more words automatically, accurately, and rapidly (learns more sight words) and becomes a more fluent reader. Researchers have found that good comprehenders (constructors of meaning) are fluent decoders (Carnine, Carnine, & Gersten, 1984; Chall, 1967; Lesgold & Curtis, 1981).

Teaching decoding systematically is a critical part of beginning literacy instruction. In order for students to independently decode words, beginning reading instruction must include systematic teaching of decoding. As readers become more fluent, they use decoding skills and strategies only when they come to words they do not recognize instantly.

Students must develop six critical elements as they learn to independently decode words. These six elements develop in an overlapping sequence: *oral language, phonemic awareness, concepts of print, letter-sound associations* (phonics/structure), *analogy,* and *learning a way to think about words.* These elements help readers become independent decoders. In addition, readers also develop a stockpile of sight words and learn a number of high-frequency words (words that occur most often in language). This combination of independent decoding and sight words helps individuals become efficient, independent readers.

Oral Language

Children begin to develop oral language the day they are born. They develop an understanding of the sounds of language (phonology); they learn how words are formed and related to each other (morphology); they learn how language conveys meaning (semantics); they develop a stockpile of word meanings and pronunciations (vocabulary or lexicon); and they learn how individuals use language to achieve certain goals (pragmatics). These aspects of language development form the foundation for reading including both decoding and comprehension. For example, if a child decodes the word *horse,* his language base serves as the checking system to tell whether the word has been decoded properly. The child's language base also serves as the basis for assigning meaning to the word *horse*.

Most children develop their use of language with ease (Snow, Burns, & Griffin, 1998). For these children, the school must provide activities that support continued language development. However, some children come from an environment with limited adult language models or have some neurological problem; they may not have a good language base. For these children, the school must provide specific instruction and activities that develop oral language. For all children, school-provided language development activities should include such things as:

▶ Good language modeling provided by teachers reading aloud to students and discussing what was read.

▶ Language lessons that model uses of a variety of types of language. For example, use a photograph as the basis for a discussion. Model expansion of language by taking children's comments and adding more description.

Child	It's a dog
Teacher	Yes, it is a big, brown dog. What else do you notice about this dog's face?
Child	A white spot.
Teacher	Yes, the big, brown dog has a white patch or spot on its face.

▶ Experiences such as field trips, class visitors, movies, videos, and CD-ROM stories that expand students' background and knowledge followed by good discussions.

▶ Opportunities for children to use language in a variety of ways. This may occur through various centers in the kindergarten and first-grade classroom.

Continued language development forms and expands the foundation for children to effectively develop their abilities to decode and comprehend. Weak or limited oral language may interfere with a child's ability to learn to read (Chard & Osborne, n.d.).

Phonemic Awareness

Directly related to oral language development is another important element that is a part of helping children develop independence in decoding—*phonemic awareness.* Phonemic awareness is the knowledge that spoken words are composed of a sequence of sounds or *phonemes*. Phonemic awareness is a part of the broader category known as *phonological awareness,* which includes all the aspects of the sounds of language separate and apart from meaning.

Research has supported the importance of phonemic awareness in relation to learning to read (Ball & Blachman, 1991) and learning to spell (Juel, Griffith, & Gough, 1986). English is an alphabetic language. This means that the sounds of the language (phonemes) are represented by symbols or alphabet (graphemes). For example, the word *cat* has three phonemes *(/c/-/ă/-/t/)* and three graphemes *c-a-t.* The word *goat* also has three phonemes /g/-/ō/-/t/ and three graphemes *g-oa-t,* but one of the phonemes, /ō/, is represented by a two-letter grapheme.

The alphabetic principle, the idea that each sound of the language is represented by a graphic symbol, is not learned naturally by most children (Eldredge, 1995). It must be explicitly taught (Adams, 1990). Phonemic awareness is a part of learning the alphabetic principle. If children have not yet acquired phonemic awareness, instruction in letter-sound associations will not be effective in helping them decode words.

Researchers have identified several aspects of phonemic awareness. Adams (1990) identifies five levels of phonemic awareness. Eldredge (1995), on the other hand, identifies six levels of phonemic awareness and notes that there is disagreement among researchers as to the *exact* levels of phonemic awareness. The elements of phonemic awareness commonly identified by multiple researchers include:

- ▶ *Rhyming Words*   being able to tell that two words rhyme (*hot-not; mat-fat*).
- ▶ *Counting Words in Sentences*   being able to tell that the following is a four-word sentence: *This is my mother.*
- ▶ *Counting Syllables in Words*   being able to tell that *horse* has one syllable, *listen* has two syllables, and so forth.
- ▶ *Counting Phonemes in Words*   knowing that *hat* has three sounds /h/-/ă/-/t/.
- ▶ *Segmenting and Blending Syllables*   hearing the word *happy* and giving the two syllables /hăp/-/ē/ is segmenting; hearing /rŭn/-/ing/ and giving the word *running* is blending.
- ▶ *Segmenting and Blending Onset and Rime*   hearing the word *brook* and identifying the onset /br/ and the rime /ook/ is segmenting; and hearing the onset /c/ and the rime /ard/ and being able to make the word *card* is blending.
- ▶ *Segmenting and Blending Phonemes*   hearing the word *hot* and giving the three phonemes /h/-/ō/-/t/ is segmenting; hearing the phonemes /p/-/ă/-/t/ and saying the word *pat* is blending.
- ▶ *Substitution of Sounds*   taking the word *hot* and substituting the sound /c/ for /h/ and saying the word *cot*.

Activities for teaching and developing phonemic awareness will be discussed later in this chapter (page 179).

Concepts of Print

As children learn to identify words as an aid to constructing meaning, they must develop some concepts about print. Clay (1985) divides these concepts into four categories: *books, sentences, words,* and *letters* (see Table 4.1).

TABLE 4.1

CONCEPTS OF PRINT

BOOKS

Knows:
- Cover
- Title, author, illustrator
- Beginning, ending
- Left-right orientation
- Top-bottom orientation
- Print tells story, not pictures

SENTENCES

Identifies:
- Sentence
- Beginning, ending of sentence
- Capital letter at beginning
- Punctuation: period, comma, question mark, quotation mark, exclamation point

WORDS

- Identifies words (knows that *day* is a word)

LETTERS

Knows:
- Letter order
- Capital and lower case

Source: Based on Clay (1985).

Beginning readers and writers must learn that books convey meaning through print. In this process they also need to know the left-right, top-bottom orientation on a page as well as facts about the book such as the cover, title, author, illustrator, beginning, and ending.

Students must also develop some understanding of the sentences on the page. They need to recognize a sentence, know that it represents a spoken message, and be able to tell the beginning and ending by recognizing the capital letters and the end punctuation. They also need some understanding of other forms of punctuation, such as quotation marks.

It is important that students develop the concept of a word and know that each word is composed of letters and that these letters appear in a certain order. Part of the learning that must take place includes knowing the difference between capital and lower-case letters. Although many children come to school understanding these concepts about print, some do not; so it may be necessary for you to help those children understand. (See Reading Routines, page 193.)

Letter-Sound Associations (Phonics and Structural Analysis)

A strong, consistent body of research has accumulated over the last thirty or more years showing that beginning readers get their best start by being *explicitly* taught letter-sound associations (Adams, 1990; Anderson, Hiebert, Scott, & Wilkinson, 1985; Chall, 1967, 1983; Snow, Burns, & Griffin, 1998). This instruction must include phonics and structural analysis. The instruction in and acquisition of phonemic awareness leads directly to teaching letter-sound associations (phonics and structural analysis).

Over the years, phonics has been a controversial issue for teachers (Allington, 1997; Flesch, 1955). Some educators and lay persons feel that phonics is the only and best way to teach children to read. Others strongly disagree. Sometimes these controversies have also involved parents, other educators, or the community at large. As a teacher, you will no doubt face these same controversies. The best way to be prepared to deal with phonics issues (or any other issues) is to:

▶ *Be Knowledgeable*   Make sure that you know what phonics is and understand the role it plays in learning to read and spell. "Word Skills: Phonics and Structural Analysis for Teachers," a special section presented at the end of this text, is designed to help you learn the basic elements about phonics and structural analysis. You may want to read this section now. See page 567.

▶ *Know the Research*   While not all teaching decisions grow out of research, there is much good research that can guide many of our decisions. Therefore, you must know and keep up with the research about phonics (and other areas). Look for patterns in such research; that is, do not depend on one isolated study to provide an answer. Throughout this text, I have tried to give patterns that are clearly documented in the research. This is important in all areas of teaching but is perhaps most important when it comes to phonics because of the often controversial and emotional nature of statements made or positions taken regarding phonics instruction.

Later in this chapter, we will look at how to teach phonics and structural analysis that lead to effective reading and spelling (see page 182).

Analogy

Analogy, when used in relation to decoding, is the process of noting similarities or patterns in words and using this to figure out an unfamiliar word. As beginning readers learn to read and spell words, they often use analogy to figure out the words (Gaskins et al., 1988). For example, if a child comes to the unknown word *ring*, she might recognize that the word looks like *sing*, a known word. Using letter-sound correspondences for the *r* and knowledge of the word *sing,* the child can make the analogy and decode the word *ring.* Analogy is *not* the process of looking for little words in big words—for example, *fat-her* in father. Such misinterpretation of analogy can lead beginning readers astray (Pinnell & Fountas, 1998).

Most readers don't use analogy immediately; they must learn some letter-sound correspondences (Ehri & Robbins, 1992) before they begin to use the process on their own. Analogy, however, becomes an important part of a reader's strategy for independently decoding words.

A Way to Think About Words

As students learn the elements of effective, independent decoding, they must develop a strategy to independently apply what they have learned in order to decode words by themselves. At the very beginning stages of reading, children are learning to "read through the word" or "sequentially decode" words. As they come to words they don't instantly recognize—for example, *horse*—they must learn to use their letter-sound correspondence knowledge to read through the word starting at the beginning—/h/-/or/-/s/—and proceeding in order.

The need for students to independently decode unknown words becomes increasingly important as they read more and read better. Students need a strategy for approaching unknown words (see Figure 4.2). Students can use this strategy well beyond beginning reading; it is based on research that shows that readers do indeed look at all the letters in words to decode them (Adams, 1990; Just & Carpenter, 1987). The following explanation will help you understand how students use the strategy presented in Figure 4.2:

▶ Students begin by looking for the largest sound chunks they recognize. This may involve an ending (*ing* or *ed*); it may be making an analogy from a known word to the unknown word (known word: *base;* unknown word: *case*); or it may be recognizing a word pattern such as *-op.* The student tries to decode the word and checks it by reading to the end of the sentence or paragraph. If this doesn't work, the student moves on to the next step.

▶ The student tries to use the individual letter-sound associations (phonics and structural analysis). The student then sequentially decodes or sounds out the word and checks it by reading to the end of the sentence or paragraph. This places context in a checking or confirming position and focuses the student initially on the letter-sound correspondences that will lead to more accurate decoding (Adams, 1990; Stanovich, 1980).

▶ Finally, if the student is unable to decode the word, he or she asks someone or refers to a dictionary as appropriate skills are learned.

The six elements in this section are critical to helping students become independent decoders. Keep in mind that while students are developing this independence in decoding, they are also learning high-frequency words and building a stockpile of sight words. Let's now focus on how to teach beginning reading so that students develop their abilities to decode and construct meaning.

FIGURE 4.2

A WAY TO THINK ABOUT WORDS

Teaching Beginning Literacy

Throughout this text we have been discussing the concept of a balanced literacy program. The beginning literacy program (kindergarten through grade 2) will have a bit more emphasis on decoding because, as we have seen, this is the bigger job of beginning reading. What exactly are the components that you should include in a Balanced Beginning Literacy Program?

A Balanced Beginning Literacy Program

Figure 4.3 shows the concept of a balanced beginning literacy program. This model will help you plan instruction and organize your classroom. The entire program must be carried out in a language-rich/print-rich environment (see Chapter 2). Each of the blocks in the balanced program has an important function to play.

▶ *Independent Reading* is the time when children have the opportunity to look at and/or read books of their own choosing. Beginning in kindergarten, children usually look at the pictures and often pretend to read the text by running their hands along the lines of print. This time establishes the habit of independent reading. As children develop their skill in reading, they begin to actually read the text.

To make this component operate effectively in your room, you will need many different books, a variety of children's and young adult periodicals, and even some newspapers. These can be displayed in the library area.

You will want to help children learn to select books for themselves. In kindergarten and the beginning of first grade, children usually make selections based on interests by looking at the covers and illustrations. As children progress in learning to read, you can help them learn to select books they can read. You may teach children a procedure used by many teachers called "Thumbs Up." Tell children to read a page in the book. Each time they come to a word they don't know, they fold a finger down on one hand. If the child's thumb is still up at the end of the page, the text is probably appropriate for the child to read. You will need to model this procedure for your students.

Independent reading at the beginning of kindergarten will usually be about 5 minutes daily. As the year goes by, this time is usually extended to 10 minutes. In first and second grades, independent reading is usually 10–15 minutes per day.

▶ *Independent Writing* is the time when children write anything they want to write. In kindergarten and the beginning of first grade, this "writing" may actually be drawing a picture with a few scribbles under it. Independent writing, like independent reading, provides students needed time to become proficient. Further, it establishes the habit of writing on a daily basis.

The amount of time for independent writing will range from 5 minutes per day at the beginning of kindergarten to 10 minutes or more by the end of the year. In first and second grade, the amount of time for independent writing is usually 10–15 minutes per day. (See Chapter 2 for a more detailed discussion of independent reading and independent writing.)

FIGURE 4.3

A BALANCED BEGINNING LITERACY PROGRAM

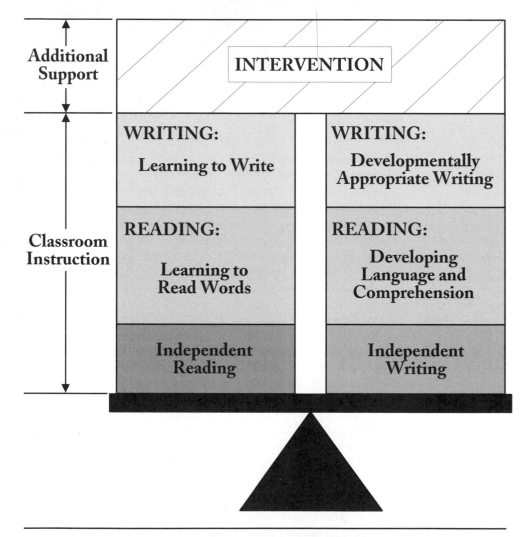

▸ **READING: Learning to Read Words** is the block where children are *systematically* and *explicitly* taught to decode words. This includes developing phonemic awareness, concepts of print, letter-sound associations, analogy, and a way to think about words. As children develop their abilities to use letter-sound associations, they *immediately begin to read little texts* that provide the opportunity to practice and apply the skills they are learning. As children increase in their abilities to read words, they should move beyond the little texts created for them to apply their beginning decoding skills to authentic literature that has been selected to help them continue to practice and apply their decoding skills. Once children develop independence in decoding, the Learning to Read Words block becomes the reading of core books (see Chapter 10).

During the Learning to Read Words block, children are also taught a number of high-frequency words. These words are also practiced and applied in the little texts being used for practice and application of decoding. Constructing meaning or comprehension is connected to the little texts after reading. A variety of teaching routines are used throughout this block. These will be presented later in this chapter.

▶ *READING: Developing Language and Comprehension* is the block that develops and expands oral language, including listening, speaking, and vocabulary. Children are taught the processes of comprehension by using rich, authentic literature for read-alouds, shared reading, and guided reading. Concepts of print are also developed through both read-alouds and shared reading. Comprehension strategies are modeled, practiced, and applied.

▶ *WRITING: Learning to Write* is the block where you teach children how to write either in groups or to the whole class. In kindergarten and first grade you begin by modeling how to form letters, words, and sentences. As students develop their abilities to write, you model spelling and grammar as you model different domains of writing. (See Chapter 7 on domains of writing.)

▶ *WRITING: Developmentally Appropriate Writing* is the block where students actually write their own pieces. In the beginning, students may only write sentences or captions for their pictures. Gradually they begin to write stories, reports, and so forth. During this block, the children write the same type of writing modeled in the Learning to Write block, although they select their own topics. Through this block, teachers provide time for the practice and application of grammar and spelling.

▶ *Intervention* is the block provided *only for students experiencing difficulty learning* and is designed to stop or prevent failure for those students. Notice that the Intervention block is held up by the six blocks of the classroom program. This shows that even students needing intervention also need strong, quality classroom instruction. (See Chapter 10 for more discussion of intervention.)

The first six blocks of the balanced beginning literacy program are for all students. The additional intervention block is only for students having difficulty learning to read.

The amount of time required for the six blocks of the balanced literacy program varies from grade level to grade level. In kindergarten, you need a minimum of 3 hours per day. In grades 1 and 2, approximately 2½–3 hours per day are needed. Any intervention instruction is in addition to these times.

The core of the balanced literacy program is the texts that are used. Can you recall the types of text introduced in Chapter 1?

Types of Text for Beginning Literacy Instruction

Beginning readers need to be completely successful as they begin the process of learning to read. They need to experience wonderful, rich literature that will excite them and motivate them to want to read more. Beginning readers, however, are often unable to read such authentic literature by themselves; they do not yet have the necessary decoding skills. Many teachers have found authentic literature too difficult for beginning readers to decode. Therefore, it is important to think about using different types of texts for different purposes.

This concept of different texts for different purposes was introduced in Chapter 1. Let's discuss decodable texts and authentic literature in more detail in relation to the balanced beginning literacy program. In addition, we will examine the need to level and sequence texts for beginning readers.

Decodable Texts

Decodable texts contain words with the phonic elements children have been taught. Such texts give beginning readers the opportunity to apply the decoding skills that they have been taught. Researchers have recommended for many years that texts for beginning reading should contain a high percentage of words reflecting previously taught phonic skills (Chall, 1967). This recommendation has been supported and documented by others over the years (Cooper, Warncke, Shipman, & Ramstad, 1979; Juel & Roper/Schneider, 1985).

Decodable texts also contain high-frequency words; if students lack the skills to decode the words or the words do not follow the regular sound patterns, they are usually taught as whole words before students read the text. There is no research at this time to support the exact percentage of words that should be decodable or the number of high-frequency words these texts should contain. The main guideline that we have from the research suggests only that the text should provide many opportunities for beginning readers to apply the decoding skills they have been taught (Juel & Roper/Schneider, 1985). Decodable texts often focus simultaneously on application of phonics and high-frequency words.

Most decodable texts are created; that is, they are written using a specific set of phonic elements and high-frequency words. Figure 4.4 shows an example of a decodable text. Over the years, many first-grade teachers have actually written little stories like these to provide students opportunities to apply specific decoding skills previously taught. A variety of guidelines have been suggested for creating decodable texts (Stahl, Duffy-Hester, & Stahl, 1998). Some researchers think it is possible to locate enough authentic literature to serve as decodable texts to provide application of the decoding skills being taught (Hiebert, 1998), but this is very difficult. Whatever the source, it seems reasonable to use *some* decodable texts for beginning reading instruction. Recently published reading programs contain decodable text as a part of decoding instruction.

As soon as children have increased their decoding abilities, their text for reading should move away from decodable, created texts to authentic literature. This usually occurs between the middle to end of first grade (Learning First Alliance,

FIGURE 4.4

SAMPLE DECODABLE TEXT FOCUSING ON SHORT *a*

Pam was going to say, "Good! I like cats."

2

But before she could say it, Sal said,

"Here is Max. Max likes rags."

3

1998). Decodable texts are used in the Learning to Read Words block of the balanced beginning literacy program.

Authentic Literature

Authentic literature, often referred to as trade books, consists of narrative and expository texts in their original forms as written by the author. Throughout this text there have been discussions and references to many pieces of authentic literature. Chapter 1 presented a detailed discussion of the merits of using authentic literature.

In the Balanced Beginning Literacy Program, authentic literature plays a critical role. First, it is used for read-alouds and shared reading in the Developing Language and Comprehension block. By listening to wonderful, rich literature and/or reading it along with the teacher, students develop listening, speaking, and vocabulary skills, and concepts of print. Using texts students have listened to or read with the teacher, comprehension skills and strategies are taught.

As students gain power in decoding, they move from reading decodable texts to reading authentic literature. By the time students move completely into authentic literature, they should have the ability to decode most words independently. However, even these students may still benefit from practice with decodable texts as new decoding elements are taught.

A combination of decodable texts and authentic literature is a powerful way to begin effective literacy instruction. However, the choice can't be random. The texts need to be leveled and organized in some way.

Leveling and Sequencing Texts

Texts used for beginning reading instruction need to be leveled or placed in a sequence of difficulty until students develop independence in decoding (Clay, 1991). The texts should move from easy to more difficult. Several different sets of guidelines have been presented for leveling texts (Fountas & Pinnell, 1996; Peterson, 1991). These criteria are helpful for leveling authentic literature and look at such factors as consistent placement of text on the page; pictures that clearly match the text; repeated words, patterns, and sentences; and use of familiar oral language structures.

Decodable texts also need to be sequenced, primarily in terms of the phonic elements taught. For example, if the initial consonants *s, m, n,* and *r* and the short vowel *a* have been taught, the words in the decodable text should use these sounds (e.g., *Sam, man, ran*). In addition to the decodable words, several high-frequency words (e.g., *the, is, on*) and story words (e.g., *Bill*) are used. As new phonic elements are taught, the number of word possibilities increases and the texts, therefore, increase in difficulty.

Most schools use a published program or several programs. Most such programs have some criteria for leveling texts. You should check out these criteria and adjust the sequencing of the books to fit your students' needs.

Your school may also have many books that have not been leveled. Therefore, it is wise to obtain a set of criteria for leveling texts and work with your colleagues to level your books. See For Additional Reading for criteria for leveling texts.

◼ **Routines for Beginning Literacy Instruction**

A routine is a set of procedures that can be used repeatedly. Within your classroom you will use and develop many routines for instruction. You have already learned a variety of routines in this text for teaching a literacy lesson, developing skills and vocabulary, and developing prior knowledge. (See Chapters 2 and 3.)

This section presents sixteen routines that are particularly effective for beginning literacy instruction. These routines, along with the others you have already learned, provide a resource from which to choose to meet the needs of your students.

Table 4.2 lists the sixteen routines. The specific functions of the routine are identified. You will note that some routines are for teaching, practicing, or applying some aspect of literacy. Others are for developing oral language or concepts of print. The remainder of this section will present each of the routines following a consistent format: PURPOSE, WHEN TO USE, DESCRIPTION/PROCEDURES, and DISCUSSION/COMMENTS. The sample literacy lesson found on page 207 will illustrate the use of some of the routines. As you study each routine, look for overlap. For example, when you are using a writing routine, you are also developing vocabulary.

Decoding Routines

Phonemic Awareness Routine

PURPOSE	Routines for phonemic awareness help children develop the awareness of sounds in words and the ability to blend sounds to make words. Since phonemic awareness involves several related components, there would be different routines involving each component.
WHEN TO USE	Phonemic Awareness Routines are used in the Learning to Read Words block of the balanced beginning literacy program. These routines can be used in kindergarten through second grade or beyond if needed.
DESCRIPTION/ PROCEDURES	Three sample routines are presented for phonemic awareness. When you use one of the routines, it should be used for short periods of time (5–10 minutes) repeatedly over several days or weeks until children have developed the component being taught. For other activities for developing phonemic awareness, see the For Additional Reading section.

Rhyming Routine

Teach:

1. Read aloud a book that contains many words that rhyme. (Use books such as *Sheep in a Jeep* [Shaw, 1986] *There's a Wocket in My Pocket* [Seuss, 1974], and *Hop on Pop* [Seuss, 1963].)
2. After reading the book, have children chant some of the lines with you:

TABLE 4.2

ROUTINES FOR BEGINNING LITERACY INSTRUCTION

ROUTINES	Teach	Practice	Apply	Develop Oral Language	Develop Concepts of Print
Decoding Routines					
• Phonemic Awareness Routine	X	X			
• Explicit Phonics Routine	X				
• Analogy Routine	X				
• Making Words Routine		X	X		
• Word Wall Routine*		X			
High-frequency Word Routines					
• Decodable Words Routine	X	X			
• Irregular Words Routine	X	X			
• Word Wall Routine*		X			
Reading Routines					
• Decodable Text Routine		X	X		
• Fluency Reading Routine		X	X		
• Read-aloud Routine	X			X	X
• Shared Reading Routine	X			X	X
• Observational Guided Reading Routine		X	X		
• Cooperative Reading Routine		X	X		
Comprehension and Writing Routines					
• Explicit Comprehension Strategy Routine	X				
• Shared Writing Routine	X				

*A word wall (a place on the wall to display words) may be used as a decoding routine and a high-frequency word routine. In this chapter it is described as a decoding routine with comments about how to use it as a high-frequency word routine.

"Beep, Beep
Sheep in a Jeep."

3. Identify several words from the text that rhyme (Example: *hop-pop*). Say the words slowly, noting that they rhyme. Give several other examples (*top-hop; pop-top*). Begin to ask children to tell whether the words rhyme.

Practice:

- Play the game STAND UP/SIT DOWN. This game is like SIMON SAYS.
- Say pairs of words that rhyme and pairs that don't rhyme. Children go from one position to the next only if the words rhyme (Sample words: *cat-hat; big-pig; cat-pig; big-jig; hat-sat; sat-rat; sat-big*). Note how children respond to tell whether they are getting the concept.
- Model and practice daily until children master the skill. Then drop the modeling, but continue to provide repeated practice.

Counting Sounds and Syllables Routine

Teach:

1. After reading aloud a favorite book to children, select a two- or three-sound word to model the number of sounds (Example: *top*).
2. Say the word slowly by stretching it out /t//ŏ→//p/; tell children that this word has three sounds. Use several other examples (*red, cat, pig*). Model the number of sounds by slowly saying the word and clapping once for each sound. Ask children to clap with you.

Practice:

- Play the CLAPPING GAME. Use only words that have three phonemes. As you say words, have children clap for each sound heard. At first, stretch the words out; as children develop their ability to do this, say the words at a more normal speed.
- Repeat this process over several days or weeks. Drop the modeling when no longer needed, and provide short daily practices until students develop the ability to hear sounds.

This same procedure may be used for counting syllables.

Segmenting and Blending Routines

Teach:

(Segmenting)

1. Select words of two syllables from a book that has been read aloud (Examples: *baby, table*).
2. Say each word, slowly stretching it out /bā→//bē→ /. Tell children that this word has two syllables (parts): *bāā* and *bēē*.
3. Repeat with several other words.

Practice:

- Play the MATCH GAME. Give each child a stack of colored tiles or colored squares of paper.
- Use five to seven two-syllable words. Say each word slowly. Direct children to place a tile or colored square on their desks for each syllable they hear in the word. In the beginning, stretch the words by saying them slowly. As children become adept at using this skill, say the words normally.

Teach:

(Blending)

1. Select several two-syllable words from a book that has been read aloud.
2. Say the words in their parts /hăp//ē/. Tell children that you can blend these syllables together to make the word *happy.* Repeat the modeling using several more examples. Gradually ask children to take over the responsibility to blend the words.

Practice:

- Play the game THREE CHEERS!
- Identify five to seven words that you will say in parts. Say each word by giving the two syllables. Ask children to say the word three times as a cheer.

Example:

Teacher: /bŏt•əl/
Children: *bottle, bottle, bottle*
This same procedure can be used for blending onset and rime.

DISCUSSION/ COMMENTS   Many different sequences have been suggested for teaching phonemic awareness; one was given earlier in this chapter (see page 168). It is important that you have a sequence to follow so that you can help children *systematically* develop phonemic awareness. All lessons for phonemic awareness should be *short, fun,* and *exciting* for children. They are much more meaningful if they are connected to books that are being read aloud. For many more activities for teaching and practicing phonemic awareness, see the For Additional Reading section.

Explicit Phonics Routine

PURPOSE   This routine provides two patterns that can be used repeatedly for explicitly teaching phonic skills and structural analysis (letter-sound associations). Two options are presented: *Option A,* Starting with Sounds, and *Option B,* Starting with Known Words. The reason for presenting two options is that though research supports explicitly and systematically teaching letter-sound associations, it does not indicate that it is better to start with sounds or with known words. You may have some children who learn phonics and structural analysis better one way than the other. Therefore, you need to know both routines.

WHEN TO USE   The Explicit Phonics Routine (Option A and/or Option B) is used in the Learning to Read Words block of the balanced beginning literacy program. Many teachers use Option B following the reading of text that contains some examples of the sound element to be taught (as Mr. Paredes did in the example at the beginning of this chapter). Others teach Option A, teaching the sounds before reading the text containing examples of the elements (as Ms. Anderson did at the beginning of this chapter).

DESCRIPTION/ PROCEDURES

This routine builds on the best research that we have to date on explicitly teaching phonics (Adams, 1990; Eldredge, 1995). It incorporates five steps: (1) *awareness*, (2) *segmentation*, (3) *association*, (4) *reading*, and (5) *spelling*.

Use the procedures outlined below to explicitly teach phonics and structural analysis. Each of the five steps is incorporated within every phonics lesson with adjustments being made to meet individual needs of students.

The following guidelines will help you plan explicit letter-sound association instruction using Option A and Option B:

Option A—Sounds First Illustration Using Short *a*

1. Awareness

a. "Today you will learn to read and spell words with the short *a* sound—/ă/. Listen to each word I say; raise your hand when you hear /ă/ (/c/•/ă/•/t/ cat; /ă/•/p/•/əl/ apple; /t/•/ă/•/p/ tap).

b. If students respond correctly, move on to the next step. If students do not respond correctly, provide more instruction in phonemic awareness. (See earlier discussion.)

2. Segmentation

a. Say, "You can hear /ă/ in the middle of *cap*. Sometimes /ă/ will be in the beginning of a word as in *at*. Model using several other words (*apple, act, pat, pass*).

b. Say, "Listen to each of these words and tell me if you hear /ă/ and whether it is the middle or beginning of the word" (*at, cap, mat, dog, ask, cast*).

If students respond correctly, move on to the next step; if they do not, provide more teaching and practice in segmentation.

3. Association

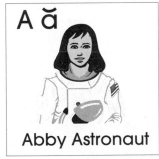

A ă

Abby Astronaut

a. Tell children that they are now going to look at the letter that stands for /ă/. Write *a* on the board. Ask children to tell what letter this is.

b. Next tell children they are going to meet a special character who will help them remember the sound for short *a*. Her name is Abby Astronaut. Ask children to repeat her name, say /ă/, and hold up the *a* letter card. Repeat two or three times.

4. Reading

a. Say, "Now let's read some words using /ă/." Print the word *mat* on the board. Remind children that they know the /m/ and /t/ sounds. Model sequential decoding saying the sounds together and showing the direction of reading by quickly moving your hand under the word:

/m//ă//t/

b. Print the following words on the board. Call on different children to come to the board and model sequential decoding, moving their hand under the word to show the direction of their reading. Remind children that they know all the sounds in the words (*at, lap, sat, Pam, man, rap, rat*).

c. Print a sentence or two on the board containing only words with sounds and high-frequency words children know. Guide individual children to read the sentences.

> Tom is a man.
> Tom sat on a mat.
> Pam sat on a mat.
> Pam has a cap.
> Tom has a cap.
> Cap! Cap!
> Rap! Rap!

5. Spelling

a. Say, "Now we will learn to spell words with /ă/." Say the word *sap* slowly. Write the letters for each sound as you say the word slowly—*sap*. Remind children that they have already learned the *s* and *p* sounds. Model spelling two or three more words with short *a*.

b. Ask children to write (using paper or magic slates) the letters for each word you say (*sat, man, tap, tan, map*).

c. Note children's performance.

Option B—Starting with Known Words
Illustration Using Initial Sound /b/

1. Awareness

a. Say, "Today you will learn to use the sound for the letter *b* to help you read and spell words."

b. "Listen to this word: /b/•/ō/•/t/." (Say it again slowly.) "How many sounds do you hear in this word?" (Students respond—three.) "What is the first sound you hear?" Repeat using words *big, boy, box*.

c. If students respond correctly, move on to the next step. If students do not respond correctly, provide more instruction in phonemic awareness. (See page 179.)

2. Segmentation

a. Say, "The first sound in box is /b/. What is the first sound in *barn*?" (Students respond—/b/.) Repeat using words *bet, bang, bake*.

b. If students respond correctly, move on to the next step; if they do not, provide more teaching and practice in segmentation.

3. Association

a. Write the words *box, boy, bear* (these words come from a book the students have listened to or read using shared

Bb

Boris Bear

reading) on the chalkboard. Underline the *b*. Say, "Each of these words begins with the same letter and the same sound. The letter is *b;* the sound is */b/.*" Say each word slowly, emphasizing the */b/* sound. Have children repeat with you.

b. Have a picture card with a bear. Show the card. Say, "This bear's name is Boris—Boris Bear. He will help us remember the sound for *b—*b/.*"

c. Write groups of words on the chalkboard. Have students read the words with you and decide which ones begin with the same letter and sound as Boris Bear.

- *band, car, bell*
- *hat, beg, big*
- *top, Bob, cap*

4. Reading

b
p̶ig

a. On the chalkboard write a word that students know—*pig*.

b. Say, "This word is *pig.* If we change the beginning letter to *b*, what sound will be at the beginning of this word?" (*/b/*) "What is the new word?" (Students respond.) Repeat using other words.

c. Say, "Now let's use what we have learned about the *b* sound to read some more words." Use only letter-sound associations students have been taught. Print each word and model sequential decoding:

bat - /b/•/ă/•/t/
ban - /b/•/ă/•/n/
bug - /b/•/ŭ/•/g/

Bab is a bug.
Bab is a big bug.

d. Write a sentence or sentences on the chalkboard using only letter-sound associations and high-frequency words students have been taught. Ask students to read, emphasizing the sound for *b*.

5. Spelling

a. Tell children that they are going to learn to spell words with */b/.* Use words starting with *b* that have ending patterns that children know. Say, "I want to spell the word *bat.* I write *b* for */b/* and *at* for */at/. b-a-t.*" Model another word—*bit*.

b. Using small chalkboards, magic slates, or sheets of paper, ask students to write the following:

- the letter you hear at the beginning of *bake*
- the letter that stands for the */b/* sound

c. Dictate several words, mixing in words that begin with other sounds students know (*bank, best, cup, zoo, box*). Have students write the words. Look for accuracy in using the *b* and any other previously taught sounds.

Follow the instruction with practice by having students read and reread decodable texts. Gradually move students to authentic literature, encouraging them to apply what they have been learning and practicing in decodable texts.

DISCUSSION/ COMMENTS

The use of routines for teaching phonics is not new (Cooper et al., 1979). Many teachers have found them effective for years. Placing a routine within the framework of a balanced beginning literacy program helps to make the program more effective. You should follow a sequence for teaching phonics. Use the one suggested in the published program your school uses or identify one from some of the sources listed in the For Additional Reading section.

Analogy Routine

PURPOSE

The Analogy Routine is designed to be used after children have learned quite a few sight words and have learned to use most letter-sound associations (Ehri & Robbins, 1992). The purpose of this routine is to teach children to look at an unknown word such as *reach* and think about it in terms of a known word (*peach*) that will help them figure out the unknown word.

WHEN TO USE

This routine is used in the Learning to Read Words block of a balanced beginning literacy program. It may also be used at other grade levels if students need to learn to use analogy to decode words.

DESCRIPTION/ PROCEDURES

With this routine, children learn how to approach an unknown word by relating it to a word they know. This becomes a part of the strategy A Way to Think About Words (see page 171).

Teach:

1. Print a sentence on the chalkboard and underline a word that is unknown.

$$\text{The } \underline{\text{goat}} \text{ drank milk.}$$

2. "Let's say I'm reading along and I come to this sentence. I read *The;* the next word I don't know." (Point to *goat.*) "It looks like a word I know—*coat.* I see the *g* at the beginning of *g-o-a-t.* I know the *g* sound is */g/.* I put the */g/* at the beginning of *oat.* I say the word *goat.* I then read the sentence and it seems to make sense."
3. Print several more words in sentences on the board and have children help you decode them and explain how they made the analogy (*lame/same; make/cake; willow/pillow*).

Practice:

• Write several sentences on the board containing one unknown word where children could make an analogy. Underline the unknown word.

Unknown	Known
lark	mark
cable	able
spot	hot

Ask children to read the sentence and explain how they thought of a known word to help them with the underlined word.

- When children are reading aloud and come to a word they cannot pronounce, prompt them to make analogies:
  - Say, "Does some part of this word look like a word you already know?"
  - "If so, say that word; then cover up the part you don't know. Say what you know. Then uncover the part you don't know. Give the sound for this part. Then blend the sound with the familiar part to pronounce the word."

- Relate the use of analogy to A Way to Think About Words strategy presented on page 171. Help children internalize this process by prompting them to use it again and again.

DISCUSSION/ COMMENTS

After children have learned to use the basic concept of analogy, teach other lessons focusing on word parts such as suffixes and prefixes. Always help students see how this skill fits into their overall strategy for independently decoding words (see page 171).

Making Words Routine

PURPOSE

Making Words (Cunningham & Cunningham, 1992) is a hands-on manipulative activity for practicing the use of letter-sound associations and word patterns to decode and spell words. Students at any level can use this routine to help them learn to more effectively decode words. The activity can be done as a whole class or as a small group activity.

WHEN TO USE

This routine fits into the Learning to Read Words block of the balanced beginning literacy program.

DESCRIPTION/ PROCEDURES

This routine may be done with the whole class using a pocket chart and large letter cards or it may be done with small groups using individual trays (like Scrabble™ letter holders) and letters. The following guidelines are for using this routine with a small group:

1. Select a target word such as *bathtub* from a book students have read. List the words you want students to make leading to the target word, progressing from two-letter words to the target word:

   -at
   -bat
   -bath
   -hub
   -tub
   -bathtub

   | bathtub | (target word)

   Print each word to be made during the lesson on a card to use for word sorting at the end of the lesson.

2. Give each student a set of letters for the target word and a tray. (Tray can be made by folding tagboard.) Make the vowels one color and the consonants another color.

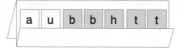

3. Before students begin, ask if anyone can guess the target word. Respond only by saying, "We'll check at the end." Ask students to make a word: *at.* Use in a sentence—"We are *at* school."

4. You make the word in your tray; show students. Say, "Does your word look like mine? If it doesn't, fix it." Have students show you their words.
5. Next, ask, "What one letter would you add to *at* to make *bat*?"
6. You make your word. Show students; have them check and show you.

7. Continue the lesson building the words you want to have made: *bath, tub, bathtub.*
8. Throughout the lesson and at the end, help students see various patterns in the word building:

   at → bat (Add one letter; make a new word; could do more rhyming here, if needed)

   bat → bath (Add one letter; make a new word; if *th* has been taught, note the digraph *th*)

   hub → tub (Change one letter; make a new word)

   bath + tub → bathtub (Compound word)

9. Using the word cards for each word made, have children sort the words into various patterns:

   at   hub   bath

   bat   tub   bathtub

10. Add any or all of the words to the word wall.
11. Finally, locate the target word in the book from which it was taken to help children build the connection between what they are learning and reading.

DISCUSSION/ COMMENTS   Even though this routine is designated as a practice routine, it is also one that teaches children about letter-sound associations and letter patterns. By continuously using this procedure, children develop their abilities to decode words independently. For more information on Making Words, see the For Additional Reading section.

Word Wall Routine

PURPOSE

Over the years, teachers have often placed words on the wall in their class-rooms in groups or categories to help children learn them. In recent years, this concept has been given more formal attention (Cunningham, 1995). When using the Word Wall Routine for decoding practice, the purpose is to help children see patterns in letter-sound associations. (When using the routine for high-frequency words, the purpose is to help children learn the high-frequency word by alphabetizing it by the initial letter.) The Word Wall Routine helps students remember the sounds and words that they are learning and use them as they read and spell.

WHEN TO USE

The Word Wall Routine is used in the Learning to Read Words block of the balanced beginning literacy program. It is especially useful at the beginning literacy levels but may also be used at other levels.

DESCRIPTION/ PROCEDURES

The Word Wall Routine for decoding is used to place words on the wall that have the same sound patterns. A picture of a key word helps children re-member the sound. The following guidelines will help you use the Word Wall Routine to reinforce the learning of letter-sound associations for both reading and writing:

1. As new letter-sound associations are taught, identify a key word that can be pictured to use as an exemplar of the sound:

   Example:

   Bb

   Boris Bear

2. Display this on a bulletin board or on the wall.
3. As children learn to read words that contain the sound, add *some* of them to the wall. These words may be selected from any texts children are reading or from their writing. When a word is added to the wall, un-derline the common sound element.
4. At least once a week or more, play short games or do activities using the words on the wall:

   Examples:
   • READ AND THINK—Call on different children to *read* all the words under a particular sound and *think* of one or more to add.

FIGURE 4.5

PARTIAL WORD WALL FOR PRACTICING LETTER-SOUND ASSOCIATIONS

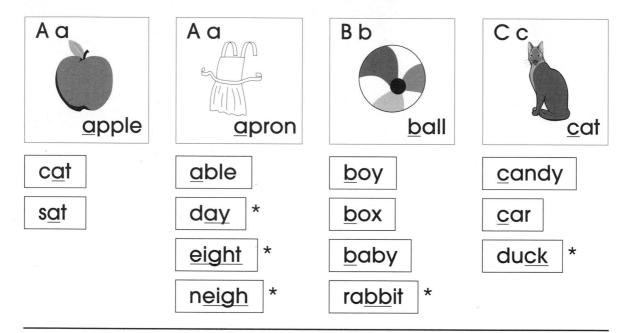

A a apple	A a apron	B b ball	C c cat
c<u>a</u>t	<u>a</u>ble	<u>b</u>oy	<u>c</u>andy
s<u>a</u>t	<u>d</u>ay *	<u>b</u>ox	<u>c</u>ar
	<u>eigh</u>t *	<u>b</u>aby	du<u>ck</u> *
	n<u>eigh</u> *	ra<u>bb</u>it *	

*These words are added as elements are taught. The most common elements are taught first. The variant spellings are not taught at the same time as the common spellings.

• FIND AND READ—Say "I'm thinking of words that start with /b/. Find the key word on the wall, read it, and read the list below."

DISCUSSION/ COMMENTS

When using the Word Wall Routine for letter-sound association instruction, group words by their common sound patterns even though the spellings are different. For example, words with the hard *c* or *k* sound as in *cat* should be grouped together or side by side to note that the same sound is represented by different letters. Print the letters representing the common sound in a bright color. Figure 4.5 shows sections of a partial word wall.

Word walls are often used for high-frequency word practice (Cunningham, 1995). These words are also put up alphabetically but not by sound patterns. The important think to keep in mind about using word walls for either letter-sound associations or high-frequency words is to remember to do follow-up activities such as "Read and Think" or "Find and Read."

High-Frequency Word Routines

High-frequency words are those that occur many more times than other words in spoken or written language. These words must be given special attention in instruction because they occur in reading and writing so frequently (Hiebert, Pearson, Taylor, Richardson, & Paris, 1998). There are many lists of high-frequency words; one of the most common is the Dolch List of 220 Basic Sight Words (Dolch, 1936).

Decodable Words Routine

PURPOSE

This routine is used to teach high-frequency words that are completely decodable (examples: *at, it*) as soon as children have learned the decoding elements involved in the word.

WHEN TO USE

This routine can be used both in the Learning to Read Words block and the Developing Language and Comprehension block of the balanced beginning literacy program. It is used to introduce new high-frequency words before children read a text.

DESCRIPTION/ PROCEDURES

The following procedures should be used (Example—teaching *an*):

1. *Review the Sounds*

   • Show the key pictures for *a* and *n*.

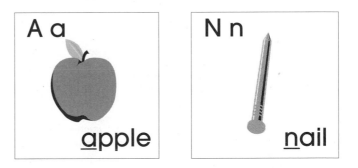

   • Ask children to give the sounds /ă/ and /n/. If they are unable to do so, use the Phonetically Unpredictable Words routine that follows and reteach the sounds later.
   • Say, "We are going to use these two sounds to read a new word."

2. *Sound and Blend*

   • Print the new word on the board:

$$an$$

   (Do not say the word.)

- Point to each letter. Ask students to give the sound. Model or coach as needed.
- Say, "Now let's blend the sounds to read the word (or let's read the word)."

Sweep your hand under the word as children blend. Model or coach as needed.

3. *Read the Word*
- Print the word in a sentence:

I see <u>an</u> apple.

(All words except *an* are known words or are decodable.)
- Ask children to read the sentence.

DISCUSSION/ COMMENTS

Following the reading of the word in the sentence, give each child a 3" × 5" card. Tell the child to copy the word on one side and the sentence on the other side. Place the word in alphabetical order in a word bank. (See Chapter 2 for discussion of words banks.) Two or three times each week, have children play games with words in their banks such as having them draw words from another person's bank and reading it or play a game like FISH.

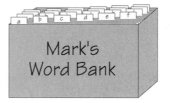

Mark's Word Bank

Phonetically Unpredictable Words Routine

PURPOSE

Use this high-frequency word routine with phonetically irregular or unpredictable words (ones that cannot be decoded, such as *the*) or with words for which children have not yet learned the necessary decoding skills.

WHEN TO USE

This routine can be used in the Learning to Read Words block or the Developing Language and Comprehension block of the balanced beginning literacy program.

DESCRIPTION/ PROCEDURES

Use the following procedures for this routine:

1. *Read the Word*
Write a sentence on the board with the word:

<u>The</u> car is red.

Read the sentence aloud to the group. Ask children to read the sentence with you.

2. *Match the Word*

   Distribute several 3" × 5" cards containing the word. Ask each child to find the word, match it by holding the card under it, and read the sentence aloud. Have the other children watching clap their hands softly if the child with the card is correct.

3. *Write the Word*

   - Hold up a word card containing the word or point to the word in the sentence. Say, "This word is *the, t-h-e.*"
   - "Now you say and spell it."
   - Ask children to write the word on their papers or slate boards, saying and spelling the word as they write.

DISCUSSION/ COMMENTS

Follow the instruction with many opportunities to read text containing the words taught. Provide repeated practice like that described in the Decodable Words Routine.

Reading Routines

Reading routines require students to read different types of texts in different ways. The modes of reading concept was introduced in Chapter 2 (see page 34). Many of the ideas related to the modes of reading concept also apply for these routines.

Decodable Text Reading Routine

PURPOSE

As discussed earlier in this chapter, decodable texts serve the purpose of providing beginning readers immediate opportunities to practice and apply in text what they are learning about decoding words and high-frequency words. Even though these very beginning texts are limited by the small number of words that can be used, they will give children a chance to experience the enjoyment and pleasure of being able to read. Remember, children will find both humor and fun in little books that may seem silly to an adult.

WHEN TO USE

This reading routine is used in the Learning to Read Words block of the balanced beginning literacy program.

DESCRIPTION/ PROCEDURES

As children are taught decoding skills, decodable text reading is provided after each two or three skills to provide immediate practice and application. There is minimal focus on comprehension. You can use the literacy lesson to carry out this routine.

1. *Introduce the Text*

   - Show the cover of the text. Tell children that they are going to read this text to practice and apply the skills they have been learning.
   - Ask children to read the title.
   - Introduce any high-frequency words needed, using one of the two routines presented earlier in this chapter.

2. *Read and Respond*
  - Direct children to read the text silently. Remind them to use the skill that has been taught. As they read, observe their behaviors and/or move from child to child asking each to read orally to you. Note their ability to apply skills.
  - After reading, discuss the story. Call on individuals to read aloud favorite parts, sentences that match illustrations, or places to prove or support their ideas.
  - Ask children to tell how they used the decoding skill being practiced or applied to figure out words.
3. *Extend the Text*
  - Provide opportunities for children to reread the text alone or use the Cooperative Reading Routine.
  - Reteach any decoding skills that seem to be causing difficulty.

DISCUSSION/ COMMENTS

The reading of decodable texts is a very short routine. In fact, at the very beginning stages of reading you may use a new decodable text each day. Keep in mind that this reading is only one part of the balanced program. Your goal is to get children to the point of independent decoding and move them quickly to reading on their own using authentic literature.

Fluency Reading Routine

PURPOSE

A major need for all children, but especially beginning readers, is to develop fluency (the ability to read texts quickly and accurately). The Fluency Reading Routine provides a procedure to help meet this goal.

WHEN TO USE

The Fluency Reading Routine is used in both the Learning to Read Words and Developing Language and Comprehension blocks of the balanced beginning literacy program.

DESCRIPTION/ PROCEDURES

The texts used for the Fluency Reading Routine may be *any* of the texts used in your program after they have been read by the students. These texts are *always* easy for children to read. Use the following guidelines to carry out this routine:

1. Select a book each child can read or have children select their own from choices you provide. Often selections are made from baskets of books that children have read previously. Usually, you will have a small group all reading the same book.
2. Have children read their books silently.
3. As children read, move from child to child asking him or her to read sections aloud to you. Note the child's fluency (i.e., speed of reading and accuracy). These observations will help you determine other things that need to be taught.

   Note: Some educators recommend timing a child's oral reading to determine fluency. I prefer to simply note whether the child is reading the words quickly and accurately without worrying about the exact time.
4. After reading, have children share and discuss their books with each other for just a few minutes.

| DISCUSSION/
COMMENTS | The Fluency Reading Routine should be done regularly in your program. In the beginning, it should be a daily routine. Often you may also use the Co-operative Reading Routine for building fluency. |

Read-Aloud Routine

| PURPOSE | The Read-Aloud Routine is designed to help children develop vocabulary, oral language, and comprehension strategies. It is a critical part of the process of helping children develop literacy. This routine utilizes wonderful, rich narrative and expository literature such as *Lucky Song* (Williams, 1997) or *Goldilocks and the Three Bears* (Marshall, 1988). Even though this routine is being introduced in the chapter on beginning reading, it can be used at all grade levels. |

| WHEN TO USE | The Read-Aloud Routine is used during the Developing Language and Comprehension block of the balanced beginning literacy program. |

| DESCRIPTION/
PROCEDURES | The format for the Literacy Lesson introduced in Chapter 2 (see page 55) can be adapted and used for the Read-Aloud Routine. You present and read aloud a wonderful book. However, here the primary focus of the routine is instructional. This routine does not replace the many times that you would read aloud to children solely for pleasure. The following suggested procedures will help you utilize this routine. |

1. *Introduce the Text*
   - Show the cover of the text and read the title; talk about other book parts. Discuss briefly to build background and concepts.
   - Ask children to *predict* what they think will happen or what they will learn or pose *questions* they think will be answered. During this time you can begin to model comprehension strategies (see Chapter 8). Record children's predictions or questions on the chalkboard or on a chart for later use.
2. *Read the Text*
   - Remind the children to think about their predictions or questions as you read the text aloud.
   - Read aloud all or part of the text following the guidelines given in Chapter 2 (page 30). Stop to discuss points or to clarify the meaning of words as needed.
   - After reading, discuss children's predictions or questions. If you are reading a story, orally model summarizing by following the story map framework. If you are reading an informational book, summarize by listing the key points presented.
   - From time to time, ask children to respond individually by drawing, or having brief discussions about favorite parts, characters, or what they learned.
3. *Extend the Text*
   - Following the read-aloud, use the text to develop oral language, vocabulary, concepts, and additional background through discussion, role playing, puppets, or other oral activities.

DISCUSSION/ COMMENTS

The Read-Aloud Routine is used for instructional purposes. Every step teaches vital comprehension strategies. Keep in mind, however, that there should also be times when reading aloud is done just for pleasure and enjoyment.

Shared Reading Routine

PURPOSE

Shared reading or the shared book experience was developed by Holdaway (1979) as a means of introducing beginners (kindergarten, first, second, and third grades) to reading using favorite books, rhymes, and poems. Shared reading may also be adapted and used with older students. With this procedure, the teacher models reading for students by reading aloud a book or other text and ultimately inviting students to join in.

Shared reading builds on children's natural desire to read and reread favorite books. The repeated reading of texts over several days, weeks, or months deepens children's understanding of them (Yaden, 1988). However, Au (1991) suggests that such reading is not just random rereading. Rather, each time a child rereads a book with the teacher, the reading should be for a different purpose: to extend, refine, and deepen the child's abilities to read and construct meaning.

WHEN TO USE

The Shared Reading Routine is used in the Developing Language and Comprehension block of the balanced beginning literacy program.

DESCRIPTION/ PROCEDURES

1. *Materials Needed*
   - One copy of the book to be read in big-book form.
   - Multiple copies of the book in little-book form for individual rereading after the big book has been read.
2. *Introducing the Book*
   - Gather the children where they can all see the big book.
   - Show and discuss the book cover; read the title, author, illustrator, and other appropriate book features.
   - Motivate children by discussing the cover and some of the pages in the book, but don't give away the entire story. This activity also encourages children to activate and develop their prior knowledge.
   - Invite children to predict what they think will happen in the book. If they have difficulty, model predicting by "thinking aloud" to show them how you would do it. Record predictions on the chalkboard or a chart for later reference. As your children gain more experience, you can formally introduce the preview and predict strategy using the poster presented in Chapter 3 (page 106). The entire process for introducing the book should take no longer than 3 to 6 minutes.
3. *Reading and Responding to the Book*
   - Read the book aloud to the children, holding it so they can see each page. Many teachers use an easel for this purpose. As you read, run your hand or a pointer under each line of print to help children develop a sense of left-to-right orientation, speech-to-

print match, and other concepts of print. If some children wish to join in, encourage them to do so, though for a first reading, many children will just listen.

- As you read, you may stop to briefly discuss the story or to respond to reactions, but you should progress through the entire book rather quickly to give children a complete sense of the story.
- At the conclusion of the reading, encourage children to respond, using questions such as the following prompts:

  Were your predictions right?
  What did you like in this story?
  What was your favorite part?
  What made you happy (or sad)?
  Who was your favorite character? Why?

- Return to the book, rereading the story and inviting children to read along. Many will feel comfortable doing this right away, but others may not join in until another day. After the second reading, many children will say, "Let's read it again." This is especially true for books, songs, or rhymes that are lots of fun. Under most circumstances, when children are excited and want to reread, you *should* reread.
- After you have read the book again, have children respond, using activities such as the following:

  –Talking with a friend about a favorite part
  –Retelling the story to a partner
  –Drawing a picture about the story and writing a word or a sentence about it
  –Drawing and writing about a favorite character
  –Writing a list of favorite characters

Help children become comfortable with making decisions about responding by giving them only a couple of choices initially.

Many of the ideas for responding suggested in Chapter 6 are appropriate to use here. The amount of time devoted to reading and responding will be from 10 to 20 minutes, depending on the book and the children.

4. *Extending the Book*

You may want to wait until children have read a book several times before extending it or wait until they have read several books within a thematic unit and combine them for extension activities.

Each time you carry out a repeated reading, you continue to model for the children. At the same time, you scaffold your instruction by transferring more and more responsibility to them. Although each repeated reading may seem to be just fun for the children, it carries very important responsibilities for learning. The following suggestions should be helpful:

- Invite children to recall the title and what the book was about. Prompt and support them if needed.
- Tell children why they are rereading the book with statements such as the following:

  "As we reread this book, let's think about who the important characters are." (comprehension)

"In our story today, notice how the author repeats lines over and over." (exploring language)

"Today, as we reread one of our favorite stories, look for places to use the phonic skills we have been learning." (decoding)

- After completing the rereading of the book, have children complete a response activity that again draws their attention to the purpose. For example:

Purpose: Comprehension

Prompt: Dramatize your favorite character.

Purpose: Explore language

Prompt: Write a group story using the story pattern. For example, after reading *Brown Bear, Brown Bear* (Martin, 1967), have children help write a story using the following pattern:

Brown Bear, Brown Bear, what do you see?
I see a redbird looking at me.

Red Bird, Red Bird, What do you see?
I see a _____ _____ looking at me.

_____ _____, _____ _____, What do you see?
I see a _____ _____ looking at me.

This response may also be done individually.

Purpose: Decoding

Prompt: List the words that have the sounds we have been learning. (Encourage children to use these words in stories they write.)

DISCUSSION/ COMMENTS

Shared reading is powerful, versatile, and flexible. The activities of shared reading will allow children to apply what they are learning in the Learning to Read Words and Text block of the balanced beginning literacy program. See For Additional Reading for books on shared reading.

Observational Guided Reading Routine

PURPOSE

I refer to this routine as Observational Guided Reading to differentiate it from Interactive Guided Reading discussed in Chapter 2. Most literacy authorities just use the term *guided reading* and don't make the distinction given here. The Observational Guided Reading Routine is designed to help children use and develop the strategies of independent reading (Fountas & Pinnell, 1996). It provides children a time to apply what they are learning in the Learning to Read Words block of the balanced beginning literacy program.

WHEN TO USE   The Observational Guided Reading Routine is used during the Developing Language and Comprehension block of the balanced beginning literacy program.

DESCRIPTION/ PROCEDURES   During Observational Guided Reading, children read texts that have a minimum of new things to learn (Fountas & Pinnell, 1996). These texts are at the students' developmentally appropriate reading level. (Texts are leveled. See the discussion on leveling texts, page 178.)

 The children read in small groups (usually 5–8) with their teacher. The following guidelines, organized around the literacy lesson concept presented in Chapter 2, should be helpful to you in learning to use Observational Guided Reading.

1. *Introduce the Book*
   - Materials: Multiple copies of the book
   - Show the book cover. Read the title. Discuss information on the cover. Ask students to *predict* what is going to happen in the text. Record the predictions.
   - Conduct a picture walk (see Chapter 3, page 122) using the book. Do not give away the ending.
2. *Read and Respond*
   - Direct students to read the book silently to see if their predictions are accurate. At the very beginning stages of reading, however, students may read aloud softly to themselves.
   - As your children read, observe their behaviors. Are some having difficulty with certain words or types of words? Are some tracking with their fingers while others are not?
   - Are children applying the decoding skills they have been taught? You can tell this when they read sections orally.
   - As you observe, look for one or two things you might help children with. For example, if several children seem to have trouble with the word *day,* print it on the board and help them sequentially decode or read through the word by identifying each sound in order if they have the skills.
   - After reading, discuss students' predictions and what happened in the text.
   - Teach any decoding or comprehension skill or strategy needed.
3. *Extending the Book*
   - Have children reread the book alone or with a partner.
   - Children may also choose to act out or role-play the story with partners.

DISCUSSION/ COMMENTS   Observational Guided Reading should be a daily routine in the balanced beginning literacy program. It allows you to see the progress of children and immediately help them correct problems. When using this routine, you should take a Running Record on each child once every couple of weeks using books they have read. (See Chapter 11 on Running Records.) For books on guided reading, see the For Additional Reading section.

Cooperative Reading Routine

PURPOSE　　The concept of cooperative reading was introduced in Chapter 2. As a routine for beginning reading instruction, cooperative reading involves partners rereading texts that have been previously read. The primary function of this rereading is to build fluency and comprehension.

WHEN TO USE　　This routine may be used in either the Learning to Read Words block or the Developing Language and Comprehension block of the balanced beginning literacy program.

DESCRIPTION/ PROCEDURES　　After the initial reading of decodable text or authentic literature, the Cooperative Reading Routine can be used to provide students practice in reading. It is best that this reading be done in partners as opposed to triads (groups of three) because with the latter there is always an odd person out. Use the following procedures with this routine:

1. Assign or have students select partners for cooperative reading.
2. Explain and model the process of cooperative reading with students:
   - Briefly discuss the book that has been previously read drawing as much as possible from the children.
   - Have children take turns reading aloud sentences, paragraphs, or pages.
3. Observe the children to note their use of decoding skills and their fluency. Coaching or supporting some children may be needed during this time.
4. Direct students to briefly discuss what they have read with their partners.

DISCUSSION/ COMMENTS　　The Cooperative Reading Routine is an effective way for children to practice reading of previously read text.

Comprehension and Writing Routines

Explicit Comprehension Strategy Routine

PURPOSE　　The Explicit Comprehension Strategy Routine provides a pattern for explicitly teaching and modeling comprehension strategies. The strategies that should be taught include identifying important information, inferencing/predicting, monitoring/clarifying, questioning, and summarizing. See Chapter 8 for a detailed discussion of each strategy and procedures for teaching.

WHEN TO USE　　This routine should be used in the Developing Language and Comprehension block of the balanced beginning literacy program.

DESCRIPTION/ PROCEDURES　　This routine involves three parts with the teacher modeling the strategy at the *concept, listening,* and *reading* levels. Use the procedures outlined below to explicitly teach comprehension strategies:

(Based on the strategy of inferencing)

1. Concept   a. Begin by developing the concept of inferencing. Use concrete materials and examples:

Say, "Look outside. Is the sun shining? Is it cloudy?" etc. (Students respond.) "What do these things indicate the weather is likely to be later in the day?" (Students respond depending on the conditions.)

b. Discuss with students how they arrived at their answer (important information they gained by looking outside, prior knowledge they had, logic). Tell students that this process is called *inferencing.*

2. Listening   a. Read aloud a short paragraph that requires students to infer.

Say, "Listen to this paragraph and tell what you think happened when Sara and Lisa went to the beach":

Sara and her friend Lisa went to the beach. They took their beach ball, a blanket, and a picnic lunch. They wanted to play in the water and lie in the sun. As soon as they put out their blanket, the sun went behind a cloud. They heard a loud clapping sound.

b. Discuss students' responses. If they have difficulty with this process, model for them using a think-aloud and repeat the process using several additional examples.

c. Talk with students about how they arrived at their conclusion.

3. Reading   a. Select a piece of text students have read that requires inferencing.

b. Model the use of inferencing with a think-aloud.

Provide repeated practice and application through reading until students are comfortable using the strategy.

DISCUSSION/   Routines for teaching comprehension have been recommended for many
COMMENTS   years and have been refined as our knowledge about comprehension has increased. In kindergarten, comprehension strategies can be modeled within the various reading routines. As texts become more challenging for readers and readers become independent decoders, a more formal approach to modeling strategies should be used (see Chapter 8).

Shared Writing Routine

PURPOSE   The Shared Writing Routine is used to model the mechanics of writing and the process of writing for children.

WHEN TO USE   This routine is used in the Learning to Write block of the balanced beginning literacy program.

**DESCRIPTION/
PROCEDURES**

The Shared Writing Routine is somewhat like Language Experience (a procedure where children dictate a text they use for reading [Allen, 1976]), except in this routine the teacher is free to put his/her own ideas into the writing. By using modeling and writing together, you will systematically teach children how to write. Use the following procedures to guide your use of this routine:

1. *Select a Topic*
   - Decide on the type of writing you want students to do—story, information, and so forth (see Chapter 7 on types of writing).
   - Tell students about the type of writing and define it.

     Example:

     "Boys and girls, we're going to learn to write a story today. Remember, stories have problems and there is a beginning, a middle, and an end."

   - Select a topic for the writing. Have children brainstorm with you and make a list of suggestions.

     Example:

     "What might we write about in our story?
        —a boy who gets lost
        —my new puppy's problem
        —our zoo adventure
     Raise your hand if you agree that the boy who gets lost will be our topic."

2. *Write Together*
   - After the topic has been selected, discuss how the type of writing might begin. Ask students to give ideas; you should feel free to add your own ideas to the writing. As students give ideas, begin to write them using the overhead, large chart paper, or the chalkboard.

     Example:

     > A little boy named Roger got lost. He was walking in the woods. He meeted a talking bear. He met a talking tree.

   - When students give an incorrect usage, you will want to add a correct example soon after. Note the meeted/met example in the story. Continue the writing until you complete the piece.

3. *Revise*

- On the same day or another day, use the piece you have written together to model ways to improve it. Ask for student input as well as giving your own.
- As students give ideas and you add ideas, write them on the original piece so that everyone can see it. Sometimes you will want to share your thinking as to why you did something. This is modeling or thinking aloud for students.

Example:

> A little boy named Roger got lost. He was
> walking in the woods. He ~~meeted~~ met a talking
> bear. The bear was big. His teeth were
> long. The boy met a talking tree. The bear
> and the tree helped him find his way home.

- Say, "I see one way we could edit our story. We should change *meeted* to *met—He met a talking bear.* To make our story interesting, we should tell some more about the bear."
- The process continues until the story is revised. Many times you will add content or ideas to the story, not just focus on usage elements.

DISCUSSION/ COMMENTS

The Shared Writing Routine is an excellent way to teach children how to write. In the process, you can also incorporate spelling and grammar (see Chapter 7). Following the shared writing, children should move to the Developmentally Appropriate Writing block and write the same type of piece on their own or with a partner.

We have looked at a variety of beginning literacy routines. You will learn many others in your classroom. The ones presented in this section give you good resources to begin to plan a balanced beginning literacy program. Let's see how this can be done.

Planning Daily Instruction Using Routines

As you plan daily instruction for your children, you will use some routines every day and others only occasionally. The following four guidelines will help you as you plan:

1. Keep in mind the model for the Balanced Beginning Literacy Program (see Figure 4.3). The six major blocks (Independent Reading, Independent Writing, Learning to Read Words, Developing Language and Comprehension, Learning to Write, and Developmentally Appropriate Writing) should be included in each day's plan. There may be rare occasions when this is not true, but for the most part, this is your goal.
2. Lay out your daily schedule in blocks following the balanced beginning literacy model. You will find, however, that there is often overlap in your blocks. (See the example of Ms. Barbizon's schedule on page 205.)
3. Vary the routines you use. While children like repetition and learn effectively when it is used, they also need some variety in their routines.
4. Select the routines you use based on students' needs. Teaching is assessment. As children respond in all teaching-related activities, note their responses and use this information to plan your instruction. For example, if during a Shared Reading Routine several children's responses show that they are not applying certain phonic elements that you have taught, you should return to the Explicit Phonics Routine and the Decodable Text Routine for reteaching and more practice.

The following lesson plan from Ms. Barbizon, a first-grade teacher, shows how she uses a variety of routines each day. I reformatted her schedule and added comments to help you see the different routines she uses. For a detailed discussion about how to organize and manage your classroom, see Chapter 10.

As You Read Ms. Barbizon's Plan

- Look for the variety of routines she uses.
- Note how she manages small groups by using independent reading and learning centers.
- Note how she gets in the blocks of a balanced beginning literacy program.

Ms. Barbizon's Schedule
(19 first graders)
November 12

- Literacy block—8:45 to 11:45 daily
- Independent work—Five learning centers for writing, vocabulary, and spelling practice

TIME	ACTIVITY	ROUTINES	COMMENTS
8:45	READING: Developing Language and Comprehension –Reread the big book *The Lady with the Alligator Purse* (Wescott, 1988). –Discussion.	• Shared Reading Routine	• This previously read book provides application of previously taught letter-sound associations and high-frequency words. This also serves as a warm-up or opening activity.
9:00	Independent Reading –Conference with Jeff, Lisa, Elaine, and Martha.		• During this time students are practicing reading. Conferences help Ms. Barbizon check for decoding and other skill application to self-selected books.
9:10	READING: Learning to Read Words –Teach digraphs *sh, ch, th.* –Practice and apply digraphs. • Read *Charlie's Shoes.*	• Explicit Phonics Routine • Decodable Text Routine • Observational Guided Reading Routine • Irregular Words Routine	• Ms. Barbizon is continuing to teach the decoding skills students need. • Ms. Barbizon combines three routines. She meets with three small groups. While she meets with one group, the other children go to an assigned learning center.
10:10	Independent Writing –Children add to journals.		• Ms. Barbizon moves from child to child to check to see how they are spelling using the letter-sound associations taught so far this year.

TIME	ACTIVITY	ROUTINES	COMMENTS
10:20	WRITING: Learning to Write –Writing a group story. –Spelling words with *sh, ch, th.* *Spelling List* • chair • show • think • much • shop	• Shared Writing Routine	• Ms. Barbizon is connecting the explicit phonics instruction with spelling. The children help her write a group story. She works the spelling words into the story.
10:40	READING: Learning to Read Words –Practice spelling words with digraphs *sh, ch, th.* –Add spelling words to word wall. –Review words on word wall.	• Making Words Routine • Word Wall Routine	• Ms. Barbizon returns to this block to provide more practice and connections for students.
11:00	WRITING: Developmentally Appropriate Writing –Children write own stories. –Encourage use of words from word wall.		• This is a follow-up to the teacher-modeled writing. Ms. Barbizon moves from student to student to provide coaching. She is looking for application of skills previously taught and evidence of students' writing abilities.
11:15	READING: Developing Language and Comprehension –Read aloud *The 500 Hats of Bartholomew Cubbins* (1938) to teach noting important details using a simplified story map.	• Read-Aloud Routine	• Ms. Barbizon is teaching listening comprehension.

TIME	ACTIVITY	ROUTINES	COMMENTS
11:15 *continued*	−Partner practice reading (select any book read).	• Cooperative Reading Routine • Fluency Reading Routine	• Children select any books they have read today or on another day. They read with a partner. Ms. Barbizon moves from pair to pair to note fluency and application of skills.
11:35	• Discuss what was learned today. Make a list on the board.		• Ms. Barbizon concludes her day by having children talk about what they learned. For example, children might say, "I learned a new word" or "I learned to read better." This helps to keep children focused and see the value of their day.

You have focused on the important components of a beginning literacy program. You have learned a variety of routines to use within this program. Now let's focus on a specific literacy lesson that can be used in the program.

Literacy Lesson

My Brown Bear Barney

This lesson was developed for a group of first graders involved in a thematic unit entitled "Special Friends." It fits into the Developing Language and Comprehension block of the balanced beginning literacy program. One of the books being read using the Shared Reading Routine was *My Brown Bear Barney* (Butler, 1988).

Before Reading the Plan

1. **Consider what you have learned about the Shared Reading Routine. Review any parts of the chapter that were not clear to you. Talk with a peer about it.**
2. **Read the text for *My Brown Bear Barney* (Butler, 1988).**
3. **Study the Teacher Preparation section on page 220 to see the planning and decision-making process that went into the development of this lesson.**

While Reading the Plan

1. **Notice how the Shared Reading Routine was carried out.**
2. **Think about how you might have changed this lesson.**

When I go shopping, I take . . . .

MY BROWN BEAR BARNEY

By Dorothy Butler
Illustrated by Elizabeth Fuller

and my brown bear Barney.

my mother, my little brother, my yellow basket,
my red umbrella

my bike, our old dog Charlie, two apples from our tree,
my boots

When I play with my friend Fred,
I take . . .

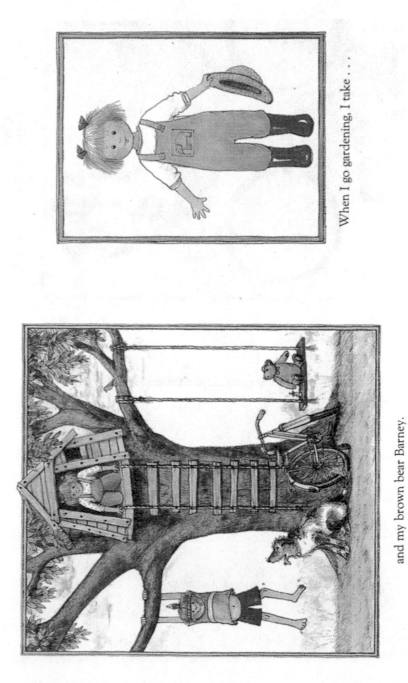

When I go gardening, I take . . .

and my brown bear Barney.

and my brown bear Barney.

my father, my straw hat, my wheelbarrow, my spade

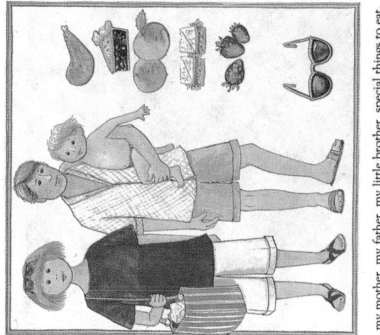

my mother, my father, my little brother, special things to eat, my sunglasses

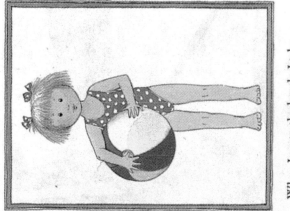

When I go to the beach, I take . . .

When I go to my grandmother's,
I take . . .

and my brown bear Barney.

and my brown bear Barney.

my pajamas in a suitcase, a flower in green paper,
a tasty tidbit for her cat, some carrots from my garden

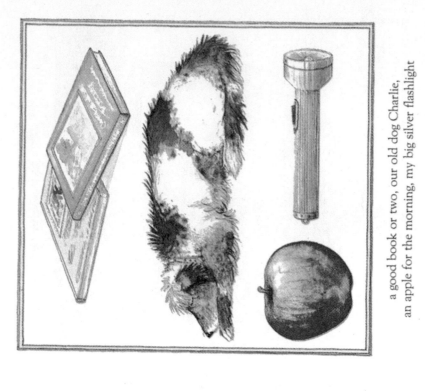

a good book or two, our old dog Charlie,
an apple for the morning, my big silver flashlight

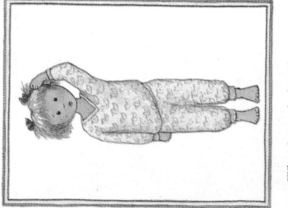

When I go to bed, I take . . .

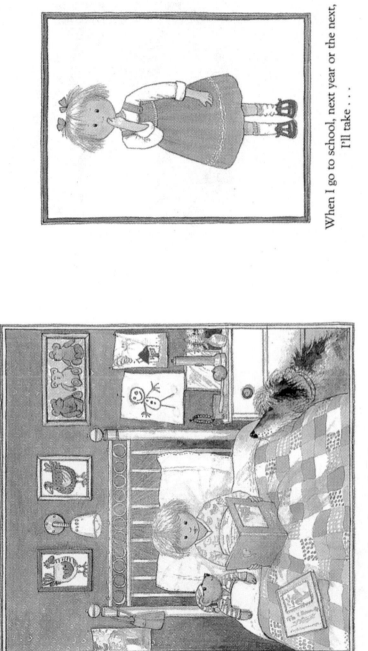

When I go to school, next year or the next, I'll take . . . .

and my brown bear Barney.

But not my brown bear Barney.
My mother says that bears don't go to school.

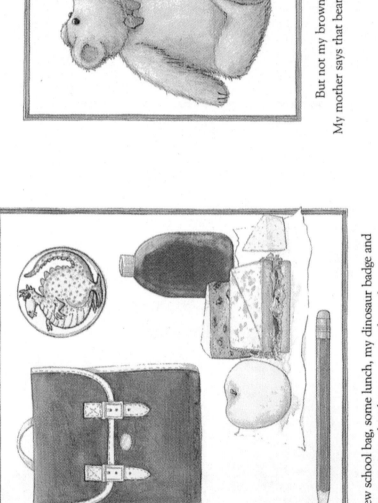

a new school bag, some lunch, my dinosaur badge and
a pencil with an eraser on the end.

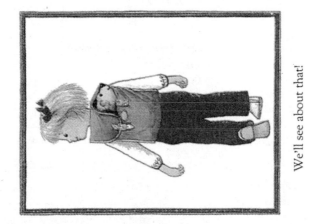

We'll see about that!

Teacher Preparation

This plan was developed for a first-grade class of twenty-three students. My preparation and decision making for the lessons went as follows:

1. After talking with the children about their interests, we decided to have a unit on "Special Friends" because almost everyone had an animal, a person, or stuffed animal as a special friend.

2. I put ten different books about special friends in the library center and noticed which books children picked up and examined. (These came from the school library, the public library, and my own collection.) Because there was so much interest in *My Brown Bear Barney* (Butler, 1988) and *Ira Sleeps Over* (Waber, 1972), I decided to use them. *My Brown Bear Barney* is a predictable, repeated-pattern book. *Ira Sleeps Over* is also about how a child finds comfort with his teddy bear. I had a copy of *Bear in Mind: A Book of Bear Poems* (Goldstein, 1989) that has good poems for chanting and opening the lessons. *The Velveteen Rabbit* (Williams, 1983) is also good for reading aloud to children during this unit. I also identified four decodable books from a published reading series to use during phonics instruction throughout the theme. These were used in the Learning to Read Words block of my program. Lessons are not illustrated here.

3. I obtained a big book for *My Brown Bear Barney* plus 15 small-book versions.

4. I reread both *My Brown Bear Barney* and *Ira Sleeps Over* to get a sense of the story lines. I then read the poems in *Bear in Mind* and marked the ones I wanted to use as chants.

5. As I read *My Brown Bear Barney*, I noticed nineteen places where the consonant *b* was used in the initial position (*bear* and *Barney* were each used six times, and *basket, boots, beach, book, bag, badge,* and *bears* once each). Since I had taught the consonant *b*, I knew this would be a good way to help children see how they can apply the skills they had been using in their decodable books.

6. I decided that my major outcomes for this unit would be as follows:

   • *Decoding:* Application of the consonant *b* in authentic literature. Continued practice of the consonants *b, r, s, m, t,* and *n* and the short vowels *a, e,* and *o.*

   • *Constructing meaning:* Use important story details to understand that favorite things often make one comfortable.

   • *Attitudes and habits:* Have fun reading, writing, and sharing books and stories about special friends.

7. I planned for this unit to last for seven to ten days, depending on student interests and responses.

The following sample presents the lesson for *My Brown Bear Barney* using the Shared Reading Routine. It focuses on application of decoding and constructing meaning.

Literacy
Lesson
continued

Introducing
My Brown Bear Barney

ACTIVITY	PROCEDURE	NOTES
Opening activity: chanting a poem	1. Display the poem from Goldstein's book (1989, p. 26) on a chart.	Warms students up for the lesson and activates prior knowledge.

MY TEDDY BEAR*

A teddy bear is a faithful friend.
You can pick him up at either end.
His fur is the color of breakfast toast,
and he's always there when you
 need him most.

Marchette Chute

---

*Source: From *Rhymes About Us* by Marchette Chute. Published 1974 by E. P. Dutton. Copyright ©1974 by Marchette Chute. Reprinted by permission of Elizabeth Roach.

2. Read the poem aloud to children, pointing to the words. Invite them to say the words with you.

3. Follow with a discussion.

ACTIVITY	PROCEDURE	NOTES
Talking about *My Brown Bear Barney* and making predictions	1. Show students the book; read the title, author, and illustrator. 2. Discuss the cover, focusing on the girl. Turn through the first two or three pages and continue discussing the pictures. 3. Have children predict what they think is going to happen. Record predictions on the chalkboard. Tell students you will return to those predictions at the end of the book.	Continues prior knowledge development for the book and creates excitement for reading. Helps children have a purpose as they read.

Literacy
Lesson
continued

Reading and Responding to *My Brown Bear Barney*

ACTIVITY	PROCEDURE	NOTES
Reading the story for interest and fun	1. Place the big book so that children can see it. Read each page aloud, sweeping your hand or a pointer under the words. Discuss the illustrations as you read. 2. Reread the story, talking about the illustrations. Invite children to read with you.	Models fluent reading.
Responding to the story: talking about things children liked or thought were funny	Invite children to share their reactions to the story.	Promotes personal responses and construction of meaning. Lets teacher know how well students understand.
Writing and drawing about the story	Have children write something about the story and draw a picture.	Ties together reading and writing. Focuses on constructing meaning.

When subsequent rereadings are done, provide many opportunities for children to build oral language through discussion and role-playing.

After Reading the Plan

1. **With a partner, talk about other ways you could have approached this lesson.**
2. **Use the routine illustrated in this lesson and the other information provided about using routines to write your own lesson using a different book. Think about other routines you might incorporate in your lesson.**
3. **Locate a primary teacher (K–2) who is using the Shared Reading Routine and other routines for instruction. Observe the class for several days. Make notes about the routines you see being used. Meet with the teacher to discuss them.**

■ Summary

This chapter developed the concept that learning to read involves two big jobs—decoding and comprehension, or constructing meaning. At the beginning stages of this process, a greater amount of instructional emphasis needs to be placed on decoding while not overlooking comprehension. Six elements were identified as ones leading to independence in decoding: oral language, phonemic awareness, concepts of print, letter-sound associations, analogy, and a strategy called A Way to Think About Words to help children become independent decoders. A model for a Balanced Beginning Literacy Program was presented. A variety of routines for instruction, practice, and application were discussed. A literacy lesson was presented showing how one routine is used in effective beginning literacy instruction.

Literature

Butler, D. (1988). *My brown bear Barney.* New York: Greenwillow Books.

Goldstein, B. S. (1989). *Bear in mind: A book of bear poems.* New York: Viking Kestrel.

Marshall, J. (1988). *Goldilocks and the three bears.* New York: Dial Books for Young Readers.

Martin, B., Jr. (1967). *Brown bear, brown bear.* New York: Henry Holt and Company.

Seuss (1938). *The 500 Hats of Bartholomew Cubbins.* New York: Vanguard.

Seuss (1963). *Hop on pop.* New York: Beginner Books: A Division of Random House.

Seuss (1974). *There's a wocket in my pocket.* New York: Random House.

Shaw, N. (1986). *Sheep in a jeep.* Boston: Houghton Mifflin.

Waber, B. (1972). *Ira sleeps over.* Boston: Houghton Mifflin.

Westcott, N. B. (1988). *The lady with the alligator purse.* Boston: Little, Brown.

Williams, M. (1983). *The velveteen rabbit.* New York: Simon & Schuster.

Williams, V. B. (1997). *Lucky song.* New York: Greenwillow Books.

For Additional Reading

Bear, D. R., Invernizzi, M., Templeton, S., & Templeton, F. (1996). *Words their way.* Columbus, OH: Merrill.

Cunningham, P. M. (1991). *Phonics they use.* New York: Harper-Collins.

Eldredge, J. L. (1995). *Teaching decoding in holistic classrooms.* Englewood Cliffs, NJ: Merrill: An Imprint of Prentice Hall.

Ericson, L., & Juliebö, M. F. (1998). *The phonologic awareness handbook for kindergarten and primary teachers.* Newark, NJ: IRA.

Fountas, I. C., & Pinnell, G. S. (1996). *Guided reading: Good first teaching for all children.* Portsmouth, NH: Heinemann.

Developing Vocabulary: Words and Meanings Beyond the Beginning Literacy Level

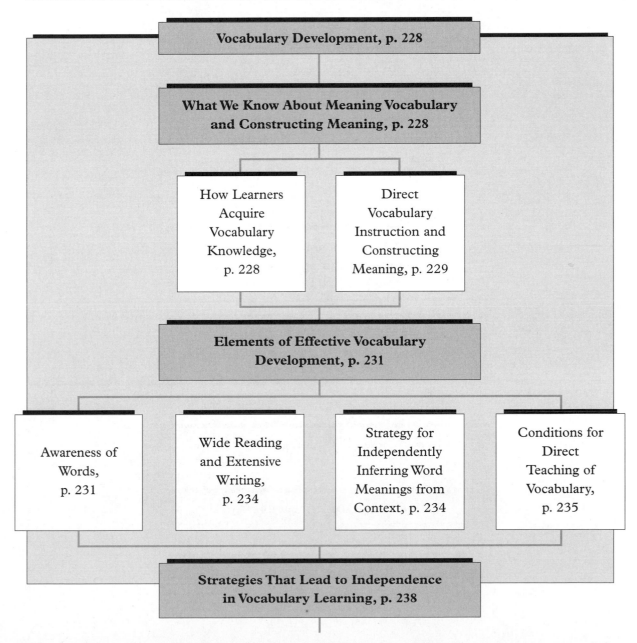

Vocabulary Development, p. 228

What We Know About Meaning Vocabulary and Constructing Meaning, p. 228

How Learners Acquire Vocabulary Knowledge, p. 228

Direct Vocabulary Instruction and Constructing Meaning, p. 229

Elements of Effective Vocabulary Development, p. 231

Awareness of Words, p. 231

Wide Reading and Extensive Writing, p. 234

Strategy for Independently Inferring Word Meanings from Context, p. 234

Conditions for Direct Teaching of Vocabulary, p. 235

Strategies That Lead to Independence in Vocabulary Learning, p. 238

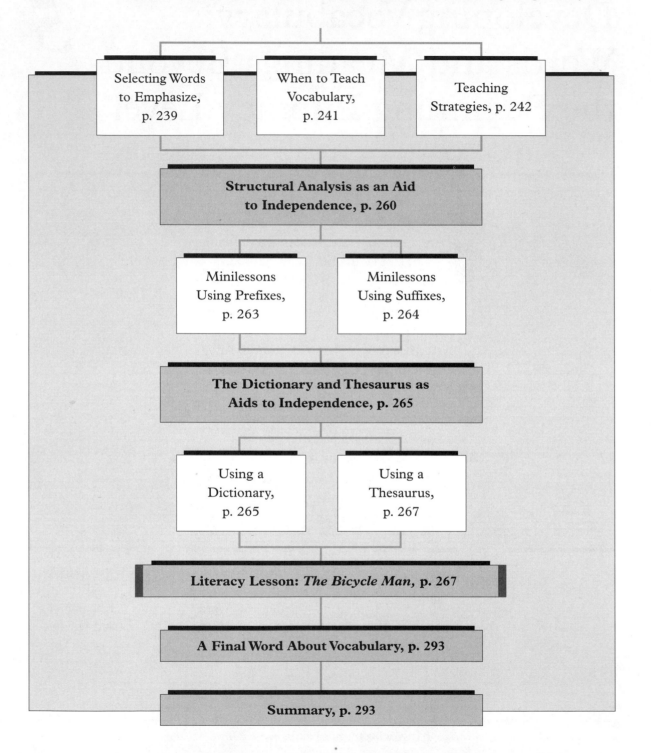

Selecting Words to Emphasize, p. 239

When to Teach Vocabulary, p. 241

Teaching Strategies, p. 242

Structural Analysis as an Aid to Independence, p. 260

Minilessons Using Prefixes, p. 263

Minilessons Using Suffixes, p. 264

The Dictionary and Thesaurus as Aids to Independence, p. 265

Using a Dictionary, p. 265

Using a Thesaurus, p. 267

Literacy Lesson: *The Bicycle Man,* p. 267

A Final Word About Vocabulary, p. 293

Summary, p. 293

FIGURE 5.1

"NEVER MINCE WORDS WITH A SHARK" BY JACK PRELUTSKY

Never Mince Words with a Shark

You may quarrel with centipedes, quibble with seals,
declaim to a duck in the park,
engage in disputes with cantankerous coots,
but never mince words with a shark.

You may rant at an anteater, banter with eels,
and haggle with gaggles of geese,
heap verbal abuse on a monkey or moose,
but a shark you had best leave in peace.

You may argue with otters, make speeches to teals,
and lecture at length to a shrew,
but a shark will deflate your attempts at debate,
and before you are done, you are through.

Source: "Never Mince Words with a Shark" from *The New Kid on the Block* by Jack Prelutsky. Copyright © 1984 by Jack Prelutsky. Reprinted by permission of Greenwillow Books, a division of William Morrow & Company, Inc.

READING POETRY SUCH AS "Never Mince Words with a Shark" (Figure 5.1) and other literature rich in language is one of the ways children develop their vocabularies. In Chapter 3, we dealt with the importance of activating and developing prior knowledge; in Chapter 4, we focused on how beginning readers and writers learn to identify words and construct meaning. In this chapter, we look at strategies and techniques for developing vocabulary beyond the beginning literacy level that continuously promote the integration of new knowledge with prior knowledge and lead to the active construction of meaning.

Vocabulary Development

As readers develop vocabulary, they learn two aspects about words: recognition and meaning (Chall, 1987); these two aspects, however, *are not* separate from each other. Children's *recognition vocabulary* consists of that body of words they are able to pronounce or read orally. Beginning literacy learners focus much of their attention on recognizing words (Chall, 1987), even though their primary focus is on meaning. Children's *meaning vocabulary* is that body of words whose meanings they understand and can use. *Recognition and meaning vocabularies develop simultaneously as students learn to read and write.*

Students' recognition vocabulary ultimately becomes sight vocabulary, or words they are able to read instantly and use in constructing meaning. Beginning readers and writers rapidly build such vocabularies through reading and writing experiences.

What We Know About Meaning Vocabulary and Constructing Meaning

Vocabulary reflects an individual's knowledge and concepts in a particular area. For example, a person knowledgeable about music will understand and use the words *meter, clef,* and *timbre* in ways that reflect musical knowledge, and an avid gardener will know and use terms such as *perennial, deciduous,* and *Gaillardia.*

The study of vocabulary has interested researchers and educators for many years (Beck & McKeown, 1991). Research clearly has established a strong relationship between the knowledge of word meanings (vocabulary) and reading comprehension (Anderson & Freebody, 1981; Davis, 1971; Johnston, 1981). In the past, the strength of this relationship led educators to recommend that students be taught crucial word meanings before reading selections (Tierney & Cunningham, 1984). Later researchers challenged the wisdom of this procedure and others related to teaching vocabulary to improve comprehension (Nagy, 1988). *Improving an individual's ability to construct meaning involves a great deal more than just teaching a few words before a selection is read.* We will address two significant issues to help you more fully understand the strong relationship between vocabulary knowledge and comprehension. First, how do learners acquire vocabulary knowledge? Second, does direct instruction in vocabulary lead to improved comprehension?

How Learners Acquire Vocabulary Knowledge

Studies of the size of children's vocabularies have given varying estimates for various grade levels (Loban, 1963; Lorge & Chall, 1963; Nagy & Anderson, 1984; Seashore, 1947). The discrepancies may have arisen because researchers used different definitions for what constituted a word, different concepts of what it means to know a word, and different bodies of words to represent English (Beck & McKeown, 1991). In light of these problems, researchers have concluded that the early estimates of vocabulary size are much too low (Nagy & Anderson, 1984). A reasonable estimate based on current research places the *average* high school senior's vocabulary at approximately forty thousand words (Nagy & Herman, 1987). When the figures on vocabulary size are compared from year to year, it appears that students must learn twenty-seven hundred to three thousand new words per year (Beck & McKeown, 1991; Nagy & Herman, 1987), or approximately seven new words per day, to achieve this forty-thousand average by the time they are seniors in high school.

The question, then, is how students acquire this astounding vocabulary. There are several plausible answers: through reading and/or listening to a wide variety of texts and other media and/or through direct instruction in word meanings. Extensive research on both of these points of view (Beck & McKeown, 1991; McKeown & Curtis, 1987; Nagy, 1988) has led to four major positions on how students acquire vocabulary (Beck & McKeown, 1991):

1. Students develop vocabulary knowledge through wide reading (Fielding, Wilson, & Anderson, 1986; Nagy & Herman, 1987).
2. Students learn vocabulary from context but need instruction about context to use it effectively (Jenkins, Stein, & Wysocki, 1984; Sternberg, 1987).
3. Students are often hindered as much as they are helped by context. Therefore, they should be encouraged to use the dictionary as an aid in acquiring word meanings (Schatz & Baldwin, 1986).
4. Students can also profit from direct instruction in vocabulary (Beck, McKeown, & Omanson, 1987; Graves, 1986, 1987; Stahl & Fairbanks, 1986).

Given the strength of the research supporting these four positions and my own experience with children, we must consider all of these proposals as viable ways for students to acquire vocabulary. The strength of the research behind the argument supporting wide reading as a means of improving both vocabulary and overall reading is very powerful and must be taken seriously. This is part of the rationale for having an independent reading and writing component in the literacy program (see Chapter 2). But while students are reading widely, they need to become independent in inferring word meanings; therefore, helping them develop an independent strategy for doing this through the use of context, the dictionary, and structural analysis will serve them well. Finally, *some students under some circumstances* may profit from the direct teaching of vocabulary; however, direct teaching is not as powerful in achieving overall growth in vocabulary and comprehension as is wide reading (Nagy & Herman, 1987). We need to carefully examine what we know about direct teaching of vocabulary to determine how and when we should do it.

Direct Vocabulary Instruction and Constructing Meaning

As noted earlier, it has been a long-standing practice to teach students words that are perceived to be crucial for understanding a selection before reading. This practice has been justified on the basis of the extensive body of research showing a strong correlation between the knowledge of word meanings and comprehension. There are two important questions to consider when thinking about the direct teaching of vocabulary: (1) Does the direct teaching of vocabulary improve comprehension? and (2) If direct teaching is used, how and when should it be done?

Direct Vocabulary Teaching and Improved Comprehension

The goal of teaching students vocabulary is to improve their overall comprehension. Early studies in this area had mixed results; some found direct teaching did improve overall comprehension, whereas others found it improved knowledge of only the specific words taught and had little or no effect on overall comprehension (Jenkins & Pany, 1981; Mezynski, 1983). However, other studies have found that the direct teaching of selected words results in small but significant improvements in comprehension (McKeown, Beck, Omanson, & Pople, 1985; Stahl, 1983; Stahl & Fairbanks, 1986; Weiss, Mangrum, & Liabre, 1986; Wixson, 1986). The determining factors seem to have been how the words were taught.

How and When Direct Teaching Is Effective

Direct teaching of vocabulary refers to activities in which information about the meanings of words is made directly available to students; this may range from very strong, teacher-led lessons to weaker forms of instruction such as having students look up words in a dictionary (Beck & McKeown, 1991). In several studies, effective instruction appears to have had several important qualities:

1. *Only a few words central to the content of the story or informational text were taught* (Beck, Perfetti, & McKeown, 1982; Wixson, 1986). In other words, the random teaching of any unknown word does not help students improve their comprehension. The words must be key-concept words.

2. *Words were taught in meaningful contexts that conveyed the particular meanings relevant to the text* (Gipe, 1978/1979; Nagy & Herman, 1987). Because words have multiple meanings, teaching a meaning that does not fit the material to be read is fruitless for students and may even hinder overall comprehension.

3. *The teaching of vocabulary was integrated with the activation and development of prior knowledge.* Vocabulary is a specialized version of prior knowledge (Nagy & Herman, 1987). In all studies that succeeded in improving comprehension by teaching vocabulary, the words taught were in some way related to the students' prior knowledge.

4. *Teachers taught words thoroughly by offering students rich and varied information about them* (Beck et al., 1987; Nagy & Herman, 1987; Stahle & Fairbanks, 1986). Simply presenting definitions is not sufficient to teach students words; the words must be related to one another and to students' experiences. When possible, they were grouped into topical or semantic categories (Stevens, 1982).

5. *Students were exposed to a word many times* (Nagy & Herman, 1987). Knowledge of word meanings is gained in increments through many experiences. Therefore, words must be used in a variety of situations, such as writing and reading, to help students achieve ownership of them.

6. *Students were actively involved in the process of learning the words* (Beck et al., 1987; Nagy & Herman, 1987). Students were not passive learners simply being told information or definitions. They verbalized what they had learned and related it to their own lives.

Although research reveals these consistent characteristics of effective teaching, *it does not show that there is any one best method for achieving these qualities* (Beck & McKeown, 1991). Rather, a variety of techniques should be used for such instruction.

Another question about direct vocabulary teaching is when to provide it—before reading, during reading, or after reading. Researchers recommend that teachers teach vocabulary before, during, and/or after reading depending on the text to be read and the students involved (Beck, McKeown, McCaslin, & Burkes, 1979).

Many researchers have looked at the effects of preteaching vocabulary on students' overall comprehension (McKeown et al., 1985; Stahl, 1983; Weiss et al., 1986; Wixson, 1986). Although they all obtained positive results, they did not compare their preteaching with the effects of vocabulary instruction provided during or after reading instruction. One researcher, Memory (1990), did look at the placement of vocabulary instruction using ninth-grade biology students, twelfth-grade government students, and twelfth-grade economics students. Students were taught technical terms at different times before, during, or after reading. Memory concluded that "this investigation failed to identify one time for teaching difficult technical terms in content area classes that is more effective than others if the objective is the learning of definitions" (p. 52). However, the teaching of definitions is not the goal of vocabulary instruction. Moreover, this conclusion was reached for high school students reading expository texts. As Tierney and Cunningham (1984) state, "These conclusions lead us to question the practice of cursorily introducing new word meanings before having students read. This practice is probably only justified when just one or two crucial words are taught at some depth" (p. 612).

Elements of Effective Vocabulary Development

As a teacher, you are responsible for implementing the literacy program in your classroom. Recall that this program should include motivation, independent reading and writing, and instruction in reading and writing; this concept of a literacy program is based on the premise that children learn to read and write by reading and writing. Throughout this process, students will vary in their need for support from their teacher and peers.

Effective vocabulary development takes place within the literacy program. It includes four important elements: awareness of words, wide reading and extensive writing, learning strategies for independently inferring word meanings from context, and *limited* direct teaching of vocabulary and vocabulary-related skills.

Awareness of Words

Considering the large number of words students encounter and the need to learn them, it is obvious that all of these words cannot be taught. Therefore, we must make students aware of learning words and create an intrinsic motivation and interest so that they will learn words independently. Teachers, peers, books, magazines, and electronic books are excellent catalysts for this motivation and interest.

Being aware of and interested in words helps students develop ownership of them. This happens when students see how a word relates to their overall backgrounds (Beck, 1984). Students develop networks of words and their relationships through repeated experiences with the words in their reading and writing and through activities specifically designed to help them build relationships among words. Thus, first encounters with a word may help students learn its meaning, but it is repeated use that develops ownership. As readers develop ownership of words, they relate them to their existing schemata and develop new schemata, thus cementing the ownership.

By making students aware of and interested in learning words, you will provide the support that helps them expand their schemata and create new ones. Many different types of activities will help to promote this awareness. Notice how all of the following suggestions are integral parts of reading and writing or extensions of reading and writing.

Noting Words in Journals

As students keep journals, have them make personal lists of words that interest them or that they would like to discuss with a group, a peer, or you. Direct students to choose words that interest or puzzle them rather than having them simply identify all the words they do not know. This places the focus of such activities on what students can do and makes it a positive learning experience. For more information on the use of journals, see Chapter 6.

Reading Aloud to Students

Reading is an excellent way to make students aware of words and expand their oral vocabulary, which is the foundation for all other vocabulary learning. As you are reading aloud a book such as *Anastasia Krupnik* (Lowry, 1979), stop periodically and discuss words such as *Hubbard Squash, ostentatious,* or other words that might be interesting, unusual, or fun for children to think about. Books that are especially written to focus on certain types of words can be read aloud before students read them independently. Some examples are *Delivery Van: Words for Town and Country* (Maestro & Maestro, 1990), *Taxi: A Book of City Words* (Maestro & Maestro, 1989), *The Weighty Word Book* (Levitt, Burger, & Guralnick, 1985), and *Murfles and Wink-a-Peeps* (Sperling, 1985). For your own reference, you might want to have available a book about word histories, such as *Word Mysteries and Histories* (Editors of the American Heritage Dictionary, 1986).

Discussion Circles

After students have finished reading a book, encourage them to get together in discussion circles to respond to the book and talk about words of interest. Even when all students have not read the same book, they enjoy sharing funny or unusual words from what they have read. (See Chapter 6 for a discussion of literature discussion circles.) This motivates other children to want to read the book and to become more interested in learning about words.

Word Banks, Word Files, and Word Books

These devices are the students' personal files of words they have learned or are interested in learning. The words can be taken from books read, from areas of study such as science, from interest areas, from writing, and from other sources, such as newspapers or from the Internet. Each word is either put on a card or written in a word book with a sentence the student has written using the word and relating it to prior knowledge. Today, word banks/word files can be created in a word processing program and saved on students' personal floppy disks. For example, a student might write the following sentence for the word *periodic:* "In my class, we have *periodic* tests in math two or three times a month." At the primary levels, the word bank idea is motivational because words and sentences can be written on cards shaped like coins and dropped into banks made of plastic bottles, boxes, or other containers. Students can then "withdraw" words from the bank and review them frequently. Always encourage students to use the banked words in their writing.

Writing

One of the best ways to make students aware of words and promote ownership is to encourage them to write. By using shared writing and minilessons, you can help children be conscious of using a variety of words and more descriptive words. Whenever students use new words in their writing, you can be sure they have started to take ownership of them.

Word Expansion Activities

After several students have read the same book or worked together in a unit on the same topic, they can use such activities as word maps, semantic maps, semantic feature analysis, or webbing to play with the words that interest them. These activities are discussed later in this chapter.

Bulletin Boards or Word Walls

Bulletin boards that students develop to display words of interest or words on a particular topic, or word walls with lists of these words, also promote awareness and ownership. Students can then be encouraged to use the words from the bulletin board or word wall in their writing.

Electronic Books and Software

At this time more and more classrooms can support current technology. If you have access to writing programs on CD-ROMs and software for student writing (see Chapter 7), take advantage of the exciting ways they support literacy development. Do not, however, feel defeated if your students do not have access to these materials.

All of these activities are based on the students' reading and writing. Words are not studied in isolation from meaningful contexts. The constant focus of these experiences is relating new knowledge to old, constantly expanding students' schemata. The benefits of awareness and ownership activities are far-reaching. They promote independence in word learning and motivate students to want to learn more about words.

Wide Reading and Extensive Writing

"Increasing the volume of students' reading is the single most important thing a teacher can do to promote large-scale vocabulary growth" (Nagy, 1988, p. 32). Writing in conjunction with reading and writing alone engages students in much more thoughtful learning and improves their ability to construct meaning (Tierney & Shanahan, 1991). Therefore, it is critical to promote wide, independent reading and self-initiated writing. Reading provides models of rich language that help students learn many new words, and writing provides an authentic reason for students to use those words and develop ownership of them. Because these two processes are so closely related and interrelated, they are mutually supportive.

Children *must* be encouraged to read self-selected books and do self-initiated writing on a daily basis. This should be a significant component of the literacy program and not something done during "extra time" or outside of class. Recall that some researchers suggest that *in-school independent reading time may be even more important to improving students' ability to construct meaning than out-of-school reading time* (Taylor et. al., 1990).

In addition to the ideas suggested in Chapter 2, try the following activities.

Book Displays

Have exciting and colorful displays of your favorite books and new books. Take a few minutes to read or tell a little about the book, just enough to get students "hooked" on reading it. Encourage students to place books they have read in the display and give a very brief comment about them. This transfers much of the ownership for learning to the students and makes them active participants.

Discussions of Interesting Words

Periodically invite children (or parents, other adults from students' homes, school custodian, and so forth) to talk about interesting or humorous words from books they have read or things they have written. By sharing the sentence in which a word appears and telling others what they think it means, children learn to apply all aspects of vocabulary learning to independent reading and writing. Such words can be placed on a class word wall for all students to use.

Many of the ideas suggested for promoting word awareness can also be used to help promote vocabulary development during independent reading and writing.

Strategy for Independently Inferring Word Meanings from Context

A necessary part of effective vocabulary development is teaching students a strategy for independently inferring word meanings (Calfee & Drum, 1986; Graves, 1987; Paris et al., 1983). If students are reading extensively and come to an unknown word, they need a plan for trying to determine its meaning. Getting students to use such a strategy is well worth the time and effort.

The student strategy presented here is based on the suggestions of Calfee and Drum (1986) and Graves (1987) and on my own experiences with students. You will need to adjust the steps to meet the varying grade levels of your students. Tell the students:

1. When you come to a word you do not know, read to the end of the sentence or paragraph to decide if the word is important to your understanding. If it is unimportant, read on.
2. If the word is important, look for base words, prefixes, or suffixes you recognize.
3. Use what you know about phonics to try to pronounce the word. Is it a word you have heard?
4. Reread the sentence or paragraphs containing the word. Try using context to infer the meaning.
5. If you still don't know the word, use the dictionary or ask someone for help.
6. Once you think you know the meaning, reread the text to be sure it makes sense.

Teach these steps in accordance with your students' level of maturity in reading. For example, a beginning reader may be mature enough to focus on only a simplified version of the strategy. Figure 5.2 shows a strategy poster you might use with primary grade children, and Figure 5.3 shows one that you could use with intermediate or higher grades. When students are learning this strategy, they should help in verbalizing the statements that go on the strategy poster; in this way, the strategy becomes theirs. They should then be reminded to refer to the poster and use the strategy as they read.

Conditions for Direct Teaching of Vocabulary

The final element of effective vocabulary development is the *limited direct teaching of words and word-related skills.* Given the mixed results of the research on direct teaching of vocabulary, it is not reasonable to consider this the major source for vocabulary learning for students. It is not possible to teach the extensive number of words one by one. Furthermore, vocabulary research shows that the direct teaching of vocabulary often helps students learn the words but does not improve comprehension.

Despite the strong research evidence that the direct teaching of vocabulary is of little value in helping students improve their meaning construction, many teachers have persisted in following this practice. But why? A number of reasons exist, *but these reasons are no longer valid.*

First, educators did not thoroughly understand the process of comprehension. They believed that meaning in a text resides in individual words. Therefore, they erroneously assumed the direct teaching of words would improve comprehension. Now, however, we know that comprehension is a process of constructing meaning by using one's prior knowledge and interacting with the text. Learning the meanings of separate, individual words has a very small relationship to this overall process. This new knowledge is slowly becoming available to more and more teachers.

FIGURE 5.2

PRIMARY-GRADE STRATEGY POSTER FOR INFERRING WORD MEANINGS

Second, educators (and publishers of basal readers) believed that teaching words before a selection is read improves comprehension for students even though no strong research base for this practice existed. Now that we have a strong research base showing that this practice is of limited value in improving comprehension, and then only under certain circumstances, educators are beginning to let go of it.

Finally, teachers did not know what to do in place of direct vocabulary teaching. Now, however, we know of many teaching strategies that help students become independent vocabulary learners and support them in developing an extensive meaning vocabulary. These strategies include independent reading and writing and the use of word maps and vocabulary self-collection, discussed later in this chapter.

FIGURE 5.3

INTERMEDIATE AND MIDDLE SCHOOL STRATEGY POSTER FOR INFERRING WORD MEANINGS

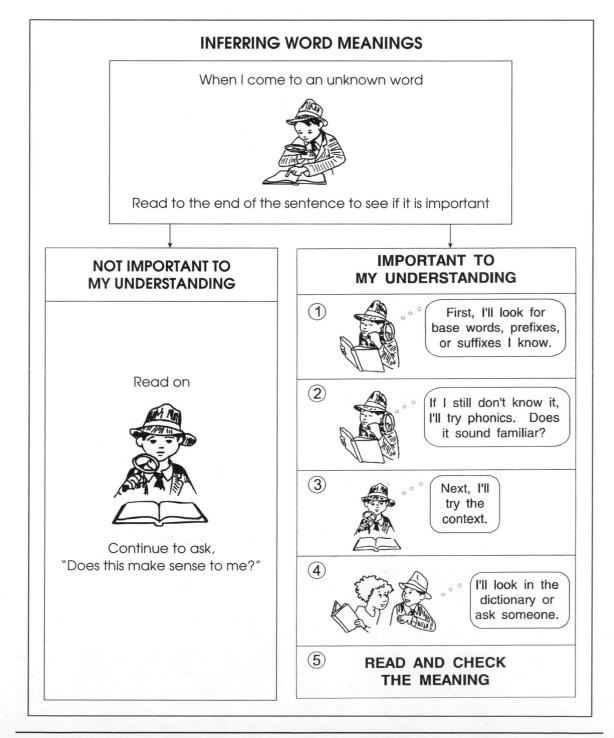

Direct teaching of vocabulary may lead to improved comprehension *only* when the following conditions are met (Stahl & Fairbanks, 1986; Snow, Burns, & Griffin, 1998):

▶ A *few* key words are thoroughly taught in meaningful context.

▶ Words are related to students' prior knowledge in ways that actively involve them in learning.

▶ Students are given multiple exposures to the words.

The teacher can use the few words that are taught to model the process of learning word meanings. Direct teaching of vocabulary-related skills, such as the use of context clues, prefixes, suffixes, base words, and the dictionary, should occupy a *very* small proportion (if any) of instructional time; incidental teaching at point of use or need may be of more value. Again, *it is more advantageous for students to spend their time reading and writing.*

Strategies That Lead to Independence in Vocabulary Learning

Although wide reading and extensive writing are the primary ways through which students develop their vocabulary knowledge, it is possible to use certain strategies and techniques that will help students become independent in their vocabulary learning and their ability to construct meaning.

Carr and Wixson (1986) give four guidelines for evaluating vocabulary instruction, all of which are based on the research conclusions discussed earlier:

1. *Instruction should help students relate new vocabulary to their background knowledge.* Because vocabulary is a specialized part of prior knowledge, students are more likely to improve their meaning construction when they do this.

2. *Instruction should help students develop extensive word knowledge.* Merely learning a definition is not learning a word (Nagy & Herman, 1987). To really learn a word and develop ownership, students must relate it to other concepts and words they know (Beck, 1984).

3. *Instruction should provide for active student involvement in learning new vocabulary.* Student-centered activities are most effective in helping students understand a word. For example, the teacher should have students take the lead in crafting their own sentences rather than simply giving them sentences.

4. *Instruction should develop students' strategies for acquiring new vocabulary independently.* Because of the large number of words in our language, students must be able to learn many words on their own. The student strategy for inferring word meanings presented earlier is one way to promote this type of learning. The types of teaching strategies and techniques the teacher uses also influence students' ability to learn words independently.

All of the teaching strategies for vocabulary instruction suggested here meet these criteria. As the teacher, you must constantly decide which words to teach, when to teach them, and which strategies to use for teaching.

Selecting Words to Emphasize

When selecting the words you will focus on during a literacy lesson, you must consider both the text and your students. The process for selecting vocabulary is similar to the process suggested in Chapter 3 for identifying prior knowledge. Figure 5.4 summarizes the decisions involved in vocabulary teaching. The first five decisions are discussed next; the remaining two decisions are discussed in the following two sections of the chapter.

1. *Review the text to identify the story line(s) or main ideas.* This information will give you a framework for identifying the important ideas in the text, which will be your basis for selecting the words for direct teaching. As we discussed in Chapters 2 and 3, this knowledge can also help you select the prior knowledge that needs to be activated or developed and decide what questions to ask if you use guided reading. Therefore, creating a story map for a narrative text or a graphic organizer for an expository text will be very helpful as you work throughout a thematic unit.

2. *Compile a list of words related to the story line(s) or main ideas.* By looking at your story map or graphic organizer, you can see the important ideas in the story or informational text and can then select words that are crucial to understanding the selection; these are your key-concept words. For example, recall the sample lesson presented at the conclusion of Chapter 3 (see pages 144–157). The graphic organizer for the first chapter of *Mummies, Tombs, and Treasure* (Perl, 1987) helped this author identify four key-concept words that seemed important to the chapter: *mummy, bacteria, decay,* and *coffin.*

   Sometimes it is easier to carry out this process with expository text such as *Mummies, Tombs, and Treasure* than with narrative text. However, it can also be done using narrative text as long as the story line is used and the terms selected focus on the problem and action within the story (Wixson, 1986). The sample lesson at the end of this chapter illustrates the complete process using a narrative text.

3. *Determine which key-concept words are adequately defined in the text.* Some of these words will be defined through context and some by direct definition. Furthermore, pronunciation guides and footnotes may be given for words that are not likely to be in the students' oral vocabularies and prior knowledge. A word usually does not have to be directly taught if the text contains adequate clues to its meaning and pronunciation, but sometimes you may want to focus on such words after reading as a way to expand vocabulary. Recall the lesson presented at the conclusion of Chapter 3; two of the words, *mummy* and *bacteria,* were defined directly in the context and were not taught directly before reading.

4. *Identify words students can determine through the use of prefixes, suffixes, root words, or base words.* Some of the key-concept words remaining on the list will include structural elements that students can use to determine pronunciation and meaning. If they can use these elements, the words containing them will not need to be taught directly. None of the words in the lesson at the end of Chapter 3 fit into this category.

FIGURE 5.4

DECISIONS TO MAKE ABOUT VOCABULARY TEACHING

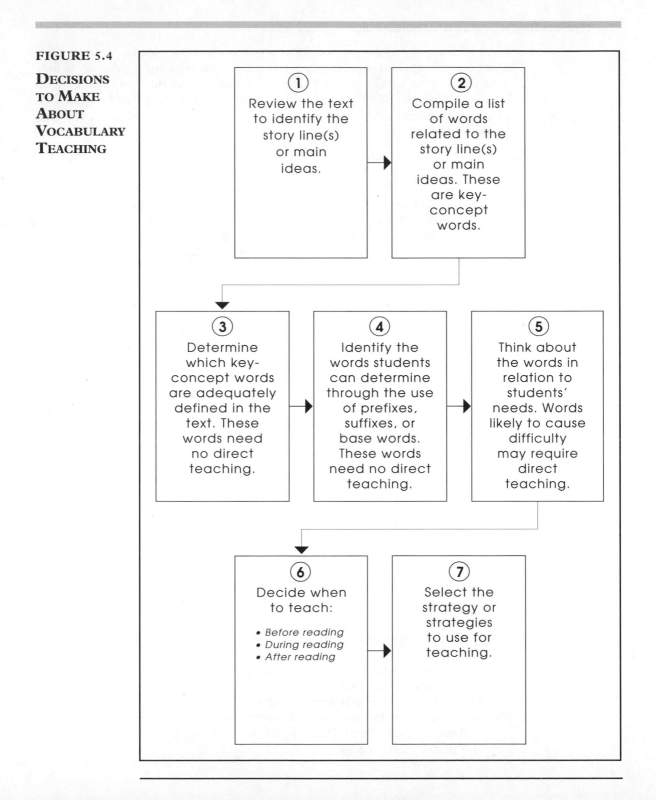

5. *Think about words in relation to students' needs.* Words likely to cause difficulty may require direct teaching. Finally, think about the words remaining on the list. If any of them are likely to be in students' prior knowledge, they need not be taught directly. Again, you might want to focus on these words after reading as a means of expanding students' vocabularies.

The words remaining on the list are those that may require direct teaching. They are unknown from students' prior knowledge and are unlikely to be learned independently through the use of context and/or structural analysis. Only two or three words should remain on the list. If the number is larger, you will probably want to consider using guided reading and divide the reading of the selection into sections so that you teach only two or three words before reading. Keep in mind that research supports teaching only a *few*, if any, key words before reading as a means of improving comprehension (Beck et al., 1982; Tierney & Cunningham, 1984; Wixson, 1986).

Now that you have identified the words that need direct teaching, you must decide when and how to teach them. A lesson illustrating this complete process for a narrative text appears at the conclusion of this chapter.

When to Teach Vocabulary

Vocabulary may be developed before, during, or after reading, depending on a number of factors. You must make decisions in relation to each instructional situation. Some students may need vocabulary support throughout their reading, and others may need no support. In the lesson at the end of Chapter 3 (pages 144–157), I chose not to teach any words before reading because the text defined the key words or students knew them from their experiences; also, I did not believe the students needed the support of preteaching vocabulary. Let's look at the conditions under which vocabulary should be taught before, during, and after reading.

Before Reading

Provide vocabulary instruction before reading in the following situations:

▶ Students are experiencing difficulty in constructing meaning and seem to have limited prior knowledge of any kind, including vocabulary. They might be second-language learners, students with learning disabilities, or students who are generally experiencing difficulty with comprehension.

▶ The text to be read contains words that are *clearly* a part of the prior knowledge students need to understand the text and you are confident students do not know these terms.

▶ The text has unusually difficult concepts; even though your students do not normally need vocabulary support before reading, they may benefit from it in these situations. For example, suppose your third graders really want to read *The Mouse Rap* (Myers, 1990), which is developmentally somewhat above their age level. Before reading the book, you introduce some of the words and concepts that you think are beyond their knowledge and experience.

▶ Students have previewed the text they are going to read and have identified words *they believe* they need to know to understand the text. Sometimes this is a good way to identify words that students really do need to know. A word that is giving them difficulty, even one that is unimportant to understanding the text, may interfere with students' overall meaning construction. Through direct teaching before reading, you can help them see that knowing this word (or every word) is not important to their overall understanding of a text. However, you have to exercise caution when teaching vocabulary before reading based on student self-selection, because you could end up devoting too much time to words that really are not important to understanding the material.

During Reading

Vocabulary support during reading is usually recommended for students who need overall teacher support through guided reading. These students are likely to be experiencing difficulty in constructing meaning or to be reading a text that has particularly difficult concepts. When you use guided reading with students, you may often find it is more appropriate to deal with words and concepts at the beginning or end of each segment of reading rather than trying to teach too many words before reading. Vocabulary support during reading has the advantage of giving students immediate opportunities to use the words.

In addition, during reading many teachers in grades 4 and above have children note interesting or unknown words in their journals. The children then bring these words to discussion groups, and the teacher uses them as the basis for vocabulary instruction.

After Reading

Vocabulary instruction after reading has two primary purposes: (1) to help students clarify the meanings of any words that were of interest to them during reading or that caused them difficulty and (2) to expand students' vocabularies by having them focus on interesting words that are related to the text they have read. For example, if first graders have read *Roundabout Cozy Cottage* (Graham, 1987), you might want to use the text and illustrations to expand their vocabularies of terms around the house. *Johnny Tremain* (Forbes, 1971), on the other hand, provides many places throughout the text to help intermediate-grade students see how an author uses rich, descriptive language. Focusing on some of these passages would be a good way to expand vocabulary and also relate the importance of descriptive language to writing.

Base decisions about when to provide vocabulary instruction and support on students' needs and the nature of the text; *sometimes no instruction will be necessary.* Table 5.1 summarizes these considerations in relation to the appropriate times to teach vocabulary.

Teaching Strategies

The final decision you must make is *how* to teach vocabulary directly (see Figure 5.4, page 240). You can use many different strategies in this process; there is no one

TABLE 5.1

WHEN TO PROVIDE VOCABULARY INSTRUCTION

	VOCABULARY INSTRUCTION		
FACTORS TO CONSIDER	**Before Reading**	**During Reading**	**After Reading**
Student considerations	*Any* students are experiencing difficulty constructing meaning.	Students are receiving guided reading support.	Students have identified words of interest or that cause difficulty.
	Students have previewed text and identified words they want to know.		Students need to expand vocabularies.
Text considerations	Text has words that are definitely keys to understanding. Text has unusually difficult concepts.	Text has words that are keys to understanding the text and are likely to cause students difficulty in constructing meaning.	Text has good opportunities for expanding vocabularies.

"best" method. However, the procedures must help students improve their ability to construct meaning and not just learn isolated words. Therefore, the strategies and techniques for supporting vocabulary development presented here are ones that help students relate new knowledge to old knowledge, actively involve students in the process of learning, help students thoroughly learn words, and support students in the process of learning to use their own strategy or strategies for independently inferring word meanings. *The ultimate goal of all vocabulary development is to help students become independent learners who have strategies for inferring the meanings of unknown words when they encounter them in reading;* furthermore, these students will have extensive vocabulary knowledge that they are able to use in constructing meaning through reading and writing.

Table 5.2 presents an overview of seven teaching strategies you can use in your literacy lessons to help students gain independence in vocabulary learning. They should *not* be used to develop isolated vocabulary lessons separate from reading and writing.

Concept of Definition Procedure (Word Maps)

Description.   Schwartz and Raphael (1985) describe a strategy known as the *concept of definition procedure,* more commonly called a *word map* strategy. The

TABLE 5.2

OVERVIEW OF VOCABULARY TEACHING STRATEGIES THAT PROMOTE STUDENT INDEPENDENCE

STRATEGY	PURPOSE	WHEN TO USE	COMMENTS
Concept of definition (word maps)	Help students become independent word learners by teaching elements of a good definition	Middle elementary and above Expository texts	Good support for strategy for independently inferring word meanings
Semantic mapping	Integrate prior knowledge and vocabulary learning	Before or after reading All texts	Develops in-depth word knowledge
Semantic feature analysis	Develop word knowledge by comparing words	Before or after reading Expository text and some narratives	Often more effective after reading
Hierarchical and linear arrays	Develop word relationships	After reading All texts	Encourages students to compare and contrast words
Preview in context	Use text context to develop word meanings	Before reading All texts	Must have text with good context clues
Contextual redefinition	Use context to determine word meaning	Before reading All texts	Useful when texts do not provide strong context clues
Vocabulary self-collection	Help students learn self-selected words	After reading All texts	Makes students responsible for own vocabulary learning

purpose of the concept of definition procedure is to help students in the middle grades and above gain control of the vocabulary acquisition process by teaching them the type of information that makes up a definition and how to use context clues and background knowledge to increase their understanding of words. This is done by using a word map (see Figure 5.5) that helps students visually depict the elements of a given concept. Each concept is composed of three types of information:

1. Class: *What is it?*
2. Properties that distinguish the concept from others: *What is it like?*
3. Examples of the concept: *What are some examples?*

Figure 5.6 shows a completed word map for the concept *ice cream.*

Procedures.   Schwartz and Raphael (1985) suggest that this strategy can be taught to students in four lessons. The following procedures are adapted from their guidelines.

FIGURE 5.5

BASIC CONCEPT OF THE WORD MAP

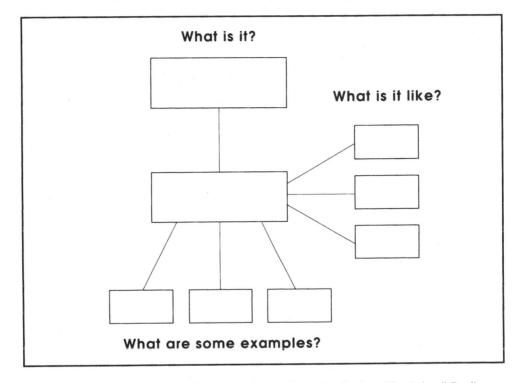

Source: Word map from "Concept of Definition: A Key to Improving Students' Vocabulary," *Reading Teacher,* Robert M. Schwartz and Taffy E. Raphael, November 1985, pp. 198–203. Reprinted with permission of Robert M. Schwartz and the International Reading Association.

Lesson 1

1. Prepare for the lesson by selecting three or more concepts children already know and developing a list of information about each; include class, at least three properties, and at least three examples. Here is a sample list for *ice cream:*

ice cream	
chocolate	frozen
cold	sweet
dessert	peach
strawberry	smooth

2. Begin by discussing the importance of being able to accurately determine word meanings to better comprehend texts. Tell students that the strategy they will

FIGURE 5.6

COMPLETED WORD MAP FOR *ICE CREAM*

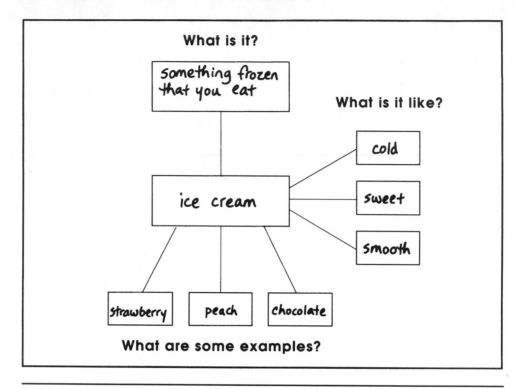

be learning during the next four lessons will help them determine whether or not they really know the meaning of a word.

3. Present students with the structure of a word map (Figure 5.5). Tell them that this map is a picture of the three things that really let us know when we understand a word. Go over each part with them.

4. Using the lists prepared for the three concepts, have students help you complete a word map for two of the concepts.

5. After students have completed the two word maps with you, have them work with a partner to complete the third. Have students share their work and discuss it.

6. Have students select a concept of their own to map, independently or with a partner.

7. Finally, have them write a definition for one of the concepts developed during the lesson. The definition for *ice cream* might be as follows:

> *A dessert that is a frozen, sweet food that you eat. It is cold. Some examples of ice cream are chocolate, strawberry, and peach.*

Lesson 2

1. Prepare for the lesson by locating or writing several sample passages that give complete information about the concepts to be discussed (class, at least three properties, at least three examples). Content textbooks are often a good source for these passages. A sample passage for the concept *flowers* might read as follows:

Flowers

Have you ever thought about plants and how they reproduce? Flowers are the parts of seed-bearing plants that help to make this happen. You may think that flowers are just pretty to look at or nice to smell. But they are important to making more plants. Each flower has special parts. You probably have noticed only the petals. Look more closely. Flowers have other important parts, such as the pistil and the stamen. Look at some of your favorite flowers such as the tulip, rose, or daisy to see if you can find these parts.

2. Present the passages along with the word map. Tell students they are to read each passage and complete the word map.
3. After they have completed the word maps, have students give oral or written definitions for the concepts presented.
4. Once students seem to understand the concept of the word map, tell them it is not necessary to limit properties and examples to three items.

Lesson 3

1. Prepare for this lesson by writing or locating several passages that are less complete in their definitions than those used in lesson 2.
2. Direct students in reading the passages and completing the word maps as they did in lesson 2. If they do not see that the information provided in the passages is incomplete, help them see this by asking such questions as "Does the passage tell you what _____ is like?" or "Does the passage give any examples of _____?"
3. Have students use other sources and their own prior knowledge to complete the word maps.
4. Complete the lesson by guiding students to the conclusion that texts do not always give complete definitions.

Lesson 4

1. Prepare for this lesson by writing or locating several more passages with incomplete contextual information for several concepts. For each concept write incomplete definitions, leaving out one or more parts of the definition developed through the use of the word map. An incomplete definition might read as follows:

A musician is a person who plays an instrument. A musician is very talented.

2. Tell students that the purpose of this lesson is for them to use what they have learned from developing word maps to decide whether some definitions are complete or incomplete.

3. Have students read the passages and evaluate the definitions for their complete-ness. Tell them to write the information that is missing from the definitions.

4. Conclude the lesson by discussing with students how they were able to tell the definitions were incomplete. Discuss how they should use this type of thinking any time they are reading and come to words they don't know.

It may be necessary to repeat one or more of these lessons several times for review purposes before students can use this procedure independently.

When to Use.   Research on the concept of definition procedure has been con-ducted using fourth and eight graders. It appears to work best with students in the intermediate and higher grades and with expository texts. Maria (1990) also re-ports that it is effective with at-risk (hard-to-teach) students in the upper elemen-tary grades. This strategy can be used in four lessons throughout a thematic unit to help students develop the understandings needed to apply the concepts in later units. The four lessons are likely to be more meaningful if they are placed after the reading of selections.

You may also use the word map portion of the lessons as a way to thoroughly develop the meanings of several related words before or after the reading of a selec-tion or at the beginning of a particular theme. For example, if you are beginning a thematic unit on space travel, you might use the word map activity to develop con-cepts such as *astronaut, space shuttle, rocket,* and *pilot.* When developing closely re-lated terms, include questioning such as that used in the rich vocabulary instruction program reported by Beck and her colleagues (Beck, McCaslin, & McKeown, 1980; Beck, McKeown, & Omanson, 1987; Beck, Omanson, & McKeown, 1982). Probe relationships by asking such questions as "Is an astronaut the same as a *pilot*?" and "Do *pilots* fly *rockets*?"

Assessment Value.   You can learn two things about your students as they learn and use this strategy: their ability to determine unknown word meanings and their prior knowledge of the concepts being developed. Schwartz and Raphael (1985) report that students who have been taught this strategy are more aware of what to do to figure out the meaning of a new word. When asked how to do this, students "indicated they would ask themselves questions and think about what they already knew. In contrast, the students without this instruction tended to answer, 'I would look it up'" (pp. 203–204).

You can determine students' knowledge and understanding of the particular concepts being developed through their responses to the structured portions of the lessons and through their answers when they generate their own words for word maps and definitions. If you are using the word map concept to develop related terms, you can tell by the responses students give to your probing questions whether they really understand the terms.

Comments.   The concept of definition procedure is excellent for preparing stu-dents to use the student strategy for independently inferring word meanings (see page 234). By using this procedure, you help students develop a concept of what they must know to understand a word and begin to think about the sources within the text that might help them define a word; that is, this strategy promotes the integration of existing prior knowledge with new knowledge. However, it requires heavy initial teacher support and guidance, and it does not work with all words; for example, it works with nouns but not with verbs.

Since many words have similar properties, Schwartz (1988) has expanded the word map concept to include the idea of comparisons. Figure 5.7 presents one such revised version. The teacher and students place a word similar to the main concept in the comparison box and discuss how this word and the main word have common properties. This procedure helps students become more precise in thinking about the properties they identify for the main concept and also helps them to further integrate knowledge within their schemata. Figure 5.8 shows a completed word map for *desert* using the revised map plan.

Be careful, however, that making word maps does not become the goal of the activity, which *must always remain the development of vocabulary knowledge to improve the construction of meaning* and independence in word learning.

Semantic Mapping

Semantic mapping, discussed in detail in Chapter 3 as an excellent strategy for activating and developing prior knowledge, uses a mapping strategy similar to the word map used in the concept of definition procedure. It can be used before reading and then expanded after reading to integrate students' new knowledge into their prior knowledge.

Semantic mapping is a time-consuming procedure. Therefore, when you use it before reading, you must be certain you have selected key-concept words for the text to be read. It is often better to use it after reading to expand vocabulary and pull together concepts students already possess.

Semantic mapping has many variations and uses; it is a good way to brainstorm for writing (see Chapter 7). For a detailed look at ideas for using semantic mapping, see Heimlich and Pittelman (1986), listed in the For Additional Reading section at the conclusion of this chapter.

Semantic Feature Analysis

Description.   With semantic feature analysis, students develop vocabulary and learn important concepts by looking at how a group of related words differ and how they are alike (Johnson & Pearson, 1984). Figure 5.9 shows how some first-grade students and their teacher set up a semantic feature analysis grid after completing a unit on gardening. They then discussed each word, indicating what they knew about the word in relation to each characteristic. This strategy has been very effective in helping students develop vocabulary and learn to construct meaning (Anders & Bos, 1986).

Procedures.   Use the following procedures to develop semantic feature grids:

1. Select a category or class of words (such as vegetables).
2. List items that fall into this category down the left side of the grid.
3. List features that some of the items have in common across the top of the grid. Sometimes you can ask students to do this.

FIGURE 5.7

BASIC CONCEPT OF DEFINITION MAP—REVISED

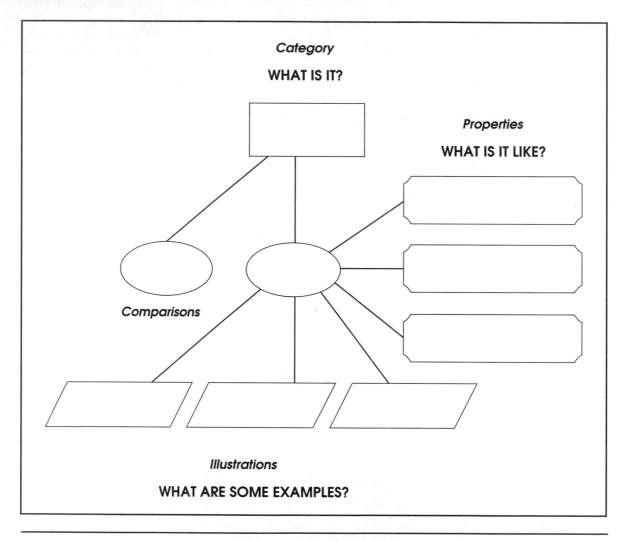

4. Have students put pluses (+), minuses (−), and question marks (?) in the squares of the grid to indicate whether the items in the category have the feature under consideration. Discuss each item, making sure students understand that some items are sometimes characterized by a feature and sometimes are not. For example, for the grid in Figure 5.9, be sure students understand that the tomato can be both green and red but is usually cooked when green.

FIGURE 5.8

COMPLETED WORD MAP FOR *DESERT*

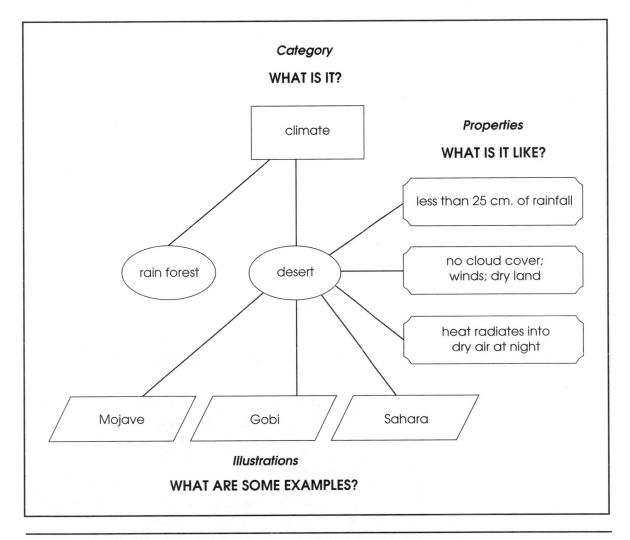

5. Add additional words and features to the grid.
6. Complete the grid and discuss each word.

Repeat the process several times, using different categories and moving from the concrete to the abstract. Encourage students to continuously look for new words to add to the grids. Students can keep grid sheets in folders or notebooks and add to them throughout the year.

FIGURE 5.9

SEMANTIC FEATURE ANALYSIS GRID

VEGETABLES	GREEN	HAVE PEELINGS	EAT RAW	SEEDS
Potatoes	−	+	+	?
Carrots	−	+	+	−
Tomatoes	− +	+	− +	+
Broccoli	+	?	+	−
Squash	+ −	+	+	+
Cabbage	+	−	+	−

After completing a semantic feature grid, students should examine the pattern of pluses and minuses to determine how the words are alike and how they differ. Question marks should serve as a basis for further research to clarify understanding of the words. This strategy will help students expand their vocabularies as well as refine the meanings of words they already know.

When to Use.   Semantic feature analysis may be used before or after reading to develop vocabulary, but it is often more effectively used after reading as a means of expanding vocabulary. It is usually most helpful with expository texts, but may also be used with some narrative texts. Finally, it is an excellent way for students to develop understanding in various content areas.

In addition to developing vocabulary, semantic feature analysis is very effective for reinforcing vocabulary and related concepts in content textbooks (Stieglitz & Stieglitz, 1981). Students at all levels can use it to review chapters before tests or to pull together concepts in concluding a thematic unit. For younger students, semantic feature grids using very simple categories and features can serve as oral language activities.

Assessment Value.   As students develop semantic feature grids, you will be able to assess their prior knowledge in relation to the categories and words being discussed. Students' responses will help you assess their understandings of word relationships as well as their thinking abilities.

FIGURE 5.10

BLANK VENN DIAGRAM

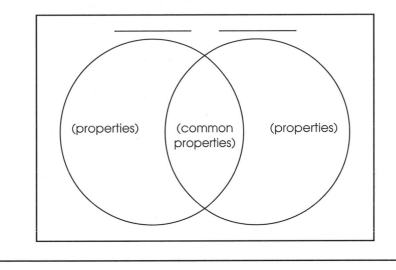

Comments.   Semantic feature analysis is one of the strategies that concentrates on helping students build relationships among concepts. Although both concept of definition procedure and semantic mapping also do this, they are not as effective. The strength of semantic feature analysis comes when students are actively involved in constructing the grids and discussing them. This, along with cooperative learning, is an excellent way to foster active participation in the process of learning.

Nagy (1988) suggests that the Venn diagram is another way to apply semantic feature analysis in the classroom. Figure 5.10 presents a blank Venn diagram. In these diagrams, two things are compared, the properties of each item are listed along the sides of the circles, and the properties common to both are listed in the intersection. For in-depth reading on semantic feature analysis, see Pittelman, Heimlich, Berglund, and French (1991) in the For Additional Reading section.

Hierarchical and Linear Arrays

Description.   Words sometimes have hierarchical relationships, for example, the names of scientific organisms (Nagy, 1988). A hierarchical array such as that in Figure 5.11 can help students understand these relationships. The exact structure of the array will depend on the concepts being analyzed.

At other times, words have a linear relationship, for example, *good, better, best; tepid, hot, scalding.* A linear array such as the one in Figure 5.12 shows this relationship.

The use of hierarchical and linear arrays helps students learn to think independently about word relationships and develop concepts.

FIGURE 5.11

HIERARCHICAL ARRAY

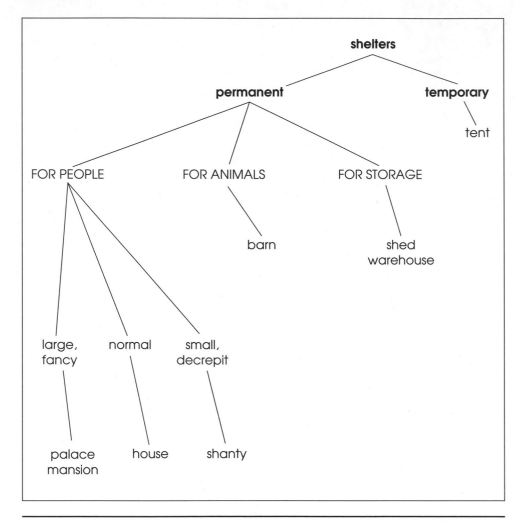

Procedures.   Use the following procedures to develop hierarchical or linear arrays with students:

1. Select a concept or group of words from literature or from students' writing for study.
2. Begin by showing students the type of array they will construct.
3. Guide students in constructing the array. Discuss the relationship among the words as the array is developed.

FIGURE 5.12

LINEAR ARRAY

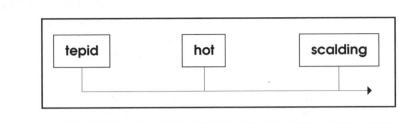

After students have had considerable experience with arrays, they can select the words for study and decide on the type of array they will use.

When to Use.   Arrays are best used after reading to help students expand their vocabularies. The visual aspect of arrays can help at-risk learners or second-language learners see the relationships among words more concretely. You can also use arrays to activate students' prior knowledge; for example, if students are going to study the places where people live, you can begin with the basic framework of the array presented in Figure 5.11 and ask students to generate the information. As the unit progresses, students can add to or change the array.

Assessment Value.   Students' responses during the development of arrays will help you assess their prior knowledge and their ability to develop relationships.

Comments.   The value of arrays is that they encourage students to compare and contrast words. Blachowicz (1986) suggests several variations called *semantic gradients* and *concept ladders*. Another variation of the hierarchial array is the "thinking tree." For a detailed discussion, see Nagy (1988) in the For Additional Reading section.

Preview in Context

Description.   The preview in context strategy, developed by Readence, Bean, and Baldwin (1981, 1985, 1989), does just what the title says: it previews words in context. With this strategy, the teacher guides students to use the context and their prior knowledge to determine the meanings of a selected set of words.

Procedures.   Use the following four steps for this strategy:

1. *Prepare.* Select the words to be taught following the procedures suggested earlier in this chapter (see Figure 5.4 on page 240). These must be key-concept words, and *you should teach no more than two or three.* Identify passages within

the text that contain strong context clues for the word. For example, we will focus on teaching *decay* and use the following passage from *Mummies, Tombs, and Treasure* (Perl, 1987):

> *Without preservation, dead animal matter usually decays very quickly. This is true of plant matter, too. A dead bird or cat, a piece of rotting fruit, can show the stages of decay. Decay is caused by bacteria.* (p. 2)

2. *Establish the context.* Present the word and the context to students; read aloud the passage as students follow along. Then have students reread it silently.

3. *Specify the word meaning.* Now lead students toward a definition of the word under study. By asking them questions, you encourage them to use their prior knowledge and clues in the text to arrive at a meaning for the word. An example of this type of questioning follows:

Teacher: What does this text tell you about the word decay?

Student: That dead animals decay.

Teacher: What happens to them when they decay?

Student: They rot.

Teacher: How could you tell from this text that *decay* means "to rot"?

Student: By what it says about rotting fruit.

4. *Expand the word meaning.* After students have a basic understanding of the word, try to deepen their understanding by discussing synonyms, antonyms, other contexts or other examples where the word might be used. The purpose of these activities is to expand students' knowledge of the word. If students have access to a dictionary or a thesaurus, they can use them. The discussion might go as follows:

Teacher: Can you think of other things that decay?

Student: Teeth. I get cavities sometimes.

Teacher: How do we prevent decay?

Student: Put something on things that keep them from decaying.

Teacher: Like what?

Student: Fluoride keeps your teeth from decaying.

Teacher: What about dead things? How do we keep them from decaying?

Student: You embalm dead people.

Teacher: So the fluid used for embalming preserves things or keeps them from decaying. Can you think of words that mean the same thing as *decay*?

Student 1: Rot.

Student 2: Spoil.

After you teach the words, encourage students to place them in their word banks or notebooks.

When to Use.   Use preview in context before reading, but *only* when the context for the word is strong. It is appropriate for all students at all grade levels but not for students who have limited prior knowledge.

Assessment Value.   As students respond in the discussions, you will be able to assess the extent of their prior knowledge and their ability to use context clues.

Comments.   The preview in context strategy is simple and easy to use. However, it is often difficult to identify contexts that contain enough clues to help students infer word meanings. Nagy (1988) points out that "context may look quite helpful if one already knows what the word means, but it seldom supplies adequate information for the person who has no other knowledge about the meaning of the word" (p. 7).

The strength of this strategy comes through the intensive discussion between the teacher and students, which deepens students' understanding. Therefore, it is important to skillfully direct the discussion with your students.

Contextual Redefinition

Description.   Since texts frequently do not provide sufficient context for students to determine the meaning of an unknown word (Schatz & Baldwin, 1986), contextual redefinition helps students use context more effectively by presenting them with *sufficient context* before reading and showing them how to use the clues to *make informed guesses* about a word's meaning (Cunningham, Cunningham, & Arthur, 1981).

Procedures.   The following five-step procedure for using contextual redefinition is adapted from Tierney, Readence, and Dishner (1990):

1. *Select unfamiliar words.* Using the procedures suggested earlier in this chapter, select two or three words to preteach. This example will use *hippophagy* and *carapace.*
2. *Write a sentence.* Write one or more sentences that provide sufficient clues to teach the meaning of the word. Try to use different types of context clues, such as direct definition, synonyms, and comparison/contrast. If the text has sufficient context clues for the word in question, use it. Here are two sample sentences:

   > The drought had been so long and severe that the cattle had died. Only the horses survived. Yet the natives were so hungry that they had to resort to *hippophagy* to avoid starvation.

   > Without its *carapace,* a turtle has no protection and is subject to certain death from its enemies or the elements.

3. *Present the words in isolation.* Using the chalkboard or overhead projector, present the words in isolation and ask students to pronounce the words, or pronounce the words for them. Then encourage students to provide a definition for each word. Wild guesses may occur; this is part of the learning process. Encourage students to come to a consensus about the meaning of each word.

4. *Present the words in context.* Using the contexts prepared for the lesson, present each word and have students read the contexts aloud, or read the contexts for them. As students discuss each word, have them come to a consensus about its meaning. Encourage guessing from the clues; in this way, at-risk students are able to participate. To help students become more attuned to the value of context, ask them to discuss the differences between trying to define the words in context and in isolation.

5. *Use a dictionary for verification.* Discuss the dictionary definition and compare it to the one developed by the students.

When to Use.   Use the contextual redefinition strategy to teach totally *new* words before reading. It is appropriate for all students who possess some skill in using the dictionary and is especially useful when the text does not provide context that will help students infer the meanings of the words selected for preteaching. Students who are having difficulty learning to construct meaning and second-language learners may profit from this strategy.

Assessment Value.   You can assess students' prior knowledge from their responses in guessing definitions in isolation and in context. The use of the context samples will let you know how well students are able to use context. Finally, dictionary verification will give you opportunities to see how effectively students use the dictionary.

Comments.   Many questions have been raised about the value of using context sentences to teach vocabulary, as we noted in the discussion of the preview in context strategy (Nagy, 1988). However, when the words to be pretaught are *carefully selected, kept to a minimum of two or three,* and *thoroughly taught,* preteaching to improve comprehension may have value (Tierney & Cunningham, 1984; Wixson, 1986). The keys to effectively using preview in context and contextual redefinition are careful word selection and thorough discussion of the words. Also, remember that students need repeated encounters with the words through reading and writing to develop ownership of them.

Vocabulary Self-Collection

Description.   Vocabulary self-collection places the responsibility for learning words on the students (Haggard, 1982, 1986). After a reading experience, students select a word they think the entire class should study. They are also encouraged to select additional words for their own personal study. This strategy has the advantages of being interactive and being based on authentic reading experiences.

Procedures.   The following procedures are based on Haggard's suggestions (1986):

1. *Select words for study.* After students have read a story or an informational text, ask them to review it and select one word for class study. They may do this as individuals, partners, or teams. You should also select one word for study so that you, the teacher, are an active learning partner and gain some

influence in the process. Encourage students to select words that seem important or interesting.

2. *Compile and define the words.* Ask each student or group to give the word selected for study and the definition (determined from context) of the word. List each word and the definition on the chalkboard or overhead; include your word as well. Use the dictionary to verify or complete definitions as needed, and encourage all students to participate in this process. With the students, agree on a final list of words and definitions.

3. *Finalize the list.* With the students, review the list to eliminate duplications, words that seem unrelated to the story or topic of study, and words that students simply do not want to study. Agree on a reasonable number (three to five) for the final list, and have students put the words and definitions in their vocabulary notebooks or journals. Some may choose to record words eliminated from the class list in their personal lists. When they write the words in their journals, ask them to write a sentence demonstrating the use of the word in their own lives or showing their understanding of it.

4. *Use and extend the words.* Encourage students to use the words in their writing and to look for them in other books they read. Plan activities that reinforce the words, such as semantic maps, semantic feature analysis, and arrays.

These procedures are based on the concept of vocabulary development after reading, but you can adapt them for use before reading by having students preview the text and select for study words that they think will be important.

When to Use.   You may use this strategy with both narrative and expository texts and with all students at any grade level. When students do not have sufficient skill to use the dictionary, you will need to provide the definitions.

Assessment Value.   This strategy gives you many opportunities to assess students' word knowledge. When students select words for study and give definitions from context, you can assess their use of context clues. As they participate in expanding definitions given by other students, you can determine the extent of their prior knowledge.

Comments.   Vocabulary self-collection has many appealing features: it is easy to implement, interactive, based on authentic reading experiences, and very versatile.

Vocabulary self-collection lends itself to the concept that children learn to read and write by reading and writing. By selecting their own words, students become active participants in their own process of learning and also learn to see the classroom as a community of learners. Some teachers may worry that students will not select important words, but remember that when the teacher participates in the process, students and teacher become partners in learning. Moreover, there is no guarantee that students will learn words the teacher selects any more readily than they will learn self-selected words. This strategy respects the students as learners and incorporates all of the ideas about authentic learning that are stressed throughout this text.

The seven strategies for developing vocabulary just discussed help students become independent vocabulary learners and constructors of meaning. All of these strategies require continual integration of new knowledge with old knowledge. Of course, no one strategy alone can meet the needs of all students and all learning situations, and *no one strategy or combination of strategies is as powerful for developing vocabulary as are wide reading and extensive writing.* Nevertheless, when used *judiciously* in combination with wide reading and extensive writing, these strategies should give students the experiences they need to develop strong vocabularies and improve their meaning construction.

■ Structural Analysis as an Aid to Independence

Recall that the goal of vocabulary development is for students to achieve independence in word learning because the number of words to be learned is too large for them to be taught individually. As was suggested, the way to achieve this independence is to make students aware of words and help them develop a strategy for independently inferring word meanings. One thing students are encouraged to do when using this strategy is to look for structural elements within the word that might help them determine its meaning. However, keep in mind that the teaching of structural elements is of limited value and should be done only under certain circumstances.

As stated throughout this text, students learn skills such as the use of structural elements through reading and writing. As they go through this process, they often require the teacher's support. You may provide this support through direct vocabulary teaching strategies or through minilessons that go back to the students' reading or writing material to focus directly or incidentally on a particular skill, such as structural analysis.

Structural analysis is the study of meaningful word parts. It may help students as they learn to recognize words (pronunciation) and as they determine the meanings of words. The following elements are usually considered part of structural analysis:

▸ *Base words:* Meaningful linguistic units that can stand alone and contain no smaller meaningful parts; also called *free morphemes* (re*sell: sell* is the base word).

▸ *Root words:* Words from which other words are derived; usually the derivational word is from another language and is a bound morpheme; that is, it cannot stand alone (*scribble* comes from the Latin root *scribere,* meaning "to write"). Teachers frequently use the terms *base word* and *root word* synonymously, but they are not the same.

▸ *Prefixes:* Units of meaning that can be added to the beginnings of base words or root words to change their meanings; these are bound morphemes and cannot stand alone (*un*happy: *un* is the prefix meaning "not").

▸ *Suffixes:* Units of meaning that can be added to the ends of base or root words to change their meanings; these are bound morphemes (tear*ful: ful* is the suffix meaning "full of ").

▸ *Inflectional endings:* Word parts that can be added to the ends of root or base words to change their case, gender, number, tense, or form; these are bound morphemes (boy*'s*: possessive case; steward*ess*: gender; tree*s*: number; walk*ed*: tense; funni*est*: form). Sometimes inflectional endings are called *suffixes.*

▶ **Compound words:** Two or more base words that have been combined to form a new word with a meaning that is related to each base word (*run + way = runway*).

▶ **Contractions:** Shortened forms of two words in which a letter or letters have been replaced by an apostrophe (*do + not = don't; there + is = there's*).

Students will become familiar with compound words and contractions through their reading and writing experiences, and for most students simply showing them what these are as reading and writing take place is usually sufficient. In some instances, however, students may need more directed support using the minilesson, as discussed in Chapter 2; but even when this is required, the lesson *always goes back to the literature* to help students see how the compound or contraction was used in context. For example, if your students have just completed reading *Aunt Flossie's Hats (and Crab Cakes Later)* (Howard, 1991) and you noticed they were having trouble figuring out compound words or contractions, you can use this story as the basis for a minilesson involving the following simple steps:

1. Go back to the story (revisit it) to identify a compound word or contraction. Read the section containing it aloud to students as they follow along. Ask them if they notice anything special about the compound word or contraction.
2. Define *compound* or *contraction*. Point out another example; then point out words that are not examples.
3. Direct students to read a page containing another example. Ask them to find the compound word or contraction.
4. Make a chart of other examples that students are able to find.
5. Conclude the lesson by discussing with students how they should use this new knowledge in reading and writing.
6. As students read and write, you may need to do periodic reviews.

Aunt Flossie's Hats (and Crab Cakes Later) is particularly good for this experience because it contains numerous examples of both compounds and contractions such as *afternoons, hatboxes, here's, she's,* and so forth.

Knowledge of the remaining elements of structural analysis also develops through reading and writing. The addition of prefixes and suffixes to words accounts for a large number of words for students in grade 4 and above (Nagy & Anderson, 1984). However, the prefixes and suffixes encountered have variant meanings, which makes it difficult for students to see a pattern (Graves, 1987). If you have to provide a minilesson, it is important to know which prefixes and suffixes to focus on and how to construct your lesson (for guidelines, see Graves, 1987; Nagy & Anderson, 1984; White, Sowell, & Yanagihara, 1989).

White, Sowell, and Yanagihara (1989) determined, on the basis of frequency of occurrence, that there are nine prefixes and ten suffixes of sufficient use to students to merit instruction (see Table 5.3). They also determined that knowing the prefixes listed would account for 76 percent of prefixed words and knowing the suffixes would account for 85 percent of suffixed words. Graves (1987) reported that knowing just four prefixes (*un-, in-*[not], *dis-, non-*) would account for nearly 50 percent of all prefixed words. Therefore, in planning minilesson support focusing on word parts, you should give greatest attention to the nine prefixes and ten suffixes listed in Table 5.3.

TABLE 5.3

Prefixes and Suffixes That Merit Instruction

PREFIXES		SUFFIXES	
[a]*un-*	Meaning "not":		Plural:
dis-	*unhappy*	*-s, -es*	*girls*
[a]*in-, im-*	*disrespectful*		Tense:
[a]*non-*	*inactive*		*jumps*
ir-	*impossible*	*-ed*	Tense:
	nonresistent		*jumped*
	irresponsible	*-ing*	Tense:
re-	Meaning "back" or "again":		*jumping*
	revisit		
[a]*un-*	Meaning "do the opposite of":	*-ly*	Meaning "like":
dis-	*untie*		*sisterly*
	disassemble	*-er, -or*	Meaning "one who performs
in-, im-	Meaning "in" or "into":		a specialized action":
	indoors		*swimmer;*
en-, em-	Meaning "into" or "within":		Used to form comparative
	entangle		degree with adjectives:
over-	Meaning "too much":		*darker*
	overdose	*-tion*	Meaning "action":
mis-	Meaning "wrong":	*-ion*	*absorption*
	misspell	*-ation*	
		-ition	
		-able	Meaning "susceptible," "capable,"
		-ible	"worth":
			debatable
		-al, -ial	Meaning "of" or "relating to":
			parental
		-y	Meaning "consisting of" or
			"inclined toward":
			sleepy
		-ness	Meaning "state," "quality,"
			"condition," or "degree":
			brightness

[a]Accounts for nearly 50 percent of all prefixed words (Graves, 1987).

Source: Based on White, Sowell, and Yanagihara (1989).

In addition to knowing which prefixes and suffixes are the most beneficial for students, you must be aware of some of the pitfalls of using prefixes as an aid to word meaning (White et al., 1989):

1. Prefixes are not consistent in their meanings; for example, *un-, dis-, re-,* and *in-* each have two meanings.

2. False analysis with prefixes often occurs. For example, removing *in* from *intrigue* leaves no recognizable base word. The prefixes *re-, in-,* and *dis-* have a particularly high risk of false analysis.

3. Looking only at word parts may mislead the reader in determining the word's true meaning. For example, *unassuming* means "modest" instead of "not supposing."

If you are aware of these possible pitfalls and know how often the affixes occur, you can plan minilessons that will help students who demonstrate the need for such support. The suggestions that follow are adapted from White et al. (1989).

Minilessons Using Prefixes

This section presents six lessons that you would teach following experiences with literature that provide examples of prefixes.

▶ *Lesson 1:* Define and teach the concept of a prefix. Create a chart such as the following:

Prefix

1. – A group of letters that go in front of a word (*un-*)
2. – Changes the meaning of a word (*kind – unkind*)
3. – When you peel it off, a word must be left. (*unkind*)

Use examples and nonexamples to teach point 3 (*unkind,* example; *uncle,* nonexample).

▶ *Lesson 2:* Negative meanings of *un-* and *dis-.* Prepare sentences containing prefixed words. Because many prefixed words also have suffixes, use familiar base words containing suffixes as well as prefixes. Have students read the sentence and look for a prefixed word; then have them "peel off" the prefix, looking for the base word. The following sample sentence could be used:

John didn't come home when he was told; he disobeyed his father.

The lesson dialogue might go as follows:

Teacher: What does *obey* mean?

(*Students reply.*)

Teacher: So what does *dis-* mean here?

(*Students reply.*)

Teacher: And *disobeyed* means what?

(*Students reply.*)

Teacher: Does this make sense?

(*Students reply.*)

Teacher: You should always check to see that the meaning makes sense.

(*Students reply.*)

Teacher: Now let's look at a word where *dis-* is not a prefix. *Discuss*—there is no base word here when we take off *dis-*. When we check the dictionary, we find that *discuss* comes from a Latin word, *discussus*.

▶ Sentences for the lessons can be written by the teacher or taken from literature students have read. After each lesson, remind and encourage students to use their knowledge about prefixes to determine the meanings of unknown words as they use the strategy for inferring word meanings. The remaining four lessons follow this pattern and focus on the following prefixes.

▶ *Lesson 3:* Prefixes *in-, im-, ir-,* and *non-,* meaning "not."

▶ *Lesson 4:* Prefix *re-,* meaning "again" or "back."

▶ *Lesson 5:* Alternative meanings of *un-, dis-, in-,* and *im-.*

▶ *Lesson 6:* Prefixes *en-, em-, over-,* and *mis-.*

Minilessons Using Suffixes

Suffixes (and inflectional endings) tend to have abstract meanings. Therefore, instruction should focus on removing the suffix and identifying the base word. The following lessons are recommended:

▶ *Lesson 1:* Teach the concept of suffixes (and inflectional endings) as was done in lesson 1 on prefixes.

▶ *Lesson 2:* Teach *-s/es, -ed,* and *-ing* with no spelling changes. Show students the suffixed word, and have them identify the suffix and define the base word (examples: *boxes, talking, lasted*).

▶ *Lessons 3–5:* Focus on three major spelling changes that occur using suffixes:

Consonant doubling: *begged, thinner, funny*

Change from *y* to *i: flies, worried, reliable*

Deleted silent *e: saved, rider, believable*

Follow the same pattern as suggested for lesson 2, but discuss the spelling change that has occurred. The suffixes used should be drawn from the list suggested in Table 5.3.

▶ *Lesson 6:* Suffixes that change the part of speech: *-ly, -er, -ion, -able, -al, -y,* and *-ness.* Again, follow the same pattern used with the other lessons. More than one lesson might be needed for this category of suffixes.

The exact grade levels for teaching prefixes and suffixes really depends on students' needs. However, it is recommended that the first three prefix lessons and the first five suffix lessons be completed by the end of grade 4. All instruction should be completed by the end of grade 5.

White et al. (1989) report favorable results with students who were taught lessons similar to those just described. They stress that "the goal of prefix and suffix instruction is *use* of word-part clues to derive the meaning of unfamiliar words" (p. 307). They believe that even in a literature-centered classroom, a "reasonable" amount of direct teaching helps students learn to use an independent strategy for inferring word meanings.

The Dictionary and Thesaurus as Aids to Independence

Two final areas of knowledge students must have to use the strategy for independently inferring word meanings and achieving independence in vocabulary learning are using the dictionary and using the thesaurus (Graves, 1987). The dictionary is an aid for reading, writing, and spelling; the thesaurus is more valuable for writing.

Using a Dictionary

The dictionary is an invaluable tool for determining both the pronunciations and meanings of words. It is especially useful when students have tried all other skills and still have not determined the meaning or pronunciation of an unknown word. Unfortunately, students are often turned off by the way they are exposed to the dictionary. Therefore, keep the following "don'ts" in mind:

▶ *Don't* give students lists of isolated words to look up and define. Words out of context have no meaning, and students will not know which definition to select. Furthermore, this type of activity becomes boring and is not good instruction.

▶ *Don't* use the dictionary as a means of punishment. Too many teachers turn to the dictionary to "punish" students by having them copy pages. Who would ever want to see a dictionary again after that?

▶ *Don't* require that every word on each week's spelling list be looked up in the dictionary and defined. This becomes a deadly, useless activity.

▶ *Don't* teach phonetic respelling except in relation to determining the pronunciations of words in the dictionary.

The "don'ts" for teaching use of the dictionary can be balanced with some very important and positive "do's":

TABLE 5.4

SEQUENCE FOR TEACHING USE OF THE DICTIONARY

1. Use picture dictionaries to introduce the concept of the dictionary in kindergarten and first grade. Have students learn to locate words in the dictionaries, and teach them to make picture dictionaries of their own.
2. As soon as students have some knowledge of the alphabet, teach them how words are arranged in the dictionary. Give them practice in locating words.
3. Show students how words in the first half of the alphabet fall in the first half of the dictionary and words in the second half fall in the second half. Point out how this knowledge can help students save time by eliminating the need to sift through lots of extra pages.
4. Introduce the concept of phonetic respelling in relation to the pronunciation key, and show students how this key can help them figure out pronunciations.
5. Teach students to locate the meanings of words by using guide words; point out that the dictionary lists more than one meaning for some words.
6. Finish teaching students how to locate words alphabetically, showing them how words are alphabetized not just through the first letter but also through the second, third, fourth, and subsequent letters.
7. Have students learn to select the correct dictionary definitions for multiple-meaning words that are presented in written context.
8. Teach the special symbols used in dictionaries, such as *n* for noun, *v* for verb, and *sing.* for singular.
9. Show students all the other types of information they can find in the dictionary, including lists of synonyms, an atlas, and geographic listings.
10. Provide students with experiences using many different dictionaries and glossaries.

▶ *Do* let students know that you, the teacher, often turn to the dictionary to check the spellings, pronunciations, and meanings of words.
▶ *Do* teach students how to use a dictionary.
▶ *Do* show students how to make use of a dictionary in their reading and writing.
▶ *Do* show students how to use a dictionary in all content areas.

Dictionary use must be taught in a manner that will leave students with positive attitudes. The teaching should begin in kindergarten and proceed through the primary grades until students know and understand the components of the dictionary and can use them effectively. The sequence in Table 5.4 should guide the use of the dictionary, which should be developed through meaningful experiences, not isolated skill lessons.

Once students have learned the basics of using the dictionary, it can become a part of their strategy for independently inferring word meanings.

Using a Thesaurus

A thesaurus such as *Roget's Thesaurus* (1965) is a dictionary of synonyms and antonyms and is very useful for helping readers and writers locate synonyms and antonyms as well as subtle shades of meaning for words. Teachers can introduce elementary-grade students to the thesaurus with *Words to Use: A Junior Thesaurus* (Drysdale, 1971).

It is much easier to learn to use a thesaurus than a dictionary. Once students know how to alphabetize and have learned the concepts of synonyms and antonyms, the rest is quite easy. They must be taught how the thesaurus is organized, how to locate a word, and how to read the synonym or antonym entries. Show students how writers use the thesaurus to locate words they want to change in their writing to avoid repetition.

After students have learned to use the thesaurus, encourage them to use it as a means of improving their writing. One very effective way to do this is through mini-lessons during the writing workshop in which you demonstrate the use of the thesaurus in a group-written story. Again, students learn best by simply *writing*.

Literacy Lesson

The Bicycle Man

This lesson illustrates the concepts of vocabulary development using a delightful book, *The Bicycle Man* (Say, 1982). You will see how words were selected for direct teaching and how the decisions were made about when and how to teach vocabulary. The plan uses the literacy lesson concept presented in Chapter 2.

Before Reading the Plan
1. **Think about what you have learned about vocabulary development from this chapter. Review any portions that you may have forgotten or that may have been unclear.**
2. **Recall the parts of the literacy lesson plan. (See Chapter 2 if you need review.)**
3. **Read *The Bicycle Man* (Say, 1982).**
4. **Read and study the Teacher Preparation section to see the decision making involved in planning the vocabulary activities for this book.**

While Reading the Plan
1. **Notice how vocabulary is developed throughout the plan and how the emphasis is on helping students achieve independence in vocabulary learning.**
2. **Think about why these particular procedures and strategies are used. Consider other strategies you might have chosen.**

THE BICYCLE MAN
by Allen Say

When I was a small boy I went to a school in the south island of Japan. The schoolhouse stood halfway up a tall green mountain. It was made of wood and the wood was gray with age. When a strong wind blew, the trees made the sound of waves and the building creaked like an old sailing ship. From the playground we could see the town, the harbor, the shining sea.

One fine spring day we had our sportsday. All the children and teachers were out in the playground long before the first bell rang.

"Did everybody remember to bring a headband?" asked Mrs. Morita. She was our first-grade teacher. Eagerly we showed her our headbands. They were red on one side and white on the other. "Remember, we're on the red team," she told us.

We swept the playground with all the brooms in the school. We tied colored flags and streamers to bamboo poles. We drew white lines on the ground with powdered chalk.

Our parents came carrying tiered lunch boxes and kettles filled with tea. They spread their straw mats and sat around the oval track.

When everything was ready Mrs. Morita rang the bell. It was nine o'clock. The principal stood on the platform and said, "Parents, children, my fellow teachers, let us remember that we are gathered here in the spirit of sportsmanship. Whether we win or lose, let us enjoy ourselves."

We cheered and clapped our hands.

The youngest children were the first to race. We lined up six at a time at the starting line.

"Ready, set, go!" Mr. Oka, the art teacher, boomed at us. We first graders leaped out and dashed around the track. Parents and teachers ran alongside of us, yelling encouragement. The older children waved flags and headbands and shouted at the top of their lungs until the mountain echoed the noise like rumbling thunder.

The winners went up to the judges' table and received prizes from the principal. The prizes were wrapped in white paper and tied with gold threads. Inside, there were oranges and rice cakes and pencils.

By the time the sixth graders finished running it was lunchtime. And that was the best part of the sportsday. My mother had cooked for two days preparing the good things to eat. The layers of lacquered boxes held pickled melon rinds and egg rolls, spiced rice and fish cakes. There were apples and peaches and sweets of all sorts.

teachers paired up and tied their ankles together with headbands and hopped around the oval. We screamed with delight when they stumbled and fell on top of one another.

We were cheering Mrs. Morita and someone's father when a hush fell on the playground. We stopped moving and talking and stared toward the gate.

In the afternoon we had the tug of war and piggyback races. After that the grown-ups had a race of their own. Parents and

Two strangers were leaning over the fence and watching us. They were American soldiers. One of them was a white man with bright hair like fire, and the other man had a face as black as the earth. They wore dark uniforms with neckties, soft caps on their heads, and red stripes on their sleeves. They had no guns.

"Look how black he is!"

"Look at the red hair!" we whispered.

The war had been over for only a short while, not even one year. American soldiers had a base in the harbor but we had never seen them in our mountain. I felt afraid.

The foreigners smiled and waved at us. When the black man cleared the fence and came toward us we all drew back and stared. He was the tallest man I had ever seen. And his clothes! Such sharp creases! And his shoes shone like polished metal.

The soldier walked in huge strides toward the school entrance where the principal's bicycle stood. He pointed at the bicycle and turned to the judges' table. The principal stood up slowly.

"He wants the bicycle," someone said.

"Maybe he doesn't know what it is."

"No, he wants to ride it."

The principal walked up to the American and bowed. He looked like a small boy greeting a giant. The tall man gave a deep bow, almost bumping heads with the principal. We started to giggle.

We watched them talk to each other with their hands. The principal pointed at the bicycle, then at the man, and nodded. Yes, you are welcome to ride my bicycle, he seemed to say. The soldier put the palms of his hands together and smiled.

The man took the bicycle by the handlebar, kicked up the stand, and rolled it out to the center of the playground. He motioned to us to make room, and then called his friend.

The other American was nearly as tall as the black man. He took off his cap and saluted us with a big bow. We giggled and bowed back. The strangers spoke to each other and nodded.

Suddenly the rider yanked on the handlebar and lifted the front wheel off the ground.

"Oh, look!" we stirred.

"How can he ride like that?"

"What an athlete!" said the art teacher.

The black man took off his jacket and handed it to the white man. Then he hoisted a long leg over the bicycle and began to pedal it round and round in a widening circle. His friend waved the jacket like a flag and cheered him to go faster.

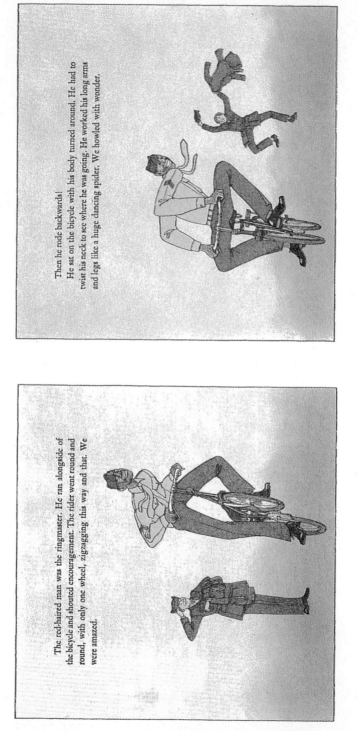

The man rode backwards, then forwards, twirling the front wheel like a spinning gyroscope. He shouted something to the ringmaster who grasped the carrier and began to push as fast as

he could. Then he let go.

The bicycle shot forward with great speed. The rider stood up on the pedals and, leaning on the handlebar, put both his feet up

on the carrier! He was in the air. His cap flew off and his necktie fluttered in the wind. He seemed to be flying free, cruising like an enormous dragonfly. "Oh, oh!" we exclaimed and gasped in turn.

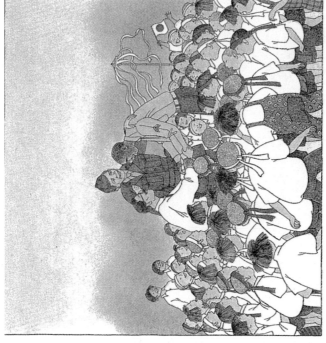

When the bicycle finally came to a stop the playground roared with wild clapping of hands and shouting. The rider panted, heaving and laughing. The ringmaster rushed up to him and lifted him in a bear hug. We mobbed around them, jumping and yelling.

The principal struggled through the crowd and the black man reached out to him. They gripped each other's arms like old friends.

The principal raised his arms to quiet us down. He took the soldiers' hands and led them to the platform. There he whispered something to Mrs. Morita and she brought him the largest box from the prize table.

The principal stood on the platform and held out the box to the Americans. He looked like the emperor awarding a great champion.

The bicycle rider received the gift with both hands and lifted it high above his head. Then he turned to the crowd.

"Ari-ga-tow, ari-ga-tow," he said. "Thank you, thank you." The whole school bowed to him, and shouted for joy.

The Americans put their caps on and walked out the gate with their prize. They went down the mountain, arm in arm, waving and laughing. We followed them with our eyes, until they disappeared around the bend in the road.

Literacy Lesson continued

Teacher Preparation

The literacy lesson for *The Bicycle Man* was developed for a class of third graders who were making good progress in developing their literacy. They often had difficulty with comprehension but were beginning to develop more independence. This book was one that I wanted the entire class to experience. A great deal of independent reading and self-initiated writing went on in this class, and the students' vocabularies were expanding because of the extensive reading and writing and the emphasis on vocabulary. My preparation for this lesson proceeded as follows:

1. I read *The Bicycle Man* and wrote out a rough story map for it:
   - *Setting:* Japanese school after World War II.
   - *Characters:* Main—person telling the story (I), the principal, Mrs. Morita (teacher), red-headed soldier, black soldier. Secondary—Mr. Oka (art teacher).
   - *Problem:* Japanese people are afraid of the American soldiers (inferred, p. 17).
   - *Action:* (1) Students prepare the school grounds for a sportsday. (2) Parents arrive with lunch boxes and kettles of food. (3) Principal, Mr. Morita, begins sportsday with a speech about sportsmanship. (4) Children have races and prizes are given to winners. (5) Children and parents have lunch. (6) Games after lunch include parents and teachers; everyone is having fun. (7) Two soldiers arrive; one has red hair and the other soldier is black. (8) Soldiers seem very tall to children; children and adults are frightened of soldiers. (9) Black soldier wants to ride principal's bike. (10) Black soldier does tricks on bicycle and delights everyone. (11) Principal awards black soldier biggest prize.
   - *Outcome:* Everyone seems less afraid of American soldiers.
   - *Theme:* Getting to know someone helps in understanding them.

2. Next, I reviewed the story with the story map in mind to identify the key-concept words. (See page 239 for a discussion of selecting words for direct teaching.) I concluded that five words were directly related to understanding the story: *sportsday, sportsmanship, foreigners, emperor,* and *champion.*

3. I then thought about these words in relation to the text and the students for whom I was preparing the lesson. I concluded that most of these students would know *emperor* because we had read *The Emperor's New Clothes* (Andersen, 1983) and champion because of all the emphasis our district places on football and basketball champions. *Sportsday* and *sportsmanship* are words children can figure out easily if they don't know them; they can use the context, their knowledge of compound words and suffixes, and their own prior knowledge. I decided that *foreigners* was the only word that needed to be developed before reading.

4. I decided to use three strategies throughout this lesson:
   - *Semantic mapping* for teaching foreigners. This strategy would help activate prior knowledge and integrate vocabulary teaching with that process (see page 249).
   - *Preview and predict* for weaving together vocabulary teaching with prior knowledge activation and purpose setting. This would work well with the preview in context strategy.
   - *Vocabulary self-collection strategy* (see page 258) for extending vocabulary after reading.

5. Finally, I decided to give students two choices for their mode of reading (see Chapter 2): cooperative and independent. I selected these two modes because some students need the support they can get from a partner and others prefer to read independently. I would be free to move around the class to offer individual support as needed, and I would begin by reading aloud a portion of the story.

Literacy
Lesson
continued

Introducing *The Bicycle Man*

ACTIVITY	PROCEDURE	NOTES
Previewing the story	1. Have students get into small groups to preview the story to see what they think it will be about. 2. Discuss group responses with the whole class.	Affords an opportunity to assess students' prior knowledge and see if they need other vocabulary and background.
Semantic mapping for foreigners	1. Place the word *foreigners* on the chalkboard. Tell students *The Bicycle Man* is about foreigners, and ask them to work with a partner to brainstorm all the words they can think of related to *foreigners*. If they don't know any examples, make some suggestions and have them use the dictionary. 2. List student responses on the board, and guide students in grouping the words and constructing the semantic map. 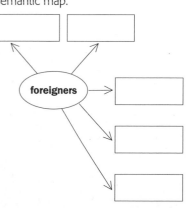 3. During discussion, stress that people are often afraid of people or things they don't know.	Activates prior knowledge and develops a key-concept word at the same time. (See Chapter 3 and page 249 for a discussion of semantic mapping.)

Literacy
Lesson
continued

ACTIVITY	PROCEDURE	NOTES
Making predictions: using preview and predict	1. Ask students to predict what they think will happen in this story.	Flows naturally from all activities that have been done.
	2. Refer students to the preview and predict poster, if needed.	See Chapter 3, page 106
	3. Have students record predictions in their journals.	Sets purpose for reading.

Reading and Responding to *The Bicycle Man*

Teacher read-aloud	1. Read aloud the first two pages as students follow along.	Gives all students the support they sometimes need to get started reading.
	2. Stop and ask students what they think is going to happen. Discuss whether they want to change any predictions.	
	3. Encourage students to make changes in their predictions.	Continues active process of predicting and confirming.
Making journal notes	Remind students to note any words or ideas they want to talk about in their journals.	Supports the process of responding during reading.
Student-selected mode of reading: Cooperative (oral or silent) Independent	1. Have students select the mode of reading they want to use for the remainder of the story.	Gives students a choice in meeting their own needs. (See Chapter 2 on modes of reading.)
	2. Remind students to continue to check whether their predictions were confirmed or changed.	Continues focus on reading for a purpose.
	3. As students read, observe each pair or trio; stop and ask questions or prompt those who need extra help.	
Individual written responses	After they complete the story, ask students to write about it in their journals. Display the following response chart for those who need more support:	Gives all students a chance for personal response. (See Chapter 6 on responding.)

Literacy
Lesson
continued

ACTIVITY	PROCEDURE	NOTES

> *Responding to* The Bicycle Man
>
> Choose *one.*
> Write about:
> • What you learned from this story
> • How this story made you feel
> • The part you liked best—why?
> • What you want to say about this story

ACTIVITY	PROCEDURE	NOTES
Whole-class discussion: Checking predictions Sharing responses Thinking critically	1. Ask students to review their predictions to note whether they were verified or changed. 2. Ask volunteers to share their responses to the story. 3. Conclude the discussion by asking students to talk about the following points: Who learned lessons in this story and why? Why was this an important experience for the Japanese people and the American soldiers in this story?	Pulls together story for all students. Promotes critical thinking.

Extending *The Bicycle Man*

ACTIVITY	PROCEDURE	NOTES
Using the vocabulary self-collection strategy	1. Divide students into groups of three, and have each group select one word that they found most interesting or important to the story. Tell them to locate the word in the story and try to define it. 2. Have each group share their word. Compile a list with definitions. 3. Contribute a word for the list (example: *lacquered boxes*). 4. Verify the definitions using the dictionary. 5. Review the list with students; have them select five to seven words for study.	Gets students involved in becoming independent word learners. Focuses on using context and prior knowledge. The teacher is part of the group and should therefore contribute a word.

Literacy
Lesson
continued

ACTIVITY	PROCEDURE	NOTES
	6. Have selected words and definitions placed in journals.	
	7. Encourage students to select any other words from the list for their own study and enter them in their journals.	Puts more responsibility for learning on the students.
Self-selected activities	Invite students to select one activity they would like to pursue with a small group: (1) Make a book about Japan, (2) plan a sportsday, or (3) make a friendship chain (a paper chain with names of students who are friends, telling why they are friends).	Extends reading, giving students choices in meeting their own needs. Promotes problem solving and thinking as well as making use of the book read. May be a long-term activity that continues while other books are being read.
	Example:	

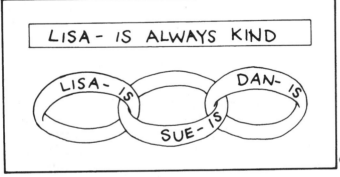

After Reading the Lesson

1. **Get together with someone else who has read the plan, and discuss it. What would you have changed, and why?**
2. **Assume you are going to use this book with more advanced students. Work with a partner to revise the plan for those students.**
3. **Meet with a partner to discuss how you might use this book to develop a more extensive unit focusing more on social studies, science, and math (see Chapter 9).**

A Final Word About Vocabulary

Learning vocabulary is a natural part of reading and writing. The more exciting reading and writing experiences children have, the more they will encounter our wonderful language. It is through these experiences that children's vocabularies grow: it is through the excitement and fun of reading and writing that they learn to read and write!

Summary

Students develop two reading vocabularies, recognition and meaning. This chapter focused on meaning vocabulary and what we know about how it grows and how it is learned.

Effective vocabulary development includes helping students become aware of words, wide reading and extensive writing, learning a strategy for independently inferring word meanings, and *limited* direct teaching of vocabulary and vocabulary-related skills. *The ultimate goal of all vocabulary development is for students to become independent word learners.*

This chapter presented suggestions and guidelines for supporting effective vocabulary growth. It suggested a strategy for independently inferring word meanings and seven strategies for direct teaching of vocabulary. The chapter's main focus, however, was that students learn vocabulary through wide reading and extensive writing.

Literature

Andersen, H. C. (1983). *The emperor's new clothes.* New York: Harper and Row.
Forbes, E. (1971). *Johnny Tremain.* New York: Dell.
Graham, F. (illus.). (1987). *Roundabout cozy cottage.* New York: Grosset & Dunlap.
Howard, E. F. (1991). *Aunt Flossie's hats (and crab cakes later).* New York: Clarion.
Levitt, P. M., Burger, D. A., & Guralnick, E. S. (1985). *The weighty word book.* Longmont, CO: Bookmakers Guild.
Lowry, L. (1979). *Anastasia Krupnik.* Boston: Houghton Mifflin.
Maestro, B., & Maestro, G. (1989). *Taxi: A book of city words.* New York: Clarion.
Maestro, B., & Maestro, G. (1990). *Delivery van: Words for town and country.* New York: Clarion.
Myers, W. D. (1990). *The mouse rap.* New York: Harper & Row.
Perl, L. (1987). *Mummies, tombs, and treasure.* New York: Clarion.
Prelutsky, J. (1984). "Never mince words with a shark." In J. Prelutsky, *The new kid on the block* (p. 89). New York: Greenwillow Books.
Say, A. (1982). *The bicycle man.* Boston: Houghton Mifflin.
Sperling, S. K. (1985). *Murfles and wink-a-peeps: Funny old words for kids.* New York: Clarkson N. Potter.

For Additional Reading

Blachowicz, C. L. Z., & Lee, J. J. (1991). Vocabulary development in the whole literacy classroom. *The Reading Teacher 45*(3), 188–195.

Heimlich, J. E., & Pittelman, S. D. (1986). *Semantic mapping: Classroom applications.* Newark, DE: International Reading Association.

Nagy, W. E. (1988). *Teaching vocabulary to improve reading comprehension.* Newark, DE/Urbana, IL: IRA/NCTE.

Pittelman, S. D., Heimlich, J. E., Berglund, R. L., & French, M. P. (1991). *Semantic feature analysis: Classroom applications.* Newark, DE: International Reading Association.

Towell, J. (1998). Fun with vocabulary. *The Reading Teacher 51*(4), 356–358.

For Exploration: Electronic Products and Resources

Use the Internet as a tool to keep up with the latest research in effective vocabulary development. The ERIC Clearinghouse on Reading, English, and Communication will offer up-to-date information as will journals and publications of such organizations as IRA, NCTE, and NECC.

Educational software companies describe and often demonstrate their vocabulary development programs on their Web sites. Start a search for effective software by visiting these sites. Look for the addresses of other software companies in journals.

The Learning Company
www.learningco.com

Mindplay
www.mindplay.com/

Sunburst
www.sunburst.com

Teacher Support Software
www.tssoftware.com

Responding and the Construction of Meaning

6

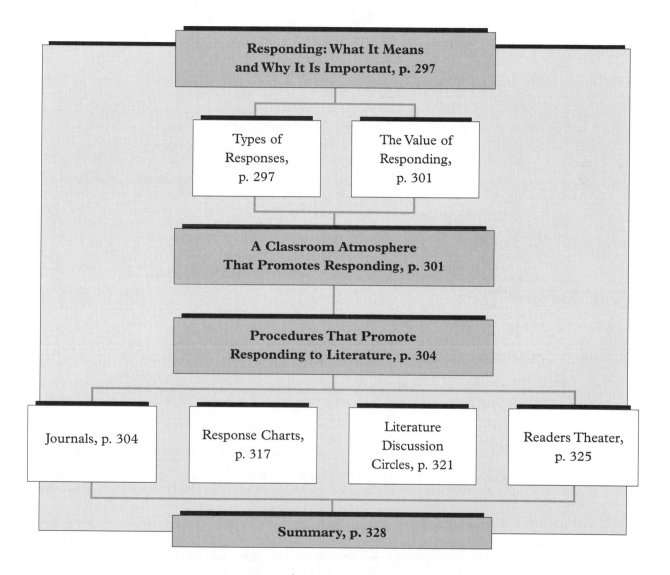

Responding: What It Means and Why It Is Important, p. 297

Types of Responses, p. 297

The Value of Responding, p. 301

A Classroom Atmosphere That Promotes Responding, p. 301

Procedures That Promote Responding to Literature, p. 304

Journals, p. 304

Response Charts, p. 317

Literature Discussion Circles, p. 321

Readers Theater, p. 325

Summary, p. 328

Let's begin by looking in on a third-grade classroom. Many different activities were taking place where Melissa and several other students were sitting at their desks reading Mississippi Bridge *(Taylor, 1990). Melissa leaned over to one of her class-mates and pointed out an illustration. They chatted for a few minutes and then returned to their reading.*

Other students worked with the book James and the Giant Peach *(Dahl, 1961). Some students were reading the book, some made notes in their journals, and one very excited young man, Mark, worked on a project. I stopped to talk to him.*

"This looks like an interesting project," I said. "Tell me about it."

Mark showed me the cover of his book. "Have you ever read it?" he asked.

"Yes, I have."

"Did you like it?"

"Yes! Did you like it?"

"I sure did! I loved when the peach started to roll away and the things that happened. I'm making a movie box about this book with my favorite parts."

In another area of the room, Mrs. Eggars, the teacher, and a group of students sat around a table discussing How Many Days to America? *(Bunting, 1988). Joe said it would be really tough to leave everything you had and go off to a new country. Maria said, "Yes, but it would be better; they might have more things, and they wouldn't be afraid of the soldiers. I'd go."*

Mrs. Eggars added, "You know, I don't know how I would feel; I've never had to leave my home like the people in our story. Do you know of anyone who has ever had this kind of experience?"

Lisa said, "Our neighbors came from Vietnam."

The discussion continued in this manner.

NOTICE WHAT WE saw in this classroom:

▶ While Melissa and her classmates were reading a book, it was very natural for them to stop and talk about some point in the story. This type of activity shows that students are taking control of and monitoring their own reading.

▶ Other students were writing in journals about their books, while one student was working on a movie box, a nonverbal response, about the same book.

▶ Some students and the teacher were a part of a discussion group. Each member participated in the discussion, no right or wrong answers were expected, and the teacher was an active participant.

▶ The teacher's role in this class was very important. Mrs. Eggars had planned the experiences that allowed and encouraged children to read, respond, and monitor their own learning. At the same time she participated in groups, modeling for students and prompting them as needed.

As all of the students in this class and their teacher show, active responding is an important element in learning to construct meaning and become literate (Hansen, 1987).

◼ **Responding: What It Means and Why It Is Important**

Responding is what one does as a result of and/or as a part of reading, writing, or listening. The children in our third-grade classroom took different actions both during and after reading. You do it all the time, too. You respond to a textbook chapter you are reading by discussing it with a peer (it was easy or too difficult), or you respond to a newspaper article on hunger and homeless people by finding out how to make food donations to a local mission. Responding is part of the natural process of constructing meaning.

When you respond to a piece of literature or to someone's writing, you are using prior knowledge to construct meaning. Therefore, each person's construction is individual and personal, the result of the transaction between the reader and the text (Rosenblatt, 1938/1976, 1991). Recall from your own college experience when you were asked to read a short story or poem and write your interpretation of it. When your paper came back, perhaps you saw you received a C because your interpretation did not agree with that of your instructor. What we know about the construction of meaning leads us to conclude that many acceptable interpretations and responses are possible from reading a single piece of literature. There is the generally accepted response, which we have always expected students to give, and there is the more personal response, which varies greatly from student to student. Even within the generally accepted responses, different interpretations often occur. Therefore, as the teacher you must be prepared to *expect, respect,* and *accept* a variety of responses from students (Martinez & Roser, 1991). These responses will help you decide what types of additional support students need.

Responding is also valuable to you, the teacher. Students' responses serve as some of the material that you use for assessment. Many school districts now have standards that call for students to respond in different formats—learning logs, projects, and so forth. For more discussion of using responses as a part of assessment, see Chapter 11.

Types of Responses

Responses to literature fall into two basic categories: personal and creative. *Personal responses* are usually oral or written. This is the type of response in which students tell how they felt about what they read, their favorite part(s) or character(s), or how what they read relates to their lives. For example, a fifth-grade student finished reading *The Lion, the Witch and the Wardrobe* (Lewis, 1950) and wrote the personal response shown in Figure 6.1 in her dialogue journal. Notice that this student responded personally by relating her book to her own life and her parents. Some personal responses are at a much simpler level, especially when students first begin responding. The second grader's response shown in Figure 6.2 consisted of nothing more than identifying his favorite story, *Skip to My Lou* (Westcott, 1989). Obviously this student needs much more support in responding.

Creative responses involve art, music, drama, and so forth. Students use what they have read in some creative way. The response shown in Figure 6.3 is a two-sided

FIGURE 6.1

PERSONAL RESPONSE TO *THE LION, THE WITCH, AND THE WARDROBE* (LEWIS, 1950)

> 10-19-99
>
> Dear Mrs. Fugler,
>
> I think The Lion, The Witch, and The Wardrobe. Was a very good book, and that you should read it some day in the class. It was a 186 pages long and has 11 chapters. Lucy in this story is kind of like me because I tell my parents but they don't believe me and I have to bother them and bother them just like Lucy did. Then they go and see for thier selfs and Then they believe her or Lucy.
>
> Sincerely
> Nichole B.
>
> Dear Nichole,
> I enjoy that book myself. Are you going to read the rest of the series? yes I am
> You did a fine job of relating Lucy to yourself. You are ready to choose your next book.
> Sincerely,
> Mrs. Fugler

poster that a student made after reading *Miss Nelson Is Missing* (Allard & Marshall, 1977).

Personal responses may be prompted by the teacher or be spontaneous on the part of the students. Personal responses are good lead-ins for discussion. Creative responses are important but sometimes overdone. It is easy to fall into the trap of spending too much time on a particular piece of literature by doing too many cre-

FIGURE 6.2

PERSONAL RESPONSE TO *SKIP TO MY LOU* (WESTCOTT, 1989)

ative activities. Keep in mind that *it is not the number of activities that makes better readers; it is the amount of reading.*

Applebee (1978) suggests another way to look at responses: he describes four types of responses, each reflecting a different level of thought processes:

▶ **Retelling:** This is a simple recall of title, beginning and ending situations, and some dialogue, with no relative importance given to any of the events.

FIGURE 6.3

CREATIVE RESPONSE TO *MISS NELSON IS MISSING* (ALLARD & MARSHALL, 1977)

> ▶ *Summary:* Events are retold in order of importance. Summaries are usually shorter than retellings.

> ▶ *Analysis:* The response to the story is personal and subjective; for example, a student responding to *Annabelle Swift, Kindergartner* (Schwartz, 1988) might say, "This story is like what happened to me in kindergarten," and then relate a similar experience.

> ▶ *Generalization:* This addresses the theme or meaning of the story; for example, a generalization of *Annabelle Swift, Kindergartner* (Schwartz, 1988) might focus on the idea that you should trust yourself and not depend on the advice of others.

Even younger children can often make limited generalizations or analyze a story to some degree (Many, 1991). Fourth graders can actively construct meaning by analyzing and evaluating literature (Kelly & Farnan, 1991).

Studies indicate that encouraging personal responses is important in helping students learn to construct meaning (Cullinan, Harwood, & Galda, 1983; Eeds, 1989; Galda, 1982, 1983; Gambrell, 1986; Hickman, 1983; Morrow, 1985; Purves,

1972). As Kelly (1990) says, "Allowing students to respond to what they read or heard from a read-aloud provided the framework for what Piaget (in Gallagher & Reid, 1983) referred to as the active involvement in learning through the construction of meaning" (p. 470). Harste, Short, and Burke (1988) maintain that "readers deepen and extend their interpretations of literature when they respond to that literature in a variety of ways" (p. 305). As responses take place and are encouraged over time, students develop more complex responses that help them become more adept at constructing meaning.

The Value of Responding

When children are given opportunities to function in a response-centered classroom, they develop a sense of ownership, pride, and respect for learning (Hansen, 1987). Because they respond to the same piece of literature their classmates do, they know their responses will be valued and accepted as much as anyone else's. In addition, when gifted students and at-risk students respond to the same piece of literature together, each responds in a manner consistent with his or her functioning level. Students learn that the teacher values their responses, and they in turn learn to value the responses of their peers. This type of respect leads to a sense of community and ownership.

Responding also helps students learn to monitor their own reading and writing. By being continuously encouraged to think about and react to what they are reading and writing, students develop their metacognitive processes, which are important in constructing meaning (Palincsar & Brown, 1986; Paris et. al., 1991). Discussion, a major form of response, helps students develop their ability to construct meaning (Sweet, 1993).

Responses also help students learn skills and strategies. Look back at the poster in Figure 6.3. This student obviously knows how to locate important information and character traits. She developed the use of these skills partly through reading and responding.

A Classroom Atmosphere That Promotes Responding

If you want students to respond to literature, you must begin by creating a classroom environment that supports and promotes responding (Harste et al., 1988). Of course, you must create a literate environment, as discussed in Chapter 2, and include extensive opportunities for students to read and write. But the response-centered classroom has many other characteristics as well.

As the teacher in this classroom, you must believe that all students have reactions and feelings that are important and valid, and students must have this belief about one another and about you. This sense of community may begin with the physical arrangement of the room, but it also includes how you treat students; if they learn that you always expect right answers or reward only thinking that you agree with, they will treat one another in that manner and strive to give only the responses they think you expect. If, on the other hand, they learn that you accept many possible answers and interpretations of what they have read, they will in turn become more tolerant and accepting of one another's ideas.

This classroom attitude evolves partly out of the way you ask and respond to students' questions. Traditionally, the teacher's role has been to ask a series of questions to determine whether students have comprehended what they have read. For example, if students have just finished reading *The True Story of the 3 Little Pigs* (Scieszka, 1989), the teacher "checks" their comprehension by asking them a series of questions such as these:

1. Who told this story?
2. What caused the wolf to go to the house of the first little pig?
3. What happened at the house of the second little pig?
4. What made the wolf angry at the third little pig's house?
5. How did you feel about the wolf's story?

Notice that only the last question begins to move students toward thinking more openly and relating what they have learned to their own experiences. Contrast these questions with the following:

1. What was different about this story and the one you already know about the three pigs?
2. Why do you suppose the wolf would choose to tell his story?
3. If you had been in the wolf's place, how would you have approached this situation?

These questions seek varied responses and say to students that it is entirely appropriate for each person to have a different response. The final difference in this second group of questions is in the way you respond to the students. If a student answers question 2 by telling you that the wolf probably told this story because he just wanted to tell another story and you say or imply that the answer is wrong, that student and others who heard your response will begin to get the message that you are looking for a correct answer, despite what you say. If, on the other hand, you say, "That is certainly a possibility; let's hear some other thoughts," students will get a totally different message from you.

There is indeed a time and a place to ask questions such as those in the first group, for example, when students need support in understanding a story during teacher-guided reading. However, when you want to prompt children's responses to reading, you should ask more open-ended, suppositional questions and then show that you accept and value a variety of responses. Table 6.1 gives some examples of questions that suit this purpose. The questions in group I specifically relate to the text being read; the questions in group II encourage deeper thinking and more comparisons.

Opportunities for students to respond to literature will come primarily in two ways: through self-selected books and materials and through those assigned by the teacher. Students may be reading self-selected literature as a part of independent reading, or you may have reached a point where you encourage self-selected reading for instructional purposes.

Many times you will want the entire class to read the same piece of literature. Obviously, students of differing abilities will approach the literature differently: some will read it independently, some cooperatively, and some supported by you

TABLE 6.1

Sample Open-Ended Questions That Promote Responses to Literature

GROUP I

1. Where and when does the story take place? How do you know? If the story took place somewhere else or in a different time, how would it be changed?
2. What incident, problem, conflict, or situation does the author use to get the story started?
3. What does the author do to create suspense, to make you want to read on to find out what happens?
4. Trace the main events of the story. Could you change their order or leave any of them out? Why or why not?
5. Think of a different ending to the story. How would the rest of the story have to be changed to fit the new ending?
6. Did the story end the way you expected it to? What clues did the author offer to prepare you to expect this ending? Did you recognize these clues as important to the story as you were first reading/hearing it?
7. Who is the main character of the story? What kind of person is the character? How did you know?
8. Are any characters changed during the story? If they are, how are they different? What changed them? Did it seem believable?
9. Some characters play small but important roles in a story. Name such a character. Why is this character necessary for the story?
10. Who is the teller of the story? How would the story change if someone else in the book or an outside narrator told the story?
11. Does the story as a whole create a certain mood or feeling? What is the mood? How is it created?
12. Did you have strong feelings as you read the story? What did the author do to make you feel strongly?
13. What are the main ideas behind the story? What makes you think of them as you read the story?
14. Is this story like any other story you have read or watched?
15. Think about the characters in the story. Are any of them the same type of character that you have met in other stories?

GROUP II

1. What idea or ideas does this story make you think about? How does the author get you to think about this?
2. Do any particular feelings come across in this story? Does the story actually make you feel in a certain way or does it make you think about what it's like to feel that way? How does the author do this?
3. Is there one character that you know more about than any of the others? Who is this character and what kind of person is he/she? How does the author reveal the character to you?

(continued)

TABLE 6.1, continued

4. Are there other characters important to the story? Who are they? Why are they important?
5. Is there anything that seems to make this particular author's work unique? If so, what?
6. Did you notice any particular patterns in the form of this book? If you are reading this book in more than one sitting, are there natural points at which to break off your reading? If so, what are these?
7. Were there clues that the author built into the story that helped you to anticipate the outcome? If so, what were they? Did you think these clues were important when you read them?
8. Does the story language seem natural for the intent of the story and for the various speakers?
9. Every writer creates a make-believe work and peoples it with characters. Even where the world is far different from your own, how does the author make the story seem possible or probable?
10. What questions would you ask if the author were here? Which would be the most important question? How might the author answer it?

Source: Group I: Reprinted by permission of the author and publisher from Sloan, Glenna Davis, *The Child as Critic: Teaching Literature in Elementary and Middle Schools,* 2d ed., pp. 104–106. (New York: Teachers College Press, 1984. © 1984 by Teachers College, Columbia University. All rights reserved.) Group II: From *Child and Story* by Kay Vandergrift (New York: Neal-Schuman Publishers, Inc., 1980). Reprinted by permission. Both cited by Harste et al. (1988).

through directed reading or read-alouds. In all instances, students will respond to the literature according to their own abilities. The literature you have students read as an entire class will usually be the materials used for your literacy lessons, which are designed to promote responding. (Recall that the parts of that lesson are introducing, reading and responding, and extending; see Chapter 2 for a detailed discussion.)

Procedures That Promote Responding to Literature

There are many different ways to encourage and support students as they respond to literature, and each procedure has a special function. This section discusses four procedures: journals, response charts, literature discussion circles, and readers theater.

Journals

Journals are booklets, notebooks, or folders in which students keep personal reflections about their reading and writing. They can range from a simple student-made booklet with a cover and pages to a spiral notebook or binder with loose-leaf pages.

Students who are involved in a writing workshop (see Chapter 10) using process writing develop fluency and confidence in their writing, and using journals extends, reinforces, and supports these skills. Journals help tie together reading and writing and give students opportunities to construct their own personal meanings (Atwell, 1987; Harste et al., 1988; Parsons, 1990; Tierney et al., 1990; Weaver, 1990a).

Basically, journals can be divided into five categories: diaries, response journals, dialogue journals, double-entry journals, and learning logs. Although these forms are similar in many ways, there are significant differences.

▶ *Diaries* are private records of personal observations or random jottings, or a daily record of thoughts and feelings. These are shared *only* if the student agrees. A diary is generally not a place where a student would respond to a piece of literature.

▶ *Response journals* are used by students to keep a record of their personal reactions to, questions about, and reflections on what they read, view, write, or listen to. Response journals are sometimes called *reading journals* or *literature logs*. They might include lists of words students want to learn, goals for reading (such as number of pages to be completed), predictions made before and during reading, notes or comments made during reading, and reactions, thoughts, or feelings recorded after reading. If you just want students to keep track of their independent reading for themselves, you may not read these journals, but if you want them to respond to literature they have read or to pieces they have written, you probably will read them. Figure 6.4 shows a sample page from a fourth grader's response journal.

▶ *Dialogue journals* have the same basic purpose response journals do, except the teacher (and sometimes peers) reads and responds in writing to the student's responses. "The major characteristic that distinguishes Dialogue Journals from other forms is the importance given to communications between the student and the teacher" (Tierney et al., 1990, p. 97). In this form of journal, the student may have a dialogue with himself or herself, with peers, and/or with the teacher. The input from others helps the student construct meaning more effectively. Figure 6.5 presents a sample page from a dialogue journal. Notice how the teacher's responses help the student think and construct meaning.

▶ *Double-entry journals* have pages that are divided into two parts. On the left-hand two-thirds of the page, students make notes, list predictions, and draw diagrams before and during reading. On the right-hand side, they write a response to their reading. If the double-entry journal is also being treated as a dialogue journal, the teacher replies on the right-hand side of the page. These journals have been recommended for use with all students, including at-risk learners (Coley & Hoffman, 1990). Figure 6.6 shows a double-entry journal completed by a seventh grader reading *The Summer of the Swans* (Byars, 1970).

Learning logs are daily records of what students have learned (Harste et al., 1988; Thompson, 1990). Figure 6.7 shows a sample entry from a third grader's learning log; this is simply a daily account of what this student has learned, with little response to the book. Sometimes, however, the learning log focuses on the learning that has taken place in a particular content area such as math, science, or social

FIGURE 6.4

PAGE FROM A FOURTH GRADER'S RESPONSE JOURNAL

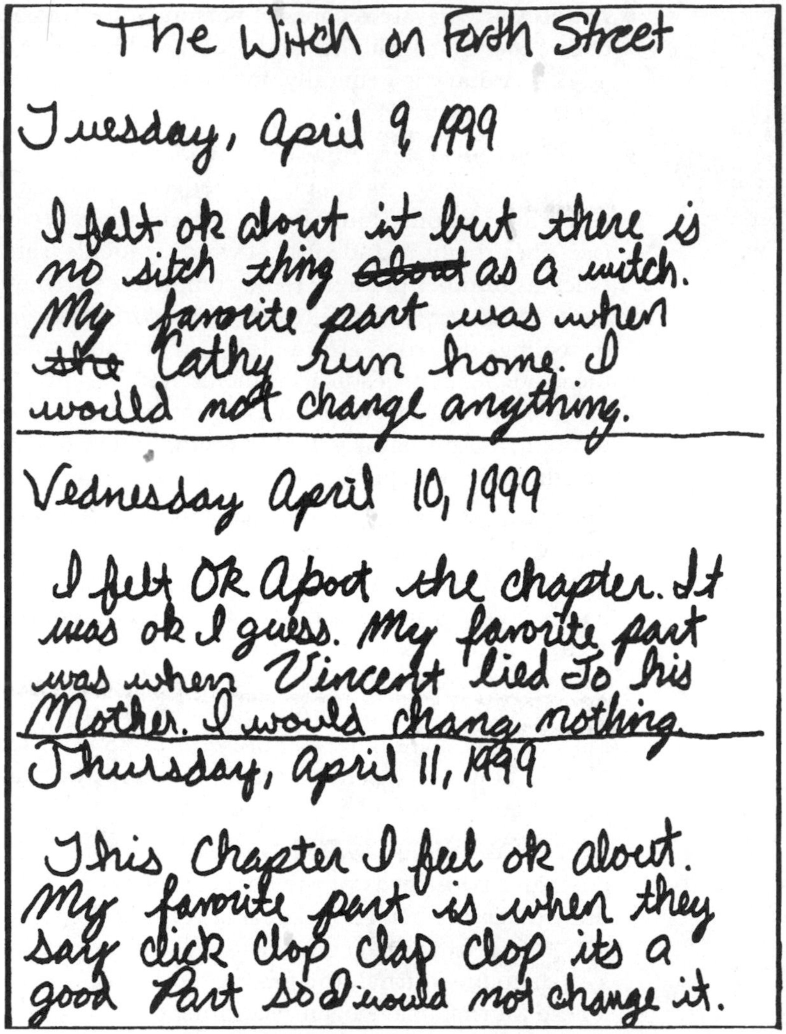

The Witch on Forth Street

Tuesday, April 9 1999

I felt ok about it but there is no sitch thing ~~about~~ as a witch. My favorite part was when ~~the~~ Cathy run home. I would not change anything.

Wednesday April 10, 1999

I felt OK apoot the chapter. It was ok I guess. My favorite part was when Vincent lied To his Mother. I would chang nothing

Thursday, April 11, 1999

This Chapter I feel ok about. My favorite part is when they say click clop clap clop its a good Part so I would not change it.

studies. Learning logs may be treated as response journals with no teacher response or as dialogue journals between the teacher and students.

Deciding Which Journal Type to Use

As you can see, many similarities exist among various types of journals. Table 6.2 summarizes their features. You must decide which type(s) you want to use, and you

FIGURE 6.5

PAGE FROM A DIALOGUE JOURNAL

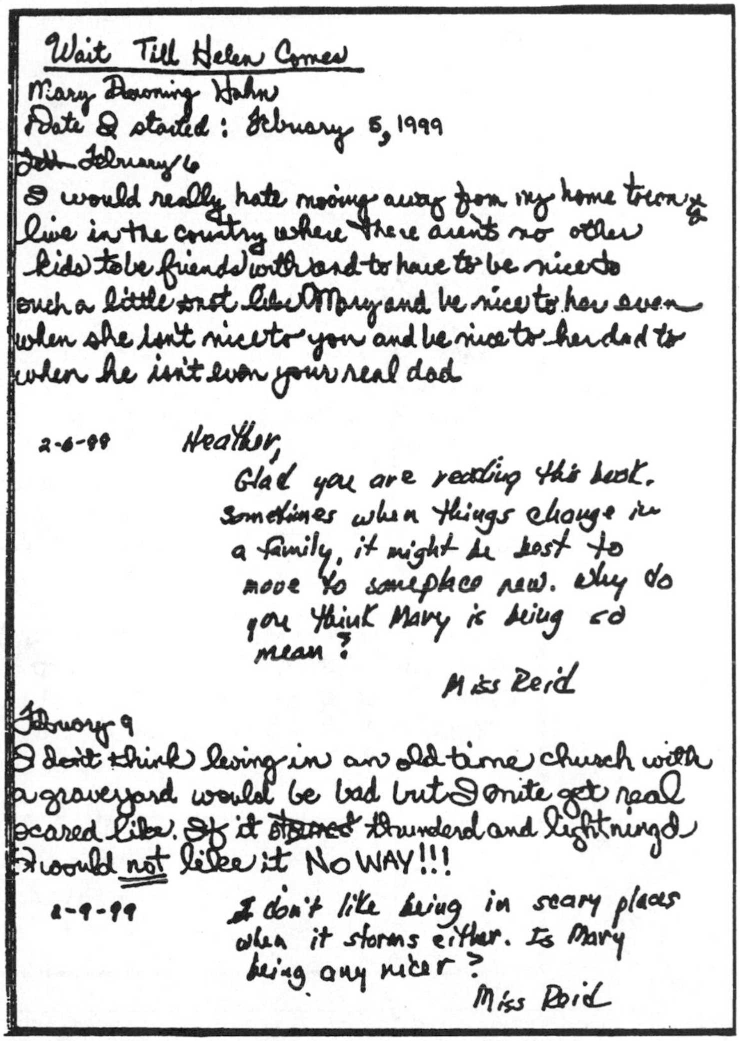

> **Wait Till Helen Comes**
> Mary Downing Hahn
> Date I started: February 5, 1999
> Jeth February 6
> I would really hate moving away from my home town to
> live in the country where there aren't no other
> kids to be friends with and to have to be nice to
> such a little snot like Mary and be nice to her even
> when she isn't nice to you and be nice to her dad to
> when he isn't even your real dad
>
> 2-6-99 Heather,
>   Glad you are reading this book.
>   Sometimes when things change in
>   a family, it might be best to
>   move to someplace new. Why do
>   you think Mary is being so
>   mean?
>   Miss Reid
>
> February 9
> I don't think living in an old time church with
> a graveyard would be bad but I mite get real
> scared like. If it stormed thundered and lightninged
> I would not like it NO WAY!!!
>
> 2-9-99   I don't like being in scary places
>   when it storms either. Is Mary
>   being any nicer?
>   Miss Reid

may find you want to use a combination. The important thing is to know why you are having students keep a journal; is it for

▶ Prompting students to reflect on their personal thoughts and feelings?

▶ Encouraging students to keep a personal record of independent reading?

▶ Encouraging students to respond to literature and/or their writing?

FIGURE 6.6

DOUBLE-ENTRY JOURNAL OF A SEVENTH GRADER

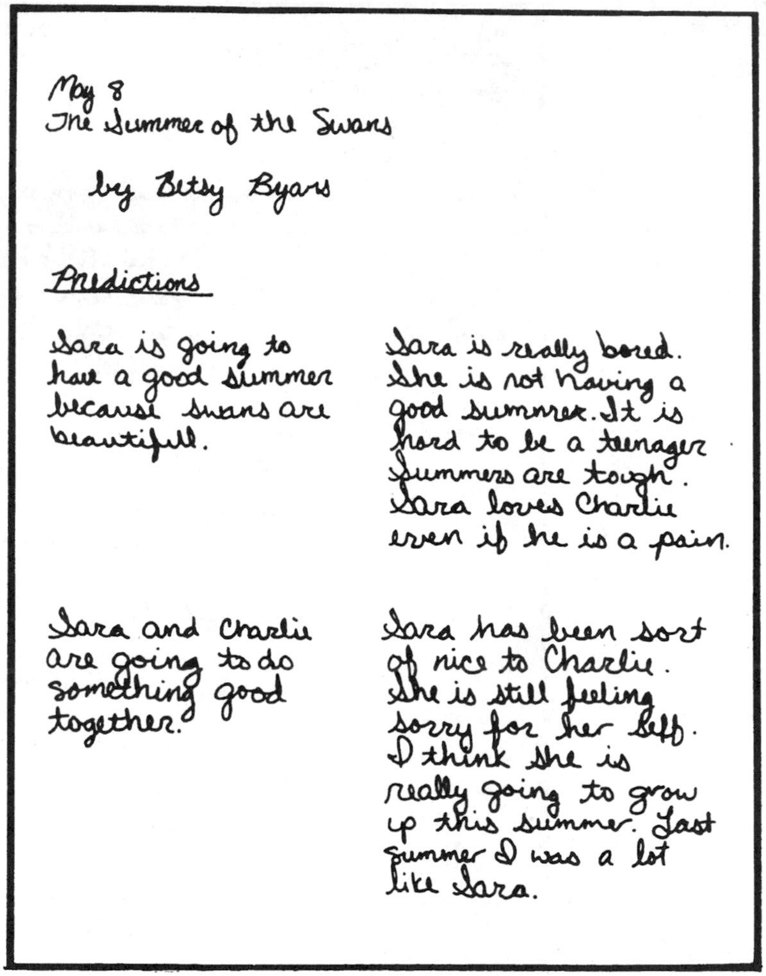

May 8
The Summer of the Swans

   by Betsy Byars

<u>Predictions</u>

Sara is going to have a good summer because swans are beautifull.	Sara is really bored. She is not having a good summer. It is hard to be a teenager. Summers are tough. Sara loves Charlie even if he is a pain.
Sara and Charlie are going to do something good together.	Sara has been sort of nice to Charlie. She is still feeling sorry for her self. I think she is really going to grow up this summer. Last summer I was a lot like Sara.

▶ Carrying on a dialogue with students to help them learn to construct meaning?

▶ Having students summarize what they have learned?

Once you have determined your purpose for using journals, you can decide on the type or combination of types you want to try. As you begin to make decisions, keep in mind that students do not have to write in their journals every day or after every piece of literature they read. Imposing such stringent requirements makes journal writing a laborious task and defeats its purpose. At first, you may have to

FIGURE 6.7

SAMPLE ENTRY FROM A LEARNING LOG, THIRD GRADE

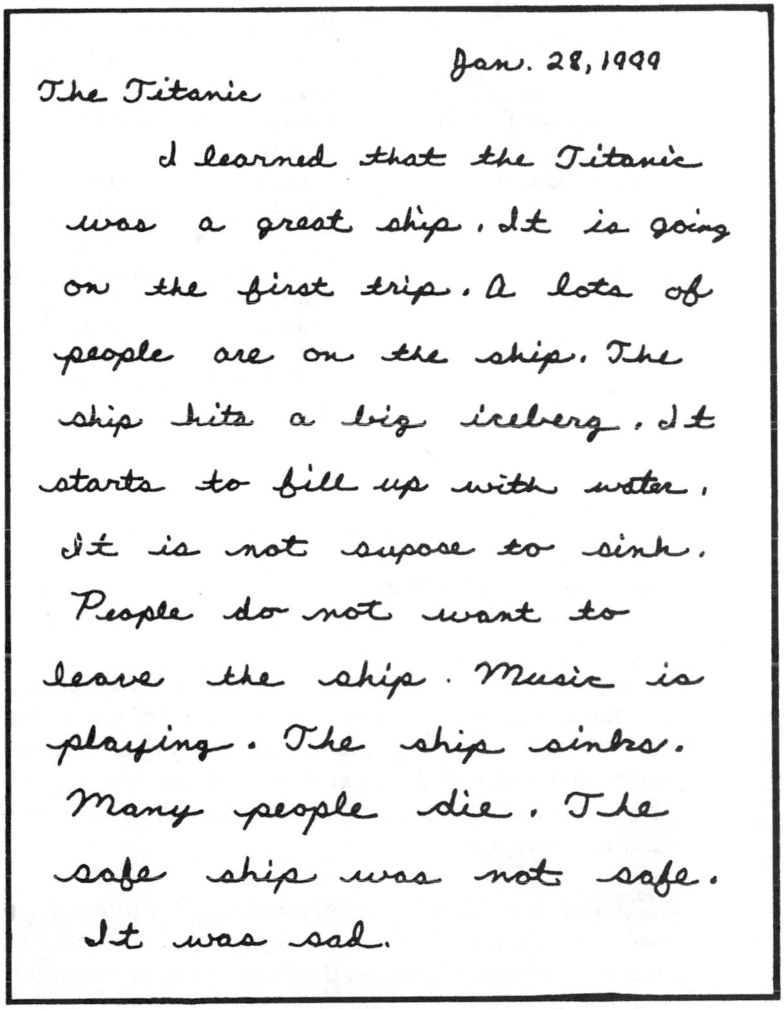

> Jan. 28, 1999
>
> The Titanic
>
> I learned that the Titanic was a great ship. It is going on the first trip. A lots of people are on the ship. The ship hits a big iceberg. It starts to fill up with water. It is not supose to sink. People do not want to leave the ship. Music is playing. The ship sinks. Many people die. The safe ship was not safe. It was sad.

nudge some students to write in their journals; however, as they become comfortable with their journals, they will write in them more readily.

Getting Started Using Journals

Once you decide which type of journal you will use, you are ready to introduce the idea to your class. Journals can be used with students at any grade level, though beginning learners are not expected to write as much as or use their journals in the

TABLE 6.2

TYPES OF JOURNALS

JOURNAL TYPE	DESCRIPTION	FEATURES
Diary	Private records of personal observations and thoughts	Not read by anyone unless student requests
Response journal (literature log or reading journal)	Reactions, questions, and reflections about what has been read	Sometimes a personal record and sometimes read by the teacher
Dialogue journal	A conversation between student and teacher about what has been read	Read by the teacher and sometimes peers; comments written by the reader
Double-entry journal	A split page on which students jot down ideas before and during reading on one side and give reactions after reading on the other side	May or may not be read by the teacher and/or peers
Learning log	A listing of what has been learned	May be treated as a dialogue journal or as a response journal

same ways older students do. You should adapt the generalized procedures and suggestions given here to your students; there are no absolute rules to follow.

Begin by making a journal of your own with some entries in it. Show your journal to the students, and discuss how all of you will keep journals in which you will write about what you have read. If you plan to read and respond to your students' journals, you should give them the opportunity to read and respond to yours. It is important that you model this process for students as well as experience what they are going through.

Explain the idea of journal writing to your class. Tell students that the purpose of journal writing is to encourage them all to think about what they are reading and to share their thoughts. If you are going to respond to students' journals, point out that this is a way for you to talk to each of them and for them to talk to you.

Talk with students about what types of entries they might make in their journals. Tell them they may write about what they have read, draw about it, make notes indicating they have shared their book in some way with another person, or perhaps decide on some idea of their own. The main thing is that they respond in some way to their reading. Stress that there is no right or wrong way to respond. Obviously, responses will vary in quality, but you will help students improve through the responses you make to their writing. Urge students to suggest how they might respond to a piece of literature, such as by telling about a character, writing about what they would have done in that situation, constructing a diorama, or relating events to their own lives.

Have students work in cooperative groups to write some journal entries. Cooperative groups support students as they begin journal writing without necessitating the use of models or samples. When this author gives samples of journal writing, students tend to copy the samples and be hampered by them. However, collaborative writing lets students see that they can create their own types of responses. Encourage students to share their responses with the class.

Talk with students about the format of their journals and how often they should write in them. Give them a simple format (or several formats) for recording such information as the date of entry, book title, author, and copyright. Then have them write whatever they want to say. If you give students some type of formula to follow or a specific outline, you will inhibit their writing. Hansen (1987) writes about a teacher who used a mimeographed form with specific elements to be covered for each entry during her first year of journal writing. The year was not successful. When the teacher dropped the form, she got much better responses from her students and became more excited about journal writing with them. If you give students several formats from which to choose, you will want to evaluate with them the one they selected and make modifications, if needed.

If students' journal entries will be read by others, encourage students to write so that others can read what they have written. However, do not focus on correct spelling yet. During the writing workshop (see Chapter 10), students will be learning about the common courtesy of writing and spelling to communicate with others. Since some journal entries are simply personal notes, words, or predictions, accuracy is less important than meaning. Moreover, if you tell students their journal entries will not be evaluated for mechanics and spelling, you will begin to free them from some of the hang-ups that might discourage writing.

Atwell (1987) tells how she uses a letter to introduce journal writing to her middle school students. A copy of a similar letter used by a third-grade teacher appears in Figure 6.8. You could adapt this idea for use at any grade level.

Use a response chart or some other device to prompt and support students who need it. Response charts were used in the literacy lessons in Chapters 2, 3, and 4 and are discussed in detail on pp. 311–321. These charts are designed to help students think of how to respond to their reading.

Plan with students a system for using and storing journals. Choose a place for storing the journals alphabetically, such as in boxes, a file drawer, or a crate. Atwell (1987) suggests having students write their names on the fronts of their journals and then arranging them alphabetically. The journals can then be numbered for easy return to the storage area.

During the initial stages of journal writing, evaluate with students how the procedure is progressing. Whenever students try something new or different,

FIGURE 6.8

LETTER FOR INTRODUCING JOURNALS TO THIRD GRADERS

Michael D. Robinson   Third Grade Teacher   ☺

Dear Girls and Boys,   August, 1999

This year you will be using your Reading Journal to write me letters about the books you are reading. I will write letters back to you as I read your letters. This will be one of the ways we talk about your books. I will also tell you about the books I am reading.

As you write each letter, tell me about your book — how you feel about it, what you like and don't like, what it makes you think about, your favorite parts, etc.... Draw pictures if you want to. I may even draw some pictures for you!

These letters will help you and me decide how you are doing with your reading and writing. We will discuss them during conferences. Here are some things for you to remember:
- date all your letters
- be sure to give the title and author
- write at least two letters each week
- tape this letter in the front of your journal

I'm excited about getting your letters. We'll learn a lot about each other.

                    Happy Reading,
                    Mr. Robinson

there are apt to be some details that need to be worked out. Therefore, it is a good idea to take time periodically to talk about how things are going and list ways to improve them.

For more detailed discussions about journal use, see the For Additional Reading section at the conclusion of this chapter.

What to Expect When Students Begin to Use Journals

Students just beginning to use journals may exhibit a number of questionable behaviors, all of which are normal. Some will show none of these behaviors, and others will exhibit many of them. Be assured, however, that all of these behaviors will fade away as students receive continued practice and support from you.

One likely response is "I don't know what to do." These students are probably insecure about their own literacy and are having difficulty constructing meaning. Some of them may simply not be comfortable with the process, but they will become more so as they gain experience. They may also respond this way if they have had many past experiences in which a right or wrong answer was expected. Writing journal responses may be totally new for students; in a sense they are redefining reading for themselves, because they are learning that a text can have multiple interpretations. For students who exhibit these behaviors, make some suggestions for possible responses. (See the discussion of response charts on pages 317–321.)

Some students will be very concerned about accuracy in spelling and usage. These students are likely to be uncertain about the language and may have been in environments that stressed correctness. Simply keep reassuring them that you are not concerned about correctness in their journals; you are concerned only about their thinking and their reactions.

Still other students may simply retell what they have read, which is another normal behavior. Students will progress beyond retelling as they gain more experience in responding, and your responses in their journals should consist of questions that focus their attention beyond this point. For example, you might write, "How would you have reacted in this situation?" or "What lesson do you think we can learn from this book?"

Some teachers encourage students to retell or summarize as one way to respond to literature. This is an effective way to help children construct meaning (Gambrell, Pfeiffer, & Wilson, 1985; Marshall, 1983; Morrow, 1985, 1989), and such responses are also easy for teachers to evaluate. Retellings and evaluation of responses are discussed more fully in Chapter 11.

Some students will immediately become comfortable with a particular mode of response and "latch onto" it, using it again and again. Your responses are important in moving these students forward. Simply asking, "Have you ever thought about the characters [or other aspects] in the stories you are reading?" will help them think of alternatives.

Finally, if you are using dialogue journals, some students may be really anxious about what you will write in their journals and what you will to think of their ideas. In these instances, you need to respond with very positive, upbeat comments that will allay these fears.

Journals are an excellent tool to use with all of your students. Barone (1990) notes that even young children begin responding by focusing on explicit story elements but soon become more interpretive, which indicates they are working through the text they are reading, focusing on more than literal comprehension and understanding the story more completely.

Responding to Students' Journals

In a response-centered classroom, both the students and the teacher are responsible for responding (Hansen, 1987). The students respond to their reading and writing and to one another's journals, including the teacher's. The teacher, in turn, responds to the students' journals, especially when dialogue journals are being used.

Teachers who want to use journals often raise two major questions: (1) "When do I find time to read all the journals?" and (2) "What exactly do I write in response to students' journal entries?" Both questions deserve serious consideration.

Finding Time to Read Journals.   You do not have to read every journal entry students make, since many entries are completely private, as with diaries. A response journal is often an individual record for the student's own use and thus requires no reading or responding by the teacher. Even when students are using journals that require you to respond, you do not have to do it every day for every entry. Dialogue journals require the most consistent form of response by the teacher because this is a major means of "talking" *with* students and helping them learn.

Finding the time to read journals is not nearly as difficult as it seems at first. Teachers often think they will have to read all the journals plus grade all the papers that normally pile up. Journals, however, replace many of the papers that have been used to try to engage students in learning and provide a much more meaningful learning task. One fourth-grade teacher said, "I read some of my students' journals during conference period if there is no one ready to talk with me. If there are any journals that I need to see on any day and haven't, I read them right after school. I rarely carry any of them home."

You may read journals at various times during the day. If you have conferences with your students, you can read some of the journals when you have no appointments. Some teachers use part of silent reading time to read students' journals. Others like to read journals just before or right after school. However you decide to proceed, your plan must fit your teaching style and needs. There is no one best way or best time to read journals.

How to Write Responses.   When you write responses in students' journals, keep in mind that you want to encourage students, guide them, refocus their responses, and make helpful suggestions.

Encouragement is your number one goal. You want to encourage students to continue to read and think about what they are reading, as well as to feel good about themselves and what they are writing in their journals. Some examples of encouraging types of responses appear on page 315.

Notice that each of these responses provides a different type of encouragement in different situations. Even though you will do more than encourage with your comments, *encouragement is essential.*

Dear Jeri,
    You are doing a very good job telling about the characters in _Now One Foot, Now the Other._ Which character do you think is most important in this story? Why? I'm looking forward to your next entry.
                                                    Mr. C

Source: Now One Foot, Now the Other (de Paola, 1980).

Dear Sam,
    The way you are retelling this story, I can tell that you are enjoying it !! Have you ever had an adventure like April's? If you have, why don't you compare your adventure to hers. Keep going! I can't wait to see what you think later in this book.
                                                    Mr. C

Source: The Egypt Game (Snyder, 1976).

Sometimes, as you are reading a student's journal, you will find that more *guidance* is needed in helping the student see important points or the big message the author is trying to deliver. This may happen frequently when you are having the entire class read the same book. For example, suppose your third graders are all reading *Fly Away Home* (Bunting, 1991) and you notice that some students are not understanding why it is important for the father and little boy not to be noticed in the airport. (This story is about a homeless father and son who make their home in a large airport, moving from terminal to terminal to keep from getting caught.) One student wrote the following:

> The boy in this story did not talk to people. He was not a friend.

The teacher might respond as follows:

> I thought the little boy really wanted to be friends. He was friends with Mrs. Medina and her family. He just couldn't be friends with everyone in the airport. Look back through the book and see if you can find places that show why he can't be friends with everyone.

At other times, students will just need to be *refocused* in their journals and in their reading. If a student always responds by drawing a picture and labeling it "My Favorite Part," you might ask the student to try a different response. For example:

> Your pictures of favorite parts are great. For your next entry, draw three pictures that show the three main events in the next chapter. Write a sentence or two about each picture.

This type of response shows how instruction and the student's growth work together. It helps the student use drawing but begins to move her or him toward looking at important events in the story. Refocusing might also be needed when students get so caught up in minute story details that they miss the real message or story line.

At other times, your responses may need to include various other kinds of *suggestions*—suggestions for other books to read, responses to try, or things to consider or think about as reading continues. Your response in the journals and the students' responses to you are a part of the running dialogue that lets you know how they are growing and gives you another way to guide them individually. Thus, the journal is both a teaching tool and a diagnostic tool. (See Chapter 11 for a discussion of using students' responses for assessment.)

You may also want to have students read and respond to one another's journals so that they will learn from one another. In "buddy journals" (Bromley, 1989), two students write back and forth to each other. At first, take time to model appropriate responses, showing that the focus should be not on rightness or wrongness but on ideas and feelings. It is best to delay using this type of journal until students have used dialogue journals with you.

Precautions When Using Journals

You need to take several precautions when using journals:

- *Beware of overuse of journals.* Sometimes teachers get so excited about journals that they use them in every subject area. Students become bored, and the journals lose their effectiveness.

- *Don't require all students to write in their journals every day.* To get everyone to write, teachers often require a daily entry. This turns students off to journals. Therefore, allow students to use journals as a choice. Some teachers require a minimum number of entries each week, especially in middle school.

- *Make sure you know your reason for having students use journals.* Be confident about why you are using journals before you begin. Avoid using journals just for the sake of using them.

- *Remember that journals are instructional tools.* Journals should replace other, less meaningful types of activities that students might do. They should not become just more "busy work" that is added on to what students already need to complete.

These precautions and the guidelines in this chapter should help you use journals effectively.

Response Charts

As students read a variety of literature, you may find they need support in learning how to respond. In such cases you can use response charts, which are simply charts with suggestions on how to respond to a given piece of literature. These devices were used in the lessons presented at the conclusion of Chapters 2, 3, and 4. Figure 6.9 presents a response chart from a sixth-grade classroom. You will notice that it is much more complex than those presented earlier. The teacher used it to get students back into journal writing at the beginning of the new school year. The response chart may also be developed by the students and teacher together before reading or after most of the reading has taken place.

Since responses to literature are personal, the goal of response activities is to get students to construct meaning by interacting with the text. It is through this interaction, or transaction, that students become better comprehenders.

FIGURE 6.9

SAMPLE RESPONSE CHART FROM A SIXTH-GRADE CLASSROOM

RESPONSE SUGGESTIONS

Before Reading

- List the title and author of the book in your journal. Give the date you started the book.

During Reading

- Note words of interest in your journal.
- Think about the story you are reading. Does it make sense? Write any questions you have in your journal.

After Reading (select one or more)

- Write a short summary of the story.
- Select your favorite character and describe his or her role in the story.
- Meet with a friend to talk about the story.
- *Other*—You decide what you would like to do.

Response charts should be useful on several occasions. First, they accustom students to the concept of responding. By giving students suggestions, you will "prime" their thinking and help them learn how to select their own modes of response. Beginning learners or those experiencing difficulty in learning often need this type of support.

Another time to use response charts is when you observe that students are not clearly understanding what they have read or are missing the entire point an author is trying to make. You can make this judgment by reading students' written responses or listening to or observing their oral or other creative responses. For example, suppose you have a group of fifth graders who have just read *The Scarebird* (Fleischman, 1987), and several students have decided to give a skit based on the book. If they portray Lonesome John as crazy instead of just lonely, you can tell they have missed the point and need support in identifying the story's problems. Therefore, you might model how you would identify the problem in this story (see Chapter 8). With the next few stories students read, you might suggest one or two ways for them to respond that would focus their attention more directly on identifying story problems, such as constructing a group story map or writing a paragraph describing the story problem.

Constructing Response Charts

Response charts are not necessary for every piece of literature students read. *Ultimately, you want students to be able to decide on their own modes of response.* However, even the best readers in a class may need some response chart support from time to time. One way to meet the individual needs of your students is to direct them to different types of response activities while still allowing choices. Therefore, to construct effective response charts, you need a variety of ideas about how students might respond to literature. In all cases, the activities on a response chart should be things students would normally do after reading a book; in other words, they should be "authentic activities."

When constructing response charts, you need to consider two factors: the type of text being read and the needs of your students. Sometimes the same response activity might work for both narrative and expository texts, but in most instances it will not. Students' needs will range from having to focus on the basic ideas in the text to having to become more inferential and evaluative in their responses. In the first case, a structured response such as a story map might be helpful; in the second case, students might think about and be ready to discuss why, for instance, the main character behaved as he or she did.

All response charts should contain one response option that says, "Other—You decide how you want to respond." Sometimes this may be the first option given. This alternative is appropriate for allowing students who don't need support to come up with their own responses. When students effectively use the "other" option, it's a good sign that they no longer need response charts. The number of options to include on a response chart should be kept small, usually three to five. For example, a new response chart might have five options, whereas one you are adding to regularly might get only three new response options at once.

Tables 6.3 and 6.4 list response options that should be helpful in constructing your own response charts for narrative and expository texts. They were developed from a variety of sources, including the works of Spritzer (1988) and Parsons (1990) and the ideas other teachers and this author have found to be effective. As you work with your students, you will develop other options that are appropriate for them.

Sometimes the response chart may include questions that cue students to respond in different ways. Parsons (1990) suggests that some students really need these aids to get them started and recommends the following questions for narrative texts:

- What surprised you about the section you read today? How does this change affect what might happen next in the story?

- What startling, unusual, or effective words, phrases, expressions, or images did you come across in your reading today that you would like to have explained or clarified? Which ones would you like to use in your own writing?

- How much do you personally agree or disagree with the way various characters think and act and the kinds of beliefs and values they hold? Where do you differ, and why?

- What issues in this story are similar to real-life issues that you've thought about or had some kind of experience with? How has the story clarified or confused or changed your views on any of these issues?

Figure 6.10 presents a sample response chart with cuing questions.

TABLE 6.3

RESPONSE OPTIONS FOR NARRATIVE TEXTS

RESPONSE OPTION	DESCRIPTION
Story mapping	Make a story map following the pattern presented on page 108.
Rewriting	Rewrite a part of the story illustrating how you would have solved the problem.
Retelling	Retell the story to a friend or small group of friends.
Illustrating	Illustrate your favorite part of important scenes from the story. Write a sentence or two about each illustration.
Sharing	Read your favorite part to a friend or group of friends. Be ready to tell why this is your favorite part. *Or* read your book to students in a grade lower than yours.
Puppetry	Use puppets to share your story with other classmates or students in another class.
Posters	Make a poster to "sell" classmates on reading this book. Remember to make it exciting so they will want to "buy" it.
Other books by the author	Select another book by this author. Read and compare the two stories.
Book talk	Give a short (3–5 minute) book talk focusing on what you feel is most exciting about your book.
Dress-up	Dress like a character from your book and act out a favorite scene for your class.
Play	Work with other students who have read the book to present a play or a readers theater presentation.
Topical study	Use the topic of your story as the basis for an informational study. For example, a child who is reading *Nine-in-One Grr! Grr!* (Xiong/Spagnoli, 1989) might do a study about the Hmong people of Laos.
Mobile	Make a mobile of important characters or events in the story.
Movie	Work with others who have read the book to make a movie using a video camera. Have a movie party to share your work with others.

For expository texts, cuing questions also need to be open-ended. Some suggested questions for expository texts are as follows:

- After reading this far in this text, what do you think you will learn about next?
- How would you feel if you were the scientist who made the discovery you just read about? Why?
- How do you feel the information in this text will be helpful in your life?
- How does the information you have just learned compare to what you already know about this topic?

You will find that you will develop your own bank of questions as you work with your students.

TABLE 6.4

RESPONSE OPTIONS FOR EXPOSITORY TEXTS

RESPONSE OPTION	DESCRIPTION	
Graphic presentation	Share the important ideas you have learned through some type of graphic device, such as a chart, timeline, diagram, or graphic organizer.	(1) Important Idea — Support / Support / Support (1) Important Idea — Support / Support / Support
Speech	Give a persuasive talk using the information you have gained about the topic of your book.	
Display	Create a display related to the book you read.	
Newspaper article	Write a newspaper article expressing your point of view about the book.	
Book	Use the information from the book you read to make a book of your own on the topic. Include text, charts, illustrations, and diagrams if appropriate.	
Debate	Have a debate with others who have read the book. Each group debating must take a different point of view.	
Bibliography	Read other books on the same topic and compile an annotated bibliography to share with others.	
Written report	Write a report about your book focusing on what you learned and how it might be helpful in the world.	
Map	Make a map to show important information you have learned. Focus on products, cities, recreation areas, and so forth.	
Experiment	Use what you have learned to conduct an experiment. Write your results.	
Newsreel	Use a video camera to make a newsreel using the information you and others have gained from their books. Write a script including facts and opinions.	

Two other forms of response can also be included on your response charts: literature circles and readers theater. These are discussed in the next two sections.

Literature Discussion Circles

Another procedure for promoting responses to literature is the literature circle (Harste et al., 1988), literature groups (Calkins, 1986; Weaver, 1990a), or literature

FIGURE 6.10

RESPONSE CHART USING CUING QUESTIONS

RESPONDING TO INDEPENDENT READING

Directions

As you read, you think about what's happening in your book in many different ways. Sometimes, questions come to your mind about some of the characters and how they are behaving. At other times, you might be impressed by the way someone or something was described. You might even be reminded of something similar that happened to you or to someone you know.

After reading independently today, try to describe the kinds of impressions and/or questions that your reading has inspired. Some people have found the following kinds of questions useful in guiding their responses. They are only suggestions. Please respond to your reading as you see fit.

- After reading this far, what more do you hope to learn about what these characters plan to do, what they think, feel, and believe, or what happens to them?
- As you think ahead to your next day's reading, what possible directions might the story take? How do you hope the story will unfold?
- If the setting and characters were changed to reflect your own neighborhood and friends and acquaintances, how would the events of the story have to change and why would that be so?
- Do you wish that your own life or the people you know were more like the ones in the story you're reading? In what ways would you like the real world to be more like the world of your book?

Source: Reprinted with permission from *Response Journals* by Les Parsons, p. 14. © Pembroke Publishers, 528 Hood Road, Markham, Ontario L3R 3K9 Canada (416) 477-0650. Available in the U.S. from Heinemann Educational Books.

discussion groups or circles. Regardless of the name(s) one uses to designate this procedure, they all have a common purpose: to get students to read and respond to literature. Having students discuss what they have read is essential to developing their ability to construct meaning.

In literature circles, children who have read the same book get together to discuss it and react to it. Initially, the teacher may start the discussion, but as students learn to function in the literature circle, they often take over this role.

The procedures for using literature circles have been described in detail by Harste et al. (1988). The guidelines given here are based on their ideas and this author's own experiences in working with children and teachers.

Guidelines for Using Literature Discussion Circles

Selecting Literature.   There are three options: one book read by the whole class, multiple books chosen by students (see Chapter 10), or individual self-selection. If several students have read or are reading the same book or selection as a part of their independent reading, these students may form a literature discussion circle of their own.

Organizing Discussion Circles.   If everyone in the class is reading the same book, establish how many circles you need to have three members in each and then have students quickly divide themselves into groups. Allowing students to select the discussion group they want to join gives them some control over their own learning and also helps to accommodate their individual needs. Many times students will sign up to be with their friends; there is nothing wrong with this. If behavior problems arise, you may have to adjust the groups, but this is usually not necessary.

If you are having the class select their reading from several different books, you can give a bit of information about each book as a teaser to spark interest and help students make their selections. Then list the titles on a chart or the chalkboard and have students sign up for the book they want to read. If more than four or five students want to read the same book, form more than one circle for that book.

The entire class may not be in literature circles at the same time. Those not involved may be doing independent reading or writing or other reading and writing activities.

Starting Discussion Circles.   Students begin by reading. If they are reading a short book or selection, they should read the entire book before coming to the circle. If they are reading a longer book, one with several chapters, they can meet in their literature circle at the conclusion of each chapter and at the end of the book. As the circle meets to discuss each chapter, the groups may decide on reading goals to be completed before the next meeting and should record these goals in their journals.

If you are working with beginning readers or students having problems reading, you can read aloud the book to that literature circle. So that students do not feel any stigma in being a part of the read-aloud group, you can announce before students sign up for their circles that a certain book will be read aloud and then invite all students to be part of this circle. Most will want to be in the listening circle from time to time. You can also provide a tape of the book in the listening center.

Promoting Discussions.   Each literature circle meeting will usually last from 5 to 10 minutes, depending on the book or selection being discussed and the students' experience in working in circles. Since the primary focus of the discussion is to bring the students and the literature together and to allow students to construct their own meanings in an authentic way, the discussion must be open-ended.

Many teachers find that using a literature circle discussion chart such as the one in Figure 6.11 helps get the groups started and keeps the discussion moving. Present the chart to students and explain it. As they become more comfortable, you will find they will start their own discussions, using the chart as a prompt. You may need to change the chart from time to time, and you can use some of the open-ended questions for cuing presented on pages 303 and 305. After students have learned to work in circles, discontinue the use of charts.

As each group carries out its discussion, move from circle to circle to monitor what is taking place. In many cases, you will want to become a member of the group

FIGURE 6.11

LITERATURE CIRCLE DISCUSSION CHART

LITERATURE CIRCLE DISCUSSIONS

1. Begin by telling the title and author of your book.
2. Talk about what you read.
   - What was your favorite part? Why?
   - How does this book relate to your life?
3. Make a list of things to discuss at your next meeting.

and add to or stimulate the discussion with questions. For example, suppose a literature circle is discussing *Regina's Big Mistake* (Moss, 1990) and you notice the discussion seems to be lagging. You might join the group by saying, "You know, when I was in school, I often felt just like Regina. I was afraid of making mistakes. What problems like that have you had in school?" In this way, you become part of the group by modeling and prompting other things to think about.

In the initial stages of using literature circles, you will need to model and demonstrate good questioning and discussion behaviors. One way is to model for the entire class using a small group. Then discuss with the class what happened and any problems they might see. You may also want to create a discussion guidelines chart such as the one presented in Chapter 3 to help students carry out their discussions.

Concluding Literature Circles. When students have completed a book, they can then decide whether they want to share it with the entire class or respond to it some other way. *It is neither necessary nor advisable for students to always complete additional activities.* The literature circle discussions may be sufficient response for most students. *Only when they are really excited about a book should they be encouraged to respond further.*

Tips for Using Discussion Circles

There is no one correct way to use discussion circles; they are a flexible tool and should be used accordingly. At the beginning, proceed slowly and carefully. Teachers have found two ways to successfully move themselves and their classes into literature circle work.

One teacher starts her class by inviting students to help select a book for the entire class. She then introduces and explains the concept of literature circles. After the circles are established, the class reads the book (or the first chapter in a longer book) and the teacher presents a literature circle discussion chart such as the one shown earlier in Figure 6.11. She poses one open-ended question to get all the groups started. As they work, she moves from circle to circle to see what is taking place, joining groups as needed. She repeats this pattern several times using different books until she is comfortable that her students understand literature circles and are working in them effectively. Then she expands to two or more books, letting the children choose which books they will read.

A second procedure for getting literature circles started is to use a small group and follow the same basic procedure as that just described. When one circle is working smoothly, you can add a second and then a third until all students are comfortable.

Regardless of the pattern you select, you will want to move slowly. When students have not had the experiences of such open discussions and have been accustomed to giving the teacher the "correct answer," they are often reluctant to talk. You may need to model open discussions several times before students are able to accept the idea that there are no absolute or correct answers.

For further reading on literature circles, see Harste et al. (1988) and Roser and Martinez (1995), listed in the For Additional Reading section.

Readers Theater

The readers theater is a form of response in which children turn a story into a play. Sloyer (1982) describes readers theater this way:

> *Readers Theatre is an interpretive reading activity for all children in the classroom. Readers bring characters to life through their voices and gestures. Listeners are captivated by the vitalized stories and complete the activity by imagining the details of a scene or action. . . . Readers Theatre becomes an integrated language event centering upon oral interpretation of literature. The children adapt and present the material of their choice. A story, a poem, a scene from a play, even a song lyric, provide the ingredients for the script. As a thinking, reading, writing, speaking, and listening experience, Readers Theatre makes a unique contribution to our language arts curriculum.* (p. 3)

This form of response allows *all* children to take part in the creative interpretation of a story. Even second-language or at-risk learners can succeed in this activity (Werthemer, 1974).

The following procedures for using the readers theater have been developed from numerous sources and my own experiences in working with children and teachers (Coger & White, 1982; Harste et al., 1988; Sloyer, 1982).

Select the Literature.   As you begin using the readers theater, you will need to help students select the literature. The stories must have lots of dialogue, strong story lines, and suspense, humor, or surprise. Discuss with students the characteristics of a good piece to use.

Read or Reread the Literature.   After reading, students should discuss the story, focusing on the characters, setting, problem, action, and outcome. Many teachers have students develop a story map (see Chapters 2 and 3). This will help students know what needs to be included in the readers theater script and what is not essential.

Develop a Script.   A good way to do this is through shared writing. Use a chart or an overhead projector, and develop the script with students. This is also a good place to refer students to the story map. Talk about the types of things that can be left out, such as the word *said* and lengthy descriptions that are not essential to the

Third graders using Readers Theater with their storybox presentation. © *Michael Weisbrot/Stock Boston*

story. Generate a list of story characters, and help students see how to identify the parts that must be read by a narrator. Figure 6.12 shows a partial script developed by some second graders and their teacher. Eventually, children will be able to do this on their own.

It is possible to purchase readers theater scripts for many pieces of literature (write to Readers Theatre Script Service, P.O. Box 178333, San Diego, CA 92117). However, one of the values of using this activity comes in developing the script. Therefore, even if you decide to purchase some scripts, you should also have students develop some of their own to give them the experience of translating a story into a script. In either case, you will need multiple copies of the script.

Discuss Props.   Only a few simple props are to be used in a readers theater presentation. These might include chairs, a stool, a yardstick for a sword, paper faces, hats, and so forth. There is no scenery. Talk with students to identify the props to use.

Prepare and Rehearse for the Presentation.   Select students to be the characters in the presentation. If you are working with the whole class, you might want to divide the class into groups so that everyone can participate in this first production; each group could give its own performance of the same program. Discuss with students how and where to stand and make hand, body, or facial gestures to convey parts of the story to their audience. Give students time to rehearse their program.

FIGURE 6.12

PARTIAL READERS THEATER SCRIPT FOR *TYE MAY AND THE MAGIC BRUSH* (BANG, 1981) DEVELOPED BY SECOND GRADERS AND THEIR TEACHER

TYE MAY AND THE MAGIC BRUSH

NARRATOR: Many years ago a cruel and greedy emperor ruled over China. His people were very poor. One of the poorest was Tye May. Her mother and father were dead and she lived alone. Every day she gathered firewood and cut reeds to sell in the marketplace. One day Tye May passed the school and saw the teacher painting. She knew right then what she wanted to do.

TYE MAY: "Please, sir, I would like to learn how to paint, but I have no money to buy a brush. Would you lend me one?"

TEACHER: (Angry) "Beggar girls don't paint. Get out of here!"

NARRATOR: But Tye May did not give up. She had an iron will. She drew pictures in the dirt when she collected wood. Her pictures looked real but she still didn't have a brush. One night when she was very tired she fell into a deep sleep.

WOMAN: "This is a magic brush. Use it carefully."

TYE MAY: "Thank you! Thank you!"

NARRATOR: The woman was gone and Tye May woke up.

Present the Program. When students have had ample time to rehearse, have the groups perform for the class. After all performances are completed, discuss with the students what was successful and what could be improved in future productions. Focus on all aspects, from selecting the literature to giving the program.

There is no one right way to use the readers theater in your class. Feel free to experiment, following your own ideas and those of your students.

■ Summary

Responding is the action one takes during or after reading or listening. This chapter focused on the importance of responding to literature in the process of constructing meaning. Students can do this in a number of verbal and nonverbal ways. The atmosphere of the classroom sets the tone that promotes and supports students' responding activities. Journals, response charts, literature circles, and readers theater are all procedures that promote responding to literature. Organizing and managing a response-centered literacy classroom is an important task for the teacher.

Literature

Allard, H., & Marshall, J. (1977). *Miss Nelson is missing!* Boston: Houghton Mifflin.

Bang, M. G. (1981). *Tye May and the magic brush.* New York: Greenwillow Books.

Bunting, E. (1988). *How many days to America?* New York: Clarion.

Bunting, E. (1991). *Fly away home.* New York: Clarion.

Byars, B. (1970). *The summer of the swans.* New York: Viking Penguin.

Dahl, R. (1961). *James and the giant peach.* New York: Viking Penguin.

de Hamel, J. (1985). *Hemi's pet.* Auckland: Reed Methuen.

de Paola, T. (1980). *Now one foot, now the other.* New York: G. P. Putnam.

Fleischman, S. (1987). *The scarebird.* New York: Greenwillow Books.

Hahn, M. D. (1986). *Wait til Helen Comes.* New York: Clarion.

Lewis, C. S. (1950). *The lion, the witch, and the wardrobe.* New York: Macmillan.

Moss, M. (1990). *Regina's big mistake.* Boston: Houghton Mifflin.

Prelutsky, J. (1988). *Tyrannosaurus was a beast.* New York: Greenwillow Books.

Schwartz, A. (1988). *Annabelle Swift, kindergartner.* New York: Orchard Books.

Scieszka, J. (1989). *The true story of the 3 little pigs.* New York: Viking Kestrel.

Snyder, Z. K. (1976). *The Egypt game.* New York: Atheneum.

Taylor, M. D. (1990). *Mississippi bridge.* New York: Dial.

Westcott, N. B. (1989). *Skip to my Lou.* Boston: Little, Brown.

Xiong, B. (told by), & Spagnoli, C. (adapted by). (1989). *Nine-in-one. Grr! Grr!* San Francisco: Children's Book Press.

For Additional Reading

Atwell, N. (1987). *In the middle.* Portsmouth, NH: Heinemann.

Fox, M. (1984). *Teaching drama to young children.* Portsmouth, NH: Heinemann.

Gambrell, L. B., & Almasi, J. F. (Eds.). (1996). *Lively discussions!* Newark, DE: International Reading Association.

Harste, J. C., Short, K. G., & Burke, C. (1988). Literature circles. In *Creating classrooms for authors* (pp. 293–304). Portsmouth, NH: Heinemann.

McMahon, S. I., Raphael, T. E., Goatley, V. J., & Pardo, L. S. (1997). *The book club connection.* Newark, DE: International Reading Association and New York: Teachers College Press.

Parsons, L. (1990). *Response journals.* Portsmouth, NH: Heinemann.

Reutzel, D. R., & Cooter, R. B., Jr. (1991). Organizing for effective instruction: The reading workshop. *The Reading Teacher, 44,* 548–554.

Roser, N. L., & Martinez, M. G. (Eds.) (1995). *Book talk and beyond: Children and teachers respond to literature.* Newark, DE: International Reading Association.

Wollman-Bonilla, J. E. (1989). Reading journals: Invitations to participate in literature. *The Reading Teacher, 43,* 112–120.

For Exploration: Electronic Products and Resources

Encouraging students to respond to literature allows them to construct meaning. This responding process is fluid, beginning before and lasting during and after reading. Exploring multimedia and hypermedia that support children in responding to literature may consume some time but it is almost sure to present its own rewards. Check the names and Web site addresses of companies and organizations listed at the end of the previous chapters in this book. Also keep an eye on postings and publications of the following:

International Society for Technology in Education
www.iste.org

International Reading Association
www.ira.org

Learning Technology Center at Peabody College
peabody.vanderbilt.edu/ltc/general/

National Council of Teachers of English
www.ncte.org

Writing and the Construction of Meaning

7

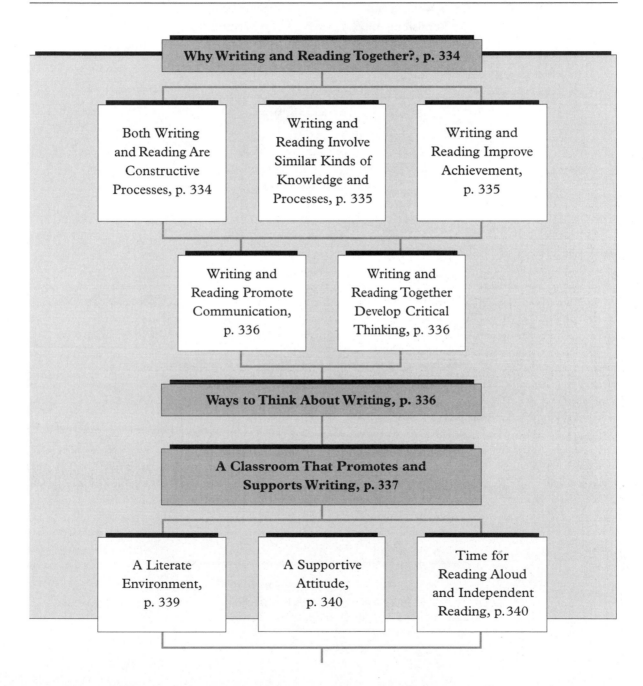

Why Writing and Reading Together?, p. 334

Both Writing and Reading Are Constructive Processes, p. 334

Writing and Reading Involve Similar Kinds of Knowledge and Processes, p. 335

Writing and Reading Improve Achievement, p. 335

Writing and Reading Promote Communication, p. 336

Writing and Reading Together Develop Critical Thinking, p. 336

Ways to Think About Writing, p. 336

A Classroom That Promotes and Supports Writing, p. 337

A Literate Environment, p. 339

A Supportive Attitude, p. 340

Time for Reading Aloud and Independent Reading, p. 340

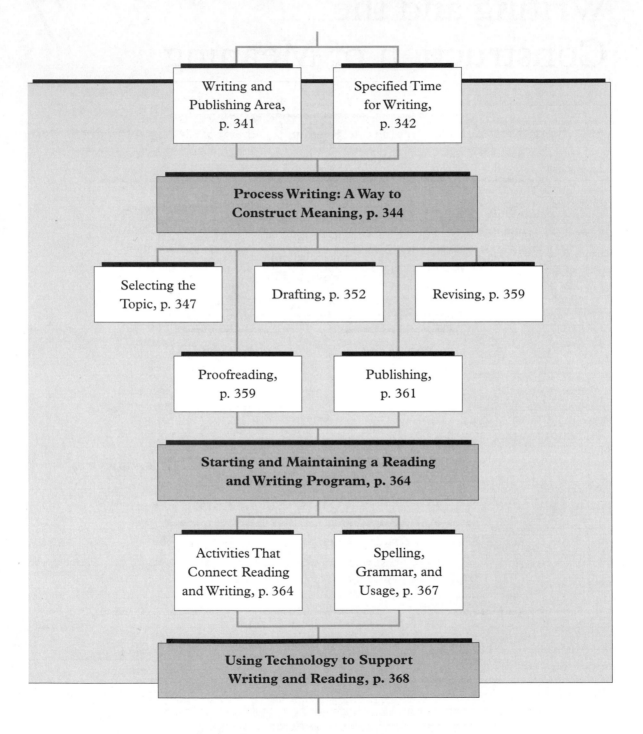

Writing and Publishing Area, p. 341

Specified Time for Writing, p. 342

Process Writing: A Way to Construct Meaning, p. 344

Selecting the Topic, p. 347

Drafting, p. 352

Revising, p. 359

Proofreading, p. 359

Publishing, p. 361

Starting and Maintaining a Reading and Writing Program, p. 364

Activities That Connect Reading and Writing, p. 364

Spelling, Grammar, and Usage, p. 367

Using Technology to Support Writing and Reading, p. 368

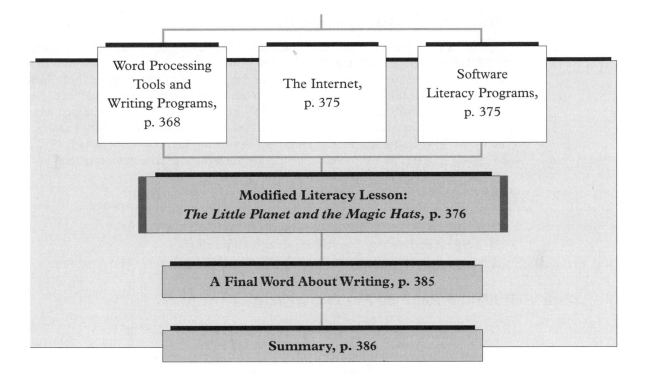

RECENTLY A THIRD-GRADE teacher and I discussed literacy and reading and writing. I asked him, "What do you think it means to develop reading and writing together?" His answer was very clear:

> Children often read books that are related to the topics they are using in writing. At the same time, they often write about what they are reading. For example, a child in my last class was reading the personal narrative Little House in the Big Woods [Wilder, 1932]; it was very natural for her to extend personal narrative into her writing. Another boy was writing a story about dinosaurs. His writing experience became the catalyst for him to read other books on dinosaurs. So you see, I can't just think of reading or writing. I think of a literacy experience or event. By giving my children support in the event they are experiencing, I am able to help them become better comprehenders; it doesn't really matter whether it is a reading focus or a writing focus. They use both of these things together.

In this chapter, we take a more detailed look at the relationships between writing and reading and how these processes develop together. A modified literacy lesson using an exemplary technology program demonstrates how the construction of meaning and story stimulate writing development.

■ Why Writing and Reading Together?

Educators have supported integrating the language arts for many years (Durkin, 1989; Loban, 1963; Moffett & Wagner, 1983). More recent research has given us a better understanding of these processes and helped us to know more about how and why they develop together (Tierney & Shanahan, 1991). In response to the question "Why writing and reading together?" several researchers have helped us to formulate a clearer (although not final) answer (Dahl & Farnan, 1998; Pearson & Tierney, 1984; Shanahan, 1990; Tierney & Leys, 1984; Tierney & Shanahan, 1991). There are at least five major reasons for teaching writing and reading together:

▶ Both writing and reading are constructive processes.

▶ Reading and writing share similar processes and kinds of knowledge.

▶ Writing and reading, when taught together, improve achievement.

▶ Reading and writing together foster communication.

▶ Combining reading and writing leads to critical thinking.

Both Writing and Reading Are Constructive Processes

The fact that reading and writing are both constructive processes is obvious from Pearson and Tierney's (1984) description of readers as composers: thoughtful readers plan reading around a given purpose; with this purpose in mind, they think about the text and begin to activate background relating to the topic. Writers go through a very similar process. They have some purpose for writing and begin to think about what they know or need to know about the topic before beginning to write.

Next, readers begin to read and construct meaning in light of their purposes and background. The cues in the text help them compose these meanings. In the same way, writers begin to write and construct meaning; their task is to compose meaning so it can be conveyed to a reader. As they write, they think about the topic and develop it; they may have a general idea when they start to write, but they really develop it only as they think more about it.

As the reading process continues, readers reread and change meaning as necessary. Again, writers do the same: they think about what they have written, reread it, and rewrite it to make it clearer.

Finally, readers reach a point where they finalize the meaning they have composed as being the best possibility for that given point in time. Writers do the same in their final copy.

Pearson and Tierney refer to each of these four phases as the *planner, composer, editor,* and *monitor* stages. Table 7.1 summarizes the similarities between the reader and the writer as composers (or constructors) of meaning. Of course, readers and writers do not proceed through these stages one after another; they go back and forth between them as they perform the overall process (Dahl & Farnan, 1998; Graves, 1984; Murray, 1985; Pearson & Tierney, 1984).

As proficient readers and writers work, they tend to use the two processes simultaneously. Think about your own experiences in writing. As you write your

TABLE 7.1

READERS AND WRITERS AS COMPOSERS OF MEANING

PROCESSES	READER	WRITER
Planner	Have purpose for reading Generate background	Have purpose for writing Generate background
Composer	Read and compose meaning	Write and compose meaning
Editor	Reread, reflect, and revise meaning	Reread, reflect, and revise
Monitor	Finalize meaning	Finalize copy

ideas, you reread them to see if they make sense. Often you turn to books or other sources to get more information to include in your writing or to make your meaning clearer. The processes of proficient reading and writing not only function in similar ways but also tend to be used together.

Teaching students to write helps them construct meaning by making them more aware of how authors organize their ideas. As they learn to write and organize their own ideas, they will have a greater appreciation and understanding of how other authors do the same.

Writing and Reading Involve Similar Kinds of Knowledge and Processes

There are other reasons reading and writing should be taught together: they naturally develop together (Baghban, 1984; Bissex, 1980; Calkins, 1983; Sulzby & Teale, 1991), and they share many of the same processes and types of knowledge (Tierney & Shanahan, 1991). Researchers have consistently found reading and writing to be highly related (Applebee, 1977; Loban, 1963; Shanahan, 1988; Shanahan & Lomax, 1988), and recently they have been able to identify some specific similarities, such as the use of similar cognitive processes (Birnbaum, 1982; Langer, 1986; Martin, 1987). But this type of research is in its infancy. Differences remain that we need to understand more thoroughly (Langer, 1986).

Writing and Reading Improve Achievement

One area researchers have studied is the effect the teaching of reading and writing together has on overall achievement. The classic U.S. Office of Education study of first-grade reading concluded that programs that incorporated writing were generally more effective in improving reading than those that did not (Bond & Dykstra, 1967). More recent research on the effects of teaching writing and reading together concludes that "studies have shown that writing led to improved reading achievement, reading led to better writing performance, and combined instruction in both led to improvements in both reading and writing" (Tierney & Shanahan, 1991,

p. 258). Caution must be exercised, however; we cannot say that simply providing instruction in one area will automatically lead to improvements in another area; it depends on how the instruction is provided. All we know is that reading and writing together have benefits that neither taught alone will convey. Also, by teaching writing and reading together, we are able to help students recognize and understand the connections between the two processes.

Writing and Reading Promote Communication

Reading and writing are not just skills to learn in order to score better on achievement tests; they are processes that help us more effectively understand and communicate with one another. Through this communication we are able to improve our world, prosper, and enjoy it. Since both communication and learning are social processes, developing reading and writing together has many social benefits.

Writing and Reading Together Develop Critical Thinking

An underlying element of all literacy learning and learning in general is "thinking." In combined writing and reading instruction, learners engage in a greater variety of experiences that lead to better reasoning and higher-level thinking than is achieved with either process alone (McGinley, 1988). Since thinking is a critical part of meaning construction, classrooms that actively foster meaning construction through reading and writing will produce better thinkers (Tierney & Shanahan, 1991).

In conclusion, let's return to the original question posed at the beginning of this section: Why writing and reading together? Reading and writing are both constructive processes that share common knowledges; while they are similar, they are not absolutely the same. Teaching reading and writing together fosters a broad perspective of literacy as a social process that results in better achievement in both activities and leads to better thinking. Tierney and Shanahan (1991) conclude, "We believe strongly that in our society, at this point in history, reading and writing, to be understood and appreciated fully, should be viewed together, learned together, and used together" (p. 275).

Even though many classrooms still focus on reading and writing as separate entities, current research makes it clear that we must view them more as a single entity called *literacy*. For more detailed discussion of the research on writing and reading, see the For Additional Reading section at the end of the chapter. In the remainder of this chapter, we focus on how to build the reading-writing connection.

Ways to Think About Writing

In Chapter 2, we discussed two different types of texts—narrative and expository— and their relationship to meaning construction. Writing can also be seen in terms of broad categories, called *domains*, that somewhat parallel the types of texts students read. There are four basic domains for writing: sensory/descriptive, imaginative/narrative, practical/informative, and analytical/expository (McHugh, 1987). Each domain represents a specific purpose for writing.

TABLE 7.2

DOMAINS OF WRITING

- *Sensory/descriptive domain:* The sensory/descriptive domain focuses on describing something in such rich and clear detail that the reader or listener can almost see or feel it. Description also incorporates the feelings of the writer.

- *Imaginative/narrative domain:* This domain focuses on telling a real or imaginary story. In incorporating some aspects of the descriptive domain, the writer learns to use the elements of a story, including setting, problem, action, and outcome or resolution.

- *Practical/informative domain:* This domain presents basic information clearly. The author provides the information without analyzing it.

- *Analytical/expository domain:* In this final domain, the writer's primary purpose is to explain, analyze, and persuade. This most abstract form of writing uses elements of all of the other forms. The difference between a report written in this domain and one written in the practical/informative domain is that this report focuses more on *why*.

Being aware of each domain and its purpose helps students clearly develop their own purposes for writing. Knowledge about domains also helps you, the teacher, plan a variety of literacy experiences. Within each domain are many possible projects for students to do that represent many of the functions and uses of literacy as identified by Heath (1983). Table 7.2 summarizes the four domains of writing. As you will see, many projects may cut across several domains.

Another way to think about writing is in terms of modes of writing (introduced in Chapter 2). There are four such modes: *independent, collaborative* (partners or a small group work together on a single writing product), *shared* (group with the teacher; this parallels shared reading [see Chapters 2 and 5]), and *write aloud* (teacher writes and verbalizes thinking aloud; students read and listen). Figure 7.1 shows an example of a collaborative story written by a group of fourth graders. Any one of the domains may be handled as independent, collaborative, or shared writing. As we have already noted, the products or projects produced within one domain may also be developed in another domain. Table 7.3 shows sample products that might be developed in each; notice how some products appear in several domains and modes.

A Classroom That Promotes and Supports Writing

Writing is a constructive process; therefore, literacy experiences that focus on writing develop students' ability to construct meaning. The research-based concept of process writing (Calkins, 1986; Dahl & Farnan, 1998; Graves, 1983, 1991; Hillocks, 1987a, 1987b) was introduced in Chapter 2 and discussed in relation to the literacy program, whose elements, as you recall, include motivation, independent reading and

FIGURE 7.1

COLLABORATIVE STORY BY A GROUP OF FOURTH GRADERS

By Ryan
and Terry
Larry and Stacy Juare;

Once upon a time there were
the martians. The first martian said,
"Let's explore that planet. Of course,
that planet was earth. When they
landed, they saw a dog and a man.
Suddenly..... the dog started to
bark. He got very mad. And
there the man saw the
martians he was scard
and he warn. The mar-
tians were scard, too...
then Suddenly..., They both ran
every which way and bumped
into each other and fell to the ground.
The martens was about to git up
and run but... The dog
caught the martions One
had a lazer gun and
shot the dog in the
nose and then... The martions
one got a gun. And shot
a cat and the cat ran
in the Haws.

TABLE 7.3

DOMAINS AND MODES OF WRITING WITH SAMPLE PRODUCTS OR PROJECTS

	DOMAIN			
MODE	Sensory/ Descriptive	Imaginative/ Narrative	Practical/ Informative	Analytical/ Expository
Independent writing	Diary Journal Letters Class notes Poems	Letters Short stories Poems	Lists Reports Letters Directions Class notes Invitations	Reports Letters to the editor Reviews Poems
Collaborative writing	Diary Journal Letters Poems	Letters Short stories Poems	Lists Reports Letters Directions Class notes Invitations	Reports Letters to the editor Reviews Poems
Shared writing	Diary Journal Letters Poems	Letters Short stories Poems	Lists Reports Letters Directions Class notes Invitations	Reports Letters to the editor Reviews Poems
Write Aloud	Any of the above	Any of the above	Any of the above	Any of the above

writing, and instruction in reading and writing. Thus, voluntary, independent reading and writing must be balanced with instruction in writing and reading, and one of the major forms of this instruction is process writing. Let's begin by looking at how to create a classroom environment that promotes and supports literacy with a greater focus on writing. We will then look at ways to develop and use process writing.

A Literate Environment

One of the major elements discussed as part of motivation in Chapter 2 is the creation of a literate environment. The classroom needs to become an exciting, stimulating laboratory for literacy experiences. The areas or centers suggested for inclusion were a library area, a writing and publishing area, a listening and viewing area, a sharing area, a creative arts area, a group meeting area, and a display area. All of these areas are essential to the overall literate environment and play a significant role in promoting and supporting writing. The creation of physical areas that support literacy is not sufficient, however, to create the overall literate environment. Within the classroom you must also develop an attitude that supports and promotes literacy.

A Supportive Attitude

A writing attitude begins with a teacher who is willing to accept the ideas students express in their writing and who shows sincere pleasure and satisfaction in what students have accomplished no matter how small the amount or insignificant the topic. Too often, students are made to feel their ideas just aren't good enough. Even if a child writes only a single sentence, it is a beginning, and the effort should be supported.

Students also need many opportunities to see the teacher write and know that the teacher writes regularly. This can be accomplished by writing notes to students, sharing some of your personal writing, such as a poem or a letter, or writing responses in students' journals (see Chapter 6 and a later section of this chapter). When students see you write, they have models for writing and develop a positive attitude about it.

Another important aspect of developing a "writing and literacy attitude" is letting students know they are partners with you in learning: "We are all learning together." Encourage students to make their own decisions concerning what to write about as well as what type of writing to use.

Finally, a writing attitude develops when students have authentic reasons to write. Just as students must have authentic reading experiences (using real literature the way real readers use it), so they must have authentic writing experiences that revolve around *real reasons to write,* not contrived ones. Some examples include the following:

- ▶ Writing a list of supplies needed for a project
- ▶ Writing an invitation to another class to see a play
- ▶ Writing a story to be published in the class newspaper
- ▶ Writing a mystery to be published
- ▶ Writing a letter to a friend

A writing and literacy attitude is clearly evident to visitors as soon as they walk through the door. They will see children writing, reading, talking, and sharing. The teacher may be hard to find; he or she may be working with a group, conferencing with an individual, or writing. Evidence of students' writing will be everywhere.

Time for Reading Aloud and Independent Reading

The importance of reading aloud to children and independent reading were discussed in detail in Chapter 2. All writing classrooms must incorporate read-aloud time and independent reading time. When children have numerous opportunities at all grade levels to hear good literature, they generally write better (Dressel, 1990). The quality of what children read also influences the type of writing they do (Eckhoff, 1983). Refer to Chapter 2 for suggestions for reading aloud and independent reading.

Writing and Publishing Area

As already mentioned, every classroom needs a writing and publishing area or center. In this center, you should have the following items to support students in their writing:

- Tables and chairs
- Paper (unlined for beginners)
- Pencils, pens, markers, crayons
- Scissors
- Tape and glue
- Construction paper and cardboard
- Old wallpaper sample books
- Yarn, brads, and staplers
- A typewriter (new or old)
- A computer
- A place to display writing
- A storage area for writing folders

The writing center can be the place where students write, meet for conferences with peers or the teacher, or do the final work on a piece of writing they wish to publish. By having this area or center in your classroom, you give significance to writing.

All students need a writing folder containing such items as a list of possible topics for writing (see Figure 7.2 for a sample form), pieces of writing in progress, and a list of pieces of completed writing (see Figure 7.3 for a sample form). Students may also choose to keep a list of words from their writing that cause them spelling problems; many teachers encourage students to do this.

Some teachers also encourage students to keep a record of the conferences they have had with peers (discussed later in this chapter). Such a record helps students prepare for their conferences with the teacher. Figure 7.4 shows a sample form that can be used for this purpose.

The writing folder is basically the student's working folder. It is brought to conferences with the teacher but is primarily for the student's use. Both the folder and the reading journal (see Chapter 6) are places where students keep their work. They are not the same thing as the literacy portfolio, which is discussed in Chapter 11.

Another record students might keep in their writing folder is a list of goals established with the teacher during a conference. These may range from general goals such as "Complete my story" or "Try a different ending" to goals that are very specific, such as "Make more use of descriptive words" or "Pay attention to capital letters and periods." After goals are set, the student and the teacher discuss the progress made and establish new goals. Figure 7.5 shows a goal sheet from a sixth grader's writing folder.

When you first begin to use writing folders with your students, keep them simple. Many students have difficulty keeping records and need help in learning

FIGURE 7.2

FORM FOR RECORDING WRITING TOPICS

their importance (Graves, 1991). Don't have students put in so many pieces that the folders lose their real purpose: as *a place to keep writing in progress.*

Specified Time for Writing

Finally, a classroom that promotes and supports writing must have identified times for writing. On the basis of his research, Graves (1983) recommends that children write every day, and more recently (1991) he has recommended that this writing time be 35 to 40 minutes per day for a minimum of four days a week. If you really believe children and young adults learn to read and write by reading and writing, there is no way to accept anything less than a plan that calls for *writing every day.*

The time provided for writing means the time for students to actually write, not the time for minilessons and other modeling or demonstrations of writing. The writing workshop plan discussed later in this chapter is a very effective way to build in times for both student writing and needed instruction. Once you become comfortable with both reading and writing workshops, you can integrate them into a literacy workshop; such a plan would be similar to the concept of integrated language arts that many teachers have tried to achieve in their classrooms (Templeton, 1991).

Creating a classroom that promotes and supports writing is critical to the success of the literacy program. Regardless of the age or grade level you teach, your classroom must be one that empowers students to take charge of their literacy. Figure 7.6 presents a checklist for evaluating your classroom's writing atmosphere.

FIGURE 7.3

FORM FOR RECORDING COMPLETED WRITING PROJECTS

WRITING RECORD

Name _____

P=Published

Date Started	Type of Writing	Title of Piece	Date Completed or Dropped

FIGURE 7.4

PEER CONFERENCE RECORD

PEER CONFERENCE RECORD

DATE	CONFERENCE WITH	WRITING PIECE	SUGGESTIONS

FIGURE 7.5

GOAL SHEET FROM A SIXTH GRADER'S WRITING FOLDER

WRITING GOALS

Name _Mark Williams_

✔ = Completed   CW = Continuing work

Date	Goal	Progress
2-5-90	_Finish my story_	✔ 2-8-90
2-8-90	_Make sentences more interesting by using descriptive words_	CW

Process Writing: A Way to Construct Meaning

Process writing (Calkins, 1986; Graves, 1983, 1991; Hillocks, 1987a, 1987b) is an approach to teaching writing that allows students to take charge of their own writing and learning. It involves five steps that were introduced in Chapter 2: selecting the topic (sometimes called *planning* or *previewing*), drafting (sometimes called composing), revising, proofreading (sometimes called *editing*), and publishing. A good way to help students become accustomed to using these steps is to display them on a classroom poster such as the one shown in Figure 7.7. Refer to the steps as writing is modeled frequently through *write aloud* and *shared writing*.

As you introduce process writing, use *write aloud* and *shared writing* to model, guide, and support each step until students take charge of their own writing. Gradually the need for modeling will diminish; however, you will always be a partner in learning with the students, interacting with them through individual and group conferences, discussing their writing ideas, having them share their own writing, and providing minilesson support as needed. Through this continuous, scaffolded support, students will grow into writers and come to think of themselves as authors, a process that further develops their ability to construct meaning.

Process writing should begin in kindergarten. At this earliest level, students will be at various developmental phases in their writing. Some will be at the *picture-writing* level, where they will simply draw a picture for their story as the student in Figure 7.8 has done. Other students will be at the *scribble-writing* phase (Figure 7.9). As students

FIGURE 7.6

CHECKLIST FOR EVALUATING THE WRITING ATMOSPHERE IN YOUR CLASSROOM

	Yes	No
1. Do you have areas or centers to promote literacy?		
Library?		
Writing and publishing?		
Listening and viewing?		
Sharing?		
Creative arts?		
Group meeting?		
Display?		
2. Does your classroom promote a writing attitude?		
Accept students' ideas?		
Students see you write?		
You write notes to students?		
Students know they are partners in learning?		
Authentic reasons for writing?		
3. Do you read aloud to your class?		
4. Is there a well-developed writing and publishing area or center?		
Appropriate supplies?		
Student writing folders?		
Storage for writing folders?		
Places to display writing?		
5. Do you have an identified time for uninterrupted student writing?		

Daily _____

If not, how often? _____

35–40 minutes _____

If not, how long? _____

Areas where I need to improve:

_____

_____

_____

progress, they will move into the *random letter* phase (Figure 7.10) and then into the *invented spelling* phase (Figure 7.11), in which they begin to associate some letters and sounds. Finally, they will reach the *conventional writing* phase, in which they will spell most words correctly. It is normal for children in any grade to be at varying points in

FIGURE 7.7

POSTER FOR PROCESS WRITING

FIGURE 7.8

PICTURE-WRITING PHASE

these stages. Beginning or less experienced writers are more likely to be at the picture, scribble, or invented spelling phases, and more experienced writers are usually closer to the conventional writing phase; in other words, it is normal to see some degree of invented spelling all the way through the elementary grades. (For more discussion of spelling, see the For Additional Reading section at the conclusion of this chapter.)

The following discussion focuses on one way to introduce process writing. As students become comfortable using the steps, teacher modeling can gradually be dropped. Adjust your suggestions to fit the grade level you teach. To begin, have a brief discussion about writing with students. Then show them a chart such as the one presented earlier in Figure 7.7 and talk briefly about each step in process writing, using the name of the step.

Selecting the Topic

As students learn the process of writing, they should begin to *select their own topics.* The teacher's role in this process is that of guide and facilitator. From the start, students must know they really can select their own topics. Take time to allow and encourage them to think of ideas on their own. You can use the following steps to help students learn this process:

FIGURE 7.9

SCRIBBLE-WRITING PHASE

FIGURE 7.10

RANDOM LETTER PHASE

FIGURE 7.11

INVENTED SPELLING PHASE

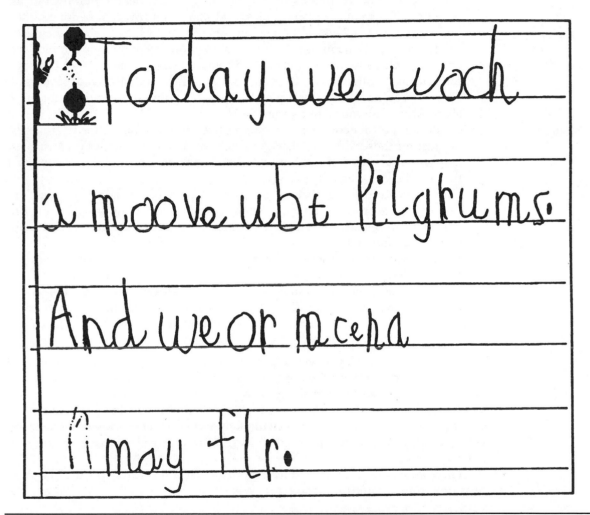

1. Give each student a blank sheet of paper, and ask the students to list anything they might like to write about. If you are focusing on the domains of writing at this point, identify the domain or product you want them to produce, for example, "Think of all the topics you would want to write a story about." As students are making their lists, you do the same, making clear that that is what

you are doing. After finishing your list, move around the room to spot any students who are having trouble. Stop and ask these students such questions as "What have you read that you would like to write about?" or "What topics are you thinking of?" Be careful not to sound critical or condescending. The object is to nudge students to think for themselves and to generate their own ideas.

After a few minutes, stop the class and share your list, commenting on the topics you selected. Next, ask for volunteers who are willing to share their lists. As students read, encourage them to comment on any of their own topics and on one another's topics. Model positive comments about their topics with such remarks as "Those are all exciting topics"; "It sounds like you have good ideas"; "You have so many topics that you are going to have to really think about which one you want to write on."

Be certain your comments are supportive and encouraging for all students, not just for those with long lists. After several students have shared their lists, help them see that it doesn't matter whether their lists are long or short; all they need is one idea to begin writing.

2. Have students look over their lists to decide if they want to add any topics. You can model the process with your own list, perhaps by adding a topic similar to one a student has selected. This lets students know that it is all right for them to get ideas from others.

3. Have students review their lists to select a topic for their first piece of writing. Suggest that they consider the following points as they make their decisions: (1) Which topic is the most interesting to you? (2) Which topic do you feel you know the most about? and (3) Which topic do you think others might enjoy reading the most? Have students circle their choices. Then share your choice with the group and have volunteers do the same.

By following these steps, you will help students select their first topic for writing. It doesn't really matter what the topics are as long as the choices are the students' and the students want to write about them.

Students should keep their lists of topics in their writing folders and should be encouraged to add to them when they think of new ideas. They should not feel they will have to write on every topic on their lists. Their ideas will change; therefore, the lists can change.

There are many other ways to have students select topics for writing. Try these ideas from time to time throughout the year:

▶ *Partners:* Have each student work with a partner to develop lists of possible topics. This is using the brainstorming strategy as suggested for activating prior knowledge in Chapter 3. It is a good strategy to use for the student who appears to have few ideas or who doesn't want to write.

▶ *Clustering:* "Clustering is a nonlinear brainstorming process akin to free association" (Rico, 1983, p. 28). Working alone, with partners, or with the teacher, students start with a topic or idea that forms the core, or nucleus, for the cluster. They then add all of the things they can think of that are related to it and select the specific topic from the cluster they wish to write about or use the ideas to develop their writing. Figure 7.12 presents a cluster on animals

FIGURE 7.12

CLUSTER ON ANIMALS DEVELOPED BY SECOND GRADERS

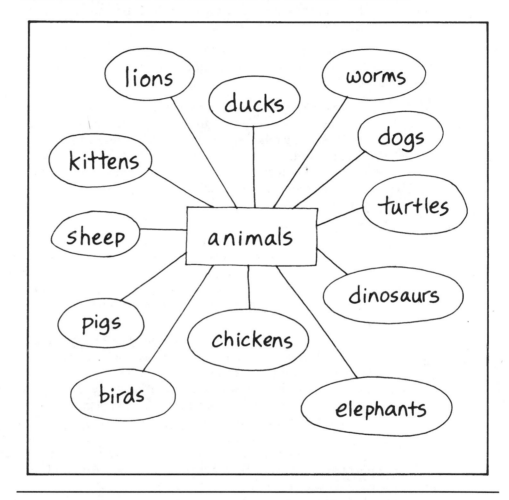

developed by a second-grade teacher and his class to get ideas for writing. Teachers report that clustering is a successful technique to use with all students, including at-risk and second-language learners (Carr, 1987; Martinez, 1987; Pierce, 1987). For more on clustering, see the For Additional Reading section at the end of the chapter.

▶ *Looking for ideas away from school:* Encourage students to look for and jot down writing ideas on the way home from school, at home, or in places they visit.

▶ *Photography ideas:* Let students use cameras to take pictures of possible topics. If possible, have them take pictures away from school as well. You can also encourage them to bring to class photographs from home that could be topics for their writing.

▶ *TV topics:* Encourage students to look for interesting topics as they watch their favorite TV shows.

Selecting topics for writing is not always easy for students. Some of the problems they encounter and suggestions for overcoming these problems include the following:

▶ *No ideas:* Some students will insist they have no ideas to use for writing. One way to help these students is to get them to talk about things they do away from school. As they talk, suggest that each of these activities could be a topic for writing. Another tactic is to ask the students to think about places they would like to go or something special they would like to do, pointing out that these too can be ideas for writing. You might serve as the students' "secretary," writing their ideas as they give them.

▶ *Too many ideas:* Some students will have so many ideas that they won't know which one to select for writing. In these cases, you can help students focus by discussing the ideas with them. If discussion doesn't work, select one of the topics for the students. One teacher who had tried other strategies to no avail finally said to a student, "Close your eyes and point to a topic. Since you like them all, write about the one you point to." That was enough encouragement to get the child started.

▶ *Don't like to write:* This problem is tougher to deal with, and there are really no easy solutions. Some students simply don't like to write and don't want to write, for a number of reasons. (Likewise, some teachers don't like to write and don't want to teach writing.) These students need to be encouraged to write and to see some of the fun of writing. You can begin by serving as the student's secretary, recording not only the topics but the first draft of the writing. Another tactic is to allow the student to dictate his or her list of topics onto a tape recorder or enter them in a computer and then write the first draft on the computer. Shared and collaborative writing are also good ways to get students started.

Selecting the topic for writing is an important part of the writing process, and students need to see that they can use their own ideas. Although there are times when students must write on assigned topics, they must be allowed to choose their own topics when they are learning "how" to write. Even in classes such as social studies, in which students are required to write reports, teachers are likely to get better products if they let students have some choice of the topic.

Drafting

Once students have selected their topics, they are ready to begin writing. The teacher and students have already modeled the process of selecting topics; now the teacher must show students how to write. Drafting includes two stages, planning and composing, both of which should be modeled as students are learning to use process writing.

Planning

Good writers think about what they are going to write and organize their ideas. To do this, they consider the purpose for their writing and the audience for whom they are writing. You should model this process using your own topic and the following steps:

1. Tell the class a little bit about your topic and what you want to write about it. Mention your audience and purpose for writing, and allow students to ask questions. Next, on the chalkboard, overhead projector, or large sheets of paper, jot down some of the ideas you have about the topic. Group ideas that go together, but don't be concerned about getting all of them organized at this point. Tell students that you now have a general plan of what you want to include in your writing and you know how you want to begin. Figure 7.13 shows the notes one teacher made while planning to write about her family's camping trip. If you are modeling expository writing, use graphic organizers like Raphael and Englert (1990) use in their Cognitive Strategy Instruction in Writing (CSIW) program. (See Figures 7.14 and 7.15.)
2. Have students work in pairs, telling each other about their topics. Afterward, have each student jot down some ideas or words about his or her topic on a sheet of paper. Volunteers should share their ideas with the class and talk about what they want to include in their writing. Help students understand that this is a beginning plan for their writing and that it will probably change as they actually write.

As students mature in their writing abilities, you can introduce outlining and include it in modeling when focusing on expository writing. Students will find outlining a useful planning tool for such activities as report writing. They may also use clustering (discussed earlier in this chapter) or semantic mapping (discussed in Chapter 3) to help them organize their ideas.

The more students mature in their writing, the less they will need to go through the planning phase as a group. However, students should be given enough teacher modeling and support to see how planning is done and how it can help them in their own writing. The more students write, the more automatically they will carry out the process of writing.

Composing

The next phase in the drafting stage is the actual composing. Students should be told to write on lined paper (unlined for beginners), using every other line to leave room for revisions. This practice helps them develop a positive attitude toward revision; it lets them know that changes can and will be made and that it is all right to make changes in their writing.

You must model this activity as well, because it is important that the students see the teacher write. Although the teacher and students can write independently

FIGURE 7.13

TEACHER'S NOTES FOR PLANNING WRITING

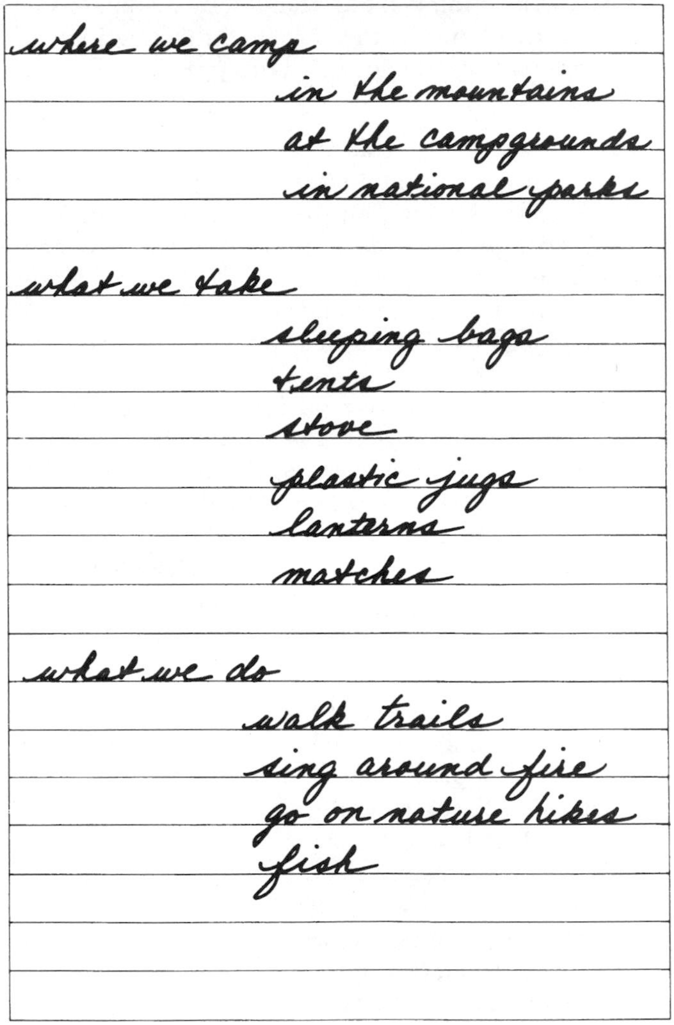

where we camp
     in the mountains
     at the campgrounds
     in national parks

what we take
     sleeping bags
     tents
     stove
     plastic jugs
     lanterns
     matches

what we do
     walk trails
     sing around fire
     go on nature hikes
     fish

and share their results later, this works best with older, more mature writers; it is less satisfactory for beginning writers, since it does not really let students see all of the process of writing. For most students, the following procedure will be most effective:

FIGURE 7.14

PLAN THINK SHEET

Author's name _____ Date _____

Topic: _____

WHO: Who am I writing for?

WHY: Why am I writing this?

WHAT: What do I already know about my topics? (Brainstorm)

1. _____

2. _____

3. _____

4. _____

HOW: How do I group my ideas?

1. Materials I'll need

_____

_____

2. Steps

_____

_____

3. Things that happened when we made it

_____

_____

4. Beginning and ending ideas

_____

_____

FIGURE 7.15

ORGANIZE THINK SHEET

What is being explained?

Who or what is needed?

Setting?

What are the steps?

First,

Next,

Third,

Then,

Fifth,

Finally,

---

1. Using the chalkboard, overhead projector, or large sheets of paper, begin to develop the topic you selected, discussing what you are doing as you go. Note the mechanics of starting a sentence and paragraph, and show students how to

organize ideas into sentences and paragraphs, asking them to suggest words or make changes in your writing. As you write, cross out some words to show students how to make changes without erasing, which often becomes a big problem for them. Don't be afraid to tell students that you don't know what to say next and that you need some help. Figure 7.16 shows a sample of a teacher's draft for modeling the family camping trip story.

2. After the initial teacher modeling, have students start their own writing. Encourage them to use the notes they made as part of their planning. While students are writing, move about the room offering guidance, assistance, and encouragement to those who need it. If some students are not writing, offer to be their secretary for the beginning few sentences of their drafts.

   If the writing is going smoothly, continue to move about the room offering assistance and support. A few minutes of talking about the topic or a few questions from the teacher are often enough to keep students writing. Give students as much time to write as the schedule will allow and as much time as they can use productively. If you see that the writing time is producing little or nothing, it is probably best to resume modeling or to stop the writing at this time.

3. If you find it necessary to resume modeling, return to your story and continue to write, explaining as you go. Continue to encourage students to help you. As you model your writing, you can note different elements of good writing. However, during the initial introduction of writing, do not overemphasize isolated mechanics.

Composing is the phase of drafting in which students develop their topics. Usually they will have received enough direction up to this point that they can proceed with their own writing without additional instruction. During this part of the writing program, students should have uninterrupted writing time to develop their ideas. Modeling occurs as the teacher moves about the room offering assistance.

In this phase of writing, the object is for students to express their ideas freely and creatively; they should not be hampered by worrying about spelling. The best way to deal with spelling is to encourage students to spell words the way they think they sound (invented spellings). This will free them to write as they realize they can take care of any spelling problems during their revision. For those students who are overly concerned about spelling words correctly or are unable to use invented spelling, provide the correct spellings by writing the words in question on a sheet of paper or the chalkboard, or tell them to pretend they are alone on an island with no one to ask. Other techniques include having one student serve as a spelling helper or having a list of troublesome words on the board or a chart. *But nothing works as well to develop a sense of spelling as having students try to spell words the way they think they sound and then make corrections during revision and proofreading.*

The amount of time allowed for the composing phase depends on the students, their writing abilities, the nature of the piece being written, and the length of time allocated to writing in the classroom. Usually the composing phase will extend over several days or writing periods. Students can place their writing in their writing folders and return to it at the next writing period or when they have some extra

FIGURE 7.16

TEACHER'S DRAFT FOR MODELING WRITING

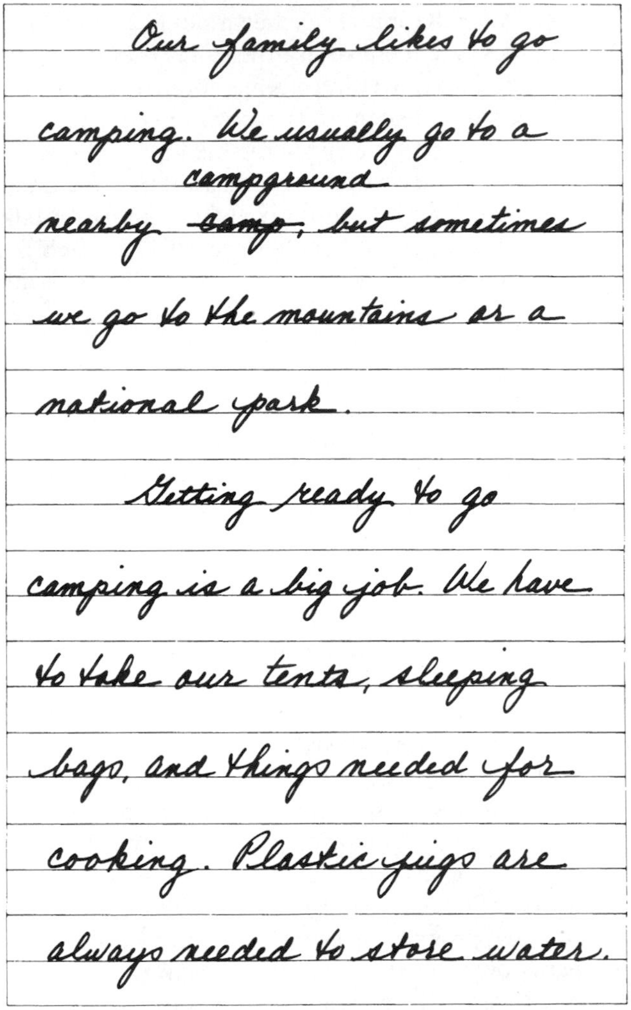

> Our family likes to go
> camping. We usually go to a
>   campground
> nearby ~~camp~~, but sometimes
> we go to the mountains or a
> national park.
>
>   Getting ready to go
> camping is a big job. We have
> to take our tents, sleeping
> bags, and things needed for
> cooking. Plastic jugs are
> always needed to store water.

time during the day. The writing, especially in the beginning stages, should be done at school.

Throughout the composing phase, you should continue to be available to help students with their writing. If students get stuck, encourage them to ask you or a peer for suggestions. For example, if a student can't think of a good word to describe his or her old dog, you might give several suggestions and let the student select the one she or he wants to use. Asking questions and offering suggestions as the students are writing is an extension of modeling and also serves as a "quick conference."

Revising

Revision, the third stage in the writing process, is the step in which the students begin to look at their work to examine content—ideas, choice of words, and so forth. Revision may involve modeling by the teacher, conferences between student and teacher or student and student, and individual student work. It is not a natural step for students to employ (Graves, 1984). Most beginning writers, especially kindergartners and first graders, are not ready for much revision; they think everything they have written is wonderful! Therefore, teachers must help students learn to appreciate the importance of revision by systematically working through this stage with them.

You can model revision by using your own writing on an overhead as an example. You and your students should first discuss what to look for when revising content:

1. Have I expressed my ideas clearly so that my audience will understand what I am saying?
2. Are there other ideas that I should add to my writing?
3. Are there other words that I can use to make my writing more exciting and interesting?
4. Are there better ways I can express my ideas?

The questions generated can be posted for students to think about as they work on their revisions. The items considered in content revision will vary according to the students' level and degree of sophistication.

After you and your students have developed guidelines for revision, show them how to go about revising their writing. Use the *write aloud* process to show how you would revise your piece. Check each of the points listed on the revision checklist and discuss problem areas with them, making changes with their help. Have them try better ways to express their ideas. Throughout the revision step, you should stress the importance of expressing oneself clearly because others will read the writing. Figure 7.17 shows a copy of the teacher's story about the family camping trip after the teacher and students revised the content.

Students are now ready to begin to work on their own revisions. At this point, they should begin to have revision conferences with one another and with you (for a discussion of writing conferences, see page 478). During these conferences, students talk about their writing and look for places where they might make changes, with you and/or other students taking on the role of an editor who asks questions and points out areas of possible improvement. Many students will already know where some of these areas are. The teacher and peers should not become the "fixers" of students' writing; rather, they should help students note places where work is needed, discuss ideas with students, and have the writers try to make the changes.

Proofreading

The fourth step in process writing is proofreading, or editing, which should take place after students have made all the content changes they believe are necessary.

FIGURE 7.17

TEACHER'S STORY USED FOR MODELING REVISION

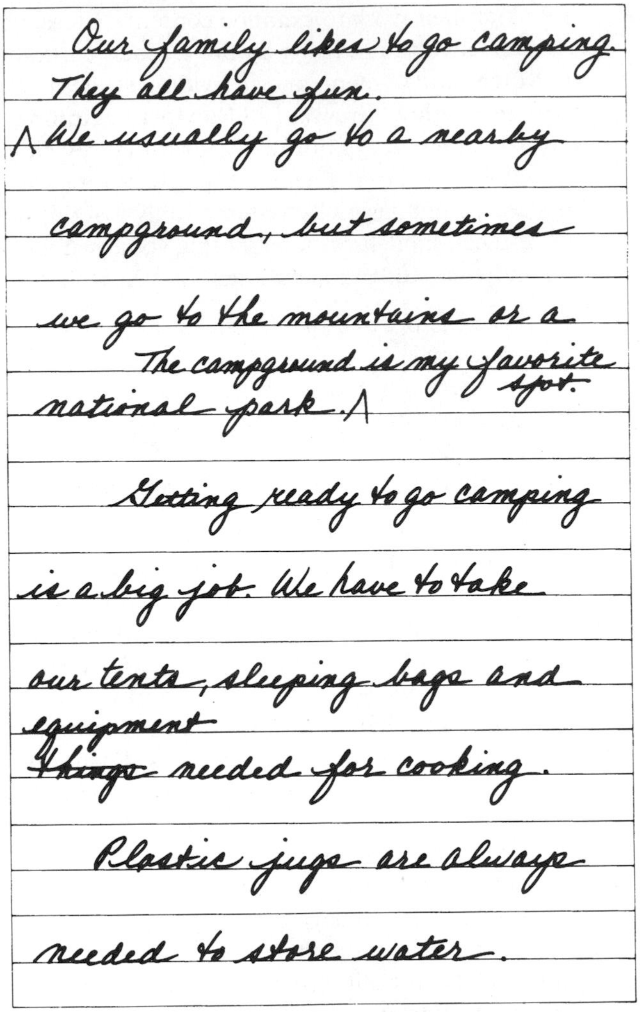

Our family likes to go camping.
They all have fun.
^ We usually go to a nearby
campground, but sometimes
we go to the mountains or a
The campground is my favorite spot.
national park. ^
Getting ready to go camping
is a big job. We have to take
our tents, sleeping bags and
equipment
~~things~~ needed for cooking.
Plastic jugs are always
needed to store water.

In proofreading, students get their writing in order for final copy, checking spelling, writing mechanics, and sentence structure. The teacher and students should work together to develop a list of things to look for in proofreading, and the list should be posted in the room so that students can refer to it as they work. In addition to spelling, the list should reflect the writing mechanics that were modeled throughout the writing. Figure 7.18 shows a proofreading checklist developed

FIGURE 7.18

PROOFREADING CHECKLIST DEVELOPED BY A FIFTH-GRADE CLASS

	Author	*Editor*
1. Sentences and questions begin with capital letters.	☐	☐
2. Sentences and questions have the correct end marks.	☐	☐
3. Paragraphs are indented.	☐	☐
4. Possible misspellings have been circled and checked.	☐	☐

Author _____

Editor _____

by a fifth-grade class and their teacher for use at the beginning of the year. This generic checklist can be used by the author (writer) or the editor (such as a peer or the teacher) for any domain of writing. As you become more comfortable with process writing, you will want to develop more specific checklists for each domain, varying the items according to the level and sophistication of the students.

Publishing

The final stage of the writing process is publishing, which has two steps: (1) making a final copy of the writing and (2) putting the writing in a form to be shared with others. Although most students will make a final copy of their writing, if they are not making progress with a piece of writing they may elect to drop it. This may occur at *any point* in the writing process. Indeed, not all writing should be published. The student, together with the teacher, should make this decision after considering both the quality of the writing and how the student feels about it. In a conference, you might ask the student such questions as "How do you think others will feel about this piece of writing?" and "Do you think it is a good idea to publish this one?" Sometimes it is appropriate for the teacher to say, "I don't think this is one of your best pieces of writing. Maybe you should just stop working on this piece or make a final copy for your file and start work on something new." If a student feels strongly about the piece being published, it is probably best to proceed, but you must always weigh the consequences of having a student publish a piece that is really inappropriate.

Publishing is important for all students, not just a special few. This phase of the writing process authenticates the reason for writing and gives students pride and enjoyment in their own work. The more students publish their writing, the more they will develop a sense of themselves as authors and grow in the writing process. One precaution: a few students will not want to create final copies or publish. You must support and guide these students until they experience the satisfaction of seeing their work published, because doing so will motivate them to write more.

When the decision is to make final copy only, the copy can be put in the student's writing folder. Even writing that is not published may be used for later review and placed in the literacy portfolio (see Chapter 11).

Producing Final Copy

After students have completed their revisions and held their initial publishing conference with the teacher, they are ready to make a final copy of their writing. In making their final copy, they should be encouraged to be as neat and accurate as possible. One way to get students to produce a good final copy is to use a computer with a word processing program, since even very young children experience success with this approach.

You and your students should work together to develop a list of guidelines to follow in making final copies, and the list should be kept where students can refer to it easily. Points such as the following can be included, but each list must reflect the needs, abilities, and level of the students:

> ### *Final Copy Guidelines*
>
> Be neat.
>
> Indent each new paragraph.
>
> Keep margins at the top, bottom, and sides of the paper straight.
>
> Check punctuation.
>
> Check spelling.
>
> Reread your final copy to be sure it is correct.

The manner in which the final copy is prepared will depend on whether it is to be published or simply filed.

Ideas for Publishing

Publishing is a very important part of the writing process (Calkins, 1986; Graves, 1983). Students need this aspect of the writing process to help them develop a sense of the importance of their writing, an understanding of why one must learn to write, and a sense of their audience.

The most common way for students to publish their writing is in book form. Individual students can produce their own books, or several students can collaborate on one. The excitement and pleasure on the faces of students after producing their first book are almost indescribable! Publishing brings closure to the students' writing experience.

Books can be produced in many forms:

▶ Construction paper covers over paper

▶ Folder books made from manila folders and paper

▶ Shape books cut to show the topic (for example, a snowman shape for a winter topic)

▶ Hardcover books made from cardboard and cloth (for directions, see Tompkins and Hoskisson [1991] in the For Additional Reading section)

Students can move from simple types of books to more complex forms as they become more practiced. They should be encouraged to include a cover page that presents their names, the illustrator's name, and the date. At the end of the book, they should place a page entitled "About the Author" where they tell about themselves and other books they have written. Also, when books are being published to be shared with other classmates, it is a good idea to include a sheet in the back where students can indicate they have read the book and comment on how they felt about it.

There are many other ways for students to share their writing without producing a book. Some of the following ideas broaden the concept of publishing to any form of sharing:

▶ **Bulletin boards:** Use a bulletin board with a catchy title and an attractive background for students to display final copies that have not been made into a book. The title might be "Great Writing from Great Kids," "Writing We Are Proud Of," "Great Writers Are Blossoming," "Award Winners," and so on. Sometimes you can attach a clothesline to the bulletin board on which students can hang their writing out for others to read.

▶ **Author's chair:** The concept of the author's chair (Graves & Hansen, 1983) was introduced in Chapter 2. This is a special chair labeled "Author's Chair." The student who has a piece of writing to share sits in the chair and reads it to the group, and a discussion of the writing follows. Usually the piece that is shared is the final copy.

▶ **Class or school newspaper:** A class or school newspaper is an excellent way to create authentic reasons for students to write. Because of the nature of a newspaper, students can get experiences with many domains of writing and numerous products—articles, stories, letters to the editor, and so forth. The newspaper can have a staff, and students can publish it using a computer.

▶ **Magazines of student-written works:** Students may also choose to submit their writing to a magazine that publishes student-written works. For a list of magazines that publish student writing, see *Magazines for Kids and Teens* (Stoll, 1997) listed in the For Additional Reading section.

▶ **Writing circles:** The concept of the literature circle was introduced in Chapter 6. You can also have a writing circle where students get together to share and discuss their writing. Also referred to as RAGs, or Read Around Groups (Olson, 1987), the writing circle consists of five or six students who sit together to read and talk about (not critique) their writing. Several writing circles may be in operation at the same time. (They may also be used for selecting and discussing a topic, revising, and proofreading. To ensure that students know the real purpose of the circle, it might be better to use the title "Writing Circle" for sharing and "RAGs" when the circle is used for other purposes.)

It does not matter how children publish and share their writing as long as they *do* it, since it is through sharing that they develop their sense of authorship and show how they have constructed meaning by conveying their ideas to others. At any grade level, sharing is an essential part of constructing meaning through writing.

Starting and Maintaining a Reading and Writing Program

The preceding discussion describes only one way to get a writing program started. You may choose to introduce process writing by having a shared writing experience with the entire class first, demonstrating each of the steps before having the students begin their own work. Some teachers, particularly those in the upper grades, simply begin with a little talk about the writing steps and then have students begin, using this initial writing experience diagnostically to determine where their students are and the type of support they need. However, if you are sure your students have little or no experience with process writing, it is better to begin with a procedure such as the one suggested here to ensure students' comfort and success.

In maintaining a reading and writing program, you should also consider activities that connect reading and writing and show how to develop grammar, usage, and spelling. Both types of activities are discussed in the sections that follow.

Activities That Connect Reading and Writing

Throughout your literacy program, you must continually help students see the connections between reading and writing and think about how each carries over to the other. The following suggestions are only a few ways to help students begin to make this explicit connection (Shanahan, 1988).

Reading Specific Types of Writing

Students need to use their writing as a springboard to reading just as they use their reading as a springboard to writing. If you have a student who has written (or is writing) a mystery, encourage her or him to read some other mysteries, such as *Encyclopedia Brown: Boy Detective* (Sobol, 1963) or *The Mysterious Disappearance of Leon (I Mean Noel)* (Raskin, 1971), to see how these authors developed their ideas.

Reading Student-Written Materials

As students begin to publish books, they can read one another's books; they will enjoy seeing what their peers have written. These books should be displayed in both the classroom and the school library and should be used as a part of the reading material for the literacy program. In many schools that do this, the student-written books are among those most frequently selected and checked out.

Developing a collection of student-written books is a simple procedure. Begin the school year by telling students that there will be a special section in the school library for books or magazines they have written. Explain that there will be a classroom library of their books and that throughout the year selected books will be placed in the school library. You and your students should develop criteria such as the following for selecting books:

1. Best written
2. Favorite topic or story
3. Topic others would most likely enjoy

4. Book student would like others to read

The student-written book collection for the library can become a schoolwide project. At the conclusion of each school year, students may donate a certain number of their books to the library, and copies should then be made so that authors can also have a copy.

As student-written books are added to the school library, special announcements should be made so that everyone in the school can see them. This can be done through a school newspaper or a bulletin board display similar to that in Figure 7.19.

Finally, a special time may be designated in the reading program for students to read the books their peers have written. For example, teachers can designate an hour every other week for this purpose and increase the time to an hour or longer each week as more books are available. Students should use this time to read the books and talk about them with their classmates. These discussions can be handled in small groups or as class discussions, but they should focus on telling about the books, not evaluating them.

Having a time in the literacy program for students to read books written by their peers gives a special importance to both reading and writing. It helps show students that these processes are related and also gives them an incentive to read and write.

Summaries

Another way to help students make the connection between reading and writing is to have them write a summary of a text they have just read (Hill, 1991). This is a skill that must be taught. The following steps for summarizing expository texts are based on research by Brown and Day (1983):

1. Determine the topic of the paragraph or text. Identify unnecessary information or trivia, and delete this information; it should not be included in the summary.
2. Look for information that is repeated; it should be included in the summary only once.
3. Note places where ideas or terms can be grouped together. For example, if the paragraph or text being summarized discusses travel by plane, ship, train, and car, all of these modes can be referred to as "transportation."
4. Identify a main-idea sentence for each paragraph, if possible. If no main-idea sentence exists, formulate one of your own.
5. Formulate your final summary, rechecking to be sure you have followed each guideline. Keep your summary short.

You should model the process of writing a summary for students using procedures similar to those suggested for teaching the writing process.

Writing summaries after reading can be handled in many creative ways. For example, you can give students such writing assignments as the following:

▶ Pretend to be newspaper reporters or TV newscasters who must present a summary of what they have read. First, write the summary; then distribute it to other students in newspaper form, or give the summary as a part of a TV news report.

▶ Maintain a log or journal that reports a summary of your readings. Write the log entries after reading your favorite selections. (Students can also be instructed to write log entries for particular selections assigned by you.)

FIGURE 7.19

**BULLETIN BOARD FOR PUBLICIZING STUDENT BOOKS
IN THE SCHOOL LIBRARY**

Summaries may also be written for narrative texts, in which case the same type of guidelines should be followed, focusing on the parts of a story map (see Chapters 2 and 3) instead of main ideas.

Story Frames

Story frames are another way to build the connection between reading and writing (Fowler, 1982). A story frame is a basic outline for a story that is designed to help readers organize their ideas about what they have read. It consists of a series of spaces hooked together by transition words; each story frame usually follows a single line of thought or aspect of a selection. Figure 7.20 presents a story frame that focuses on a particular character from a selection.

After students read a selection, you can use the story frame as an oral discussion starter. You should encourage students to fill in the slots in the frame, basing their re-

---

FIGURE 7.20

SAMPLE STORY FRAME FOCUSING ON A CHARACTER

This story is about _____.

_____ is an important character.

_____ tried to _____.

The story ends when _____

_____.

---

sponses on their reading; however, you should also encourage them to express the ideas creatively in their own words. When students have become familiar with the concept of using story frames, you can use story frames in written activities following reading.

Although story frames can be written for specific selections, some of the basic patterns can be used repeatedly. Figure 7.21 presents three additional story frames focusing on setting, plot, and character comparison.

Spelling, Grammar, and Usage

We discussed the importance of writing in helping children learn to spell in Chapter 4. Writing is also important in helping students learn the various conventions of our language.

Formal grammar teaching as a way to promote meaning construction through writing is not considered a useful activity for students. As Hillocks and Smith (1991) state, "Why does grammar retain such glamour when research over the past 90 years reveals not only that students are hostile toward it, but that the study of grammar has no impact on writing quality?" (p. 602). They also state that "the grammar sections of a textbook should be treated as a reference tool that might provide some insights into conventions of mechanics and usage" (p. 602).

The basic premise that children learn to read and write by reading and writing while receiving instruction as needed also applies to grammar, usage, and spelling. Repeated opportunities to write help children learn the conventions of writing and also help them construct meaning through reading. Minilessons held during conferences or in small groups are good ways to support students in learning mechanics, usage, and spelling, and these lessons can be built around a demonstrated need in students' writing. Figure 7.22 shows the steps for using students' writing as a basis for minilessons. This model is based on the work of Wilde (1990, 1996), Gentry (1997), and Gentry and Gillet (1993).

Figure 7.23 presents a sample spelling lesson and Figure 7.24 shows a sample grammar lesson.

FIGURE 7.21

SAMPLE STORY FRAMES

Setting Frame

This story takes place _____

_____. I can tell this because the

author uses such words as _____

_____to tell

where this story happens.

Plot Frame

This story begins when _____

_____. Next,

_____.

Then _____

_____. The story ends when

_____

_____.

Character Comparison Frame

_____ and _____are

two characters in our story. _____ is

_____, whereas _____is

_____. For instance, _____

tries to _____ and

_____ learns a lesson when _____

_____.

Using Technology to Support Writing and Reading

Technology is increasingly common in classrooms. Three important types of technology that especially support writing and reading include (1) word processing and writing programs, (2) the Internet, and (3) software literacy programs.

Word Processing Tools and Writing Programs

Research has shown that the use of word processing leads students at all levels to write longer pieces and to revise more (Dahl & Farnan, 1998). The teacher still plays a critical role in the process by serving as a monitor and a coach for

FIGURE 7.22

SIX STEPS TO MEANINGFUL TEACHING OF GRAMMAR AND SPELLING BASED ON WRITING

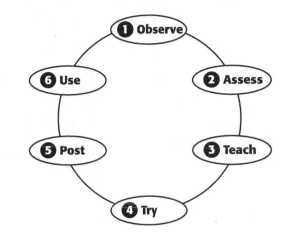

Each step is described below:

❶	**Observe**	• Examine students' writing. • Identify strengths in spelling or grammar. *AND* • Identify needs in spelling or grammar.
❷	**Assess**	• Have students write some words using the spelling pattern or grammar convention. *OR* • Have students write a sentence using the grammar convention. • Note how they do.
❸	**Teach**	• Teach a minilesson on the spelling pattern or grammar convention. • Draw examples used in minilessons from literature being read.
❹	**Try**	• Have students write some words or a sentence or more using what they learned. *OR* • Repeat the assessment used in Step 2. • Compare to students' performance in Step 2, Assess.
❺	**Post**	• Write the grammar convention or spelling generalization or pattern on a chart with examples and post on the wall. • For spelling patterns, add lists of words to the word wall.
❻	**Use**	• Encourage students to use the spelling pattern or grammar convention in their writing. • Remind students to refer to wall postings as needed.

FIGURE 7.23

SAMPLE SPELLING LESSON

❶ **Observe**   • Several students have written sentences in their stories like the following:

The dog had muddy feet. He jumped on the chair seet to get the met on the table.

Major Strengths
- Knows beginning consonants *d, m, f, j, s, t*
- Knows high-frequency words *the, had, he, on, to, get*
- Knows the double consonant pattern *dd.*

Needs
- Needs to learn long *e* pattern *ee* and *ea.*
- Needs to learn *ed* ending.

> ✪   Start by teaching a lesson on *ee, ea* words.

❷ **Assess**   • Ask students to write four words on their papers before you teach a minilesson—*beat* (My team will beat your team.), *keep, seat, tree.*

Examples of Students' Second Answers		
1	**2**	**3**
beat	*beat*	*beet*
keep	*ceep*	*keep*
seat	*seat*	*seet*
tree	*tree*	*tree*

❸ **Teach**   • Write the following list* of words on the board:

see	eat
three	meat
sleep	bead

* (*Note:* Words should be taken from literature students are reading.)

• Have students underline what is the same in each column.

s<u>ee</u>	<u>ea</u>t
thr<u>ee</u>	m<u>ea</u>t
sl<u>ee</u>p	b<u>ea</u>d

Figure 7.23 continued

- Read aloud each list (or have the list read aloud).
- Ask what vowel sound you hear in each column of words (long *e*).
- Point out that long *e* may be spelled *ee* or *ea*.

❹ **Try** • Repeat the assessment used in Step 2.

Examples of Students' Second Answers		
1	**2**	**3**
beat	beat	beet
keep	ceep	keep
seat	seat	seet
tree	tree	tree

- Student 1 has the knowledge to spell words using *ea* and *ee*.
- Student 2 understands the *ea/ee* patterns but needs to work on the *k*.
- Student 3 understands the *ee* pattern but needs more work with *ea*.

❺ **Post** • Make a chart.

Spelling

The long *e* may be spelled *ee* or *ea* in words.

Examples: meat
keep

- Add to the word wall.

Long e

ea	ee
sea	see
meat	tree
seal	sleep
meal	keep

- Continue to add other words over time.

❻ **Use** • Remind students to check the posting on the chart and the word wall to check their spelling as they write.
- Observe students' writing to see if they are using the *ee*, *ea* spelling patterns correctly.

FIGURE 7.24

Sample Grammar Lesson

❶   **Observe**   • Several students have written sentences like the following:

Student 1

My dad drives a dodge ram truck. His name Harry. The truck is red.

Student 2

We went to california on a Vacation. We had fun and saw

the golden gate bridge.

Student 3

I live in kentucky near Barkley lake. I like to
fish and catch perch.

Major Strengths
  – Capitalizes beginning of sentences.
  – Uses correct end punctuation.
  – Uses nouns.

Needs
  – Does not know difference between common and proper nouns.
  – Does not capitalize nouns correctly.

✪   Teach a lesson on common and proper nouns.

---

❷   **Assess**   • Dictate the following sentences to students:

Mr. Brown likes ice cream. His favorite brand is Blue
Bunny which really is nonfat yogurt.

Figure 7.24 continued

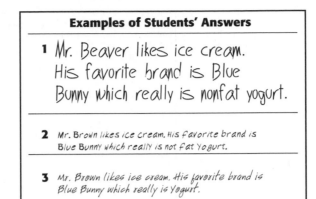

Examples of Students' Answers

1 Mr. Beaver likes ice cream.
His favorite brand is Blue
Bunny which really is nonfat yogurt.

2 Mr. Brown likes ice cream. His favorite brand is
Blue Bunny which really is not fat Yogurt.

3 Mr. Brown likes ice cream. His favorite brand is
Blue Bunny which really is Yogurt.

❸　**Teach**　• Write the following on the board:

> ● A _noun_ is the name of a person, place, or thing.
>
> ● A _common noun_ names any person, place, or thing.
>
> ● A _proper noun_ is a particular person,
> place, or thing. Capitalize proper nouns.

• Have students open a book that the whole class is reading. Locate examples of common and proper nouns. Make a list of them.

Common Nouns	Proper Nouns
airplane	Boeing 747
ship	the Queen Elizabeth
submarine	Bob Marshall
mountain	Mt. Hood
book	Bridge to Terabithia

• Ask students what they notice about the two groups and how they are capitalized. (Point out if not given.)
• Note that little words like *to* in *Bridge to Terabithia* are not capitalized.

❹　**Try**　• Repeat the assessment used in Step 2.

(continued)

Figure 7.24 continued

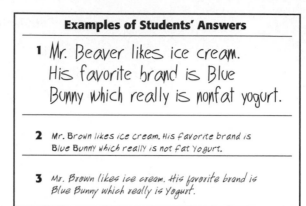

- • All students have learned to differentiate between common and proper nouns. Students 2 and 3 need to focus on the word *nonfat*.

❺ Post • Make a chart for the wall about common and proper nouns. Add to the list over time.

Nouns
Names of persons, places, or things

dog, baby, house, automobile, airplane, Maple Tree, The White House, table, zoo, The Brookfield Zoo.

Common Nouns	**Proper Nouns**
Names of any person, place, or thing	Name of particular persons, places, or things. Capitalize proper nouns except for little words in the middle.
dog baby house automobile airplane table zoo	Maple Tree The White House The Brookfield Zoo

❻ Use • Remind students to check the posting and use what they have learned in their writing.
          • Observe students to see if they are using common and proper nouns appropriately in their writing.

students. Following is a list of some of the more popular software programs for word processing:

The Children's Writing & Publishing Center, The Learning Company
Great Beginnings, Teacher Support Software
Kid Pix Studio, Broderbund
Kid Words 2, Davidson & Associates
Kid's Media Magic, Humanities Software
Magic Media Slate, Sunburst
MediaWeaver, Humanities Software
Microsoft Works, Microsoft
The Scholastic Process Writer, Scholastic
Storybook Weaver, MECC
Student Writing Center, The Learning Center
Write Away!, Sunburst
Amazing Writing Machine, Broderbund

The Internet

Web sites on the Internet are another important way to enhance the writing program. Even though Web sites come and go, Dahl and Farnan (1998) identify four related to writing that they feel would be interesting for both teachers and students:

www-gse.berkeley.edu/Research/NWP/nwp.html

This is the home page for the National Writing Project. It helps teachers stay abreast of research and new ideas on writing.

www.inkspot.com

This site is for young writers and teachers. Students can get advice about their writing as well as get their writing published on the Web.

www.writes.org/netscape/about_wp/guide.html

This site for adolescents ages 12 to 19 is know as Writes of Passage. It is an electronic literary journal that allows students to interact with famous published writers.

www.kidpub.org/kidpub/intro.html

This site, known as KidPub, is a place where young writers can read stories written by kids from all over the world. They can also submit their own words for publication.

Software Literacy Programs

Software programs that support effective literacy learning are becoming more available for classroom use. One series, The Little Planet Literacy Series (1996), a research-based program, develops writing, listening, viewing, reading, and thinking together. Its approach provides varying entry to and paths through the program for children of all literacy skills levels. The program consists of CD-ROMs, videos, full color story cards, and instructions for the teacher, both in a

notebook binder and CD-ROM format. Students thus may enter by listening to
and viewing the "anchor story" (Bransford, Sherwood, Hasselbring, Kinzer, &
Williams 1990), and build literacy skills by discussing, retelling, creating, and
writing their own books and then sharing their books with others. Lessons can be
done by whole class, cooperative learning groups, or individual students. Little
Planet programs are well-supported technically and theoretically, and include a
CD component with background on its research-base and use, and a Web site at
www.littleplanet.com. Following this brief introduction is a modified literacy lesson showing one way Little Planet Literacy Series' programs can be introduced
in kindergarten or first grade.

Modified
Literacy
Lesson

The Little Planet and the Magic Hats, Volume 1, The Anchor Story

This modified literacy lesson starts with viewing, listening, and thinking. It was designed for use
with kindergartners or first graders. This is the first lesson students would complete using the
Little Planet Literacy Series. The outcome of the entire series of lessons would be a student-
written, multimedia book.

Before Reading the Plan
1. **Think about what you have learned about the importance of teaching reading
    and writing together. Review any parts of the chapter that were unclear. Talk with
    a peer about it.**
2. **Review the seven storyboard cards (pages 378–384), which depict major scenes
    from the "anchor story" movie *The Little Planet and the Magic Hats* and read the
    story summary.**

Anchor Story Summary

The animals are in a cave telling stories. Wongo comes along and tells them he is a wizard and
says he has magic hats. All the animals buy one hat except Ribbit. Wongo is really not a wizard
and the hats are not magic.

While Reading the Plan
1. **Think about different ways you might introduce this story.**
2. **Think about how you might find time in your classroom to use this technology
    program at least two days per week with children.**

*Modified
Literacy
Lesson
continued*

Teacher Preparation

1. I read the teacher's material for teaching *The Little Planet and the Magic Hats* (pages 7–12).
2. I developed a plan for having children use the computer two days per week during center time for the Little Planet Series.
3. I checked the computer and made sure the CD-ROM worked appropriately.

Introducing *The Little Planet and the Magic Hats*

ACTIVITY	PROCEDURE	NOTES
Looking at character storyboards	1. Present Storyboard Card #3. Say: Here are some of the characters we will meet in *The Little Planet and the Magic Hats*. This is Baldy with his new hat. Is he a real animal? How do you know?	This activity builds background for the story.
	2. Present Storyboard Card #4. Say: This is Ribbit. Is he a real animal? How can you tell? Does he look like any other animals you've seen?	
	3. Continue with Storyboard #6 (Owly-Bear) and Storyboard #2 (Wongo).	
Predicting real or make-believe	1. Ask children whether they think this story really happened based on the characters they have met. Why or why not?	Sets purpose for viewing.
	2. Tell children to view the story to see if their predictions were correct. Tell them to listen for the challenge to them at the end of the story.	

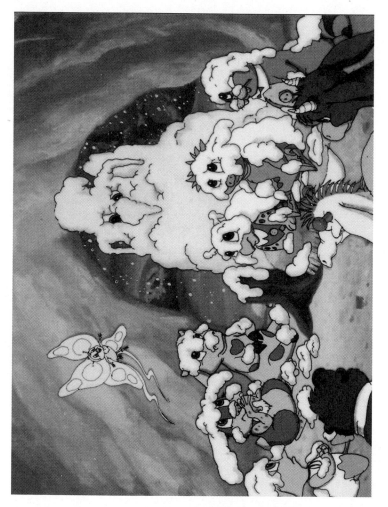

Storyboard #1

Storyboard #2

Storyboard #3

Storyboard #4

Storyboard #5

Storyboard #6

Storyboard #7

Modified Literacy Lesson continued

Viewing and Responding—*The Little Planet and the Magic Hats*

ACTIVITY	PROCEDURE	NOTES
Viewing on CD-ROM or video	Use the CD-ROM or video to have students view the story.	
Checking predictions/ discussing	1. Ask students if their predictions were correct. Discuss.	Helps children construct meaning.
	2. Discuss the story. Ask such questions as:	
	• Who was your favorite character?	
	• What types of things would you include in your book?	

Extending *The Little Planet and the Magic Hats*

Preparing for writing	Tell children that they will help the animals write their story. Over the next several days, we will review our story using other lessons from *The Little Planet.*	Helps children prepare for writing.

Note: Other lessons from *The Little Planet* will follow.

After Reading the Plan
1. **Locate the Little Planet Series and use the CD-ROM and video.**
2. **Discuss with a peer other ways you might use software to stimulate writing and reading.**

A Final Word About Writing

So much has been written about writing, and this chapter has presented only a basic overview of how writing and reading work together to help students learn to construct meaning. I encourage you to read more extensively about writing using some of the suggestions in the For Additional Reading section.

■ Summary

This chapter stressed that writing and reading should be taught together because both are constructive processes, share similar types of knowledge and processes, improve achievement in both areas, foster communication, and together produce outcomes that are not achievable by either alone. The chapter emphasized the importance of establishing a classroom that promotes and supports writing and provided suggestions for creating such a classroom.

Process writing was developed as a major procedure for helping students learn to construct meaning through writing. The chapter discussed ways to use minilessons to teach spelling and grammar on the basis of writing. A modified literacy lesson showed how to use technology as a basis for connecting reading and writing.

Literature

Raskin, E. (1971). *The mysterious disappearance of Leon (I mean Noel)*. New York: E. P. Dutton.

Sobol, D. J. (1963). *Encyclopedia Brown: Boy detective*. New York: Lodestar Books.

Wilder, L. I. (1932). *Little house in the big woods*. New York: Harper.

For Additional Reading

Calkins, L. M. (1986). *The art of teaching writing*. Portsmouth, NH: Heinemann.

Gentry, J. R. (1987). *Spel . . . is a four-letter word*. Portsmouth, NH: Heinemann.

Gentry, J. R. & Gillet, J. W. (1993). *Teaching kids to spell*. Portsmouth, NH: Heinemann.

Graves, D. H. (1983). *Writing: Teachers and children at work*. Exeter, NH: Heinemann.

Graves, D. H. (1991). *Build a literate classroom*. Portsmouth, NH: Heinemann.

Graves, D. H. (1994). *A fresh look at writing*. Portsmouth, NH: Heinemann.

Raphael, T. E., & Englert, C. S. (1990). Writing and reading: Partners in constructing meaning. *Reading Teacher, 43,* 388–400.

Shanahan, T. (Ed.). (1990). *Reading and writing together: New perspectives for the classroom*. Norwood, MA: Christopher-Gordon.

Stoll, D. R. (ed.). (1997). *Magazines for kids and teens*. Newark, DE: International Reading Association.

Tierney, R. J., & Shanahan, T. (1991). Research on the reading-writing relationship: Interactions, transactions, and outcomes. In R. Barr, M. L. Kamil, P. Mosenthal, & P. D. Pearson (Eds.), *Handbook of reading research* (Vol. 2, pp. 246–280). White Plains, NY: Longman.

Tompkins, G. E., & Hoskisson, K. (1991). Directions for making hardcover books. In G. E. Tompkins & K. Hoskisson, *Language Arts* (p. 251). New York: Merrill.

For Exploration: Electronic Products and Resources

Authoring software ranges from word processing programs that offer standard word processing capabilities to programs that allow students to create and publish multimedia projects and interactive Web pages. All software for student writing requires careful evaluation. What age student is it for? Is it instructionally sound? Does it present content that is part of your curriculum? Will it motivate students? Is it more effective than other approaches to the content and to the goals of the writing assignment? Always answer these questions yourself. Product information may give you some answers, but it will not tell you everything you need to know.

Explore these sites to learn about the range of authoring software.

Sunburst

www.sunburst.com
Magic Media Slate, Write On!

Pierian Spring Software

www.pierian.com
Digital Chisel, An Odyssey of Discovery: Writing for Readers

Humanities Software

www.humanitiessoftware.com
MediaWeaver, The Multimedia Writing Tool, Bilingual: English and Spanish, Kid's Media Magic, The Reading, Writing, Multimedia Machine, Write On!

MECC

www.mecc.com
Storybook Weaver

Mindplay Company

www.mindplay.com
Cotton Tales

Teacher Support Software

www.tssoftware.com
Reading Realities At-Risk Series, Language Experience Recorder, Great Beginnings, Sentence Starters, Read-A-Logo

Broderbund

www.broderbund.com/education
Kid Pix Studio, Amazing Writing Machine

Teaching Strategies for Constructing Meaning

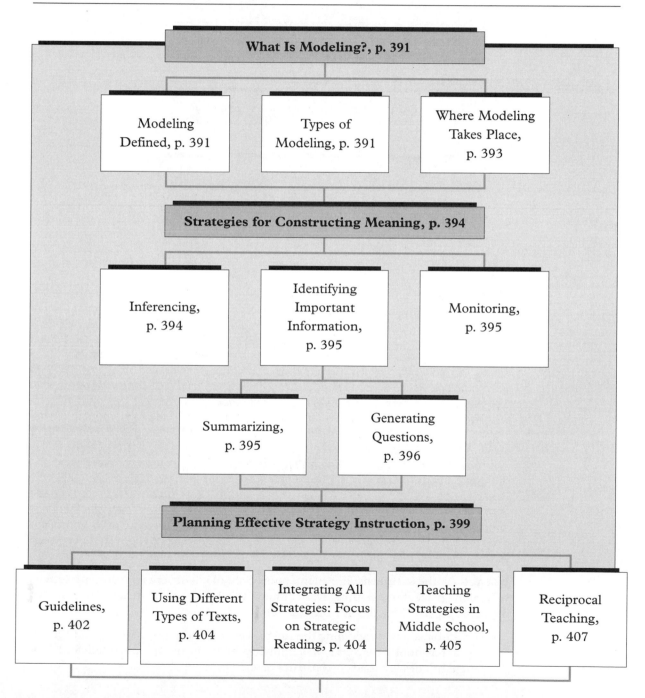

What Is Modeling?, p. 391

Modeling Defined, p. 391

Types of Modeling, p. 391

Where Modeling Takes Place, p. 393

Strategies for Constructing Meaning, p. 394

Inferencing, p. 394

Identifying Important Information, p. 395

Monitoring, p. 395

Summarizing, p. 395

Generating Questions, p. 396

Planning Effective Strategy Instruction, p. 399

Guidelines, p. 402

Using Different Types of Texts, p. 404

Integrating All Strategies: Focus on Strategic Reading, p. 404

Teaching Strategies in Middle School, p. 405

Reciprocal Teaching, p. 407

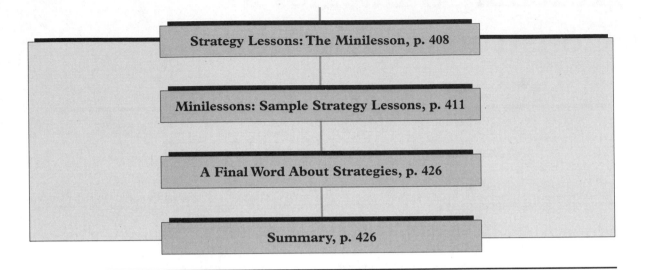

*L*et's walk through Brownsville Elementary School to see what is happening in three different classrooms.

Mr. Robinson was reading the big book Pretend You're a Cat *(Marzollo, 1990) with his first graders. As he read aloud each page, he invited the children to join in whenever they felt comfortable doing so. After reading the entire book aloud once, he briefly discussed with the children what they liked in the story. Then he immediately read aloud each page of the book again, stopping to have the children read the page with him.*

Farther down the hall, Ms. Garza's third-grade class was finishing story time. She had just read aloud Princess Furball *(Huck, 1989), after which all the students had returned to their seats and immediately started independent reading time. Ms. Garza stayed in the library area and read a section in her own book,* Complete Guide to Gardening *(Better Homes and Gardens, 1979). Everyone in the room was actively engaged in reading his or her own book.*

Upstairs, Mr. Lee was showing his fifth graders a strategy poster for previewing and self-questioning. The class was looking at the book Lurkers of the Deep: Life Within the Ocean Depths *(Robison, 1978). Mr. Lee was saying, "As I look through this book, I can see from the section headings and photographs that it is going to give me a lot of information about light in the ocean. One question I would like to answer as I read this book is: How does the light in the ocean affect life there? What question might you want to answer?" Terri volunteered that she would like to know how plants and animals grow in the dark.*

IN EACH OF these Brownsville Elementary School classrooms a different activity was taking place, but one thing was common to all of them: the teacher was modeling some aspect of reading for the students.

▶ Mr. Robinson was modeling the full process of reading by reading and rereading a big-book story. He was showing how words are decoded and how language cues are used to construct meaning.

▶ Ms. Garza had just completed a read-aloud period, which is also a form of modeling. During uninterrupted reading time, she also modeled reading as she read her own book. Finally, the students modeled reading for one another as they read their own books.

▶ Mr. Lee was modeling a particular strategy, preview and self-question, to help students do what expert readers do: determine their purpose for reading. By sharing his thinking as he used this strategy, Mr. Lee was making his mental processes public to help the students think about this strategy.

These three classroom scenes show the variability in the processes of modeling. Sometimes teachers serve as models for students by simply providing day-to-day opportunities in which students see them read and write and have natural language interactions. Ms. Garza was providing this type of modeling. At other times, modeling is used as an instructional technique to show students a process or a strategy, as Mr. Robinson and Mr. Lee were doing.

If you have been reading the chapters in this text in the sequence presented, you have already encountered both concepts of modeling. Shared reading, an important modeling strategy, was discussed in Chapter 4. Modeling is also a scaffolding technique that supports children as they develop literacy. Chapter 7 explored the use of modeling in developing students' ability to write. In this chapter we explore the concept of modeling in detail, with emphasis on its use with reading strategies.

What Is Modeling?

Literacy learning is an interactive, constructive process. In essence, children develop literacy (writing, reading, speaking, listening, viewing, and thinking) by having real literacy experiences. However, as they have these experiences, they need carefully scaffolded instruction (Dole, Duffy, Roehler, & Pearson, 1991). Modeling is an important form of such support.

Modeling Defined

Modeling is the process of showing or demonstrating for someone how to use or do something she or he does not know how to do; most human behaviors are acquired in this way (Bandura, 1986). Modeling can also be described as the process by which an expert shows students (nonexperts) how to perform a task so that they can build their own understanding of how to complete that task (Collins et al., 1986). With literacy learning, this expert may be an adult outside of school, an adult in school (usually the teacher), or a peer. When a child sees a parent writing a letter or reading a book, modeling is taking place. When Mr. Lee talked aloud using previewing and self-questioning, he was modeling. When a child sees a friend successfully complete a piece of writing and share it, modeling has occurred.

Types of Modeling

As you can see from the examples already presented, modeling can be implicit or explicit (Roehler & Duffy, 1991). *Implicit* modeling takes place when the processes or ideas being modeled occur as a part of an experience and are *not directly* identified or stated. Reading aloud to students and letting students see you write a letter are examples. Implicit modeling always occurs within the context of the complete process of reading and writing. *Explicit* modeling involves directly showing and talking with students about what is being modeled. Roehler and Duffy (1991) have identified two types of explicit modeling: talk-alouds and think-alouds.

In a *talk-aloud,* the teacher presents students with a series of steps for completing a task or a process and then asks questions to guide them through the process. For example, Baumann and Schmitt (1986) describe using a talk-aloud approach to teach students how to locate main ideas. A portion of that procedure follows:

> *Here are three steps we will use to figure out unstated paragraph main ideas. [Teacher displays these on a chart or a transparency.]*
>
> 1. *First, decide what the* topic *of the paragraph is. The topic is like a short title and is usually one or two words that tell what the whole paragraph is about.*
> 2. *Next, decide what is said about the topic. Read through the paragraph to see what the rest of the sentences tell you about the topic. Then write a sentence that includes the topic and what is said about the topic. This will be the* main idea.
> 3. *Then, check yourself. Go through each of the sentences in the paragraph. Ask yourself for each sentence "Does this sentence go with or support the main idea?" If it does, it is a* detail *that supports the main idea. If you find several sentences that do not support or go with your main idea, go back to Step 1 and start over.* (p. 642)

As the steps are presented, the teacher talks the students through them to determine the main idea. The emphasis is on the procedural steps and not on any thinking that takes place in using the steps.

Think-alouds are a second type of explicit modeling (Clark, 1984; Meichenbaum, 1985). In this approach, teachers actually share with students the cognitive processes, or thinking, that they go through. Compare the following partial think-aloud for learning to infer main ideas with the talk-aloud presented earlier:

> *As I read through this paragraph, I can immediately tell that the topic of it is space travel because it mentions outer space, rockets, and planets. Even though mention is made of early pioneers, I can see that this is only a point of comparison. I notice that all of the points compared show me how early pioneer travel and space travel have been similar.*

Notice that the teacher is sharing his thinking to reveal the process one goes through in formulating or inferring a main idea.

An inherent danger in explicit modeling is that the activities will become nothing more than the modeling of an isolated skill, which is not effective in helping students construct meaning (Pearson, Roehler, Dole, & Duffy, 1990). *Explicit modeling must be done within the context of a specific text* (Duffy et al., 1987; Roehler & Duffy, 1991). All examples of modeling presented in this chapter and throughout the text adhere to this important guideline. Table 8.1 summarizes different types of modeling.

Table 8.1

SUMMARY OF TYPES OF MODELING

TYPE	DESCRIPTION	EXAMPLE	COMMENTS
Implicit modeling	Takes place as part of an experience; not directly identified	Reading aloud to a child Writing a group story Shared reading	Has the advantage of always being in the context of the actual process
Explicit modeling	Directly showing or talking students through a process; two types		Should always be done within the context of the process.
Talk-aloud	Presents a series of steps for completing a process or task	Demonstrating the steps in using a dictionary	There is a very fine line between talk alouds and think alouds.
Think-aloud	Presents the thinking one goes through in performing a process or task	Presenting the thinking involved in inferring from text	Helps students learn strategies and processes

Where Modeling Takes Place

Modeling can occur at numerous points throughout the literacy program:

▶ *During daily activities:* Although the daily activities of the literacy program will afford many opportunities for both implicit and explicit modeling, most of the modeling will be *implicit*. Read-aloud times, shared writing experiences, periods for independent, self-initiated reading and writing, and cooperative reading are just a few examples. Because the literacy-centered classroom operates on the premise that children learn to read and write by reading and writing, all of the activities associated with real reading and writing play a significant role in the modeling of these processes.

▶ *Process writing:* This is another important point where modeling occurs. The process of writing, shared writing, and writing conferences present many opportunities for both implicit and explicit modeling (see Chapter 7).

▶ *Literacy lessons:* The literacy lesson consists of three parts (see Chapter 2): introducing, reading and responding, and extending. Within introducing and reading and responding, there will be opportunities for explicit modeling of prior knowledge, vocabulary, and particular strategies that students need to construct meaning. Implicit modeling by the teacher and peers will occur in all three parts of the lesson, including extending.

▶ *Minilessons:* Minilessons, developed on the basis of students' needs, afford the most opportunities for explicit modeling of strategies for both reading and writing.

These lessons can be developed around the framework presented in Chapter 2. They may take place during your reading workshop or your writing workshop (see Chapter 10). Later in this chapter, we will look at specific strategies for reading and how to model them.

Modeling helps students become more expert readers and writers and gives them better control over their metacognitive processes (Paris et al., 1991). However, the teacher must effectively balance implicit and explicit modeling. In the remainder of this chapter, we will focus on how to model strategies that help students construct meaning.

Strategies for Constructing Meaning

Research has clearly shown that reading (comprehension) is a constructive process in which individuals construct meaning by interacting with the text (Pearson et al., 1990). This constructive interaction involves the individual's prior knowledge, the text, and the reading situation or context (Lipson & Wixson, 1986). As discussed in Chapter 7, this constructive process also takes place through writing.

Expert readers have strategies or plans to help them solve problems and construct meaning before, during, and after reading (Paris et al., 1991). Although the number of these strategies is small, they should be thoroughly developed (Pearson et al., 1990). Even though many unanswered questions remain and much research needs to be done in this area (Dole et al., 1991), you must address two major questions:

1. What strategies do my students need as they become expert constructors of meaning?
2. How are these strategies best developed in the literacy program?

We will examine both of these questions in the remainder of this chapter.

Volumes of research have attempted to identify the strategies used by expert constructors of meaning (Baker & Brown, 1984a, 1984b; Dole et al., 1991; Paris et al., 1991; Pearson, Roehler, Dole, & Duffy, 1992; Pressley, Johnson, Symons, McGoldrick, & Kurita, 1989). When these studies are examined as a group, five important strategies emerge:

1. Inferencing, including prediction
2. Identifying important information (story line in narrative texts and main ideas in expository texts)
3. Monitoring
4. Summarizing
5. Generating questions

Although the research discusses many other strategies, these five appear to have the greatest support for inclusion in the literacy program.

Inferencing

Inferencing, the process of judging, concluding, or reasoning from some given information, is the heart of meaning construction for learners of all ages (Anderson &

Pearson, 1984). Even very young readers and readers performing a simple task such as reading a sentence use inferencing to supply information that is not given (Kail, Chi, Ingram, & Danner, 1977). When students make predictions before or during reading, they are inferencing: using available information and prior knowledge to construct meaning (recall the preview and predict strategy discussed in Chapter 3). A strategy poster such as the one in Figure 8.1 can be used to help students think about this process as they read.

Identifying Important Information

Strategic readers identify the important information in what they read. In narrative texts or stories, they identify or infer the story line or story grammar (see Chapters 2 and 3; also, see Mandler, 1984); in expository texts, they identify or infer the main ideas (Baumann, 1986). Although identification is similar in both types of texts, the task differs because the structures of the texts are different. Whatever terminology is used to describe this process, we know that meaning construction can be improved when students learn a strategy for identifying important information in each type of text (Baumann, 1984; Short & Ryan, 1984; Winograd & Bridge, 1986). Figures 8.2 and 8.3 present strategy posters you can use to help students learn this important strategy for narrative and expository texts. A sample minilesson for modeling this strategy for narrative text is presented on page 411.

Monitoring

Monitoring, sometimes called *clarifying,* is the process of knowing that what you are reading is not making sense and then having some plans for overcoming this problem. This is an important part of students' metacognitive development (Baker & Brown, 1984a, 1984b; Brown, 1980) and is a developmental process that improves with age (Paris et al., 1991). Expert constructors of meaning are able to anticipate problems in reading and correct them as they occur. This "fix-up" process may involve rereading, reading ahead, raising new questions, changing predictions or making new ones, evaluating what is read, using strategies for identifying words (see Chapter 4), looking up words, or seeking help from an outside source. Figure 8.4 presents a strategy poster you can use in teaching students how to use a monitoring strategy known as "stop and think." A sample lesson for modeling this strategy appears on page 417.

Summarizing

Summarizing is the process of pulling together the essential elements in a longer passage of text. Effective constructors of meaning are able to use this strategy; research has shown that certain guidelines can help students develop this skill (Brown & Day, 1983; also, see the discussion on writing summaries in Chapter 7). Although much of this training research has focused on expository texts, the same types of guidelines can be applied to narrative texts using the story grammar concept already discussed. Figures 8.5 and 8.6 present strategy posters to use in teaching summarizing. A sample lesson using informational text is presented on page 420.

FIGURE 8.1

STRATEGY POSTER FOR INFERENCING

Generating Questions

A final strategy readers can use to improve their meaning construction is generating their own questions (self-questioning) to be answered from reading (Davey & McBride, 1986; Singer & Donlan, 1982). This process involves teaching students how to generate questions that require them to integrate information and think as they read. For example, a good "think" question might be "Why did the dinosaurs

FIGURE 8.2

STRATEGY POSTER FOR IDENTIFYING IMPORTANT INFORMATION IN NARRATIVE TEXT

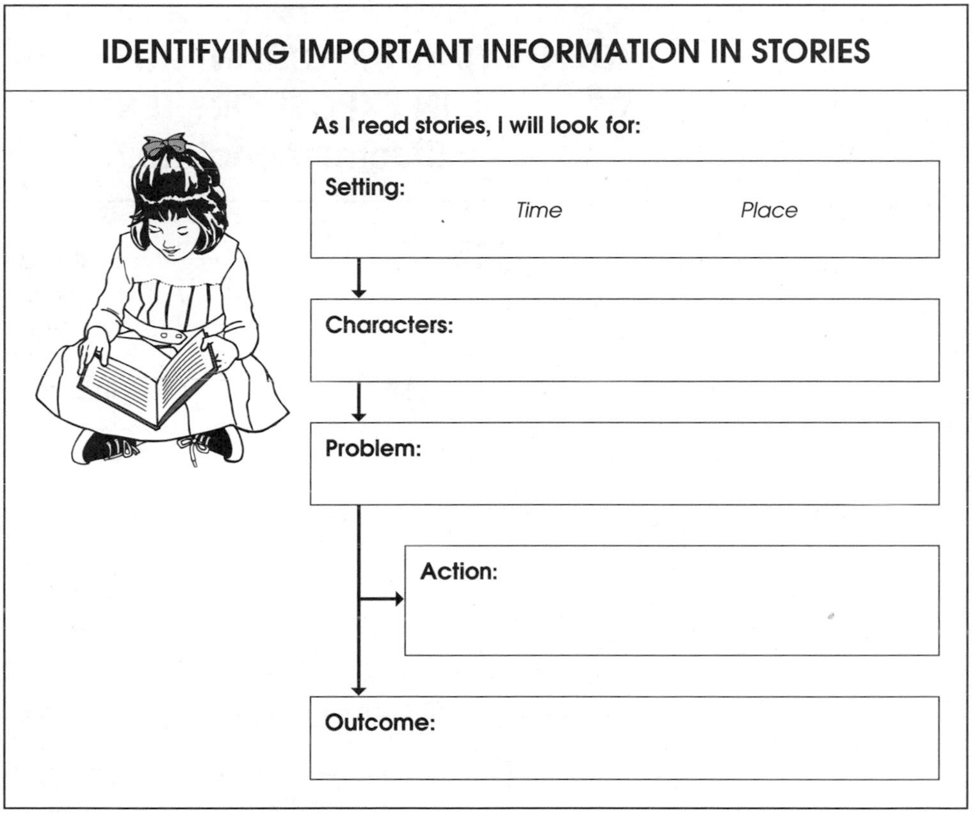

IDENTIFYING IMPORTANT INFORMATION IN STORIES

As I read stories, I will look for:

Setting:
    Time   Place

Characters:

Problem:

Action:

Outcome:

become extinct?" This question helps focus the reader's thinking on much more than just specific facts. Figure 8.7 presents a poster for this strategy using expository text.

Ongoing research should add to our understanding of how the literacy learner uses various strategies. However, the current level of our knowledge supports helping readers learn to use the five strategies just discussed. Generating questions may have little value unless it is taught thoroughly (Denner & Rickards, 1987; Pressley et al., 1990). However, if well taught, this strategy may be the most useful one for promoting meaning construction before, during, and after reading (though all five strategies do this in some way). Table 8.2 shows when each strategy would fit into an individual's reading.

FIGURE 8.3

STRATEGY POSTER FOR IDENTIFYING IMPORTANT INFORMATION IN EXPOSITORY TEXT

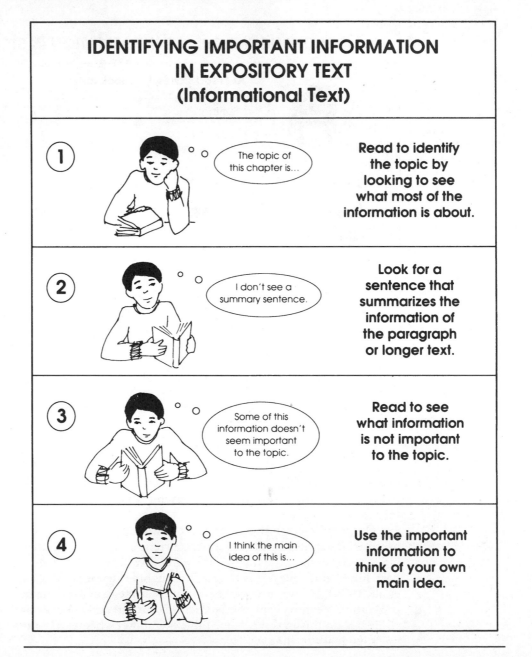

FIGURE 8.4

STRATEGY POSTER FOR STOP AND THINK

Planning Effective Strategy Instruction

Modeling is one way to support children in their learning. Much of the time this modeling may be *implicit,* but in most circumstances it should be *explicit.* If reading or writing performance indicates the need for support using a given strategy, a mini-lesson with explicit modeling should be provided.

FIGURE 8.5

STRATEGY POSTER FOR SUMMARIZING NARRATIVE TEXT

SUMMARIZING STORIES
(Narrative Text)

1. Read your story to find the important parts:
   • Setting
   • Characters
   • Problem
   • Action
   • Outcome
   Make notes.

2. Look over your notes and decide what can be left out.

3. *First I will tell the title and author. Then I'll tell...*

   Think about how you will tell or write your summary to make it clear.

4. Tell or write your summary.

FIGURE 8.6

STRATEGY POSTER FOR SUMMARIZING EXPOSITORY TEXT

FIGURE 8.7

STRATEGY POSTER FOR QUESTION GENERATING

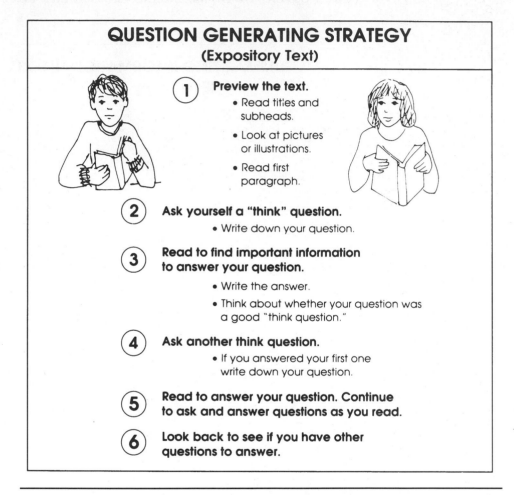

Guidelines
==========

A great deal is known about effective strategy instruction (Duffy, 1993; Pressley & Harris, 1990). The following guidelines should be helpful in developing this instruction within your classroom.

Determine the need for strategy instruction on the basis of student performance. Students will learn some strategies through their reading and writing experiences. When you observe that their meaning construction would be enhanced

TABLE 8.2

POINTS WHERE STRATEGIES MAY HELP STUDENTS CONSTRUCT MEANING

	READING		
STRATEGY	Before	During	After
Inferencing (including predicting)	✓	✓	
Identifying important information	✓	✓	✓
Monitoring		✓	
Summarizing		✓	✓
Generating questions	✓	✓	✓

by a minilesson involving modeling, provide it. *Students' needs should be the primary determining factor in using explicit modeling.*

Introduce only one or two strategies at a time. This allows you to thoroughly teach the strategy by making certain students have *repeated* opportunities to use it in real reading situations. At first students may seem uncomfortable or uncertain with the strategy, but this uncertainty will fade.

Model and practice the strategy in the meaningful context of a reading experience. This is a critical issue, because an inherent danger in strategy instruction is that the strategies will remain isolated. When strategies fail, it is often because they have been taught and practiced as isolated elements. A real reading experience means students will (1) work with a text where the strategy would be useful, (2) use that text as the basis for having the strategy modeled by the teacher, and (3) use additional texts for practicing the strategy. No fill-in-the-blank, mark, circle, or underline types of exercises should be used, because such activities isolate the strategy.

Model each strategy at the point where it is most useful. Make the modeling of a strategy as authentic as possible by doing it when students are most likely to use it in reading. For example, model preview and predict before reading a text and then follow it up after reading.

Be sure that modeling and practicing are interactive and collaborative activities. Strategy learning and use is most effective when students are active participants and work alongside their peers. For example, students learning to summarize may first work together to help the teacher construct a summary and later work with a partner to write a collaborative summary chart of a story they have read.

Gradually transfer modeling from yourself to the students. This is the scaffolding of instruction. Once you have modeled a strategy enough times for students to begin using comfortably, have students model it for one another and use it on their own. If you see that more modeling is needed, provide it and then begin to release responsibility to the students again.

Help students experience immediate success with each strategy. Nothing encourages students more than success. Have them explain how the strategy helped them, and point out successes you have seen. If you find a particular strategy is not working for a student, discontinue using it and move on to another one.

Encourage the use of a strategy across the curriculum. Once students have started to use a strategy, model its use in other curricular areas such as science and social studies. As students use strategies in these areas, have them reflect on and discuss how the various strategies helped them more effectively understand what they read. This will help them see the value of the strategy and will interest them in learning additional strategies.

Guide students to become strategic readers. Once they are familiar with each strategy, model and encourage the use of all strategies together. See below for a discussion of how to do this.

These guidelines will be applied in the sample minilessons beginning on page 411.

Using Different Types of Texts

When planning effective strategy instruction, you must consider the types of texts students will be reading. You have learned about the differences between narrative texts and expository texts; narrative texts contain the elements of a story grammar (characters, setting, problem, action, and outcome) and expository texts are organized around main ideas and supporting details using different text structures (see Chapter 3 for a discussion of text structures). Sometimes authors combine narrative and expository structures in the same text. For example, *The Popcorn Book* (de Paola, 1978) tells a story and at the same time presents information. This type of book is sometimes known as an *informational story.*

Content texts used in such classes as health, science, history, and so forth are usually expository texts. However, these books often combine several text structures; for example, a U.S. history chapter may have passages presenting sequence combined with passages showing cause/effect; these passages may be combined with some narration that explains how things fit together.

In planning strategy lessons, you should consider how to adjust the strategies for the type of text to be read. Table 8.3 shows the type of text and circumstances under which the five strategies discussed earlier work best. Remember that all strategies work with any type of text; however, some modifications are needed to adjust to the different types of texts.

Integrating All Strategies: Focus on Strategic Reading

When people read a text, they use several strategies simultaneously. Therefore, as strategies are taught, it is important at some point to pull all the strategies

TABLE 8.3

STRATEGY USE IN DIFFERENT TYPES OF TEXTS

STRATEGY	NARRATIVE TEXTS	EXPOSITORY TEXTS	COMMENT
Inferencing	Yes	Sometimes	Since expository texts present factual information, too much inferencing in a text reduces the text's quality.
Identifying important information	Yes, focus on story elements	Yes, focus on main ideas and supporting details	Must adjust strategy to structure of text.
Monitoring	Yes	Yes	Adjust the monitoring strategies to the type of text.
Summarizing	Yes, focus summary on story elements	Yes, focus summary on main ideas and details	Must adjust strategy to structure of text.
Generating questions	Yes, focus questions on story elements	Yes, focus questions on main ideas and key concepts	Must adjust strategy to structure of text.

together and focus students' attention on being strategic readers by learning to select the strategy or strategies that will best help them construct meaning within what they read.

A good way to accomplish this focus on strategic reading is to first teach students all of the strategies quickly, using suggestions and guidelines presented in this text. Then use the posters for the various strategies along with a poster such as that in Figure 8.8 to remind students about all of the strategies. Before students read any text, discuss with them which strategies they might use as they read. If you are guiding or coaching the reading, periodically model and discuss the use of various strategies during reading. After reading, have students reflect on how the use of various strategies helped them construct meaning. At any point before, during, or after reading, you may need to model the concept of strategic reading by modeling the use of one or more of the strategies.

Teaching Strategies in Middle School

Middle school students need to learn and use all five strategies for constructing meaning. The goal for middle school needs to be to help students be strategic

FIGURE 8.8

POSTER PROMOTING THE USE OF ALL STRATEGIES TOGETHER

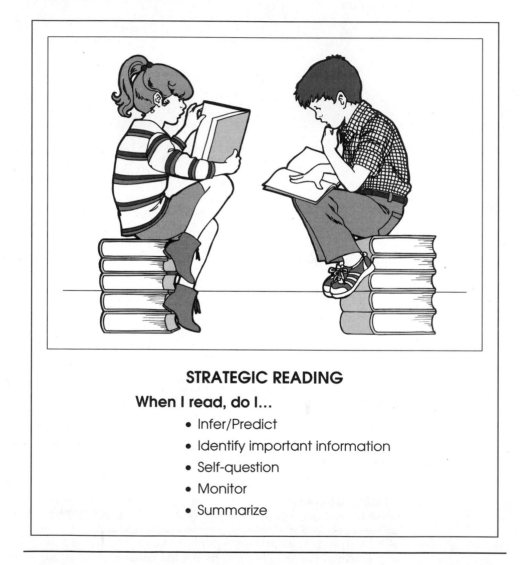

STRATEGIC READING

When I read, do I...

- Infer/Predict
- Identify important information
- Self-question
- Monitor
- Summarize

readers every time they read. Therefore, the strategies for constructing meaning should be taught and used in all classes, not just reading or language arts.

To accomplish this goal, place the focus on strategic reading. Use a checklist such as the one in Figure 8.9 to get students to focus on using all of the strategies

FIGURE 8.9

CHECKLIST TO HELP STUDENTS FOCUS ON USING ALL STRATEGIES IN ALL SUBJECT AREAS

My Strategic Reading Guide

As I read, do I . . .

1. *Infer/predict*
   - Look for important information?
   - Look at illustrations?
   - Think about what I know?
   - Think about what may happen or what I want to learn?

2. *Identify important information*
   - Look for story elements?
   - Look for main ideas and important details?

3. *Self-question*
   - Ask questions and look for answers?

4. *Monitor*
   - Ask: Does this make sense to me?
     Does it help me meet my purposes?
   - Try fix-ups?
     - Reread
     - Read ahead
     - Look at illustrations
     - Ask for help
     - Think about words
   - Evaluate what I read?

5. *Summarize*
   - Summarize after I read?
     - Stories—think about story parts
     - Informational texts—think about main ideas and important details

together in all subject areas. Again, continue to model strategies as needed and have students reflect on how they have used various strategies to construct meaning. The primary focus of the modeling should be on using all of the strategies together.

Reciprocal Teaching

An excellent way to develop the use of strategies in upper elementary and middle school students is through the use of reciprocal teaching (Palincsar & Brown, 1986). Reciprocal teaching is an interactive process where the teacher and students take turns modeling four strategies after reading a meaningful chunk of text—*predict, question, clarify,* and *summarize.* This reciprocal modeling process takes the place of the typical discussion that follows reading.

Research has demonstrated that reciprocal teaching is effective in helping all students increase their comprehension ability. However, it is most effective in helping below-level readers accelerate their reading in a short amount of time (Rosenshine &

Meister, 1994). (See Chapter 10 for more detail on the use of reciprocal teaching for below-level readers.)

Strategy Lessons: The Minilesson

As noted earlier in this chapter, explicit modeling may take place within the literacy lesson or through minilessons. For example, if, as part of a literacy lesson, you see the need to help students summarize stories, the most logical place to do this will be at the conclusion of the lesson, after a story has been read. Students will then practice using the strategy in the meaningful context of reading the next selection.

This section presents three sample strategy lessons organized around the minilesson concept. These lessons may be taught before or after the literacy lesson or as part of it, depending on the particular strategy and where it needs to be placed.

The minilesson is a very flexible plan for developing strategy lessons based on the principles of effective instruction using explicit, or direct, teaching and effective strategy learning. The parts of the plan should flow into an interactive dialogue that makes up the entire lesson. As the name *minilesson* implies, the lesson is short and focused, lasting from 5 to 10 minutes and rarely longer than 15 minutes. Some lessons may need to be taught several times, depending on the students' level and how they respond, and some lessons may not work for certain students and should be discontinued as you move on to more effective experiences. The four parts of the minilesson are (1) introduction, (2) teacher modeling, (3) student modeling and guided practice, and (4) summarizing and reflecting. The three parts of the follow-up to the minilesson are (1) independent practice, (2) application, and (3) reflection. The first four parts constitute the brief minilesson. The remaining three parts can take place over several days or more.

1. *Introduction:* During this portion of the lesson, you let students know what they are going to learn and relate it to reading or writing and their prior knowledge. You may talk directly with them and point out relationships, or you may draw information from them through an interactive discussion. For example, when teaching a lesson on inferencing, you might say:

   Tell me some examples in the last book we read where the author gave clues about something but didn't tell you directly what was intended. [Students respond.] *This happens many times in books. When you figured out information from the clues, you were using a strategy called* inferencing. *Today we are going to think more about inferencing.*

   This very focused introduction should take just a few minutes.

2. *Teacher modeling:* During this part of the lesson, you show students how to *use* and how to *think about* the strategy being taught by "thinking aloud" with them. As you do this, you want to make certain students have the concept of the strategy. For example, with inferencing you might start with something concrete, such as a text illustration, and talk about what it shows and what you can infer from clues such as facial expressions or objects pictured. You should always use a piece of text as the basis for your modeling, and you should make this part of the lesson interactive by drawing students into the modeling. After

you have modeled for students, gradually transfer the modeling to them and help them "think aloud" about how they are using the strategy as they read the text. This process flows naturally into the next part of the lesson.

3. *Student modeling and guided practice:* Students are now using the strategy under your guidance, usually within the same text where the strategy was originally modeled. For example, if you are using a short story to model inferencing, you might have students continue through the story to find other places to use inferencing, all the while encouraging them to think aloud as they work. In some cases, you will need to prompt students with questions, examples, or additional modeling. Throughout, give students feedback about how they are doing in using the strategy. The teacher modeling, student modeling, and guided practice flow together so closely that it is often difficult to tell where one begins and the other ends. The purpose of this portion of the lesson is to ensure that students are able to use the strategy before releasing them to practice it independently.

4. *Summarizing and reflecting:* Finally, prompt students to summarize what they have learned and get them to reflect on how and where they might use the strategy. Use prompts such as the following:

   ▸ How did we make inferences in this story?

   ▸ What did we use besides story information?

   ▸ Where do you think you will use this strategy?

   Remember that *students* need to verbalize what they have learned and where and how they might use it.

The follow-up to the minilesson consists of opportunities to practice, apply, and think about how the strategy has been useful to the student. This consists of (1) independent practice, (2) application, and (3) reflection.

1. *Independent practice:* This is the time when students use the strategy in authentic reading or writing situations that are very similar to those in which the strategy was developed and taught. For example, if you have modeled inferencing in a mystery, you can have students read additional mysteries and ask them to write solutions to the mysteries in their journals to show how they have used this strategy. Since each strategy must be thoroughly taught, many students will need repeated practice before they are comfortable applying it on their own. Keep in mind, however, that students have been using inferencing throughout their lives. Therefore, they are merely transferring to reading something they already know how to do.

2. *Application:* Now students will use their newly learned strategy in a totally different situation than the one in which they have learned it. For example, for the inferencing strategy they might self-select mysteries to read or write a mystery in which they provide clues, leaving the solution up to their readers. You may check application during conferences or group discussions. The application phase creates conditions that encourage transfer of the strategy to other areas.

3. *Reflection:* As students are practicing and applying the strategy, encourage them to look back and think about how they have used it. Encourage them to talk

TABLE 8.4

SUMMARY OF MINILESSON AND FOLLOW-UP PLAN FOR DEVELOPING MEANING CONSTRUCTION STRATEGIES

	PURPOSE	POSSIBLE ACTIVITIES
Minilesson		
Introduction	Let students know what they will learn. Relate it to prior knowledge and reading and writing.	Interactive discussion led by teacher
Teacher modeling	Show students how to use and think about the strategy.	Teacher-led "think-alouds" Student "think-alouds"
Student modeling and guided practice	Students gradually take charge of the strategy. Students try the strategy under teacher direction.	Student "think-alouds" Cooperative groups
Summarizing and reflecting	Pull together what has been learned. Think about when it might be useful.	Teacher-prompted discussion Cooperative groups
Follow-up		
Independent practice	Try the strategy.	Reading in text similar to type used in modeling Writing
Application	Use the strategy in a new situation.	Self-selected books Writing Content-area work
Reflection	Think about how the strategy has been useful.	Student-teacher discussion

about ways to improve and other times and places where they might use the strategy. This activity helps students make the strategy their own and also helps them see how they have succeeded.

The minilesson with follow-up affords a flexible plan for helping students learn to use strategies to construct meaning. These procedures must be viewed as basic; that is, they may need to be adapted and adjusted to fit the strategy being taught. Table 8.4 summarizes the parts of the minilesson and follow-up.

Sample Strategy Lessons

The following sections present minilessons dealing with three of the strategies suggested for helping students construct meaning: identifying important information in narrative text, monitoring, and summarizing expository text. Each lesson should be viewed as a *generic model* to help you plan lessons of your own. Although parts of the lessons are scripted to show you the types of things you might say, they are *only examples* to help you plan. The lessons may be read as a group or used selectively to meet your needs. The follow-up portions merely suggest the direction you might take and are not presented in their entirety.

Before Reading the Lessons
1. **Review this chapter to clarify any questions you have on modeling or minilessons.**
2. **Read the introduction and text on which each lesson is based. All of these texts were presented at earlier points in this book.**

While Reading the Lessons
1. **Think about how each element of the minilesson was developed.**
2. **Think about how you might change the lesson.**

*Mini-
Lesson #1*

Identifying Important Information in Narrative Text

Introduction

Purpose: To identify the important information in a story using a story map

Level: Primary (first or second grade)

Text: Jamaica Tag-Along (Havill, 1989; text located on page 61)

Students will have read and responded to this story before you teach the lesson. If the story map prediction strategy discussed in Chapter 3 was used when introducing the story, the reading of the story and this lesson can be closely tied together.

ACTIVITY	PROCEDURE	NOTES
Introduction	1. Tell students that to understand stories, they need to be able to identify the important information in them.	Lets students know what they will learn.
	2. Ask students to recall the story they have just read, *Jamaica Tag-Along.* Discuss it briefly.	Relates lesson to a story students already know.

Mini-lessons *continued*	ACTIVITY	PROCEDURE	NOTES
	Teacher modeling	1. Display the strategy poster in Figure 8.2 (page 397) and tell students these are the main parts to *all* stories. Briefly discuss each part.	Identifies story parts. If story map prediction was used, it should be related here. Teacher shares thinking.
		2. Show students how to identify the setting using the following think-aloud:	

> *Teacher Think-Aloud*
>
> ``First, I want to think about the setting. This includes the time and place of our story. Starting on pages 1–2, I can tell that this story takes place in Jamaica's neighborhood because it says that Ossie wants to play basketball with his friends. You usually play in your own neighborhood. After reading pages 6–9, I am sure this story is taking place in Jamaica and Ossie's neighborhood. It is also taking place during warm weather because you don't play outside without jackets during winter.''

| | | 3. Record the time and setting on the chart. | |
| | Student modeling and guided practice | Ask students to go through the remainder of the text, identifying other places that would help them identify the setting. Each time they identify a place, ask them to share how this helped them determine the setting. | Gives students a chance to practice and ``think aloud'' about what they have just learned. |

ACTIVITY	PROCEDURE	NOTES
Teacher modeling	1. Tell students that another part of the story is the characters—the people or animals in the story.	Focuses students on the next part.
	2. Tell them that a story may have several characters, some more important than others.	Teacher continues to share thinking with students.
	3. Use the following "think-aloud" to show students how you would identify the main character:	

> **Teacher Think-Aloud**
>
> ``The title of the story tells me right away that Jamaica must be an important character in the story. When I read pages 1, 2, and 5, I see that Ossie is also important because Jamaica wants to tag along with her brother.''

	4. Record Jamaica and Ossie on the chart.	
Student modeling and guided practice	1. Ask students to continue looking through the story to identify other important characters. As they identify each, ask them to read the page or pages that made them think this character was important. Prompt and guide students with such questions as the following: Who else took an active part in the story besides Jamaica and Ossie? Were there other characters who were just in there but really didn't do much?	Students try out what they just learned. Teacher prompting may be needed. Some students may need help recognizing why Berto is important to the story.
	2. Record students' responses on the chart.	

ACTIVITY	PROCEDURE	NOTES
Teacher modeling	1. Tell children that the next part of the story to consider is the problem. Talk with them about the problem, explaining that it is the big question or situation that runs through the story.	Focuses students' attention on the next element.
	2. Tell children that you will show them how to figure out the problem. Have them use their books as you ``think aloud'' to show how to figure out the problem:	

> *Teacher Think-Aloud*
>
> ``On pages 1 and 2, I can tell that Jamaica wants to go with her brother. On page 5, Jamaica says that she doesn't want to tag along. She wants to play. I can tell that Ossie doesn't want to be bothered because she is younger. The problem is that Jamaica wants to play with her older brother, but he doesn't want her to. I know that this is the way some older boys and girls are about their younger brothers and sisters.''

	3. Record the problem on the chart.	
Student modeling and guided practice	Ask students to find other places in the story that show the problem, sharing their thinking as they proceed.	

	ACTIVITY	PROCEDURE	NOTES
Mini-lessons *continued*	Teacher modeling	1. Tell students that the next part of the story to consider is the action or events that take place as a result of the problem and that lead to the solution. Point out that they need to notice only the most important things. 2. Use the following ``think-aloud'' to show students how to identify the action:	

> *Teacher Think-Aloud*
>
> "After Jamaica knew that Ossie wasn't going to let her play, she followed him to the playground on her bike. She didn't want him to know she was there. On pages 6–7, I can tell this because of words like *hide* and *crept.*" (Record the event on the chart under "Action.") ``On page 8, I learn that Jamaica tries to get in the game." (Record the second event on the chart.)

	ACTIVITY	PROCEDURE	NOTES
	Student modeling and guided practice	Ask students to continue finding important events and telling why they selected each one. Help them select the following events: • The boys still won't let Jamaica play (page 11). Jamaica goes to the sandlot to play by herself (page 13). As Jamaica swings, a little boy (Berto) gets in her way, and she doesn't like it (page 15).	Students will want to identify every little detail. Encourage them to focus only on the important things.

	ACTIVITY	PROCEDURE	NOTES
Mini-lessons *continued*		• Berto tries to help Jamaica build her sandcastle, but she doesn't like it (pages 16–17). • Berto's mother tells him to leave Jamaica alone, and Jamaica realizes that's how her brother Ossie hurts her feelings (pages 18–21). • Jamaica lets Berto help her build the sandcastle (page 23).	
	Teacher modeling and student modeling	1. Record students' responses on the chart. 2. Tell students that the final important part of the story is the outcome. Tell them they know how this story ends and you want them to help you ``think aloud'' to tell how they could identify the outcome. 3. Talk students through the outcome, and record it on the chart. (Ossie joins Jamaica and Berto; Jamaica doesn't even mind if Ossie tags along.)	By this time, all students will know the story. Therefore, let them help identify the outcome.
	Reviewing the story	Use the completed story map and have children retell the story. Point out each part of the story as they retell it.	Pulls the story together for the students.
	Summarizing and reflecting	1. Ask students to explain what they should look for to identify the important information in stories. 2. Ask them when they will be able to use this strategy. 3. Remind them that the strategy poster will be available to help them recall the important parts of a story.	

Mini-lessons
continued

Discussion

This minilesson would be followed by many opportunities to read other stories. Before each reading, remind students to think about the story parts by referring them to the strategy poster.

There are many ways to develop this lesson. For some students, it might be helpful to focus on one story element at a time. However, I have found that children learn this strategy much more readily if you introduce the whole concept at once and then focus on each element in detail as needed. Also, notice in this lesson how the teacher modeling was alternated with the student modeling and guided practice. This shows the flexibility of this plan to fit students' needs and the strategy being taught.

As subsequent stories are read, you will want the modeling to become more student directed and less teacher directed. Even young children can begin to verbalize their thinking as they identify story elements. Research has shown that teaching students to identify the important information in stories does help them construct meaning (Pressley et al., 1989).

It is important not to allow strategy instruction to destroy the story. Keep the learning light and fun; even though you focus on the strategy, the content of the story will be of most interest to the children.

As mentioned earlier, you could combine this strategy with story map prediction (see Chapter 3), which you could start before reading and use after reading to teach the strategy for identifying important information. After reading, you would return to the predictions students made to help them identify the important information in stories. These two strategies flow nicely into teaching students to summarize stories.

Mini-Lesson #2

Monitoring
(Self-Monitoring or Clarifying)

Introduction

Purpose: To use the monitoring strategy of ``stop and think'' to improve meaning construction

Level: Third or fourth grade

Text: The Bicycle Man (Say, 1982; text located on page 269)

Monitoring is the heart of the meaning construction process because it brings together many strategies and processes. It is a strategy that students acquire gradually and will need to be taught, or at least reviewed and expanded, numerous times. One version I like to use is ``stop and think.'' Figure 8.4 (page 399) presents a basic poster for this strategy. When using stop and think, students periodically stop and say, ``Does this make sense to me?'' If it does not, they try a number of ``fix-up'' techniques such as rereading, reading ahead, looking up words, or seeking help from another source.

This strategy is best taught by introducing it before reading and then modeling it during teacher-directed reading, with teacher and students taking turns modeling. (This type of instruction is similar to the process used in reciprocal teaching; see Palincsar & Brown, 1984a, 1984b.)

	ACTIVITY	PROCEDURE	NOTES
Mini-lessons *continued*	Introduction	1. Display the strategy poster in Figure 8.4 (page 399). Explain to students that good readers ``stop and think'' about their reading to be sure it is making sense. Explain each step on the poster, and tell them they will learn to use this strategy as they read *The Bicycle Man.*	Lets students know what they are going to learn.
		2. Introduce the book, using some of the procedures suggested earlier in this text. Have students predict what they think will happen in the story.	
	Teacher modeling	Read aloud the first three pages (two with text, one with picture); then stop and use the following think-aloud:	You have to create a problem so you can model the process.

> *Teacher Think-Aloud*
>
> "This is a good place for me to stop and ask myself, *Does this make sense?* I understand that the author is telling this story and it takes place in a school in Japan. I'm not sure if I know what a sports-day is. I think I'll reread page 3." (Reread page 3 aloud.) "A sportsday must be like our field day where we have different events. So far I haven't learned much about my prediction about the bicycle man."

*Mini-
lessons
continued*

ACTIVITY	PROCEDURE	NOTES
Student modeling and guided practice	1. Direct students to silently read the next two pages to see if they make sense. Tell them you will call on one of them to be teacher and talk about what she or he did when stopping to think.	The first few times students do this, you may need to prompt them. They will become comfortable with this procedure over time.
	2. If needed, prompt students as they play the role of teacher: Were there any words you didn't know? What parts would you reread? What did you learn about your predictions from these two pages?	
Teacher modeling	1. Direct students to continue silently reading the next three pages to see what they learned about their predictions. Then use the following ``think-aloud'':	Teacher models another ``fix-up'' strategy.

> *Teacher Think-Aloud*
>
> "The story is making sense to me, but there was one word I didn't know. Do any of you know this word?" (Write *lacquered box* on the board. Ask students for help. After they respond, continue.) "When I stop and think about the word *lacquered,* the clues in the text tell me it is some type of box. The exact type of box seems unimportant, so I wouldn't look this word up in the dictionary. I still haven't learned much about my prediction and the bicycle man. So, I'll read on."

*Mini-
lessons*
continued

ACTIVITY	PROCEDURE	NOTES
	2. Continue alternating with teacher modeling and student modeling and guided practice until the story has been completed.	
Discussing the story	Encourage students to respond to the story by telling how they felt about it and what they learned.	Pulls the story together.
Summarizing and reflecting	Display the strategy poster and ask students to tell what they learned about stop and think and to talk about how and when they could use this strategy.	Helps students make the strategy their own.

Discussion

Students will practice and apply this strategy as they read other books. Most children require several modeling experiences before they learn to use stop and think. For younger students, it is often helpful to model only one ``fix-up'' procedure at a time.

Once you have introduced the strategy, you should concentrate on it over a block of days to allow students to become comfortable with it. The procedure of alternating modeling between yourself and the students is a very effective way to make the strategy a natural part of students' reading. Another approach is to have them use cooperative reading and take turns being the teacher. If the entire class is doing this, you can move through the class to monitor student progress and provide additional support by joining any pairs of students who might need more help.

*Mini-
Lesson #3*

Summarizing Expository Text

Introduction

Purpose: To summarize informational (expository) text

Level: Intermediate and higher

Text: ``The First Egyptian Mummies,'' from *Mummies, Tombs, and Treasure* (Perl, 1987; text located on page 144)

Summarizing informational or expository text requires students to focus on different elements than those in narrative text. The strategy presented here is based on rules developed by Brown and Day (1983) and successfully researched by others (Bean & Steenwyk, 1984). The rules are as follows:

1. Delete trivial information.
2. Delete redundant information.
3. Substitute superordinate terms for lists of terms.
4. Integrate a series of events with a superordinate action term.
5. Select a topic sentence.
6. Invent a topic sentence if there isn't one.

It is best to teach this strategy after students have learned to identify important information in expository text. Your first lessons would focus on summarizing paragraphs; later lessons would be extended to longer texts. You would teach this lesson after students had read ``The First Egyptian Mummies''; it is assumed they already know how to summarize paragraphs.

ACTIVITY	PROCEDURE	NOTES
Introduction	Ask students to recall the strategy they have learned for summarizing paragraphs. Tell them they are going to learn how to apply this to longer texts.	Relates what students will learn to what they already know.
Teacher modeling	1. Display the strategy poster shown in Figure 8.6 (page 401). Review each step with students.	Focuses students' attention on what they will learn.
	2. Ask students to recall ``The First Egyptian Mummies,'' and briefly discuss it.	
	3. Tell students you are going to show them how to apply the summarizing informational text strategy to more than a paragraph. Use the following think-aloud, along with a transparency of the text. As you use the think-aloud, mark out the text and make notes in the margin. Figure 8.10 shows how one page would look.	Shows students how to think through the steps of the strategy.

FIGURE 8.10

MARKED PAGE FOR MODELING SUMMARIZING

sues of once-living things, returning them to nature in other forms.

But sometimes nature springs a surprise or two on us. One such surprise took place long ago in the vast North African desert country of Egypt. Before the beginning of recorded history — perhaps seven or eight thousand years ago — people began to settle on the banks of the Nile River, which runs through the Egyptian desert. The ribbons of well-watered land that bordered the Nile provided precious soil for growing food crops. So, in selecting a place to bury their dead, the Egyptian farming people avoided the river shore. They chose instead the hot, barren sands that lay beyond it.

Shows that these mummies were not planned

The people dug small shallow graves. Usually they buried their dead in a crouched position. They placed them on their sides with their knees drawn up to their chests. That way their bodies took up as little space as possible.

The Egyptians hoped that in some magical way the dead were not really dead. Perhaps their spirits lay beneath the sand along with their limp, unclothed bodies. Perhaps a spirit might wish to eat or drink just as the living did. So the families of the dead included some clay pots of food and jars of water in the shallow pit graves. And sometimes they added a man's favorite tool or spear of sharpened stone, a woman's beads of shell or bone, or a child's toy.

Interesting but not important to our summary

Then the family covered the grave with sand and piled some rocks on top of it. The rocks helped to mark the grave. They also made it difficult for jackals and other wild animals of the desert to reach the body inside it.

Delete for summary

Most of this page not important to our summary

3

Teacher Think-Aloud

''First, when we read this chapter we determined that the topic was mummies. We decided there were three parts to the topic: (1) mummies, (2) combining upper and lower Egypt, and (3) man's attempt to improve mummies. The text related to the first topic ends at the top of page 6. So we have completed the first part of step 1–identify the topic. Now we need to delete the trivial information and use steps 2 and 3.

''It seems to me that most of pages 1 and 2 are additional explanations of details that can be grouped together; they relate to the definition of a mummy:

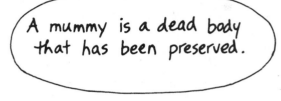

A mummy is a dead body that has been preserved.

''Pages 3 and 5 have many ideas relating to how the first mummies came to be. These can be grouped together; also, there is additional information about the Nile that could be deleted. We could list these ideas for our summary:

Egyptians buried people in hot sands.

Hot sands preserved the bodies by taking out the moisture.

Dry cold also preserved bodies of the Incas in the Andes Mountains of South America.

ACTIVITY	PROCEDURE	NOTES

``In step 4, we need to look for a main-idea statement. The closest thing we have to one is the first sentence in paragraph 2 on page 5, but this doesn't really give the main idea. It only tells part of the information presented. We will have to go to step 5 and formulate our own main-idea sentence. Based on the important information we have, I think this is the best statement for this part of our text:

> The first mummies were accidents of nature.

``Now we are ready to put our summary together using the ideas we have identified with this strategy:''

> A mummy is a dead body that has been preserved. Egyptians buried bodies in hot sand. The sands preserved the body by taking out moisture. Dry cold also preserved the bodies of the Incas in the Andes Mountains of South America. The first mummies were accidents of nature.

4. Discuss the summary paragraph. Point out that the summary for this chapter should probably have three paragraphs, since three parts to the topic were identified.

Pulls together ideas modeled.

Mini-lessons *continued*

ACTIVITY	PROCEDURE	NOTES
Teacher-student modeling and guided practice	1. In using the strategy, direct students to summarize pages 6–8, which is the text related to the second part of the topic. 2. Use a transparency of the pages and have students mark out information and make notes as they ``think aloud'' about the process. 3. Prompt them as needed: What happened to bring Egypt together? What information can be deleted or grouped? Combining upper and lower Egypt created the need for what? 4. Assist students in writing their summary.	Begins to release responsibility to students.
Student modeling and guided practice	1. Using a transparency of pages 8, 9, 10, and 11, have students mark out material and make notes as they ``think aloud'' to summarize this last part of the chapter. 2. Have students work with a partner to develop the summary for the last part.	Lets students try the strategy with teacher support if needed.
Creating a final summary	Put all three parts of the summary together, and have students check to see if changes need to be made.	Pulls all parts of the summary together.
Summarizing and reflecting	Prompt students to summarize the parts of the strategy and talk about its uses: What steps do you follow when summarizing longer text? What is different when summarizing longer text instead of paragraphs? How and when do you think you might use this strategy?	Helps students see what they have learned and why it is important.

*Mini-
lessons
continued*

Discussion

This lesson would be followed by having students read the next chapter, ``Why the Egyptians Made Mummies,'' and practice using the summarizing informational text strategy. Most students will need repeated teacher modeling and guided practice. They could begin summarizing Chapter 2 in cooperative pairs; this would allow you to observe what they have learned and how they are using the strategy.

Since summarizing is difficult for students to learn, lessons are much more effective if they are kept short and focused, with emphasis on meaning construction; in other words, the most important thing is to respond to and understand the text. They will learn to use the strategy best through repeated meaningful experiences with the text along with modeling support from the teacher.

You should use the poster for this and other strategies to keep students aware of the strategies, displaying the posters where they can be easily seen and used. Periodically, invite students to reflect about how they are using the strategy and talk about how they can use it more effectively.

After Reading the Plans

1. **Select any strategy lesson plan presented in this chapter. Working with a partner, develop several more ``think-alouds'' that you would use to model the strategy.**
2. **Working with a partner, select any strategy you would like to teach and prepare a lesson on it. Teach the lesson to a small group, and discuss the results.**
3. **Select a grade level of your choice and observe for an hour or two, looking for evidence of students using the strategies mentioned in this chapter. Talk with the teacher to see how the children learned them. Were they taught? Did the students learn them through their literacy experiences?**

■ A Final Word About Strategies

The strategy lessons just described should serve as models to help you develop your own lessons. Although research supports the inclusion of the five strategies discussed here, remember that this is not the last word. *Many students may do just as well by reading, writing, and interacting with their peers and you about their reading and writing.* Children will improve at reading and writing only if we allow them to read and write. Teaching strategies may be a helpful form of support for some students, but not for others. Only the wise, informed, observant teacher can decide whether students are profiting from strategy instruction. You must be that teacher!

■ Summary

This chapter focused on modeling as one aspect of scaffolded instruction. Modeling is the process of showing someone how to use or do something he or she does not know. It may be *implicit* or *explicit*. Explicit modeling may involve "talk-alouds," in which steps are described, or "think-alouds," in which cognitive processes are shared.

Five strategies were suggested for helping students improve their meaning construction: inferencing, identifying important information, monitoring, summarizing, and generating questions. Finally, the chapter presented guidelines for planning strategy instruction and three sample lessons.

Literature

de Paola, T. (1978). *The popcorn book.* New York: Holiday House.

Havill, J. (1989). *Jamaica tag-along.* Boston: Houghton Mifflin.

Huck, C. (1989). *Princess Furball.* New York: Greenwillow Books.

Marzollo, J. (1990). *Pretend you're a cat.* New York: Dial.

Perl, L. (1987). *Mummies, tombs, and treasure.* New York: Clarion.

Robison, B. H. (1978). *Lurkers of the deep: Life within the ocean depths.* New York: David McKay.

Say, A. (1982). *The bicycle man.* Boston: Houghton Mifflin.

For Additional Reading

Pressley, M., Burkell, J., Cariglia-Bull, T., Lysynchuck, L., McGoldrick, J. A., Schneider, B., Snyder, B. L., Symons, S., & Woloshyn, V. E. (1990). *Cognitive strategy instruction that really improves children's academic performance.* Cambridge, MA: Brookline.

Pressley, M., & Harris, K. R. (1990). What we really know about strategy instruction. *Educational Leadership, 48,* 31–34.

Constructing Meaning Across the Curricum

9

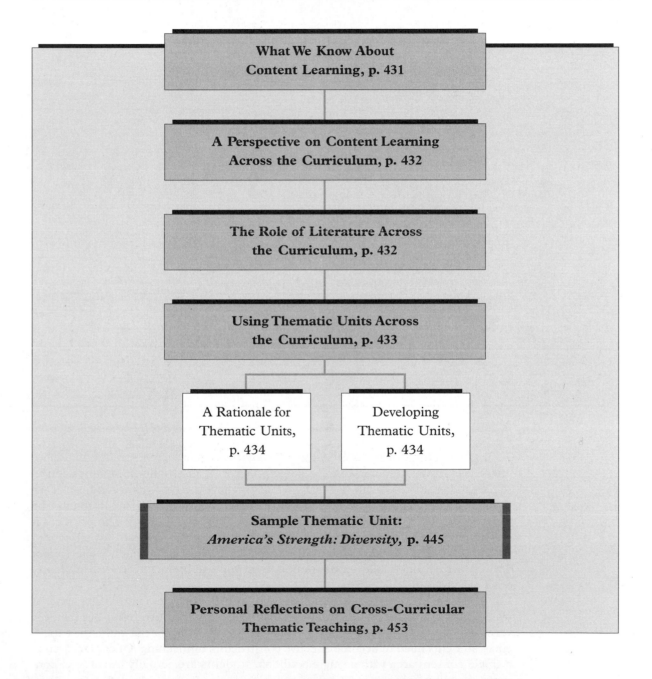

What We Know About
Content Learning, p. 431

A Perspective on Content Learning
Across the Curriculum, p. 432

The Role of Literature Across
the Curriculum, p. 432

Using Thematic Units Across
the Curriculum, p. 433

A Rationale for
Thematic Units,
p. 434

Developing
Thematic Units,
p. 434

Sample Thematic Unit:
America's Strength: Diversity, p. 445

Personal Reflections on Cross-Curricular
Thematic Teaching, p. 453

429

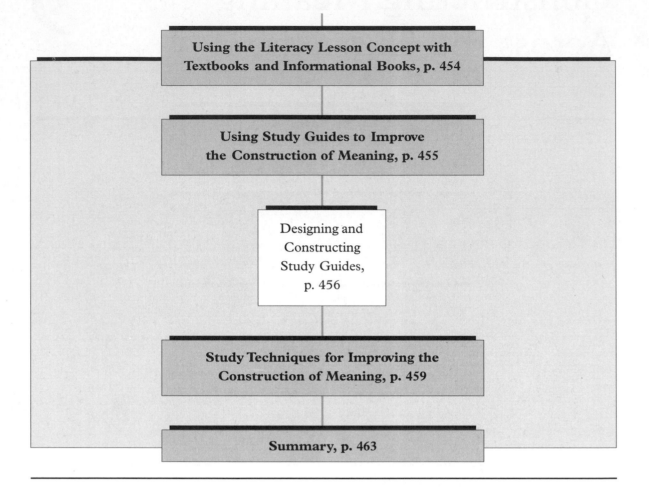

Using the Literacy Lesson Concept with Textbooks and Informational Books, p. 454

Using Study Guides to Improve the Construction of Meaning, p. 455

Designing and Constructing Study Guides, p. 456

Study Techniques for Improving the Construction of Meaning, p. 459

Summary, p. 463

TRADITIONALLY, EDUCATORS HAVE first thought about reading instruction and language arts instruction and then, at some other time, instruction in math, science, social studies, and so forth. Typically educators have said that children first "learn to read" and then are able to "read to learn." This line of thinking led us to talk and think about an area known as *content reading* (Herber, 1978, 1984). Though there is indeed a time when students are more focused on "learning to read," which gradually gives way to "reading to learn," the two tasks are neither mutually exclusive nor entirely sequential. Children develop literacy and use literacy to learn simultaneously (Wells, 1986).

All of the ideas and principles presented in earlier chapters of this text apply as we begin to think about constructing meaning across the curriculum. In fact, the various content areas of the school curriculum are the basis for the authentic experiences students need to become effective constructors of meaning. Of course, even in a single content area with a single textbook, students are actually learning to construct meaning.

What We Know About Content Learning

The process of constructing meaning has many of the same features in various content areas:

▶ Students construct meaning by having authentic experiences within the content areas.

▶ These experiences involve and integrate all aspects of the language arts.

▶ When using *any* text, students construct meaning by activating their prior knowledge and interacting with the text.

▶ As students construct meaning, they build relationships between old knowledge and new knowledge. Learning in one curricular area is enhanced when relationships can be built between that area and others.

▶ When learning in any curricular area, students need scaffolded support from the teacher and peers to help them construct meaning.

Although all content areas share these features, they also have their differences, such as different text structures and terminology.

Armbruster (1991) makes six recommendations for improving learning in content areas and the ability of students to construct meaning:

1. Integrate reading (and all aspects of literacy) with content instruction. This integration should take place across disciplines and should focus on more holistic learning as opposed to the learning of isolated facts. This type of learning is in line with what we know about schema theory and how students construct meaning. It helps students build relationships and leads to greater transfer of knowledge and skill from one discipline to another.

2. Increase opportunities for students to read informational texts throughout *all levels of schooling.* Students are very interested in such texts, but need more experience with reading and meaning construction in these different text structures.

3. Provide students with experiences that will help them become strategic readers by scaffolding instruction and gradually releasing them to be responsible for their own reading. Model strategies using informational texts.

4. Keep students actively learning by helping them focus on what to do before reading, during reading, and after reading. Help them learn to monitor their reading, build connections with old knowledge, and use writing to improve their construction of meaning.

5. Increase opportunities for collaborative learning.

6. Modify teacher education to ensure that *all* teachers gain the knowledge and learn the techniques needed to make these five things happen.

In the remainder of this chapter, we focus on how to improve students' ability to construct meaning in all content areas across the curriculum. The emphasis is on two approaches:

1. Using thematic, cross-curricular units to plan and organize for literacy learning and content learning.

2. Applying principles and techniques for successful meaning construction by focusing on how to use textbooks and other resources more effectively.

A Perspective on Content Learning Across the Curriculum

In far too many classrooms, content knowledge is isolated into separate disciplines that fail to promote broad understandings and relationships. Learning is assumed to take place through primarily one avenue—the textbook—and students frequently do not read it (Armbruster, 1991); the teacher tells or reads aloud the information.

In contrast, learning across the curriculum is interactive, allowing students to construct meaning through a variety of problem-solving experiences that use many types of literature and other resources such as films, resource persons, CD-ROMs, the World Wide Web, and hands-on projects and experiments. For example, the concepts to be learned in science and math are *not* most effectively learned by reading a book or an article, which is only *one* source of information. Authentic learning in science and math takes place through hands-on experimentation and problem solving.

This text takes the point of view that the ability to both construct meaning and gain content knowledge is enhanced by thinking about and engaging in cross-curricular learning. Even if you are in a teaching situation that focuses on a separate subject, you can enhance learning by building connections between the subject you are teaching and other disciplines.

The Role of Literature Across the Curriculum

The textbook has been assumed to be the centerpiece for learning throughout our educational system, particularly in content areas such as math, science, and social studies (Elliott, 1990). This assumption creates two major problems. First, as already noted, the textbook is only one source of information. Second, textbooks have numerous shortcomings that often hinder meaning construction:

- ▶ *Textbooks are often unappealing to students* (Elliott, 1990). Many textbooks, in an effort to avoid controversy, do not present material that is of interest to students.

- ▶ *Textbooks are often too difficult for the grade level for which they are assigned* (Chall & Conrad, 1990). Even though many textbooks have been improved, some are still too complex and problematic in structure.

- ▶ *Textbooks are often inconsiderate* (Anderson & Armbruster, 1984a). They are often written with an organization and style that fail to help students construct meaning.

- ▶ *Textbooks often cover many topics in a cursory manner* (Tyson & Woodward, 1989). As a result, students cannot study a topic in depth. Many authors have tried to correct this problem, however.

- ▶ *Textbooks used in schools are often dated* (Tyson & Woodward, 1989). When schools are unable to buy new textbooks often enough to keep the curriculum up to date, students have to use textbooks that contain dated or inaccurate information.

- ▶ *Textbooks are developed by publishers for a national marketplace* (Elliott & Woodward, 1990). This means schools that depend solely on textbooks are unable to focus on the specific concerns of their curricula. They are bound to this "national curriculum."

Even though textbook publishers have made strides in improving their products and addressing many of these concerns (Elliott & Woodward, 1990), they have not totally overcome some of these problems. Therefore, one very good way for schools to deal with this dilemma is to use the textbook as only *one resource* and to build their curricula around a variety of quality literature and other "real-world" resources such as magazines, newspapers, online sources, and so forth.

Research has shown that literature has educational value for content-area learning (Hickman & Cullinan, 1989). Students can "read, hear, and discuss biographies, myths, fairy tales, and historical tales to fire their imagination and to whet their appetite for understanding how the world came to be as it is" (History–Social Science Curriculum Framework and Criteria Committee, 1988, p. 5). Therefore, the use of all types of literature to complement textbooks has been strongly recommended as a way to improve students' learning and meaning construction (History–Social Science Curriculum Framework and Criteria Committee, 1988; Moss, 1991).

The literature to be used across the curriculum should be both fiction and nonfiction, although some topics may lend themselves only to nonfiction. For example, an upper-grade or middle school class studying medieval times might read historical fiction pieces such as *Knight Prisoner: The Tale of Sir Thomas Malory and His King Arthur* (Hodges, 1976) or *A Connecticut Yankee in King Arthur's Court* (Twain, 1987), as well as such nonfiction pieces as *Age of Chivalry* (Wright, 1988), *Luttrell Village: Country Life in the Middle Ages* (Sancha, 1983), and *Castle* (Macaulay, 1977). All of these books, both historical fiction and nonfiction, could support and extend the chapters on medieval times provided in the social studies text. They could bring the period to life, broadening students' sources of information and enlivening their study.

From the kindergarten level to the upper grades, literature can be a vital part of the materials students use to construct meaning. It motivates students, extends textbooks, and makes learning more authentic and exciting.

In the next section, we focus on how to develop a thematic unit using textbooks, literature, and other real-world resources. Then we will use the literacy lesson concept to see how to use all types of text resources to further develop students' abilities to construct meaning.

Using Thematic Units Across the Curriculum

Thematic units (see Chapter 2) are frameworks for planning and organizing learning experiences around common bodies of knowledge, thinking, or concepts that cut across many curricular lines, such as language arts, science, art, or music. They provide an organization and structure that create communities of learners who continue to construct meaning and knowledge (Fredericks, Meinbach, & Rothlein, 1993; Pappas et al., 1990).

Even when thematic units are used to integrate only the language arts, many other curricular areas come into play. These cross-curricular or interdisciplinary connections are "real" only when they are meaningful and relevant to the curriculum and students' lives (Routman, 1991). Thus, although you may begin using thematic units as a way to integrate the language arts, you will soon begin to see how the important curricular concepts from many disciplines can be developed through these units.

A Rationale for Thematic Units

From the beginning, every chapter in this text has promoted a rationale that supports the use of thematic units as a way to organize for effective learning. These units build on students' interests and prior knowledge by focusing on topics that are relevant to students' lives. They build knowledge relationships and allow for authentic learning by encouraging problem solving that cuts across curricular lines. They also support students in a variety of interactive and collaborative ways.

Developing Thematic Units

Developing thematic units is not a complicated process and should be kept as simple as possible, especially in the beginning stages. It can be divided into three stages: planning, implementing, and culminating (Pappas et al., 1990; Routman, 1991; Walmsley, 1994). Figure 9.1 shows these three stages with the activities that take place within each. There is no one correct way to carry out this process.

Planning the Theme

Planning a thematic unit involves four activities: (1) choosing the theme, (2) identifying what students might learn, (3) selecting resources, and (4) selecting activities and developing a timeline. The planning process is interactive; as you think about a particular theme or consider certain resources, you will get other ideas about themes or other activities that you might add.

Many teachers carry out the planning process alone, especially as they begin to use thematic units. However, it is possible and more authentic to involve students whenever appropriate. Sometimes several teachers at a grade level collaborate, and sometimes collaborations are schoolwide. In some cases, you may want to collaborate with other teachers in a listserver discussion group on the Internet. In the middle school, teachers may use an interdisciplinary team approach to plan. This team might include a teacher from each of several disciplines, such as English, social studies, science, and so forth.

Choosing the Theme.   You may think about such things as student interests, what you want students to learn, what is developmentally appropriate, or topics you are responsible for within the curriculum. The theme should be broad enough to allow you to involve several different curricular areas but not so broad that students will lose sight of it and fail to make the connections. Also, selecting a topic that is too broad or unmanageable will discourage you and cause students to lose interest.

As you begin to use themes more extensively in your classroom, you may become concerned about how to keep track of the various concepts you have developed across the curriculum. Some teachers find a form such as the one in Figure 9.2 helpful.

FIGURE 9.1

DEVELOPING A THEMATIC UNIT

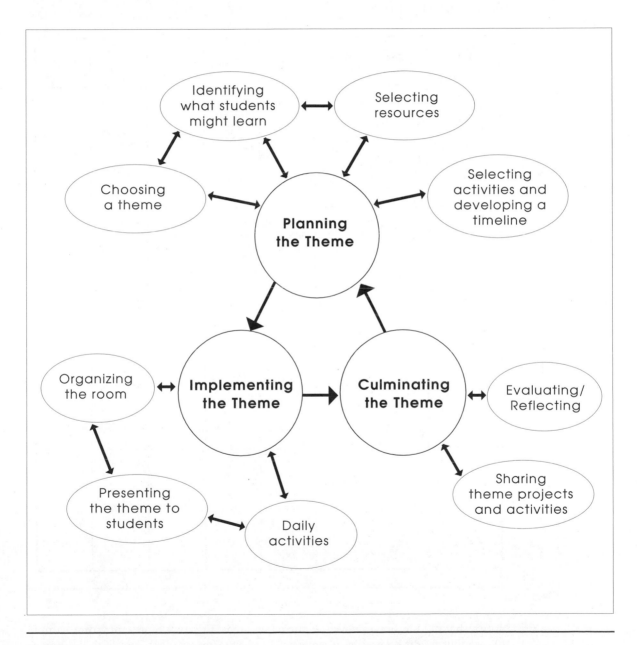

FIGURE 9.2

FORM FOR KEEPING TRACK OF THEMES AND CURRICULAR AREAS

Curricular Area / Theme	Language Arts	Social Studies	Science	Math	Health	Art Music Drama PE	Other
Helping Out	• Decodes words independently • Retells stories	• Has a concept of helper		• Uses addition to keep simple records		• Art— Uses form and color	
Baby Animals	• Identifies important information • Writes simple reports		• Understands the importance of animals	• Keeps records and compares growth—weight	• Good food important to animals and people		

Notice that not all themes cover all curricular areas. Figure 9.3 presents some sample themes that might be used at various grade levels. However, any one of these themes could be covered at any grade level.

FIGURE 9.3

SAMPLE THEMES AT VARIOUS GRADE LEVELS

K   Colors of the seasons
1   Preparing for winter
2   A favorite author or illustrator (choose any author or illustrator)
3   Fairy tales
4   Prehistoric animals
5   Space travel
6   Science fiction
7   Understanding the environment
8   The cost of pollution

Identifying What Students Might Learn.   While you are selecting a topic, or right after you have selected it, you need to think in general terms about what students might learn during the unit. Recall from Chapter 2 the major outcomes related to attitudes and habits and constructing meaning. These same two categories can be used for cross-curricular units. Following are examples of the outcomes developed for a unit on foods:

▶ *Attitudes and habits*

1. Develops an improved attitude about proper foods to eat

2. Appreciates the planning and preparation required to prepare a healthy meal

▶ *Constructing meaning*

1. Knows the important food groups and can choose a balanced daily diet

2. Identifies the procedures in planning a basic meal

3. Understands the processes required in growing food for a country

In addition to major outcomes, you may identify specific strategies and skills students might develop within the unit. For example, for the foods unit, you might choose to focus on such strategies and skills as the following:

▶ Selects appropriate book sources for a report

▶ Identifies important information in text

▶ Takes notes

▶ Writes a report

▶ Uses simple addition

Of course, many other skills and strategies will also develop as a result of the unit experiences, but these are the ones you plan to focus on. Identifying what students

TABLE 9.1

CATEGORIES OF THEME RESOURCES

RESOURCE	EXAMPLES
Print resources	Literature Textbooks Newspapers and magazines Encyclopedias and reference books Primary source materials (notes from observations, interviews, letters, etc.) Brochures
Electronic resources	The Internet World Wide Web Books on CD-ROMs Software programs
Hands-on resources	Old pottery Tools Appliances Clothing Masks Toys
Community resources	People Museums Libraries Parks Chambers of Commerce
Arts	Paintings Samples of architecture Sculpture Graphic and decorative arts and crafts Music Theater Television, videos, film Records, tapes, compact discs, CD-ROMs

might learn forms part of the foundation for assessment and evaluation, both throughout and at the conclusion of the thematic unit.

Selecting Resources. These can include print resources, hands-on resources, community resources, and the arts.

The Internet is also an excellent resource for materials for thematic units. Many schools now have this computer capability. Through the Internet, students can visit such places as museums, the White House, and many others. Students and teachers can share ideas. Publishers such as Houghton Mifflin and Scholastic have online services to help students and teachers keep abreast of new ideas. See the For Exploration section at the end of this chapter.

FIGURE 9.4

FORM FOR PLANNING THEMATIC UNIT ACTIVITIES

Activities	Independent/ Individual	Cooperative/ Small Group	Whole Class	Self-Selected	Teacher Assigned	Teacher Directed
Initiating activities						
Developing activities						
Culminating activities						

Again, there is no one right set or type of resource to use. Your decision depends on the thematic unit and the level for which you are developing it. Table 9.1 presents several examples of theme resources.

When making your selections, remember to maintain a balance of types of resources. You will nearly always use print resources, but other resources may not be available for all themes. Try to think about which ones will create the most authentic learning experiences and provide the greatest motivation as students continue to develop their ability to construct meaning.

Selecting Activities and Developing a Timeline.   This is the last part of your planning process. Remember that your purpose is to help students understand the theme and continue to learn to construct meaning. You will need three categories of activities: activities for initiating the theme, developing the theme, and culminating the theme. Although you may preplan certain activities, you will add or change others as the unit progresses and as you assess students' progress. Figure 9.4 presents a form with categories of activities.

Third graders create a display as an initiating activity for their theme. © *Michael Zide*

Activities for the theme should involve such things as problem solving; reading; writing reports; making charts, graphs, or timelines; creating Web pages; projects; art; music; drama; and so forth. Your role as the teacher will be to direct some groups, monitor others, and participate in still others. Sometimes you will be working with small groups or having individual conferences, and at other times you may be conducting a whole-class activity. Several books listed in the For Additional Reading section provide many ideas. You may also choose to use strategies such as K-W-L, discussed in Chapter 3.

In planning and selecting activities for a theme, give special attention to those used to initiate the theme. These should be interactive and should do three very important things for students:

1. Motivate students and get them excited about the theme
2. Activate prior knowledge and develop background needed for the theme
3. Set the tone for the theme by helping students take ownership of their learning as the unit progresses

Since a great variety of initiating activities are possible for any theme, you must select ones that best meet your students' needs and the theme you are developing. Initiating activities may include such things as drama, group discussions, displays of artifacts or other items to motivate interest, reading aloud a good piece of literature, music (good source books are *The Raffi Singable Songbook* [Raffi, 1980] and *Go In and Out the Window* [Fox & Marks, 1987]), and art. Sometimes you will use several initiating activities; at other times you will need only one. Just be sure to get the unit off to an exciting start!

As you proceed, you can enhance your planning by using a technique known as *webbing* (Norton, 1982; Pappas et al., 1990). Once you have selected the thematic unit you want to develop, you proceed as follows:

1. Make a list of ideas you think of in relation to your chosen theme and the outcomes you desire.
2. Begin to group the ideas into categories and create a web.
3. Think specifically about what students might accomplish in the thematic unit.
4. Make lists of resources and activities you might use.
5. Group ideas, resources, and activities and continue to add them to your web.

This planning process is dynamic; your ideas and thoughts will constantly change. A sample thematic unit is provided later in this chapter to illustrate the complete process; you may wish to refer to that theme at this point (see page 445).

Culminating activities should pull together the ideas and concepts developed in the unit, as well as give students a time to share what they have done and use what they have learned. Culminating a unit should be fun. It should also include some time for reflecting on the unit and on each student's individual goals and activities.

Finally, you must develop a timeline for your thematic unit. Units may last for a few days, several weeks, or, in some classes with upper-grade students, up to a month. Relevant factors to consider in determining the length of the unit include the scope of the theme, your instructional objectives, student interests and motivation, and how involved students become in certain activities. As you become comfortable using thematic units, you will find it easier and easier to adjust your time schedule. An initial timeline for a unit might be just a simple daily listing of the major activities you plan to accomplish. For example, the theme on foods discussed earlier might be planned for two weeks, and the rough timeline might look as follows:

September 23	Introduce theme and brainstorm with students
September 24	Select project and begin individual work
September 25	Begin literacy lesson using book to be read by whole class
September 26	Have discussion circles to review what has been learned conduct individual project work
September 27	Begin small-group projects
October 1	Work on individual projects and reports and conferences
October 2	Work on individual projects and reports and conferences
October 3	Work on individual projects and reports and conferences
October 4	Culminate the unit and share projects

Kindergartners and their teacher reflect on theme learnings. © *Michael Zide*

Implementing the Theme

Implementing the theme involves organizing the room, presenting the theme to students, and carrying out daily activities. This phase will cover most of the time allotted for the theme.

Organizing the Room.   This involves planning and setting up appropriate centers and areas to support the theme. Chapter 2 discussed setting up a literate environment in detail (see page 27); you may want to reread that section now. It is important to create the atmosphere for the unit, because this helps to get students motivated and excited. Moreover, the various areas and centers provide the vehicles for managing the daily schedule as the theme develops.

Presenting the Theme.   This involves motivating and exciting students with an initiating activity or activities, sharing and developing the theme plans with students, and helping students decide which activities they will do. By presenting the theme, you activate prior knowledge and develop background, which is vital to the construction of meaning.

During this time, you must help students begin deciding and planning what they will do. As you share the theme activities with them, point out where they have choices to make. Some teachers use a bulletin board; some post charts in the room; and some give a printed outline to each student. Some teachers also like to use a form such as the one in Figure 9.5 to help students make decisions and keep track of their work. This form may become a part of their literacy portfolio (see Chapter 11).

Carrying Out Daily Activities.　This final portion of implementing the theme requires that you work out a daily and weekly time schedule that allows you to get in your theme activities. These activities provide ongoing instruction and evaluation throughout the theme. You may choose to build in the concepts of the reading workshop or writing workshop, discussed in Chapter 10. Figure 9.6 shows a possible daily time schedule for teachers who use cross-curricular thematic units. Chapter 10 provides more information on planning daily schedules.

Culminating the Theme

In this final stage, you will use the culminating activities you developed as you planned your theme. Students will share theme projects and activities and evaluate and reflect on the results of the theme.

Sharing Projects and Activities.　Sharing is critical to helping students construct meaning and feel a sense of community and ownership. During this time students give talks, show their work, and talk with one another about the theme activities. Sharing may take the form of a special day, event, or activity devoted to pulling together what has been learned, having a play or a fair, putting on some type of display, inviting students from other classes, and so forth. An entire day or more may be devoted to culminating the theme if there are enough activities to make it worthwhile.

Evaluating and Reflecting.　This is also an important culminating activity. Throughout the theme, you and your students will have been assessing progress, and at this point you want them to return to their theme plan and talk about how they have done on the theme activities. You may use small-group discussions and circulate to talk with each group, or you may use individual conferences. Students should talk about how they have done in relation to the theme goals, focusing on what they have done well and what they might do better in the next unit. This should not become a "heavy time" for "grading"; rather, it should be a natural time in which you and the students reflect and take stock of how things have gone as well as which strategies and skills have helped them construct meaning and accomplish their goals. From the kindergarten level on, this can be a positive, constructive time that helps all students grow in their own literacy abilities.

As the teacher, you will also want to reflect on the unit. Was the length of time appropriate? How did the unit go? What would you change? How have your students grown? How have you grown? These and many other questions will help you use cross-curricular thematic units more and more effectively.

FIGURE 9.5

STUDENT RECORD SHEET FOR A THEME PLAN

THEME PLAN

Name _____ Theme _____

Date started _____ Date completed _____

THEME GOALS	
What I Want to Accomplish	How I Did
1.	
2.	
3.	

MY OWN PROJECT(S)			
Focus	Started	Completed	Comments

OTHER ACTIVITIES				
Activity	Done With	Started	Completed	Comments

FIGURE 9.6

A DAILY TIME SCHEDULE FOR CROSS-CURRICULAR TEACHING

Daily Schedule

8:30	Opening Exercise
8:40	Warm Up/Sharing
8:50	Reading Workshop
10:15	BREAK/RECESS
10:35	Whole-Class Activities
11:15	LUNCH
11:45	Teacher Read-Aloud
12:00	Writing Workshop
1:10	Small Group/Independent Projects
2:00	Specials (Music, PE, Art)*
2:40	Sharing/Celebrating the Day
3:00	Dismissal

* Some teachers still have specials, but the specials build on the class theme.

In summary, developing a theme involves planning, implementing, and culminating the theme. Each of these stages is very fluid and interactive and should be adjusted to fit your needs and the needs of your students. The following section presents a sample cross-curricular theme entitled "America's Strength: Diversity."

Sample Thematic Unit

America's Strength: Diversity

The sample theme presented in this section was developed for use in a fifth-grade class with a wide range of abilities. Both the planning process and the theme outline are presented.

Before Reading the Thematic Unit
1. **Review the portion of this chapter focusing on developing thematic units.**
2. **Discuss any questions you have with a peer or your instructor.**
3. **Read the planning process for the theme.**

While Reading the Thematic Unit
1. **Think about why certain activities might have been selected.**
2. **Think of other ways you might have developed the theme.**
3. **Keep in mind that there is no ``right way'' to develop a theme. You have many alternatives.**

Sample Thematic Unit **continued**

Planning Process for the Theme

Basically, I planned this theme using the process described in this chapter.

1. I considered many different topics by brainstorming a list of ideas. I finally settled on ``America's Strength: Diversity'' because this idea would allow me to make many connections across the curriculum. This is also a theme that could go in many different directions or could be the focus of study for an entire year.
2. Next, I began to brainstorm learning goals, resources, and activities. The rough web shown in Figure 9.7 helped me focus and limit the theme.
3. I decided to focus first on my major outcomes: attitudes and habits and constructing meaning. Since I could use this theme early in the year, I wanted to develop the idea that America's strength comes from its diversity of cultures. More in-depth study would come in later themes.

   In terms of skills, I wanted to stress things that would be basic throughout the year: gathering information, presenting information, and measuring and understanding proportions.
4. I identified many resources, including all types of literature, reference sources, some Internet Web sites, and a social studies text, *America Will Be* (Armento, Nash, Salter, & Wixson, 1991); the first chapter in this book was appropriate. The literature selected represented a wide range of cultures, interests, and difficulty levels. I also identified some community resources. The focus of my outcomes helped me keep the number of resources reasonable.
5. I generated possible activities that were appropriate for a three-week theme, which was the amount of time I planned for the unit. I focused on initiating, developing, and culminating activities. I also thought about possibilities for assessment and evaluation throughout the theme as well as at its conclusion.
6. After completing my basic plans, I worked out a timeline, a pacing chart, and a daily schedule. I knew that daily plans would change as students carried out their activities.
7. Finally, I analyzed my unit in terms of cross-curricular learning.

Thematic Unit: America's Strength: Diversity

Major Outcomes, Strategies, and Skills

Attitudes and Habits
- Appreciate the cultural diversity of America
- Relate cultural diversity to one's own life

Constructing Meaning
- Understand culture and diversity of cultures
- Understand how different cultures have contributed to America
- Know that the strength of America lies in diversity
- Begin to understand the challenges of living in a culturally diverse society

Strategies and Skills
- Gathering information (reference books, literature, and textbooks; interviews)
- Presenting information (reports, oral and written; charts and graphs; timelines)
- Math (percentage and proportion, measuring)

FIGURE 9.7

ROUGH PLANNING WEB FOR THEMATIC UNIT "AMERICA'S STRENGTH: DIVERSITY"

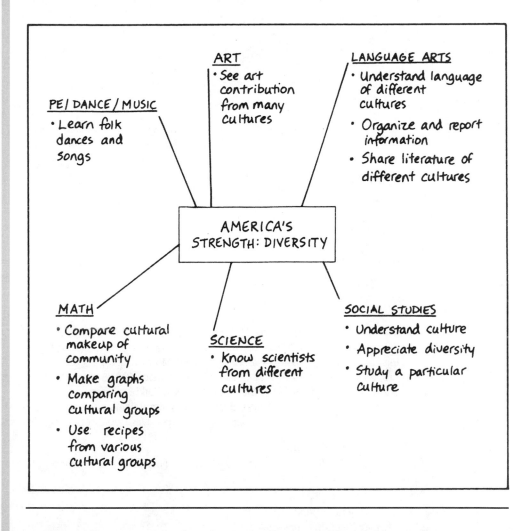

Resources

Possible Theme Literature: These books will be used for self-selected reading, group projects, and individual activities. Other books may also be located in the library.

<u>Nonfiction</u>

Ashabranner, B. (1984). *To live in two worlds.* New York: Dodd, Mead.
Dolphin, L. (1991). *Georgia to Georgia: Making friends in the U.S.S.R.* New York: Tambourine Books.

Sample Thematic Unit
continued

Feelings, M. (1971). *Moja means one: Swahili counting book.* New York: Dial.
Feelings, M. (1974). *Jambo means hello: Swahili alphabet book.* New York: Dial.
Freedman, R. (1980). *Immigrant kids.* New York: E. P. Dutton.
Garza, C. L. (1990). *Family pictures.* San Francisco: Children's Book Press.
Jacobs, W. J. (1990). *Ellis Island: New hope in a new land.* New York: Scribner's.
Perl, L. (1989). *The great ancestor hunt: The fun of finding out who you are.* New York: Clarion.

Biography

Mitchell, B. (1987). *Raggin': A story about Scott Joplin.* Minneapolis: Carolrhoda Books.
Roberts, M. (1986). *Henry Cisneros: Mexican American mayor.* Chicago: Childrens Press.
Say, A. (1990). *El Chino.* Boston: Houghton Mifflin.
Walker, A. (1974). *Langston Hughes, American poet.* New York: Crowell.

Poetry

Adoff, A. (1982). *All the colors of the race.* New York: Lothrop, Lee & Shepard.
Katz, J. B. (1980). *This song remembers.* Boston: Houghton Mifflin.
Schon, I. (Ed.) (1983). *Doña Blanca and other nursery rhymes and games.* Denison.

Folktales

Griego, Y., Maestas, J., & Auaya, R. A. (1980). *Cuentas: Tales from the Hispanic southwest.* Santa Fe: The Museum of New Mexico.
Hamilton, V. (1985). *The people could fly.* New York: Knopf.
Mendez, P. (1989). *The black snowman.* New York: Scholastic.
Young, E. (1989). *Lon Po Po.* New York: Philomel.

Realistic Fiction

Baylor, B. (1976). *Hawk, I'm your brother.* New York: Scribner's.
Bunting, E. (1988). *How many days to America? A Thanksgiving story.* New York: Clarion.
Galarza, E. (1971). *Barrio boy.* Notre Dame, IN: University of Notre Dame Press.
Haugaard, E. C. (1991). *The boy and the samurai.* Boston: Houghton Mifflin.
Hurwitz, J. (1990). *Class president.* New York: Morrow Junior Books.
Lord, B. B. (1984). *In the year of the boar and Jackie Robinson.* New York: Harper & Row.
Politi, L. (1949). *The song of the swallows.* New York: Scribners.
Say, A. (1982). *The bicycle man.* Boston: Houghton Mifflin.
Taylor, M. D. (1990). *Mississippi bridge.* New York: Dial Books for Young Readers.

Textbooks and References

- *America Will Be,* Chapter 1, by Armento, Nash, Salter, and Wixson (1991), pp. 2–27
- *The World Book Encyclopedia*
- *The World Almanac*
- Daily newspapers
- Weekly news magazines
- *Community Resources*
- Persons from different cultural groups
- Chamber of commerce
- Local cultural centers

Theme Activities

ACTIVITIES	INDEPENDENT/ INDIVIDUAL	COOPERATIVE/ SMALL GROUP	WHOLE CLASS	SELF- SELECTED	TEACHER ASSIGNED	TEACHER DIRECTED
Initiating activities:						
Teacher read-aloud *How Many Days to America?*, Bunting			X			X
Small-group discussions using K-W-L *Focus:* What we know about different cultures in America		X			X	
Start a family tree (complete throughout unit)	X				X	
Complete theme goal sheet *Focus:* • Unit options • What I want to learn	X					
Developing activities:						
Write a make-believe personal journal *Topic:* My trip to America	X				X	
Read books reflecting the literature of different cultural groups	X			X		
Literature circles *Focus:* • Discussing literature of various cultures • Comparing literature of various cultures		X		X		
Lessons on graphs			X			X

*Sample
Thematic
Unit*
continued

ACTIVITIES	INDEPENDENT/ INDIVIDUAL	COOPERATIVE/ SMALL GROUP	WHOLE CLASS	SELF- SELECTED	TEACHER ASSIGNED	TEACHER DIRECTED
Keep a daily learning log	X				X	
Study a cultural group and write a report *Focus:* • Language • Important people • Foods • Customs • Architecture	X			X		
Develop timeline of cultural growth in *our* community *Focus:* • Events • Causes			X			X
Read Chapter 1 in *America Will Be*			X			X
Make graphs showing cultural diversity in our • country • state • city or town • school • classroom		X		X		
Math lessons on • percentage • proportion			X			X
Make posters about famous American scientists from other cultures	X ....*OR*.... X			X		
Make a recipe collection *Focus:* Recipes of different cultural groups		X		X		
Learn authentic folk dances			X			X

ACTIVITIES	INDEPENDENT/ INDIVIDUAL	COOPERATIVE/ SMALL GROUP	WHOLE CLASS	SELF-SELECTED	TEACHER ASSIGNED	TEACHER DIRECTED
Make a cultural map of the country *Focus:* • Where various groups settled • Where groups came from and why • Where groups have moved within the country		X				X
Interview a person from another culture	X			X		
Culminating activities: Share reports and projects	X ····· *OR* ····· X					
Festival of our culture *Focus:* • Literature (drama, storytelling) • Foods • Dances, songs, games			X			
Panel discussion and interviews *Focus:* How different cultural groups have contributed to America's strength		X				
Complete and discuss K-W-L chart		X			X	
Reflect on the unit *Focus:* • Self-evaluation • Ways to improve			X			X

Sample
Thematic
Unit
continued

Plan for Implementing the Unit

Timeline and Pacing

Total days: 15
Days 1 and 2:   Initiating activities
Days 3–13:   Developing activities
Days 14 and 15:   Culminating activities

Daily Schedule

8:30	Opening activities (teacher read-aloud, song, or student sharing)
8:50	Reading workshop

    8:50   Minilesson
    9:00   State-of-the-class conference
    9:05   Teacher-assigned reading and responding
    9:30   Self-selected reading and responding

10:05   Sharing
10:15   Morning break
10:40   Writing workshop

    10:40   Minilesson
    10:50   State-of-the-class conference
    10:55   Writing and conferring
    11:30   Sharing

11:45   Lunch and recess
12:30   Teacher read-aloud
12:45   Small-group and independent project time
1:30   Whole-group progress report
1:40   Whole-class instruction or small-group
            instruction and independent work
2:25   Review the day
2:35   Prepare for dismissal
2:45   Dismissal

Evaluation

Self-Evaluation

• Using K-W-L chart
• Theme goal sheet

Daily Observations

• Teacher's log on individual students

Portfolios (discussed in Chapter 11)

• Work samples (teacher selected and student selected)
• Records of independent reading
• Teacher-developed unit test

Sample Thematic Unit continued

Theme Analysis

THEME	LANGUAGE ARTS	SOCIAL STUDIES	SCIENCE	MATH	ART	MUSIC/PE
America's Strength: Diversity	Gather information: Reference Books Interviews Textbooks Literature Present information: Reports Charts and graphs Oral reports	Culture Diversity Maps Population	Famous inventors and their inventions	Percentages Proportion Measurement	Art forms of different cultures	Songs and dances from different cultures

After Reading the Thematic Unit
1. Working with a partner, discuss how you would have changed this theme.
2. Select a topic and develop a theme of your own.

Personal Reflections on Cross-Curricular Thematic Teaching

Many years ago, when I was a beginning teacher, I was assigned a combination fifth- and sixth-grade class, and I approached it as I had been taught to do in college. In the process of trying to teach separate subjects to each grade level, I almost decided I didn't want to teach. However, I had a wonderful supervisor, Dr. Grace Champion, who suggested that I forget the subjects and plan a unit in which my students could study different problems.

Under Dr. Champion's direction, I planned my first integrated unit. It had a "living things" focus, which I chose because it was a topic in the curriculum common to both fifth and sixth grade. My students read many books about living things, and I had many basal readers from which to choose. We found all the stories that related to our theme and read them, I brought in books from the public library. We planned and completed projects, wrote reports, created many displays, and used materials from our science texts, encyclopedias, and any other available sources.

When students needed special help with something, I formed small groups and taught them what they needed, whether how to locate information, how to write a paragraph, how to use a certain math concept needed to make a graph, or just how to read and discuss certain chapters in a book that was causing them difficulty.

From this point on, I taught my combination class in thematic units. There were many things I didn't know (and still don't know), but I stumbled forward. Each unit got better and better. At the end of the year, *all* of my students made substantial gains on their achievement tests, despite my (then) rather unorthodox way of teaching.

During the next few years, I used cross-curricular units in every grade I taught. Students went to the library. They read; they wrote; they solved problems. My classes always scored very high on their achievement tests.

Over the years, as I became a reading specialist and went to graduate school, I got farther and farther away from my thematic teaching. Only through further study, research, and working in classrooms over the past ten years have I come to realize what I had and what I left behind. Dr. Champion, who had also been my first-grade teacher and college professor in children's literature, had launched me in a positive direction that I now know was important.

Cross-curricular teaching is not easy at first, but it is possible for all teachers. It is a matter of good planning and letting go of preconceived ideas about what classrooms ought to be. The rewards come in seeing children who are excited, who want to learn, and *who do learn!*

Each person grows into this ability to do integrated, cross-curricular teaching in many different ways. No one ever completely integrates everything, and each teacher must handle it differently. However, if you want to help students at all grade levels and in all subject areas learn to construct meaning more effectively, take the ideas about integrated, cross-curricular teaching to heart. It has taken me thirty years to get these ideas together, and I am still learning every day!

Using the Literacy Lesson Concept with Textbooks and Informational Books

One problem in content-area teaching is how students and teachers use textbooks (Armbruster, 1991). To improve this situation, scaffolded support should be provided for students who need it before, during, and after reading. You can apply the literacy lesson concept you have learned to use throughout this text to help students become more active constructors of meaning in content classes and in cross-curricular learning situations. As you recall, the literacy lesson consists of three parts: introducing, reading and responding, and extending.

When *introducing* a chapter in a textbook or other informational book, you activate students' prior knowledge and background for the chapter. Sometimes this may include developing a *few* key concept terms before the chapter is read. At the same time, students must develop purposes for their reading.

In a *well-written* informational text, the key concepts and main ideas are clearly evident, and therefore it is often easier to identify the key background concepts and key terms than in a story or narrative selection. If you develop key terms when introducing a chapter, follow the guidelines and suggestions given in Chapter 5.

Reading and responding to the text means students must read the chapter and *actively* respond to it by doing something with what they have learned. Depending on the grade level, students' abilities, and the text they are reading, many students will be able to read the textbook or other text resource independently, but some will need more support provided by cooperative reading, shared reading, teacher-guided reading, or teacher read-alouds.

A variation of teacher-guided reading that is often used with textbooks is a study guide, which gives students a set of questions or activities to help them through the text. The guide serves as a partial replacement for the teacher and it supports students as they work independently or with a partner. Study guides are discussed in more detail later in this chapter.

Responding should involve students in a variety of authentic activities, including discussion, retelling, summarizing, and writing about what they read (see Chapter 6). Answering the end-of-chapter questions provided in most textbooks is *not* appropriate responding, although questions may be used to focus a discussion group.

Another part of responding should be completely individual and personal. Students might use a learning log or some other device or activity to respond to the textbook chapter or informational book that is the focus of the literacy lesson (see Chapter 6).

Extending is the final part of the literacy lesson, the time when students take the meanings they have constructed and use them in some way. For example, if students have just learned some information about how to perform an experiment in science, a natural way to extend their learning would be to have them perform an experiment. If the literacy lesson is part of a thematic unit, extending should always tie back to the unit.

Since textbooks contain a variety of text structures (see Chapter 3), it is often necessary to vary the literacy lesson to accommodate text differences and student needs. For example, students reading a social studies text may need to focus on the sequential or cause-effect development of historical events, and students reading a science text may need to focus on major ideas and the cause-effect relationships in nature.

The literacy lesson format is very flexible. You can use it with any textbook or informational text to help students learn to construct meaning. Within a thematic unit, it is not necessary to have a literacy lesson for all texts students read: they will receive much of the support they need through other theme activities and the use of self-selected books and materials. In the next section, we look at how to use study guides as a part of the literacy lesson.

Using Study Guides to Improve the Construction of Meaning

As noted earlier, a study guide may be used as an alternative to teacher-guided reading in the literacy lesson. Researchers have found that study guides help students set purposes as they read content text (Armbruster, Anderson, & Osterlag, 1989; Wood, Lapp, & Flood, 1992). A study guide, as its name implies, is a guide for studying and is similar to the monitoring guide discussed in Chapter 2. It is a set of activities and questions that direct students through the reading of a textbook or other informational text.

Study guides can fulfill at least three purposes:

1. They can provide support for students who need help in constructing meaning in textbooks and informational texts. The more structured and directive the guides, the more support they will provide.

2. They can stimulate thinking by providing thought-provoking questions and/or activities.

3. By changing the design and construction of the study guide, you can meet a broad range of literacy needs within your classroom.

Use of study guides does help students construct meaning (Alvermann & Moore, 1991). They may be used in very simple forms in grades 2 and 3, but are usually most effective in grade 4 and above.

Designing and Constructing Study Guides

Use the following eight guidelines when constructing a study guide.

Determine your purpose.   Is your purpose to give students the scaffolding they need to more effectively construct meaning, to stimulate thinking, or to do both?

Decide on the amount of support you want to provide.   Once you have determined your purpose for the guide, this decision usually follows rather readily. For students who are having difficulty constructing meaning, you need to provide a lot of support. For example, you may use activities such as the following:

❱ Identify the two main causes of air pollution.

_____

_____

❱ List three factors that contribute to lung disease:

1. _____

2. _____

3. _____

When putting the study guide together, follow the flow of the chapter. Since the activities and questions should help students actively construct meaning, it is important to focus on ideas in the order they appear.

Include opportunities for students to write.   An important part of constructing meaning is expressing what you have learned in your own words. Activities such as the following can help accomplish this task:

❱ Write one or two sentences telling why insects are helpful to people.

_____

_____

_____

_____

Incorporate opportunities for students to make predictions and monitor their reading.   Activities such as the following will help with both of these processes:

▶ *Previewing and predicting:* After looking through this chapter, what do you think you will learn? List two things.

_____

_____

▶ *Stop and think:* How do pulleys help people?

_____

_____

_____

or

▶ Have your predictions changed? If so, why?

_____

_____

_____

Provide questions and activities that bring out key concepts or main ideas. Too often study guide questions or activities focus on trivial information and fail to lead students to main ideas and/or concepts developed in the text. Questions or activities such as the following are more likely to help students construct meaning:

▶ Complete the following graphic organizer showing how the discovery of the atom has helped people:

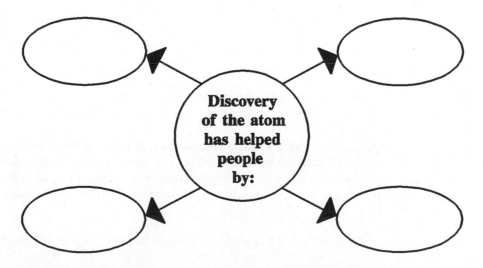

Three Ideas for Good Health	
Ideas	*How I Feel About These Ideas*
1.	
2.	
3.	

▶ Write a sentence or two telling how the Mayflower's voyage changed the world.

_____

_____

_____

_____

Include activities and questions on all study guides that require students to "think" and make use of what they have read. Even students who are having difficulty constructing meaning are able to think and need to think. Activities such as the following are good ones to incorporate into a study guide.

▶ Complete the above chart:

How will the information in this text help you in your lifetime?

_____

_____

_____

_____

Provide activities and questions that will help students pull together or summarize the text. By providing questions or activities that follow the flow of the chapter and bring out key ideas, you will lead students to formulate a summary. A final activity for the study guide should require students to do some type of summarizing. Here is an example:

▶ Look back at the first three guidelines. Now write a sentence or two telling the big ideas you have learned in this text.

_____

_____

_____

_____

These eight principles can serve as a basis for developing a study guide. Figure 9.8 shows an example of a partial study guide written to go with the informational book *Voyager to the Planets* (Apfel, 1991).

Study Techniques for Improving the Construction of Meaning

As students learn to construct meaning across the curriculum, they must develop techniques that will help them study, think about, and remember information. Teachers in many curricular areas frequently encourage students to use a number of techniques, such as underlining, note taking, summarizing, outlining, mapping, making some type of graphic organizer to show information they learned, and student questioning. We discussed the value of summarizing and student questioning in detail in Chapter 8. Now let's examine what we know about these other techniques.

The following conclusions are based on the very thorough and critical reviews of research by Anderson and Armbruster (1984b) and Alvermann and Moore (1991):

▶ *Underlining:* With this technique, students underline information they believe is important or should be remembered. In fact, you may be doing this as you are reading this chapter. Research suggests that underlining is no more effective than any other study technique in helping students learn and remember information (Anderson & Armbruster, 1984b). In fact, Alvermann and Moore (1991) conclude that it is no better than simply having students read for understanding and recall. Remember, however, that the number of studies focusing

FIGURE 9.8

PARTIAL STUDY GUIDE THAT PROVIDES HEAVY SUPPORT FOR STUDENTS

STUDY GUIDE
FOR
VOYAGER TO THE PLANETS

Name _____ Date _____

① *Preview and predict:* Look through the book at the photographs. Read the captions. Predict two or three things you think you will learn in this book; write them below.

_____

_____

_____

_____

_____

② pages 7–9
    What was the purpose for Voyager I and Voyager II?

    Voyager I _____

    _____

    Voyager II _____

    _____

FIGURE 9.8 *Continued*

③ pages 10–11
Describe how Voyager looked.

_____

_____

_____

_____

Now you think: Why did Voyager look this way?

_____

_____

_____

_____

What problem did Voyager have?

_____

_____

_____

_____

Now you think: Why was it important to correct this problem?

_____

_____

_____

_____

FIGURE 9.8   *Continued*

④ pages 12–15
   Complete this chart showing what Voyager learned about Jupiter.

Things Learned About Jupiter
Temperature
Clouds
Jupiter's Solar System

on underlining is small because students are discouraged from marking in their textbooks. The real value in underlining is most likely to come from the process of deciding what information is important in the text, not the underlining itself. Therefore, the strategies for identifying important information in Chapter 8 are probably more important for students than underlining.

▶ *Note taking:* This is the technique of writing down ideas or information that one believes is important. The research in this area (Alvermann & Moore, 1991; Anderson & Armbruster, 1984b) shows that note taking is an effective study technique if it involves thinking about the text as opposed to just writing down isolated facts or insignificant information. The value in note taking, as with underlining, comes in the process of thinking and deciding what is important. Here again we see the importance of the strategies discussed in Chapter 8.

▶ *Outlining:* Outlining involves writing a verbal sketch showing the main points and supporting information in a text. For this technique to help students construct meaning, it must be thoroughly taught (Anderson & Armbruster, 1984b; Alvermann & Moore, 1991). Students must not only learn the various forms of outlining but also learn how to identify the information that is important and the ideas that support this information. Again, this goes back to the strategies developed in Chapter 8.

▶ *Mapping or graphic organizers:* This technique involves showing the information gained from a text in some visual way. (See Chapter 3 for examples.) Again, research shows that for this technique to be helpful, it must be thoroughly taught over the long term. Students must be able to identify the important information in a text and the relationships among pieces of information. The process of deciding what information is important and how to construct the graphic organizer is the type of active involvement students must have to ensure that they construct meaning. Research also suggests that it is better for students to construct the organizer themselves than to have the teacher supply a prepared organizer.

In conclusion, all of the techniques reviewed here revolve around the strategy of identifying important information discussed in Chapter 8. To use any of these techniques, students must know how to use that strategy.

All of the techniques must be thoroughly taught and modeled. No one technique appears to be significantly better than another for helping students construct meaning. Rather, each person finds his or her own best way to study and remember information. Some people use one technique, some use another, and still others combine techniques or create their own. Therefore, it is best to give students experiences with all of these techniques and allow them to find the one (or ones) that works best for them.

Summary

This chapter focused on how students construct meaning across the curriculum. In this process, students learn to build relationships among various curricular areas, each of which provides the basis for the content students actually use for

constructing meaning. Textbooks are only one resource. A variety of types of literature used in conjunction with textbooks create many more authentic and exciting
opportunities for learning.

The chapter suggested that using cross-curricular thematic units is an effective
way to improve students' meaning construction and overall learning. It discussed
and illustrated the process of developing a thematic unit and the use of the literacy
lesson concept for textbooks and informational texts. Study guides were suggested
as a strategy to incorporate into the literacy lesson.

The chapter also summarized reviews of research on various techniques for
studying. Basically, all techniques for studying involve the strategy of identifying
important information in texts. No one technique for studying appears to be better
than another.

Literature

Apfel, N. H. (1991). *Voyager to the planets.* New York: Clarion.

Fox, D., & Marks, C. (1987). *Go in and out the window: An illustrated songbook for
young people.* New York: Henry Holt.

Freedman, R. (1987). *Lincoln: A photobiography.* New York: Clarion.

Hamilton, V. (1985). *The people could fly.* New York: Knopf.

Hodges, M. (1976). *Knight prisoner: The tale of Sir Thomas Malory and his King
Arthur.* New York: Farrar, Straus and Giroux.

Macaulay, D. (1977). *Castle.* Boston: Houghton Mifflin.

Raffi. (1980). *The Raffi singable songbook.* New York: Crown.

Sancha, S. (1983). *Luttrell Village: Country life in the Middle Ages.* New York:
HarperCollins.

Twain, M. (1987). *A Connecticut Yankee in King Arthur's court.* New York: Morrow.

Wright, S. (1988). *Age of chivalry.* New York: Watts.

For Additional Reading

Fredericks, A., Meinbach, A., & Rothlein, L. (1993). *Thematic units.* New York:
HarperCollins.

Moore, D. W., Readence, J. E., & Rickelman, R. J. (1989). *Prereading activities for
content area reading and learning* (2nd ed.). Newark, DE: International Reading
Association.

Norton, D. E. (1991). Nonfiction: Biographies and informational books. In D. E.
Norton (Ed.), *Through the eyes of a child: An introduction to children's literature*
(3rd ed., pp. 607–677). New York: Macmillan.

Pappas, C. C., Kiefer, B. Z., & Levstik, L. S. (1990). *An integrated language
perspective in the elementary school: Theory into action.* New York: Longman.

Walmsley, S. (1994). *Children exploring the world: Theme teaching in elementary school.*
Portsmouth, NH: Heinemann.

Ward, G. (1988). *I've got a project on . . .* Australia Primary English Teaching
Association, distributed by Heinemann, Portsmouth, NH.

Wood, K. D., Lapp, D., & Flood, J. (1992). *Guiding readers through text: A review of study guides.* Newark, DE: International Reading Association.

For Exploration: Electronic Products and Resources

Integrating educational technology across the curriculum can range from connecting your class through e-mail and shared Web pages with other classes studying the same theme to using software that helps students practice content area skills or access information. Keeping track of possibilities and resources requires time and focus, but one way you can keep up is by reading journals devoted to informing educators about classroom applications of technology. Journals often offer valuable reviews of software. They also present articles about how other teachers and students are applying technology. Check these journals, some of which are online only, and see if there is one that matches your styles and needs:

CD-ROM Today

Computers in the Schools

From Now on: The Educational Technology Journal
www.fromnowon.org/

The Electronic School
www.electronic-school.com/

Learning and Leading with Technology
www.iste.org/L&L/

Electronic Learning

TC World
www.tcworld.com/

These are a mere handful. Search for other journals at newstands or on the Web.

Remember that you can access information about software directly from company Web sites. All of the following create software that students can use in individual content areas or in cross-curricular learning:

Broderbund
www.broderbund.com/education

The Learning Company
www.learningco.com

Maxis
www.maxis.com/

MECC

www.mecc.com/

Optical Data Corporation

www.opticaldata.com/

Panasonic Interactive Media Company

www.panakids.com

Sunburst

www.sunburst.com

Organizing and Managing the Balanced Literacy Classroom

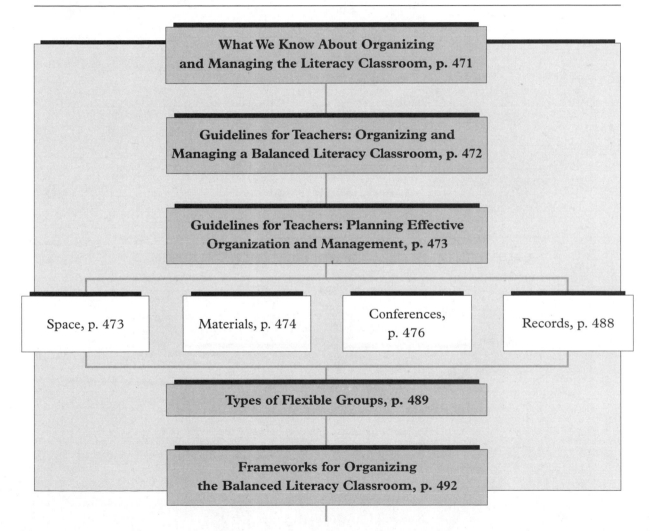

What We Know About Organizing and Managing the Literacy Classroom, p. 471

Guidelines for Teachers: Organizing and Managing a Balanced Literacy Classroom, p. 472

Guidelines for Teachers: Planning Effective Organization and Management, p. 473

Space, p. 473

Materials, p. 474

Conferences, p. 476

Records, p. 488

Types of Flexible Groups, p. 489

Frameworks for Organizing the Balanced Literacy Classroom, p. 492

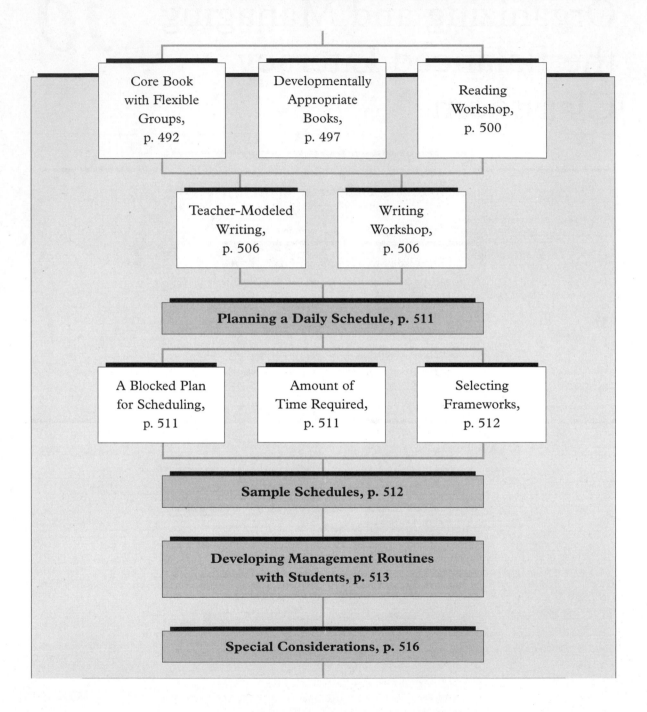

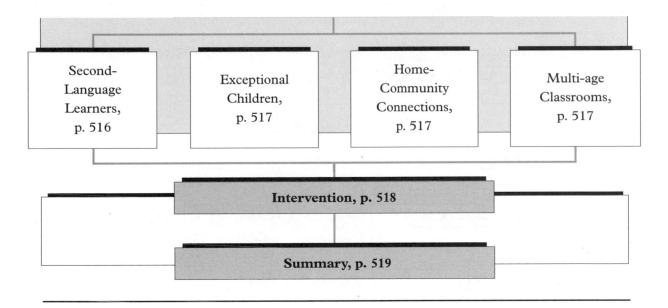

Y ou have learned a great deal about literacy and how children construct meaning. Now your challenge is to take all of your knowledge and begin to plan, organize, and manage your classroom to provide your students with balanced literacy experiences. A short visit to Mrs. Dopheide's second-grade class on Monday morning showed you how she accomplished this task.

As we entered the room, the last student was sharing what she had written over the weekend; she was reading aloud to the class a note she had written to her friend who had moved to another state. Each Monday morning, Mrs. Dopheide takes about 15 minutes to invite boys and girls to share reading and writing experiences they have had at home. She told us this activity builds good relationships with the home and helps the children see how much they use reading and writing in their lives.

"Boys and girls, we need to talk for a few minutes about what we will be doing this week," Mrs. Dopheide began. Then she pointed to a chart entitled "Our Weekly Plans" (Figure 10.1) and continued, "We are all going to read a wonderful new book, Too Many Tamales [Soto, 1993], which goes with our Family theme. Of course, we will have our Writing Workshop to continue work on our personal narratives that we are writing for our Families book. We have to get started on planning for our family fair. Can you think of any other things we need to do this week?"

"What about conference time? I need to talk with you about my new book," said Larry.

"Yeah, me too," added Rosie.

"Aren't we having Reading Workshop this week?" asked Sonja.

"Yes, we are," replied Mrs. Dopheide.

"What new books do you have for us?" asked Eric.

"It's a surprise; you'll have to wait until Wednesday when we start our Reading Workshop."

"Oh, come on," groaned nearly everyone.

Mrs. Dopheide added children's suggestions to the chart and then said, "Let's begin our morning with Writing Club." She then showed children the day's schedule and began the Writing Club, the class time for independent writing.

FIGURE 10.1

WEEKLY CLASS PLAN

FROM THIS BRIEF visit to Mrs. Dopheide's class, you can see that she does many different things in organizing and managing a balanced literacy classroom:

▶ She makes strong connections between her classroom and her students' homes. By inviting those who wish to do so to share their reading and writing experiences from the weekend, she demonstrates the importance of literacy at home and brings students' homes into the classroom community of learners.

▶ Children are an integral part of the process of planning. By sharing her plans with the class and asking for their suggestions, Mrs. Dopheide makes everyone feel he or she is part of the learning process.

▶ Mrs. Dopheide uses many different organizational frameworks and concepts to organize her class: Reading Club (independent reading), Writing Club (independent writing), Writing Workshop, Reading Workshop, books for the whole class, conferences, and so forth. A balanced literacy classroom requires a variety of organizational structures.

Throughout this chapter you will learn many different frameworks, organizational techniques, and procedures that will help you organize and manage a balanced literacy classroom. All of the ideas suggested here are based on one body of knowledge: *how children and young adults develop literacy.*

What We Know About Organizing and Managing the Literacy Classroom

Recall the reading and writing instruction you had when you were in elementary school. Did you have reading groups? Did you spend much time writing, or did anyone teach you how to write? Were you in the same reading group all the time? Was English or language arts instruction generally taught from an English textbook, with units on various parts of speech or writing conventions such as punctuation, with little time for writing? Chances are you recall some or all of these things from your own educational experiences. In addition to all we have learned about literacy learning, we have learned a great deal about organizing the classroom for literacy instruction.

For years, most elementary teachers divided their classes into three reading groups (Barr & Dreeben, 1991). Sometimes classes were tracked; that is, all students at one ability level were assigned to one teacher for all or part of the day. Both of these patterns of instruction were generally referred to as "ability grouping" or "tracking" (Cunningham & Allington, 1994). This concept of organizing for instruction has come under considerable criticism (Allington, 1983; Dawson, 1987; Harp, 1989; Hiebert, 1983; Slavin, 1986; Sorensen & Hallinan, 1986). Research has shown that these types of ability groupings do not lead to success or prevent failure for students (Allington & Walmsley, 1995). Therefore, some other types of organizational structures are needed.

One of the most important things we have learned about reading and writing is *who* can learn to do it. For many years, teachers often thought that students who were having difficulty learning were "slow" or just unable to learn to read and write. Many different types of programs were provided for these students, who were often referred to as "remedial" or "at risk." None of these programs worked effectively (Allington & Walmsley, 1995; Cunningham & Allington, 1994). More recently, however, effective programs such as Reading Recovery (Clay, 1985; DeFord, Lyons, & Pinnell, 1991) and small-group intervention plans (Hiebert & Taylor, 1994) have demonstrated that nearly *all* children can learn to read and write. For detailed descriptions of these programs, see Hiebert and Taylor (1994) in the For Additional Reading section at the conclusion of this chapter.

A related issue is the pace of instruction. For years, the prevailing belief was that instruction for students having difficulty should be given at a slower pace or in smaller pieces (Allington & Walmsley, 1995). However, existing evidence indicates this is not true (DeFord et al., 1991; Allington & Walmsley, 1995). Students who are having difficulty learning actually need instruction that is paced *faster* to help them catch up. In fact, I believe *all* students need instruction that is appropriately fast paced. When instruction is paced too slow, many students lose interest and fail to learn.

Students having difficulty learning often need extra support to help them catch up. This can be delivered through strong early intervention programs such as Reading Recovery and small-group intervention models. However, the key to having successful literacy programs for *all* students is to create classroom instruction that is oriented toward success for all students.

We need to know how to organize classrooms that prevent failure and promote success! To accomplish this, we need to use the concepts about literacy learning developed in this text and in other sources and organize our classrooms based on what we know about how children and young adults learn.

Guidelines for Teachers: Organizing and Managing a Balanced Literacy Classroom

Regardless of the grade level you teach, you will find it easier to organize and manage a literacy-centered classroom that promotes success by considering the following ten guidelines:

1. *Provide an exciting classroom environment that supports many literacy activities.* See Chapter 2 for a detailed discussion of this classroom.
2. *Provide daily times for independent reading and writing.* Guidelines for these blocks of time were provided in Chapter 2.
3. *Base your organization on students' interests and literacy strengths.* Find out what students can do and what their interests are. For example, if you have many students who are very good oral readers but poor constructors of meaning, have them do readers theater and other types of activities involving oral reading. Chapter 11 gives suggestions for determining students' interests and strengths.
4. *Make students a part of the decision-making process.* This involves having students set goals for themselves and helping to set goals for the class. Within the literacy activities of the classroom, students should be given choices as to what they read, how they read, and how they respond and share and what they write, how they write, and how they publish and share. By giving students choices, you are better able to accommodate individual needs and encourage students to take ownership of their own learning. The choices provided are not free-rein choices but are often formulated and guided by the teacher. (See Chapter 11 for a discussion of the use of portfolios.)
5. *Provide blocks of time for direct instruction as needed.* A well-balanced literacy program includes both direct and indirect instruction. Utilize small groups for directly teaching skills and strategies as needed.

6. *Provide blocks of time when* all *students can be successful at reading and writing.* Provide some times when everyone in the class has the opportunity to experience or read the same book and do the same type of writing. This helps to build self-esteem and lets all students in the class know they can do some of the same things others can do.

7. *Provide blocks of times when* all *students have the opportunity to receive instruction with books that are developmentally appropriate for them.* Students need to have times when they select the books they will read from a group of titles that represent a range of difficulty levels. This allows students to get instructional support with books they can read.

8. *Provide blocks of time when students receive instructional support as they write on products and topics of their own choosing.* During this time, you can provide specific instructional support in writing.

9. *Keep in contact with students' homes.* Have activities that encourage home-school cooperation (Boyer, 1995). These might include home read-aloud programs, writing, and other activities.

10. *Keep the pace of instruction appropriately fast for all students.* Instruction needs to be delivered at a pace that holds students' attention. Often in literature-based classrooms, students are asked to do too many activities with one book. The number of activities does not make the difference in how well students read and write; the amount of actual reading and writing they do is what matters.

11. *Be flexible.* Try many different organizational techniques and procedures. Don't latch on to one procedure and use it all the time, or you will risk losing sight of students' needs. Remember that a variety of patterns will be needed to accommodate students' needs.

No set of guidelines can make classroom organization and management foolproof. However, keeping these eleven points in mind can help you grow in your ability to make good decisions and develop a success-oriented classroom that runs smoothly.

Guidelines for Teachers: Planning Effective Organization and Management

Effective organization and management depend on careful, ongoing planning. As you begin to plan your classroom, you need to consider four factors: *space, materials, conferences,* and *recordkeeping.*

Space

Of course, classrooms vary in the amount of space available for the students and instructional activities, and teachers vary in the ways they want their classrooms organized and arranged. The main goal is the same for everyone: to make sure the room arrangement promotes and supports the community of literacy learners and contributes to an exciting, literacy-centered atmosphere.

Use the following steps to organize your classroom space:

1. Take an inventory of what you have available—desks, tables, bulletin boards, bookcases, storage areas, electrical outlets, a water source, chalkboards, and other equipment such as computers, tape players, an overhead/screen, and so forth. Think about which things are fixed in place and which are movable.

2. Think about the things you want in your classroom—centers or areas (see Chapter 2), small- and large-group instructional areas, bulletin boards students can use, storage areas for student work, a place for teacher materials, and space to store extra materials. Take some time just to sit and look around your room and think about how you want to arrange it.

3. Draw a quick sketch of the layout to get you started. Here are some tips to keep in mind as you make your plans:

   • Pushing desks together promotes conversation and interaction, an important goal of a literacy-centered classroom.

   • Some students need a space away from other students where they can work alone. Use movable bookshelves to section off the room.

   • Art and science areas need access to water.

   • The teacher's desk or work table is often best placed off to the side where the teacher can also hold conferences with students.

   • Areas where students are likely to be talking together are best placed away from an instructional area where you will be meeting with small groups.

   • Centers or areas requiring electrical equipment or computers need to be placed near outlets.

4. Once you have your plan in mind, begin to arrange your room. If you have time before students arrive, live with the arrangement for a few days as you do other things.

5. After students arrive, try out your arrangement for several days. If you discover certain things aren't working, change them.

Materials

As you organize and arrange your classroom, consider the books, magazines, newspapers, and other instructional materials you will be using. Obviously there will be lots of books; some will be in the classroom library, and others may be in sets for instructional use.

Library Area

The library area was discussed in Chapter 2. If you have a good central library in your school where children can come and go freely to check out materials, it is not as important to have a full classroom library; just having a space to keep classroom collections of books will suffice.

When you are working with emergent, or beginning, readers, it is useful to have lots of little, easy-to-read books. Many teachers organize these books in baskets, boxes, or barrels that are color coded for difficulty. For example, the easiest "Basket of Books" might be yellow, with each book having a yellow dot; red might be average; and green might be more challenging. This coding helps students select books, but students can move from one color to the next color when they feel ready.

Kindergarten and first-grade students work together in a learning center. © *Bohdan Hrynewych/Stock Boston*

The books in the baskets can be trade books or may come from the many collections of books for emergent readers published by such companies as Houghton Mifflin, Rigby, and the Wright Group.

As students become more mature readers, they will need to be taught how to select books for themselves that they are comfortable reading. One way to do this is to teach them the "thumbs up" test. You open a book and read a page aloud or to yourself. If you come to a word you don't know, you put down a finger. If you finish the page and your thumb is still up, the book is probably right for you. Of course, there will be many times when a student will really want to read a book even if it contains more than five unfamiliar words on a page. In such a case, you should encourage the student to try the book.

The library area materials require a simple checkout system; a card with the book title and a place for students to write their names will work. Letting different students take turns being the librarian helps develop responsibility and provides an opportunity for students to learn more about "real-world" literacy.

Instructional Materials

You will need class sets of books, sets of decodable texts for your beginning literacy program, multiple copies of single titles, and a variety of single titles. If you are using a published reading/language arts program, you may have an anthology that you will use primarily as your class set of books. However, an anthology alone is

A sixth-grade classroom has special work areas even with limited space. © *Michael Zide*

not enough. You will also need sets of trade books covering a wide range of interests and difficulty levels.

Class sets or multiple copies of trade books may be stored in a central location within the school to facilitate wider use. Rolling carts will make it easier to move sets of books in and out of classrooms. Teachers at each grade level usually agree that certain pieces of literature are core. For example, fourth-grade teachers might agree that *Big Boy* (Mollel, 1995) would be a core piece for their level. This helps to prevent students reading the same books over and over again.

Conferences

In literacy-centered classrooms, conferences may take place between students or between the teacher and students. Reading or writing conferences take place when the teacher and student(s) engage in a conversation about a book or books or about a student's piece of writing. Conferences play an important role in all aspects of literacy learning (Calkins, 1986; Graves, 1983, 1991). Graves (1991) maintains that "the conference—the listening stance—is the heart of good teaching" (p. 89).

Conferences may be formal, planned events or informal ones that take place any number of times during the day—in the hallway, in the lunchroom, on the playground, or during any part of the daily classroom routine. Some educators refer to informal conferences as *miniconferences* or *on-the-spot conferences* (Tompkins & Hoskisson, 1991).

These conferences are really nothing more than times when you stop to chat and listen carefully to what students are saying; good teachers do this all the time.

During informal miniconferences, you might ask children such questions as "What are you reading?", "How do you like this book?", or "What writing piece are you working on now?" For example, Mrs. Laird, a fourth-grade teacher, stopped by the desk of one student:

Mrs. Laird: What have you been reading lately? *— assessed*

Mark: I'm still reading the same book I got last week.

Mrs. Laird: How do you like it?

Mark: I don't.

Mrs. Laird: Why don't you stop reading this book and select another one?

Mark: I don't know.

Mrs. Laird: Don't you like dinosaurs? *— redirecting coach role*

Mark: Yes!

Mrs. Laird: I saw a great dinosaur book in the reading center this morning. You'll love it! It's called *Tyrannosaurus Was a Beast* [Prelutsky, 1988]. Try that one. *knowledge base literacy strategist*

In this brief discussion, Mrs. Laird was able to determine that her student was bogged down with a book he didn't like and then direct him to an area of his interest. Even though informal conferences may last only a minute or two, they yield valuable information about how students are doing and enable the teacher to provide on-the-spot support.

After this brief encounter, Mrs. Laird wrote a note about this miniconference on the student's page in her notebook. Sometimes she relies on memory and makes notes later. However, it is not always necessary to make notes about a miniconference. The one presented here just happened to be one where the teacher gathered some valuable information about the student that she felt needed to be recorded. Some teachers carry self-adhesive notes that they write on and date; later they stick them on the students' pages in their notebook.

Purposes of Formal Teacher-Student Conferences

Formal literacy conferences may have several purposes. First, they may be held for *sharing and discussing a book*. The teacher and the student talk about a book the student is reading or has completed, and the student may read favorite parts. The teacher might share thoughts or feelings about the book or make suggestions for other books the student might want to consider. If the students are keeping journals, responses might be shared and discussed, or questions about the book or words of concern to the student might be reviewed.

Second, conferences may be used for the teacher and student(s) to *discuss some aspect of the student's writing* and for the teacher to *ask probing or guiding questions* that will help the students formulate their ideas. This is a time for modeling and coaching to help students develop their writing.

Third, the literacy conference may be used to *provide a minilesson on a particular strategy or skill* that seems to be causing the student(s) difficulty—perhaps a problem with phonics, an aspect of punctuation, or comprehension. During this conference, the teacher would use the minilesson concept and model the particular strategy or skill needed. (See Chapters 2 and 8 for details about minilessons and modeling.)

Finally, literacy conferences may be held to *assess students' progress.* By having students share their responses to a piece of literature, the teacher can tell how well students are able to comprehend or construct meaning. Oral reading gives clues to the students' decoding abilities, and written responses in journals provide evidence about spelling, grammar and usage, and comprehension.

One conference might have several purposes. For example, students might be sharing a book at the same time the teacher is assessing progress. It is important to have a single conference serve as many purposes as possible. The following suggestions should be helpful in planning your conferences:

- *When you begin to use conferences, explain their purpose and procedures to students.* Role-play several conferences to establish routines and guidelines for behavior.
- *Keep conferences short and focused.* Graves (1991) notes that conferences need to be brief and focused. If students don't need a conference, don't have one; their time would be better spent reading or writing.
- *Maintain a positive, interactive environment.* Use probing questions and statements that encourage students to think about and talk about their writing.
- *From time to time, have group conferences during which you talk with several students about their writing.* This is an especially useful procedure if students are doing similar types of writing or appear to have similar needs for support.
- *Keep a simple record sheet for each student.* Figure 10.2 shows a sheet you can use for writing. This will tell you what students are doing and what needs they have.

Scheduling Conferences

Literacy conferences seldom last more than 5 to 10 minutes. It is best to keep conferences as short as possible and focused on your purpose.

Students should sign up for their conferences on a sign-up sheet or a section of the chalkboard. (Sometimes you will also request to see a student.) Figure 10.3 shows a conference sign-up chart used by a second-grade teacher. Notice that on Friday no one requested a conference, so the teacher had extra time to meet with those she has not seen recently. A good rule of thumb is to hold conferences with students at least once a week for first, second, and third grades and once every other week for fourth grade and above. However, students' needs should be the major determining factor in deciding frequency of conferences.

Each teacher must work out the best time during the daily schedule to hold conferences. Some prefer to schedule a few each day, and others schedule on designated days such as Monday, Wednesday, and Friday.

Preparing for Conferences

To ensure successful conferences, you must be certain that both you and the students are prepared and understand how and why conferences take place. The best

FIGURE 10.2

RECORD SHEET FOR KEEPING TRACK OF STUDENTS' WRITING

Name _____ Grade _____

Date	Writing Piece	Suggestions	Minilesson Needs	Goals/Comments

way to do this is to role-play and model a conference period so that students see what happens and know how it occurs.

When teachers first begin to use conferences, they are often concerned about what the rest of the class does while one or two children are in conference. A chart such as the one shown in Figure 10.4 lists options students have during the conference period. Once students become comfortable with conference times, a chart is usually not needed.

Students also have to prepare themselves for the conference. Figure 10.5 shows a conference chart that many teachers find helpful in directing students in this process. After a week or so of conferencing, *you and the class* should evaluate how things are going and make adjustments as needed.

Finally, you must prepare yourself for the conferences. You will need some type of loose-leaf notebook with a section for each student. On the first page write the student's name, age, and grade, and also list the student's interests and any pertinent information about his or her reading and writing strengths. One of these pages

FIGURE 10.3

CONFERENCE SIGN-UP CHART

READING CONFERENCES

	Student Requested	Teacher Requested
Monday	Leo Susan Lisa Joan Jeff	
Wednesday	Terri Frank Joey Sid	Tim Mike
Friday		Sara Mary Anne Bill

might look like Figure 10.6. Following the opening page, you will need several blank pages on which to record your observations and comments from the conference and any goals you and the student agree on to be accomplished before the next conference. Keep the page simple, such as that shown in Figure 10.7.

Have some ideas about questions or statements you might use to prompt students to discuss the book they are reading (you might consult the lists of open-ended questions presented in Chapter 6). In addition, Veatch (1966, 1978) suggests that individual conferences should explore four areas with students: personal involvement of the child with the book, ability to read and understand, sheer mechanical reading ability, and oral reading. Veatch said many years ago that hundreds of questions can be asked in each of these areas. Here are some of her samples:

1. Area of personal involvement

    Teacher: *Why did you choose this story? Do you know anyone else in this class that would like it also?*

FIGURE 10.4

**CHART SHOWING STUDENTS WHAT TO DO WHILE
TEACHER IS IN CONFERENCE**

THINGS TO DO DURING
CONFERENCES

- Read your book or selection
- Write in your journal
- Work on your writing project
- Meet with a Literature Circle
- OTHER- You decide on something
  worthwhile to do
- Work in the Listening Center
- Prepare for your conference

Why do you think you are more interested in this kind of story than others in this class?

Would you like to be this character? Why?

2. Area of critical reading or general comprehension

Teacher: *What kind of a story is this? Real?*

or

Could this story have happened? Why? Or why not?

Tell me the story rapidly.

If this character did so and so, would you think he would get in trouble?

At the time this story was supposed to have happened, what was going on in our country that was very important?

3. Area of mechanical skills

Teacher: *What words did you have trouble with?*

FIGURE 10.5

CHART FOR HELPING STUDENTS PREPARE FOR A CONFERENCE

BEFORE YOUR READING CONFERENCE

(1) Have your book.

(2) Be sure your journal is up to date.

(3) Make a list of things you want to discuss.
Put them in your journal.

or

Here are two words that look very much alike. Tell me how you know the difference.

or

Let me point to several words in your story. Tell me what they are and what they mean.

4. Area of oral reading

Teacher: *Which part of the book have you chosen to read aloud to me?*

Make your voice go up and down.

Make your voice spooky, or scary, or sad, or mean, or whatever the story calls for. (Veatch, 1978, p. 69)

FIGURE 10.6

PARTIAL TEACHER'S NOTEBOOK PAGE FOR EACH STUDENT

Name *Lisa Smith*   Age *8*   Grade *3*

Interests: *horses, roller skating,*

making clay figures

Reading Strengths	Writing Strengths
- *Rereads when things aren't clear* - *Always previews her book*	- *Loves to write* - *Uses descriptive words*

OTHER OBSERVATIONS

The questions you ask during a writing conference should help students reflect on their writing (think about it critically), expand their writing, and select ways to improve their writing (Millett, 1986). The following questions are from Millett (1986, pp. 27–29):

Reflecting Questions

▶ What part is most interesting to you?

▶ What feeling do you want your reader to have?

▶ Is this the idea that you wanted me to get?

FIGURE 10.7

SAMPLE CONFERENCE PAGE FROM NOTEBOOK

Date	Comments	Goals for Next Conference
9/7	Terri had finished reading *Jam*. She loved the story and said her uncle was like Mr. Castle. She thought it was OK for dads to stay home. No problems with vocabulary or comprehension. Excellent oral reading. Needs to select more challenging book.	1. Select a more challenging book. 2. Use different responses in journal other than drawing.

Expanding Questions

❱ That's interesting—would you like your reader to know about that?
❱ Can you tell more about . . . ?
❱ Is that important to add?

Selecting Questions

Phrase questions that relate to focus *and* order:

❱ Which part is *most* important?
❱ Where could this new idea go?

▶ Which parts talk about the same thing?

▶ How might you put these parts together?

Ask questions about beginnings *and* endings:

▶ Which of three or four titles did your partner like best? Why?

▶ Can you turn your topic sentence beginning into a more interesting lead?

▶ Do you end with the most important thing you want your readers to know or feel?

▶ Does your ending repeat what you said in the beginning, or does it say the same thing in a different way? Which kind of ending is better for this piece? Why?

Ask questions about sentences:

▶ How many of your sentences begin the same way?

▶ How else could you start two or three of these sentences?

▶ Could you break this long sentence into shorter ones?

▶ How might you combine two or three short sentences?

Ask questions about wording *and* phrasing:

▶ Which sentences do the best job of showing, not just telling?

▶ Where else could you use words that show instead of tell?

▶ Many of the ideas discussed in Chapter 11 on assessment can easily be incorporated into conference sessions.

Conducting Conferences

During literacy conferences, you will talk with students about books they have read independently or pieces they are writing or have written. Conferences may also be about books you have assigned for the whole class to read, but these are usually dealt with through literature circles or whole-class discussions.

The conference time with each student should be a relaxed, pleasant experience. You can just let the conference evolve naturally, but it may also be a good idea to have a plan in mind. Here is one possible sequence for a reading conference:

▶ What would you like to focus on today?

▶ Tell me about your book.

▶ What have you written in your journal that you would like to share?

▶ Read aloud the part that you liked best.

▶ Let's talk about what you think our goals should be for next time.

You will also need a plan for writing conferences. If the student asked for the conference, begin by having the student tell what he or she wants to discuss. Then proceed from there. A simple basic plan that works well for many teachers is as follows (Calkins, 1986; Graves, 1983; Millett, 1986):

1. *Opening:* The student reads his or her draft. You listen or read along as the student reads.

2. *Discussion:* Talk about the content and sequence of ideas, unless the student has some other specific purpose. Ask questions that get the student to talk about the piece of writing.
3. *Closing:* Help the student focus attention on *one* thing to do to improve the writing. This will help the student realize quick success.

Every conference will be different, but having a plan such as one of these in mind will be helpful in the beginning. As you and your students have more experiences with conferences, you will devise a plan that works best for you.

Many teachers are afraid to try reading conferences because they haven't read every book in the library. The solution is to just tell students if you don't know the book they are reading; they will enjoy sharing something new with you. It is easier to talk about a book if you have read it, but you can talk about any book by using very general questions:

▶ Tell me about your book.
▶ Who are the characters?
▶ Where does it take place?
▶ What happened?
▶ How did the story end?

You will notice that this line of questioning follows the story map concept discussed earlier in this text. You can also develop very general questions for expository texts:

▶ What is the topic of your book?
▶ What are the big ideas the author tells you?
▶ Find me a place to read aloud that supports one of the author's big ideas.

Sometimes you will find it helpful to have conferences with two students at the same time. This is always possible when you have assigned a book for the entire class to read or when students have read the same book or are reading books that are closely related. With two students, you can encourage higher-level thinking by comparing and contrasting books.

Peer Conferences

Peer conferences are another good way for students to have a conversation with someone about their writing or reading (Dahl, 1988). Students need to know the purposes of the conference. However, they also need to know what is expected of them and what they should do during the conference. Peer conferences are often held in preparation for a teacher conference.

An effective way to get peer conferences started is to develop with the class a set of guidelines to follow, such as those for writing from a third-grade class shown in Figure 10.8. Similar guidelines can be developed for reading. Adjust the guidelines for your grade level. Teacher conferences can serve as models for peer conferences. It is also a good idea to role-play peer conferences and talk with students about how to improve them.

FIGURE 10.8

PEER CONFERENCE GUIDELINES FROM A THIRD-GRADE CLASS

Our Peer Conference Guidelines

- Remember that your friend's writing is his/her own work. Don't try to rewrite it.
- Let the writer read the piece of writing aloud.
- Talk about the things you like.
- Ask questions about things you don't understand.
- Make one or two suggestions for improving the writing.
- If you are proofreading, also read it silently.

Evaluating Conferences

As you work with conferences, you and your students should take time to evaluate them. Together you should talk about such things as the following:

1. How are our conferences working?
2. What is especially good about our conferences?
3. What problems do we have?
4. What can we do to improve our conferences?

If your students are new to conferences, you will probably need to do this several times during the beginning of the year until everything is running smoothly.

You must also evaluate your own ability to handle conferences. The more experience you have, the better you will be at this activity. Here is a list of questions to ask yourself:

1. How are my conferences going overall?
2. Are they too long or too brief?

3. Am I asking questions that prompt children to think?
4. Is the conference truly a discussion, or am I testing?
5. Am I getting helpful information about my students' abilities to use reading and writing?
6. Are the other students in the class engaged in productive activities while I am conferencing?

A good way to evaluate your conferences is to tape-record one or two and listen to them. This will help you see how you can improve and will suggest many more questions than those raised here. Conference procedures may change from year to year, because new circumstances will arise with each new class.

Records

An important part of keeping your classroom running smoothly is keeping sufficient records of what is happening and what individual students are doing. Teachers must develop ways to do this that suit their own circumstances. Consider several options as you decide on the types of records you want to keep.

Teacher Notebook or Portfolio

The teacher notebook or portfolio is an excellent way to organize a lot of information in one location. You use a large three-ring binder with dividers. Here are some possible sections for your teacher notebook or portfolio:

▶ *Theme plans:* This section contains a simple outline plan for the theme you are covering. It may also include themes that have been completed or that you are planning. Chapter 9 provides information to help you in working out this plan.

▶ *Schedules/lesson plans:* Daily or weekly schedules and lesson plans are kept here. Your lesson plans may take on many different forms. Some teachers like to keep their lesson plans separate from this notebook, whereas others like to include as much information as possible in one place.

▶ *Book lists:* Lists of books you want to use or obtain for your class are compiled here. These may be books you want for a particular theme, want to order through the librarian, or want to purchase with funds you have available. A simple list with title, author, publisher, and ISBN number will give you the information you need to obtain the book when the time comes.

▶ *Student information:* This section would contain a separate tab for each student. It would include copies of forms such as those shown in Figures 10.9 and 10.10 to record pertinent observations and conference information. A page such as the one in Figure 10.11 would be for parent conferences.

Other Ways to Keep Records

Not all teachers like the teacher notebook or portfolio concept. Some teachers prefer to keep separate folders or spiral notebooks for each student. The same types of information described above would be kept here. Other teachers use 5" × 8" cards to make notes of observations and conferences. They then rely more heavily on the student portfolio concept, which is discussed in Chapter 11.

FIGURE 10.9

STUDENT DATA SHEET FOR TEACHER NOTEBOOK

Name _____Birthdate _____Age _____

Address _____Telephone_____

Parent(s)/Guardian _____

Reading Data

Writing Data

Listening, Speaking, and Viewing Data

_____

The important thing is to remember that there is more than one way to keep records. You should choose the method that best helps you monitor and adjust your classroom organization.

Types of Flexible Groups

An important teaching and organizational strategy is using *flexible groups* in contrast to whole-class and individual activities. As the name implies, these are groupings that change continually. Flexible groups may consist of two, three, or more students working together to accomplish a specific purpose. Unlike the old concept of reading groups where students were assigned to a group for a long period of time (often the entire school year), flexible groups may change every day or may last for several days. The size of a group depends on the purpose. For example, literature discussion groups (see Chapter 6) are usually most successful when they contain three to five students. This allows for interaction but is small enough to ensure that

FIGURE 10.10

SHEET FOR RECORDING OBSERVATIONS AND STUDENT CONFERENCE RESULTS

Name		Grade	
Date	Observation	Date	Observation

FIGURE 10.11

SHEET FOR RECORDING OBSERVATIONS AND PARENT CONFERENCE RESULTS

Name			Grade	
Date	Parent Comments	Teacher Comments	Student Comments	Actions

everyone gets to participate. The rule of thumb is to keep the group small enough to accomplish the intended purpose.

▶ Use *interest groups* any time you want students of similar interests to work together for discussion, completing a project, or having a lesson. For example, if you have several students who have very strong interests in science, you could pull them together to teach them how to perform a particular experiment, or they might complete a project together.

▶ *Strengths and needs groups* build on students' strengths or help them learn something they need. For example, after students have read and discussed the book *Pelicans* (Patent, 1992), you might bring together students who had trouble identifying the main ideas. This needs group would also be a minilesson group and would receive direct instruction on main idea. At other times, you might have a support-in-advance activity (see page 492) to build background by mixing students who have some background with those who have little background.

▶ *Minilesson groups* are for teaching lessons needed by certain students, as discussed earlier. Many times these groups will be used for direct instruction with a specific skill or strategy. However, minilessons are not always based on need. Some are taught simply because there is something you want a group or the class to learn. For example, you may teach a minilesson at the beginning of the year to the whole class on how to select books that are appropriate for them. Some minilessons may be taught several times throughout the year. For example, you may need to teach a minilesson on adjectives every time some students are writing description.

▶ *Discussion groups* are used following the reading of parts of books or complete books. These groups may be formed by students electing to work together, by the teacher, or by a combination of the two. Discussion groups may also be used for writing; students meet to share their writing or to get peer reactions. In one sixth-grade class this author recently visited, discussion groups were being held for students to read aloud and talk about mysteries they had written.

▶ *Project groups* may be formed for long- or short-term projects related to any aspect of the curriculum. For example, a first-grade class may be making a mural about seasons that is developed throughout the year; different groups are responsible for different seasons. Often project groups are composed of students with differing abilities and needs.

▶ *Modeling groups* may be used any time students need more modeling of reading, writing, or other skills or strategies. This modeling may involve students, the teacher, or another adult as a model. For example, fourth graders who need extra support in reading might prepare a book to read aloud to a group of first graders. The first graders get good models, and the fourth graders build their confidence and skill in reading.

The important thing to keep in mind about these various types of groups is that they are *flexible;* they are always changing based on students' strengths, needs, interests, and various purposes for learning. Flexible grouping is one of the most useful tools you will have for creating and maintaining a success-centered literacy classroom.

Frameworks for Organizing the Balanced Literacy Classroom

Organizing and managing a balanced literacy classroom that promotes success for all students requires a balance of activities. A model for a beginning balanced literacy program was presented in Chapter 4 (see page 174). The model in Figure 10.12 shows the activities of a balanced literacy program for grades 3–8:

- ▶ Daily independent reading and writing
- ▶ Core reading instruction and developmentally appropriate reading instruction
- ▶ Teacher-modeled writing and developmentally appropriate writing
- ▶ Intervention for those students having difficulty learning and needing more support

The model in Figure 10.12 shows the three primary goals for this organizational structure—power and practice, instruction, and additional support. Independent reading and writing provide the power and practice. These concepts were discussed in detail in Chapter 2.

This section of the chapter will discuss five frameworks that will help you plan the instruction in your classroom: (1) core books with flexible groups, (2) developmentally appropriate books, (3) reading workshop, (4) teacher-modeled writing, and (5) writing workshop. Intervention, the part of the program where you provide additional support, is discussed at the conclusion of this chapter on page 518.

Core Book with Flexible Groups

This framework for organizing the classroom is often referred to as *whole-class instruction*. Figure 10.13 shows how this framework operates. A better name for this pattern is *core book with flexible groups* because the only thing that is really whole-class is the fact that everyone has experiences with the same text.

Description

Everyone in the class will read the same piece of text. This could be the grade-level anthology or a trade book such as *Head for the Hills!* (Walker, 1993), which is the story of the Johnstown flood. *Each student needs a copy of the book being read.*

Begin by activating prior knowledge and developing background for the piece of literature (see Chapter 3). Some students may have limited prior knowledge for the book. For them, you need to provide a preview or develop key concepts to provide a stronger base for what the whole class will read. This concept is known as *support in advance* or *jump starting*. This is a flexible group combining both student strengths and needs. Using any of the techniques for activating prior knowledge and developing background discussed in Chapter 3, support in advance may be provided by the classroom teacher or a support teacher such as Title I. Then, when

FIGURE 10.12

A BALANCED LITERACY PROGRAM FOR GRADES 3–8

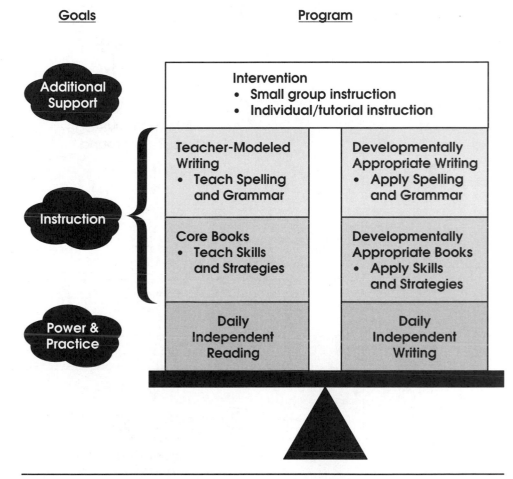

the whole class begins the book, a different prior-knowledge activity is used; the students who were given support in advance are now able to function more successfully with the whole class.

After prior knowledge has been activated and developed, students are ready to read. You accommodate individual differences among students by using different modes of reading (see Chapter 2). Either you and/or the students decide how the piece will be read. By giving students choices in how they will read, you will accommodate individual needs. Keep in mind, however, that when less able readers are given choices, they often select the choice that allows them to "hide" because

FIGURE 10.13

Core Book with Flexible Groups

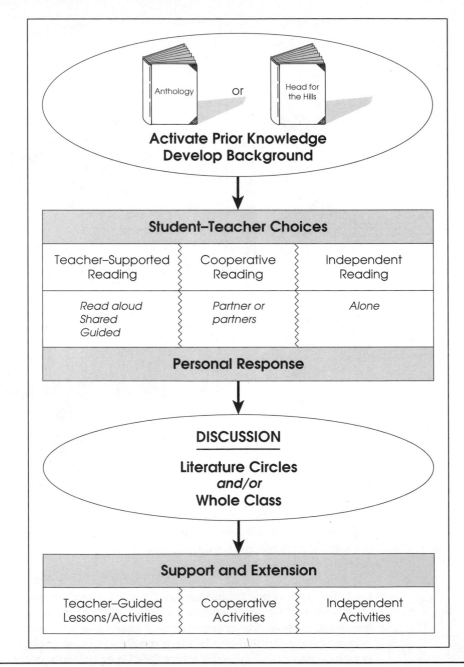

they don't want to reveal that they need help (Johnston & Allington, 1991). You must be alert to this situation and help these students believe it is okay for them to get support. You may do this by having very strong readers and those needing help come together with you.

You may give the students two or three choices, for example: "Today you may read the first two chapters independently or come to the table and I will guide you through the chapters." If you see that students are not making good choices, you guide them to better decisions. It is not necessary to always offer students three choices, and sometimes you may decide how the whole class will read the book. A critical element in making this pattern of instruction work is varying the modes of reading to accommodate individual needs. Kindergarten and first-grade teachers are likely to conduct most of their initial readings as teacher-supported reading. After students have read the piece of literature, they should make a personal response to what they have read. Usually this is done in writing (see Chapter 6).

Personal response is followed by discussion, which is another form of response. Traditionally, discussion has been teacher directed, with students simply answering the teacher's questions. Research has demonstrated the importance of students discussing what they have read as a way to develop their ability to construct meaning (Sweet, 1993). For discussion, you should use the literature discussion circle concept introduced in Chapter 6, giving students the option to decide with whom they will meet to discuss what they have read. The literature discussion circles may be followed by whole-class discussion to pull together the ideas of various groups. During the discussion circles, you should pay close attention to how students respond. This information will help you plan the support and extension activities students need. (For more information on observing students during responses, see Chapter 11.) For example, if during response you notice that some students reading *Head for the Hills!* are missing important details, you might provide a minilesson on details using the chapters students have read.

The final step in the core book framework is providing support and extension. This is where you teach skills and strategies and do other types of activities that extend students' reading.

Support and extension activities may consist of teacher-guided lessons or activities, cooperative activities, or independent activities. It is not necessary to do all of these; you select what you believe is needed to thoroughly develop the students' abilities to construct meaning. For example, after reading the first two chapters in *Head for the Hills!,* you may just teach a needed skill lesson and do other activities when the book is completed. In addition to minilessons, support and extension activities may include such things as more creative responses, vocabulary activities such as making word maps or word webs, writing, art, and so forth. You have probably already recognized how you have utilized all of the parts of the literacy lesson concept you have been learning throughout this text.

An important question to address is how much time this framework requires. Obviously the answer depends on the text being read and the students themselves. However, the following guidelines should help you in planning to use this framework:

▶ Activating prior knowledge should be done quickly. If support in advance is done, it is likely to be completed on a day prior to beginning the literature with the whole class. Therefore, the whole-class prior-knowledge activity should last no longer than 10 to 15 minutes. After students start reading, you may discover they need more prior-knowledge support; therefore, you provide it at the time needed. *Remember, students* want *to read!* Don't wear out the book with too much prior-knowledge work.

▶ The amount of time allotted to reading each day will vary according to the book and the grade level. This time period may range from 15 to 30 minutes.

▶ Discussion circles should be kept short to keep students focused and on task. In kindergarten and first grade, these discussions may last only a matter of seconds. Beyond these levels, 5 to 10 minutes is usually long enough for the discussion.

▶ The amount of time for support and extension activities depends on the nature of the activities. Minilessons may last only 5 to 10 minutes, whereas other types of activities may last longer.

The important thing to bear in mind about time is to keep the pace of instruction *appropriately fast*. The pace of instruction should be based on students' strengths and needs. It is important to keep students reading, not spending too long on one book doing too many activities. A chapter or two in a book such as *Head for the Hills!* should take one or two blocks of class time. More will be said about time in the section on scheduling.

Benefits of the Core-Book Framework

This framework offers many benefits. First, it puts everyone in the class on a level playing field. All the students believe they are able to read the same types of books everyone else in the class can read; this reduces the stigma that has been attached to ability grouping.

Second, it provides a way to teach key skills and strategies. Students then apply these when they read developmentally appropriate books.

Third, this framework promotes and supports discussion involving *all* students. This is very important in helping students construct meaning.

A final benefit is flexibility; this framework is not linear. You may start by activating prior knowledge, having students read, and then having them discuss. You may reserve the support and extension for later. The next day you may continue the book by doing just reading because no prior knowledge is needed.

Problems to Avoid

While this is a very strong framework for promoting success, it can have many problems and pitfalls, especially if the plan is misused. First, this plan *must be balanced* with the developmentally appropriate books plan described in the next section. *All students must be given instruction with books that are developmentally appropriate.* (See Chapters 2, 4, and 11 on determining developmental appropriateness of books.)

Second, the plan can fail if all students are treated exactly the same. In other words, you must vary the modes of reading, the discussion groups, and the support and extension activities. You can't just have the whole class read the book independently, answer questions, and complete one activity. Finally, *choice for students is critical.* You must allow some student choice to truly accommodate individual needs.

A final pitfall to avoid is having everyone in the class read the same book but dividing the class into several reading groups by ability level. This does *not* achieve the goal of a success-centered classroom, because the focus is only on students' levels. The one-book framework should allow *all* students to experience success with the same text.

Developmentally Appropriate Books

The developmentally appropriate framework is based on the idea that all students need books that are appropriate for their reading ability. Figure 10.14 shows how this framework operates.

Description

You begin by selecting several books that cover a range of reading levels. In the example described here, we are looking at books that would be used in a first-grade classroom. You may use two or more books; usually four is about the most teachers want to use at one time. The easiest book in the diagram is *Sheep in a Jeep* (Shaw, 1986), and the most difficult is *Clean Your Room Harvey Moon* (Cummings, 1991). The other two books, *The Wonderful Pigs of Jillian Jiggs* (Gilman, 1988) and *Mommy Doesn't Know My Name* (Williams, 1990), fall in between. If you are using only two books, one of them must be easy enough for students who need easy reading material. When using the developmentally appropriate books framework, you need enough copies of each book so that each student can have one.

You designate one of the books the "teacher book." This means that students who read this book will work with you for part of the book or throughout the whole book. The teacher book gives students who need teacher support a place to go. Sometimes the teacher book is a very challenging book for which any student would need teacher support.

Sometimes you will assign students to the book you want them to read and at other times you should allow student choice. If students are going to select their book, begin by introducing each book to the class. Read aloud just a portion to activate prior knowledge and give students a sense of the book. Tell students which book is to be the teacher book. Give students a few minutes to look at the books, select the one they want to read, and decide how they will read it. Remind them to use "thumbs up" (see page 475) to select the book that is right for them.

If you are working with older students and longer books, you might display the books for several days, allowing students to look them over and sign up for the book they want to read. Students may make a second choice in case too many sign up for the same book.

After students make their selection, they read the book in the mode they have decided to use. Since the books in this example are short, they will easily be completed in about 20 minutes or so. After students complete their reading, they do their personal responses and then have a literature discussion circle with others who have read the same book. To prompt the discussion, you can use a generic response chart such as the one in Figure 10.15. As students discuss their books, you move from group to group to participate in or monitor the discussions.

FIGURE 10.14

DEVELOPMENTALLY APPROPRIATE MODEL

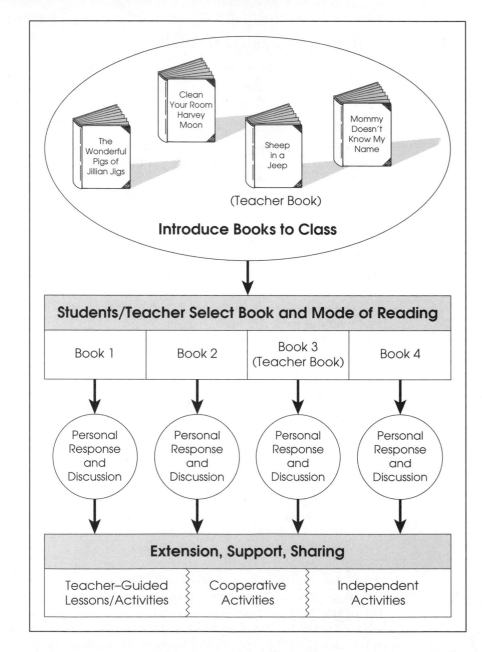

Fifth graders have time to study and select the book they want to read. © *Michael Zide*

Finally, you provide one or more activities that all students can do to extend and support the books and allow students to share. For example, with the four books suggested in Figure 10.14, each group of students might complete a story map as a way to share their books with one another; this would also help them focus on constructing meaning for their books. The extension and support may also include minilessons or other types of activities as described in the previous framework for support and extension.

The amount of time required to complete this framework using these four books is approximately 60 to 80 minutes for a first-grade class. If you are using chapter books such as *The Summer of the Swans* (Byars, 1970) or *Number the Stars* (Lowry, 1989), this process may last several weeks. When using this framework with four books in first grade, the books may be used over three or four days. Often students will reread the same book several times. This is fine as long as students don't get stuck on one book and fail to move on; if students do get stuck, you can remove the book and/or add new ones to the group and entice them to try a new one.

The developmentally appropriate book framework is effective at all grade levels. Figure 10.16 shows it being used with three chapter books, *The Summer of the Swans* (Byars, 1970), *Number the Stars* (Lowry, 1989), and *The Kid in the Red Jacket* (Park, 1987); the last is the easiest of the three. When using this framework with chapter books, the books may last a week or longer. Discussion does not necessarily take

FIGURE 10.15

GENERIC RESPONSE CHART FOR PROMPTING DEVELOPMENTALLY APPROPRIATE BOOK DISCUSSIONS

Discussion
1. Retell what you read.
2. Tell your favorite part or character.

place at the end of each chapter, and the teacher book rotates from book to book to allow teacher interaction for each book.

Benefits of the Developmentally Appropriate Books Framework

The major benefit of the developmentally appropriate books framework is that it allows all students to have instructional support with books that are appropriate to their reading ability. In these books, students can apply the skills and strategies they learned in the core book. By incorporating the element of student choice with a range of teacher-selected books, you are able to more effectively accommodate students' individual needs. Many teachers use the developmentally appropriate books framework with trade books and the core-book framework with anthologies.

Problems to Avoid

Teachers repeatedly report that the biggest problem with the developmentally appropriate books framework is management. It is often difficult to have so many books going at one time. Once you are using the core-book framework effectively, slowly begin the developmentally appropriate books approach using just two books.

Another problem is the teacher's reluctance to allow students choice some of the time. Teachers are often afraid that students will select a book that is not appropriate to their level of reading. If you see that students are always selecting books they are unable to read, conference with and guide them to better selections.

Finally, you and your school will need to build collections of books with multiple copies at a wide range of levels. Centralized book collections facilitate the developmentally appropriate books process.

Reading Workshop

The reading workshop is a third framework you can use to organize and manage the literacy-centered classroom. Atwell (1987) discusses the reading workshop as a way to approach reading in her middle school classes. The workshop is a time when the entire class is engaged in reading, responding, and sharing books with the

FIGURE 10.16

DEVELOPMENTALLY APPROPRIATE BOOKS—UPPER-GRADE FRAMEWORK

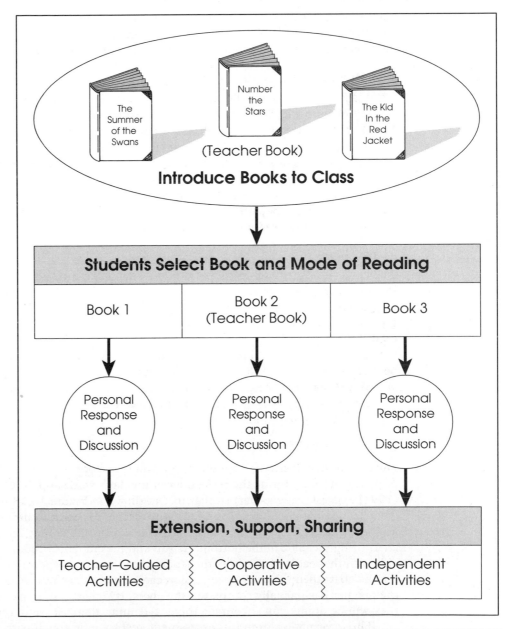

teacher and with peers. Although it provides time for the teacher to help students improve their construction of meaning, the heart of the reading workshop is time for reading. Reutzel and Cooter (1991) have adapted the reading workshop as proposed by Atwell for use in elementary grades 2 through 5.

Description

The reading workshop consists of five main components: teacher sharing time, minilesson, state-of-the-class conference, self-selected reading and responding, and student sharing time. These are outlined in Figure 10.17, along with suggested times.

Teacher Sharing Time

The teacher uses this initial sharing time to motivate or excite children about literature. For example, you might use a short story such as *Hemi's Pet* (de Hamel, 1985) to introduce children to a series of books on pets or one of Jack Prelutsky's poems from *Tyrannosaurus Was a Beast* (Prelutsky, 1988) to excite children about the study of dinosaurs. This sharing takes from 5 to 10 minutes and serves to warm up the class. Holdaway (1979) describes this process for kindergarten and first grade. Older students also profit from teacher sharing time. Many teachers allow students to share a poem they have read or written or to tell a story. You can use this sharing time to lead into your minilesson.

Minilesson

The concept of the minilesson was introduced in Chapter 2 and discussed in detail in Chapter 8. This lesson on a strategy or a skill is designed to meet a need based on students' responses to reading or to provide prereading support such as background or vocabulary for a particular piece of literature that students are about to read. This lesson using direct instruction incorporates the skill or strategy within the context of a piece of literature students have already read or listened to. It may be done with the whole class or a small group.

Minilessons may be drawn from teachers' resource books or developed by the teacher. However, skills from a published curriculum guide or teacher's manual should be taught *only* if a real need exists.

State-of-the-Class Conference

During this brief period (5 minutes), you will take stock of what students are doing or planning to do during the remainder of the day's workshop. Reutzel and Cooter (1991) suggest using a chart similar to that shown in Figure 10.18 to keep track of what each student is doing. Initially, many teachers keep this chart on a clipboard and simply ask each student what he or she is doing on that day. They complete the chart using the code at the bottom. As you and the students become more comfortable with the reading workshop, the students can assume responsibility for completing the chart themselves. A large version can be posted each week. In Figure 10.18, the teacher has partially completed the chart. By having students announce what they will be doing, you encourage them to commit themselves to a particular task.

The information from this assessment keeps you in touch with what students are doing and lets you know which students may need a conference or other teacher

FIGURE 10.17

READING WORKSHOP PLAN

- **Teacher Sharing Time** (5–10 minutes)
  A time when the teacher shares some literature to spark students' interests and motivate them for independent reading

- **Minilessons** (5–10 minutes)
  A teacher-directed lesson focusing on prereading activities that activate and develop prior knowledge for a particular piece of literature or a skill or strategy needed.

- **State-of-Class Conference** (3–5 minutes)
  Each student tells the teacher and the rest of the class what he or she is doing that day. The teacher records on the state-of-the class chart. This lets the teacher determine needs for conferences, etc.

- **Reading and Responding** (40–60 minutes)
  Alternative A
    During this time, students engage in several possible activities:
    - Self-selected reading (10–20 minutes)
    - Literature circles (20–30 minutes)
    - Conferences with the teacher (20 minutes)
  Alternative B
    A variation of this plan requiring 60 minutes is often used.
    - Whole-class reading and responding (10–20 minutes)
    - Self-selected reading and responding (10–20 minutes)
    - Literature circles (10–20 minutes)
    - Conferences with the teacher, held during teacher-assigned reading or only on selected days (10 minutes)

- **Student Sharing Time** (5–10 minutes)
  Students share what they are doing or have done. This may be done in sharing circles or as a whole class. The teacher may comment about activities or commend students who participated in conferences.

---

support. For example, if you notice that a student has been reading the same book for several days with no response group activity, you know you may need a special meeting with the student to find out what progress has been made and to set new goals or change existing ones.

Reading and Responding

This is the core of the reading workshop, the time when students read and respond to books. There are two alternatives for using this time. Alternative A has three basic

FIGURE 10.18

STATE-OF-THE CLASS CHART

STATE-OF-THE-CLASS					
Name	M	Tu	W	Th	F
Ann	SSR	J		~	
Beth	LC-D	SSR			
Bill	SSR	LC-D			
Carl	J	SSR			
Cathy	LC-DNR	SSR			
Darin	R	SSR			
David	SSR	SSR			

CODE   SSR - Self-Selected Reading   LC - Literature Circle Meeting
        J   - Journal   D   - Discussing
        R   - Response Activity   G   - Setting Goals
        RK - Record Keeping   DNR - Determining New
                                                 Response

types of activities: self-selected reading, literature responses, and individual reading conferences. Usually this portion of the workshop lasts from about 40 to 60 minutes, depending on the age level of your students.

Self-selected reading usually lasts from 10 to 20 minutes, depending on the grade level. During this time, the students read independently or with a partner. You should also read for some portion of the time to serve as a model, but you should also circulate to hold individual miniconferences, keep students motivated and encouraged, and do on-the-spot, incidental teaching. Throughout this time, students may also make entries in their journals.

Literature responses can involve a number of activities, such as writing in journals or meeting with a literature circle. During this time, you continue to circulate and confer with individuals, or meet with a literature circle to participate in the discussion or serve as a recorder. Some students may continue their silent reading while others are meeting in literature circles, working in journals, or doing some other response activity. If students have not chosen to meet with a literature circle, they should always be encouraged to respond in some other way, such as by sharing with a friend or completing a project about the book they have read.

Individual reading conferences with students who are not in literature circles make up the last 10 minutes of the period. During these conferences, other students may complete a literature circle or continue with self-selected reading. Usually two or three conferences are held each day.

If you want the whole class or a selected group of students to read the same book, you will use alternative B. You can assign the book and provide the appropriate activities for a literacy lesson. You also include time for self-selected reading, and you adjust the code for the state-of-the-class chart to RT—Reading Time, SS—Self-Selected, and AR—Assigned Reading (see Figure 10.17). You can adjust the times for the other activities according to students' needs.

If you decide to move into the reading workshop gradually, you can schedule two days for the workshop and use the remaining days for other reading activities. Then you can expand the reading workshop to your full program.

You may be in a school that uses a literature anthology. If so, you can use the anthology for students to select what they want to read or combine the reading workshop framework with the core-book framework discussed earlier. Lessons suggested in the teacher's resources may be used selectively for minilessons. Basically, this pattern is alternative B suggested in Figure 10.17. You will have to adjust the code for your state-of-the-class chart to go with this combined approach.

Student Sharing Time

During the last 5 to 10 minutes of the reading workshop, students share books they have read and report their progress on literature projects or other response activities. Sharing time "advertises" the excitement of literacy learning and helps to promote the class as a community of readers. During this time, students may ask one another for ideas to improve what they are doing. Some teachers often divide the class into small sharing groups (three to five students) to allow for greater student involvement. The teacher then circulates among the groups, commenting or just listening. Longer sharing times may be scheduled when certain literature circles have a special activity or project to share, such as a readers theater performance or a puppet play.

Benefits of the Reading Workshop

The reading workshop provides an effective framework for systematically developing the reading block in your balanced literacy classroom. If you use alternative B as outlined in Figure 10.17, you are also able to incorporate both core-book supported reading and developmentally appropriate reading.

Problems to Avoid

If you choose to use the reading workshop as a totally self-selected reading block (alternative A), you may risk overlooking the need for more instruction and in-depth discussion that comes when all students experience the same book (framework 1) or when they self-select from a controlled set of books (framework 2). One problem with the individualized reading approach (Veatch, 1978) was that students all read different books and did not get enough discussion to develop their ability to effectively construct meaning. This problem can be easily avoided by going to alternative B for the reading workshop.

Another problem with the reading workshop is starting it without appropriate student preparation. Atwell (1987) suggests that you develop and clarify rules of the workshop with students before you begin and during its initial use.

Teacher-Modeled Writing

The teacher-modeled writing framework provides you with an effective way to model writing using the shared writing mode discussed in detail in Chapter 7.

Description

This framework begins by having the whole class (or a large group) work with the teacher to develop a common piece. The teacher or students may actually write the text. At another time, the teacher conducts a minilesson using the group-written piece to revise and improve the particular type of writing. The teacher elicits ideas from the students and models various elements to help students see how to write in the domain (see Chapter 7) or product being modeled. Depending on their needs, students move to either supported writing or independent writing; if students go to supported writing, they will later move on to independent writing.

Benefits of Teacher-Modeled Writing

This framework provides a sound way for you to model writing for your students; by having students move from shared to guided, collaborative/cooperative, and independent writing, you scaffold instruction and gradually release responsibility to students.

In addition, this framework can be easily combined with the writing workshop, the next framework discussed. By combining the two frameworks, you achieve a balance of modeled writing and developmentally appropriate writing.

Problems to Avoid

The most significant problem in using the teacher-modeled writing framework is moving students too quickly or too slowly through the various stages of writing. Providing either too little or too much modeling can cause problems for students. The most important thing to remember is that once students know how to write in the particular domain or for the particular product, the way they develop and become mature writers is by *writing*. Even when students move to independent writing, you need to keep in mind that through conferencing you continue to model for students and support them in their growth as writers.

Writing Workshop

The writing workshop, which is similar to the reading workshop, has been recommended by numerous researchers and writing specialists (Atwell, 1987; Calkins,

1994; Hansen, 1987). It is a very flexible plan that places students and teacher in a partnership for learning.

Description

The writing workshop consists of four basic parts: minilessons, state-of-the-class conferences, writing and conferring, and group sharing. Each part flows into the next to make up the block of time allocated for writing. The ideas and suggestions given here are based on the work of Atwell (1987), Calkins (1994), and Hansen (1987) and my own experiences in working with children and teachers.

Minilesson

The minilesson is done with the whole class and usually lasts from 5 to 10 minutes. The content of the minilesson is determined by student needs as evidenced during a previous writing workshop. The guidelines presented in Chapter 2 also apply here.

Since the minilesson content is based in part on student needs, the topics covered may range from how to select a topic to how to write a business letter. Following is a list of possible topics for minilessons:

- Procedures for the writing workshop
- Writing an opening paragraph
- Punctuating items in a series
- Selecting words to show fear, suspense, bravery, or other characteristics
- Selecting topics
- Writing a friendly letter
- Examples of humor from a piece of literature
- Correct use of paragraph form
- Outlining for a report
- Writing description
- Punctuating dialogue

There are many more possible topics for minilessons. Some days no minilesson is needed; this time may be used for more sharing or writing.

State-of-the-Class Conference

The state-of-the-class conference, a very brief activity, helps to ensure that you know exactly what all students are doing during each writing workshop. Atwell (1987) uses a clipboard and chart similar to the one in Figure 10.19 to keep track of students each day.

After you have completed the minilesson, take 5 minutes to ask students to identify what they will be doing during the day's workshop. Use codes such as those shown in Figure 10.19 to record each student's reply. By examining your chart, you can tell who might need some extra conference time or just a quick visit from you during writing. As you become more comfortable with this procedure, you might

FIGURE 10.19

PARIAL STATE-OF-THE-CLASS CHART

State of Class Chart					
Names	M	T	W	Th	F
Lisa	①	Ⓒ	②	RV	PR
Ted	①	①	Ⓒ	②	②
Larry	②	Ⓒ	RV	PR	P
Susan	Ⓒ	P	Ⓢ ①	①	Ⓒ
Mike	②	PR	P	Ⓢ	①

Code

① – First Draft
② – Second Draft
Ⓒ – Conference
RV – Revising
PR – Proofing
P – Publishing
Ⓢ – Shaving

choose to make a large state-of-the-class chart and have students complete it each day as the writing workshop begins.

The state-of-the-class conference builds in a "comfort factor" for you. It lets you know what students are doing and gives you a way to know what is happening over the week. Teachers who use the writing workshop indicate repeatedly that this portion of the workshop gives them the control they feel they need but still encourages student independence.

Writing and Conferring

Writing and conferring is the core of the writing workshop and usually lasts from 30 to 40 minutes, depending on the grade level. During this block of time, students are writing; you may be writing yourself or holding conferences with students.

Since students will be at various stages in developing their writing piece, you will need to do a variety of things, depending on their needs. Some of the time you will be working on some writing of your own, thus modeling adult writing and expressing that you value this activity. At other times you will be circulating through the class, talking with individual students, reading portions of their writing, prompting and encouraging them, and offering whatever support they need. These brief encounters may be viewed as miniconferences or just times to talk with, guide, and support students. During this time, you will gain valuable information that will help you plan minilessons and assess students' progress. You will want to carry note cards, a pad, or adhesive labels so that you can make notes for future use in planning and/or for insertion into your notebook page for each student.

During this time, students may be holding a peer conference, working on revision, editing, planning a new piece, or just getting topics for writing. You might stop to visit, but remember that these are *peer* conferences. You will have a time to meet with students later.

During writing and conferring, you will also hold formal group and/or individual conferences with students. Using a sign-up chart or an area of the chalkboard, students should sign up in advance of conference time to meet with you, either at the beginning of each day's writing workshop or the day before you announce you will hold conferences. You need to be flexible about this.

Group Sharing

Group sharing is just like an individual or peer conference, except that the whole group reacts to a piece of writing. This portion of the writing workshop usually lasts 5 minutes or longer, depending on your schedule and what needs to take place. During this time, you might incorporate the concept of the author's chair discussed in Chapter 2.

Group sharing is not just a show-and-tell time; it is a time for students to talk about their writing with peers and get some additional reactions, as well as a time to celebrate their successes by sharing finished products. All of this sharing promotes the classroom as a community of writers, a place where writers discover how well they have constructed meaning. For example, if a student gives a report on dinosaurs, other students might ask questions about things they don't understand or think are incorrect, or even suggest another book on dinosaurs that the author should read before finishing the piece.

Some teachers divide the class into two or three sharing groups so that more individuals can share at one time. Some teachers tend to skip sharing time or cut it short. However, you should avoid doing this, because sharing time provides so many benefits:

- It provides students with authentic reasons for writing and gives them the audience writers need.
- It brings closure to the construction of meaning by having both readers and writers discover whether they have successfully accomplished their purpose.
- It helps students grow in both their writing and reading by getting feedback from peers and having to respond to that feedback.

▶ It is another point in the development of literacy where reading and writing are integrated into one process within the community of learners.

Benefits of the Writing Workshop

The writing workshop is a flexible, manageable framework that allows you to meet individual needs. It is possible to combine the writing workshop with the teacher-modeled writing framework to provide balanced writing instruction. The teacher-modeled writing piece can be inserted into the minilesson slot of the writing workshop, thereby giving you a way to model writing while at the same time having students write independently. You might do one shared piece each week or on a regular cycle, using the remaining time to have students do guided, collaborative/cooperative, or independent writing.

Problems to Avoid

It takes time to move effectively into the use of the writing workshop framework. Therefore, if you plan to use this framework you need to develop a systematic plan for its use and try it out gradually. It is especially important to share the framework with students, discussing each section. As you work with students in the writing workshop, it is useful to periodically evaluate how things are working. Teachers at various grade levels have found the following procedures very helpful in starting the writing workshop:

1. *Familiarize yourself with the writing workshop plan.* Think about how you will use it in your classroom.
2. *Think through procedures you will want to use.* The state-of-the-class chart, conference scheduling, and simple recordkeeping for your conferences are enough to get started. Gradually add other procedures you have learned from this text and other sources.
3. *Talk with your students about the workshop.* Make a chart showing the parts of the plan, and use it as a guide for you and your students.
4. *Designate a day to begin.* This may take place at the beginning of the year or at any point during the year. Students may have pieces of writing in progress, or you may want everyone to start with a new piece of writing. Teachers find both approaches successful.
5. *Use your first few minilessons to establish basic routines.* After the first day, you will begin to know what types of support your students need with procedures and routines. (There really aren't many to be concerned about.)
6. *Evaluate what is happening with your students.* Talk about the writing workshop. Ask students for suggestions to make it better.
7. *Trust your judgment.* You are a professional and know how to make decisions. If something feels right, do it; if it feels wrong, don't do it. However, give things time to work; don't just drop something after one attempt.

Now that you are familiar with the five frameworks for organizing and managing a success-centered literacy classroom, we will focus on how to plan daily routines and schedules using these frameworks along with time for independent reading and writing.

Planning a Daily Schedule

Regardless of the type of program you have in your school—*separate subjects program* (separate times for reading, English, math, and so forth), *integrated language arts program* (all of the language arts taught together), or a *cross-curricular program* (thematic units are developed that cut across curricular lines)—you must have a daily plan that will help you manage the instruction and activities of your classroom. There is *no one right schedule* that works for all teachers. However, if you have a system for thinking about your schedule, it makes planning easier and more efficient for you.

One of the most effective models for planning a schedule that has evolved over the last decade is a blocked scheduling plan. Researchers have found that this type of blocking leads to improved student achievement and more effective and efficient use of student and teacher time (Cunningham, Hall, & Defee, 1998). First, we will look at a blocked scheduling concept and related issues and then review some examples of several blocked plans.

A Blocked Plan for Scheduling

When you use a blocked scheduling plan, you think about the big jobs that need to be included in effective literacy instruction. The jobs include:

- Reading
- Word Work
- Writing/Language

Each block is given varying amounts of time depending on what needs to be done.

Reading is the block that includes self-selected independent reading, and reading, rereading, and responding to texts used for instructional purposes. This involves both core books and developmentally appropriate books.

Word Work is the block where you teach and students practice all skills and strategies related to decoding and spelling of individual words.

Writing/Language includes independent writing, teacher-modeled writing, developmentally appropriate writing, and the teaching of grammar, usage, and mechanics.

The values of thinking about your literacy program schedule in these types of blocks are four-fold:

1. It gives you a way to organize and plan systematic daily instruction.
2. It helps you avoid skipping things because you know that each block is generally included every day.
3. It allows you to effectively plan for and use any support staff you may have (aides, reading specialist, resource teachers, and volunteers).
4. It helps students participate more fully in their literacy program because they know what is to come and what to expect each day.

Amount of Time Required

A daily blocked plan will work from kindergarten through grade 8. Research does not give us answers as to the exact amounts of time that should be devoted

TABLE 10.1

MINIMUM AMOUNTS OF TIME FOR A DAILY BLOCKED LITERACY SCHEDULE

GRADE LEVELS	MINIMUM TIMES
Kindergarten	3 hours*
Grades 1–2	2–3 hours
Grades 3–5	$1^1/_2$–2 hours
Grades 6–8	1–2 hours

*Most half-day kindergartens don't have this much time.

to literacy instruction in general or to each block specifically. However, through years of working with teachers and students, I would suggest that the times presented in Table 10.1 are the minimums that you need at each grade level to have an effective literacy program. How do the suggested times stack up against what you know about the amount of time teachers usually have for literacy instruction? If you find yourself saying, "I (or teachers I know) usually have more time," *great.* If you find yourself saying, "No way, I (or teachers I know) don't have this much time," you really need to do some rethinking and discussing of the amount of time available for literacy instruction. Remember, it *takes time* to provide quality literacy instruction that prevents student failure.

Selecting Frameworks

We have looked at a daily blocked plan plus five frameworks for organizing a balanced literacy day (see pages 492–510). As you plan your daily schedule, you will want to incorporate the various frameworks as needed. A look at some sample schedules from several teachers will help you see how they incorporate the frameworks in their blocked schedule and get in all the necessary components of a balanced literacy program.

Sample Schedules

Figures 10.20, 10.21, 10.22, and 10.23 present sample schedules from four teachers. Figures 10.20 and 10.21 follow the beginning balanced literacy program model presented in Chapter 4 (see page 174) and Figures 10.22 and 10.23 follow the model presented in this chapter for grades 3–8. Read and study all the schedules with the following points or questions in mind:

▶ Does each teacher get in the daily three blocks? How do they vary the way it is done?

FIGURE 10.20

Ms. Barnett's Kindergarten Schedule

8:30   Arrival and Sign-in

8:45   Warm-up/Daily Interview/Daily News

   Reading

   • Reread a previously read book (developing language and comprehension block)

   • Respond (discussion/writing)

   • Small groups—decodable books routine or observational guided reading routine (learning to read words and text block or developing language and comprehension block)

   • Independent reading/Conferences

9:25   Word Work

   • Decoding skill instruction (learning to read words and text block)

   • Word games

9:40   Center Time (math, science, social studies)

10:00   BREAK/RECESS/SPECIALS (art, music, computer lab)

10:30   Writing/Language

   • Independent writing/conferences (in journals)

   • Teacher-modeled writing

   – Minilesson (some days)

   • Developmentally appropriate writing (students write what teacher modeled, selecting own topic)

11:10   Sharing

11:30   Dismiss

▶ How do these teachers' time allotments compare to the times given in Table 10.1?

▶ How does each teacher start the day? What is their purpose with this type of activity?

Developing Management Routines with Students

In order to manage your classroom effectively, you must develop routines with your students. There are four critical steps in the process of developing management routines:

1. ***Develop a daily schedule***   We have discussed this in detail in the previous section. Review any parts of that section now if you need to do so.

2. ***Identify independent activities for students to do***   Students need to know what to do when they have completed any of their work and are not

FIGURE 10.21

MR. LOPEZ'S FIRST-GRADE SCHEDULE

8:45   Opening exercise/Morning message

9:00   Word Work

- Phonemic awareness/Phonics/Word skills (learning to read words and text block)
- Independent practice using decodable books (learning to read words and text block)
- Spelling

9:30   Reading

- Independent reading
- Reading decodable book, shared reading routine, or observational guided reading routine (learning to read words and text block or developing language and comprehension block)
- Responding activities (discussion/writing)

10:20   BREAK

10:30   Writing/Language

- Independent writing
- Teacher-modeled writing
- Grammar minilesson or spelling lesson
- Developmentally appropriate writing

11:10   Morning share

11:15   LUNCH

11:45   Math

12:20   Art (M)/Music (W)/ PE (T-Th-F)

1:10   Teacher read-aloud time

1:25   Science/social studies/health

2:05   Project time

2:30   Prepare to go home

2:45   Dismiss

---

working with you. Therefore, you should always have a variety of activities students can do when work is completed. Table 10.2 lists possible activites you can use. You will have many others as you develop your teaching skills. These activities need to change frequently. They should be posted somewhere in the room so that students can refer to them.

3. ***Develop and discuss routines with students***   To help students feel comfortable working in groups and working independently, you need to develop

FIGURE 10.22

Ms. Sanders's Fifth-Grade Schedule

8:30   Making daily plans

10:30 Writing/Language
- Independent writing
- Teacher-modeled writing (M and T as needed)
- Grammar lesson (M and T as needed)
- Developmentally appropriate writing/writing workshop (T–F)

9:20   Reading
- Reading club (independent reading)
- Comprehension strategy lesson (M and W)
- Core book (M–T)
- Developmentally appropriate books (W-Th-F)

10:10 BREAK

10:20 Word Work
- Spelling
- Word skill lessons
- Vocabulary expansions

10:50 Project time/Independent work

11:30 Math

12:20 LUNCH

12:50 Teacher read-aloud

1:05   Specials (art [M], music [W], PE [T-Th], computer lab [F])

1:40   Social studies/science units

2:30   Health (T-Th)/PE (M-W-F)

3:00   Prepare to dismiss

3:15   Dismiss

routines within the classroom. The following steps have been used effectively by many teachers:

- Develop with students a set of classroom guidelines for general behavior. Post these where they can be easily seen (see Figure 10.24). Notice that there is space left to add new guidelines.

- Appoint one or two student monitors each week. These are the persons students can go to with questions if you are busy with a group.

FIGURE 10.23

**MR. BURGESS'S EIGHTH-GRADE SCHEDULE
(60-MINUTE PERIOD)**

Writing Workshop—M-T-W (Writing/Language—Word Work)
Reading Workshop—Th-F (Reading—Word Work)

Upon arrival	• State-of-class check
5 minutes	• Group sharing
10 minutes	• Minilesson
30 minutes	• Read/Write/Confer
10 minutes	• Partner/Class share
5 minutes	• Goal setting/Close

> ● Present and post your daily schedule for students to see. Discuss what will be happening throughout each day.

> ● Role-play the schedule and procedures with students. Create situations where problems are likely to arise (need to go to the restroom; student doesn't know a word, and so forth). Discuss and evaluate the role-playing. This may need to be done several times at the beginning of the year.

4. *Try your plans and revise as needed*   After using your schedule and routines for a few days, discuss with students how things are going. Ask for suggestions for improving or changing the schedule or any routines. Talk about how monitors are being used.

Using these four steps should help you develop an effecient management plan.

▊ Special Considerations

The four classrooms and schedules just reviewed show you a variety of ways teachers schedule. There are, however, four special considerations you must also address in scheduling: second-language learners, exceptional students, home-community connections, and multi-age classrooms.

Second-Language Learners

All four of the teachers reviewed earlier have students who are second-language learners. These students learn language just as all other students do. While they often require more patience and extra support, second-language learners participate in the same literacy learning experiences other students do. The ideas presented throughout this text work equally effectively with second-language learners.

TABLE 10.2

INDEPENDENT ACTIVITIES FOR STUDENTS TO DO WHEN WORK IS COMPLETED

- Independent reading
- Independent writing
- Response activity for a book
- Vocabulary games
- Computer activities
- Listen to tapes
- Complete other work
- Map activities
- Work on a project
- Learning centers

Exceptional Children

Our four teachers have children who are exceptional. Some have been included in the regular classroom from special education, some are gifted and talented, and others have learning disabilities. In all cases, the teachers used flexible grouping along with the various frameworks and a variety of teaching strategies to meet the needs of all students.

Home-Community Connections

Our four teachers maintain close ties with students' homes and communities. They do this by drawing on community resources, having students share at home books they have read and pieces they have written in school, and maintaining constant communications with families through conferences and newsletters. Having a continuous connection with the home is critical to the effective literacy classroom.

Multi-age Classrooms

None of the classrooms reviewed earlier are multi-age classrooms. However, many schools are moving toward the multi-age concept, whereby several ages are placed in the same class (Chapman, 1995). These classes are sometimes called "families." Within each family, students usually study a common theme. Within this theme, the teacher can use the same five frameworks described in this chapter to organize and manage instruction.

FIGURE 10.24

CLASSROOM BEHAVIOR CHART

During work times we will . . .

* Work quietly

* Go to our weekly monitors for help if Miss Janes is busy.

* Select an independent activity to do when my work is finished

Frameworks such as the developmentally appropriate books approach, reading workshop, and writing workshop are very effective in organizing the multi-age classroom. If you look back over the schedules of the first three teachers presented in the previous section, you can easily see that they could also be used for a multi-age class. The biggest mistake often made in multi-age classes is treating each age as a separate group. This is contrary to theory and research behind the multi-age concept. For more information on multi-age classrooms, see Chapman (1995), listed in the For Additional Reading section.

Intervention

The final piece in organizing a balanced literacy program is intervention. Intervention is additional instruction (usually in reading) that prevents or stops reading failure. Research has clearly demonstrated that some students will never achieve complete success in reading without additional instructional support that is given *in addition to the balanced classrooom program* that everyone receives (Snow, Burns, & Griffin, 1998).

There are many very successful intervention programs that have documented success in the research. The scope of this text does not allow full discussion of these programs. Listed below are brief descriptions of several of these programs with references as to where you can get more information about them:

EARLY INTERVENTION IN READING (E.I.R)*

A small-group intervention model for first-grade children.

Taylor, B. M., Frye, B. J., Short, R., & Shearer, B. (1992). Classroom teachers prevent reading failure among low-achieving first-grade students. *The Reading Teacher, 45,* 592–597.

READING RECOVERY*

A one-on-one tutorial program for first-grade children.

Clay, M. M. (1985). *The early detection of reading difficulties* (3rd ed.). Portsmouth, NH: Heinemann.

Pinnell, G. S., Fried, M. D., & Estice, R. M. (1990). Reading recovery: Learning how to make a difference. *The Reading Teacher, 43,* 282–295.

FACILITATING READING FOR OPTIMUM GROWTH (F.R.O.G.)

A small-group intervention program for first and second grade children.

Allington, R. L., & Walmsley, S. A. (eds.). (1995). *No quick fix: Rethinking literacy programs in America's elementary schools* (p. 148). New York: Teachers College Press.

RIGHT START*

A small-group intervention program for first-grade children.

Hiebert, E. H., Colt, J. M., Catto, S. L., & Gury, E. C. (1992). Reading and writing of first-grade students in a restructured Chapter I program. *American Educational Research Journal, 29,* 545–572.

SOAR TO SUCCESS

A small-group intervention program utilizing reciprocal teaching for students in grades 3–6.

Cooper, J. D., Boschken, I., McWilliams, J., & Pistochini, L. (1998). *Soar to Success: The intermediate intervention program,* Levels 3–6. Boston: Houghton Mifflin Company.

Cooper, J. D., Boschken, I., McWilliams, J., & Pistochini, L. (1997). *A study of the effectiveness of an intervention program designed to accelerate reading for struggling readers in the upper grades—Final report.* Available from Houghton Mifflin Company, Boston, MA.

*This book contains references to all starred programs:

Hiebert, E., & Taylor, B. (Eds.). (1994). *Getting reading right from the start: Effective early literacy interventions.* Needham Heights, MA: Allyn & Bacon.

■ Summary

This chapter focused on developing a balanced literacy classroom. Such classrooms promote success and prevent failure. Organizing and managing the balanced literacy classroom should be based on what we know about how students develop literacy.

Effective organization and management considers space, materials, conferences, and records to be kept. Flexible grouping is a key technique that should be used in the five frameworks presented for organizing the balanced literacy classroom. The chapter also presented sample schedules and a system for developing management routines.

Literature

Byars, B. (1970). *The summer of the swans.* New York: Viking Penguin.

Cummings, P. (1991). *Clean your room Harvey Moon.* New York: Bradbury Press.

de Hamel, J. (1985). *Hemi's pet.* Auckland: Reed Methuen Publishers.

Gilman, P. (1988). *The wonderful pigs of Jillian Jiggs.* New York: Scholastic Inc.

Lowry, L. (1989). *Number the stars.* Boston: Houghton Mifflin.

Mollel, T. M. (1995). *Big boy.* New York: Clarion.

Park, B. (1987). *The kid in the red jacket.* New York: Random House.

Patent, D. H. (1992). *Pelicans.* New York: Clarion.

Prelutsky, J. (1988). *Tyrannosaurus was a beast.* New York: Greenwillow Books.

Shaw, N. (1986). *Sheep in a jeep.* Boston: Houghton Mifflin.

Soto, G. (1993). *Too many tamales.* New York: G. P. Putnam's Sons.

Walker, D. R. (1993). *Head for the hills!* New York: Random House.

Williams, S. (1990). *Mommy doesn't know my name.* Boston: Houghton Mifflin.

For Additional Reading

Allington, R. L., & Walmsley, S. A. (Eds.). (1995). *No quick fix: Rethinking literacy programs in America's elementary schools.* New York: Teachers College Press.

Chapman, M. L. (1995). Designing literacy learning experiences in a multiage classroom. *Language Arts, 72*(8), pp. 416–428.

Cunningham, P., & Allington, R. L. (1994). *Classrooms that work: They can all read and write.* New York: HarperCollins.

Hiebert, E., & Taylor, B. (Eds.). (1994). *Getting reading right from the start: Effective early literacy interventions.* Needham Heights, MA: Allyn & Bacon.

Assessment and Evaluation in the Balanced Literacy Classroom

11

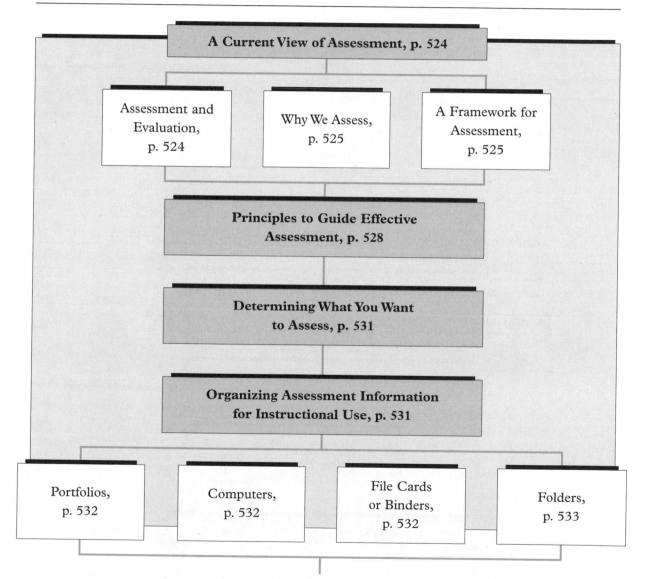

A Current View of Assessment, p. 524

Assessment and Evaluation, p. 524

Why We Assess, p. 525

A Framework for Assessment, p. 525

Principles to Guide Effective Assessment, p. 528

Determining What You Want to Assess, p. 531

Organizing Assessment Information for Instructional Use, p. 531

Portfolios, p. 532

Computers, p. 532

File Cards or Binders, p. 532

Folders, p. 533

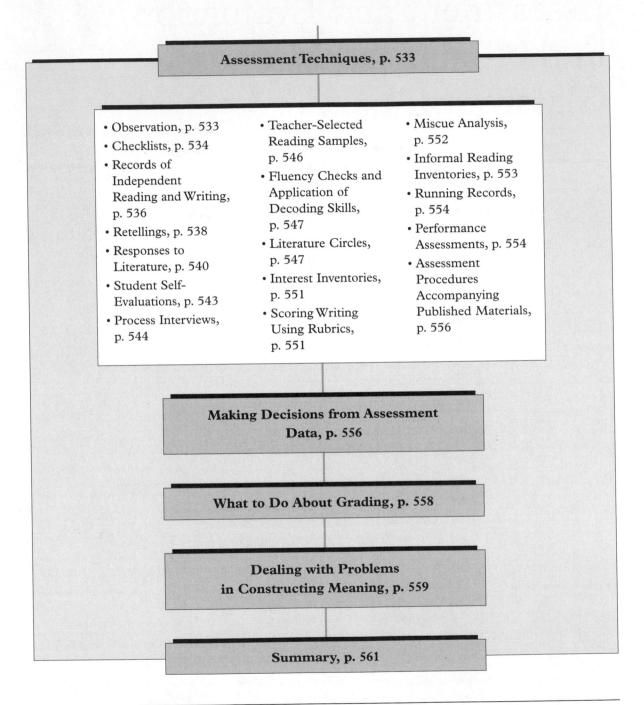

Assessment Techniques, p. 533

- Observation, p. 533
- Checklists, p. 534
- Records of Independent Reading and Writing, p. 536
- Retellings, p. 538
- Responses to Literature, p. 540
- Student Self-Evaluations, p. 543
- Process Interviews, p. 544

- Teacher-Selected Reading Samples, p. 546
- Fluency Checks and Application of Decoding Skills, p. 547
- Literature Circles, p. 547
- Interest Inventories, p. 551
- Scoring Writing Using Rubrics, p. 551

- Miscue Analysis, p. 552
- Informal Reading Inventories, p. 553
- Running Records, p. 554
- Performance Assessments, p. 554
- Assessment Procedures Accompanying Published Materials, p. 556

Making Decisions from Assessment Data, p. 556

What to Do About Grading, p. 558

Dealing with Problems in Constructing Meaning, p. 559

Summary, p. 561

Mr. Ryan is a second-grade teacher who is very concerned about the growth his students are showing in learning to construct meaning. A look at some of the activities that take place in his classroom will give us a sense of how Mr. Ryan assesses students' progress in literacy.

As we entered Mr. Ryan's second-grade classroom, we saw that the class was divided into four small literature discussion circles, each group discussing the same book, Ira Says Goodbye *(Waber, 1988). Three discussion points were listed on the chalkboard:*

1. Why Reggie acted as he did
2. Your favorite part
3. How you would feel

Mr. Ryan was seated with one of the groups, listening. At one point he joined in by saying, "When my best friend moved away, I wouldn't talk to anyone about it. How would you act if you had been in Ira's place, Lisette?"

Mr. Ryan was carrying a clipboard and a pad of adhesive notes. As he moved from one circle to the other, he jotted down observations on the adhesive papers and stuck them on sheets on the clipboard.

After the literature circles were completed, the class began self-selected, independent reading time. When it was over, some students went to a box marked "Reading and Writing Portfolios" and recorded the book they had just read.

At the end of the day, Mr. Ryan looked over the notes he had placed on the clipboard throughout the day. He had a notebook with a section for each student, and he placed some of the adhesive notes on students' pages, reading and discarding others. Then he quickly looked through the portfolios to see how much independent reading students had done and whether they had added any other pieces of writing to their portfolios.

From his notes and his examination of the portfolios, Mr. Ryan saw that all students except one were doing a lot of independent reading, so he made a note to have a conference with her as soon as possible. After seeing that several students did not seem to understand the story Ira Says *Goodbye, he listed their names so he could form a group where he will teach the skill of noting details using a story map and the text students have read.*

THINK ABOUT THIS classroom in terms of assessment, and list all the places where you thought assessment was taking place. Then compare your list to the following discussion.

Some observers may see no evidence of assessment in Mr. Ryan's classroom: what you "see" depends on your perspective on assessment and literacy learning. However, Mr. Ryan obviously believed children learn to read and write by reading and writing, and assessment was an integral part of his instructional activities. Look at all the places where this was evident:

▶ Mr. Ryan was participating in the literature circles and so was able to observe students' actual responses to *Ira Says Goodbye.*

▶ Mr. Ryan made notes as he observed various aspects of students' reading. Later he reviewed those notes and placed some of them in his notebook for use in planning future instructional activities.

▶ Students participated in their own assessment by recording books in their reading and writing portfolios that they had completed during independent reading time. Independent reading is an important part of literacy learning and assessment.

▶ At the end of the day, Mr. Ryan reviewed his notes and reviewed students' portfolios to assess their progress and plan future activities.

▶ Mr. Ryan was assessing students against their previous performances, comparing performances on current work to those on work already in their portfolios.

▶ Mr. Ryan used his observations to determine skills that should be taught.

Although this was only a small part of the overall assessment plan in Mr. Ryan's room, we begin to get a picture of how he viewed and approached assessment. In this chapter, we examine some basic ideas about how to develop assessment that are in line with the overall concept of the balanced literacy program stressed throughout this text. We will focus on the classroom, giving only minor attention to the overall school literacy program. *The material in this chapter should be viewed as a basic framework for thinking about assessment in the balanced literacy classroom.*

A Current View of Assessment

Over the last twenty to thirty years, assessment in reading has focused primarily on measuring students' performance on skill elements. For example, it has been the normal practice to give students tests to determine whether they have mastered certain skills. These practices were based on the belief that students learn to read and write only by learning a collection of skills that were viewed as integral parts of reading and writing and could be taught and tested.

The constructive, interactive view of literacy learning has given us different views on assessment. Practices in literacy assessment are beginning to reflect what we know about literacy learning. Because of Mr. Ryan's view of literacy learning, he was developing a different perspective on assessment.

Assessment and Evaluation

Although the terms *assessment* and *evaluation* are often used interchangeably within the field of education and especially within the field of literacy, they really represent different aspects of related processes (Bertrand, 1991). *Assessment* is the process of gathering information about something (getting students to respond), and *evaluation* is the process of judging that information (judging students' responses) to determine how well individuals are achieving or have achieved what they or someone else expects them to achieve. For example, asking a student to retell a story is assessment; you are asking that student to respond. Then, when you judge the accuracy of the retelling and give it a score or a grade, you are evaluating the response.

In the balanced literacy classroom, procedures for assessment and evaluation are not as cut and dried as they were in classrooms where teachers often gave students a test and expected students to achieve a score of at least 80 percent. If they achieved that score, it was assumed they knew whatever the test was supposed to measure. If they came up short, teachers simply retaught what the test was claimed to measure and then retested the students. However, teachers often saw students who could pass the skills tests but could not read or write, and vice versa. What was being assessed and evaluated in this classroom clearly was not reflecting the full processes of reading and writing.

Assessment and evaluation must go together in the balanced literacy classroom: one has no value without the other. A beginning step in planning for assessment in your classroom is to think about why you are assessing students.

Why We Assess

Many educators have strong negative feelings about many or all aspects of assessment and evaluation. Among their concerns are (1) procedures that do not assess what is being taught, (2) separation of assessment from instruction, (3) misuses of assessment data, and (4) cultural biases of tests. Even in light of these and other issues, there are still some strong reasons for having assessment and evaluation procedures in all classrooms, and especially in the balanced literacy classroom.

First, all teachers need ways to determine what students are learning and the progress they are making. This information provides the basis for making decisions, planning instructional activities and experiences, and distinguishing effective from ineffective procedures. Assessment must be viewed as something that goes hand in hand with instruction (Boyer, 1995). Second, effective assessment helps students take ownership of their learning, seeing and planning ways to foster their own literacy growth. When students think about and reflect on their learning, they become more active participants in the process. Finally, good assessment procedures signal to the community that schools are doing an effective job of helping children develop literacy.

A Framework for Assessment

As you begin to think about assessment in your classroom, you will need to understand a number of concepts and terms. Table 11.1 presents a selected list of these terms and their definitions. Most of them will be discussed in more detail throughout this chapter. You may want to review these terms before reading further.

Assessment may be considered in terms of two broad categories: informal and formal. *Informal assessment* utilizes observations and other nonstandardized procedures; *formal assessment* utilizes standardized procedures or procedures carried out under controlled conditions (Harris & Hodges, 1995). Examples of informal assessments include the use of checklists, observations, and performance assessments or tasks. Informal assessments are clearly and easily made a part of instruction. Formal assessments include such tests as state tests, standardized achievement tests, or tests accompanying a published program. These formal types of assessment are not embedded in instruction, but they *must reflect* the *instruction* to be of value in assessing students' literacy development. The standardized achievement test is most useful in evaluating overall program growth as opposed to evaluating individual student progress or determining instructional needs.

Standardized tests have been widely criticized for a number of reasons (Tyler & White in Farr and Carey, 1986):

1. Tests do not reflect the full range of student cultural backgrounds and thus lead to decisions that are often unfair to minority students.

TABLE 11.1

ASSESSMENT TERMINOLOGY

TERM	DESCRIPTION
Authentic assessment	Assessment activities that reflect literacy in the community, the workplace, and the instructional activities of the classroom. *Example:* Students write a letter to the editor about an environmental problem; the letter may be used to assess and evaluate students' writing abilities and skills. (See also *performance assessment.*)
Benchmarks (standards)	Statements of expectations of what students are to learn, usually given grade by grade or age by age. *Example:* Firsts graders will orally read age/grade appropriate text with 90% accuracy.
Checklist	A form that lists targeted behaviors as indicators of achievement, knowledge, or skill. *Example:* An oral language checklist that a kindergarten teacher might use.
Formal assessment	A test or task utilizing procedures that are carried out under controlled conditions. *Example:* A state-level competency test.
Grade score/grade equivalent	A score transformed from a raw score on a standardized test that is the equivalent earned by an average student in the norming group; these scores are *not* recommended for use because they may be misleading. *Example:* A grade 3 student scores 7.1 on a reading comprehension test but was never tested on passages at the grade 7 level.
Informal assessment	Observations or other nonstandardized procedures. *Example:* A teacher-made checklist.
Informal reading inventory (IRI)	A series of graded passages used to determine students' levels of reading and strengths and needs in decoding and comprehension. (See also *miscue* and *running record.*) *Example:* Most published reading series have passages that correlate with their materials.

Miscue	An oral reading response that differs from the text; may be analyzed to assess a student's reading development. (See also *informal reading inventory* and *running record.*)
	Example: A student reads the following sentence with the miscues noted:
	
	      pony
	The horse/ galloped so
	     (1)
	fast that the man was thrown
	           ark night
	through the air/ at lightning/
	        (2) (3)
	 sky
	speed/.
	 (4)

TABLE 11.1

ASSESSMENT TERMINOLOGY, *continued*

TERM	DESCRIPTION
	Miscue 1 does not change meaning; miscues 2, 3, and 4 do change meaning and should be analyzed further.
Percentile	A score on a scale of 100 showing the percentage of a distribution that is equal to or below it. *Example:* A score at the 70th percentile is equal to or better than 70 percent of the scores of others on whom the test was normed.
Performance assessment	A task that requires the student to demonstrate his or her level of knowledge and skill by making a response such as that required in instruction or the real world. (See also *authentic assessment.*) *Example:* A student is asked to construct a model of a catapult. The task requires the student to demonstrate such abilities as reading, following directions, and so forth.
Reflection	The process by which students and/or the teacher look back at what they have learned, discussing how it has helped them, where they might use it, and what they might concentrate on next. *Example:* After students have read a text with emphasis on certain strategies, they discuss with the teacher and peers how the strategies helped them construct meaning.
Rubric	A set of guidelines or acceptable responses for the completion of a task. *Example:* A rubric for assessing the writing quality of a story would include being able to identify the story elements (setting, character[s], problem, action, outcome) and a 4-point scale in which 4 is high, 3 is average, 2 is low, 1 is inadequate, and 0 indicates insufficient material.
Running record	A written record of a student's oral reading in which a blank sheet of paper rather than a copy of the actual text is used in coding. *Example:* A first-grade teacher has a student read aloud a previously read book, noting the correct and incorrect words.
Standard score	A score that tells how far an individual is from the average score (mean) on a test in terms of the standard deviation. Standard scores are most commonly used on standardized tests. *Example:* A student scores 60 on a test; the standard deviation is 5, and the average (mean) score is 55. This student is one standard deviation above average.
Standardized test	A test given under specified conditions allowing comparisons to be made; a set of norms or average scores are given to allow comparisons. *Example: Metropolitan Achievement Tests; Iowa Test of Basic Skills*

2. Current standardized tests have only limited value for holding teachers, schools, and school systems accountable for the quality of education.
3. Tests impose a limiting effect on classroom teaching.
4. Tests are too narrow in scope to provide fair evaluation of new approaches to teaching. (p. 11)

Although these criticisms were made about standardized tests in general, they also apply to tests that have been used to assess and evaluate literacy learning and construction of meaning. The problems with existing standardized testing, combined with what we have learned about how children actually develop literacy, have led some educators to conclude that norm-referenced tests were of little instructional value to teachers (Harp, 1991).

Even in light of these criticisms, many educators recognize that school districts will continue to use norm-referenced, standardized tests to evaluate literacy programs (Pikulski, 1990b). However, these tests are being changed to better match what we know about learning (Pikulski, 1990b). Changes are occurring in state competency tests and in the National Assessment of Educational Progress (NAEP, 1990a, 1990b). Some of the changes being made include

▶ Not testing isolated skills

▶ Using full-length, authentic texts to assess meaning construction

▶ Accounting for students' prior knowledge before reading

▶ Incorporating a broader concept of assessment by collecting samples of student work

▶ Incorporating some type of student self-assessment

Although these changes will not perfect the various tests used throughout our educational systems, they will begin to move assessment closer to what we know about literacy learning and effective literacy instruction. At some point in the near future, teachers may even be able to use the new norm-referenced tests to help them plan instruction.

It is critical that we prove to our communities that our programs are successfully helping students develop literacy, especially as we try new instructional techniques. Failure to do this will result in a return to practices that we have learned are not as valuable to students as we once thought. The only way to prevent this return to the past is to "move assessment activities closer to the actual work of teachers and children; we must make classrooms the starting points for linking learning to large educational and social purposes" (Perrone, 1991, p. 164).

Principles to Guide Effective Assessment

As you begin to plan for informal and formal assessment in your classroom, you should consider the eight principles outlined in this section. Numerous researchers and educators have developed guidelines for balanced literacy assessment (Farr & Tone, 1994; Harp, 1991; Valencia, 1990a, 1990b; Valencia, Hiebert, & Afflerbach, 1994). The principles presented here are based in part on their ideas and this author's personal interpretations of this research while working with teachers.

1. Assessment should be an ongoing process.   Literacy assessment is not a test given at the end of a unit or a block of study, separate from the ongoing daily activities of instruction. Instead, assessment should take place every time a child reads, writes, speaks, listens, or views something. When assessment is viewed as an ongoing part of instruction, it becomes natural and expected.

2. Effective assessment is an integral part of instruction.   The best forms of assessment are the routine daily activities of instruction, which tell us exactly how our students are performing. By comparing the work of individual students over time, we can determine patterns of growth. When a student writes a story about her trip to visit friends, you can assess her ability to organize ideas, express herself, and use the various conventions of language. Overall, you get a picture of how effectively she constructs meaning through writing. Throughout my years of teaching and working with teachers, many teachers have said, "There was no reason to give that test. I already knew what my kids could do from their daily activities." In other words, we must learn to trust our judgments as we make them from evidence gathered during instruction.

3. Assessment must be authentic, reflecting "real" reading and writing.
For years, I have asked teachers in workshops and classes, "If you want to know how well children read and write, what do you need to have them do?" They have always replied in unison, "Have them read and write." The tasks of assessment in a balanced literacy classroom must reflect and honor the "wholeness" of language (Harp, 1991). It is possible for learners to be very effective readers and writers and not do well on a test covering an isolated piece of the process. For example, when a student reads the wonderful Roald Dahl book *Esio Trot* (1990), and writes a response to it, it is possible to authentically assess his or her ability to construct meaning.

4. Assessment should be a collaborative, reflective process.   It should not be viewed as something the teacher does *to* the students. We know learning is a collaborative process; we learn alongside and with our students and our peers (Collins, Brown, & Newman, 1986). If this is true for learning, it is also true for assessment. As students collaborate with their teacher on assessment, they reflect and ask themselves, "How have I done?" "What can I do to improve?" "How can I use what I have learned?" Thus, students should help you assess and evaluate their own progress in literacy. I learned this the hard way many years ago from a fifth-grade student named Paul. Paul was an excellent student. He could read and critically discuss anything I put in his hands. However, I often asked Paul to read aloud because he wasn't a good oral reader. I then decided he needed to be placed in a lower-level book group, but he still couldn't read aloud. Finally, I asked Paul what he thought his problem was. He was not only very intelligent but also very outspoken. He said, "I don't have a problem. When are you going to learn that I don't like to read out loud?" Needless to say, I learned pretty fast! It turned out that Paul could construct meaning better than any other fifth grader I had that year.

Collaboration means students sometimes help select *what* they want evaluated. This becomes a joint effort in which teacher and students work and think together, and should also involve parents and other caregivers (Dillon, 1990). When students, teacher, and parents collaborate on evaluation, the responsibility is shared, as it should be.

5. Effective assessment is multidimensional.   Quality assessment should use several different tasks, such as samples of writing, student retellings, records of independent reading, self-evaluations, and checklists. In making these choices, you need to trust your own intuition based on your knowledge and observations about students. More formal types of assessments have proclaimed their validity and reliability using various statistical procedures. Although many of the techniques being suggested today are more informal, we must still know that they are *trustworthy* (Valencia, 1990a), and one way to determine this is to use multiple tasks to get a consistent pattern of performance. Cambourne and Turbill (1990) argue that data generated from multiple sources using teacher observations and judgments are just as trustworthy and "scientific" as those generated by what have been called "measurement-based" approaches to assessment.

6. Assessment should be developmentally and culturally appropriate.   We know children develop literacy and their ability to construct meaning by "trying out" their reading and writing and making approximations. Therefore, tests or procedures that require absolute mastery at a given level or complete mastery of a given set of words before moving to a new book are *completely contrary* to how we know children learn. We must select assessment tasks that honor children's developmental levels of learning.

At the same time, we must consider the cultural diversity of our classrooms. Children from different cultures have not only different language bases but also different patterns and styles of learning (Au, 1993; Garcia, 1994). We must take these into consideration as we plan our assessment procedures.

7. Effective assessment identifies students' strengths.   Children learn to construct meaning by doing what they already know how to do and by getting support in gaining new strategies and techniques. Effective assessment therefore must help us identify what our students do well. For many years, we have given students tests to find out what they do *not* know; then we proceeded to plan lessons totally around these weaknesses. This is contrary to how students acquire language and contrary to how they learn to construct meaning.

8. Assessment must be based on what we know about how students learn to read and write.   This entire text has focused on how students learn to read and write and construct meaning. Clearly, we know assessment has not kept pace with our knowledge about reading and writing. We know the two processes are similar but different. We also know they develop together and produce benefits that are attainable by neither one alone (Tierney & Shanahan, 1991). And we know reading and writing are both constructive processes. As we plan assessment tasks, we must keep this knowledge in mind, incorporating new knowledge as it becomes available.

We should always remember that we are a part of our students' learning processes. We are working *with* them, not *on* them. In the remainder of this chapter, we focus on ideas and techniques for applying these eight principles to the balanced literacy classroom.

Determining What You Want to Assess

Assessment must be based on goals. What do we want students to do? How will we know if they are learning to do it? What is the overall goal of the balanced literacy classroom? We want students to develop their ability to construct meaning through reading and writing and to assume responsibility for their own learning. Therefore, this is what we want to assess.

Since students in the balanced literacy classroom are writing and reading every day, it should be easy to assess this activity. Assessment can be an integral and natural part of instruction (what Cambourne and Turbill [1990] call a "natural" theory of assessment) in which the routine daily activities of reading and writing also serve as the assessment activities.

Au, Scheu, Kawakami, and Herman (1990) have taken the idea of what to assess in a balanced literacy classroom one step further. Maintaining that the overall goal of the literacy program is effective construction of meaning through reading and writing, they have identified a literacy curriculum framework that contains six aspects: (1) ownership, (2) reading comprehension, (3) writing process, (4) word identification, (5) language and vocabulary knowledge, and (6) voluntary reading. They believe that "students' ownership of literacy is the overarching goal in the framework, and its position highlights the affective dimension of literacy development" (Au et al., 1990, p. 575).

On the basis of these aspects of literacy, Au and her colleagues have identified everyday instructional experiences that can serve as assessment tasks. Designated tasks become a part of each student's literacy portfolio (discussed later in this chapter) and are used by the teacher to determine each student's growth in literacy development.

Another concern is deciding what to expect of students each year in school. These yearly expectations, referred to as *benchmarks* (Cambourne & Turbill, 1990) or *performance standards,* serve as guideposts to help the teacher determine the progress students are making in literacy development. Many states and school districts are identifying benchmarks as guideposts for instruction and assessment (Garrett, 1993). For a detailed look at how to use standards and benchmarks to plan instruction, see *Literacy Assessment: Helping Teachers Plan Instruction* (Cooper & Kiger, in press) listed in For Additional Reading.

Organizing Assessment Information for Instructional Use

The primary reason for assessing what students have done is to help you plan the instructional activities and experiences you will need to provide to help students continue to improve their literacy development. Instruction is assessment; in other words, every instructional activity is an assessment activity. By looking at how students perform during instruction, you are able to get a sense of what they are learning and using in terms of reading, writing, speaking, listening, thinking, and viewing. Many times your observations during instruction become your best assessment tools.

There are three guiding principles that will help you use assessment information for instructional purposes:

1. *Organize.*   For the information you gather to be helpful to you in planning instruction, it must be organized in a way that is useful to you. It doesn't matter how you organize it. It only matters that you *do organize it.*

2. *Review.*   You must review the information on a regular basis. A regular basis means daily or weekly. This means that you are constantly looking at how students are performing and deciding what needs to happen next. This is what Cooper and Kiger (in press) call assessment-based literacy instruction.

3. *Update.*   Updating information is really a part of the reviewing process. As you are continuously reviewing how students are performing, you should also add new information and/or revise information you have. We often think we will remember what students have done. It is easy to forget, especially when dealing with large numbers of students.

The remainder of this section will present four alternatives for organizing assessment information. This is followed by a section on assessment techniques. You should select the organizational procedure and techniques that will work best for you.

Portfolios

Portfolios are collections of an individual student's work gathered over time. Many schools have moved to a portfolio concept for organizing all of their assessment data. These portfolios are passed on from teacher to teacher. The primary purpose of the portfolio is to present a picture of each student's performance and progress over time.

Many schools have a master version of the portfolio that is passed on from year to year. Individual teachers keep more specific daily instructional information in one of the other forms described in the following sections. For more information on portfolios, see For Additional Reading.

Computers

With the increasing use of computers comes new ways to organize information for quick retrieval and use. Individual teachers and entire school systems are making more use of the computer as a way to organize and store assessment data. You will want to explore whether such options are available in your school and/or district.

File Cards or Binders

Many teachers like to use 5" × 8" file cards or binders to keep records of students' performance. The type of information you keep is structured by a checklist of some type (see the section on assessment techniques). Each student is assigned a file card or a section in the notebook. The teacher can then refer to it easily on a daily basis.

Folders

Teachers have for years used folders of work to keep track of how each student is performing. This is much like using a portfolio. Like the portfolio, for this technique to be effective, it must have an organizational structure. This is usually done using some type of checklist.

Assessment Techniques

Assessment as discussed in this chapter is a dynamic and interactive process that is an integral part of instruction. Instruction and assessment blend into one ongoing activity. You can use many different techniques as part of this process. Many blend naturally into instruction; others give you a somewhat more formal way to assess student progress.

Since the overall goal of literacy learning is meaning construction, the techniques suggested in this section look at either the process as a whole or an important aspect of the process. Most of them can be easily used on the basis of the information given here; appropriate references are given for those that require more detailed study. As you study and review these techniques, you should be thinking about those that will be most advantageous to you in your classroom and those you need to learn more about. *You do not need to use them all.*

Observation

In balanced literacy classrooms, assessment and evaluation are based on a combination of formal and informal techniques, and many of these are highly dependent on observing students as they read and write. "Kid watching" (Goodman, 1986), as it is frequently described, is the process of observing students as they perform authentic literacy tasks or looking at the results of those tasks.

You learn to be an observer of children by first realizing that observation is a powerful and reliable part of your assessment and evaluation process. Observations must be based on what you know about how children learn to read and write. Therefore, you need to understand what responses are expected and typical and what responses might indicate a need for more or different support. For example, the first grader who writes a sentence about his *dg* is not misspelling the word *dog*; rather, he is making an approximation that shows he is learning the spelling pattern in the word *dog*. Therefore, this student would benefit from more shared reading experiences with natural, repetitive language and words following the type of spelling pattern found in the word *dog*, as well as many opportunities to continue writing his own stories.

As a teacher, you must develop the habit of always looking, thinking, and asking, "What does this mean?" Opportunities to observe students are unlimited and include

▶ Listening to a student read aloud

▶ Watching students give a play

▶ Reading and noting how a student has written a response to a story

▶ Analyzing a student's written report

▶ Listening to and studying what students say as they give oral reports

▶ Listening to dialogue between two students waiting in line for lunch

Nearly every classroom activity can be used for some form of observation of literacy learning, and all of these observations can become the data on a checklist or a note placed in a literacy portfolio.

When you observe, you must keep in mind that good assessment is multidimensional. Therefore, one observation is not sufficient: you must look at several observations over time, watching for patterns of performance. It is from these patterns that you can assess and evaluate students' ability to construct meaning.

Many techniques can be combined with observation or used in addition to observation to help you become an effective observer. As you gain more experience with observation, you will become more and more comfortable. You will soon realize that instruction and assessment are really one ongoing process. Figure 11.1 shows some sample observation notes made by Mrs. Ehrman in her third-grade class. She used self-adhesive notes and put the student's initials and the date on each. These notes could then be easily transferred to the student's portfolio.

Checklists

Checklists are an excellent tool for observing various aspects of your students' ability to construct meaning. They may be developed in general areas related to meaning construction, such as reading, writing, speaking, listening, and viewing, or be developed for specific aspects of literacy learning, such as concepts of print or story retelling.

Each checklist should contain the qualities or traits you are looking for and some procedure for recording what you observe. Sometimes the checklists can be developmental (Cockrum & Castillo, 1991), particularly if they are language-related checklists. Other checklists simply help you look for the presence or absence of the traits.

The checklist shown in Figure 11.2 for assessing ownership can be used at any grade level. The teacher indicates the presence of a particular trait and comments on it or on the students' overall development of ownership. Checklists may be compared over time to see how the students' ownership or attitudes and habits change.

More general checklists, such as that shown in Figure 11.3, may also be used. This list, which would be included in the literacy portfolio, has four places to record observations during the school year. It can be completed by the teacher, the student, or both.

You will often want to develop your own checklists for the particular thing(s) you want to observe. There are many sources of checklists, including curriculum guides, textbooks, and journal articles. You can take an existing checklist and adapt it to fit your needs. Some checklists can be developed for group observations (Figure 11.2) and others for individual observations (Figure 11.3).

FIGURE 11.1

OBSERVATION NOTES FROM MRS. EHRMAN'S THIRD-GRADE CLASS

10/14 M. R. Asks for help when a word is not known; does not try his own strategies.	10/14 M.L.C. Self corrects many temporary spellings during revision.
10/14 I.S. Could use a mini-lesson on quotations; experimented with them in writing.	10/14 R.B. Referred to glossary for word meanings and spellings during reading and writing. Much improved.
10/14 B.T. Is having trouble selecting appropriate books; needs guidance.	10/14 R.M. Retelling showed much improvement in story comp. Needs more exp. text.

FIGURE 11.2

CHECKLIST FOR OWNERSHIP OF READING

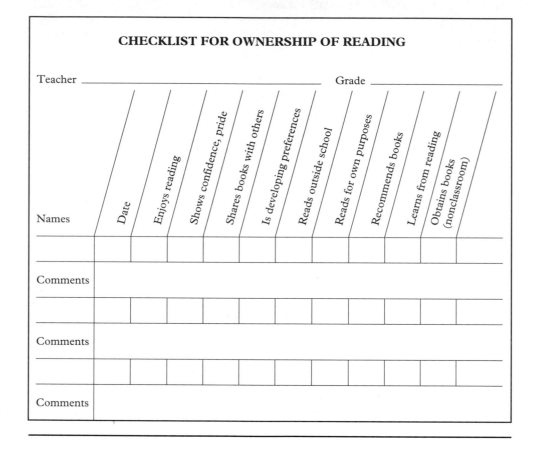

Checklist for ownership from "Assessment of students' ownership of literacy," Kathryn H. Au, Judith A. Scheu, and Alice J. Kawakami, *The Reading Teacher*, October 1990. Reprinted with permission of Kathryn H. Au and the International Reading Association.

Records of Independent Reading and Writing

An important factor to consider in assessing students' meaning construction is the amount of self-selected, independent reading and writing they do. These records may be kept in journals or learning logs where students record their independent reading or do their writing. However, it is often useful to have a form that summarizes this information to place in the student's literacy portfolio. Figures 11.4 and 11.5 present forms you can use to record independent reading.

FIGURE 11.3

CHECKLIST FOR MEANING CONSTRUCTION

Construction of Meaning

Name _____

Date	1	2	3	4
Retells stories and text accurately				
Gives responses to stories and text that show understanding				
Conveys meaning through written stories and reports				
Conveys meaning through spoken language				

Comments:
CODE:
+ = very effectively
√ = effectively
− = needs improvement
NO = Not Observed

FIGURE 11.4

INDEPENDENT READING RECORD

Name _____

Date Completed	Title and Author	Comments

Chapter 7 contains forms for summarizing writing pieces that have been started, completed, and published.

Retellings

Retellings are powerful tools because they are one of the most authentic techniques you can use for both instructional and assessment purposes (Gambrell, Pfeiffer, & Wilson, 1985; Marshall, 1983; Morrow, 1989). Though retellings integrate instruction and assessment, here we focus only on using them as assessment tools.

"Retellings are postreading or postlistening recalls in which readers or listeners tell what they remember either orally or in writing" (Morrow, 1989, p. 40). By studying the students' retellings, you can gain insights into their thinking, organization, and general understanding of what they have read or listened to. For instance, you can learn how they identify important information, make inferences, and summarize information. This is one of the most effective techniques for holistically assessing the process of meaning construction.

Retellings can be used with both narrative and expository texts. By comparing students' retellings over time, you can determine their progress in learning to construct meaning. In addition, each retelling can be used diagnostically to help you develop support activities.

Morrow (1989) has given very complete guidelines for using retellings as assessment tools. The following guidelines are based on her suggestions as well as on my own experiences in working with children and teachers.

FIGURE 11.5

MORE ELABORATE FORM OF RECORDING INDEPENDENT READING

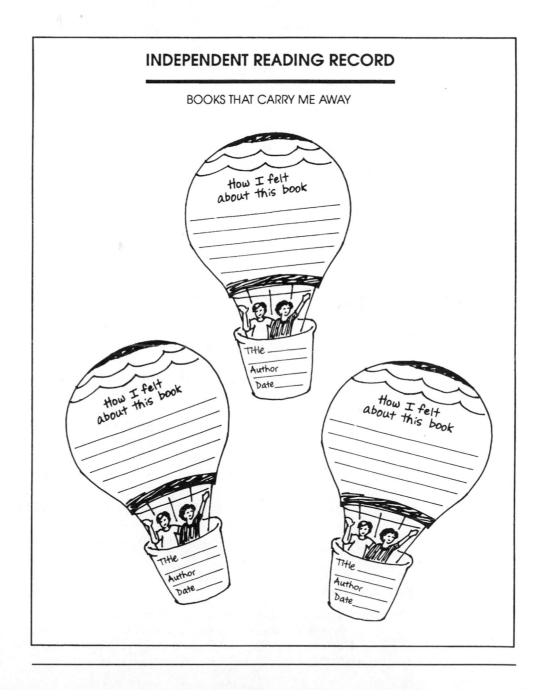

INDEPENDENT READING RECORD

BOOKS THAT CARRY ME AWAY

Guidelines for Using Retellings for Assessment

Selecting the Text.   Select the story or informational text (expository text) that students are to read, or have students make the selection. If you are comparing students' retellings over time, use the same type of texts each time; for example, compare narrative with narrative and expository with expository. As texts are selected, examine them to be sure their conceptual difficulty is not drastically different. In other words, don't compare retellings from a simple text such as *Cranberries* (Jaspersohn, 1991) with a more complex text such as *Franklin Delano Roosevelt* (Freedman, 1990).

Preparing the Text.   Read the text yourself. With stories, identify the setting (place and time if important), characters, problem, action (events leading to outcome), and outcome or resolution. For informational texts, identify the topic, purpose, and main ideas. List this information on a sheet of paper.

Reading and Retelling the Text.   Have the student read the text silently. (If you are using this as a listening experience, read the text to the students.) This should be treated as a routine instructional activity. Immediately following the reading, ask the student to retell the story or text. Do not prompt initial retellings, except for generic prompts such as "Tell me more" or "Keep going; you're doing a nice job."

As students give their retellings, check off the ideas given on the paper you prepared earlier. After they have completed their unprompted retellings, you may then prompt them with questions about specific parts of the story or text that they did not include in their unprompted retellings.

Summarizing and Evaluating the Retelling.   Figures 11.6 and 11.7 present sheets you can use for summarizing each student's retelling. Each retelling has a possible score of 10, and the guidelines for scoring each retelling are basically the same. One point is given for correct responses, and exceptions to this rule are given on the summary sheets. In scoring retellings, use your own judgment and your observations.

After scoring each retelling, you can examine it to determine whether the student understands the story or text, has ideas well organized, or has used various strategies. You will then want to discuss and review the retelling with the student. This information can help you develop instructional experiences. As Morrow (1989) notes, retellings can develop essentially the same skills and processes they assess.

Responses to Literature

The importance of students' responding to literature was discussed in Chapter 6. The type of response given *may* help indicate how the student has constructed meaning. For example, the student who continuously says or writes such things as "I liked it," "It was funny," or "The best part was _____" may not be

FIGURE 11.6

RETELLING SUMMARY SHEET FOR NARRATIVE TEXT

Story Retelling Summary Sheet

Name _____ Date _____

Title _____

Student selected _____ Teacher selected _____

	Scores	
	Unprompted	*Prompted*

Setting:
  Begins with introduction (1 pt.)   _____   _____

  Gives time and place (1 pt.)   _____   _____

Characters:
  Names main character (1 pt.)   _____   _____

  Identifies other characters (1 pt.)   _____   _____

      Gives names _____
      Gives number _____
      Actual number _____
      Number given _____

Problem:
  Identifies primary story problem (1 pt.)   _____   _____

Action:
  Recalls major events (1 pt.)   _____   _____

Outcome:
  Identifies how problem was solved (1 pt.)   _____   _____

  Gives story ending (1 pt.)   _____   _____

Sequence:
  Retells story in order (2 pts. = correct;   _____   _____
  1 pt. = partial, 0 = no evidence of sequence)

                          TOTAL SCORE   _____   _____
                          (10 pts. possible)

Observations/comments:

Analysis:

Source: Adapted from L. M. Morrow, Using story retelling to develop comprehension, in K. D. Muth, ed., *Children's comprehension of text: Research into practice,* pp. 37–58 (Newark, DE: International Reading Association, 1989).

FIGURE 11.7

RETELLING SUMMARY SHEET FOR INFORMATIONAL TEXT

Informational Text Retelling Summary Sheet

Name _____ Date _____

Title _____

Student selected _____ Teacher selected _____

	Scores	
	Unprompted	*Prompted*
Introduction:		
Identifies topic (1 pt.)	_____	_____
Gives some purpose or focus (1 pt.)	_____	_____

Main Ideas:
    Number given _____
    Actual number _____
    (6 pts. = all correct; 4 pts. = 2/3 correct;
    2 pts. = 1/3 correct; 0 pts. = none correct)

| Shows logical understanding of how ideas are related; explains ideas (2 pts. = relates all ideas; 1 pt. = relates some ideas; 0 pts. = shows no relationship of ideas) | _____ | _____ |

TOTAL SCORE   _____   _____
(10 pts. possible)

Observations/comments:

Analysis:

---

processing or understanding what was read, or perhaps has not learned to respond to literature and needs more support and prompting from the teacher (see Chapter 6). The student who gave the following response to *Where the Red Fern Grows* (Rawls, 1974) demonstrated in her journal that she had constructed appropriate meaning from this book:

> Billy's love for his dogs is like my love for my cat Prince. I had to work hard to get Prince. I love him so much. Billy learned how important love was. I did to. Everybody needs somebody to love.

As you encourage students to respond to literature, you will need to develop some criteria for evaluating those responses. The following questions should be helpful:

1. Does the response show that the student knows the story line (narrative) or main ideas (expository) of the text?
2. Did the student simply retell the text or relate it to his or her own experiences?
3. Does the response show that the student is thinking clearly and logically?
4. Does the response show that the student is using any skills or strategies?

How would you evaluate the response given to *Where the Red Fern Grows* using these questions?

Many teachers use a simple form such as the one in Figure 11.8 to evaluate students' responses to literature. They then attach the evaluations to the response and place it in the portfolio. Teachers also use this evaluation for grading purposes.

Student Self-Evaluations

Student self-evaluations have been recommended as a vital part of assessing and evaluating meaning construction (Flood & Lapp, 1989; Tierney, Carter, & Desai, 1991). You can promote these evaluations very easily by asking students to write in their journals about the progress they are making in reading and writing. Self-evaluation can be prompted by such questions as the following:

- How do you feel you are doing in reading/writing?
- What are your strengths in reading/writing?
- What do you enjoy the most about reading/writing?
- What do you feel you need to do to improve your reading/writing?

FIGURE 11.8

FORM FOR EVALUATING RESPONSES TO LITERATURE

Constructing Meaning Evaluation

Name _____ Date _____

Title _____

Circle one:

$+$	$\sqrt{}$	0
Shows thorough understanding	Shows some understanding	Needs support in developing understanding

Comments:

Another way to get students to evaluate their construction of meaning is by giving them a form such as the one in Figure 11.9 to evaluate their understanding of what they read. The form can be completed periodically and placed in the literacy portfolio. Similar types of self-evaluation forms may also be completed for writing.

Self-evaluation is important in helping students learn to monitor their own reading and writing. The actual process of self-evaluation needs to be taught to students as they use it. For example, they can use a checklist such as the one in Figure 11.10 to evaluate how they have used various strategies as they read a text. As a part of the teaching, you would model the process for students. This type of checklist can be shortened to include only those strategies students have learned.

Process Interviews

Learning more about students' metacognitive development, or how they "think about their reading," is important in helping them learn to construct meaning (Baker & Brown, 1984a, b; Brown, 1980). To assess students' thinking about their reading, Paratore and Indrisano (1987) developed a procedure known as the *process interview,* sometimes called a *reading interview.* It consists of the following questions:

1. *How do you choose something to read?*
2. *How do you get ready to read?*

FIGURE 11.9

FORM FOR SELF-EVALUATION OF READING

Self-Evaluation of Reading

Name_____ Date_____

Book read_____

Mark the scale below:

|—————————————————|—————————————————|—————————————————|

I feel that   I don't
I thoroughly   feel that
understood   I understood
this book.   this book.

Why I marked the scale as I did:

_____

_____

_____

_____

3. *When you come to a word you can't read, what do you do?*

4. *When you have a question you can't answer, what do you do?*

5. *What do you do to help remember what you've read?*

6. *How do you check your reading?*

7. *If a young child asked you how to read, what would you tell him or her to do?* (Paratore & Indrisano, 1987, p. 782)

After a student orally answers the questions and you record the responses, you analyze them to see what type of support the student needs. For example, a student who answers question 6 even after prompting by saying that she "looks for pictures" does not have a good set of monitoring strategies. It might be helpful to teach this student to use a strategy such as stop and think, focusing on rereading, reading ahead, and other techniques for monitoring reading.

A process interview for writing may be done using questions that follow a pattern similar to those used for reading. Since this is an informal procedure, questions for either the reading or writing interview can be rephrased or changed to

FIGURE 11.10

STUDENT SELF-MONITORING CHECKLIST

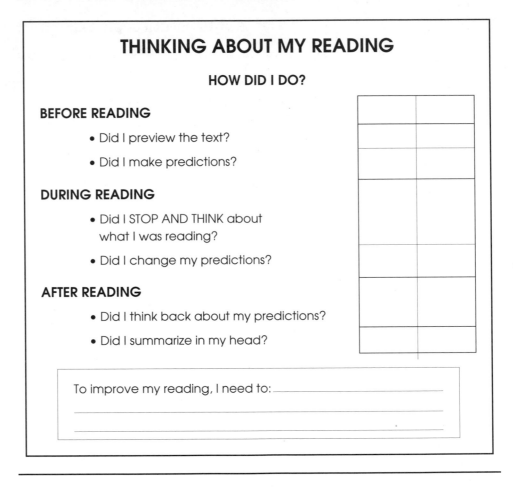

THINKING ABOUT MY READING

HOW DID I DO?

BEFORE READING

- Did I preview the text?

- Did I make predictions?

DURING READING

- Did I STOP AND THINK about what I was reading?

- Did I change my predictions?

AFTER READING

- Did I think back about my predictions?

- Did I summarize in my head?

To improve my reading, I need to: _____

_____

_____

ensure that students understand them. Interviews of this type can be conducted with students of all ages as long as the questions are worded appropriately.

Teacher-Selected Reading Samples

One of the most important criteria for assessing and evaluating students' progress is that the materials used be books and texts that students read every day. Select a book, a chapter of a book, or a short story or text you want students to read, and introduce the material as you would in a literacy lesson (see Chapter 2). Have students read the text silently, and then ask them to complete a task appropriate to their grade level that will let you see how effectively they have constructed meaning. These tasks could include the following:

- Completing a story map
- Listing the most important or main ideas in the text
- Writing a summary (this is a very sophisticated process and should be reserved for the upper elementary and middle school levels)
- Answering questions that focus on the story elements
- Answering questions that draw out the main ideas of the text

All tasks except the summary can be scored by determining the percentage of items correct. The summary has to be scored more holistically by giving it a rating such as the following:

1 = All major ideas included

2 = Most major ideas included

3 = Many major ideas missing

Samples of reading can be taken over time and compared to determine student progress.

Fluency Checks and Application of Decoding Skills

Many teachers find it helpful to use teacher-selected or student-selected samples for oral reading. After students practice their passages, they read them aloud into a tape recorder or to the teacher. The teacher takes several passages over time and compares them to show student development in decoding; effective constructors of meaning know how to decode words automatically (see Chapter 5). This technique differs from the miscue analysis (discussed later), because in miscue analysis students do not prepare their passages. This procedure would let you compare a student's "best" performances over time.

You can analyze these taped passages by looking at the patterns of students' responses to determine students' ability to decode words. Many teachers find it useful to make the tape recordings a part of the students' portfolios. In this way, students can compare their passages to determine their own growth in decoding; the tapes can also be used during parent conferences to help parents determine the progress their children are making. Figure 11.11 shows a passage a first grader read from *Fix-It* (McPhail, 1984). The teacher's markings and notes show what the student read and how the teacher judged the student's decoding abilities.

Literature Circles

The literature circle (see Chapter 6) presents a good opportunity to observe students' ability to construct meaning and react personally in an authentic literacy experience. Wood's (1988) procedure for assessing and evaluating comprehension during a group discussion involves looking at nine behaviors related to meaning construction as students discuss what they have read: making predictions, participating in discussion, answering questions on a variety of levels, determining word

FIGURE 11.11

First Grader's Marked Oral Passage

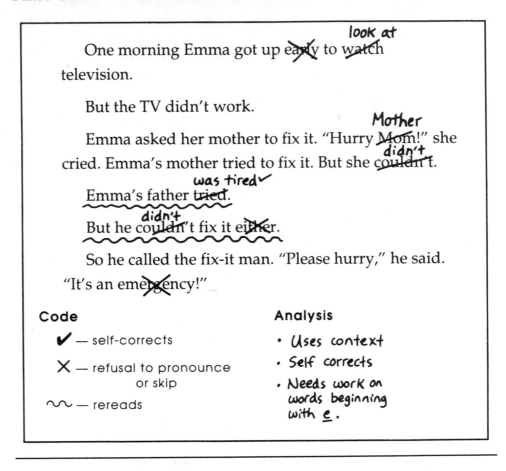

Code

✔ — self-corrects

✗ — refusal to pronounce or skip

〜 — rereads

Analysis

- Uses context
- Self corrects
- Needs work on words beginning with *e*.

meaning through context, reading smoothly and fluently, retelling selections in own words, comprehending after silent reading, reading between the lines, and having a broad background knowledge. A grid is used to record students' responses using a simple code: Often= +, Sometimes = S, Seldom = –, and Not Observed = N.

I have found that teachers are able to use the literature circle to assess and evaluate meaning construction. However, like Paradis et al. (1991), I have also found that teachers need to develop (or adapt from some other source) their own specific procedures and indicators. The following general guidelines should help you accomplish this purpose.

Guidelines for Developing Procedures for Observing Literature Circles

Select indicators for meaning construction.   Use the information in this text and other sources to help you decide what indicators you should look for to tell you that your students are effectively constructing meaning. In the beginning keep the number small, remembering the importance of strategies such as predicting, confirming and/or changing predictions, inferencing, and summarizing. Following are examples of indicators you might use:

General indicators

- Participates in discussion
- Listens to responses of others
- Builds own response on ideas of others

Indicators for narrative texts

- Identifies important parts of story (setting, characters, and so forth)
- Identifies favorite parts or characters
- Relates story to own experiences
- Compares to other stories

Indicators for expository texts

- Identifies topic
- Identifies main ideas
- Sees relationships in text
- Shows signs of using knowledge gained
- Can relate information to own life

Develop a procedure for recording information.   You can use a simple grid such as the one in Figure 11.12 with a code similar to the one developed by Wood (1988), discussed earlier. This grid contains a space for comments or observations.

Designate a time for observation.   It is not necessary to observe every literature circle for assessment purposes; use selected ones. You may either participate in the discussion or sit off to the side to observe. Teachers who become accustomed to this procedure report that they find themselves always observing even when they are just participating in the circles. This activity becomes a natural part of teaching.

Review the data for yourself and with students.   After you have completed your observation, study the data you have collected to see what your students' strengths are. Think about ways to use these strengths and also provide ongoing

FIGURE 11.12

GRID FOR OBSERVING CONSTRUCTION OF MEANING DURING A LITERATURE DISCUSSION CIRCLE

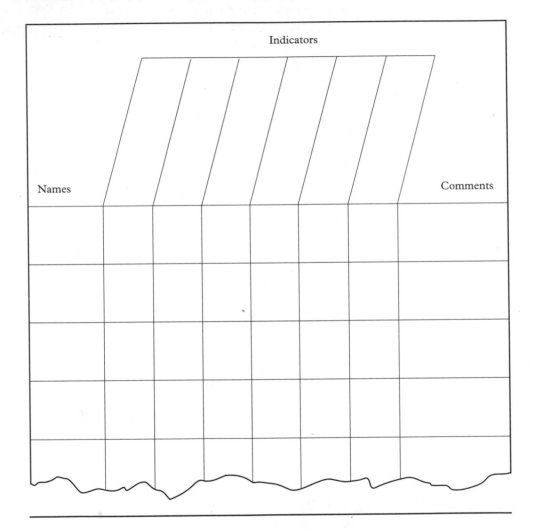

support. For example, if you observe that several students are very good at predicting but have difficulty summarizing, have them make predictions using story map prediction. Then use their story map predictions to lead into the summarizing stories strategy (see Chapters 3 and 8). Take time to review and discuss your observations with students, asking them for their perceptions and reactions.

Interest Inventories

Another important assessment and evaluation technique is the interest inventory. The information obtained may be useful to you in a number of ways:

- Choosing book collections from the library to bring into the classroom
- Ordering books
- Planning thematic unit topics
- Creating study groups
- Conferring with individual students or groups of students

There are many different forms of interest inventories, but they generally consist of a number of statements that students respond to orally (during conferences or interviews) or in writing. Often these are incomplete statements that students are asked to complete; see Figure 11.13 for examples.

Scoring Writing Using Rubrics

Holistic scoring is a widely used procedure to assess and evaluate a student's ability to construct meaning through writing. It involves looking at a piece of writing in its entirety and assigning it a score, using a set of guidelines called a *rubric* (Cockrum & Castillo, 1991). This process is generally used on instructional writing tasks rather than on self-initiated writing or written responses to literature. Holistic scoring assumes all aspects of writing are related and must be viewed in their entirety (Patchell, 1986).

When using the holistic procedure, the teacher reads the piece of writing and assigns it a score from 0 to 4. Although a detailed discussion of holistic scoring is beyond the scope of this text, the following scale (or rubric) from Millett (1986) may give you a sense of how this procedure is used:

0   *Papers in this category cannot be scored for one reason or another. Papers that are blank, that respond to an assignment different from the one given, that merely comment on the assignment ("This topic is silly"), that only copy or rephrase the assignment, or that are illegible would all be included in this category.*

1   *Papers in this category attempt to deal with the assignment, but they fail to do so adequately. These papers are too general, abrupt, or refer to the assignment only indirectly.*

2   *Papers in this category respond to the task set up in the assignment, but they do so in a way that is sketchy, inconsistent, and incomplete. There are gaps or other problems in the organization. Vocabulary may be too general and the paper lacking in the detail necessary to convey the purpose clearly and exactly. The reader has a basic idea of what the writer is trying to say but has to make many inferences.*

3   *Papers in this category fulfill the requirements of the assignment although the reader might encounter a little confusion from time to time. The paper is generally well organized so that the reader does not need to make a lot of inferences. These papers include sufficient details so that the reader understands the writer's message.*

FIGURE 11.13

COMPLETION STATEMENTS FOR AN INTEREST INVENTORY

Directions: Use these statements to develop an interest inventory. Add your own ideas.

Read the statements aloud and ask the student to complete them orally or have students read and complete them in writing.

1. I enjoy _____.

2. My favorite subject in school is _____.

3. When I read, I like to read _____.

4. My favorite thing in the world is _____.

5. I like to spend time _____.

6. My hobbies are _____.

7. I like to write about _____.

8. When I finish school, I want to be _____.

9. My favorite television shows are _____.

10. I would like to learn more about _____.

11. I would like to spend more time in school _____.

---

4   *Papers that merit this highest score are well organized, complete, and explicit. These papers include all of the strengths of the 3 category, but they are more clearly and consistently presented. The reader grasps the writer's message easily without having to make inferences. The writer uses a varied and exact vocabulary that enhances as well as clarifies the message.* (pp. 51–52)

Miscue Analysis

Miscue analysis is a procedure that lets the teacher "get a window on the reading process" (Goodman, 1965). A miscue is an oral response that is different from the text being read. For example, if the text reads, "Billy rode his horse around the ranch," and a child reading this says, "Billy rode his pony around the ranch," this miscue shows that the child has constructed the appropriate meaning for this sentence even though she didn't say the exact words. Sometimes miscues are referred to as *unexpected responses* or *errors*.

Goodman (1965) concluded from his research that by studying a student's miscues from an oral reading sample, the teacher could determine the cues and strategies the student was using or not using in constructing meaning. This procedure attempts to look at the process of reading holistically.

On the basis of Goodman's research, the reading miscue inventory (Goodman & Burke, 1972) was developed. Although this analysis is normally reserved for students who are having difficulty constructing meaning, the classroom reading miscue assessment (CRMA), a simplified version of miscue analysis (Rhodes & Shanklin, 1990), can be used with all students in a classroom. The CRMA takes from 10 to 15 minutes per student. Rhodes and Shanklin (1990) indicate that it "helps teachers gather important instructional information by providing a framework for observing students' oral reading and their ability to construct meaning" (p. 254).

All of the variations of miscue analysis require additional study on your part as a teacher. See the For Additional Reading section for suggestions.

Informal Reading Inventories

The informal reading inventory (IRI) consists of a series of samples of text organized in increasing difficulty; students individually read the texts orally and/or silently. By studying their oral reading patterns and their responses to comprehension questions, the teacher can get a picture of how they analyze words in context, how they construct meaning, and what their approximate levels of reading are. This procedure has been used in assessing and evaluating reading since the 1920s (Beldin, 1970). IRIs usually consist of four types:

1. *Teacher constructed* using materials from which students will be reading
2. *Publisher constructed* to match series of texts to be used for reading instruction
3. *Generic IRIs* using samples of a variety of types of texts
4. *Group IRIs* that have been adapted from the individual IRI concept; these are usually teacher made

One major advantage of using IRIs has always been that students' reading was actually being used as the basis for seeing how well they could read. Their ability to analyze words was determined by looking at how they actually carried out this process in context. Applying some of the concepts of miscue analysis to the analysis of oral reading improved the process. Even when much controversy surrounds reading assessment, the use of IRIs remains a very popular procedure (Pikulski, 1990a).

For a fuller explanation of the procedures for using IRIs, see Cooper & Kiger, (in press), listed in the For Additional Reading section. As you learn to use this widely used procedure, keep the following questions in mind:

1. Does the reading of samples or portions of text give you the same picture of students' ability to construct meaning that the reading of complete texts does?
2. Is it really possible to identify precise levels of text and determine students' reading levels using these texts?
3. In general, are the procedures used to administer, score, and interpret the IRI consistent with what we know about how children develop literacy?

These questions should help you to be a more critical (evaluative) user of the IRI. The value of IRIs is enhanced when miscue analysis is used to analyze oral reading or when the running record (see the next section) concept is applied to the IRI.

Running Records

Another procedure for analyzing a student's reading is the running record (Clay, 1985), which is similar to miscue analysis. In this procedure, students read complete texts or samples of text. By looking at the students' responses, you are able to see their strengths and weaknesses in using various reading strategies and cuing systems (see Chapter 4). Running records are an important part of the assessment and evaluation used in the Reading Recovery Program in New Zealand and the United States (Clay, 1985; Pinnell, Fried, & Estice, 1990). They are also very useful for classrooms with beginning literacy learners.

The following guidelines should be helpful in learning to take a running record. You should refer to Clay (1985) for more detailed discussions of the procedures. Teachers in kindergarten through third grade should find this technique useful in determining students' progress as they develop what Clay (1992) calls a "self-extending system," or independence in using reading strategies (though these procedures may also be used at upper levels with students developing beginning reading strategies). The guidelines are as follows:

1. Choose or have the child choose a book (or selection) she or he has read previously. For longer books, use a sample containing at least one hundred words.
2. Have the child read aloud the text. As the child reads, make a check mark on a blank sheet of paper for each word called correctly. (See Figure 11.14, which shows a sample running record taken by a first-grade teacher using the book *My Five Senses* [Miller, 1994].)
3. If the child makes miscues, mark as follows:
   - *Misreads word:* Write the word with the error above it (see Figure 11.14 [p. 2]).
   - *Omits word:* Write the word and circle it (p. 4).
   - *Self-corrects:* Write the word with SC above it (p. 2).
   - *Teacher tells word:* Write the word with *T* above it (p. 19).
4. To score, use the following formula:

$$\frac{\text{Total Words Read Correctly*}}{\text{Number of Words in Book/Sample}} \times 100 = \_\_\_\%$$

   * Self-corrections are correct

5. Ninety percent accuracy or higher is considered good progress.
6. Look at student's miscues to determine strategies used and those not used. (For a detailed discussion, see Clay [1985], listed in the For Additional Reading section.)

Performance Assessments

Performance assessments are tasks that require students to demonstrate their literacy knowledge and skills by making real-world responses. Research has shown that such tasks are effective instructional tools (Khattri, Kane, & Reeve, 1995). Performance assessments include such devices as reports, posters, construction projects, plays, and so

FIGURE 11.14

RUNNING RECORD SUMMARY SHEET

Lisa S.   11-21-99

My Five Senses

p. 2 ✓ ✓ ✓ ✓ ✓ ✓ nose ^noise SC

p. 3 ✓ ✓ ✓ ✓ ✓ ✓

p. 4 ✓ ✓ ✓ ✓ ✓   (myself)

p. 5 ✓ shadow ^shoe

p. 6 ✓ ✓

p. 7 ✓ ✓ ✓

p. 8 ✓ ✓ ✓ ✓ ✓ ✓

p. 9 ✓ ✓

p. 10 ✓

p. 11 ✓ ✓

p. 12 ✓ ✓ ✓ ✓ ✓ ✓

p. 13 ✓ ocean ^sea

p. 14 ✓

p. 15 ✓ ✓ ✓

p. 16 ✓ ✓ ✓ ✓ ✓ ✓ ✓

p. 17 ✓ ✓ ✓

p. 18 ✓ ✓

p. 19 ✓ whispered ✓

p. 20 ✓ ✓ ✓ ✓ ✓ ✓

p. 21 ✓

p. 22 ✓

p. 23 ✓ ✓

p. 24 ✓ ✓ ✓ ✓ ✓ ✓ ✓

$$\frac{81}{85} \times 100 = \underline{95}\%$$

Good progress; good use of strategies

forth, all of which require students to demonstrate what they have learned. There are several important criteria to consider as you develop performance assessments:

▶ Identify the specific strategies, skills, and knowledge you want students to learn.

▶ Be sure the performance task selected actually requires the use of the strategies, skills, and knowledge identified.

▶ Develop a rubric for evaluating the task.

Assessment Procedures Accompanying Published Materials

For many years, the publishers of basal readers have produced different types of tests to accompany their materials. Many publishers are moving more and more toward authentic literature and real books as resources for literacy development and are including in their packages a variety of suggestions and procedures for more authentic assessment and evaluation. If you are using one of these published resources, you should keep in mind what you have learned about effective literacy learning and assessment and select only those procedures that fit your needs and the needs of your students.

Making Decisions from Assessment Data

Table 11.2 summarizes the assessment techniques discussed in the previous section; it can serve as a reference guide for your use. Each technique can be used in the balanced literacy classroom and reflects what we know about literacy learning and assessment at this time. As mentioned earlier, *no classroom needs all of these techniques all of the time.* You must become a selective user of the various techniques. Consider the following points as you decide which techniques to use:

▶ *How children develop literacy:* This is paramount to everything we have discussed in this text. Any assessment technique used should be in line with what we know about how children learn and develop literacy.

▶ *Principles for effective assessment:* Continuously refer to these principles and ask yourself whether the techniques you are using are consistent with them (see page 528).

▶ *Trust your judgment:* If you know or believe a technique is inappropriate, question it; maybe you shouldn't use it. Consider another alternative. However, give a technique several trials before discarding it.

▶ *Start small:* Select one or two techniques to use, and try them out. Add others if necessary.

▶ *Evaluate techniques:* As you use various assessment techniques, evaluate them. Are they assessing what you want to assess? *If they don't inform instruction and help you and your students improve literacy learning, they shouldn't be used.* Talk with your colleagues to come up with alternative techniques.

As you gather assessment information from students' literacy activities, you should use it to make decisions about instruction for and with your students. The following scenarios illustrate how assessment and evaluation help with instructional decisions:

TABLE 11.2

REFERENCE GUIDE TO ASSESSMENT TECHNIQUES

TECHNIQUE	PURPOSE	COMMENTS
Observation or "kid watching" (p. 533)	Watch students' performance in authentic learning situations	An essential procedure for good classroom assessment and evaluation
Checklists (p. 534)	Guide observations	May be used to guide observations in many areas related to literacy learning
Records of independent reading and writing (p. 536)	Keep track of independent reading and writing	Should be used at all levels; gives insights about students' attitudes and habits
Retellings (p. 538)	Assess meaning construction	One of the best procedures to assess construction of meaning
Responses to literature (p. 540)	Assess meaning construction, levels of thinking, and use of strategies	Shows how students use what they have read and integrate ideas into their own experiences
Student self-evaluations (p. 543)	Determine students' perceptions of their own reading and writing	Helps students take ownership of learning
Process interviews (p. 544)	Gain insight into students' metacognition processes	Individual procedure that should be used selectively
Teacher-selected reading samples (p. 546)	Assess meaning construction Assess decoding, if done orally	Informal procedure; may be collected and compared over time
Fluency checks (p. 547)	Check decoding	Checks application of decoding in context
Literature circles (p. 547)	Assess meaning construction	Integrates instruction and assessment
Interest inventories (p. 551)	Determine students' interests	Provides a basis for planning learning activities
Scoring writing using rubrics (p. 551)	Evaluate meaning construction through writing	Provides a way of judging writing by looking at the entire piece
Miscue analysis (p. 552)	Assess decoding and use of strategies	Procedure requires detailed training (see For Additional Reading)
Informal reading inventories (p. 553)	Assess meaning construction and decoding	Procedure requires detailed training (see For Additional Reading) Use judiciously
Running records (p. 554)	Assess use of decoding strategies	Procedure requires detailed training (see For Additional Reading)
Performance assessments (p. 554)	Assess application of all strategies, skills, and knowledges	Makes assessment an integral part of instruction
Assessment procedures accompanying published materials (p. 556)	Varies according to publisher	Should be used selectively

▶ As you observe a group of six students reading a little version of a big book, you notice that four of them have not developed fluency with the text. Therefore, you decide to reread the big book, using sentence strips and word cards to reconstruct the book in the pocket chart. You will also have children add words to the word wall (see Chapter 4).

▶ During writing workshop, many students are still having trouble writing persuasive paragraphs. Therefore, you decide that tomorrow you will conduct a minilesson on persuasive writing using the shared writing technique. This will be followed by collaborative or cooperative writing to provide continued scaffolding for those who need it (see Chapter 7).

▶ After having seven students retell a story they have read, you note that all of them have good understanding of story elements and concepts. Therefore, you decide they are ready for more challenging chapter books.

The use of assessment and evaluation data as described in the preceding examples shows how assessment and instruction truly go hand in hand.

What to Do About Grading

One issue continues to frustrate many teachers: grading. Nearly all schools continue to give grades after adopting a portfolio concept, and in most instances the report card system does not match the assessment plan they have implemented. Grading has always been an issue in reading instruction. Why, however, does it appear to be a more significant issue with the portfolio concept of assessment?

Under the old concept of assessment, teachers could easily take numerical grades from worksheets, workbooks, and tests, place them in a grade book, total them, and average them for a grade. They could then show the students, parents, and administrators their "proof" for the grades given without feeling they had to judge or evaluate what the students had actually done. This was a very comfortable position, but it did not really reflect what the students were doing.

The report card systems in place in many schools (A-B-C letter grading) simply do not match the view of assessment developed in this chapter (Cockrum & Castillo, 1991; Tierney, Carter, & Desai, 1991). Therefore, most schools need to rethink and evaluate the report card system.

If letter grades must be given in a balanced literacy classroom, evaluation must be viewed as being more subjective. Therefore, there are a number of factors to consider.

First, written descriptions (or rubrics) for each letter grade should be developed that vary by grade level and school and are based on the overall school objectives. The descriptions could include some of the benchmarks discussed earlier. For example, an A at grade 3 might read as follows: "A = Reads many self-selected books with understanding. Is able to compare books and draw conclusions. Shows a thorough understanding of what has been read." These letter descriptions would guide the assessment.

Second, a rating scale might be used to evaluate written and/or oral responses to literature. For example, "A = Response indicates *thorough* understanding of what was read; B = Response shows some understanding of what was read"; and so forth.

Third, students should participate in their own grading. After discussing your grading criteria with them, ask them to determine their own grades and place their grades in their portfolios with written justification.

You will find that establishing your own criteria for grading will make the job of grading far less difficult than most people make it out to be. Use the principles for assessment discussed earlier in this chapter. These principles, along with your criteria for grading, should help to make this difficult task easier.

Dealing with Problems in Constructing Meaning

When you use various instructional and assessment techniques, you will find that some students are encountering problems in meaning construction. Years ago, teachers looked at these students and asked, "What skills are they lacking?" or "What types of comprehension questions are they unable to answer?" What we have learned about the process of constructing meaning and literacy learning leads us to look at these problems in other ways, to ask different questions and use different techniques to support students in this situation. The following six questions should help you in thinking about and analyzing students who are having problems with meaning construction.

Does the student's behavior indicate a "real" problem" with meaning construction, or is it a normal expectation or one specific to one situation? Often young readers exhibit reading behaviors that are normal aspects of their literacy development and do not reflect any problems. For example, a first or second grader reading books such as *Jillian Jiggs* (Gilman, 1985) or *The Lady with the Alligator Purse* (Westcott, 1988) may not recognize every word but may have a thorough understanding of the stories. It is normal to expect that students at the early levels of literacy learning will not know by sight all of the words in every story they read. A sixth grader reading an informational book about prehistoric animals may miss an important point because he does not know one or two unusual key-concept words in the text. This is a specific situation and does not indicate a major problem in constructing meaning.

To determine whether students are having genuine problems in learning to construct meaning, look for *patterns* of behaviors. Ask whether these patterns are normal occurrences in literacy learning, are specific to one type of situation, or are "real" problems for the student.

Is the problem one of understanding the text or of decoding individual words? Sometimes students will read a text and be unable to respond to it personally, retell it, or answer questions posed by the teacher. When you examine the situation further, you may find such a student is unable to read the text aloud—in other words, to decode the words. Perhaps the student has not learned the letter-sound relationships of the language and does not know phonics and the other cuing systems that would help develop this ability. This student should receive support such as the following:

▶ *Direct Instruction in Decoding Skills and Strategies:* Provide systematic, explicit instruction in needed decoding skills and strategies. This instruction should be preceeded by a careful diagnosis to determine students' strengths and needs (see Cooper & Kiger, in press).

▶ *Shared and repeated readings:* Engage the student in shared and repeated readings using texts that have strong, rhythmic patterns; this is also appropriate for older students. Use the texts to point out decoding clues such as context, structural elements, and phonic elements (see Chapter 4).

▶ *Make lists of patterned words to be used in writing:* Brainstorm with students to create a list of words that follow a particular phonic or structural element, and encourage them to use these words in their writing.

Examples:

c*at*	c*ap*
m*ap*	n*ap*
b*at*	l*ap*

before
*before*hand
*fore*tell
*un*safe
*un*happy
*un*tied

▶ *Involve students in writing:* Have students do shared, collaborative, and independent writing, encouraging them to spell words as they think they sound (see Chapters 2 and 7).

▶ *Teach students a strategy for inferring word meanings:* A strategy such as the word detective strategy (see Chapters 4 and 5) helps students relate decoding and meaning.

There are many other techniques you might use in this situation. These are the types of support that are consistent with what we know about how students learn to decode words in a meaningful way (see Chapter 4).

If you determine that the student's problem is one of constructing meaning, continue to ask the following questions before deciding on a plan of support.

Does the reader have sufficient prior knowledge (schema, background) for the text being read?   Because this is so important to successful meaning construction, you should examine the status of the student in these areas. Observation is the best technique for doing this. Some students often need more detailed activation of prior knowledge and background to gain a framework for meaning construction, and many teachers report that more thorough development of background is helpful. See the strategies and techniques discussed in Chapter 3.

Is the text clearly written?   Sometimes readers have the background needed to read and understand a text, but the text is not clearly written or the author has not given enough information or background to get the ideas across. In these cases, you must carefully examine the text to see if lack of clarity is part of the difficulty. For example, a reader may have trouble understanding a particular author's writing style or a particular type of text.

If the text to be read is a major part of the problem, there are several ways you can provide support for the student:

▶ Change the text.

▶ Use a mode of reading that is more structured, such as teacher-guided reading (see Chapter 2).

▶ Use graphic organizers before and after reading to help students identify the important information in the text (see Chapters 3 and 8).

Does the reader know the key-concept vocabulary needed to construct meaning from the text? In some instances, particularly with expository texts, readers may have difficulty because they do not understand key-concept words. Many of the suggestions presented in Chapter 5 may be helpful in these situations.

Can the reader use strategies such as predicting, self-questioning, monitoring, and summarizing? These strategies are important to constructing meaning (see Chapter 8). If you are able to tell through observing students' responses to reading that they cannot use these strategies, you may need to provide more support for them. Ideas discussed in Chapters 3 and 8 should help you in developing a stronger strategic support system for students.

Monitoring is often a problem for students who are having difficulty constructing meaning. A good way to tell whether readers are able to monitor their own comprehension is to have them read and answer questions about the text and then ask them to tell whether they think their answers are correct. Good comprehension monitors know when their answers are correct but may think some of their answers are wrong when they are actually correct. Poor comprehension monitors will think their answers are right when they are really wrong (Palincsar & Brown, 1984).

Analyzing students' problems is not a simple task, but as we continue to learn more about the process of constructing meaning we can become more effective in locating the possible causes of problems and find better ways to provide support for students.

Summary

This chapter focused on a new concept of assessment for the balanced literacy classroom. Eight principles for effective assessment were suggested:

1. Assessment should be an ongoing process.
2. Effective assessment is an integral part of instruction.
3. Assessment must be authentic, reflecting "real" reading and writing.
4. Assessment should be a collaborative, reflective process.
5. Effective assessment is multidimensional.
6. Assessment should be developmentally and culturally appropriate.
7. Effective assessment identifies students' strengths.

8. Assessment must be based on what we know about how students learn to read and write.

The chapter discussed four ways to organize assessment information to make it useful for helping make instructional decisions.

The chapter then presented a variety of assessment techniques that are consistent with these principles. These include observation, checklists, records of independent reading and writing, retellings, responses to literature, student self-evaluations, process interviews, teacher-selected reading samples, fluency checks, application of decoding skills, literature circles, interest inventories, scoring of writing using rubrics, miscue analysis, informal reading inventories, running records, performance assessments, and assessment procedures accompanying published materials. The need to use these techniques selectively and as a basis for making instructional decisions was stressed.

The chapter concluded with a brief discussion of grading and a series of questions to use in thinking about and analyzing problems in the construction of meaning.

Literature

Dahl, R. (1990). *Esio trot.* New York: Viking.

Freedman, R. (1990). *Franklin Delano Roosevelt.* New York: Clarion.

Gilman, P. (1985). *Jillian Jiggs.* New York: Scholastic.

Jaspersohn, W. (1991). *Cranberries.* Boston: Houghton Mifflin.

Miller, M. (1994). *My five senses.* New York: Simon & Schuster.

McPhail, D. (1984). *Fix-it.* New York: Dutton Children's Books, a Division of Penguin.

Rawls, W. (1974). *Where the red fern grows.* New York: Bantam.

Waber, B. (1988). *Ira says goodbye.* Boston: Houghton Mifflin.

Westcott, N. B. (1988). *The lady with the alligator purse.* Boston: Little, Brown.

For Additional Reading

Au, K. H., Scheu, J. A., Kawakami, A. J., & Herman, P. A. (1990). Assessment and accountability in a whole literacy curriculum. *The Reading Teacher, 33,* 574–578.

Clay, M. M. (1985). *The early detection of reading difficulties* (3rd ed.). Auckland, New Zealand: Heinemann.

Cooper, J. D., & Kiger, N. (In press). *Literacy assessment: Helping teachers plan instruction.* Boston: Houghton Mifflin.

Farr, R., & Tone, B. (1994). *Portfolio and performance assessment: Helping students evaluate their progress as readers and writers.* Orlando: Harcourt Brace College Publishers.

Farr, B. C., & Trumbull, E. (1997). *Assessment alternatives for diverse classrooms.* Norwood, MA: Christopher-Gordon.

Goodman, Y., Watson, D., & Burke, C. (1987). *Reading miscue inventory: Alternative procedures.* New York: Richard C. Owen.

Harp, B. (1996). *The handbook of literacy assessment and evaluation.* Norwood, MA: Christopher-Gordon.

Hill, B. C., & Ruptic, C. (1994). *Practical aspects of authentic assessment: Putting the pieces together.* Norwood, MA: Christopher-Gordon.

Johnson, M. S., Kress, R. A., & Pikulski, J. J. (1987). *Informal reading inventories* (2nd ed.). Newark, DE: International Reading Association.

Tierney, R. J., Carter, M. A., & Desai, L. E. (1991). *Portfolio assessment in the reading-writing classroom.* Norwood, MA: Christopher-Gordon.

Valencia, S. W., Hiebert, E. H., & Afflerbach, P. P. (Eds.). (1994). *Authentic reading assessment: Practices and possibilities.* Newark, DE: International Reading Association.

For Exploration

NCTE

www.ncte.org

IRA

www.ira.org

Epilogue: Success-Centered Literacy Instruction

In his famous poem Langston Hughes says, "Hold fast to dreams, for if dreams die; life is a broken winged bird that cannot fly . . ." The dream of all teachers is that *every child* will achieve success in literacy learning. But this goal does not have to be a dream. Clearly, based on what we know about literacy learning today, *failure is preventable* for the vast majority of students.

Attaining this dream requires that we create balanced literacy classrooms that provide a variety of types of instruction that build on students' strengths. Throughout this process, the focus must be on *what students can do!*

Creating balanced literacy classrooms that yield success for all students requires that we do the types of things this text has suggested consistently and systematically. When students are given good instruction that is appropriately paced and tailored to their needs, they learn! Let's not just dream about preventing failure; let's make it a reality for *all* students!

Word Skills:
Phonics and Structural
Analysis for Teachers

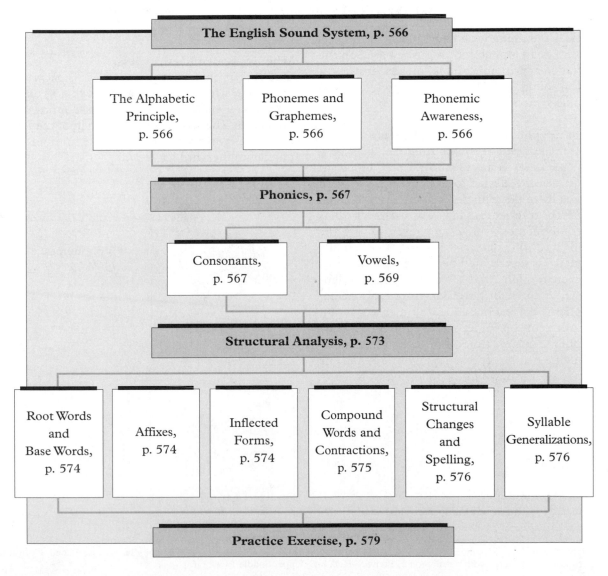

The English Sound System, p. 566

The Alphabetic Principle, p. 566

Phonemes and Graphemes, p. 566

Phonemic Awareness, p. 566

Phonics, p. 567

Consonants, p. 567

Vowels, p. 569

Structural Analysis, p. 573

Root Words and Base Words, p. 574

Affixes, p. 574

Inflected Forms, p. 574

Compound Words and Contractions, p. 575

Structural Changes and Spelling, p. 576

Syllable Generalizations, p. 576

Practice Exercise, p. 579

This handbook resource is designed to help you develop a basic knowledge about phonics and structural analysis. *It is not intended in any way to provide complete coverage of all the technical aspects of the structure of language and/or phonology.*

Read pages 566–570 using the imbedded questions to guide your reading. After reading, complete the practice exercise on pages 579–581. Check your answers.

THE ENGLISH SOUND SYSTEM

What is the alphabetic principle?
English is an alphabetic language based on the alphabetic principle. This means that each speech sound of the language is represented by a graphic symbol.

What are phonemes and graphemes?
The smallest unit of speech sound in language is the *phoneme.* The symbols that represent phonemes are referred to as *graphemes.* The word *cat* has three phonemes—/c/ /ă/ /t/—represented by three graphemes. The word *deep* also has three phonemes—/d/ /ē/ /p/—even though the word has four letters—d-e-e-p. The middle phoneme is represented by two letters—*ee.*

Even though English is an alphabetic language, it does not have one-to-one phoneme-grapheme correspondence. In other words, not all phonemes are represented by the same grapheme every time. For example, the /f/ phoneme can be represented by more than one grapheme, as shown in the following words:

/f/   *ph*one
       *f*ork
       pu*ff*
       rou*gh*

What is phonology?
Phonology is the study of speech sounds. *Phonological awareness* is the knowledge that words

have separate parts. There are three ways to look at the parts of words:

syllables: *look* (one syllable)

onsets and rimes: *look*
/l/ = onset
/ŏŏk/ = rime
or
brick
/br/ = onset
/ick/ = rime

phonemes: /l/ /ŏŏ/ /k/

What is phonemic awareness?
One part of phonological awareness is *phonemic awareness,* which is the awareness that spoken words are made up of speech sounds or phonemes. Think of the word for each of the following pictures and think of the number of phonemes the word has:

= 3 phonemes
/d/ /o/ /g/

= 3 phonemes
/h/ /ou/ /s/

*Adapted from J. D. Cooper, E. W. Warncke, & D. Shipman. (1988). *The What and How of Reading Instruction,* 2nd ed. Copyright © 1988. Reprinted with permission of Prentice-Hall, Inc., Upper Saddle River, NJ.

What are segmenting and blending?

There are two major processes involved in phonemic awareness—segmenting and blending. *Segmenting* is the process of hearing a spoken word and being able to identify its phonemes; for example, *boat* has three phonemes—/b/ /ō/ /t/. *Blending* is the process of hearing the phonemes and being able to put them together (blend) to tell what the word is; for example, /s/ /ŏ/ /k/ is *sock*. Phonemic awareness is a prerequisite to learning phonics. Children are able to perform segmenting and blending tasks without being able to name the letters.

PHONICS

What is phonics?

Phonics is the study of the relationships between the speech sounds (phonemes) and the letters (graphemes) that represent them. Phonics is sometimes called *decoding*. It is the sounding out of unknown words. The amount of phonics instruction needed by individual learners varies greatly.

Phonics produces *only* pronunciation, or an approximate pronunciation, of the unknown word. The pronounced word must be in the reader's oral language, both to check the accuracy of the decoding process and to check the meaning of the word in its contextual usage. For example,

Pitta are almost extinct because of acid rain.

Although readers may be able to say "pitta," they may not understand the above sentence. No real reading has taken place unless the author's meaning has been conveyed to the reader, even if the decoding was perfect! The reader may infer that "pitta" is plural because of the word *are* and a living thing because *extinct* is a term used with creatures. Therefore, some meaning has been conveyed. It is just not complete. (By the way, pitta are brightly colored birds found in southern Asian and Australian forests.)

Consonants

What is a consonant?

There are two basic categories of sounds in English, consonants and vowels. A *consonant* is a speech sound (phoneme) in which the flow of breath is constricted or stopped by the tongue, teeth, lips, or some combination of these. The letters (graphemes) representing such speech sounds are also called consonants. Most single consonants are regular in sound in that they represent only one sound no matter where they appear in a word.

*b*oy	ta*b*	ra*b*id (*b*s all sound alike)
*d*og	ha*d*	ra*d*ar (*d*s all sound alike)

What sounds are expected for *c* and *g*?

There are several notable exceptions to consistent single consonant sounds. Consonants *c* and *g* have hard and soft sounds. The grapheme *c* is expected to have its hard sound /k/ when it is followed by the vowels *a, o, u,* or by another consonant. The hard sound of *c* is the sound usually associated with the letter *k*.

*c*at	*c*ot	*c*ut	*c*lass	al*c*ove

The soft sound of *c* is the sound heard in *city*. The soft sound of *c* occurs when the *c* is followed by *e, i,* or *y*.

*c*ell	*c*ider	*c*ycle

The hard and soft *g* generalization is not as consistent as the hard and soft *c* generalization. The grapheme *g* is expected to have its hard sound when it is followed by the vowels *a, o, u,* or another consonant. The hard sound of *g* is the guttural sound that is heard in the following words:

*g*ate	*g*ot	*g*um	*g*lad	ra*g*

The soft sound of *g*—/j/—is expected when it is followed by the vowels *e, i,* or *y*. The soft sound of *g* is the sound usually associated with the letter *j* as in the following words:

gentle   giant   gym

What sounds are associated with *s*?

The letter *s* has four different sounds. There is no generalization covering when the reader should expect each sound. The sounds represented by *s* are illustrated by:

see – /s/

sure – /sh/

ha*s* – /z/

trea*s*ure – /zh/

What are some other exceptions to consistent consonant sounds?

The following exceptions to consistent single consonant sounds are far less common than those noted above. They are presented here to illustrate that there are other exceptions and as a caution to teachers to think carefully before requiring learners to decode phonetically unpredictable words.

Grapheme	Phoneme	Word
f	/v/	o*f*
x	/ks/	e*x*it
x	/z/	*x*ylophone
qu	/k/	anti*que*
qu	/kw/	*qu*iz

What are consonant clusters, and what else may they be called?

Consonants may also appear in *clusters* in words; that is, more than one consonant may come together before a vowel or between vowels in a word. Some materials for reading instruction refer to all groups of consonants as consonant clusters. Other materials divide them into two categories: consonant digraphs and blends.

What are digraphs?

Consonant Digraphs. A consonant digraph is two consecutive consonants (in a word or syllable) that represent one speech sound. In other words, two graphemes represent just one phoneme. The word digraph means (di) two (graph) letters. In fact, the word digraph contains a digraph, *ph*. There are essentially three kinds of digraphs:

1. **New Sound.** Some consonant digraphs represent a new sound that is unlike the sound of either of the single consonants or any other consonants. This type of consonant digraph may have more than one sound.

Digraph	Word	Phoneme
sh	*sh*ut	/sh/
th	*th*is	(voiced *th*)
	*th*in	(unvoiced *th*)
wh	*wh*en	/hw/
	*wh*o	/h/
ch	whi*ch*	/ch/
	*ch*asm	/k/
	*ch*ef	/sh/

2. **Either Sound.** Some consonant digraphs represent the sound of one of the single consonants contained in the digraph.

Digraph	Word	Phoneme
ck	ki*ck*	/k/
kn	*kn*ot	/n/
wr	*wr*ite	/r/
gn	*gn*at	/n/
pn	*pn*eumatic	/n/
gh	*gh*ost	/g/

3. **Another Sound.** Some consonant digraphs represent the sound of another grapheme.

Digraph	Word	Phoneme
gh	lau*gh*	/f/
ph	*ph*one	/f/

Other consonant clusters often referred to as digraphs include *nk* as in ba*nk; ng* as in si*ng;* and double consonants as in mi*tt*en, su*mm*er, and ru*dd*er.

What are consonant blends?

Consonant Blends. A consonant blend is two or three consonant sounds clustered together in a word or syllable, where all consonant sounds are heard. The phonemes merge in speech sounds. The reader produces a speech sound for each consonant seen. The word *blend* contains two blends, *bl* and *nd*. There are three major categories of blends.

1. Blends beginning with the letter *s:*

str *str*ong	sc *sc*ab	sn *sn*ail
spl *spl*ash	sk ri*sk*	sp wa*sp*
scr *scr*eam	sl *sl*ow	st la*st*
spr *spr*ing	sm *sm*og	sw *sw*an

2. Blends concluding with the letter *r:*

br *br*oth	fr *fr*esh	tr *tr*out
cr *cr*owd	gr *gr*ass	spr *spr*ay
dr *dr*aft	pr *pr*ove	str *str*aw

3. Blends concluding with the letter *l:*

bl *bl*ue	gl *gl*ass	cl *cl*ose
pl *pl*ace	fl *fl*ip	sl *sl*ave

The *lp* in he*lp,* the *tw* in *tw*in, the *dw* in *dw*arf, and the *nd* in sa*nd* are all examples of other consonant blends. Remember, whenever each consonant in a cluster can be heard, the cluster is called a blend.

Why are consonant sounds important?
Consonant sounds are more consistent than vowel sounds. There is less deviation in the sounds of consonants, whether they are single or in clusters. Therefore, a few consonants, along with a vowel, are usually taught first so children can begin to build words.

Vowels

What is a vowel? What are the categories of vowel sounds?
A vowel is a speech sound in which the flow of breath is relatively unobstructed. The letters representing such sounds are also called vowels. The letters *a, e, i, o,* and *u* always function as vowels. The letter *y* is sometimes a consonant (as in *y*ell) and sometimes a vowel (as in b*y* and ma*y*). The letter *w* functions as a vowel in combination with another vowel (as in la*w*). The categories of vowel sounds are short vowels, long vowels, vowel digraphs, diphthongs, the schwa sound, exceptions to expected vowel sounds, and *y* and *w* functioning as vowels.

What are short vowels?

Short Vowel Sounds. Short vowel sounds are sometimes referred to as unglided. The five short vowel sounds are represented in the following words:

/ ăt/   /ĕd/   / ĭt/   /ŏx/   /ŭp/

The breve (brĕv), or curved line over a vowel (ă), is the diacritical marking used to indicate the short vowel sound in phonetic respellings. Sometimes dictionaries make no mark for the short vowel sound.

Two other vowel sounds also referred to as short vowel sounds are the /aw/ sound as represented by the *a* in c*a*ll, the *ou* in c*ou*gh, the *au* in c*au*ght, and the *aw* in l*aw;* and the short *oo* sound /o͝o/ as in l*oo*k and g*oo*d.

What are long vowels?

Long Vowel Sounds. Long vowels are those in which the name of the letter is heard. These sounds are sometimes referred to as the glided sounds. There are five long vowel sounds in English, as represented in the following:

Word	Pronunciation
ate	/āt/
eat	/ēt/

ice   /īs/
open   /ō•pən/
use   /ūz/ v.
           /ūs/ n.

The macron /mā´-krŏn/, a straight line over the vowel (ā), is the diacritical mark used to indicate the long vowel sound in phonetic spellings. Another vowel of this type is the long *oo* sound /o͞o/ as heard in r*oo*m and c*oo*l.

What are vowel digraphs?

Vowel Digraphs. Vowel digraphs, like consonant digraphs, occur when two adjacent vowels in a syllable represent one speech sound; that is, two vowel letters only evoke one phoneme and are, therefore, considered one grapheme. The most frequently occurring vowel digraphs are:

Vowel Digraph	Word	Vowel Phoneme
ee	s*ee*d	/ē/
oa	g*oa*t	/ō/
ea	s*ea*t	/ē/
ai	p*ai*n	/ā/
ay	d*ay*	/ā/

The most usual sound of these vowel digraphs is the long sound of the first vowel. However, there are exceptions; for example:

Vowel Digraph	Word	Vowel Phoneme
ea	br*ea*k	/ā/
ea	br*ea*d	/ĕ/
ie	p*ie*ce	/ĕ/
oa	br*oa*d	/aw/

What are diphthongs?

Diphthongs. Diphthongs, like consonant blends, consist of two vowels in one syllable where two sounds are heard. In some reading materials, diphthongs are called vowel blends. The most frequently occurring diphthongs are:

Diphthong	Example Word
oi	*oi*l
oy	*oy*ster
ou	h*ou*se
ow	n*ow*

What vowel combinations can be either diphthong or digraph?

Two other vowel combinations function sometimes as digraphs and sometimes as diphthongs: *ou* and *ow*. The *ou* in *out* is a diphthong; in *brought* it is a vowel digraph. The *ow* in *now* is a diphthong; in *show* it is a vowel digraph. When teaching the phonemes to be associated with these graphemes, it is necessary to teach that each has two distinct sounds.

ou

Digraph	Diphthong
c*ou*gh /aw/	c*ou*ch /ou/
thr*ou*gh /o͞o/	
t*ou*gh /ŭ/	

ow

Digraph	Diphthong
sn*ow* /ō/	c*ow* /ou/

What is a schwa?

Schwa. The schwa sound of a vowel is known as the softened or indeterminate sound. It sounds like a short *u* and frequently occurs in the unstressed or unaccented syllable of a word. It may be spelled with any vowel or combination of vowels. The diacritical mark representing the schwa sound is often an upside down and backward *e* (ə).

Vowel	Example of Schwa Sound	
a	above	/ə•buv´/
e	craven	/krā´•vən/
i	beautiful	/byoo´•tə•fəl
o	committee	/kə•mit´•ē/
u	cherub	/chĕr•əb/

The schwa sound may be represented sometimes by two vowels as shown with the *io* in the word por*tio*n /pôr´•shən/.

What are the exceptions to expected vowel sounds?

Exceptions to Expected Vowel Sounds. Short vowel sounds are the most common vowel sounds in words. The short vowel is expected in a closed syllable, a syllable (or word) ending with one or more consonants. For example, *cat* and *at* are closed syllables; they end with a consonant. There are four standard exceptions to the expected short vowel sounds in a closed syllable.

1. When a vowel is followed by *r*, the vowel sound is not short; rather, it is called an r-controlled vowel.

   ar c*ar*   er h*er*   ir f*ir*
   or f*or*   ur f*ur*

Notice that the *er, ir,* and *ur* all sound the same. The *ar* sounds like the letter name *r*, and the *or* sounds like the word *or*.

2. When the vowel *a* is followed by *l*, it usually represents the /*aw*/ phoneme.

   s*al*t (*sôlt*)
   t*al*k (*tôk*)
   b*al*l (*bôl*)

3. When the vowel grapheme *o* is followed by *lt* or *ld*, it has the long *o* phoneme.

   b*ol*t g*ol*d

4. When the vowel grapheme *i* is followed by *gh, ld,* or *nd,* it usually has the long *i* phoneme (exception wĭnd).

   n*igh*t s*igh* w*il*d m*in*d

When do *y* or *w* serve as vowels?

Y as a Vowel. The letter *y* functions as a vowel when it represents either the short or long sounds of the letter *i*, or is part of a digraph or diphthong. The short *i* sound of *y* is expected in a closed syllable.

   g*y*m g*y*p s*y*mbol

The long *i* sound of *y* is expected when it occurs alone in an open syllable; that is, one ending with a vowel, in this case *y*.

   m*y* d*y*namic p*y*thon

When *y* is preceded by the vowels *a* or *e*, it functions as the second vowel of a vowel digraph.

   d*ay* th*ey* k*ey*

When *y* is in the final position in words of two or more syllables, it usually represents the long *e* sound.

   part*y* assembl*y*

(Note: In some dialects, this final *y* sound is the short *i*. Some dictionaries mark its pronunciation both ways.)

There are two infrequent patterns in which *y* also represents a vowel: when *y* is preceded by *u* or followed by *e*.

   g*uy* b*ye*

W as a Vowel. The letter *w* functions as a vowel only when it is in combination with another vowel: as part of a digraph when preceded by *a, e,* or *o;* as part of a diphthong when preceded by *o* (sometimes).

   W as Part of a Digraph
   p*aw*
   bl*ow*
   gr*ew*

W as Part of a Diphthong
>   cl*ow*n

What generalizations govern vowel sounds?

Vowel Sound Generalizations. There are no hard and fast rules for the expected vowel sounds, only generalizations. The generalizations are quite interrelated. Only those generalizations determined to be the most consistent and applicable are presented in this text (Bailey, 1967; Clymer, 1963/1996; Emans, 1967).

- **The most common vowel sound generalization relates to the short vowel sound.** This sound is expected in a closed syllable, one ending with a consonant. This kind of syllable is sometimes referred to as the CVC pattern (C = Consonant, V = Vowel, C = Consonant). The consonants may be single or in clusters, and it is not mandatory to have a consonant in the initial position of such a syllable or short word. The following words follow the CVC pattern:

>   rag (CVC)
>   shot (CCVC)
>   wish (CVCC)
>   at (VC)

The CVC generalization is useful in pronouncing one-syllable words as well as the individual syllables of polysyllabic words. The following words all contain closed syllables with a short vowel sound:

hamlet	/hăm•lĭt/
fancy	/făn´•sē/
section	/sĕk´•shən/

- **There are three generalizations for when to expect long vowel sounds.** The first is the sound expected in an open syllable, one that ends in a vowel. It is sometimes referred to as the CV pattern (C = Consonant, V = Vowel). There may or may not be a consonant before the vowel. The following words and syllables within words follow the CV pattern:

m*e*	/mē/
*o*pen	/ō•pən/
h*o*tel	/hō•tĕl´/
m*u*sic	/myoo´•z ĭk/

The CV generalization is useful in pronouncing one-syllable words as well as individual syllables of polysyllabic words. The following words contain open syllables with long vowel sounds:

m*u*sic	/myoo´•z ĭk/
prem*o*lar	/prē•mō´•lər/
r*o*mance	/rō•măns´/
T*i*tanic	/tī•tan´•ik/
m*e*ter	/mē´•tər/

- **A long vowel sound is also expected with certain vowel digraphs.** When the vowel digraphs *ee, oa, ea, ai,* and *ay* are in the CVVC pattern, the first vowel often represents its long sound, and the second vowel is not sounded. The following words follow the CVVC pattern:

b*oa*t	s*ay*	str*ai*n	*ea*t	s*ee*
c*oa*st	del*ay*	p*ai*nt	tr*ea*t	sl*ee*p

- **A long vowel sound is also expected in the CVCe (the *e* is usually shown in lower case) pattern.** This is sometimes referred to as the final *e* pattern. The final *e* serves to indicate that the preceding vowel should probably represent the long sound. It occurs most frequently in one-syllable words. The following words follow the CVCe pattern:

>   ate   make   rebate   stroke   fine

Summary

What is the key to a reader using phonics effectively?

It is important to remember that when a reader uses phonics, it will have value only if the word to be decoded is in the reader's oral language. Once phonic generalizations have been applied to an unknown word, the reader has to test it against his or her oral vocabulary to recognize whether the decoding process has resulted in a recognizable English word. In effect, the reader pronounces a sound(s) and asks: Is this a word I know? The reader will also need to use context clues to decide whether the decoded word makes sense in the sentence.

Phonics is one of several word recognition skills students need in order to learn to read. Phonics is not the goal of reading instruction. It serves as a means to an end: the construction of meaning. Some learners may have dif-ficulty learning phonics; if so, other word recognition skills such as context should be taught.

STRUCTURAL ANALYSIS

What is structural analysis?

Structural analysis is a word recognition skill in which knowledge of the meaningful parts of words aids in the identification of an unknown written word. A reader may use structural analy-sis either as an aid to the pronunciation of an unknown word or as an aid to understanding the meaning of an unknown word. Structural analysis may be considered both a word recog-nition and a comprehension skill. A mature reader may use structural analysis for both pur-poses simultaneously.

Structural analysis requires the reader to look at meaningful units or parts of words in order to decode a word or to decide what a word means. The following diagram shows you the relation-ships among the parts of structural analysis that will be discussed in this section.

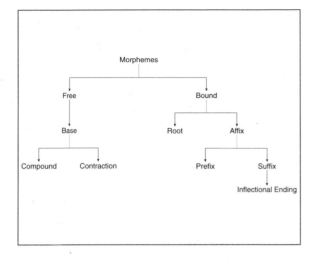

What are morphemes?

The meaningful structural parts of words are called *morphemes*. A morpheme is the smallest unit of meaning in a word. Any unit of meaning in a word is a morpheme.

Cat is a single morpheme.

Cats is two morphemes.

The *s* added to the word *cat* means more than one cat, so it is a second meaning unit added to the meaning unit *cat*.

What are the two types of morphemes?

There are two types of morphemes: bound mor-phemes and free morphemes. A bound morpheme must be attached to another morpheme in order to carry meaning. A free morpheme can stand alone, as a word, in the English language. The *s* in *cats* has no meaning unless it is attached to a word; it is a bound morpheme. The word *cat* can stand alone; it is a free morpheme. The following words illustrate bound and free morphemes.

Unhappy has two morphemes. (*un* is bound; *happy* is free)

Redoing has three morphemes. (*re* and *ing* are bound; *do* is free)

Disagreeable has three morphemes. (*dis* and *able* are bound; *agree* is free)

Desk has one morpheme. (it is free)

Root Words and Base Words

What are root words and base words?

Every word has a major meaning-bearing morpheme. This morpheme may be either a bound or a free morpheme, and is either a root word or a base word. Root words come from or are derived from another language and will not stand alone in English; they are bound morphemes. Base words are English words and will stand alone; they are free morphemes. Following are examples of root words:

Root Words

con*tain*	de*tain*	re*tain*
re*fer*	con*fer*	de*fer*
con*cede*	re*cede*	

Notice that *tain, fer,* and *cede* are the major meaning-bearing parts of these words, but are not English words. An English word is formed only when other bound morphemes are added to these roots. Each of the above words contains two bound morphemes.

Following are examples of base words:

Base Words

girl	*girls*
comfort	un*comfor*table
mark	re*mark*ing

Notice that the base word remains a free morpheme even when one or more affixes have been added to it.

Affixes

What are affixes?

An affix is any morpheme attached to the main meaning-bearing part of a word. Affixes are prefixes, suffixes, and inflectional endings and are bound morphemes. An affix may either precede or follow the root or base word or both. Base and root words may have more than one affix. Root words must have at least one affix.

What is a prefix?

A *prefix* is a bound morpheme added to the beginning of a word. Prefixes add to and change the meaning of the base or root word.

Prefix	Meaning	Example
dis	not	disable
	remove, to make not	disappear
	undo, reverse	disassemble
ex	out	exhale
	beyond	expand
re	back	revert
	again	remake

What is a suffix?

A *suffix* is a bound morpheme added to the end of a word. Suffixes add to and change the meaning of the base or root word.

Suffix	Meaning	Example
er	one who has to do with	laborer
	resident of	southerner
	performs an action	worker
ness	condition of being	fullness
less	without	powerless
	beyond the range of	sightless

Words formed by the addition of prefixes or suffixes to base or root words are known as *derived words,* or derivatives. A different meaning has been derived, or obtained, from the meaning of the original root or base word.

Inflected Forms

What are inflectional endings?

Inflectional endings are a special set of suffixes. They, like other suffixes, are added to the end of a root or base word. Inflectional endings change the number, case, or gender when added to nouns; tense when added to verbs; and form when added to adjectives and adverbs.

Group

n.	Number:	cat*s*	more than one
n.	Case:	child*'s*	shows owner-ship
n.	Gender:	host*ess*	changes to female
v.	Tense:	help*ed*	past tense
adv/adj	Form:	tall*er*	compares two things

The most common inflectional endings are:

Nouns

- **Number** *s* and *es* when affixed to nouns to indicate plurality, as in *toys* and *dresses.*

- **Case** *'s* when attached to nouns to indicate possession, as in "John's ball is red."

- **Number and case** *s'* to indicate plurality and possession, as in "It is the girls' recess time."

- **Gender** *ess* when attached to nouns to indicate change of gender, as from *steward* to *stewardess.*

Verbs

- **Tense** *ed* and *ing* when attached to verbs to indicate, respectively, past tense and present participle, as in *walked* and *walking* and *s* to verbs to indicate agreement with third-person singular nouns, as in "Mary works."

Adjectives/Adverbs

- **Form** *er* and *est* when affixed to adjectives or adverbs to indicate, respectively, comparative and superlative forms, as in *faster* and *fastest.*

When new words are formed by the addition of inflectional endings, they are called inflected forms of the words. The *er* in *taller* is an inflectional ending because it changes the form of the word, but *er* in *helper* is not an inflectional ending because it does not change the tense, case, number, form, or gender of the word. (The *er* in *helper* is a suffix; it changes the verb *help* into a noun—one who helps.)

It is possible for a word to be both derived and inflected. Any word that has had a prefix or suffix added to it is a derived form of that word. The addition of an inflectional ending produces the inflected form.

Independent is a derived form of *depend.* (prefix *in* + *depend* + suffix *ent*)

Unhappier is both derived and inflected. (prefix *un* [not] + *happy* [base word] + inflected ending *er* [comparative])

Compound Words and Contractions

What are compound words and contractions? Two other types of words are formed by the combination of meaningful structural units, or morphemes: compound words and contractions. *Compound words* are a combination of two free morphemes. The meaning of the new word must retain elements of both meanings and pronunciation of the two previous morphemes in order to be classified as a compound word. *Dollhouse, racetrack,* and *bathroom* are compound words: *office, target,* and *together* are not compound words.

Contractions are formed by combining two free morphemes into a shortened form by the omission of one or more letters and the insertion of an apostrophe where those letters were omitted.

are + *not* form the contraction *aren't*
they + *are* form the contraction *they're*
he + *will* form the contraction *he'll*

Without the use of context clues, confusion may arise with the use of *'s* with singular nouns. The word *boy's* could be the contracted form of *boy* + *is* or it may be a change of case and the possessive form of boy.

John's sister can't say what John's going to do.

In this sentence, the first *John's* is possessive while the second one is the contracted form of *John is*.

Structural Changes and Spelling

What are the important structural changes in a word that influence spelling?

Structural analysis can be helpful, but sometimes beginning readers find the addition of a structural part to a known word confusing. The word may look so different that they are unable to recognize the derived word. This is especially true when a spelling change occurs in the base word.

The following generalizations should be taught to aid in the reader's recognition of base words and derived words as well as to aid in the spelling of such words.

1. When a word ends with *e*, the *e* is dropped before adding an inflectional ending that begins with a vowel.

   bake + *ing* becomes *baking*

   hope + *ed* becomes *hoped*

2. When a word ends with a single consonant, that consonant is doubled before adding *ing* or *ed*.

   hop + *ed* becomes *hopped*

   begin + *ing* becomes *beginning*

3. When a word ends with *f* or *fe* (with a silent *e*), the *f* is usually changed to *v* before the ending is added.

   calf + *es* becomes *calves*

   wife + *es* becomes *wives*

4. When a word ends in *y* preceded by a consonant, the *y* is usually changed to *i* before endings are added, unless the ending begins with *i*.

   dry + *ed* becomes *dried*

   party + *es* becomes *parties*

   sorry + *est* becomes *sorriest*

   cry + *ing* becomes *crying*

5. When a word ends with *y* preceded by a vowel, no change is made in the base word before adding endings.

   boy + *s* becomes *boys*

   stay + *ed* or *ing* becomes *stayed* or *staying*

6. When the base word ends with *s*, *ss*, *ch*, *sh*, or *x*, the inflectional ending *es* is added, rather than *s*; when the word ends in *f/fe*, change to *v* and add *es*; when the word ends in *y*, change to *i* and add *es*.

   focus becomes *focuses*

   mess becomes *messes*

   lunch becomes *lunches*

   dish becomes *dishes*

   box becomes *boxes*

   half becomes *halves*

   cry becomes *cries*

Syllable Generalizations

What is a syllable, and how does knowledge of syllables aid in word pronunciation?

A syllable is an oral language unit in which a vowel sound is heard. There are as many syllables in a word as there are vowel sounds. In word recognition, we don't worry about conventions of "correct" division of words; rather we divide in order to deal with the pronunciation of one-syllable units at a time. A syllable may or may not contain a consonant sound.

a, my, ate, dog, boat (these are monosyllabic words)

dis-con-tin-ue, re-lat-ed (these are polysyl-labic words)

Knowledge governing vowel sounds (discussed earlier) applies whether to a one-syllable word or a polysyllabic word.

The primary reason for teaching or learning how to divide words into syllables for reading or decoding purposes is to give the reader clues to the possible pronunciation of vowel sounds in unknown words.

What are the generalizations concerning syllable division?

Generalizations for syllabic division of words give the reader possibilities to chunk an unfamiliar word so that he or she may decode it by applying phonic and structural analysis. (Syllabication is *not* used for dividing words in writing. The dictionary should be used for this purpose. Therefore, students must be taught to read phonetic respellings.) If the decoded word is in the reader's oral language, this serves as the reader's check on the accuracy of the generalizations that have been applied. Structural elements of the word are dealt with first; then phonic generalizations are applied as needed.

What are three structural generalizations for dividing words into syllables?

The first three generalizations for syllables deal with the structural parts of unknown words, that is, bases, roots, and affixes. Whenever readers are being taught to divide words into syllables, they should first look for meaningful chunks of the unknown word.

1. Almost all affixes form separate syllables. In the word *rewrite,* *re* is a separate syllable; in the word *useless,* *less* is a separate syllable. Exceptions to this include the inflectional endings *'s, s,* and *ed* except when *ed* is preceded by *d* or *t.*

    books is one syllable
    Sue's is one syllable

    chained is one syllable
    wanted is two syllables
    loaded is two syllables

2. The two words of a compound word form separate syllables, even if there are additional syllables in one or both of the words used to form the compound word.

Word	Morphemes	Syllables
cowboy	*cow + boy*	2 syllables
lumberjack	*lumber + jack*	2 + 1 = 3 syllables
policewoman	*police + woman*	2 + 2 = 4 syllables

3. The contracted form of two words sometimes produces just one syllable because it is a vowel that has been deleted to form the contraction. Sometimes it produces two:

    can't is one syllable
    they'll is one syllable
    couldn't is two syllables
    wasn't is two syllables

The next five syllabication generalizations help readers apply phonic generalizations by dividing long words into syllables (chunking).

1. When two consonants occur between two vowels, the syllabic division is usually *between the two consonants.* (Do not divide consonant digraphs and blends; they are treated as single consonants.) This pattern is known as the -VCCV- pattern. There may or may not be other consonants preceding or following this pattern.

bargain	bar-gain
circus	cir-cus
enter	en-ter
entertain	en-ter-tain

2. In the -VCCV- pattern, divide *before or after the blend or digraph.* (Exception: double consonants; many experts treat double consonants as digraphs.)

letter   lett-er
graphic   graph-ic
doctrine   doc-trine

3. When one consonant occurs between two vowels, the syllabic division may put the consonant with *either the first or second vowel.* This is known as the -VCV- pattern. There may or may not be other consonants preceding or following this pattern.

a. When the consonant goes with the first vowel, the first syllable is closed, and the first vowel sound is expected to be short (VC-V).

riv-er   ex-it   liz-ard

b. When the consonant goes with the second vowel, the first syllable is open and the first vowel is expected to be long (V-CV).

ma-jor   ho-tel   ba-con

First, try the consonant with the first vowel and check against oral language. If this seems incorrect, try the consonant with the second vowel.

There are a few words in our language with the -VCV- pattern that actually appear to divide both ways. These words are called *homographs* because they are spelled the same. However, they are two different words with different pronunciations and meanings. The contextual usage of the words and the reader's oral language are the only checks on the correct pronunciation. The words don't actually divide differently; the accent is placed differently.

record (rē-cord´ rĕ´-cord) Be sure to record record low temperatures.

present (prē-sent´ prĕ´-sent) Will you present the present to our guest?

4. When a word ends in *le* preceded by a single consonant, the final syllable usually consists of the *consonant plus the le.*

cradle   cra-dle   (krā-dəl)
trifle   tri-fle   (trī-fəl)

If two consonants precede the *le,* usually divide *after the second consonant* to prevent splitting blends and digraphs.

rattle   ratt-le
ankle   ank-le

5. The vowel sound in an unstressed or unaccented syllable is often the schwa sound. Any vowel may have the schwa sound, which sounds like the short *u.*

com-mit´-tee   (kə•m ĭt´•ē)
a-gain   (ə•gĕn´)
dem´-*on*-strate (dem´•ən•strāt)

Summary

The division (or chunking) of unfamiliar words is guided by generalizations or possibilities, not by rules. These generalizations must be used in conjunction with each other and with phonics. Because many words in the English language are not phonetically regular, sometimes it is necessary to check the pronunciation of a word in the dictionary. Before requiring students to sound out words, teachers must be sure that the words follow accepted generalizations for their pronunciations. The following steps summarize how to apply generalizations for dividing words into syllables or chunks:

1. Separate affixes.

2. Follow generalizations to divide base or root words.

3. Apply phonic generalizations.

4. Try alternates if the first attempt doesn't result in an acceptable word for the context.

	onset	*rime*
street	_____	_____
day	_____	_____
race	_____	_____

PRACTICE EXERCISE

Directions

This series of exercises is designed to help you practice and check the knowledge you gained from this resource. Complete each exercise; then check your answers with those on page 583.

PART I

Write the answer on the line for each question.

1. How many sounds do your hear in [cat image] ? _____

2. Write the word for these sounds: /h/ /ou/ /s/. _____

3. Identify the onset and rime in the following words:

Part II

Classify the italicized letters in the following words as (a) diphthong, (b) vowel digraph, (c) consonant digraph, or (d) consonant blend. Write the correct letter in the blank to the left of each word.

_____ 1. *bl*ack

_____ 2. *oy*ster

_____ 3. *sh*ine

_____ 4. t*oi*l

_____ 5. *br*ight

_____ 6. *dw*indle

_____ 7. *pn*eumatic

_____ 8. *g*oat

_____ 9. *ea*se

_____ 10. h*ow*

_____ 11. *gn*aw

_____ 12. p*ai*l

_____ 13. br*ough*t

_____ 14. wre*ck*

_____ 15. t*ow*

_____ 16. thi*ng*

_____ 17. cra*ft*

_____ 18. n*ee*d

_____ 19. *str*ing

_____ 20. l*ay*

PART III

From among the four words in each list, select the one that *does not* conform to the phonics generalization that the other three do. Write the letter of the exception on the line to the left. Then write the generalization to which the other words conform on the next line. If all words conform, choose "e," no exception.

Example:

__c__   a. bait   b. sail   c. said   d. bail   e. no exception

_____ *CVVC generalization - ai digraph* _____

___ 1.   a. rate   b. line   c. mete   d. seem   e. no exception

___ 2.   a. gin   b. gift   c. gym   d. gem   e. no exception

___ 3.   a. cup   b. pin   c. slur   d. get   e. no exception

___ 4.   a. eat   b. seat   c. coat   d. seem   e. no exception

___ 5.   a. be   b. no   c. music   d. me   e. no exception

___ 6.   a. fir   b. fur   c. order   d. me   e. no exception

PART IV

From column B select the synonym, example, or definition that best fits the term in column A. Then write the letter of the synonym, example, or definition on the line to the left.

Column A	Column B	Column A	Column B
___ 1. grapheme	a. *can't*	___12. diphthong	i. *meaner*
___ 2. morpheme	b. blended vowel sound	___13. contraction	j. two letters representing one phoneme
___ 3. derived word	c. *inhospitable*	___14. inflected word	
___ 4. phoneme	d. letter	___15. phonemic awareness	k. *tablecloth*
___ 5. digraph	e. clues provided by sentence meaning		l. *women's*
___ 6. compound			m. study of phoneme-grapheme relationships
___ 7. phonics	f. speech sound		
___ 8. basic sight word	g. merging consecutive consonant sounds, each retaining its own identity		n. *an*
___ 9. affixes			o. major meaning-bearing unit
___10. base word			p. prefixes, suffixes, inflectional endings
___11. possessive	h. meaningful structural unit		q. awareness of sounds in spoken words

PART V

Divide each of the following nonsense words in syllables, and mark the vowels with diacritical marks. Be ready to state your reasons for syllabication and for vowel sounds. Where two possibilities for division exist, give both.

1. ekon

2. roashing

3. whochment

4. sluppelgug

5. presilnapishment

6. drackle

7. mastle

8. kromsul

9. bleting

PART VI

Choose the best answer among the stated possibilities.

1. The study of the phoneme/grapheme relationship in English is called

   a. phonetics.

   b. phonics.

   c. linguistics.

   d. both a and b

2. The word pronounced by the use of phonics must be in the reader's oral language in order to

   a. check the accuracy of the pronunciation.

   b. check the accuracy of phonics rules.

   c. check the contextual meaning of a word.

   d. All of the above.

3. The sounds of *c* and *g* may be identified as

   a. hard and soft.

   b. short and long.

   c. hiss and guttural.

   d. None of the above.

4. Which of the following words contains a digraph?

   a. blind

   b. must

   c. kick

   d. gram

5. Which of the following words contains a consonant blend?

   a. wash

   b. letter

   c. ship

   d. stripe

6. The sounds of *s* may be

   a. c, st, sh, s

   b. s, sh, z, zh

   c. k, c, z, s

   d. gz, ks, s, c

7. In which of the following groups of words are all three exceptions to vowel generalizations?

   a. sir, cat, bake

   b. colt, see, out

   c. car, find, old

   d. vie, sigh, my

8. Which of the following words would you *not* expect to see on a list of basic sight words?

   a. the

   b. play

   c. with

   d. certainly

9. Which of the following words is probably correctly divided into syllables?

a. mis-thez-ment

b. bomn-y

c. ci-mtor

d. ba-tmle

10. Which of the following words contains a schwa?

a. again

b. cart

c. book

d. below

See page 583 to check your answers.

ANSWER KEY

PART I

1. three

2. house

3. *str   eet*

   d   ay

   r   ace

PART II

1.	d	11.	c
2.	a	12.	b
3.	c	13.	b
4.	a	14.	c
5.	d	15.	b
6.	d	16.	c
7.	c	17.	d
8.	b	18.	b
9.	b	19.	d
10.	a	20.	b

PART III

1. d—final *e* or CVCe generalization

2. b—soft *g* generalization or

   e—CVC generalization

3. c—CVC generalization

4. e—CVVC generalization

5. e—if only first syllable of music is considered; c—if second syllable is—open syllable generalization

6. d—r-controlled vowel sound

PART IV

1.	d	9.	p
2.	h	10.	o
3.	c	11.	l
4.	f	12.	b
5.	j	13.	a
6.	k	14.	i or l
7.	m	15.	q
8.	n		

PART V

1. ē•kŏn, ĕk•ən

2. rōash•ĭng

3. whŏch•mənt

4. slŭp•pĕl•gŭg, slŭpp•əl•gəg

5. prē•sĭl•năp•ĭsh•mĕnt, prē•sĭl•nā•pĭsh•mənt

6. drăck•əl

7. măs•təl, măst•le

8. krŏm•sŭl

9. blĕt•ing

PART VI

1.	b	8.	d
2.	a	9.	a
3.	a	10.	a
4.	c		
5.	d		
6.	b		
7.	c		

References

Adams, M. J. (1990). *Beginning to read: Thinking and learning about print.* Cambridge, MA: MIT Press.

Adams, M., & Bertram, B. (1980). *Background knowledge and reading comprehension. Reading Education Report No. 13.* Urbana, IL: Center for the Study of Reading, University of Illinois. (ERIC Document Reproduction Service ED 181 431).

Allen, R. V. (1976). *Language experiences in communication.* Boston: Houghton Mifflin.

Allington, R. L. (1977). If they don't read much, how they ever gonna get good? *Journal of Reading, 21,* 57–61.

Allington, R. L. (1983). The reading instruction provided readers of differing reading abilities. *Elementary School Journal, 83,* 548–559.

Allington, R. L. (1997). Overselling phonics. *Reading Today,* August/September, 15–16.

Allington, R. L., & Walmsley, S. A. (Eds.). (1995). *No quick fix: Rethinking literacy programs in America's elementary schools.* New York: Teachers College Press.

Alvermann, D. E., Dillon, D. R., & O'Brien, D. G. (1987). *Using discussion to promote reading comprehension.* Newark, DE: International Reading Association.

Alvermann, D. E., & Hynd, C. R. (1987, December). *Overcoming misconceptions in science: An on-line study of prior knowledge activation.* Paper presented at the meeting of the National Reading Conference, St. Petersburg, FL.

Alvermann, D. E., & Moore, D. W. (1991). *Secondary schools.* In R. Barr, M. L. Kamil, P. B. Mosenthal, & P. D. Pearson (Eds.), *Handbook of reading research* (Vol. 2, pp. 951–983). New York: Longman.

Alvermann, D. E., Smith, L. C., & Readence, J. E. (1985). Prior knowledge activation and the comprehension of compatible and incompatible text. *Reading Research Quarterly, 20,* 420–436.

Anders, P., & Bos, C. (1986). Semantic feature analysis: An interactive strategy for vocabulary development and text comprehension. *Journal of Reading, 29,* 610–616.

Anderson, R. C., & Freebody, P. (1981). Vocabulary knowledge. In J. T. Guthrie (Ed.), *Comprehension and teaching: Research reviews.* Newark, DE: International Reading Association.

Anderson, R. C., Hiebert, E. H., Scott, J. A., & Wilkinson, I. A. G. (1985). *Becoming a nation of readers: The report of the Commission on Reading.* Washington, DC: National Institute of Education.

Anderson, R. C., & Pearson, P. D. (1984). A schema-theoretic view of basic processes in reading comprehension. In P. D. Pearson (Ed.), *Handbook of reading research* (pp. 255–291). New York: Longman.

Anderson, R. C., Reynolds, R. E., Schallert, D. L., & Goetz, E. T. (1977). Frame-works for comprehending discourse. *American Educational Research Journal, 14,* 367–381.

Anderson, R. C., Wilson, P. T., & Fielding, L. G. (1988). Growth in reading and how children spend their time outside of school. *Reading Research Quarterly, 23*(3), 285–303.

Anderson, T. H., & Armbruster, B. B. (1984a). Content area textbooks. In R. C. Anderson, J. Osborn, & R. J. Tierney (Eds.), *Learning to read in American schools* (pp. 193–226). Hillsdale, NJ: Lawrence Erlbaum.

Anderson, T. H., & Armbruster, B. B. (1984b). Studying. In P. D. Pearson (Ed.), *Handbook of reading research* (pp. 657–679). New York: Longman.

Applebee, A. N. (1977). Writing and reading. *Journal of Reading, 20,* 534–537.

Applebee, A. N. (1978). *The child's concept of story: Ages two to seventeen.* Chicago: University of Chicago Press.

Armbruster, B. B. (1991, May 5). *Content area reading instruction.* A presentation given at the Conference on Reading Research, Las Vegas, NV.

Armbruster, B. B., Anderson, T. H., & Osterlag, J. (1989). Teaching text structure to improve reading and writing. *Reading Teacher, 43,* 130–137.

Armento, B. J., Nash, G. B., Salter, C. L., & Wixson, K. (1991). *America will be.* Boston: Houghton Mifflin.

Association for Supervision and Curriculum Development. (1994). The online classroom. *Update, 36*(10), 1.

Atwell, N. (1987). *In the middle.* Portsmouth, NH: Heinemann.

Au, K. H. (1979). Using the experience-text-relationship method with minority children. *The Reading Teacher, 32,* 677–679.

Au, K. H. (1993). *Literacy instruction in multicultural settings.* Orlando: Harcourt Brace.

Au, K. H., Mason, J. M., & Scheu, J. A. (1995). *Literacy instruction for today.* New York: HarperCollins.

Au, K. H., Scheu, J. A., Kawakami, A. J., & Herman, P. A. (1990). Assessment and accountability in a whole literacy curriculum. *The Reading Teacher, 43,* 574–578.

Baghban, M. (1984). *Our daughter learns to read and write: A case study from birth to three.* Newark, DE: International Reading Association.

Baker, L., & Brown, A. L. (1984a). Metacognitive skills in reading. In P. D. Pearson (Ed.), *Handbook of reading research* (pp. 353–394). New York: Longman.

Baker, L., & Brown, A. L. (1984b). Cognitive monitoring in reading. In J. Flood (Ed.), *Understanding reading comprehension* (pp. 21–44). Newark, DE: International Reading Association.

Bailey, M. H. (1967). The utility of phonic generalizations in grades one through six. *The Reading Teacher, 20,* 413–418.

Ball, E. W., & Blachman, B. A. (1991). Does phoneme segmentation training make a difference in early word recognition and development spelling? *Reading Research Quarterly, 26,* 49–66.

Bandura, A. (1986). *Psychological modeling: Conflicting theories.* Chicago: Aldine-Atherton.

Barone, D. (1990). The written responses of young children: Beyond comprehension to story understanding. *New Advocate, 3,* 49–56.

Barr, R., & Dreeben, R. (1991). Grouping students for reading instruction. In R. Barr, M. L. Kamil, P. Mosenthal, & P. D. Pearson (Eds.), *Handbook of reading research* (Vol. 2, pp. 885–910). New York: Longman.

Barrera, R. B. (1983). Bilingual reading in the primary grades: Some questionable views and practices. In T. H. Escobedo (Ed.), *Early childhood bilingual education* (pp. 164–184). New York: Teachers College Press.

Bartlett, F. C. (1932). *Remembering.* Cambridge, U.K.: Cambridge University Press.

Baumann, J. F. (1984). The effectiveness of a direct instruction paradigm for teaching main idea comprehension. *Reading Research Quarterly, 20*(1), 93–115.

Baumann, J. F. (1986). *Teaching main idea comprehension.* Newark, DE: International Reading Association.

Baumann, J. F., & Schmitt, M. C. (1986). The what, why, how, and when of comprehension instruction. *The Reading Teacher, 39,* 640–647.

Beach, R., & Appleman, D. (1984). Reading strategies for expository and literary text types. In A. C. Purves & O. Niles (Eds.), *Becoming readers in a complex society* (pp. 115–143). Eighty-third Yearbook of the National Society of Education. Chicago: University of Chicago Press.

Bean, T. W., & Steenwyk, F. L. (1984). The effect of three forms of summarization instruction on sixth graders' summary writing and comprehension. *Journal of Reading Behavior, 16,* 297–306.

Beck, I. L. (1984). Developing comprehension: The impact of the directed reading lesson. In R. C. Anderson, J. Osborn, & R. J. Tierney (Eds.), *Learning to read in American schools: Basal readers and content texts* (pp. 3–20). Hillsdale, NJ: Lawrence Erlbaum.

Beck, I. L., McCaslin, M., & McKeown, M. (1980). *The rationale and design of a program to teach vocabulary to fourth-grade students.* Pittsburgh: University of Pittsburgh, Learning Research and Development Center.

Beck, I. L., & McKeown, M. G. (1981). Developing questions that promote comprehension: The story map. *Language Arts, 58,* 913–918.

Beck, I. L., & McKeown, M. (1991). Conditions of vocabulary acquisition. In R. Barr, M. L. Kamil, P. Mosenthal, & P. D. Pearson (Eds.), *Handbook of reading research* (Vol. 2, pp. 789–814). New York: Longman.

Beck, I. L., McKeown, M. G., McCaslin, E. S., & Burkes, A. M. (1979). *Instructional dimension that may affect reading comprehension: Examples from two commercial reading programs.* Pittsburgh: University of Pittsburgh, Learning Research and Development Center.

Beck, I. L., McKeown, M. G., & Omanson, R. C. (1987). The effects and uses of diverse vocabulary instructional techniques. In M. G. McKeown & M. E. Curtis (Eds.), *The nature of vocabulary acquisition.* Hillsdale, NJ: Lawrence Erlbaum.

Beck, I. L., Omanson, R. C., & McKeown, M. G. (1982). An instructional redesign of reading lessons: Effects on comprehension. *Reading Research Quarterly, 17*(4), 462–481.

Beck, I. L., Perfetti, C. A., & McKeown, M. G. (1982). Effects of long-term vocabulary instruction on lexical access and reading comprehension. *Journal of Educational Psychology, 74,* 506–521.

Beldin, H. O. (1970). Informal reading testing: Historical review and review of the research. In W. K. Durr (Ed.), *Reading difficulties: Diagnosis, correction, and remediation* (pp. 67–84). Newark, DE: International Reading Association.

Bertrand, J. E. (1991). Student assessment and evaluation. In B. Harp (Ed.), *Assessment and evaluation in whole language programs* (pp. 17–33). Norwood, MA: Christopher-Gordon.

Better Homes and Gardens. (1979). *Complete guide to gardening.* Des Moines: Meredith Corporation.

Birnbaum, J. C. (1982). The reading and composing behavior of selected fourth- and seventh-grade students. *Research in the Teaching of English, 16,* 241–260.

Bissex, G. L. (1980). *Gnys at wrk: A child learns to read and write.* Cambridge, MA: Harvard University Press.

Blachowicz, C. L. Z. (1986). Making connections: Alternatives to the vocabulary notebook. *Journal of Reading, 29,* 643–649.

Bond, G. L., & Dykstra, R. (1967). The cooperative research program in first-grade reading instruction. *Reading Research Quarterly, 2,* entire issue.

Boyer, E. L. (1995). *The basic school.* Princeton, NJ: The Carnegie Foundation for the Advancement of Teaching.

Bransford, J. Sherwood, R., Hasselbring, T., Kinzer, C., & Williams, S. (1990). Anchored instruction: Why we need it and how technology can help. In D. Nix & R. Spiro (Eds.), *Cognition, education and multimedia: Exploring ideas in high technology* (pp. 115–141). Hillsdale, NJ: Lawrence Erlbaum.

Bridge, C. A., Winograd, P. N., & Haley, D. (1983). Using predictable materials vs. preprimers to teach beginning sight words. *The Reading Teacher, 36*(9), 884–891.

Bromley, K. D. (1989). Buddy journals make the reading writing connection. *The Reading Teacher, 43,* 122–129.

Brown, A. L. (1980). Metacognitive development and reading. In R. J. Spiro, B. C. Bruce, & W. F. Brewer (Eds.), *Theoretical issues in reading comprehension* (pp. 453–481). Hillsdale, NJ: Lawrence Erlbaum.

Brown, A. L., & Day, J. D. (1983). Macrorules for summarizing texts: The development of expertise. *Journal of Verbal Learning and Verbal Behavior, 22*(1), 1–14.

Burns, P. C., Roe, B. D., & Ross, E. P. (1988). *Teaching reading in today's elementary schools* (4th ed.). Boston: Houghton Mifflin.

Cain, K. (1996). Story knowledge and comprehension skills. In C. Cornoldi & J. Oakhill (Eds.), *Reading comprehension difficulties: Processes and interventions* (pp. 167–192). Mahwah, NJ: Lawrence Erlbaum.

Calfee, R. C., & Drum, P. A. (1986). Research on teaching reading. In M. C. Wittrock (Ed.), *Handbook of research on reading* (3rd ed.) (pp. 804–849). New York: Macmillan.

Calkins, L. M. (1983). *Lessons from a child on the teaching and learning of writing.* Exeter, NH: Heinemann.

Calkins, L. M. (1986). *The art of teaching writing.* Portsmouth, NH: Heinemann.

Cambourne, B. (1988). *The whole story: Natural learning and the acquisition of literacy in the classroom.* New York: Ashton-Scholastic.

Cambourne, B., & Turbill, J. (1990). Assessment in whole language classrooms: Theory into practice. *Elementary School Journal, 90,* 337–349.

Carnine, L., Carnine, D., & Gersten, R. (1984). Analysis of oral reading errors made by economically disadvantaged students taught with a synthetic phonics approach. *Reading Research Quarterly, 19,* 343–356.

Carr, E., & Wixson, K. K. (1986). Guidelines for evaluating vocabulary instruction. *Journal of Reading, 29,* 588–595.

Carr, M. (1987). Clustering with nonreaders/writers. In C. B. Olson (Ed.), *Practical ideas for teaching writing as a process* (pp. 20–21). Sacramento: California State Department of Education.

Cazden, C. (1972). *Child language and education.* New York: Holt, Rinehart and Winston.

Center for the Study of Reading. (n.d.). *Suggestions for classroom: Teachers and independent reading.* Urbana, IL: Center for the Study of Reading, University of Illinois.

Chall, J. S. (1967). *Learning to read: The great debate.* New York: McGraw–Hill.

Chall, J. S. (1983). *Learning to read: The great debate* (rev. ed.). New York: McGraw-Hill.

Chall, J. S. (1987). Two vocabularies for reading: Recognition and meaning. In M. G. McKeown & M. E. Curtis (Eds.), *The nature of vocabulary acquisition* (pp. 7–17). Hillsdale, NJ: Lawrence Erlbaum.

Chall, J. S., & Conrad, S. S. (1990). Textbooks and challenge: The influence of educational research. In D. L. Elliott & A. Woodward (Eds.), *Textbooks and schooling in the United States* (pp. 42–55). Chicago: National Society for the Study of Education.

Chapman, M. L. (1995). Designing literacy learning experiences in a multiage classroom. *Language 145, 72*(8), 416–428.

Chard, D., & Osborne, J. (n.d.). *Guidelines for examing phonics and word recognition instruction in early reading programs.* Austin, TX: Texas Center for Reading and Language Arts.

Chomsky, C. (1965). *Aspects of the theory of syntax.* Cambridge, MA: MIT Press.

Clark, C. M. (1984). Teacher planning and reading comprehension. In G. G. Duffy, L. K. Roehler, & J. Mason (Eds.), *Comprehension instruction: Perspectives and suggestions* (pp. 58–70). New York: Longman.

Clark, M. M. (1976). *Young fluent readers.* London: Heinemann.

Clay, M. M. (1967). The reading behavior of five-year-old children: A research report. *New Zealand Journal of Educational Studies, 2,* 11–31.

Clay, M. M. (1979). *Reading: The patterning of complex behavior* (2nd ed.). Auckland, New Zealand: Heinemann.

Clay, M. M. (1982). *Observing young readers: Selected papers.* Exeter, NH: Heinemann.

Clay, M. M. (1985). *The early detection of reading difficulties* (3rd ed.). Portsmouth, NH: Heinemann.

Clay, M. M. (1991). *Becoming literate: The construction of inner control.* Portsmouth, NH: Heinemann.

Clymer, T. (1968). What is "reading"? Some current concepts. In H. M. Robinson (Ed.), *Innovation and change in reading instruction.* Sixty-seventh Yearbook of the National Society for the Study of Education. Chicago: University of Chicago Press.

Clymer, T. (1963/1996). The utility of phonic generalizations in the primary grades. *The Reading Teacher, 16,* 252–258. (Reprinted in *The Reading Teacher, 50,* 182–187, 1996)

Cockrum, W. A., & Castillo, M. (1991). Whole language assessment and evaluation strategies. In B. Harp (Ed.), *Assessment and evaluation in whole language programs* (pp. 73–86). Norwood, MA: Christopher-Gordon.

Coger, L. E., & White, M. R. (1982). *Readers theatre handbook: A dramatic approach to literature.* Glenview, IL: Scott, Foresman.

Cohen, D. (1968). The effect of literature on vocabulary and reading achievement. *Elementary English, 45,* 209–213.

Coley, J. D., & Hoffman, D. M. (1990). Overcoming learned helplessness in at-risk readers. *Journal of Reading, 33,* 497–502.

Collins, A., Brown, J. S., & Newman, S. E. (1986). *Cognitive apprenticeship: Teaching the craft of reading, writing and mathematics.* Report No. 6459. Cambridge, MA: BNN Laboratories.

Cook-Gumprez, J. (Ed.). (1986). *The social construction of literacy.* Cambridge, U.K.: Cambridge University Press.

Cooper, J. D. (1986). *Improving reading comprehension.* Boston: Houghton Mifflin.

Cooper, J. D., & Kiger, N. (In press). *Literacy assessment: Helping teachers plan instruction.* Boston: Houghton Mifflin.

Cooper, J. D., Warncke, E. W., & Shipman, D. (1988). *The what and how of reading instruction,* 2nd ed. Columbus, OH: Merrill.

Cullinan, B., Harwood, K., & Galda, L. (1983). The reader and the story: Comprehension and response. *Journal of Research and Development in Education, 16,* 29–38.

Cunningham, P. M. (1995). *Phonics they use.* New York: Harper-Collins.

Cunningham, J. W., Cunningham, P. M., & Arthur, S. U. (1981). *Middle and secondary school reading.* New York: Longman.

Cunningham, P., & Allington, R. L. (1994). *Classrooms that work: They can all read and write.* New York: HarperCollins.

Cunningham, P. M., & Cunningham, J. W. (1992). Making words: Enhancing the invented spelling-decoding connection. *The Reading Teacher, 46* (2), 106–115.

Cunningham, P. A., Hall, D. P., & Defee, M. (1998). Nonability grouped, multilevel instruction: Eight years later. *The Reading Teacher, 51* (8), 652–664.

Dahl, K. L. (1988). Peer conferences as social contexts for learning about revision. In J. E. Readence & R. S. Baldwin (Eds.), *Dialogues in literacy research* (pp. 307–315). *Thirty-seventh yearbook of the National Reading Conference.* Chicago: National Reading Conference.

Dahl, K. L., & Farnan, N. (1998). *Children's writing: Perspectives from research.* Newark, DE: International Reading Association, and Chicago, IL: National Reading Conference.

Davey, B., & McBride, S. (1986). Effects of question generating training on reading comprehension. *Journal of Educational Psychology, 78*(4), 256–262.

Davis, F. (1971). Psychometric research in reading comprehension. In F. Davis (Ed.), *Literature of research in reading with emphasis on models.* Brunswick, NJ: Rutgers University Press.

Dawson, M. M. (1987). Beyond ability grouping: A review of the effectiveness of ability grouping and its alternatives. *School Psychology Review, 16,* 348–369.

DeFord, D. E., Lyons, C. A., & Pinnell, G. S. (1991). *Bridges to literacy: Learning from reading recovery.* Portsmouth, NH: Heinemann.

Delpit, L. (1995). *Other people's children.* New York: The New Press.

Denner, P. R., & Rickards, J. P. (1987). A developmental comparison of the effects of provided and generated questions on text recall. *Contemporary Educational Psychology, 12,* 135–146.

Dillon, D. (1990). Editorial. *Language Arts, 67,* 237–239.

Dillon, J. T. (1984). Research on questioning and discussion. *Educational Leadership, 42,* 50–56.

Dolch, E. W. (1936). A basic sight vocabulary. *Elementary School Journal, 36,* 456–460.

Dole, J. A., Duffy, G. G., Roehler, L. R., & Pearson, P. D. (1991). Moving from the old to the new: Research on reading comprehension instruction. *Review of Educational Research, 61,* 239–264.

Dole, J. A., & Smith, E. L. (1989). Prior knowledge and learning from science text: An instructional study. In *Cognitive and social perspectives for literacy research and instruction* (pp. 345–352). *Thirty-eighth Yearbook of the National Reading Conference.* Chicago: National Reading Conference.

Dressed, J. H. (1990). The effects of listening to and discussing different qualities of children's literature on the narrative writing of fifth graders. *Research in the Teaching of English, 24,* 397–414.

Driver, R., & Erickson, G. (1983). Theories in action: Some theoretical and empirical issues in the study of students' conceptual frameworks in science. *Studies in Science Education, 10,* 37–60.

Duffy, G. G. (1993). Rethinking strategy instruction: Four teachers' development and their low achievers' understandings. *Elementary School Journal, 93*(3), 231–247.

Duffy, G. G., Roehler, L., Sivan, E., Rackliffe, G., Book, C., Meloth, M., Vavrus, L., Wesselman, R., Putnam, J., & Bassiri, D. (1987). Effects of explaining the reasoning associated with using reading strategies. *Reading Research Quarterly, 22,* 347–368.

Durkin, D. (1966). *Children who read early.* New York: Teachers College Press.

Durkin, D. (1978). What classroom observations reveal about reading comprehension instruction. *Reading Research Quarterly, 14*(4), 481–533.

Durkin, D. (1981a). Reading comprehension instruction in five basal reader series. *Reading Research Quarterly, 16*(4), 515–544.

Durkin, D. (1981b). What is the value of the new interest in reading comprehension? *Language Arts, 58*(1), 23–43.

Durkin, D. (1989). *Teaching them to read* (5th ed.). Boston: Allyn and Bacon.

Durkin, D. (1990). Dolores Durkin speaks on instruction. *The Reading Teacher, 43,* 472–476.

Eckoff, B. (1983). How reading affects children's writing. *Language Arts, 60,* 607–616.

Editors of the American Heritage Dictionary. (1986). *Word mysteries and histories.* Boston: Houghton Mifflin.

Eeds, M. (1989). Grand conversations: An exploration of meaning construction in study groups. *Research in the Teaching of English, 23,* 4–29.

Eldredge, J. L. (1995). *Teaching decoding in holistic classrooms.* Englewood Cliffs, NJ: Merrill: An Imprint of Prentice Hall.

Elley, W. B., & Mangubhai, F. (1983). The impact of reading on second language learning. *Reading Research Quarterly, 19*(1), 53–67.

Elliott, D. L. (1990). Textbooks and the curriculum in the postwar era: 1950–1980. In D. L. Elliott & A. Woodward (Eds.), *Textbooks and schooling in the United States* (pp. 42–55). Chicago: National Society for the Study of Education.

Elliott, D. L., & Woodward, A. (1990). Textbooks, curriculum and school improvement. In D. L. Elliott & A. Woodward (Eds.), *Textbooks and schooling in the United States* (pp. 222–232). Chicago: National Society for the Study of Education.

Emans, R. (1967). The usefulness of phonic generalizations above the primary grade. *The Reading Teacher, 20,* 419–425.

Farr, R., & Carey, R. F. (1986). *Reading: What can be measured?* (2nd ed.). Newark, DE: International Reading Association.

Farr, R., & Tone, B. (1994). *Portfolio and performance assessment: Helping students evaluate their progress as readers and writers.* Orlando: Harcourt Brace College Publishers.

Farris, P. (1987). Promoting family reading through magazine packs. *The Reading Teacher, 40,* 825–826.

Feitelson, D., Kita, B., & Goldstein, Z. (1986). Effects of listening to stories on first graders' comprehension and use of language. *Research in the Teaching of English, 20,* 339–356.

Fielding, L. G., Anderson, R. C., & Pearson, P. D. (1990). *How discussion questions influence children's story understanding.* Tech. Report No. 490. Urbana, IL: Center for the Study of Reading, University of Illinois.

Fielding, L. G., Wilson, P. T., & Anderson, R. C. (1986). A new focus on free reading: The role of tradebooks in reading instruction. In T. E. Raphael (Ed.), *Contexts of school-based literacy* (pp. 149–160). New York: Random House.

Flesch, R. (1955). *Why Johnny can't read.* New York: Harper & Row.

Flesch, R. (1981). *Why Johnny still can't read.* New York: Harper & Row.

Flood, J., & Lapp, D. (1988). Conceptual mapping strategies for information texts. *The Reading Teacher, 41,* 780–783.

Flood, J., & Lapp, D. (1989). Reporting reading progress: A comparison portfolio for parents. *Reading Teacher, 42*(7), 508–514.

Fountas, I. C. & Pinnell, G. S. (1996). *Guided reading: Good first teaching for all children.* Portsmouth, NH: Heinemann.

Fowler, G. L. (1982). Developing comprehension skills in primary grades through the use of story frames. *The Reading Teacher, 36*(2), 176–179.

Fredericks, A., Meinbach, A., & Rothlein, L. (1993). *Thematic units.* New York: HarperCollins.

Freedle, R. P. (1979). *New directions in discourse processing.* Hillsdale, NJ: Lawrence Erlbaum.

Freeman, E. B., & Hatch, J. A. (1989). Emergent literacy: Reconceptualizing kindergarten practice. *Childhood Education, 66*(1), 21–24.

Freppon, P. (1991). Children's concepts of the nature and purpose of reading in different instructional settings. *Journal of Reading Behavior, 23*(2), 139–163.

Fries, C. (1962). *Linguistics and reading.* New York: Holt, Rinehart and Winston.

Galda, L. (1982). Assuming the spectator stance: An examination of the responses of three young readers. *Research in the Teaching of English, 16,* 1–20.

Galda, L. (1983). Research in response to literature. *Journal of Research and Development in Education, 16,* 1–7.

Gambrell, L. B., & Palmer, B. M. (1993). Children's metacognitive knowledge about reading and writing in literature-based and conventional classrooms. In C. K. Kinzer & D. J. Leu (Eds.), *Literacy research, theory, and practice: Views from many perspectives* (pp. 215–223). Chicago: National Reading Conference.

Gambrell, L. B., Pfeiffer, W., & Wilson, R. (1985). The effects of retelling upon reading comprehension and recall of text information. *Journal of Educational Research, 78,* 216–220.

Gambrell, T. (1986). Growth in response to literature. *English Quarterly, 19,* 130–141.

Garcia, G. E. (1994). Assessing the literacy development of second language students: A focus on authentic assessment. In K. Spangenberg-Urbschat & R. Pritchard (Eds.), *Kids come in all languages: Reading instruction for ESL students* (pp. 180–205). Newark, DE: International Reading Association.

Garrett, S. (1993). *A core curriculum for our children's future: Priority academic students skills.* Oklahoma City: Oklahoma State Department of Education.

Gaskins, I. W., Downer, M. A., Anderson, R. C., Cunningham, P. M. Gaskins, R. W., Schommer, M., & the Teachers of Benchmark School. (1988). *A metacognitive approach to phonics: Using what you know to decode what you don't know* (Tech. Rep. No. 424). Champaign: University fo Illinois at Urbana–Champaign, Center for the Study of Reading.

Gentry, J. R. (1987). *SPEL . . . Is a four-letter word.* Portsmouth, NH: Heinemann.

Gentry, J. R. (1997). *My kid can't spell.* Portsmouth, NH: Heinemann.

Gentry, J. R., & Gillett, J. W. (1993). *Teaching kids to spell.* Portsmouth, NH: Heinemann.

Gipe, J. P. (1978/1979). Investigating techniques for teaching word meanings. *Reading Research Quarterly, 14,* 624–644.

Goldenberg, C. (1991). Learning to read in New Zealand: The balance of skills and meaning. *Language Arts, 68,* 555–562.

Goodman, K. S. (1965). A linguistic study of cues and miscues in reading. *Elementary English, 42,* 639–643.

Goodman, K. S. (1986). *What's whole in whole language.* Portsmouth, NH: Heinemann.

Goodman, K. S., Freeman, Y. S., Murphy, S., & Shannon, P. (1988). *Report card on basal readers.* New York: Richard C. Owen.

Goodman, K. S., & Goodman, Y. M. (1991). Consumer beware! Selecting materials for whole language readers. In K. S. Goodman, L. B. Bird, & Y. M. Goodman (Eds.), *The whole language catalog* (p. 119). Santa Rosa, CA: American School Publishers.

Goodman, Y. M. (1986). Children coming to know literacy. In W. H. Teal & E. Sulzby (Eds.), *Emergent literacy: Reading and writing* (pp. 1–14). Norwood, NJ: Ablex.

Goodman, Y. M., & Burke, C. (1972). *Reading miscue inventory manual: Procedures for diagnosis and evaluation.* New York: Richard C. Owen.

Grabe, M., & Grabe, C. (1998). *Integrated technology for meaningful learning.* Boston: Houghton Mifflin.

Graves, D. H. (1983). *Writing: Teachers and children at work.* Exeter, NH: Heinemann.

Graves, D. H. (1984). *A researcher learns to write.* Exeter, NH: Heinemann.

Graves, D. H. (1991). *Build a literate classroom.* Portsmouth, NH: Heinemann.

Graves, D. H., & Hansen, J. (1983). The author's chair. *Language Arts, 60,* 176–182.

Graves, M. F. (1986). Vocabulary learning and instruction. *Review of Research in Education, 13,* 91–128.

Graves, M. F. (1987). The roles of instruction in fostering vocabulary development. In M. G. McKeown & M. E. Curtis (Eds.), *The nature of vocabulary acquisition* (pp. 165–184). Hillsdale, NJ: Lawrence Erlbaum.

Graves, M. F., & Cooke, C. L. (1980). Effects of previewing difficult short stories for high school students. *Research on Reading in Secondary Schools, 6,* 28–54.

Graves, M. F., Cooke, C. L., & LaBerge, H. J. (1983). Effects of previewing difficult and short stories on low-ability junior high school students' comprehension, recall and attitude. *Reading Research Quarterly, 18,* 262–276.

Guthrie, J. T., & Greaney, V. (1991). Literacy acts. In P. Barr, M. L. Kamil, P. Mosenthal, & P. D.

Pearson (Eds.), *Handbook of reading research* (Vol. 2, pp. 68–96). New York: Longman.

Guthrie, J. T., & Wigfield, A. (Eds.). (1997). *Reading engagement: Motivating readers through integrated instruction.* Newark, DE: International Reading Association.

Haggard, M. R. (1982). The vocabulary self-collection strategy: An active approach to word learning. *Journal of Reading, 27,* 203–207.

Haggard, M. R. (1986). The vocabulary self-collection strategy: Using student interest and world knowledge to enhance vocabulary growth. *Journal of Reading, 29,* 634–642.

Halliday, M. A. K. (1975). *Learning how to mean.* New York: Elsevier North-Holland.

Hansen, J. (1981a). The effects of inference training and practice on young children's reading comprehension. *Reading Research Quarterly, 16,* 391–417.

Hansen, J. (1981b). Inferential comprehension strategy for use with primary grade children. *Reading Teacher, 34,* 665–669.

Hansen, J. (1987). *When writers read.* Portsmouth, NH: Heinemann.

Harp, B. (1989). What do we know about ability grouping? *The Reading Teacher, 42,* 430–431.

Harp, B. (1991). Principles of assessment in whole language classrooms. In B. Harp (Ed.), *Assessment and evaluation in whole language programs* (pp. 35–50). Norwood, MA: Christopher-Gordon.

Harris, A. J., & Sipay, E. R. (1985). *How to increase reading ability* (8th ed.). New York: Longman.

Harris, T. L., & Hodges, R. E. (1981). *A dictionary of reading and related terms.* Newark, DE: International Reading Association.

Harris, T. L., & Hodges, R. E. (Eds.). (1995). *The literacy dictionary.* Newark, DE: International Reading Association.

Harste, J. C., Short, K. G., & Burke, C. (1988). *Creating classrooms for authors.* Portsmouth, NH: Heinemann.

Harste, J. C., Woodward, V. A., & Burke, C. L. (1984). *Language stories and literacy lessons.* Portsmouth, NH: Heinemann.

Heath, S. B. (1983). *Ways with words.* Cambridge, U.K.: Cambridge University Press.

Herber, H. L. (1978). *Teaching reading in content areas* (2nd ed.). Englewood Cliffs, NJ: Prentice-Hall.

Herber, H. L. (1984). Subject matter texts—Reading to learn: Response to a paper by Thomas H. Anderson and Bonnie B. Armbruster. In R. C. Anderson, J. Osborn, & R. J. Tierney (Eds.), *Learning to read in American schools: Basal readers and content texts* (pp. 227–234). Hillsdale, NJ: Lawrence Erlbaum.

Herber, H. L., & Nelson, J. (1975). Questioning is not the answer. *Journal of Reading, 18,* 512–517.

Hickman, J. (1983). Everything considered: Response to literature in an elementary school setting. *Journal of Research and Development in Education, 16,* 8–13.

Hickman, J., & Cullinan, B. E. (1989). A point of view on literature and learning. In J. Hickman & B. E. Cullinan (Eds.), *Children's literature in the classroom: Weaving Charlotte's web* (pp. 3–12). Needham Heights, MA: Christopher-Gordon.

Hiebert, E. H. (1983). An examination of ability grouping for reading instruction. *Reading Research Quarterly, 28,* 231–255.

Hiebert, E. H. (1998). Selecting texts for beginning reading instruction. In T. E. Raphael & K. H. Au (Eds.), *Literature-based instruction: Reshaping the curriculum* (pp. 195–218). Norwood, MA: Christopher-Gordon.

Hiebert, E. H., & Taylor, B. (Eds.) (1994). *Getting reading right from the start: Effective early literacy interventions.* Needham Heights, MA: Allyn and Bacon.

Hiebert, E. H., Pearson, P. D., Taylor, B. M., Richardson, V., & Paris, S. G. (1998). *Every child a reader.* Ann Arbor, MI: Center for the Improvement of Early Reading Achievement (CIERA).

Hill, M. (1991). Writing summaries promotes thinking and learning across the curriculum—but why are they so difficult to write? *Journal of Reading, 34,* 536–539.

Hillocks, G., Jr. (1987a). What works in teaching composition: A meta-analysis of experimental treatment studies. *American Journal of Education, 93,* 133–170.

Hillocks, G., Jr. (1987b). Synthesis of research on teaching writing. *Educational Leadership, 44,* 71–82.

Hillocks, G., Jr., & Smith, M. W. (1991). Grammar and usage. In J. Flood, J. M. Jensen, D. Lapp, & J. R. Squire (Eds.), *Handbook of research on teaching the English language arts* (pp. 591–603). New York: Macmillan.

History–Social Science Curriculum Framework and Criteria Committee. (1988). *History-social science framework.* Sacramento: California State Board of Education.

Holdaway, D. (1979). *The foundations of literacy.* Sydney: Ashton Scholastic, distributed by Heinemann, Portsmouth, NH.

Holmes, B. C., & Roser, N. L. (1987). Five ways to assess readers' prior knowledge. *The Reading Teacher, 40,* 646–649.

Huck, C. S. (1989). No wider than the heart is wide. In J. Hickman & B. E. Cullinan (Eds.), *Children's literature in the classroom: Weaving Charlotte's web* (pp. 252–262). Needham Heights, MA: Christopher-Gordon.

Huck, C. S. (1991). Literature in the whole language classroom. In K. S. Goodman, L. B. Bird, & Y. M. Goodman (Eds.), *The whole language catalog* (p. 188). Santa Rosa, CA: American School Publishers.

Huey, E. B. (1908/1968). *The psychology and pedagogy of reading.* Cambridge, MA: MIT Press.

Hynd, C. R., & Alvermann, D. E. (1986). Prior knowledge activation in refutation and non-refutation text. In J. A. Niles & R. V. Lalik (Eds.), *Solving problems in literacy: Learners, teachers, and researchers* (pp. 55–60). *Thirty-fifth Yearbook of the National Reading Conference.* Rochester, NY: National Reading Conference.

Jenkins, J. R., & Pany, D. (1981). Instructional variables in reading comprehension. In J. T. Guthrie (Ed.), *Comprehension and teaching: Research reviews.* Newark, DE: International Reading Association.

Jenkins, J. R., Stein, M., & Wysocki, K. (1984). Learning vocabulary through reading. *American Education Research Journal, 21,* 767–788.

Johnson, D. D., & Pearson, P. D. (1984). *Teaching reading vocabulary* (2nd ed.). New York: Holt, Rinehart and Winston.

Johnston, P. (1981). *Prior knowledge and reading comprehension test bias.* Unpublished doctoral dissertation, University of Illinois, Champaign, IL.

Johnston, P., & Allington, R. (1991). Remediation. In R. Barr, M. L. Kamil, P. Mosenthal, & P. D. Pearson (Eds.), *Handbook of Reading Research* (Vol. 2, pp. 984–1012). New York: Longman.

Juel, C., & Roper/Schneider, D. (1985). The influence of basal readers on first grade reading. *Reading Research Quarterly, 20,* 134–152.

Just, M. A., & Carpenter, P. A. (1987). *The psychology of reading and language comprehension.* Boston: Allyn & Bacon.

Kail, R. V., Chi, M. T. H., Ingram, A. L., & Danner, F. W. (1977). Constructive aspects of children's reading comprehension. *Child Development, 48,* 684–688.

Kelly, P. R. (1990). Guiding young students' response to literature. *The Reading Teacher, 43,* 464–470.

Kelly, P. R., & Farnan, N. (1991). Promoting critical thinking through response logs: A reader response approach with fourth graders. In S. McCormick & J. Zutell (Eds.), *Learner factors/teacher factors: Issues in literacy research and instruction,* 40th Yearbook of the National Reading Conference (pp. 277–284). Chicago: National Reading Conference.

Khattri, N., Kane, M. B., & Reeve, A. L. (1995). How performance assessments affect teaching and learning. *Educational Leadership, 53*(3), 80–83.

Klare, G. R. (1984). Readability. In P. D. Pearson (Ed.), *Handbook of reading research* (pp. 681–744). New York: Longman.

Lamme, L. L. (1990). Exploring the world of music through picture books. *The Reading Teacher, 44,* 294–300.

Langer, J. A. (1986). Reading, writing and understanding: An analysis of the construction of meaning. *Written Communication, 3,* 219–267.

Learning First Alliance. (1998, June). *Every child reading: An action plan of the Learning First Alliance.* Washington, DC: Author.

Lenneberg, E. (1967). *Biological foundations of language.* New York: Wiley.

Lesgold, A. M., & Curtis, M. E. (1981). Learning to read words efficiently. In A. M. Lesgold & C. A. Perfetti (Eds.), *Interactive processes in reading.* Hillsdale, NJ: Lawrence Erlbaum.

Lipson, M. Y. (1982). Learning new information from text. The role of prior knowledge and reading ability. *Journal of Reading Behavior, 14,* 243–261.

Lipson, M. Y. (1984). Some unexpected issues in prior knowledge and comprehension. *The Reading Teacher, 37,* 760–764.

Lipson, M.Y., & Wixson, K. K. (1986). Reading disability research: An interactionist perspective. *Review of Educational Research, 56,* 111–136.

Loban, W. D. (1963). *The language of elementary school children.* Champaign, IL: National Council of Teachers of English.

Lorge, I., & Chall, J. S. (1963). Estimating the size of vocabularies of children and adults: An analysis of methodological issues. *Journal of Experimental Education, 32,* 147–157.

Mandler, J. M. (1984). *Stories, scripts and scenes: Aspects of schema theory.* Hillsdale, NJ: Lawrence Erlbaum.

Many, J. E. (1991). The effects of stance and age level on children's literary responses. *Journal of Reading Behavior, 23,* 61–85.

Maria, K. (1988, December). *Helping fifth graders learn with science text.* Paper presented at the meeting of the National Reading Conference, Tucson, AZ.

Maria, K. (1990). *Reading comprehension interaction: Strategies and issues.* Parkton, MD: York Press.

Marino, J. L., Gould, S. M., & Haas, L. W. (1985). The effect of writing as a prereading activity on delayed recall of narrative text. *Elementary School Journal, 86,* 199–205.

Marshall, N. (1983). Using story grammar to assess reading comprehension. *The Reading Teacher, 36,* 616–620.

Martin, S. (1987, December). *The meaning-making strategies reported by provident readers and writers.* Paper presented at the National Reading Conference, St. Petersburg, FL.

Martinez, E. B. (1987). It works! In C. B. Olson (Ed.), *Practical ideas for teaching writing as a process* (p. 23). Sacramento: California State Department of Education.

Martinez, M. G., & Roser, N. L. (1991). Children's responses to literature. In J. Flood, J. M. Jensen, D. Lapp, & J. R. Squire (Eds.), *Handbook of research on teaching the English language arts* (pp. 643–654). New York: Macmillan.

Mason, J. M., & Au, K. H. (1990). *Reading instruction for today* (2nd ed.). Glenview, IL: Scott, Foresman.

McCormick, S. (1977). Should you read aloud to your children? *Language Arts, 54,* 139–143.

McGinley, W. (1988). *The role of reading and writing in the acquisition of knowledge: A study of college*

students' reading and writing engagements in the development of a persuasive argument. Unpublished doctoral thesis, University of Illinois at Urbana–Champaign.

McHugh, N. (1987). Teaching the domains of writing. In C. B. Olson (Ed.), *Practical ideas for teaching writing as a process* (pp. 81–87). Sacramento: California State Department of Education.

McKenzie, M. (1985). *Shared writing. Language matters.* London: Inner London Educational Authority.

McKeown, M. G., Beck, I. L., Omanson, R. C., & Pople, M. T. (1985). Some effects of the nature and frequency of vocabulary instruction on the knowledge and use of words. *Reading Research Quarterly, 20*(5), 522–535.

McKeown, M. G., & Curtis, M. E. (1987). *The nature of vocabulary acquisition.* Hillsdale, NJ: Lawrence Erlbaum.

McNeil, D. (1970). *The acquisition of language: The study of developmental psycholinguistics.* New York: Harper & Row.

McNeil, J. D. (1987). *Reading comprehension: New directions for classroom practice* (2nd ed.). Glenview, IL: Scott, Foresman.

Meichenbaum, D. (1985). Teaching thinking: A cognitive behavioral perspective. In S. Chapman, J. Segal, & R. Glaser (Eds.), *Thinking and learning skills: Current research and open questions* (Vol. 2, pp. 407–426). Hillsdale, NJ: Lawrence Erlbaum.

Memory, D. M. (1990). Teaching technical vocabulary: Before, during or after the reading assignment. *Journal of Reading Behavior, 22,* 39–53.

Menyuk, P. (1984). Language development and reading. In J. Flood (Ed.), *Understanding comprehension* (pp. 101–121). Newark, DE: International Reading Association.

Meyer, B. J. F. (1975). *The organization of prose and its effects on memory.* Amsterdam: The Hague North-Holland Press.

Meyer, B. J. F., & Freedle, R. O. (1984). Effects of discourse type on recall. *American Educational Research Journal, 21,* 121–143.

Mezynski, K. (1983). Issues concerning the acquisition of knowledge: Effects of vocabulary training on reading comprehension. *Review of Educational Research, 53,* 253–279.

Mier, M. (1984). Comprehension monitoring in the elementary classroom. *The Reading Teacher, 37*(8), 770–774.

Millett, N. C. (1986). *Teaching the writing process: A guide for teachers and supervisors.* Boston: Houghton Mifflin.

Moffett, J., & Wagner, B. J. (1983). *Student-centered language arts and reading, K-13* (3rd ed.). Boston: Houghton Mifflin.

Moore, D. W., Readence, J. E., & Rickelman, R. J. (1989). *Prereading activities for content area reading and learning* (2nd ed.). Newark, DE: International Reading Association.

Morrow, L. M. (1985). Retelling stories: A strategy for improving children's comprehension, concept of story structure, and oral language complexity. *Elementary School Journal, 85,* 647–661.

Morrow, L. M. (1987). Promoting voluntary reading: The effects of an inner city program in summer day care centers. *The Reading Teacher, 41,* 266–274.

Morrow, L. M. (1989). Using story retelling to develop comprehension. In K. D. Muth (Ed.), *Children's comprehension of text: Research into practice* (pp. 37–58). Newark, DE: International Reading Association.

Morrow, L. M., & Weinstein, C. S. (1982). Increasing children's use of literature through program and physical design changes. *Elementary School Journal, 83,* 131–137.

Morrow, L. M., & Weinstein, C. S. (1986). Encouraging voluntary reading: The impact of a literature program on children's use of library centers. *Reading Research Quarterly, 21,* 330–346.

Moss, B. (1991). Children's nonfiction trade books: A complement to content area texts. *The Reading Teacher, 45,* 26–32.

Murray, D. M. (1985). *A writer teaches writing* (2nd ed.). Boston: Houghton Mifflin.

Nagy, W. E. (1988). *Teaching vocabulary to improve reading comprehension.* Newark, DE/Urbana, IL: International Reading Association/National Council of Teachers of English.

Nagy, W. E., & Anderson, R. C. (1984). How many words are there in printed school English? *Reading Research Quarterly, 19,* 304–330.

Nagy, W. E., & Herman, P. A. (1987). Breadth and depth of vocabulary knowledge: Implications for acquisition and instruction. In M. G. McKeown & M. E. Curtis (Eds.), *The nature of vocabulary acquisition* (pp. 19–35). Hillsdale, NJ: Lawrence Erlbaum.

National Assessment of Educational Progress. (NAEP). (1990a). *Assessment and exercise specifications.* 1992 National Assessment of Educational Progress in Reading, March 28, 1990. (Mimeographed document.)

National Assessment of Educational Progress (NAEP). (1990b). *Reading framework: 1992 National assessment of educational progress reading assessment.* 1992 NAEP Consensus Planning Project, March 28, 1990. (Mimeographed document.)

Neuman, S. (1988). Enhancing children's comprehension through previewing. In J. E. Readence & R. J. Baldwin (Eds.), *Dialogues in literacy research* (pp. 219–224). *Thirty-seventh Yearbook of the National Reading Conference.* Chicago: National Reading Conference.

Norton, D. E. (1982). Using a webbing process to develop children's literature units. *Language Arts, 59,* 348–356.

Norton, D. E. (1991). *Through the eyes of a child— An introduction to children's literature* (3rd ed.). New York: Macmillan.

Noyce, R. M., & Christie, J. F. (1989). *Integrating reading and writing instruction in grades K-8.* Boston: Allyn and Bacon.

Ogle, D. M. (1986). K-W-L: A teaching model that develops active reading of expository text. *The Reading Teacher, 39*(6), 564–570.

Olson, C. B. (1987). *Practical ideas for teaching writing as a process.* Sacramento: California State Department of Education.

Otto, W., et al. (1977). *The Wisconsin design for reading skill development: Comprehension.* Minneapolis: NCS Educational Systems.

Pace, A. J., Marshall, N., Horowitz, R., Lipson, M. Y., & Lucido, P. (1989). When prior knowledge doesn't facilitate text comprehension: An examination of some of the issues. In *Cognitive and social perspectives for literacy research and instruction* (pp. 213–224). *Thirty-eighth Yearbook of the National Reading Conference.* Chicago: National Reading Conference.

Palincsar, A. S., & Brown, A. L. (1984a). *A means to a meaningful end: Recommendations for the instruction of poor comprehenders.* Reprint. Champaign, IL: Center for the Study of Reading.

Palincsar, A. S., & Brown, A. L. (1984b). Reciprocal teaching of comprehension-fostering and comprehension-monitoring activities. *Cognition and Instruction, 2,* 117–175.

Palincsar, A. S., & Brown, A. L. (1986). Interactive teaching to promote independent learning from text. *The Reading Teacher, 39*(8), 771–777.

Pappas, C. C., Kiefer, B. Z., & Levstik, L. S. (1990). *An integrated language perspective in the elementary school: Theory into action.* New York: Longman.

Paradis, E. E., Chatton, B., Boswell, A., Smith, M., & Yovich, S. (1991). Account–ability: Assessing comprehension during literature discussion. *The Reading Teacher, 45,* 8–17.

Paratore, J. R., & Indrisano, R. (1987). Intervention assessment of reading comprehension. *The Reading Teacher, 40,* 778–783.

Paris, S. G., Cross, D. R., & Lipson, M. Y. (1984). Informed strategies for learning: A program to improve children's reading awareness and comprehension. *Journal of Educational Psychology, 76,* 1239–1252.

Paris, S. G., Lipson, M. Y., & Wixson, K. K. (1983). Becoming a strategic reader. *Contemporary Educational Psychology, 8,* 293–316.

Paris, S. G., Wasik, B. A., & Turner, J. C. (1991). The development of strategic readers. In R. Barr, M. L. Kamil, P. Mosenthal, & P. D. Pearson (Eds.), *Handbook of reading research* (Vol. 2, pp. 609–640). New York: Longman.

Parsons, L. (1990). *Response journals.* Portsmouth, NH: Heinemann.

Patchell, G. (1986). Holistic scoring in the classroom. In C. B. Olson (Ed.), *Practical ideas for teaching writing as a process* (pp. 185–187). Sacramento: California State Department of Education.

Pearson, P. D. (1985). Changing the face of reading comprehension instruction. *The Reading Teacher, 38,* 724–738.

Pearson, P. D., & Dole, J. A. (1987). Explicit comprehension instruction: A review of research and a new conceptualization of instruction. *Elementary School Journal, 88*(2), 151–165.

Pearson, P. D., et al. (1979). *The effect of background knowledge on young children's comprehension of explicit and implicit information.* Champaign, IL: Center for the Study of Reading, University of Illinois.

Pearson, P. D., & Johnson, D. D. (1978). *Teaching reading comprehension.* New York: Holt, Rinehart and Winston.

Pearson, P. D., Roehler, L. R., Dole, J. A., & Duffy, G. G. (1990). *Developing expertise in reading comprehension: What should be taught? How should it be taught?* Technical Report No. 512. Champaign, IL: Center for the Study of Reading.

Pearson, P. D., Roehler, L. R., Dole, J. A., & Duffy, G. G. (1992). Developing expertise in reading comprehension. In S. J. Samuels & A. E. Forstrup (eds.), *What research has to say about reading instruction* (pp. 145–199). Newark, DE: International Reading Association.

Pearson, P. D., & Tierney, R. J. (1984). On becoming a thoughtful reader: Learning to read like a writer. In A. C. Purves & O. Niles (Eds.), *Becoming readers in a complex society. Eighty-third Yearbook of the National Society of the Study of Education* (pp. 144–173). Chicago: University of Chicago Press.

Pehrsson, R. S., & Robinson, H. A. (1985). *The semantic organizer approach to writing and reading instruction.* Rockville, MD: Aspen Systems Corporation.

Perfetti, C. (1985). *Reading ability.* New York: Oxford University Press.

Perrone, V. (1991). Toward more powerful assessment. In V. Perrone (Ed.), *Expanding student assessment* (pp. 164–166). Alexandria, VA: Association for Supervision and Curriculum Development.

Peterson, B. (1991). Selecting books for beginning readers. In D. E. DeFord, C. A. Lyons, & G. S. Pinnell (Eds.), *Bridges to literacy: Learning from reading recovery* (pp. 119–147). Portsmouth, NH: Heinemann.

Peterson, P., Wilkinson, L., & Hallinan, M. (1984). *The social contexts of instruction: Group organization and group processes.* Orlando, FL: Academic.

Piaget, J., & Inhelder, B. (1969). *The psychology of the child.* New York: Basic Books.

Pierce, K. (1987). Clustering in first grade. In C. B. Olson (Ed.), *Practical ideas for teaching writing as a process* (pp. 22–23). Sacramento: The California State Department of Education.

Pikulski, J. J. (1990a). Informal reading inventories. *The Reading Teacher, 43,* 514–516.

Pikulski, J. J. (1990b). The role of tests in a literacy assessment program. *The Reading Teacher, 43,* 686–688.

Pinnell, G. S., & Fountas, I. C. (1998). *Word matters.* Portsmouth, NH: Heinemann.

Pinnell, G. S., Fried, M. D., & Estice, R. M. (1990). Reading recovery: Learning how to make a difference. *The Reading Teacher, 43,* 282–295.

Pressley, M., Burkell, J., Cariglia-Bull, T., Lysynchuck, L., McGoldrick, J. A., Schneider, B., Snyder, B. L., Symons, S., & Woloshyn, V. E. (1990). *Cognitive strategy instruction that really improves children's academic performance.* Cambridge, MA: Brookline.

Pressley, M., & Harris, K. R. (1990). What we really know about strategy instruction. *Educational Leadership, 48,* 31–34.

Pressley, M., Johnson, C. J., Symons, S., McGoldrick, J. S., & Kurita, J. A. (1989). Strategies that improve children's memory and comprehension of text. *Elementary School Journal, 90,* 3–32.

Purves, A. C. (1972). *How porcupines make love: Notes on a response–centered curriculum.* New York: Wiley.

Raphael, T. E., & Englert, C. S. (1990). Writing and reading: Partners in constructing meaning. *The Reading Teacher, 43,* 388–400.

Readence, J. E., Bean, T. W., & Baldwin, R. S. (1981, 1985, 1989). *Content area reading: An integrated approach.* Dubuque, IA: Kendall/Hunt.

Reutzel, D. R., & Cooter, R. B., Jr. (1991). Organizing for effective instruction: The reading workshop. *The Reading Teacher, 44,* pp. 548–554.

Reutzel, D. R., & Fawson, P. C. (1990). Traveling tales: Connecting parents and children through writing. *The Reading Teacher, 44,* 222–227.

Rhodes, L. K. (1981). I can read! Predictable books as resources for reading and writing instruction. *The Reading Teacher, 34,* 511–518.

Rhodes, L. K., & Shanklin, N. L. (1990). Miscue analysis in the classroom. *The Reading Teacher, 44,* 252–254.

Ribowsky, H. (1985). *The effects of a code emphasis approach and a whole language approach upon emergent literacy of kindergarten children.* Unpublished paper presented at the National Reading Conference.

Rico, G. L. (1983). *Writing the natural way.* Los Angeles: J. P. Tracher, Inc. Distributed by Houghton Mifflin, Boston.

Rigg, P., & Allen, V. G. (1989). *When they don't all speak English.* Urbana, IL: National Council of Teachers of English.

Robinson, H. A., Faraone, V., Hittleman, D. R., & Unruh, E. (1990). In J. Fitzgerald (Ed.), *Reading comprehension instruction 1783–1987: A review of trends and research.* Newark, DE: International Reading Association.

Roehler, L. R., & Duffy, G. G. (1991). Teacher's instructional actions. In R. Barr, M. L. Kamil, P. Mosenthal, & P. D. Pearson (Eds.), *Handbook of reading research* (Vol. 2, pp. 861–883). New York: Longman.

Rosenblatt, L. (1938/1983). *Literature as exploration.* New York: Modern Language Association.

Rosenblatt, L. (1978). *The reader, the text and the poem.* Carbondale, IL: Southern Illinois University Press.

Rosenblatt, L. (1991). Literary theory. In J. Flood, J. M. Jensen, D. Lapp, & J. R. Squire (Eds.), *Handbook of research on teaching the English language arts* (pp. 57–62). New York: Macmillan.

Rosenshine, B. V. (1980). Skill hierarchies in reading comprehension. In R. J. Spiro et al. (Eds.), *Theoretical issues in reading comprehension* (pp. 535–554). Hillsdale, NJ: Lawrence Erlbaum.

Rosenshine, B. V., & Meister, C. (1994). Reciprocal teaching: A review of research. *Review of Eductaional Research, 64*(4), 479–530.

Routman, R. (1988). *Transitions: From literature to literacy.* Portsmouth, NH: Heinemann.

Routman, R. (1991). *Invitations.* Portsmouth, NH: Heinemann.

Ruddell, R. B. (1963). The effect of the similarity of oral and written patterns of language structure on reading comprehension. *Elementary English, 42,* 403–410.

Rumelhart, D. E. (1980). Schemata: The building blocks of cognition. In R. J. Spiro et al. (Eds.),

Theoretical issues in reading comprehension (pp. 33–58). Hillsdale, NJ: Lawrence Erlbaum.

Sanders, M. (1987). Literacy as "passionate attention." *Language Arts, 64,* 619–633.

Sawyer, W. (1987). Literature and literacy: A review of research. *Language Arts, 64*(1), 33–39.

Schatz, E. K., & Baldwin, R. S. (1986). Context clues are unreliable predictors of word meanings. *Reading Research Quarterly, 21,* 439–453.

Schmitt, M. C. (1990). A questionnaire to measure children's awareness of strategic reading processes. *The Reading Teacher, 43*(7), 454–461.

Schwartz, R. (1988). Learning to learn vocabulary in content area textbooks. *Journal of Reading, 32,* 108–118.

Schwartz, R. M., & Raphael, T. E. (1985). Concept of definition: A key to improving students' vocabulary. *The Reading Teacher, 39,* 198–203.

Seashore, R. H. (1947). How many words do children know? *Packet, 2,* 3–17.

Secretary's Commission on Achieving Necessary Skills (SCANS). (1991). *What work requires of schools.* Washington, DC: U.S. Department of Labor.

Shake, M., & Allington, R. (1985). Where do teacher's questions come from? *The Reading Teacher, 38,* 434–438.

Shanahan, T. (1988). The reading writing relationship: Seven instructional principles. *The Reading Teacher, 41,* 636–647.

Shanahan, T. (1990). Reading and writing together: What does it really mean? In T. Shanahan (Ed.), *Reading and writing together* (pp. 1–18). Norwood, MA: Christopher-Gordon.

Shanahan, T., & Lomax, R. (1988). A developmental comparison of three theoretical models of the reading–writing relationship. *Research in Teaching English, 22,* 196–212.

Short, E. J., & Ryan, E. B. (1984). Metacognitive differences between skilled and less skilled readers: Remediating deficits through story grammar and attribution training. *Journal of Educational Psychology, 76,* 225–235.

Simons, H., & Ammon, P. (1989). Child knowledge and primerese text: Mismatches and miscues. *Research in the Teaching of English, 23*(4), 380–398.

Singer, H., & Donlan, D. (1982). Active comprehension: Problem-solving schema with question generation for comprehension of complex short stories. *Reading Research Quarterly, 17,* 166–186.

Slavin, R. E. (1986). *Ability grouping and student achievement in elementary schools: A best evidence synthesis.* Report No. 1. Baltimore, MD: The Johns Hopkins University Center for Research on Elementary and Middle Schools.

Slavin, R. E. (1990). *Cooperative learning: Theory, research and practice.* Englewood Cliffs, NJ: Prentice-Hall.

Sloyer, S. (1982). *Readers theatre: Story dramatization in the classroom.* Urbana, IL: National Council of Teachers of English.

Smith, F. (1971). *Understanding reading.* New York: Holt, Rinehart and Winston.

Smith, N. B. (1965). *American reading instruction.* Newark, DE: International Reading Association.

Snow, C., Burns, M. S., & Griffin, P. (Eds.). (1998). *Preventing reading difficulties in young children.* Washington, DC: National Academy Press.

Sorensen, A., & Hallinan, M. (1986). Effects of ability grouping on growth in academic achievement. *American Educational Research Journal, 23,* 519–542.

Spiro, R. J. (1979). *Etiology of comprehension style.* Champaign, IL: Center for the Study of Reading, University of Illinois.

Spritzer, D. R. (1988). Integrating the language arts in the elementary classroom using fairy tales, fables, and traditional literature. *Oregon English, 11,* 23–26.

Stahl, S. A. (1983). Differential word knowledge and reading comprehension. *Journal of Reading Behavior, 15,* 33–50.

Stahl, S. A., Duffy-Hester, A. M., & Stahl, K. A. D. (1998) Everything you wanted to know about phonics (but were afraid to ask). *Reading Research Quarterly, 33,* 338–355.

Stahl, S. A., & Fairbanks, M. M. (1986). The effects of vocabulary instruction: A model-based meta-analysis. *Review of Educational Research, 56* (1), 72–110.

Stahl, S. A., Osborn, J., & Lehr, F. (1990). *Beginning to read: Thinking and learning about print, by M. Adams, A Summary.* Champaign, IL: Center for the Study of Reading.

Stahl, S. A., & Vancil, S. J. (1986). Discussion is what makes semantic maps work in vocabulary instruction. *The Reading Teacher, 39,* 62–67.

Stanovich, K. E. (1980). Toward an interactive-compensatory model of individual differences in the development of reading fluency. *Reading Research Quarterly, 16,* 32–71.

Stanovich, K. E. (1986). Matthew effects in reading: Some consequences of individual differences in the acquisition of reading. *Reading Research Quarterly, 21,* 360–407.

Stauffer, R. G. (1969). *Teaching reading as a thinking process.* New York: Harper & Row.

Sternberg, R. J. (1987). Most vocabulary is learned from context. In M. G. McKeown & M. E. Curtis (Eds.), *The nature of vocabulary acquisition* (pp. 89–105). Hillsdale, NJ: Lawrence Erlbaum.

Stevens, K. C. (1982). Can we improve reading by teaching background information? *Journal of Reading, 25,* 326–329.

Stieglitz, E. L., & Stieglitz, U. S. (1981). SAVOR the word to reinforce vocabulary in the content areas. *Journal of Reading, 25,* 46–51.

Strickland, D. S. (1990). Emergent literacy: How young children learn to read and write. *Educational Leadership, 47*(6), 18–23.

Strickland, D. S., & Cullinan, B. (1990). Afterword. In M. J. Adams, *Beginning to read: Thinking and learning about print* (pp. 426–433). Cambridge, MA: MIT Press.

Strickland, D. S., & Taylor, D. (1989). Family storybook reading: Implications for children, families, and curriculum. In D. S. Strickland & L. M. Morrow (Eds.), *Emerging literacy: Young children learn to read and write* (pp. 27–34). Newark, DE: International Reading Association.

Sulzby, E. (1985). Kindergartners as writers and readers. In M. Farr (Ed.), *Advances in writing research* (Vol. 1). Norwood, NJ: Ablex.

Sulzby, E. (1989). Assessment of writing and of children's language while writing. In L. Morrow & J. Smith (Eds.), *The role of assessment and measurement in early literacy instruction* (pp. 83–109). Englewood Cliffs, NJ: Prentice-Hall.

Sulzby, E., & Teale, W. (1991). Emergent literacy. In R. Barr, M. L. Kamil, P. Mosenthal, & P. D. Pearson (Eds.), *Handbook of reading research* (Vol. 2, pp. 727–757). New York: Longman.

Sweet, A. P. (1993). *State of the art: Transforming ideas for teaching and learning to read.* Washington, DC: U.S. Department of Education, Office of Research.

Taba, H. (1967). *Teacher's handbook for elementary school social studies.* Reading, MA: Addison-Wesley.

Taylor, B. M., & Beach, R. W. (1984). Effects of text structure instruction on middle-grade students' comprehension and production of expository text. *Reading Research Quarterly, 19*(2), 147–161.

Taylor, B. M., Frye, B. J., & Maruyama, G. M. (1990). Time spent reading and reading growth. *American Educational Research Journal, 27*(2), 351–362.

Taylor, D., & Dorsey-Gaines, C. (1988). *Growing up literate.* Portsmouth, NH: Heinemann.

Taylor, D., & Strickland, D. S. (1986). *Family storybook reading.* Portsmouth, NH: Heinemann.

Teale, W. H., & Sulzby, E. (1986). *Emergent literacy: Writing and reading.* Norwood, NJ: Ablex.

Templeton, S. (1991). *Teaching the integrated language arts.* Boston: Houghton Mifflin.

Terry, A. (1974). *Children's poetry preferences: A national survey of upper elementary grades.* Urbana, IL: National Council of Teachers of English.

Thomas, R. L. (1989). Knowing poetry: Choosing poetry for children. In J. Hichman & B. E. Cullinan (Eds.), *Children's literature in the classroom: Weaving Charlotte's web* (pp. 161–172). Needham Heights, MA: Christopher-Gordon.

Thompson, A. (1990). Thinking and writing with learning logs. In N. Atwell (Ed.), *Coming to know: Writing to learn in the intermediate grades* (pp. 35–51). Portsmouth, NH: Heinemann.

Thornburg, D. (1992). *Edutrends.* San Carlos, CA: Starsong Publications.

Tierney, R. J., Carter, M. A., & Desai, L. E. (1991). *Portfolio assessment in the reading-writing classroom.* Norwood, MA: Christopher-Gordon.

Tierney, R. J., & Cunningham, J. W. (1984). Research on teaching reading comprehension. In P. D. Pearson (Ed.), *Handbook of reading research* (pp. 609–655). New York: Longman.

Tierney, R. J., & Leys, M. (1984). *What is the value of connecting reading and writing?* Reading Education Report No. 55. University of Illinois at Urbana–Champaign.

Tierney, R. J., Readence, J. E., & Dishner, E. K. (1990). Reader's theater. In *Reading strategies and practices: A compendium* (3rd ed.) (pp. 190–195). Boston: Allyn and Bacon.

Tierney, R. J., Readence, J. E., & Dishner, E. K. (1990). *Reading strategies and practices: A compendium* (3rd ed.). Boston: Allyn and Bacon.

Tierney, R. J., & Shanahan, T. (1991). Research on the reading-writing relationship: Interactions, transactions, and outcomes. In R. Barr, M. L. Kamil, P. Mosenthal, & P. D. Pearson (Eds.), *Handbook of reading research* (Vol. 2, pp. 246–280). New York: Longman.

Tompkins, G. E., & Hoskisson, K. (1991). *Language arts: Content and teaching strategies.* New York: Merrill, an imprint of Macmillan.

Tompkins, G. E., & Weber, M. (1983). What will happen next? Using predictable books with young children. *The Reading Teacher, 36,* 498–502.

Trelease, J. (1989). *The new read-aloud handbook.* New York: Penguin.

Tunnell, M. O., & Jacobs, J. S. (1989). Using real books: Research findings on literature based instruction. *The Reading Teacher, 42*(7), 470–477.

Tyson, H., & Woodward, A. (1989). Why students aren't learning very much from textbooks. *Educational Leadership, 47,* 14–17.

Valencia, S. W (1990a). A portfolio approach to classroom reading assessment: The whys, whats and hows. *The Reading Teacher, 43,* 338–340.

Valencia, S. W. (1990b). Alternative assessment: Separating the wheat from the chaff. *The Reading Teacher, 44,* 60–61.

Valencia, S. W., Hiebert, E. H., & Afflerbach, P. P. (Eds.). (1994). *Authentic reading assessment: Practices and possibilities.* Newark, DE: International Reading Association.

Veatch, J. (1978). *Reading in the elementary school* (2nd ed.). New York: Wiley.

Vukelich, C. (1984). Parents' role in the reading process: A review of practical suggestions and ways to communicate with parents. *The Reading Teacher, 37,* 472–477.

Vygotsky, L. S. (1978). *Mind in society.* Cambridge, MA: Harvard University Press.

Walmsley, S. (1994). *Children exploring the world: Theme teaching in elementary school.* Portsmouth, NH: Heinemann.

Walmsley, S. A., & Walp, T. P. (1990). Integrating literature and composing into the language arts curriculum: Philosophy and practice. *Elementary School Journal, 90*(3), 251–274.

Ward, G. (1988). *I've got a project on . . .* Australia: Primary English Teaching Association, distributed by Heinemann, Portsmouth, NH.

Weaver, C. (1990a). *Understanding whole language.* Portsmouth, NH: Heinemann.

Weaver, C. (1990b, March 28). Weighing claims of "phonics first" advocates. *Education Week,* p. 32.

Weaver, C. S., III, & Kintsch, W. (1991). Expository text. In R. Barr, M. L. Kamil, P. Mosenthal, & P. D. Pearson (Eds.), *Handbook of reading research* (Vol. 2, pp. 230–245). New York: Longman.

Weber, R. (1991). Language diversity and reading in American society. In R. Barr, M. L. Kamil, P. Mosenthal, & P. D. Pearson (Eds.), *Handbook of reading research* (Vol. 2, pp. 97–119). New York: Longman.

Weisberg, R. K., & Balajthy, E. (1985, December). *Effects of semantic mapping training on disabled readers' summarizing and recognition of expository text structure.* Paper presented at the National Reading Conference, San Diego, CA.

Weiss, A. S., Mangrum, C. T., & Liabre, M. M. (1986). Differential effects of differing vocabulary presentations. *Reading Research and Instruction, 25,* 265–276.

Wells, G. (1986). *The meaning makers: Children learning language and using language to learn.* Portsmouth, NH: Heinemann.

Wells, G. (1990). Creating the conditions to encourage literate thinking. *Educational Leadership, 47*(6), 13–17.

Werthemer, A. (1974). Story dramatization in the reading center. *English Journal, 64,* 85–87.

White, R. E. (1981). The effects of organizational themes and adjunct placements on children's prose learning: A developmental perspective. *Dissertation Abstracts International, 42,* 2042A-2043A. (University Microfilms No. 81–25, 038).

White, T. G., Sowell, J., & Yanagihara, A. (1989). Teaching elementary students to use word-part clues. *Reading Teacher, 42,* 302–308.

Wigfield, A., & Asher, S. R. (1984). Social and motivational influences on reading. In P. D. Pearson (Ed.), *Handbook of reading research* (pp. 423–452). New York: Longman.

Wilde, S. (1990). A proposal for a new spending curriculum. *Elementary School Journal, 90,* 275–289.

Wilde, S. (1996). The minilesson and assessment: From writing to spelling and back again. *Primary Voices K–6, 4*(4), 16–18.

Winograd, P. N., & Bridge, C. A. (1986). The comprehension of important information in written prose. In J. B. Baumann (Ed.), *Teaching main idea comprehension* (pp. 18–48). Newark, DE: International Reading Association.

Winograd, P. N., Wixson, K. K., & Lipson, M. (Eds.). (1989). *Improving basal reading instruction.* New York: Teachers College Press.

Wixson, K. K. (1986). Vocabulary instruction and children's comprehension of basal stories. *Reading Research Quarterly, 21,* 317–329.

Wood, K. D. (1988). Techniques for assessing students' potential for learning. *Reading Teacher, 41,* 440–447.

Wood, K. D., Lapp, D., & Flood, J. (1992). *Guiding readers through text: A review of study guides.* Newark, DE: International Reading Association.

Yaden, D. (1988). Understanding stories through repeated read-alouds: How many does it take? *The Reading Teacher, 41,* 556–560.

Author/Source Index

Delpit, L., 26
Denner, P. R., 397
Desai, L. E., 543, 558
Dillon, D. R., 114, 530
Dillon, J. T., 114
Dishner, E. K., 35, 129, 255
Dolch, E. W., 191
Dole, J. A., 14, 60, 92, 142, 143,
    144, 391, 392, 394
Donlan, D., 396
Dorsey-Gaines, C., 9, 141
Dreeben, R., 471
Dressel, J. H., 30, 340
Driver, R., 96
Drum, P. A., 232, 233
Duffy, G. G., 391, 392, 394, 402
Duffy-Hester, A. M., 176
Durkin, D., 5, 9, 10, 30, 34, 40,
    114, 334
Dykstra, R., 15, 335

E
Eckhoff, B., 340
Eeds, M., 298
Ehri, L. C., 171, 186
Eldredge, J. L., 165, 168, 183
Elley, W. B., 47
Elliot, D. L., 432, 433
Emans, R., 572
Englert, C. S., 353
Erickson, G., 96
Estice, R. M., 554

F
Fairbanks, M. M., 227, 228, 236
Faraone, V., 5
Farnan, N., 298, 334, 337, 368,
    375
Farr, R., 525, 528
Farris, P., 52
Fawson, P. C., 52
Feitelson, D., 30
Fielding, L. G., 47, 104, 227
Flesch, R., 14, 170
Flood, J., 142, 455, 543
Fountas, I. C., 35, 171, 178, 198,
    199
Fowler, G. L., 366

Fredericks, A., 433
Freebody, P., 226
Freedle, R. O., 100
Freedle, R. P., 98
Freeman, E. B., 7
Freeman, Y. S., 87
French, M. P., 251
Fried, M. D., 554
Fries, C., 5
Frye, B. J., 47

G
Galda, L., 298
Gallagher, J. M., 299
Gambrell, L. B., 311, 538
Gambrell, T., 298
Garcia, G. E., 530
Garrett, S., 531
Gaskins, I. W., 170
Gentry, J. R., 367
Gersten, R., 166
Gillet, J. W., 367
Gipe, J. P., 228
Goetz, E. T., 94
Goldenberg, C., 122
Goldstein, Z., 30
Goodman, K. S., 5, 9, 84, 87,
    552–553
Goodman, Y. M., 5, 84, 533,
    553
Gough, P. B., 168
Gould, S. M., 121
Grabe, C., 4, 28
Grabe, M., 4, 28
Graves, D. H., 48, 50, 334, 337,
    342, 344, 359, 362, 363,
    476, 478, 485
Graves, M. F., 104, 227, 232,
    233, 259, 260, 263
Greaney, V., 6
Griffin, P., 4, 47, 167, 170, 236,
    518
Griffith, P. L., 168
Guthrie, J. T., 6, 24

H
Haas, L. W., 121
Haggard, M. R., 256

Haley, D., 84
Hall, D. P., 47, 511
Halliday, M. A. K., 6, 10
Hallinan, M., 471
Hansen, J., 48, 50, 104, 294,
    299, 309, 312, 363, 507
Harp, B., 471, 528, 529
Harris, A. J., 55
Harris, K. R., 402
Harris, T. L., 93, 525
Harste, J. C., 9, 297, 300, 301,
    317, 318, 325
Harwood, K., 298
Hasselbring, T., 376
Hatch, J. A., 7
Heath, S. B., 6, 9, 337
Heimlich, J. E., 247, 251
Herber, H. L., 40, 430
Herman, P. A., 227, 228, 236,
    531
Hickman, J., 298, 433
Hiebert, E. H., 13, 122, 170,
    176, 191, 471, 528
Hillocks, G., Jr., 48, 337, 344,
    367
History–Social Science
    Curriculum Framework and
    Criteria Committee, 433
Hittleman, D. R., 5
Hodges, R. E., 93, 525
Hoffman, D. M., 303
Holdaway, D., 29, 41, 196, 502
Holmes, B. C., 103, 104, 114,
    118
Horowitz, R., 96
Hoskisson, K., 363, 476
Huck, K. S., 16, 25
Huey, E. B., 5
Hynd, C. R., 96, 142

I
Indrisano, R., 544, 545
Ingram, A. L., 395
Inhelder, B., 9

J
Jenkins, J. R., 227, 228
Johnson, D. D., 123, 247, 394

Subject Index

for prior knowledge activation,
144–157
reading and responding to
literature in, 55–56
sample, 61–83
summary of, 58
using computer program for,
376–386
using textbooks in, 454–455
for vocabulary development,
265–290
literacy program, balanced
defined, 2, 26
independent reading/writing
in, 47–53
lesson format for, 53–83
motivation in, 26–32
and reading aloud, 30–32
reading/writing instruction in,
32–46
selecting literature for,
84–87
thematic units in, 53–55
literate environment, 27, 472
checklist for evaluating, 31
and promoting writing,
339–340
role of responding in, 299–302
and thematic units, 442
literature
authentic, 15–16
in beginning literacy program,
176, 178
in cross-curriculum learning,
432–433, 454–455
developmental appropriateness
of, 84–85, 497–498
extending, 56–58, 455
guidelines for selecting, 84–87
organizing and managing
classroom, 474–476
reading and responding to,
55–56
student selection of, 497–498
See also text(s)
literature discussion circles,
319–325. *See also* discussion
circles

literature log, 303

M

magazines, for student writing,
363
Making Words Routine, 187–188
management. *See* organization
and management
mapping
semantic, 116, 123–126
as study technique, 463
See also story maps; word
maps
mature reading, emphasis in,
165, 166
meaning, constructing
and authentic literature, 15–17
comprehension as, 12–13
dealing with problems in,
559–561
in literacy learning, 8, 9
strategies for, 394–399
and study guides, 455–463
and vocabulary knowledge,
226–229
and word identification, 14–15
See also strategies, for
constructing meaning
meaning vocabulary, 226
metacognition
assessing, 544–546
defined, 14
monitoring of, 395
miniconferences, 476–477
minilesson group, 491
minilessons, 59–60
description of, 407–410
follow-up to, 407, 409–410
modeling in, 59, 393–394
in reading workshop, 502
for strategy teaching, 407–426
on word structures, 261–263
using conferences as, 477–478
in writing workshop, 507
misconceptions, in prior
knowledge, 95–96, 142–144
miscue analysis, 552–553
modeling, 33

defined, 391
guidelines for, 402–404
in minilessons, 393–394,
408–409
sample lesson for, 411–426
in strategy lessons, 408–409
student, 407, 409
types of, 391–393
when to use, 393–394
in writing instruction, 46, 344,
358, 360, 393
modeling groups, 491
monitoring, as reading strategy,
394, 395, 399
sample lesson for, 417–420
monitoring guides, 41, 42
morphemes, 573–574
motivation
in literacy programs, 26–32
parent and teacher role in, 32
and prior knowledge, 140
and reading aloud, 30–32
and real literature, 15–16
multi-age classrooms, 517–518

N

narrative text, 13–14
description of, 97–99
and prior knowledge
activation, 140
reading strategies for, 397,
404, 405
response options for, 317–318
retelling of, 540, 541
structured preview for,
130–131
summarizing, 395, 400
See also text(s)
nativist theory, of language
acquisition, 9
needs groups, 491
newspaper, for sharing writing,
363
note taking, 463

O

observation, in assessment,
533–534, 535
observational guided reading, 35

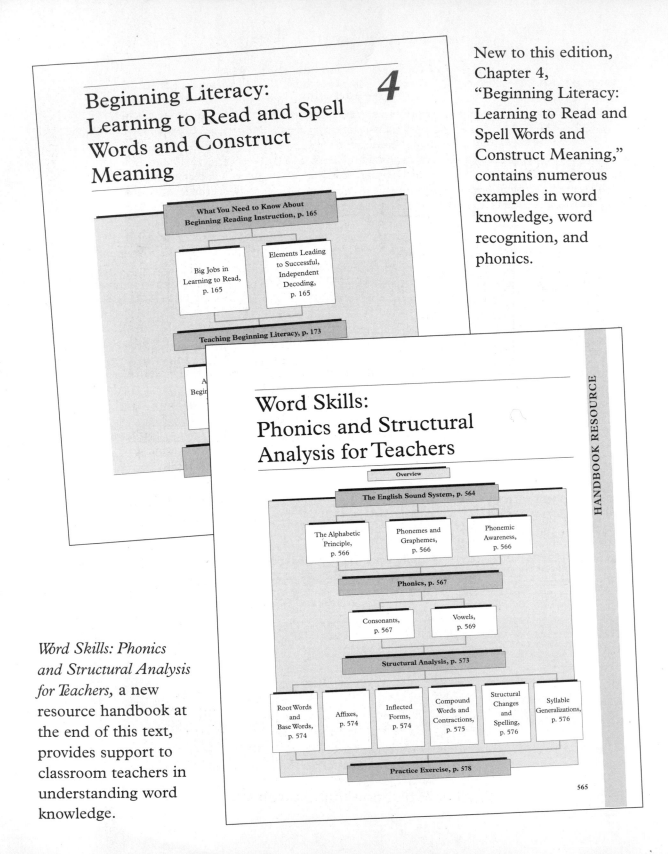

New to this edition, Chapter 4, "Beginning Literacy: Learning to Read and Spell Words and Construct Meaning," contains numerous examples in word knowledge, word recognition, and phonics.

Beginning Literacy: Learning to Read and Spell Words and Construct Meaning

4

What You Need to Know About Beginning Reading Instruction, p. 165

Big Jobs in Learning to Read, p. 165

Elements Leading to Successful, Independent Decoding, p. 165

Teaching Beginning Literacy, p. 173

A
Begin

Word Skills: Phonics and Structural Analysis for Teachers, a new resource handbook at the end of this text, provides support to classroom teachers in understanding word knowledge.

Word Skills: Phonics and Structural Analysis for Teachers

Overview

The English Sound System, p. 564

The Alphabetic Principle, p. 566

Phonemes and Graphemes, p. 566

Phonemic Awareness, p. 566

Phonics, p. 567

Consonants, p. 567

Vowels, p. 569

Structural Analysis, p. 573

Root Words and Base Words, p. 574

Affixes, p. 574

Inflected Forms, p. 574

Compound Words and Contractions, p. 575

Structural Changes and Spelling, p. 576

Syllable Generalizations, p. 576

Practice Exercise, p. 578

565